BEER, BRATS, AND CHEESE

BEER, BRATS, AND CHEESE

A Wisconsin Road Trip

Heather Kerrigan

THE UNIVERSITY OF WISCONSIN PRESS

Publication of this book has been made possible, in part,
through support from the Anonymous Fund of the College of Letters
and Science at the University of Wisconsin–Madison.

The University of Wisconsin Press
728 State Street, Suite 443
Madison, Wisconsin 53706
uwpress.wisc.edu

Printed in the United States of America
This book may be available in a digital edition.

Library of Congress Cataloging-in-Publication Data

Names: Kerrigan, Heather, author.
Title: Beer, brats, and cheese : a Wisconsin road trip / Heather Kerrigan.
Description: Madison, Wisconsin : The University of Wisconsin Press, 2025. | Includes bibliographical references and index.
Identifiers: LCCN 2024014090 | ISBN 9780299349844 (paperback)
Subjects: LCSH: Breweries—Wisconsin—Guidebooks. | Bars (Drinking establishments)—Wisconsin—Guidebooks. | Cheese shops—Wisconsin—Guidebooks. | Beer—Wisconsin—Guidebooks. | Bratwurst—Wisconsin—Guidebooks. | Cheese—Wisconsin—Guidebooks. | Wisconsin—Guidebooks.
Classification: LCC TX907.3.W6 K47 2025 | DDC 917.7504—dc23/eng/20240405
LC record available at https://lccn.loc.gov/2024014090

To my husband, my forever adventure partner and expert navigator,
and our daughter, whose patience and unwitting humor kept me
grounded as I wrote—and finished—this book.

Wisconsin is always a good idea.

Contents

Illustrations

MAPS

PHOTOGRAPHS

Preface

I don't quite remember when I first decided that I wanted to take a road trip around my home state, sampling all the beer, brats, and cheese I could. But I do remember the excitement. The more I researched, the more obsessed I became with learning everything I could about these quintessential—albeit, maybe a bit cliché—Wisconsin foods: how they're made, why they're here, what makes them such a big part of Wisconsin life, and, most important, where to get the best.

Months of research and planning—and replanning after COVID-19 shuttered many a store, restaurant, and brewery—resulted in one epic twenty-six-hundred-mile road trip over the course of four weeks. Was it crazy? In more ways than one. Did I question my life choices? Maybe just a few times. But was it worth it? Undoubtedly, 100 percent yes. Across miles and miles of county roads, Rustic Roads, and interstates, I was reintroduced to the resplendent beauty of America's Dairyland. On barstools, benches, folding chairs, and lawns, I sampled the best beer, brats, and cheese I've ever had. At countless tables, registers, information counters, and on shop floors, I talked to and learned from the backbone of the state's food and beverage industry. And all along the way, my passion for the state where I was raised grew.

I could never imagine keeping everything I learned before, during, and after the trip to myself—from where to get the best brats in Mauston to which blends of pasture grass produce buttery-yellow cheese curds to why extra head on a glass of beer enhances the taste. So, in the pages that follow I've shared what makes Wisconsin tick. The craft brewers, production brewhouses, butchers, dairy farms, creameries, brewpubs, taprooms, and restaurants perfecting their craft. There's also a little about the past, present, and future of Wisconsin beer, brats, and cheese, and the spots and events where you can indulge a bit more in the Wisconsin experience.

Whether you call the Badger State home or just love a good road trip, I hope this book inspires you to get out and explore the culinary world of Wisconsin.

Happy travels.

BEER, BRATS, AND CHEESE

Introduction

BECOMING AMERICA'S DAIRYLAND

While Wisconsin has been producing cheese for some 180 years, dairy hasn't always been an agricultural staple. Native Americans gathered from and farmed on the land for thousands of years before the arrival of the first trader, missionary, or European settler. Oneida, Ho-Chunk, Ojibwe, Menominee, Potawatomi, and other nations and tribes that called the area home grew white corn, beans, and squash, cultivated wild rice, and harvested cranberries. The Indigenous population worked with the environment in the land that would become Wisconsin, and relied on the bounty that grew in and around the area's grasslands, prairies, forests, streams, and marshes.

After achieving territory status in 1836, the Wisconsin area began attracting new settlers from the eastern United States in search of natural resources—first mineral wealth and then fertile farmland. The immigrants who would arrive in the ensuing decades, primarily from Europe, found pristine land that was perfect for bountiful wheat production. In the early days of the state's history, more effort went into growing crops, and any dairy produced on a farm fed the farmer's family.

By the latter half of the nineteenth century, however, farmers had overworked the land, and soil leaching and invasive bugs severely limited wheat production. In turn, Wisconsin wheat farmers were forced to find new agricultural pursuits. Several turned to what they knew best from their original homelands: dairy farming and cheese production.

There is some debate over who opened the first cheese factory in the state, though many credit Charles Rockwell, who started a small operation in the southeastern part of Wisconsin near Fort Atkinson in 1837, as well as Anne Picket, who opened a cheese factory in 1841 in Lake Mills, using milk from her neighbor's cows. In 1844, John J. Smith moved near Sheboygan Falls from New York, the top cheese-producing state at the time, and started a wheat farm that would later incorporate dairy. Despite his efforts, Smith was perhaps surprised to be turned away when he tried to market his wares in Illinois, where buyers believed Wisconsin cheese was inferior to what was coming from New York.

To help combat this public perception, in 1872, dairy farmers came together to establish the Wisconsin Dairymen's Association, which was responsible for helping farmers work together to market their products and encourage more Wisconsinites to pursue dairy farming. The association also pushed for higher quality milk and more standardized dairy products. In part, the Dairymen's Association did this by educating farmers on the importance of cleaning their equipment and proper dairy storage. Cleaner, fresher dairy would produce a more uniform product, which could help raise Wisconsin's cheese profile and bring in a higher price at market.

In the late nineteenth century, however, in an effort to make more money, some cheesemakers created an adulterated cheese that had water or skim milk added in. While the taste was similar to regular cheese when fresh, this so-called filled cheese quickly lost its flavor, and Wisconsin's cheesemaking reputation again suffered. Shortly thereafter, official quality standards were implemented, and the position of dairy and food commissioner was created to put a stop to the tainted cheese production. In 1915, Wisconsin became the first state to implement a license for cheesemakers, factories, and creameries. Just a few years later, in 1921, the state instituted mandatory grading standards for certain cheese varieties.

These collective efforts were successful in helping grow the number of creameries and ensure the public knew that they could expect only the highest quality cheese from Wisconsin. Wisconsin overtook New York as the nation's top cheese-producing state in 1910, and by 1920 there were only three counties—Iron, Oneida, and Pepin—that did not have a cheese factory within their borders. In 1922, to keep up with nationwide demand, the state boasted its record-high 2,807 commercial cheese-making factories.

While the number of cheese factories would decline over the next several decades due to the Great Depression and World War II, factory consolidation, and more efficient technology for shipping milk longer distances, cheese production soared. In 1995, Wisconsin produced more than 2 billion pounds of cheese, but in that same year, there were only 142 cheese factories. By 2022, Wisconsin had 124 cheese factories—from major, national companies to co-ops to small mom-and-pop operations—and had topped 3.5 billion pounds of cheese per year, thus solidifying its place as the number-one cheese-producing state (interestingly, California produces more milk, but Wisconsin makes around 1 billion more pounds of cheese annually).

Today Wisconsin continues to cement its reputation for world-class cheese. It remains the only state in the country with a Master Cheesemaker program—and in fact offers the only such program outside of Europe. Since its creation in 1994, more than ninety individuals have graduated from the intensive, three-year course and apprenticeship open only to those who have held a Wisconsin cheesemaker's license for at least a decade. Master Cheesemakers are certified in a specific type of cheese (and must have been producing that product for at least five years before applying), and once certified, can add the Master's Mark to their products, denoting that they've achieved the highest level of cheese expertise in the state.

Wisconsin's cheesemakers are also branching out to innovate products to meet public demand. They include new varieties of cheese made with sheep's and goat's milk, as well as Hispanic-style cheeses like queso fresco, oaxaca, chihuahua, cotija, and quesadilla. Wisconsin boasts nearly two dozen plants making Hispanic-style cheese, including southwestern Wisconsin's W&W Dairy, Wisconsin Cheese Group, Mexican Cheese Producers, and V&V Supremo. In 2022, Wisconsin was second in the nation in its production of Hispanic-style cheese, with approximately 1.28 million pounds produced annually, or 33 percent of the US total (California was the top producer at 1.66 million pounds).

In the decades since the first cheesemakers made their way to the rolling hills and prairies of Wisconsin, the state has set itself apart as a cheesemaking powerhouse. Wisconsin produces more varieties of cheese and more sheep's milk and goat's milk cheese than any other state, and its cheeses have won more than seventy-three hundred awards—more than any other state or country. Its climate, luscious green pastures, and copious amounts of natural limestone water make it the perfect spot for pasture raising cows, sheep, and goats to produce high-quality milk that can be turned into award-winning cheese.

PUTTING WISCONSIN ON THE MAP

You could argue ad nauseam about whether it was cheese or beer that put Wisconsin on the country's culinary radar. In reality, they grew side by side, as both farmers and brewers found ways to use the state's natural resources to their advantage.

Enterprising settlers have been brewing beer in Wisconsin since before it became a state, or even a territory. The Europeans who moved into present-day Wisconsin before the 1830s brewed ales at home, which at one time was a standard household chore for women. There is also some evidence that these home brews may have been not only shared with local friends and family but also sold to those moving into or traveling through the area on their way west. The first commercial brewery opened in 1835 near southwestern Wisconsin's Mineral Point, and was soon followed by another in nearby Elk Grove, both areas where the mining industry was centered and beer was likely in high demand among laborers.

At around the same time, lager was gaining a foothold, replacing ale as a favorite beverage of the working class for its smoother, more refreshing taste. Because of the way lager is crafted, it requires dark, cool spaces to age. Enter Milwaukee, the perfect spot to site caves that could draw on nearby ponds and lakes for water and ice. Setting up operations along Lake Michigan also ensured brewers had easy access to fresh water and transport routes, and nearby fertile farmland meant hops, barley, and other critical ingredients were simple to acquire. With an influx of German immigrants and their taste for lager beers that reminded them of home, the city quickly became Wisconsin's brewing capital—and it never looked back. The *Milwaukee Sentinel* in 1892 boasted that the city was known throughout the world for its lager beer expertise (though at that time, Milwaukee was still lagging behind the brewing dynamos of New York, Chicago, and St. Louis).

Breweries began springing up along Lake Michigan's shoreline, both north and south of Milwaukee, in cities large and small, with Green Bay becoming one of the last European settlements of the mid-1800s to have a brewery. As time went on, intrepid brewers began to move west, setting up anywhere they could find fresh water, which mainly meant along the streams and rivers that make up Lake Michigan's tributaries. By the time Wisconsin became a state, in 1848, there had been around three dozen commercial breweries, some of which were already closed. Most were located in and around Milwaukee, but a few had pushed out as far as present-day Monroe County.

During the Civil War, the growth of breweries in Wisconsin slowed, as supplies and equipment became harder to procure. Existing breweries found their place as important community centers, however, giving those both for and against the war a spot to meet, share their grievances, and decide how to react to the news of the day.

After the war, brewing again took off, and many individuals interested in setting up their own commercial operations started looking for sites away from Milwaukee and other large cities, to avoid competition from established brewers. No matter where they were, breweries were big business in Wisconsin's early days as a state, because their establishment sometimes encouraged local farmers to grow barley, hops, and other beer staples that they could sell to the brewery. The brewery would then provide the spent grain back to the farms as animal feed. The growth of breweries also meant the need for other services, and soon more people moved into these villages, towns, and cities, and they expanded around the brewery operation. Breweries often resulted in road and rail improvements as well, allowing brewers to bring in supplies and send out products more easily. Some breweries persuaded railroad companies to add a spur to their line simply to pick up the company's products. It would still be many decades, however, before Wisconsin beers were shipped much farther than neighboring midwestern states with some exceptions; Kenosha's New Era Brewing Company shipped all the way to Georgia in the late 1880s.

Prohibition, of course, put a damper on further expansion, just as the state's beer powerhouses, such as Pabst and Schlitz, were looking for new methods to market their products far and wide. Some breweries looked for creative ways to continue operation without drawing attention from authorities. They included brewing near beer, a fermented malt beverage with a low alcohol content, distributing underground, and shipping beer in barrels that had near beer in the top half where inspectors would look and actual beer in the bottom. Other companies, such as Potosi, moved at least in part to dairy, after recognizing that many of the large pieces of equipment used in the brew operation were easily modified for dairy production. Pabst did the same (though the family had already been involved in smaller scale cheese production), creating its line of Pabst Wonder Process Cheese. Because Prohibition didn't outlaw home brewing for personal consumption, other breweries, including G. Heileman in La Crosse, sold products to home brewers, sometimes marketed as baking supplies.

After the 1933 ratification of the Twenty-First Amendment ended Prohibition, some breweries never reopened or came back to their full capacity, and those that did were in for another round of constraints with the start of World War II. The traditional male-driven brewery labor force dwindled, as did grain, packing supplies, and even space in railcars, all in the name of supporting the war effort. Breweries were encouraged to shift from selling bottled beer, so the metal that would go toward caps could instead go to war production, and the industry suggested brewers move away from beers like bocks that require more grain for production.

The postwar decades were ones of expansion, contraction, and consolidation. The huge breweries that dominated the nationwide scene bought up small rivals and either adopted their flavors and brands or scrapped their products entirely. Breweries also began experimenting with new varieties, including light beer, ice dry, and nonalcoholic styles to continue to attract new audiences. By 1975, three of the five largest breweries in the country were located in Wisconsin: Schlitz, Pabst, and Miller.

A piece of legislation in 1978 helped spark the latest round of growth in the Wisconsin beer scene. That was the year President Jimmy Carter signed a bill that included an amendment to legalize at the federal level home brewing for personal and family consumption. It was an important turning point because many of the breweries and brewpubs that exist today started as apartment, garage, and kitchen home-brewing experiments that would eventually turn into some of the beers that have proliferated across the state.

Today brewpubs, breweries, microbreweries, nanobreweries, and the like continue popping up around Wisconsin, and the state's largest craft brewers still dominate nationally. According to the Brewers Association, as of 2022, New Glarus Brewing Company, Minhas Craft Brewery, and Stevens Point Brewery ranked twelfth, fifteenth, and nineteenth, respectively, in a list of the nation's top-producing craft-brewing companies. Certainly, some brewers have struggled to find a place in a crowded market, while others gain a cult following or expand into regional or national distribution. Breweries across Wisconsin are as varied as the styles of beer on tap: no two are alike.

KING OF SAUSAGE

Bratwurst is believed to have originated in the 1300s in what would eventually become eastern Germany. Its name is derived from the German words *braten* (to fry or to roast) and *wurst* (sausage). In its early days, the cased veal product was traditionally consumed for breakfast because it spoiled quickly.

Sausage making in Wisconsin dates to the first people to live in the area. Native Americans throughout the land that would become Wisconsin crafted pemmican, a sausage-like smoked protein cake, made by combining wild game, corn, wild rice, cranberries (another Wisconsin staple), fat tallow, and other available ingredients.

Fast forward to the early 1800s, and millions of immigrants from Germany began flooding into the United States. Many of them came to settle in Wisconsin; in fact, at one point the future state marketed itself as the perfect location for German immigrants. Those who came sometimes set up farms, where brats and other sausages were a staple food because they were cheap, easy to make, portable, and could be enjoyed quickly between work tasks. It was around this time that more farms began making their brats out of pork, rather than the more traditional veal, reportedly because pork was cheaper.

While brats were regularly enjoyed at home and could be found in some butcher shops, it wasn't until the mid-1900s that its mass popularity exploded. In 1945, Ralph F. and Alice Stayer opened a butcher shop named after their small community of Johnsonville. Their early focus was on beef, but Ralph soon decided that he could make a better tasting brat from premium cuts of pork, rather than the leftover pieces that were more typically used to produce the sausage.

Today Sheboygan is known as the Bratwurst Capital of the World. Why Sheboygan and not Johnsonville? Johnsonville is an unincorporated area within the town of Sheboygan Falls, which is located within Sheboygan County, of which the county seat and largest city is Sheboygan. The sausage title could just as easily have gone to Bucyrus, Ohio, which also tried to crown itself, but in 1970, Judge John Bolgert declared that it was in fact the Wisconsin city that deserved this distinction. In 1997, the Wisconsin Senate went so far as to issue Senate Joint Resolution 20, which noted that "the flavorful, delicious Sheboygan double bratwurst on a hard roll, with the works . . . is declared the ultimate state sandwich and that citizens of Wisconsin and other states are invited and encouraged to experience and enjoy this culinary, ethnic delight."

Sheboygan truly embraces its sausage heritage, and its tourism bureau website has a brat oath, which reads, in part, "With resolution I proclaim the promise to always fry brats, to always serve them on a hard roll and to always protect them from non-sanctioned preparation techniques. I hereby swear that I denounce pre-boiling. I denounce overdressing with pickled cabbage and other offensive forms of condimentation. I denounce the oblong bun, and I will deny all temptation to engage in inter-relations between brat and cheese rituals." It concludes, "I shall never, even in the shadow of the face of death, deny a brat eater a beer."

However, while the city might be famous for brats, they aren't exclusive to Sheboygan. Stores and restaurants around the state are crafting these fresh sausages, which have become a staple at cookouts, civic club fundraisers, tailgates, and church brat fries. And it isn't just the big players like Johnsonville where revelers get their meats: small towns all over Wisconsin still have butchers making freshly ground brats out of everything from chicken and beef to veal and pork, in both traditional and nontraditional flavors.

As you may have guessed from the oath, Wisconsinites take their brats seriously, but they disagree about how the sausage should be prepared and served. In Sheboygan, a brat is grilled over charcoal, served on a split hard roll called a semmel, and then topped with brown mustard and onions. In other parts of the state, brats are parboiled in beer and onions to prevent them from exploding on the grill (some residents will tell you they prevent brat explosions by skipping parboiling then cooking the brats away from the coals and turning frequently with tongs or fingers, the latter of which will prevent piercing the sausage casing and letting the juice escape). Brats might even be topped with sauerkraut or spicy mustard. In a pinch, nonconformists will serve their brats on glorified hot dog buns, though most Wisconsinites would probably recommend against it because such buns can't hold up to the juiciness of a perfectly grilled (or, in Wisconsin-ese, fried) brat.

HOW TO USE THIS GUIDE

It would be easy—and fun—to spend years cruising around Wisconsin, stopping at every creamery, cheese shop, taproom, butcher shop, market, dairy, restaurant, brewery, and brewpub you can find. To save time, this book offers a sampling of locations where you can try some of the state's best beer, brats, and cheese. It is not an exhaustive list of every location in Wisconsin, but rather a highlight reel.

The book is divided into five parts, with each chapter reflecting a specific region of the state. Chapter 1 covers southeastern Wisconsin, including the major cities of Milwaukee, Kenosha, and Racine. Chapter 2 begins in Madison and continues south and west toward the Mississippi River, before heading north to La Crosse. Chapter 3 takes you to the west central part of the state and the cities of Eau Claire, Wausau, and Chippewa Falls. Chapter 4 explores Up North Wisconsin and the Northwoods, while Chapter 5 covers Green Bay, Door County, Sheboygan, and the surrounding region.

Each chapter is made up of one long road trip that begins at the first location and ends with the final one, though you can easily break up each section into multiple road trips and begin anywhere along the route. The road trip in each chapter is not circular; instead, the next chapter begins near where the previous one ended, allowing you to move from region to region and combine the shorter trips into one epic adventure!

Within each chapter, you'll see special boxed features. Pit Stops provide an overview of annual, local events that celebrate beer, brats, and cheese. Detours are nearby stops on your route that might not be beer, brat, or cheese related but offer some additional local color. WisconsInsights are fun facts about the state's beer, brat, and cheese culture.

If you flip quickly through the book, you might find that many of the locations are breweries. But this doesn't mean you'll be sampling only beers. Because brats and cheese are such a staple in Wisconsin's food culture, some of their best varieties can be found at breweries and brewpubs. So, while some breweries do in fact have only beer, at others you can enjoy gourmet brats, gooey fried cheese curds, creamy mac and cheese, cheese curds topped with brats, and much, much more.

Finally, please enjoy your road trip safely, and never drink and drive. Plan your trip with plenty of time to enjoy, drink responsibly, take a designated driver, or call an Uber. If worse comes to worst, the Tavern League of Wisconsin offers the SafeRide program, which gives free rides to patrons of member breweries. There are more than five thousand members across the state, so if you need a ride ask your bartender or visit the Tavern League of Wisconsin website for a directory of resources.

A FINAL NOTE

This guidebook is based on a road trip that took place in the summer of 2022 and is not meant to be exhaustive, nor can it document all of the newcomers, closures, events, current hours, and days of operation. For the most up-to-date information, check each location's website or social media page (see the appendix for a list), or follow along on Instagram @somelikeitbrat or online at www.hkerrigan.com.

CHAPTER 1

Milwaukee and Southeastern Wisconsin

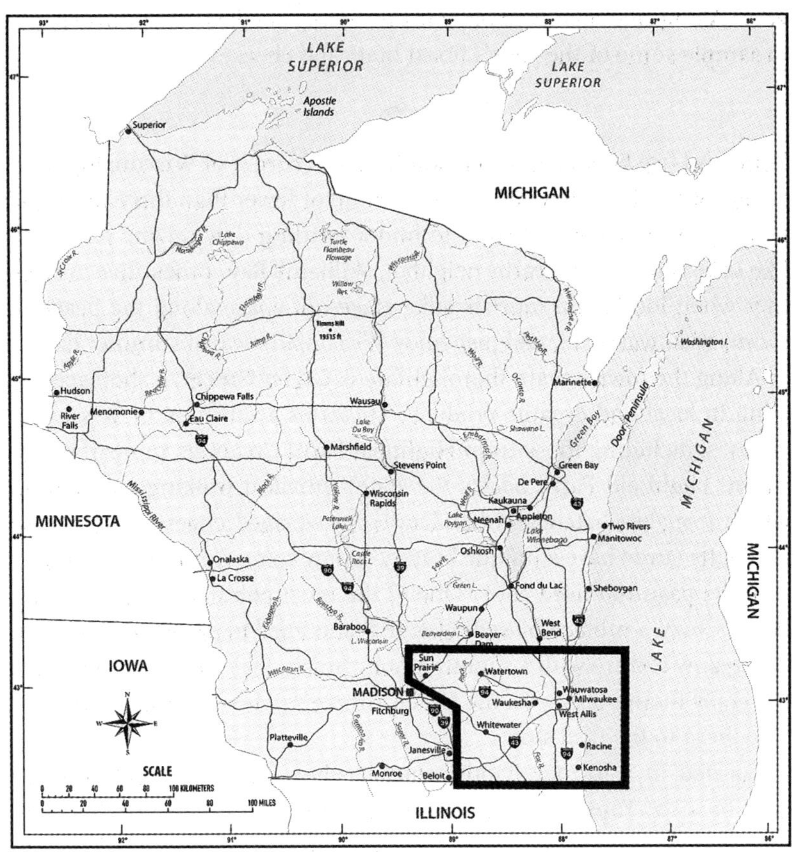

The boxed region indicates the approximate Milwaukee and southeastern Wisconsin area covered in this chapter.

Southeastern Wisconsin has long been a favorite locale for brewers. In decades past, they relied on easy access to ports and rail corridors to ship their products throughout the Midwest, as well as the small inland lakes and streams that provided water and ice for chilling barrels of beer. Today Lake Michigan is a source of the copious amounts of fresh water required for the brewing process. In fact, the lake's high-quality water offers the right mix of minerals that breweries need as a blank slate for their creations. As you drive throughout this part of Wisconsin, you'll spot dozens of large brew operations and small craft breweries. Alongside them (and often inside them), you'll also have the chance to sample some of the state's finest brats and cheeses.

~

Your road trip begins in the far southeastern corner of Wisconsin, in the village of Williams Bay. With a population of fewer than three thousand people, you may be surprised to find a bustling downtown. Yet, much like Lake Geneva, its nearby neighbor, Williams Bay comes alive in summer when locals and tourists alike stake out space along the beach to swim, boat, water-ski, and just enjoy Wisconsin's warm summer days.

Along the town's main thoroughfare is **Green Grocer**, a shop specializing in local and organic products. It carries a selection of Wisconsin cheeses, including those from Highfield Farm Creamery in nearby Walworth. Highfield Farm boasts the state's smallest milking parlor from which it makes batches of handcrafted, cave-aged cheeses and cheese curds. Its curds have a unique buttery-yellow color, from the use of milk from its pasture-raised cows. One of the most popular cheese varieties is Stir Crazy, a mild colby-style cheese that is aged to produce a semifirm yet creamy texture with a slightly smoky finish. Pick up some cheeses to try, enjoy them outside on the Green Grocer's patio or along the lake, or take them to the next stop.

Located in a former Baptist church whose current structure dates back to 1910, **Topsy Turvy Brewery** was born out of the owner's love of the state's craft-brewing history. Here, among stained-glass windows and cathedral ceilings, you can try hazy IPAs, wheat beers, blonde ales, stouts, and sours, many bearing names that celebrate all things Wisconsin, such

Green Grocer, Williams Bay

as Wisconsin Big Buck IPA and Geneva Beach Blonde. The brewery has a small menu that includes fresh cheese curds from Lake Geneva's Hill Valley Dairy and a brat from Lake Geneva Country Meats, but guests are also welcome to bring in their own food. Topsy Turvy Brewery frequently has live music and other events, and has an outdoor beer garden that is dog friendly.

About four blocks north along Broad Street sits **Hill Valley Cheese Bar & Shop**. Thursday through Monday afternoons, you can check out the company's cheddar, gouda, and curds, all made with milk from the

WisconsInsights

Dairy farms inject more than $86,000 per minute into the state's economy.

Henningfeld family's sixty-five milking cows. The cheese isn't made at the Lake Geneva storefront, but is actually crafted in Milwaukee. In addition to a mild, medium, and sharp cheddar, Hill Valley produces specialty cheddars—such as bacon, whiskey, and habanero—a whiskey gouda, and flavored cheese curds.

From Lake Geneva, head forty-five minutes east along Highway 50 toward the city of Kenosha. Situated halfway between Chicago and Milwaukee, Kenosha, known as Southport in the early to mid-1800s, was the site of a number of brewing innovations. Conrad Muntzenberger ran one of the state's first steam-powered breweries, and his son Adolph invented and patented a barrel washer that quickly gained popularity around the country.

WisconsInsights

The first brewpub in the Upper Midwest, Brewmasters' Pub, opened in Kenosha in 1987, thanks to the efforts of a group of home brewers.

Since the Chrysler engine plant shut down in 2010, Kenosha has been a city in transition. Part of its rebirth included a burgeoning craft beer scene. **R'Noggin Brewing Company** opened its doors in 2016, when two brothers took their garage brewing operation mainstream. Since then, the brewery has been charming locals with its craft brews and gaining attention for its unique can designs. In addition to the lineup of beers that range from malty to barrel-aged to sour to easy drinking, the brewery has pizza and pretzels—plus the occasional food truck—but invites guests to bring in their own snacks or order delivery.

If you're looking for a full meal, nearby is **Brat Stop**. Located right off Highway 50 and just minutes from the Wisconsin-Illinois border, the restaurant has been serving a selection of wursts and other Wisconsin favorites to locals and travelers since 1961. Get some brats and curds to go, or take a seat in the dining room and select from an array of brat flavors, including jalapeño cheddar, veal, Cajun, traditional, and garlic.

Brat Stop, Kenosha

If you're itching to get back on the road, call ahead and Brat Stop will have your goodies packaged and ready for pickup.

Kenosha's newest entrant into the craft beer scene, **Kenosha Brewing Company**, is southwest of the city's downtown, in the same location as the Midwest's first brewpub after Prohibition. Local monks even perfected their own craft brewing in the building nearly a century ago. Today the menu includes not only fried cheese curds but also upscale and not-your-typical bar food, like Saganaki made from an imported kasseri cheese set aflame to produce a crisp crust, and served with pita bread. It's definitely one of the more unique cheese presentations at a brewery. As far as the beer goes, Kenosha Brewing Company has its own line of hard seltzers, plus wheat beers, IPAs, porters, and ales, along with guest taps featuring pours from various Wisconsin and midwestern breweries.

Now venture into the heart of downtown Kenosha. Grab a street parking spot anywhere you can find one and stop by **Rustic Road Brewing**

Pit Stop

In mid-May, Kenosha hosts Craft Beer Week. The city's four breweries and tourism bureau put together a number of events, such as block parties, breakfasts, live music, and food and drink specials.

Company, which calls itself "Kenosha's oldest operating brewery" (a title it holds by only three months over its nearby competitor, PUBLIC Craft Brewing Co.). The business opened in 2012, the brainchild of owner Greg York, who first started brewing beer in his college apartment. The brewery takes its name from the Wisconsin Rustic Roads program that over the past four decades has designated more than 120 roads as a unique way to explore the state's scenic countryside. Rustic Road has a cozy location, with bar seating and a few tables both inside and out. The intimate setting reflects the brewery's small-batch operation, which is on full display the moment you enter the taproom. Rotating taps include a farmhouse ale, porter, fruited gose, milkshake IPA, and kölsch. If you're hungry, dig into the brewery's menu for garlic cheese curds and craft brats. The brat offerings change frequently, meaning you can try

Detour

As of 2023, there are more than seven hundred miles of designated Rustic Roads across sixty-one Wisconsin counties. Each is marked with a brown-and-yellow sign for easy identification. These roads may be dirt, gravel, or paved and are lightly traveled. Each includes natural features, such as native plants and animals, or agricultural vistas. As you plan your route, or even while driving, consider detouring down one of these unique roads. And don't worry: each Rustic Road is often either a closed loop or connected to highways at both sides, so you won't come to a dead end.

different flavors—from bacon cheddar to mac and cheese stuffed and everything in between—each time you visit.

Full of beer and brats, stroll toward **PUBLIC Craft Brewing Co.**, located around the block from Rustic Road. PUBLIC's motto is Beer for the People, and its focus is on feeding and entertaining everyone who comes through the doors. From the outside, you might be fooled into believing that the taproom is a furniture store, but the window displays are actually seating areas surrounding the large open taproom and its central bar. Turntable Tuesday is a local favorite, when you can bring your own vinyl and receive half off your first beer. Other events include trivia nights, college nights, guest tap features, and live music. PUBLIC has an extensive tap list with lighter drinking beers as well as IPAs, bocks, Belgian dubbels, and sours. While chicken wings and sandwiches are the specialties, the menu also features fried cheese curds, bacon beer cheese mac bombs, and rice bowls.

PUBLIC Craft Brewing Co., Kenosha

Pit Stop

When you find yourself in Kenosha in early September, get tickets to the Great Lakes Brew Fest. For one price, you get unlimited samples of some 300 craft beers, ciders, and hard seltzers, many of which are Wisconsin made. Live music and food vendors—including the Wisconsin Fried Cheese Curds concession stand—also make an appearance.

While you're downtown, and if you're still hungry, within easy walking distance of both PUBLIC and Rustic Road is **Century Pub & Eatery**. Here you'll find standard pub fare, including burgers, sandwiches, wraps, wings, cheese curds, and a Friday fish fry, along with a juicy brat, all at prices that can't be beat. Pro tip: customers rave about the totchos, a multi-person platter of Tater Tots smothered with nacho toppings.

No trip to the Kenosha area would be complete without a visit to **Mars Cheese Castle**, a popular stop for tourists entering the state on I-94. Located in a castle-esque building with an entrance that mimics a drawbridge, Mars Cheese Castle has an abundance of cheese varieties to choose from, whether you favor a Wisconsin-made baby swiss or sharp cheddar, a bag of fresh squeaky cheese curds, or even a chocolate cheese fudge. Or treat yourself to a cheese spread and pick up a box of crackers to nibble along the day's journey. If you're hungry, Mars Cheese Castle

Pit Stop

At the end of April, Kenosha holds the Dairy State Cheese & Beer Festival, an afternoon event that benefits Boys & Girls Club of Kenosha. A ticket gets you four hours of unlimited beer and cheese samples, live music, and a souvenir glass. Tickets can be purchased online in advance or at the door. If you plan early enough, take advantage of the event's Black Friday ticket special, to save a few dollars.

has cheesy breakfast sandwiches, melty grilled cheese, Usinger's brats, the self-described "world's best" fried cheese curds, and a variety of other deli offerings. Before you leave, don't forget to pick up some Wisconsin gifts, a Cheesehead hat, or a case of local beers.

Next, it's time to head toward another of southeastern Wisconsin's major cities: Racine. As you travel northeast from Kenosha—and if you're taking this drive on a summer afternoon—swing by the **Petrifying Springs Biergarten**. Located inside Petrifying Springs Park, the annual event has rotating local craft beer taps and German exports, with a side of live music and trivia. Hungry? Brats served up on a pretzel roll are on the menu, along with other snacks, sausages, and the fan favorite Wisconsin Pretzel Board, which includes a large soft pretzel, fresh cheese curds, sausage bites, and a side of mustard and Obatzda, a German beer cheese spread. Pro tip: The biergarten accepts only cash, and there is an ATM on-site. Another pro tip: Come armed with sunscreen. There are

Petrifying Springs Biergarten, Kenosha

very few shaded seating areas within the biergarten, and those summer afternoons can get toasty.

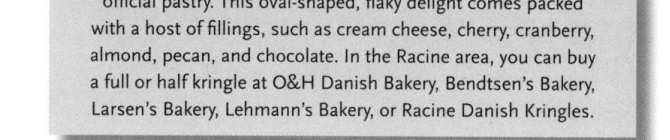

Continuing north, you'll reach Racine. In the early 1800s, the city was expected to become the largest port on the western part of Lake Michigan. However, a number of devastating fires—including one in 1882 that burned for days and required Chicago firefighters to take the train to town to help fight the blaze—rendered most of the buildings completely unusable. Without the necessary infrastructure, Racine never became the large port it was supposed to be.

Now, two Racine residents are hoping to use their award-winning home-brew knowledge to elevate the city's beer profile. Mark and Chris Flynn had long been fixtures on the home-brewing scene, establishing the Belle City Homebrewers Club and opening their own brewing and winemaking supply store, Hop To It. But in 2011, their hard work came under fire when Racine enforced an old Wisconsin law restricting home-brew consumption to the home where it was made. Only establishments with a liquor license were allowed to distribute home brew under the law, even samples. With the help of other beer clubs and home brewers around the state, Mark successfully lobbied the Wisconsin legislature to change the law. Thanks to their hard work, new rules were put in place to support home brewers by allowing them to share their products with family, friends, local home-brew clubs, and even enter them in competitions. Fast forward and today you can enjoy the Flynns' creations at **Littleport Brewing Company**. The taproom is located in a renovated building that once served as a livery where horses and hearses were kept (ask the bartenders and they'll gladly tell you some ghost stories,

Detour

While in Wisconsin, be sure to sample a kringle, the state's official pastry. This oval-shaped, flaky delight comes packed with a host of fillings, such as cream cheese, cherry, cranberry, almond, pecan, and chocolate. In the Racine area, you can buy a full or half kringle at O&H Danish Bakery, Bendtsen's Bakery, Larsen's Bakery, Lehmann's Bakery, or Racine Danish Kringles.

including one where the fire department was called to investigate the sound of a woman singing). Littleport has twenty-one taps, including its own brews and some other Wisconsin favorites. From blonde ales and cream ales to seltzers, witbiers, and IPAs, the wide range of offerings means everyone is likely to find something they enjoy. A few snacks, including frozen pizzas and stuffed pretzels, are available, along with chips, beef jerky, and beer nuts.

Just east of Littleport is **Reef Point Brew House**, the city's go-to spot for classic American comfort food. While overlooking Lake Michigan, tuck into any one of its BBQ platters, chophouse specials, or sandwiches, such as the Wisconsin burger, with beef and brat patties plus cheddar cheese and bacon sandwiched into a pretzel bun.

Pit Stop

Beer and bacon lovers rejoice! Each November, Racine is home to the Beer & Bacon Walk, a five-hour stroll through the city's downtown to sample craft brews and bacon-infused snacks (like a maple bacon cake pop or bacon-wrapped sausage). Tickets can be purchased online in advance, and each includes twenty three-ounce beer samples, twenty bacon food samples, a commemorative pint glass, and a sixteen-ounce full pour.

From downtown Racine, head west. If you're making your journey during summer, be sure to stop at Racine County's **Franksville Craft Beer Garden**. Located in Franksville Memorial Park, this community gathering spot is open from mid-May until late October. At any time, Franksville has a selection of around twenty Wisconsin beers, plus cider and wine, food trucks (including Das Brat & Pretzel, a beer garden favorite for savory quarter-pound brats served on a pretzel bun), live music, fish fry Fridays, and various activities for kids and adults.

Continue to the city of Burlington, located along Racine County's western edge. Although it once billed itself as Chocolate City USA because of the Nestlé factory within its borders (when the wind is blowing right, it still makes the city smell like warm brownies), it also has a long history in commercial brewing. In the early 1850s, Jacob Muth set up Burlington's first commercial brewery, and over time that flagship establishment was turned into a malthouse and eventually sold to a theater group. Since then, a series of beer makers, including the Wisconsin Brewing Company, have come and gone through Burlington, fighting through Prohibition and World War II by looking for new income streams and cheaper ways to acquire much-needed supplies. During the war, one of these breweries reportedly tried to strike a deal with the city to get certain tin cans that it could repurpose into bottle caps, but the city refused and instead gave the brewery the opportunity to dig through the trash dump and take what it wanted for six dollars per ton. By the late 1950s, brewing dried up and for decades the city didn't have a commercial brewer.

That's changing, and two breweries are working to make the city a destination for craft beer lovers.

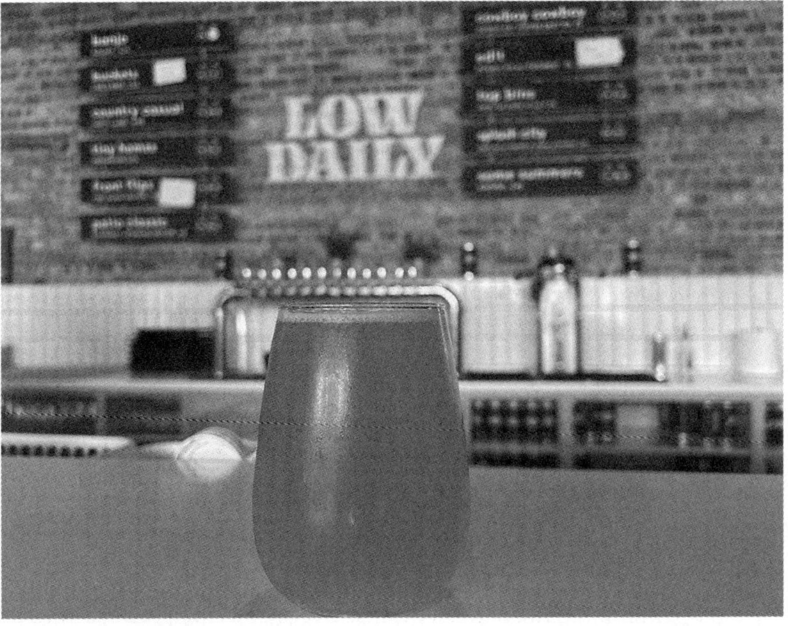

Low Daily, Burlington

Located in a former Milwaukee Electric Railway & Light Co. depot, **Low Daily** is the city's newest brewery (though it's only a few months younger than its nearby competitor). The old ticket counter and waiting room is now the taproom, and the brewhouse stands in what was once an open-air area through which trolleys would pass. The brewery's large outdoor patio is located where the boarding platform once was. The taproom carries a selection of lagers, IPAs, saisons, and stouts, plus some seltzers. If you're feeling peckish, there's a small selection of snacks (think meat, cheese, crackers, and popcorn) and food trucks on occasion.

Just a couple of blocks away is **The Runaway Micropub & Nanobrewery**. At the time of its opening, the single-room space was the first brewery in more than sixty-five years in Burlington. With a small-batch focus, The Runaway has an ever-changing lineup of brews (and some guest taps), including ales, seltzers, and IPAs. It also has a rotating food menu that relies on locally sourced ingredients. Featured items include a cheddar sausage from East Troy's Hometown Sausage Kitchen and a creamy mac and cheese. The taproom, which has a small indoor seating area and outdoor patio, has live music on Saturdays.

From the center of Burlington, head due west then straight north to the town of East Troy. Right on the downtown square is **East Troy Brewery**. Located in what was once a bank (take a walk around the vault before you leave, where mug club members can store mugs in their very own safety deposit box!), the brewpub has a large menu, including two cheese-centric snacks: a soft pretzel with beer cheese and fried cheese

Pit Stop

Each May, East Troy holds its annual Brewfest, spotlighting dozens of craft beers from area breweries. It is traditionally held in conjunction with the East Troy Area Chamber of Commerce three-day Corn & Brat Roast, where you can enjoy Hometown Sausage Kitchen brats and live entertainment. The event also includes a home-brew competition and samples. Tickets can be purchased in advance or at the door (for a slight upcharge), and each ticket includes tasting samples and a souvenir glass.

East Troy Brewery, East Troy

curds from Hill Valley. The latter comes with a curry tomato ketchup that perfectly balances the creaminess of the curds. Both the large indoor taproom and outside patio fill up quickly on the weekends, so you may find yourself waiting. But the food and the beers—including stouts, wheats, lagers, ales, and IPAs—are worth the time.

At nearby **Hometown Sausage Kitchen**, two chefs are making fresh, small-batch artisan sausages with locally procured ingredients and meat raised by local farmers. The store carries traditional brat flavors ready for your next cookout, but if you're looking to be a bit more adventurous, get a pack of the spicy Thai, chili dog, Hungarian, or breakfast brat with just a hint of maple to complement your morning meal. Or opt for the best-selling Packer brat, stuffed with bacon, cheddar, and spinach.

Now, it's time to wend your way up Highway 43 toward Milwaukee, where you could easily spend a month or more touring all the restaurants serving up the best brats and cheese, not to mention the breweries and taprooms. For decades, Milwaukee was the epicenter of brewing

Detour

Whether you're in East Troy to visit the East Troy Brewery or heading to Brewfest, plan a stop at The Hive Taproom just west of the downtown core. The Hive has more than a dozen session meads on tap, all made from local raw honey. The knowledgeable staff behind the bar can help you find a mead that suits your preferences, whether you're typically a beer, wine, cocktail, or mocktail drinker. The team bringing their smooth and not-overly-sweet mead to southeastern Wisconsin is a husband-wife pair. He is the brewer and she is the beekeeper.

in Wisconsin, and to some degree, it still is today. Immigrants from Europe and the eastern United States moved to the area—with beer knowledge and, sometimes, equipment in tow—because it was easy to reach. With access to inland fresh water, shipping ports, and rail hubs, they used their brewing expertise to create a solid product and distribute it throughout the Midwest and, eventually, around the country. Whether or not you're a beer drinker, names like Pabst, Miller, Schlitz, and Blatz probably ring a bell.

These days, Miller is the only one of the brewing powerhouses of the past to continue making its beer in Milwaukee. Blatz was the first to bow out in 1959, followed by Schlitz, which closed its Milwaukee operations in 1981 and is now brewed by Pabst. Pabst stuck around until 2020, when it moved its base to San Antonio. However, you can still visit some of the historic Pabst brewery's buildings, tour the Pabst mansion, and even stay in the Brewhouse Inn & Suites, a boutique hotel housed in the original Pabst plant. Or, if you're looking for something a little spookier, you can see the final resting place of many members of the Pabst family, along with other early beer barons, at the Forest Home Cemetery on Milwaukee's South Side. In fact, the cemetery can organize a private beer barons tour if you're so inclined.

Pit Stop

Milwaukee County Parks operates one traveling and six permanent beer gardens. If you visit in summer, take a look at the county parks website to see where and when you can sample a local beer in the fresh air.

With the brewing giants gone, Milwaukee's beer scene is now largely dominated by craft brewers, including **Sprecher Brewing Co.**, Milwaukee's oldest craft brewery and one of the few in the United States using a fire-brewing method. Founder Randy Sprecher first fell in love with German beers while serving in Germany during the Vietnam War. On his return to the United States, he studied fermentation science at the University of California at Davis, before taking a position as supervisor of brewing operations with Pabst. In the mid-1980s, Sprecher decided to open his own brewery and built a lot of the equipment by hand with friends. In addition to its lineup of lagers, IPAs, and ales, Sprecher makes root beer (with Wisconsin honey) that was named by the *New York Times* as the best in the country. The brewery was among the first to make alcoholic pops, and today has various flavors in that line. Sprecher has a taproom where you can try a flight, sip a full pint, fill a growler, and nosh on some local snacks. You can also watch the brewing operation from the indoor beer garden, or, if you have the time, take a tour.

Pit Stop

Every weekend in September and the first weekend in October, Bavarian Bierhaus hosts Oktoberfest in Milwaukee's Heidelberg Park. For more than sixty years, locals and travelers have flocked to the family-friendly event to sip German beers, sample delicious foods (including cheese-stuffed pierogi, bier cheese fries, and cheese curds), and try their hand at the midway games. Event organizers recommend securing tickets and table reservations online early, because the event frequently sells out.

Head next to **Gathering Place Brewing Company**, located in Milwaukee's Riverwest neighborhood. The owners set out to create a community-centric brewery, which is reflected in the name that comes from the Native Potawatomi word "Milwaukee" meaning "gathering place by the waters." The intimate taproom is the perfect place to meet old friends or make new ones while you sample the year-round, seasonal, and specialty brews. You'll find primarily European-style beers with a local flair, and even those crafted with Wisconsin ingredients, such as the Limb Shaker, a Belgian-style tripel brewed with cherries from Door County.

One block south is **Amorphic Beer**, a great stop for any science nerd (said with complete affection; the brewery offers beer science tours once a month and nerd bingo every Thursday). Most of Amorphic's beers have an ABV above 6 percent, and you can expect hoppy brews, lagers, and some sours on the menu. Both Gathering Place and Amorphic Beer often have food trucks on-site if you need a bite.

WisconsInsights

As of 2022, Wisconsin ranks thirteenth in craft breweries per capita in the United States, but seventh in craft beer production per adult, pumping out 7.6 gallons per person of legal drinking age in the state.

In the Riverwest neighborhood are two other breweries, each offering a slightly different atmosphere and beverage lineup. If you're hungry, **Company Brewing** is a solid pick. This brewery and restaurant has a wide-ranging menu that includes burgers, a Friday fish fry, and even vegan- and vegetarian-friendly options. The cheesiest option on the menu is the Popper Grilled Cheese, which showcases two Wisconsin cheeses: Widmer's brick cheese and Sartori's parmesan frico. Most of the sandwich's other ingredients are local as well. Company is also slinging fried cheese curds, made from local Silver & Lewis cheese and served with a side of house-made ranch. If you happen in on a Saturday or

Sunday before 3 p.m., brunch is offered (specials are often full of local cheese). Of course, Company also has its own brews. Lighter lagers and pilsners are poured alongside many fruity goses, hoppy IPAs and double IPAs, and strong imperial stouts and porters. Company has a music venue on-site, and any time there's a show, it's open until 2 a.m.

If you're instead on the hunt for a strong brew, stop by **Black Husky Brewing**. Most of its beers—from a few pale ales to a double IPA to the seasonal lineup—have an ABV well above 6 percent. Each beer brewed here is associated with one of the dogs in the cofounders' son's sled dog kennel. For example, there's Vain, a pale ale with citra hops, that honors Shad, a dog that ran the Iditarod sled race and can be a bit arrogant. Since they started brewing in a small log cabin in the Northwoods in 2010, the cofounders have tried to keep things small and simple. They still deliver their own brews around town and even bottle by hand. As you may have guessed, Black Husky is dog friendly, both in the taproom and on the patio. While the brewery doesn't have its own kitchen, it does offer delivery from a local restaurant as well as some snacks (think popcorn and chips). Pro tip: if you're heading to Black Husky on a Friday, wear flannel and you'll get one dollar off per pint.

Continue traveling south into the Brewer's Hill neighborhood, home of **Lakefront Brewery**. The owners, a pair of brothers, got their start home brewing beer, attempting to one-up each other with a tastier beverage. Today they sell their products to the public in an early twentieth-century

Detour

Want to get out and stretch your legs? Hop on Milwaukee's Beerline trail, so named because many of the city's biggest breweries were built nearby. The trail runs north to south along the western side of the Milwaukee River for 3.7 miles. Its southern edge is near the Milwaukee Riverwalk, from which you can reach the downtown location of The Tap Yard, a summer beer garden that sets up in Schlitz Park. The summer gathering spot has twenty-four craft beers on tap, live music, games, and food trucks.

building that once housed the Milwaukee Electric Railway & Light Company's coal-fired power plant. Lakefront's beer hall has multiple unique chandeliers that at one time hung in a space intended to be the Plankinton Hotel's beer hall. According to Lakefront, no beer hall was ever opened on the site because the hotel broke ground on the day World War I started, then Prohibition followed. The fixtures hung in the hotel's restaurant until the city took ownership of them before the hotel was destroyed. Lakefront's owners eventually reached a deal with Milwaukee to purchase and restore them. In addition to its touchpoints with Milwaukee history, the brewery is responsible for firsts in the beer industry. It created the first beer in the country to be brewed entirely from ingredients grown in state (including yeast), was the first certified organic brewery, and made the first government-certified gluten-free beer. Lakefront was also one of the first breweries in the country since Prohibition to produce a pumpkin beer (you can still try it today, from August through

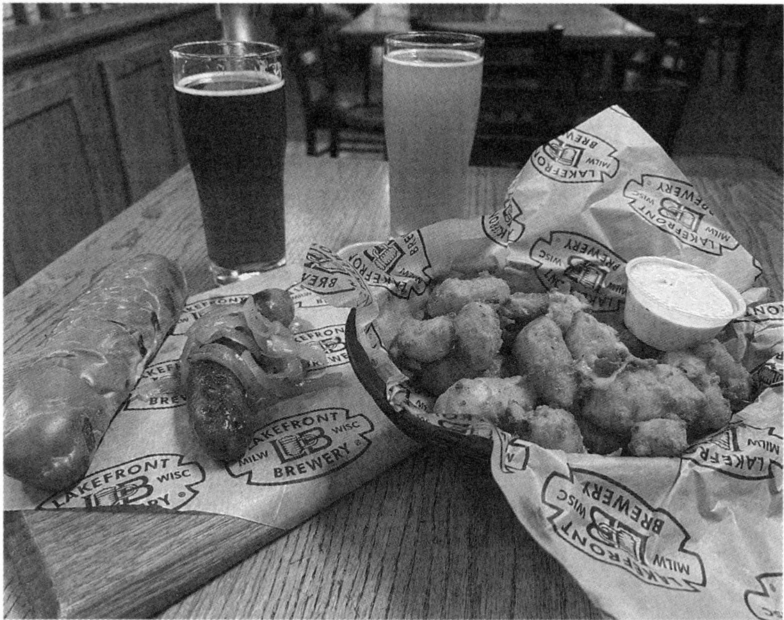

Lakefront Brewery, Milwaukee

October). In fact, it's one of the few pumpkin lagers available in the world. It's easy to understand why tens of thousands of visitors flock to Lakefront every year. If you're one of them, consider a tour (offering samples before and during the tour), then pop into the beer hall for dinner. The beer-battered fried cheese curds are the perfect accompaniment to the sausage flight. Three different locally made sausages are available (a brat, hot dog, and kielbasa), and you can pick as many as you like (each sausage is priced individually). On Thursdays, Lakefront has a Curd of the Day, and on Friday, Saturday, and Sunday (weather permitting), the Curdwagon is out on the patio, cooking fried cheese curds and beer brats. Try stopping by the weekend Curdwagon for a basket of fried cheese curds "Milwaukee Style," topped with a beer reduction, sauerkraut, Polish mustard, shredded cheddar, and deep-fried brat crumble.

Almost directly east from Lakefront (but on the other side of the river) is **Eagle Park Brewing and Distilling Company**. Located on Milwaukee's Lower East Side (with a second location in Muskego), Eagle Park is housed in a 1920 Cream City brick building that was once the garage for a tannery. Here the star is the cheese curds, a half pound of lightly battered and fried Wisconsin curds, served with a choice of sauce (pro tip: the garlic aioli really makes these curds sing). The full menu also has a gooey grilled cheese and a Smashburger, plus giant Milwaukee Pretzel Company pretzel sticks served with beer cheese. Looking for something to wash it down? Eagle Park has an extensive beer list, offered as flights along with full and half pours. Its focus is on IPAs, but you can find plenty of other styles too. Notably, in mid-2022, Eagle Park acquired the popular (but closing) Milwaukee Brewing Company's intellectual property, branding, and recipes. While you can no longer visit Milwaukee Brewing Company's brewery or taphouse, you can try many of its most popular beers, including Outboard Cream Ale and Louie's Demise (a red ale), at Eagle Park.

Wend your way back across the river to **Milwaukee Brat House**'s downtown location (there's also a restaurant in Shorewood). Here you can sample Usinger's Famous Sausage. For 140 years, the Usinger family has been making truckloads of all types of sausage at its nearby factory.

Eagle Park Brewing and Distilling Company, Milwaukee

The Brat House carries Usinger's brats, Italian sausage, and Polish sausage. Enjoy your brat topped with Wisconsin cheddar, jalapeños, and bacon; go classic with sautéed onions and fresh sauerkraut; or choose the Farwell, loaded with sautéed onions, roasted poblano peppers, diced bacon, pesto, and melted gouda. The brat also comes as a patty. There's a sausage sampler if you can't decide, and, of course, there's a basket of fried Wisconsin cheese curds with a side of ranch.

Still hungry? Grab a quick bite at **3rd Street Market Hall**, which has been welcoming visitors since October 2021 to sample some of the city's eclectic cuisine. There are myriad vendors, offering everything from beer, soups, and tortas, to arepas, ramen, and acai bowls. Multiple stalls take advantage of Wisconsin's wide selection of cheese to round out the menu, and you can imbibe at a self-tap beer wall with two dozen local options to try.

WisconsInsights

Milwaukee-based Usinger's made the hot dogs for the 2002 Winter Olympics.

The next few locations will keep you primarily south of I-94. Start off at **Wizard Works Brewing**, which has magic-inspired beers, brewed by a performing magician. Easy drinkers are the name of the game here, including a blonde ale, Czech pilsner, and Irish red ale, with an IPA, English strong ale, and porter available for good measure. If you're struggling to decide which beer to pick, you can quite literally roll the dice. Should you arrive at this cozy space in Milwaukee's Third Ward at the right time, the owner might be around to do some magic tricks or read your mind.

If baseball is your favorite pastime, visit **Broken Bat Brewing Co.** This small taproom serves baseball-themed beers, including Harry Cherry, a cherry hefeweizen, and Batter's Rye, a rye IPA. In summer, Broken Bat runs its Concession Stand Series, fruity sours with flavors reminiscent of ballpark snacks, such as super ropes and lemon ice. If you're with a group, consider booking the brewery's indoor Wiffle ball field. For $160 an hour, twenty people can take the field, or just enjoy a Broken Bat beer while cheering from the benches.

Head next to **Indeed Brewing Company**. Indeed was born in Minneapolis but established a taproom and pilot brewery in Milwaukee, where it carries its regular lineup of beers as well as some brews you can find only in Wisconsin. The vibe is wonderfully eclectic, dogs are welcome in the attached patio, and light snacks are available (or you can bring in

WisconsInsights

Each year, Wisconsin's dairy industry generates $45.6 billion. That's more than the value of Florida citrus and Idaho potatoes combined.

your own food). Most of the beers (except those with honey) are vegan friendly, and Indeed even offers a gluten-free hard kombucha. As for the beer, there are many easy-drinking, low ABV offerings, including a pistachio cream ale, Italian-style pilsner, American light lager, and a Mexican honey light lager. Malt- and hop-forward brews are available for those seeking a stronger beverage.

Located right off I-94, **Third Space Brewing** has a large indoor/outdoor taproom where you can enjoy the weather, watch the trains pass, play a board game, or catch the brew operation in action. Since being named one of the fifty fastest-growing craft breweries in the United States in 2018, Third Space has won multiple awards for its ales and IPAs. With year-round beers and seasonal and special releases, it's easy for everyone to find something to enjoy. Third Space has some snacks available for purchase and also has a Peruvian food truck on-site Tuesday through Sunday. If you're looking for entertainment, Third Space regularly holds

Indeed Brewing Company, Milwaukee

events, including yoga, live music, and craft workshops. Once a month, the brewmaster leads a beer school, offering participants the chance to learn about different beer styles while sampling corresponding brews (pro tip: beer school books up more than a month in advance, so make your plans early). Wondering where the name comes from? The owners first met at summer camp, which they called their "third space."

WisconsInsights

As of 2022, the five biggest breweries in Wisconsin, by barrels of beer produced within the state, were Miller and Leinenkugel's producer Molson Coors, 6.4 million barrels; New Glarus Brewing Company, 233,947; Minhas Craft Brewery, 162,278; Octopi, 160,000; and Stevens Point Brewery, 150,000.

Nearby at **City Lights Brewing Co.** you'll find yourself in a historic coal gasification plant where the locals punch in on a vintage timecard machine (the person with the most hours at the bar gets a prize). The owners maintained much of the industrial charm of the building, including a crane that dates back to 1899 and now secures the milled grain. City Lights' award-winning lineup includes a hazy IPA, coconut porter, and Mexican lager that are available year-round, as well as some seasonal and special release offerings, such as an Irish red ale, stout, and Oktoberfest lager. Hungry? Go for the cheese curds, smoked gouda mac and cheese bites, or the Pritzlaff brat, served with mustard, onions, and sauerkraut. If you're on your way to a Brewers game, City Lights is a great stop beforehand, and even offers a shuttle to American Family Field.

Leaving the Milwaukee city limits and venturing into Wauwatosa, stop at **Big Head Brewing Co.** Choose a beer (the blonde ale, hazy IPA, and raspberry cream ale are some of the most popular) and get ready for some friendly competition. Cornhole, pinball, giant Jenga, shuffleboard, darts, and more are available. And if it's Wednesday, it's trivia night. When you're feeling hungry, you can order a cheesy pizza or get delivery

City Lights Brewing Co., Milwaukee

from any number of local restaurants. If you happen to be traveling with your kids (furry or otherwise), Big Head is both child and dog friendly.

Just up the street from Big Head Brewing Co. is **Outpost Natural Foods**'s Wauwatosa location (Outpost also has one store in Mequon and two in Milwaukee). The company is committed to sourcing organic, local, and fair-trade products, and local in Wisconsin = cheese. One of Outpost's producers is Cesar's Cheese, located in Sheboygan Falls. While you can't visit Cesar's headquarters, you can pick up some of its award-winning Hispanic-style cheese at Outpost. If it's your style, go for the queso oaxaca, a hand-stretched string cheese that won best of class, second award, and third award in the string cheese category at the 2023 US Championship Cheese Contest.

If you don't find the Wisconsin cheeses you're looking for at Outpost, try **The Village Cheese Shop**, a mere two minutes away. Owner Sabrina

Magyar handpicks the best of Wisconsin, midwestern, and European cheeses to stock her Wauwatosa store. Each cheese you select is cut and wrapped on the spot, and if you come on a Saturday, you can try the fresh mozzarella. For something a bit more substantial, a small menu of sandwiches, salads, and cheese boards is available. Pro tip: the store is closed on Sunday and Monday.

Pit Stop

If you find yourself in Milwaukee during baseball season, a visit to American Family Field is in order. The home of the Milwaukee Brewers, affectionately referred to as the Brew Crew, offers not only hours of entertainment (including racing sausages) but also fantastic beer, brat, and cheese options.

You can opt to buy a ticket for the game with seating at the stadium's J. Leinenkugel's Barrel Yard (note: the restaurant is also open on non–game days), which has a menu inspired by the Northwoods. Past entrées have included a wurst platter and four-cheese baked macaroni. The restaurant also has fried cheese curds with peppers, sour cream, and onion aioli; a soft pretzel duo with beer cheese; a Wisconsin meat and cheese board; and a beer cheese soup. As expected, Barrel Yard has an extensive list of Leinie's beers on tap, plus some that are brewed in a pilot brewery at American Family Field and available only on-site.

If you select stadium seating, there is a plethora of Wisconsin offerings to tickle your tastebuds. Local brands abound, and food options include Johnsonville brats, fried cheese curds, and a sandwich called the Dog 'n' Brat Show that has brat strips, sauerkraut, spicy mustard, and cheese sauce. Pro tip: using the MLB Ballpark app, you can locate beer, brats, and cheese curds in the section nearest to your seat. Another pro tip: you'll likely get a more authentic Wisconsin brat experience at a stadium parking lot tailgate than inside the stadium.

Whether you need a quick pick-me-up or a beer, travel northeast to **Vennture Brew Co.**, a hybrid brewery, coffee roaster, taphouse, and café. Vennture's beers are available both in cans and on tap, and multiple brews are a twist on sweet treats, such as a barrel-aged imperial stout that tastes like crullers, a pastry stout that mimics a pączki, and an imperial oat ale meant to remind you of Fruity Pebbles. Free Wi-Fi makes Vennture a popular place for people to come for a morning coffee and stay into the afternoon and evening for an adult beverage. An interesting fact about the company name: the owners chose *venn*, as in Venn diagram, to start the moniker, where one circle is the coffee, another the beer, and the intersection is the community the owners sought to create, envisioning a place that crossed the atmosphere of a cozy coffee shop with a friendly neighborhood bartender.

WisconsInsights

According to the National Hot Dog and Sausage Council, American Family Field is the only stadium in Major League Baseball where sausages outsell hot dogs.

The next stop of the day is for brats. Whether you need a quick bite or a pack of brats to take home, **Bunzel's Meat Market** won't disappoint. The daily deli menu features a homemade brat (pro tip: the deli is closed every Sunday), while the fresh and frozen brat packs include such options as kraut and onion, beef, jalapeño cheddar, and honey mustard. The market also has a large bakery, produce, and grocery selection so you can pick up whatever you need before you hit the road again.

For another brat option, just down West Burleigh Street is Wauwatosa's **Good City Brewing** (locations also in Mequon, downtown Milwaukee's Deer District, and Milwaukee's East Side) delivering all the Wisconsin favorites. Start your meal with some deep-fried cheese curds, before tucking into the double brat burger. With two brat patties, American cheese, ale mustard, and sport pepper relish, you won't be leaving hungry. Not feeling meaty? Go for the mac and cheese, with a beer cheese sauce

Good City Brewing, Wauwatosa

made from Good City's pilsner and local Deer Creek aged white cheddar. Good City also has a wide-ranging beer list, seltzers, and various nonalcoholic options. Pro tip: not all locations have the same menu, so if you're after something specific, be sure to check in advance.

Hop back in the car and head south, past the Wisconsin State Fairgrounds, over to **Ope! Brewing Co.** in Milwaukee's near western suburb of West Allis. A newcomer to the local beer scene, Ope! has a tap list featuring beers with regular availability, plus seasonal and experimental offerings. Just as the brewery's name reflects an often-used midwestern word (*ope* = *excuse me* or *sorry*!) the beer names here are a similar play on cheesehead lexicon: Jeet Yet?, an oatmeal stout, and Let Me Sneak Past Ya, a hazy IPA, are just two examples. While Ope! doesn't have a kitchen, food trucks are often available. If it's summer, sit inside or outside and enjoy the laid-back, family- and dog-friendly vibe.

If you're local or have the equipment to cook your own dinner, stop next at **Becher Meats** butcher shop. While the brats aren't ready to eat, you can pick them up fresh or frozen to take home and prep to your liking. If brats truly aren't your style, Becher has various cuts of meat and some local sauces for flavoring.

WisconsInsights

Wisconsin's cheeses have won more than seventy-three hundred awards as of 2023, more than any other state or country.

While you're in the neighborhood, walk across the street to **West Allis Cheese and Sausage Shop**. The Wisconsin fries, topped with a brat, caramelized onions, and cheese sauce, are a must-have (and a great accompaniment to the Becher Meats brat served on a pretzel bun). If you haven't quite met your daily cheese quota, fried cheese curds and Wisconsin cheese soup are also on the menu. Once you've had your fill, you can pop into the shop, which sells a wide variety of Wisconsin cheeses and other local snacks (including Steinke's Gourmet Wisconsin beer cheese popcorn—a great car snack, as long as you brought napkins!).

From West Allis, start working your way west toward Waukesha. On the way, ask yourself, What do you get when you combine two doctors, a professional cyclist, and a local entrepreneur? Answer: the family-friendly, dog-friendly (on the patio at least) **Raised Grain Brewing Company**. Limited releases and seasonal brews join a lengthy list of pale ales, pilsners, and IPAs with year-round availability. Pro tip: many of the options are on the higher end of the ABV scale for their style. If beer isn't your thing, the brewery has taps with its own line of hard seltzer. When the weather is nice, relax on the patio and order via the QR code at your table. If you're hungry, Raised Grain has house-made food, including beer cheese nachos and the Brewmaster Mac & Cheese pizza, covered with cheddar, candied bacon, parmesan Béchamel sauce, parmesan, hot sauce, and, of course, macaroni!

About fifteen minutes away is the small city of Delafield, found within the Kettle Moraine, an area of southeastern Wisconsin created more than ten thousand years ago when two lobes of glacial ice collided. As the sediment receded, it left behind lakes, wetlands, valleys, and hills that make up a scenic landscape perfect for outdoor recreation. On the outskirts of the city's charming downtown is **Delafield Brewhaus**, a restaurant, brewery, and banquet facility. Delafield was one of the first brewpubs in the state to craft a purpose-built location for the business. The food menu consists of cheese curds with a pale ale beer batter served with ranch dipping sauce, a house-made beer cheese soup, a Wisconsin grilled cheese, mac and cheese, and a mac and cheese pizza topped with bacon crumbles. You can also try out the sausage platter, where weisswurst and ring bologna join a brat. Kids can partake in the cheese fest, too, with a kids' mac and cheese or quesadilla. As the name implies, this is also a great stop for beer. Delafield Brewhaus's five beers with year-round availability include a kölsch, wheat beer, pale ale, amber ale, and porter. Delafield also brews up a handful of seasonal beers, including a warm weather favorite, Bomb Pop, a blue-tinged malt beverage that tastes like summer in a glass.

WisconsInsights

Brats have been served at the Brewers' home games since 1953, back when they were the Milwaukee Braves.

Travel a few miles northwest to Oconomowoc, where the first barrel of beer made in the city limits was sold in 1868 by City Brewery. Nowadays, you can tuck into some beer and food at the veteran-owned **SteelTank Brewing Co.** Before ever opening their doors to the public, SteelTank's owners, a pair of engineers, were distributing wholesale beer they contract-brewed in Waukesha County. When a one-time Harley-Davidson dealership became available, the owners jumped on the chance to bring their beer to the masses. The taproom's orange-and-black color scheme harkens back to its past life (as does the former parts counter that serves as the bar), while each of the brews honors the military background of the owners. These military-inspired names include Hop 2-3-4, an American IPA; Special 'H'ops, a hazy IPA; and Tracer Rounds, a red ale. One of the stars here is the food. Try out the Howitzer, a flight of beer cheese served with herbed pretzel crostini. Or go for the more traditional Wisconsin cheese curds, a giant soft pretzel with beer cheese for dipping, or a poutine covered with fresh curds. Be sure to save room for one of SteelTank's brats: The Narco Tank is covered in a chili-chorizo beer cheese, while the M-4 Sherman comes topped with sliced corned beef, swiss cheese, sauerkraut, and Thousand Island dressing.

Staying in Oconomowoc, stop by **Brewfinity Brewing Company**, formerly named Sweet Mullets Brewing Co. (after the founder's hair style in the 1980s). Brewfinity's taps have a good mix of light lagers, hoppy IPAs, and heavier porters and stouts. The Killin' Me S'mores, an easy-drinking

SteelTank Brewing Co., Oconomowoc

porter with chocolate, marshmallow, and graham flavors, won the silver medal at the 2020 US Beer Open. Looking to the food menu, you have a wide cheese selection, with mac and cheese bites, a crispy, gooey delight served with a side of ranch, or some beer-battered mozzarella sticks. (Pro tip: build your own pizzas are available on Fridays, but only until the toppings run out.) When visiting on a summer Sunday, take advantage of the brewery tours. For ten dollars you can learn about the brew operation and sample assorted beers. Be sure to check the brewery's website before your summertime visit to find out whether Brewfinity is set up at the local traveling beer garden, Pints in the Park.

Continuing northwest along Highway 16, you'll reach the city of Watertown. **Kraemer Wisconsin Cheese** began as a dairy business in the 1920s, and by the 1970s became a dairy store selling some of the state's best varieties of cheese and sausage. Today the shop has many cheese styles from around the state as well as Kraemer originals, including thirteen varieties of cheese spreads made in small forty-pound batches to ensure the highest quality product. On Wednesdays and Fridays, you can stop in for a grilled cheese and a milkshake.

The final leg of the southeastern Wisconsin road trip takes you toward Madison along one of two different routes. If you head north from Watertown, you'll reach the town of Theresa, where you can watch the cheesemaking process in action at **Widmer's Cheese Cellars** from 7:00 a.m. to 11:30 a.m. on weekdays, or catch the informative video if you come another day or time. In the nearby retail area, treat yourself to some samples of Widmer's cheeses (it specializes in brick, cheddar,

WisconsInsights

The first Wisconsin state fair was held in 1851 and featured seven cheesemakers. The modern-day fair receives upward of three hundred individual entries annually for its dairy products contest, in which contestants compete in more than forty classes to see who has the best cheese, sour cream, butter, yogurt, and milk.

and colby) or pepper the staff with all of your burning cheesemaking questions. The plant, adorned in Swiss district flags, has been keeping locals well fed since 1922 and today is in its third generation of family ownership. Under the direction of Master Cheesemaker Joe Widmer, the cheese is still made the old-fashioned way, where carefully tended curds are hand scooped into forms before the whey is pressed out.

Next, travel toward Beaver Dam, home of **Ooga Brewing Company**. The business is located on the site of a former used-car lot and auto shop, which gave the owners the idea to name the business after the noise an old-time car horn makes (*ah-oo-gah*). The taproom is low-key, and the brewers are focused on illuminating the best of Wisconsin, with locally sourced ingredients and equipment, collaborative brews with nearby businesses, and rotating guest beers from in-state breweries. On tap you'll find the 2022 World Beer Cup gold medal winning Holla!, a spin on a classic cream ale infused with fresh jalapeños. With a small-batch operation, the taps are always changing, but you might find IPAs, wheats, and kölsches.

Now, traveling southwest down Highway 151 you'll come to **Cercis Brewing Company** in Columbus. Surrounded by unique local shops and historic landmarks, Cercis has been brewing IPAs, ales, and porters since 2018. If you need something cheesy, Cercis has you covered, whether you want nachos, a cheese board, or even just chips and cheese. For something a bit more substantial, check out the Wisconsin Artisan Grilled Cheese, a sandwich smothered with sharp cheddar, aged brick cheese, grilled seasoned mushrooms, and white onions.

About thirty minutes north of Madison is **Sassy Cow Creamery**. All of the milk used by the creamery to craft its different cheese products comes from the cows on its two adjacent farms. At the store, you can buy milk, ice cream, and try out Sassy Cow's grilled cheese sandwiches, each of which comes with a side and chocolate or white milk. A number of traditional and signature grilled cheeses are on the menu, including the chicken, bacon, ranch, and a triple cheese with Sassy Cow cheddar, havarti, and muenster. In summer, you can take a farm tour Thursday, Friday, and every other Saturday, so long as you book online in advance. Each thirty-minute tour includes a pint of milk.

If you instead choose to head south from Watertown, you'll stop first at **Tyranena Brewing Company**, the social hub of Lake Mills. Tyranena made a name for itself both within and outside the state when its brewers focused on aggressively hopped beers in the early 2000s, as opposed to other craft brewers at the time who were making lighter beers they thought had wider appeal. Tyranena's best known beer, Bitter Woman IPA, is indicative of that hop-forward taste. The other flagship beers, including Chief BlackHawk Porter and Mangy Fox Copper Ale, pay tribute to the Native people who inhabited the Lake Mills area centuries ago as well as its present-day community happenings. The brewery has an indoor taproom and a large outdoor beer garden, with frequent live music and food trucks. Pro tip: If you want to bring your four-legged friend to the brewery, be sure to call ahead and get permission from the staff. Tyranena has a strict pet policy and, based on the crowd or event occurring on the day of your visit, may not allow your dog to accompany you.

WisconsInsights

A whopping 48 percent of all US specialty cheese is made in Wisconsin.

Not far from Tyranena is **Sunshine Brewing Company**, where the cheese comes in the form of Mexican food. Tacos, burritos, nachos, and quesadillas dominate the menu and serve as a complement to the fruit-forward blonde ale, hard seltzer, and Dutch kuyt. Those searching for something a little heavier can look to the Belgian tripel and stout.

Whether you chose the northern or southern route, you'll wind up at **Full Mile Beer Company & Kitchen** in Sun Prairie. Cheese and brats are both on the menu, and you might have a tough time choosing your meal with the delicious scents wafting throughout the space. Choose from a beer cheese soup, wurst platter, cream ale–battered Ellsworth Creamery cheese curds, or any one of the wood-fired pizzas. The comfort food leaving the kitchen pairs well with the small-batch beers that

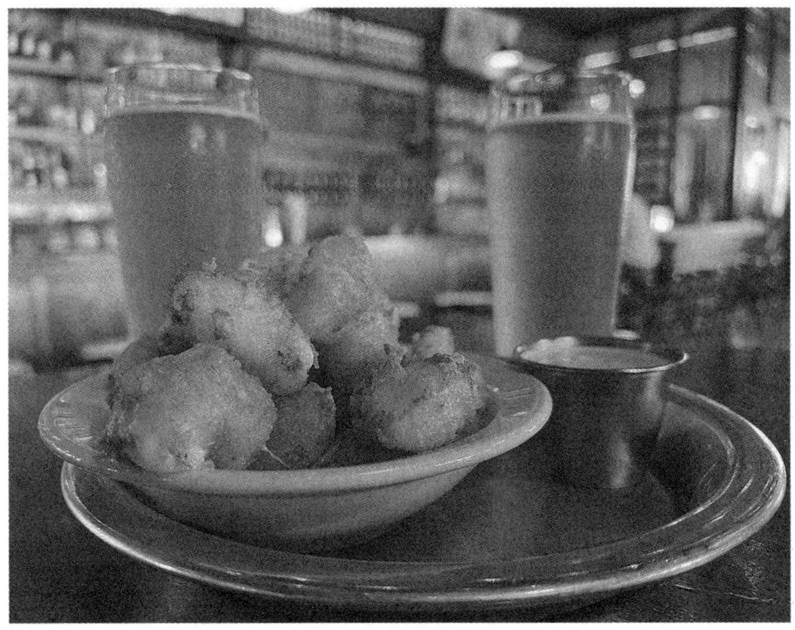

Full Mile Beer Company & Kitchen, Sun Prairie

run the gamut from light cream ales to heavy dark lagers. Full Mile also has house-made seltzers and a local bottled cider and gluten-free beer. If you're passing through on a Thursday or Saturday, chances are you'll catch some live music. Full Mile brings in acts to please everyone's tastes, from bluegrass to rock to polka to country and everything in between.

CHAPTER 2

Madison and South Central Wisconsin

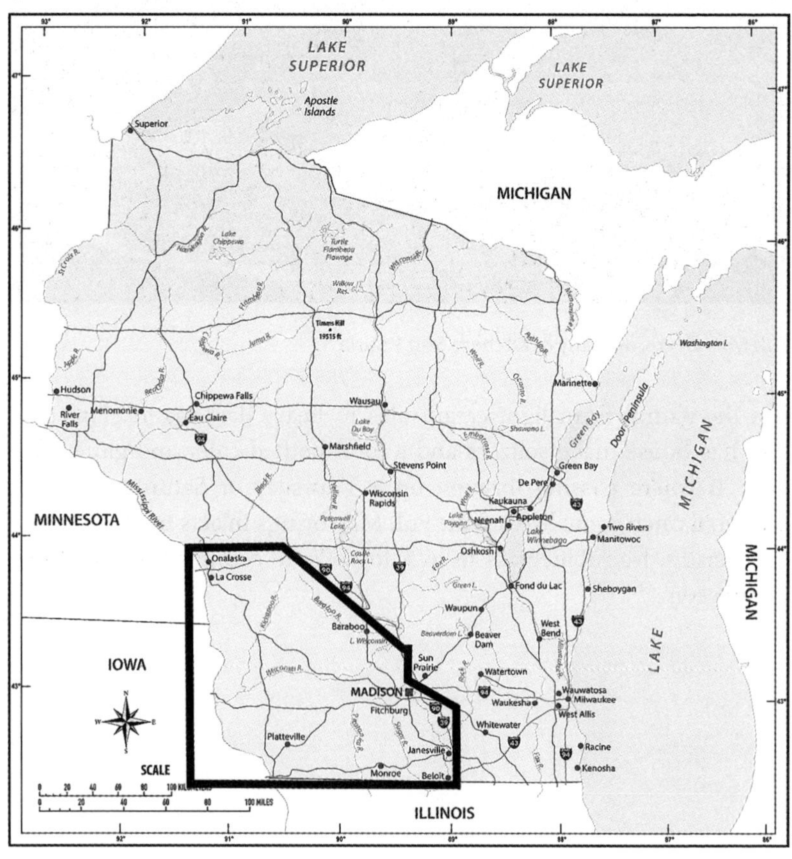

The boxed region indicates the approximate Madison and south central Wisconsin area covered in this chapter.

If cheese is your reason for heading out on this road trip, you're in luck. Since before statehood, the southwestern and south central portions of Wisconsin have been dotted with dairy farms and creameries. Get ready to bite into some of the freshest, squeakiest curds, hold your nose for limburger, and wash it all down with a few brewskis.

~

Get things started at **Karben4**, a company that was once a fifteen-barrel draft-only start-up brewpub on Madison's East Side and today distributes its product to many parts of the state. It's almost the antithesis of a craft brewery that's trying to create a serious experience for the cultured, in-the-know beer aficionado. Instead, Karben4 is bringing fun into the taproom and beer, with brews named Midwesty (a pilsner), Threat Level: Midnight (a s'mores stout), and Stroop! There It Is! (a stroopwafel-flavored beer available in winter). The carefree atmosphere is accentuated by food truck popups, trivia, live music, and more.

Nearby, try **ALT Brew**, a 100 percent gluten-free nanobrewery. Whether you prefer a dry-hopped IPA or a smooth-drinking ale, ALT Brew delivers it all without using barley, wheat, or rye. Like many businesses, the brewery grew out of necessity. When brewmaster Trevor Easton's wife was diagnosed with a gluten intolerance, he wanted to maintain their shared love of sampling craft beers, just without any adverse reactions. Unhappy with what he found, Easton set out to make his own gluten-free beer.

Pit Stop

If it's Memorial Day weekend in Madison, it's time for Brat Fest, dubbed the world's largest bratwurst festival. The event has been in operation since 1983, and is facilitated by a nonprofit and powered by volunteer workers. Event staff "earn" ten dollars per hour, which is then donated to the charity of their choice. More than a hundred local charitable organizations benefit from Brat Fest funds. The event itself is free (and so are the concerts offered all weekend), but once you're in the gates, you can purchase brats, local beers, or an ice cream for dessert.

Karben4, Madison

And yes, even the equipment is used only for gluten-free production, so patrons don't have to worry about any traces of gluten showing up in the beer. ALT Brew's offerings range from farmhouse ale to porter to pumpkin to sours and just about anything else you can think of. Of the three dozen or so beers ALT Brew has developed so far, many are on tap and in cans or bottles at breweries and restaurants around Wisconsin, giving gluten-free customers a malty beverage option. The taproom is open only Thursday through Saturday, so be sure to check the website or social media pages before your visit to verify the hours. While ALT Brew doesn't have a kitchen, it does offer packaged gluten-free snacks. You'll have to ask the staff about ordering or bringing in any food, and if they give you the go-ahead, it must be gluten free.

For the chance to try multiple Wisconsin cheeses all in one store, stop by **Mousehouse Cheesehaus** in Windsor. The stock comes from Wisconsin creameries, and it's all available for sampling to help you choose

WisconsInsights

The terms *brewery, brewpub, taproom, craft brewery, microbrewery,* and *nanobrewery* are sometimes used interchangeably but actually have different definitions. Generally speaking, brewpubs are breweries with restaurants that sell around one-quarter of its beer on-site. Taprooms are like brewpubs but have far fewer food options. Breweries are huge operations that produce more than six million barrels of beer per year. Craft breweries produce no more than six million barrels of beer annually and must be independent, that is, less than 25 percent owned or controlled by a non–craft brewer. A microbrewery makes fifteen thousand barrels of beer or fewer per year, and three-quarters or more of that must be sold off-site. Nanobreweries are the smallest of the bunch and typically make beer in three-barrel batches or less.

exactly what you like. The offerings cover nearly every type of cheese imaginable, and some you've probably never even dreamed of (like a morel mushroom and leek monterey jack). If you need more than a snack, get a sandwich at the deli, then select a spot in front of the viewing windows to watch cheese being cut and wrapped (if you're lucky, you might even get to see Mousehouse's famous fudge being produced).

Nearby, in Waunakee, **Octopi** is a highly unique brewery in that it not only brews its own beer but also is a contract brewer, meaning that it makes beer for other big- and small-name breweries, plus grocery stores. In fact, it was opened primarily to contract-brew and is actually one of the largest breweries in the state. Contract brewing itself isn't all that unique, but the majority of contract brewers don't keep their spaces

WisconsInsights

Nearly 40 percent of all dairy companies in Wisconsin are multigenerational, and some go back as far as four generations.

open to the public. Now, you won't necessarily be able to try everything Octopi is brewing, nor will you know all the breweries it works with (due to confidentiality agreements). While you're in the taproom, you can try labels including Octopi, Untitled Art, and Dachs (German for *badger*). The in-house beers include a pilsner, juicy IPA, seltzer, stout, amber ale, session IPA, and some other varieties. Octopi also keeps pop and non-alcoholic beer in cans and bottles (plus juice boxes for the kids). The food is a huge draw here, and once you've walked into the taproom, you'll know why: the scent of the burgers, tacos, sandwiches, and sides (including fried cheese curds) will have your mouth watering.

Pit Stop

One of the newest Wisconsin events that celebrates cheese is Madison's Art of Cheese Festival. The three-day artisan cheese event includes tours in the Monroe and Driftless regions, a cheesemaking minicourse, pairing and cooking classes, brunch, yoga, a walking tour, and the Wisconsin Cheese Ball, where you can dance the night away while nibbling cheese samples. Event organizers hope to hold the festival every other year in late September/early October.

Hopefully you'll still have an appetite by the time you reach the next destination, a mere two miles away: **The Lone Girl Brewing Company**, a family-friendly brewpub with an amazing rooftop deck. Yes, Lone Girl has beer. But the food menu is an absolute symphony of cheesy good flavors. The restaurant is frying up cheese curbs (yes, with a *b*, muenster cheese curbs to be specific) in its own signature beer batter alongside cheese-stuffed meatballs, mac and cheese, and the "world famous" brewben, a sandwich featuring beer-braised corned beef, swiss cheese, beer mustard, sauerkraut, and caramelized onions. If that's not enough, Lone Girl also has a host of sandwiches and burgers, and even a cheesecake on the dessert menu that comes infused with its Towhead Belgian Blonde Ale. When it comes to beer, Lone Girl has around a dozen on tap, including an array of light, dark, hoppy, and smooth. From Friday to Sunday, Lone Girl often has a special event, like tableside family-friendly magic, local music acts, and bingo, plus a once-a-month meat raffle.

WisconsInsights

The crowler, a thirty-two-ounce aluminum can used to hold tap beer, wasn't introduced in Wisconsin (that distinction belongs to Colorado), but the cap-sealing machine that makes it all possible was created in Manitowoc at Wisconsin Aluminum Foundry.

Make your way from Lone Girl around the west side of Lake Mendota to the Madison suburb of Middleton. There, for more than three decades, **Capital Brewery** has been keeping Madisonians full of craft beer. From May to October, you can join the locals in Middleton's Backyard, as the brewery refers to its biergarten, for a Wisconsin Amber, Mutiny IPA, Special Pilsner, or any number of regular and seasonal beers. In winter, the drinking moves inside to the brewery's taproom. Capital Brewery holds the distinction of multiple firsts, including filling Wisconsin's first growler and brewing one of the first commercial beers using wild rice.

Continuing that circular route along the lake, head into downtown Madison. Across from the state capitol sits **Fromagination**, a cheesemonger founded in 2007 to showcase Wisconsin's artisan cheeses. Cheeses can be cut to order or selected prewrapped, and many are out around the store for sampling among the various local and Wisconsin-themed products. The store sells multiple raw milk cheeses, made with unpasteurized milk that must be aged for at least sixty days to be legally salable in the United States. The raw milk cheese available in store comes in a unique array of flavors and is produced mostly at small operations by Wisconsin cheesemakers. As the knowledgeable staff will tell you, this type of cheese is incredibly difficult to make because of the variation in flavor of the raw milk. If you have the time, feel free to ask

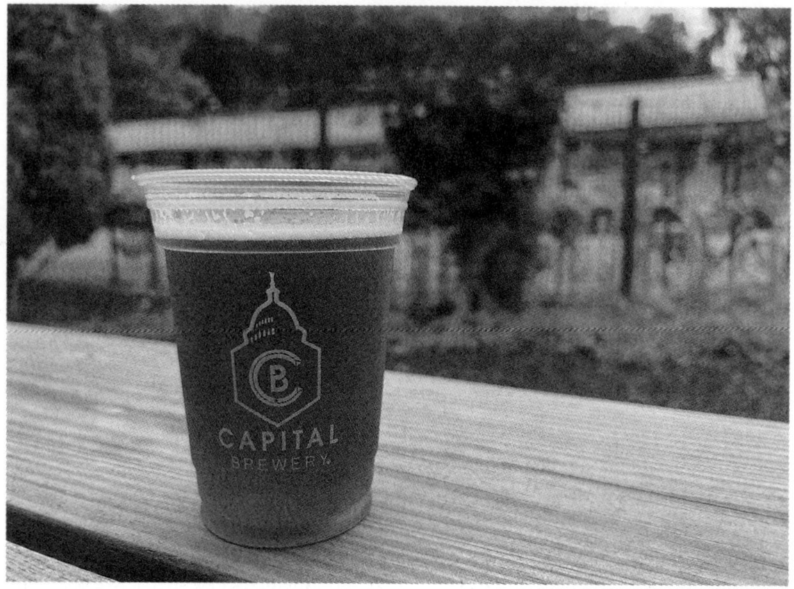

Capital Brewery, Middleton

the staff questions to find the perfect cheese for your palate. If you're short on time, visit Fromagination's website for videos and courses about cheese, pairings, and even creating the perfect cheese board.

Walk to the other side of the capitol complex to **Young Blood Beer Company** on King Street. If the weather is favorable, try out the patio (and feel free to bring your dog for some scratches and treats). Billing itself as "an oasis of life and leisure," there's a dozen or so beers to try, including everything from double and triple hazy IPAs, to multiple sours, and a pilsner. The menu doesn't strike the typical taproom chord. Instead, Young Blood has global offerings, such as a banh mi, barbacoa nachos, a halloumi cheese crunchwrap, elote hot dogs, and poutine topped with squeaky fresh cheese curds (available in both a personal and party size).

Work your way along East Main Street, between two of Madison's lakes, until you reach South Brearly Street, then hang a right. A pink door is your gateway to **Giant Jones Brewing**, a woman-owned business and the first certified organic craft brewery in Madison. The focus is on

Pit Stop

If you're in Madison on a Wednesday or Saturday, be sure to swing by the Dane County Farmers' Market, the largest producers-only farmers' market in the United States. Open year-round (pro tip: the location changes depending on the season, so check the website before you visit), it's a great place to sample some of Wisconsin's finest cheeses.

At the market, seek out Capri Cheese, a one-man micro-operation on a farm that was the first organically certified homestead goat dairy in the Midwest. The company grew out of necessity, when the owner started making goat's milk products because his son was extremely allergic to cow's milk. Today the farm produces goat and mixed milk cheeses, of which its fetas and gouda-style products are the most popular. Another booth is operated by Darlington's Brunkow Cheese, known for its Brun-uusto (its take on juusto, the Scandinavian baked cheese), and one of its varieties won Best of Class at the World Championship Cheese Contest. Keep an eye out for Hook's, a world champion cheesemaker that produces aged cheddars (including a fifteen-year aged cheddar); cow, goat, and sheep cheese; blue cheese; swiss; and gouda. In 1982, Hook's colby won Best in Class and the World Champion Award at the World Championship Cheese Contest. Producer Julie Hook is the only woman ever to win the World Champion Award for colby.

Other producers include Forgotten Valley Cheese, Bleu Mont Dairy, Murphy Farms, McCluskey Brothers, and Crème de la Coulée Artisan Cheese, all offering various forms of block and wedge cheese, curds, and spreads. The market has a waiting list one to two years long for new vendors, so you never know what else might show up when you visit.

strong, flavorful beers, so expect something a bit on the heavier side, like a stout with hints of dark chocolate and espresso or a double international pale ale with a malty, dry finish. In addition to the tap list, Giant Jones has bottles of its own beers and some other Wisconsin brands available in the cooler. Most days of the week, the taproom doesn't offer food on-site, but you're welcome to carry something in or have it delivered. On Wednesdays, however, you can take part in pizza night, a Giant Jones partnership with ORIGIN Breads, a Madison-area company known for its sourdough breads made primarily from grains grown and milled in Wisconsin's Driftless region.

Next up is **Working Draft Beer Company**, where it's easy to unwind with the selection of board games, or even get some work done (conveniently placed outlets are all over the taproom so you can stay all day and never worry about running out of juice). The taproom seeks to bring together and honor the community it calls home. In doing so, the owners repurposed lanes and pin decks from Village Lanes, a bowling alley that served the area for nearly sixty years, into the taproom's bar top and common tables. The brewery also boasts an artist-in-residence program that invites artists of all types to share their works, whether music, painting, poetry, or another medium. The bartenders are fully Midwest Nice, are happy to let you sample, and will make recommendations until you find the beer for you. The taps run the gamut from light, low ABV pilsners and amber lagers to hard seltzers to IPAs to scotch ales. Working Draft also has Wisconsin guest taps, and while it doesn't have a full kitchen, you can buy beef sticks, nuts, pretzels, and chocolate at the bar.

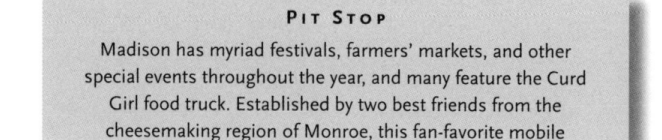

Pit Stop

Madison has myriad festivals, farmers' markets, and other special events throughout the year, and many feature the Curd Girl food truck. Established by two best friends from the cheesemaking region of Monroe, this fan-favorite mobile establishment has freshly fried squeaky curds and homemade dipping sauces. Check the website, Facebook, or Instagram pages while you're in town to see where you can catch them.

Stay on Madison's East Side to visit **Starkweather Brewing Company**, named in honor of a nearby creek. The taproom is new to Madison's beer scene, opening in February 2022, but has already built a loyal fan base. Starkweather regularly has a cream ale, wheat ale, and an IPA on tap, but the brewmaster is always looking to play with flavors, so expect to find new tastes and inventive brews each time you visit. Pro tip: depending on the day you stop by, you might have the chance to chat with the brewmaster, Peter Schroder, a native of the Netherlands who bartends regularly. If you're hungry, the taproom has a small menu, offering a Johnsonville brat, Landjaeger, and a few other hot items and bar snacks. The fried cheese curds from Decatur Dairy are always a solid choice, especially served alongside Starkweather's house-made ranch.

If you found a parking space near Starkweather, you might want to walk to the next stop, at the corner of Atwood Avenue and Dunning Street, where you can get a cold brew (coffee) to go with your cold brews. **Forward Craft & Coffee** puts a little twist on the traditional taproom, offering both beer and coffee drinks. The location is perfect, whether you want to meet with friends in the main room or just need to get some work done in a quiet space. The establishment is committed to keeping things local, so expect regionally sourced snacks, roasted coffee, and flavored cold brew. While Forward doesn't brew its own beer, many of the taps are dedicated to Wisconsin offerings. Flights are available, and customers are invited to mix and match beer and coffee. In terms of food, you'll find coffeehouse offerings, like scones, granola, and muffins, plus some charcuterie.

Time to do a bit of backtracking toward the University of Wisconsin–Madison campus for a stop at **State Street Brats**, which will give you that college-town bar vibe while you dig into tasty food and a cold beer. State Street Brats serves up its own take on fried cheese curds: cubes of garlic white cheddar, beer battered, deep fried, and served with a side of ranch. Kick it up a notch with the Sconnie Style Poutine, french fries topped with the cheese cubes and melted white cheddar. True to its name, the restaurant also has brats. The regular menu has two options: the red brat, a smoked beef and pork sausage, and the white brat, its award-winning all-pork brat from Bakalars Sausage Company in La Crosse. If

Detour

The University of Wisconsin–Madison has undoubtedly played an important role in the state's cheesemaking history. It was the site of the first dairy school in the United States and of the invention of the Babcock test, which accurately measures milk fat content and is a critical tool for dairies as they select the best milk for cheese production. Today the university continues its cheese legacy, serving as the home of the Wisconsin Master Cheesemaker Program, offering short courses in dairy topics, and housing the Center for Dairy Research, a technical resource for those in the cheese community. What's more, a team of student interns work under cheesemakers to learn the craft of making cheese. The students produce some forty thousand pounds each year, of around two dozen varieties, including brick, cheddar, gouda, marbled colby jack, havarti, Dutch käse, monterey jack, and baby swiss. You can sample some of their work at the Babcock Dairy Store on the university campus, which also has sandwiches and ice cream.

you can't decide, go for the Wisconsin Sampler and you'll get one of each plus a basket of cheese cubes. Or go all in on the Tourist Special, a red brat, cheese cubes, and a New Glarus Spotted Cow. State Street Brats often has a brat special with unique toppings. Keep in mind that the restaurant restricts entry to those age twenty-one and older after 9 p.m., unless accompanied by an adult (who must leave their ID with the bouncer at the door).

Now head south, wending your way out of downtown Madison to **Black Rose Blending Co.**, where the focus is on making experimental, small-batch beers, wines, and cider. The tasting room (with varied hours depending on the season) has a limited draft list, but it regularly includes some of Black Rose's own beers plus guest taps. Food options include a Wisconsin cheese plate with three artisan cheeses paired with

State Street Brats, Madison

Pit Stop

Be sure to check out the brat fry at Bavaria Sausage in Fitchburg, Friday afternoons from Memorial Day to Labor Day (weather permitting). The Facebook page has more information on this summertime event.

flatbread crisps and stone-ground mustard. The brewery, a member of the Craft Beer Pinball League, boasts six pinball machines for patrons, and monthly high scores are eligible for prizes.

About two miles away is **Delta Beer Lab**, the perfect spot for those who consider themselves science nerds on the inside (or outside). From the lab tables and chairs to the beakers used for tastings and even the brew names, Delta Beer Lab has the science lab ambiance perfected. On tap, you can find West Coast and Midwest IPAs, gose, a cider/beer hybrid named Pi (Caramel Apple Pi), a porter, and some lighter golden and amber ales. As for food, you're welcome to bring in your own, try out a food cart (check the website or social media for details), or tuck into a cheesy pizza from Pep's Drafthaus, which you crisp up yourself at the pizza station. If you're looking for something to do, Delta has darts, a shuffleboard table, and card and board games (in addition to live entertainment and trivia on various nights each month). Pro tip: While you're welcome to tip, it isn't expected. The taproom prices cover operating costs, including full wages and revenue sharing for employees. Any additional amount you tack onto your bill will go to a local organization.

When you're ready for a snack, make your way toward Stoughton for a bit of Norwegian history and a lot of cheese. With a large selection of Wisconsin cheeses (and some from around the world), **Cheesers LoKal Market** is perfect, whether you're looking for picnic options, a quick bite, or even a gift. Since 1995, the shop owners have been carefully curating their in-store selection, and even visit local creameries when on vacation to pick the best to stock. Some of the most popular cheeses include Milton Creamery Prairie Breeze, Roth butterkäse, Wood River roasted red

Delta Beer Lab, Madison

pepper cheddar, and Kindred smoked gouda. In addition to the cheeses, Cheesers has a wide selection of other local products, including crackers, meats, honey, wine, and spreads. If you're coming from out of town, be sure to ask for a pin to place in the shop's map of visitors. Seating is available upstairs if you want to sample a bit of your cheese stash before heading out, and complimentary wine tastings take place each Thursday afternoon. Pro tip: while you're at Cheesers, ask if the shop has anything in stock from Uplands Cheese Company, a creamery in the Driftless region of southwestern Wisconsin that is known for its Pleasant Ridge Reserve, the most-awarded cheese in US history.

WisconsInsights

Just how much of a powerhouse is Wisconsin cheese? You can find it in 98 percent of the nation's grocery stores.

Located just across the street from Cheesers is **Viking Brew Pub**, a Scandinavian themed restaurant with a Viking ship–shaped bar. (Despite what you might have assumed, the brewery is actually named after the co-owner, Vik Malling.) The venue has a lengthy menu chock full of pub grub and Scandinavian cuisine offerings, including cheesy favorites Valhalla Dip served with house-made chips, a jumbo soft pretzel with beer cheese sauce, fried cheese curds, a mac and cheese flatbread, a BBQ mac, a wrap with mac and BBQ pulled pork, and a burger smothered in beer cheese sauce. To accompany your meal? Viking has its own line of brews, including the Uff Da, a Belgian tripel; the Saison d'Stoughton, a farmhouse ale; and Sigurd the Mighty Strong Scotch Ale.

WisconsInsights

Viking Brew Pub was the first brewery to open in Stoughton, a place that embraced teetotaling for much of its history.

Your trip next heads toward the Wisconsin-Illinois border with a quick stop in the heart of Janesville. Here in the historic Carriage Works building is **Rock County Brewing Company**, the city's first nanobrewery. Everything is brewed in small batches, but you'll still find a ton of variety on tap. Rock County offers seltzers, sours, cream ales, hefeweizens, IPAs, and even stouts. Come on Friday for trivia night, and if you're hungry, tuck into a Milwaukee Pretzel Company pretzel served with cheese. The small taproom takes advantage of the historic building's structure, with exposed brick walls complemented with rustic wooden tables, barrels, and seating.

Even farther south, in Beloit you can get your brat fix, courtesy of **G5 Brewing Company** and its G5 Mac & Cheese, a steamy bowl of noodles swimming in a smoked gouda cheese sauce and topped with a brat and grilled onions. Of course, G5 also has beer, so since you're there for the brat mac, have a crisp kölsch, a peanut butter and chocolate stout, a light pilsner, or any one of its IPAs. G5 has a consistently changing lineup of brews, all made using Wisconsin-built equipment.

Until **CheezHEAD Brewing** came along, downtown Beloit didn't actually have a brewery. But in 2020, CheezHEAD threw open its doors in honor of all things Wisconsin and beer. In both the taproom and beer garden (weather permitting) you can find CheezHEAD's unique small-batch beers, alongside some Wisconsin taps. House selections include a vanilla cream ale, a peanut butter porter, a Mexican lager, a couple of spicy beers brewed with habanero, an IPA, and a farmhouse ale. Not sure what to get? Try a flight, which comes on a board shaped like a giant wheel of cheese. The CheezHEAD kitchen menu pays homage to Wisconsin's dairy industry. Choose from cheese curds (plain or jalapeño), a selection of cheese spreads with crackers, soft pretzels with hot beer cheese dip, or a beer cheese soup (the brewery has noncheese appetizers and entrées as well). If you arrive in spring, summer, or fall and snag a seat in the beer garden, cornhole is out to keep you entertained.

From Beloit, it's time to head to Green County, arguably the state's biggest cheesemaking hub, with sixteen area cheese factories that pump out more than two hundred million pounds of cheese per year. Long ago, the factories in this southwestern part of the state made limburger, brick, block swiss, and wheel swiss cheese, but today the county produces around a hundred varieties of cheese. Many of these cheeses are crafted by the award-winning cheesemakers from Chalet Cheese Cooperative, Decatur Dairy, Edelweiss Creamery, Emmi Roth USA, Grande Cheese Company, Klondike Cheese Company, Silver & Lewis, Wisconsin Cheese Group, and W&W Dairy, Inc., among others. Green County is home to the National Historic Cheesemaking Center and has several Master Cheesemakers in its borders. The county seat's high school mascot is a mouse and its teams are the Cheesemakers.

Start off at **Decatur Dairy**, which has been making award-winning havarti and muenster cheese since the 1940s. And while the factory is located in the small town of Brodhead, the popularity of Decatur's products means you can find it in many stores, restaurants, and breweries around Wisconsin. Led by a Master Cheesemaker, the Decatur co-op also manufactures a swiss cheese, a colby-swiss marbled cheese, brick, farmers cheese, butterkäse, and queso blanco. The Brodhead store serves grilled cheese sandwiches every day until 4:30 p.m., on sourdough with a secret sauce. Varieties include the Smokey Bandit, made with smoked butterkäse; On Wisconsin!, with beer cheddar and beer mustard; and Dilly, with dill havarti and dill pickles. The shop has tables both in and outside if you don't want takeout.

Pit Stop

Every other September in even-numbered years, the streets of Monroe come alive for Green County Cheese Days, one of the oldest and largest cheese celebrations in the country. First held in 1914, the event was inspired by a local businessperson who traveled by train with a small group to visit Sauerkraut Days in Forreston, Illinois. The men returned home convinced that if a village could celebrate fermented food, certainly a town full of dairies could have a cheese festival. The event includes yodeling, alphorns, cheesemaking demonstrations, and Wedgie, the Cheese Days mascot. Throughout the festival, you'll have many opportunities for sampling cheese in myriad forms—deep-fried cheese curds, raclette sandwiches, grilled cheese, and cheesecake on a stick.

Ready for a quick drink? Head into Monroe, the heart of cheese country and home of **Bullquarian Brewhouse**, a two-barrel nanobrewery that serves ten different beers and its own homemade pizzas. Among the taps at this comfy, café-esque spot, you'll often find a couple of easy drinkers, plus some hop-forward IPAs. If you're hungry, the homemade pizza is a great option, and if you're there at the right time of year, you can pair an Oktoberfest beer with the Oktoberfest pizza, topped with a local three-cheese swiss blend plus brats.

Given the strong link between beer and Wisconsin, it is perhaps unsurprising that the nation's second-oldest brewery is located in the state. **Minhas Craft Brewery** has been in operation for more than 160 years (much of that time under the name of owner Joseph Huber), owned over time by first- and second-generation immigrants from Switzerland, France, Great Britain, Germany, and Denmark. Today the brewery crafts its own beer, spirits, cream liqueurs, and old-fashioned pop. On your visit, you can choose to take a tour (offered daily) that ends with a twenty-minute all-you-can-drink tasting. Or just go for the tasting. No matter which you pick, when your twenty minutes are up, head to the gift shop for a bit of browsing, but don't forget to grab your complimentary five-pack of either house-made pop or craft beer. You even get to keep your tasting glass. The brewery is home to the nation's largest beer memorabilia museum, which consists of advertising artifacts, beer growlers from around the world, model trucks and trains, toy cars, and other beer-related items.

Minhas is conveniently located near Monroe Courthouse Square, where you'll discover an assortment of local shops and eateries, including **Baumgartner's Cheese Store & Tavern**, Wisconsin's oldest cheese

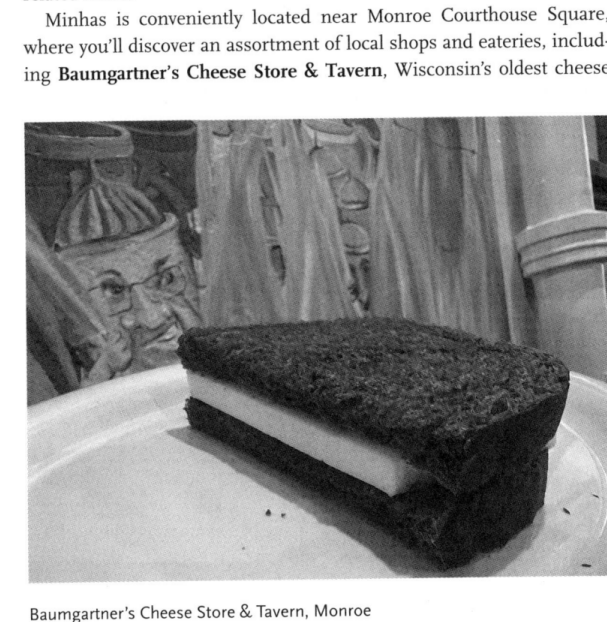

Baumgartner's Cheese Store & Tavern, Monroe

store. Since 1931, Baumgartner's has offered the finest Wisconsin cheese to locals and tourists—butterkäse, havarti, farmer cheese, gouda, muenster, blue cheese, stilton, aged cheddars, multiple swiss varieties, apple jack, raclette, and more. A tavern adjoins the store, where you can enjoy local beers and a classic cheese sandwich, a no-frills, room-temperature delight with two slices of soft bread and a thick piece of cheese in the middle. Choose from brick, cheddar, swiss, or limburger—which comes with some onions and a mint.

WisconsInsights

As of 2021, Hispanic cheese accounted for 3.2 percent of all cheese made in Wisconsin, up from 2.2 percent in 2011.

On the northern outskirts of Monroe is **Alp and Dell Cheese Store**. Located at the Emmi Roth plant, the shop offers more than one hundred varieties of cheese, including those from Emmi Roth, imports, and offerings from around Wisconsin. Alp and Dell also has a huge stock of curds in many flavors, such as garlic dill and white cheddar. While you're there, sample some cheese (especially the world champion Grand Cru Surchoix or Canela, a Spanish-style hard cheese rubbed with cinnamon and paprika that has won the American Cheese Society competition many years in a row), and pick up a selection of cheeses to munch on the way to the next stop. If you want more than just a snack for the road, the shop will also cut bulk cheese to your specifications.

If you're driving north and start wondering, What's that smell?, you'll know you've reached **Chalet Cheese Cooperative**, the only factory in the United States that still produces limburger cheese. Founded in 1885, it is one of the oldest cheese cooperatives still in operation. Today the Master Cheesemaker–led co-op gets its milk fresh each day from fourteen dairy farms in Green County, providing the backbone for its high-quality product. While you're in the shop, if you can't quite stomach the thought of limburger, Chalet Cheese also has baby swiss, brick, cheddar, and a selection of specialty cheeses available.

Alp and Dell Cheese Store, Monroe

Continue north along County Road N until you reach the town of New Glarus, home of **New Glarus Brewing Company**. The brewery distributes only within the state, which is why its tagline is “Only in Wisconsin,” and why it's such a hot commodity for out-of-staters. (New Glarus did attempt distribution into Illinois at one point, but decided it was detracting from serving hometown customers.) The company dates back to June 1993, when Deborah Carey and her husband, Dan, converted an abandoned warehouse into a brewery; the first barrels rolled off the line that November. Notably, Deborah was the first woman in the United States to found and operate a brewery. Today the husband-and-wife team oversee an operation that produces more than two hundred thirty thousand barrels per year, all crafted with 100 percent natural ingredients. Since its inception, New Glarus has made nearly one hundred types of beer, of which its most recognizable is Spotted Cow, a naturally cloudy farmhouse ale originally brewed with a bit of corn to honor Wisconsin's farmers (it's now all malt to avoid GMOs). No matter where

DETOUR

Among Green County's many cheese claims to fame is the National Historic Cheesemaking Center. Located in a restored 1888 Chicago, Milwaukee & St. Paul railroad depot is a small museum (open Thursday through Sunday, May through October) where for five dollars knowledgeable guides will share colorful stories and bring to life the history of cheesemaking in Wisconsin from the late 1800s to today. Once your guided or self-guided tour is complete (and you've collected your gift bag), stop by the gift shop to stock up on books about the history of cheese and Green County and other cheese-related goodies (just know that there is no actual, edible cheese sold at the shop, though the tour guides are happy to share their favorite spots with you). The property also contains the Imobersteg Farmstead Cheese Factory, an authentic cheese production building and equipment from the late 1800s that was relocated and restored in 2010. The factory holds an annual demonstration where a giant wheel of swiss cheese is made over the span of a few hours using original methods from the 1800s. Both retired and Master Cheesemakers participate in the event. If you can't make it to the museum, keep your eyes peeled around Monroe for the center's concession trailer, which serves up grilled cheese and fresh cream puffs.

you're coming from, the brewery is definitely worth a stop whether you want to tour, taste, or traipse through the property. (Pro tip: it's open only Monday through Friday.) If you're looking to sample, buy a wristband at the gift shop counter for eight dollars and you'll receive three tasters of your choice, a souvenir tasting glass, and a token good for a New Glarus at select restaurants and bars in town. Tastings are free if you have a military ID. You can also buy a pint to sip while you explore the gift shop, sit outside on the patio, or walk through the museum. Free brewery

New Glarus Brewing Company, New Glarus

self-tours take you through nearly all of the brewing, canning, and bottling process. Check the New Glarus website before you visit if you're interested in booking a hard-hat tour, a behind-the-scenes look at both the current and original breweries. The three-hour tour includes a private beer and cheese pairing. Before you leave New Glarus's sprawling property, pick up a six-pack, twelve-pack, or case of your favorite beer, or, if you're feeling brave, go for a quarter or half barrel!

While you're in New Glarus (the town, not the brewery), swing by **Glarner Stube** for dinner. The inside is reminiscent of a Swiss chalet, which is a perfect complement to the food. On the menu are numerous Swiss offerings and some Wisconsin favorites, such as a veal brat from Hoesley's Meats, served as either a sandwich or smothered in a brown onion gravy. (Hoesley's is located nearby and a great stop if you're looking for fresh or frozen brats to cook at home. The many flavors at the butcher shop include swiss and mushroom, cajun, pizza, Italian, jalapeño, cheddar, smoked, veal, and beer and bacon.) If you're in the mood, Glarner Stube also has a cheese fondue served with bread for dipping and cheese curds battered with New Glarus Spotted Cow.

Pit Stop

Each June, New Glarus is home to the Beer, Bacon, and Cheese festival. Tickets usually go on sale in April and often sell out. A ticket entitles you to unlimited samplings of craft beer, specialty meat, and artisan cheeses around New Glarus.

Heading north to Paoli, stop at **Landmark Creamery**, where the focus is on making unique cheeses from sheep's and grass-fed cow's milk. The styles include pipit, a sweet, creamy sheep's milk cheese that melts well on a burger, and Rebel Miel, a semifirm beer-washed cheese. Landmark also sells a shredded mac and cheese blend, sheep's milk fondue, and the award-winning Pecora Nocciola, a pecorino-style cheese made from sheep's milk. The friendly owners are glad to help you choose a pairing for your next meal, and if you want something more than sliced cheese for the road, the shop also has grilled cheese sandwiches and custom cheese boards.

You might be surprised to learn that Wisconsin is home to the Troll Capital of the World, but that's the self-proclaimed nickname embraced by Mount Horeb. What's up with the trolls? The moniker owes itself to the steady stream of Norwegians who moved to the area in the late 1800s and brought along their troll mythology. The life-size troll statues and pictures around town, however, didn't start showing up until the 1970s. The Mount Horeb Area Chamber of Commerce website has a downloadable troll map to help you locate each one. While you're on the hunt, pop into **Grumpy Troll Brew Pub**, located in the former Mount Horeb Creamery and Cheese Company building that dates back to 1916, and try one of its award-winning ales and lagers (or the in-house root beer) or sample the cheese on the menu. Start off with either the beer cheese soup or deep-fried cheese curds (made with cheese from Monticello), and follow it up with the Cheese Lovers Mac & Cheese (tossed in homemade beer cheese sauce).

As you meander your way toward the Wisconsin Dells, stop in Baraboo, a town known for its circus history. In the late 1800s, the Ringling brothers established a circus here, and many others would eventually make their way to town too. Today you'll find the Circus World Museum and the home of Albert Ringling, one of the Ringling Bros. Circus founders. That mansion is attached to the aptly named **AL. Ringling Brewing Co.** taproom, with a circus motif that pays exceptional attention to detail (try to spot all the elephants around the bar), complete with a calliope that plays at the end of each tour of the mansion. Year-round taps include the Prohibition-style low ABV Ringling Original beer, a pilsner, honey blonde ale, Irish red ale, and English porter. You might also see Cow Pie!, a chocolate pecan dessert stout brewed in collaboration with the Baraboo Candy Company, manufacturer of the Cow Pie! candy. AL. Ringling releases limited brews throughout the year as well. While the menu (served from the pie car) is mainly Paraguayan, there is a giant soft pretzel with beer cheese dipping sauce and fried cheese curds with the quintessential side of ranch for dipping.

> **WisconsInsights**
>
> It isn't all about the cheese—Wisconsin is also trying to mold the nation's best butchers through its Master Meat Crafter Program, a two-year intensive that started in 2008 at the University of Wisconsin–Madison. Candidates must complete workshops, a research project, and even mentor an individual on meat science and processing.

Next up is **Tumbled Rock Brewery & Kitchen**. Depending on what time of day you arrive, you can sit either inside or out on the restaurant's patio or choose a spot at the adjacent brewhouse. No matter where you land, make sure you come with your appetite. The menu is lengthy, with plenty of cheesy options to choose from. It includes fried curds,

Tumbled Rock Brewery & Kitchen, Baraboo

a bologna sandwich with mustard cheese sauce, a pulled ham and gruyère sandwich, and a diner favorite, the Mac Daddy, a pizza topped with homemade mac and cheese, thick slices of bacon, and a bit of sriracha. You can also get the mac and cheese (or a lobster mac and cheese) as an entrée. Of course it's a brewery, so you'll have plenty to wash down your meal, especially more traditional styles, like English ales and German lagers. Among the flagship beers is Udder's Up, a cream ale; Sarrington Road, an English IPA; Devil's Doorway, a double IPA; Chuck Brown Dog, an English brown ale; and the Dutch Farmer, a Dutch lager. Seasonal beers are also available. If you need to stretch your legs after your visit, you're in luck. The north entrance to Devil's Lake State Park is nearby.

Every year, around four million people visit the Wisconsin Dells. Ask a Wisconsinite about it, and you'll likely get mixed reviews. For some, it's a tourist trap full of people from Illinois, but for others it harkens back to childhood memories of family trips to the water parks and wax museum, a ride on a Duck, and a treat at the fudge shop grabbed just early enough to catch Aqua the waterskiing clown. Believe it or not (Ripley's museum is also in town), the Dells is a natural wonderland. Located on the Wisconsin River, the Dells offers towering sandstone cliffs, slot canyons, trails, rolling hills, and more. It's also a perfect stop for cheese, beer, and brats.

Kick off your Dells visit at **Market Square Cheese**, located next to the outlet mall. Since 1969, the store has been making sure locals and tourists get their cheese and sausage fix. Each year, the store sells more than a hundred tons of Wisconsin cheese, with varieties ranging from gouda and cheddar to blue cheese, flavored curds, string cheese, cheese spreads, and even cheese shaped like cows and Wisconsin to take home to your friends. The store also has plenty of other local snacks—including fudge and a wide selection of root beer—and souvenirs.

WisconsInsights

In 2022, Wisconsin's craft breweries boosted the state's coffers to the tune of more than $2.5 billion.

When you need a more substantial bite, head up Wisconsin Dells Parkway to **Brat House Grill**, a sports bar-esque venue with pull tabs to set your happy hour price. As the name implies, this is the place you come for brats, and they're served in several ways: on top of french fries, in a beer cheese soup, as a burger patty, over macaroni smothered in a house-made six-cheese sauce, with a multi-meat platter, and as a regular old brat on a bun (though even that last option has options: with cheddar, a chicken brat stuffed with feta and swiss, or one smothered with swiss and mushrooms). And yes, Brat House Grill has a plain brat, too, just in case. You can sample all that inside a historic building, constructed in 1850 as a one-room Baptist Boys School House. Since then, it's been a Methodist church, Grand Army of the Republic hall, antique mall, and, finally, the place you go in the Dells for brats.

Brat House Grill, Lake Delton

Pit Stop

Each year in mid-October, the Dells takes a day to honor Wisconsin's brewing heritage with the Dells on Tap event, where attendees have the chance to sample dozens of Wisconsin beers. This adults-only affair also presents the opportunity to participate in a mustache and beard competition, if you're so inclined. Tickets for Dells on Tap go on sale in August and tend to sell out fast.

If you're looking for something a little different, the Dells is full of other restaurants to try. Consider **Edge-O-Dells Bar & Restaurant**, a campground open only to those aged twenty-one and up (kids are welcome at the restaurant though!). Among its lengthy menu of wraps, wings, sandwiches, and dinner plates is the Sconnie Burger, a half pound of beef topped with cheddar curds and sliced cheese (with the option to add bacon). Or unleash your inner Viking at **Asgard Axe and Tap**, where you can not only munch on a brat, pizza fries, or grilled cheese but also toss axes and play arcade games.

In an unassuming business park, **Bevy Brewery & Winery** is resurrecting a local favorite: a honey blonde ale once brewed by Port Huron Brewing, which closed in 2021. Alongside this easy drinker, guests will find Bevy's other beers—ranging from the top-selling juicy pale ale to a pilsner—ciders, meads, and wines, many of which are crafted with Wisconsin ingredients. Sample your way through the selection while pouring your own beverages at the tap wall, then pay on your way out.

Leaving the tourist haven of the Dells, head along Highway 13 toward Mauston. On the outskirts of town, and way up there on the Midwest Nice scale, is **Wisconsin River Meats**. The butcher shop located in the Wisconsin River valley is well-known among locals and those in the military and diplomatic communities abroad who rely on shipments of brats, bacon, cheese, and other smoked meats for a little taste of home. Although it's not a restaurant where you can pop in and grab a brat to go, you can get some to take home (Wisconsin River Meats offers original, mushroom swiss, cheddar, cranberry, and jalapeño in traditional links and also brat patties) or buy local Wisconsin cheeses and beef sticks and have yourself a little car picnic. The people behind this store truly know what they're doing: Owners John Hamm and David Mauer have dozens of years of experience in the meat industry, and Dave is a graduate of the University of Wisconsin–Madison Master Meat Crafter Program. If you really want to dig into their meat knowledge, they're happy to chat, share their know-how, and find out what brought you to their place.

While you're in Mauston, stop by **Gravity Box Brewing Company**. With sixteen rotating taps, all made on-site right behind the brewery windows, everyone in your group will find something to enjoy. Expect to see an IPA, light lager, stout, hard seltzer, amber, farmhouse ale, wheat beer, pale ale, and more. Have a seat in the cozy taproom or at the bar. If it's nice, take your beer to the beer garden. If you're wondering about the brewery's name: a gravity box is an efficient means to transport grain from a field to a farm or a grain elevator. You can see part of one right behind the bar, holding the taps. Even the tap handles celebrate the strong farming community in the area and are made out of farm equipment. Gravity Box has some flatbreads available but is also a BYO food establishment, so you're welcome to bring your cheese and snacks from Wisconsin River Meats, order from a local restaurant, or check out one of its food trucks.

On the way to Hillsboro, you may feel like you're in the middle of nowhere, but that's Wisconsin for you. You'll know you're in the right place, though, when you see the large Land O'Lakes plant. Next door, **Hillsboro Brewing Company** is a beer lovers' (and cheese lovers') dream. If the weather is nice, opt for outdoor seating on the patio. Or head into the restored, turn-of-the-century building, where you can belly up to the bar or settle into a booth right next to the brew tanks. Hillsboro boasts

WisconsInsights

Wisconsin produces about 3.5 billion pounds of cheese per year, which equates to about one of every four pounds of cheese in the United States.

more than forty beers and seltzers on tap, and you'll note everything from cream ales to milk stouts. Foodwise, go for one of its two types of cheese curds: a standard, fried curd or the dill pickle fried curd, both served with a side of ranch. If you're looking for something bigger, Hillsboro also has several pizzas and burgers, plus a house-made queso and some brisket nachos if you're feeling cheesy.

Right nearby Hillsboro Brewing Company is **The Cheese Store and More**. This family-owned shop has an assortment of Wisconsin cheeses, all cut to order, including garlic cheddar, raclette, cheddar blue, maple bacon cheddar, and everything in between. The shop also has cheese curds, spreads, shredded varieties, and many other unique Wisconsin-made cheeses and local items. If you want something sweet, the hand-scooped ice cream is a town favorite.

Detour

If you need some time out of your car, consider hitting the Cheese Country Recreation Trail. This forty-seven-mile path stretches from Mineral Point to Monroe and winds through three counties' worth of historic communities, bars, restaurants, cheese stores, and more. The route is heavily trafficked by ATVs and other motorized vehicles (in fact, you'll note in many of the towns of Cheese Country that even the roads are ATV friendly), but horses, bikes, and skis are welcome. Just know that some of the surface portions aren't bike friendly.

Tucked just outside of Richland Center's downtown, where Highway 80 meets Highway 14, is **Mel's Micro**, the home of unpretentious small-batch craft beers, including a stout, IPA, amber ale, and brown ale. The bar also has some local and national taps to try, plus golden fried curds. On any night of the week, you'll see locals playing pool, watching the game, or just shooting the breeze.

Head south along Highway 80, and when you cross the Wisconsin River you'll reach **Meister Cheese**. The company has been crafting blocks

Mel's Micro, Richland Center

of cheddar, monterey jack, havarti, colby, and more for one hundred years, and in that time it's focused on making its cheese with milk sourced only from humanely raised cows (that means no artificial hormones or unnecessary antibiotics, spacious animal housing, vegetarian feed, and around-the-clock access to the pasture). You can sample its "cows first, cheese second" wares at the small retail store in Muscoda, near the company's headquarters and processing facility.

About thirty minutes northeast, in the tiny town of Plain, visit one of the oldest cheesemakers in Wisconsin. The family-owned **Cedar Grove Cheese** opened its original factory in 1878. Today it gets its milk from thirty-five family-owned farms, most within twenty miles of the factory. Other than longevity, how do you know the product is good? Sales of Cedar Grove's fresh curds can exceed twenty-six thousand pounds per week during peak season. Cedar Grove is also home to many firsts. In 1993, it became the first in the nation to declare that all of its products are rBGH free. And it was the first cheese plant in the nation to install a wastewater treatment facility. There, Cedar Grove treats the wastewater byproduct of cheese production before emptying it into the Wisconsin River basin. When you visit, you can check out the Living Machine to see how the water gets cleaned. If you ask in advance, you might get a tour. If not, the staff is always happy to answer questions and discuss their cheesemaking operation.

WisconsInsights

If Wisconsin were a country, it would rank fourth in cheese production worldwide, behind the United States, Germany, and France.

Turn south again, back into the Wisconsin River valley, for a stop at **Arena Cheese**, the home of the original colby jack, a yellow-and-white speckled creation that blends together—you guessed it—colby and monterey jack cheeses. If you visit Monday through Friday, you might see Arena's cheese being made, and you can sample fresh curds every day

Pit Stop

Every April, Dodgeville celebrates the state's dairy farmers with the Wisconsin Grilled Cheese Championship. The late Lorin Toepper, a local resident, came up with the idea to hold an event to bring more awareness to the role dairy farmers play in the state economy. When he saw that California had a grilled cheese championship, he knew that was the right choice because, as Toepper explained, Wisconsin has superior cheese. In multiple rounds, competitors, from amateurs to professionals, compete in timed events to make the best cheesy sandwich. Tickets can be purchased on the event website, and in addition to grilled cheese, you will find many local food trucks to fill your belly.

of the week. In addition to a lengthy lineup of cheeses made by both Arena and other Wisconsin cheesemakers, you'll find cheese spread, cheese fudge, and some sausage to balance out the perfect cheese board.

As you continue your journey southwest, you'll pass a number of popular Wisconsin attractions, including the House on the Rock (it's exactly what it sounds like) and Governor Dodge State Park. After Highway 23 crosses Highway 18, you'll hit **Schurman's Wisconsin Cheese** in Dodgeville. The store carries around eighty varieties of cheese, including some Wisconsin award winners, like Pleasant Ridge Reserve and Roth Grand Cru, and a slew of cheddars. Fresh curds are available on Monday and Friday, but you're likely to find something to like no matter when you visit.

Whether you need a place to stay, a place to eat, or a place to drink, the next stop at **Commerce Street Brewery & Hotel** in Mineral Point has it all covered. The small combination B&B, taproom, and restaurant is

Commerce Street Brewery & Hotel, Mineral Point

housed in a repurposed limestone warehouse that dates to 1854, is listed on the National Register of Historic Places, and was originally used to store supplies unloaded from the railway that runs nearby (today you can visit the Mineral Point Railroad Museum in Wisconsin's oldest surviving depot, just up the street). Among the various menu items, Commerce Street has fried jalapeño cheese curds (which aren't overly spicy) and (if you're lucky) the Brewben Sandwich, a pretzel bun topped with swiss cheese, brats, sauerkraut, and Thousand Island dressing. On tap, Commerce Street brews a cream ale, coffee stout, saison farmhouse ale, Irish stout, and a couple of other beers, and also has some Wisconsin brews in cans and bottles. When you're ready to rest your head for the night, you can stay in one of the five guest rooms (as long as you've booked well in advance—they tend to fill up quickly), with exposed limestone walls, whirlpool tubs, fireplaces, and luxury amenities.

About fifteen miles down Highway 23 is Darlington's **City Service Brewing**, which serves craft brews in a 1930s service station. From the decor to the beer names, City Service is nostalgia at its best. Vintage gas pumps, oil cans, and signage litter the small taproom. The bar was crafted from a 1962 Lincoln Continental, and the taps run through large gasoline barrels. There's even an antiques and collectibles shop (Ted's Stuff) located in the back room. In summer, outdoor patio seating appears along Main Street, and live music fills the air most weekends. As for the beer, select from the flagship Red Line Irish Red, a medium-bodied, low hop red ale, and some rotating offerings, like Piston Wheat, Lowrider Mexican Lager, and Road Trip Mild English Bitter Ale. City Service also has some Wisconsin guest taps, along with its own root beer and pop. Pro tip: the hours can be somewhat inconsistent, so it's best to check the Facebook page ahead of your visit to verify that the brewery will be open.

Heading southwest toward the Mississippi River, make a quick detour for some cheese at **Shullsburg Creamery**, a company that's been producing award-winning Wisconsin cheese since 1934. Every day of the week, the shop welcomes visitors to sample its many varieties, such as soft colby, Jack 'N Dill monterey jack, and blueberry cheddar.

Cheese in hand, you're off to **Potosi Brewery**, in "Beer's Hometown." The Potosi Brewing Company was founded in 1852 and grew to become

Pit Stop

On the first Saturday in October, along the city's historic Water Street, stop by Shullsburg Cheesefest, a free, family-friendly event that has cheese tastings, vendors, the fire department's annual breakfast, main stage events, raffles, activities for kids, and even a Test Your Cheese IQ quiz show. No tickets are needed, and up-to-date information is available on the Cheesefest Facebook page and by emailing shullsburgcheesefest@gmail.com.

the fifth-largest brewery in the state. It remained in continuous operation until 1972—even surviving Prohibition. The brewery reopened in 2008, under the ownership of the nonprofit Potosi Brewery Foundation. You can visit the brewery any day of the week and dine and sip in either the restaurant or the beer garden (open spring, summer, and fall); tours of the production facility are available on weekends. The menu here is full of Dairy State favorites. Beer-battered white cheddar curds, beer bread, a local cheese and sausage platter, beer cheese soup, the brat patty sandwich, a brat burger, a Wisconsin grilled cheese, and a mac and cheese made with Wisconsin cheese and local bacon all grace the menu. Bacon cheddar tots—a golden fried delight stuffed with tons of bacon and cheddar—are available as a side and shouldn't be missed. And to accompany it, the brewery has a rotating selection of craft beers, including experimental brews, ales, stouts, IPAs, shandies, and radlers. If you're looking for a little history with your meal, within the Potosi facility you can stop by the ABA National Brewery Museum, the Great River Road Interpretive Center, and the Transportation Museum. Between the beer memorabilia, stories about the scenic byway that runs near Potosi, and information on the role of transportation in brewing, you'll walk away knowledgeable about the history of beer making and the place Potosi calls home.

From Potosi, head straight north for about a half hour. Driving through the quaint downtown of Fennimore, you'll be greeted by Igor, a large

Potosi Brewery, Potosi

cement mouse and mascot of this **Carr Valley Cheese** location (Carr Valley also has retail outlets in La Valle, Mauston, Mazomanie, Sauk City, and the Wisconsin Dells). The company started making cheese in 1902 and since 1986 has been owned by Master Cheesemaker Sid Cook, who has won more top international and national awards than any other North American cheesemaker. After snapping a few pictures with Igor (who can resist?), head inside and sample some of the cheese before picking

Pit Stop

If you didn't get enough beer memorabilia at Potosi, every March you can catch the Port of Potosi Breweriana & Collectibles Show where more than one hundred booths are set up for you to buy, sell, and trade old beer and brewery items. Food is available for purchase during the event, and attendees can get a special deal for a National Brewery Museum tour.

your favorites. It'll be tough, considering that Carr Valley is one of the most award-winning cheese companies in the world, taking home more than seven hundred awards for everything from its Ba Ba Blue and Black Sheep Truffle to the Snow White Goat Cheddar and Gran Canaria. Some of the varieties are available only seasonally, like the winter solstice cheddar and wildflower cheddar. Top sellers include the apple smoked cheddar, aged asiago spread, spicy beer spread, and cranberry chipotle cheddar. Fresh curds are also for sale, plus spreads, butters, snacks, and gifts. If you're interested in seeing Carr Valley craft its cheeses, you'll have to visit the La Valle or Mauston plants—just be sure to arrive early.

Continue north just a bit for another cheese stop. **Udder Brothers' Creamery** in Boscobel considers itself an ice cream shop (and there are a ton of delicious varieties to choose from), but it's so much more. Inside are dozens of cheese varieties from Kindred Creamery, Käse Meister, Pine River, Vern's, and Udder Brothers' own cheddar made from its cows' milk, alongside eggs, beef, milk, and fresh sandwiches.

After you leave Udder Brothers, follow the Wisconsin River west until it meets the Mississippi River in Prairie du Chien, once a major trading center for the area's Native peoples and European immigrants. Today the town is host to a bunch of historical landmarks and events celebrating its time as a fur-trading hub and fort, along with shops, restaurants, scenic overlooks along the river, and an annual Oktoberfest (complete with plenty of brats and favorite Wisconsin games like cornhole and euchre). Among the many destinations in town, **Fort Mulligan's Grill Pub** is celebrated among locals and travelers for its cheese curds. Made with locally produced cheese, then beer battered and deep fried, these golden nuggets could be a meal in itself. But they're also a wonderful accompaniment to the burgers, sandwiches, wraps, dinner plates, and salads on the full menu.

From Prairie du Chien, head into Wisconsin's Driftless region, so named for its topography formed not by glacial drift and the rock and sediment it left behind, but by the lack thereof. During the last Ice Age, an area covering twenty-four thousand square miles across Wisconsin, Minnesota, Iowa, and Illinois was left completely untouched by glacial erosion. Unlike the broad, flat prairies and rolling hills found throughout much of the state, this area has a rugged landscape with steep hills, deep river valleys, tall bluffs, and forested ridges, making it popular for outdoor recreation.

Detour

Looking for a sweet break? Carr Valley (and many other companies featured in this guide) sells treats from Valley Fudge & Candy. A favorite is the Cookie Butter Crunch Fudge, made with Biscoff Cookie Butter and vanilla fudge, crafted with Wisconsin butter.

Stop first in Viroqua's **Driftless Café**, what amounts to a love letter to the region of Wisconsin it calls home. Under the direction of co-owner Luke Zahm, host of the PBS show *Wisconsin Foodie*, the restaurant writes its menu each day in order to take advantage of the freshest ingredients it gets from local suppliers. While a lot of times that means vegetable or protein-forward dishes—and Driftless Café does not disappoint in that regard—the chef is also incorporating some of Wisconsin's finest cheeses. You might, for example, get the chance to try the Baked Wisconsin Mac and Cheese, made with Uplands Pleasant Ridge Reserve, Westby cheddar, Sartori sarvecchio parmesan, and other cheeses from local creameries. Or sample a local cheese board or the loaded grilled cheese. The beer garden, open in warmer months, sometimes has truffle fries sprinkled with Pleasant Ridge Reserve. The innovative menu pays homage to the more than two hundred certified organic farms in and around the Driftless area, and a chalkboard inside the intimate café has a list of the local producers and farmers whose ingredients are on the menu.

Still hungry in Viroqua? Then **Noble Rind Cheese Company** is conveniently right next door. Opened in early 2022, the husband-and-wife team behind the shop curates American farmstead cheeses and some international varieties to offer customers as wedges, on cheese or charcuterie boards, and on sandwiches. Many of the sandwiches are served on house-made milk bread and focaccia, and Noble Rind even makes the American cheese that graces its grilled cheese sandwiches. There are all manner of other snacks in store, including crackers, nuts, jams, and salami, the last of which is sourced from Driftless Provisions in Viroqua. The shop offers special tastings and can also be found handing out samples at community events around town.

WisconsInsights

According to Google data mapped by Nathan Yau, the state of Wisconsin has almost three times more bars than grocery stores.

If you feel like you're having a cheesy day, you aren't wrong. This part of Wisconsin is covered with dairy farms and, by extension, creameries. The next one on your route is **Nordic Creamery** in Westby, whose award-winning cheese comes from Bekkum Farmstead, now in its fourth generation of family ownership. Pick up sheep, goat, and cow milk cheeses, including the Blazing Billy jalapeño-infused goat cheese, a semi-hard cellar-aged goat cheese, a raw milk goat cheddar, raw milk sheep cheddar, and raw milk feta. If you have some time, browse the selection of regionally produced food and gifts, try a homemade ice cream, or (from May through September) visit the free petting zoo. If you can't make it to the store but happen to be in the area in December, Nordic Creamery runs a pop-up shop at Valley View Mall for all your holiday entertaining and gift-giving needs.

Just up the road is **Westby Cooperative Creamery**, which has been making cheese and other dairy products in small batches since 1903. The co-op is owned by more than one hundred farmers who supply their milk each day to the creamery, which then turns out fresh cottage cheese, sour cream, yogurt, cream cheese, and other dairy products. Westby cheese varieties include cheddar, colby, colby jack, grated parmesan, traditional and smoked string cheese, and yellow, white, and pepper curds. In addition to its own products, the Westby Cooperative store carries Wisconsin cheese brands, such as Sartori, Pine River, and Jim's

Cheese. Pro tip: The Westby retail shop is not located at the corporate office, so be sure to choose the right location (206 South Main Street in Westby) when you set your GPS. You'll know you've found the spot when you reach a quaint town full of small shops.

Next, enjoy a scenic drive into the heart of Amish country, home of **Pasture Pride Cheese**. As you pull up, the first thing you'll notice is the giant mouse statue and the cow bench, but don't take a seat just yet. Get yourself inside to pick up a bag of fresh curds, then settle into the cow seat and watch the world go by as you listen to the quiet "squeak" with each bite. Pasture Pride's team produces cow, goat, and mixed milk cheeses with milk that comes in small batches from local Amish dairies. The cheese crafted from the milk these animals produce takes on a different flavor because the cows are often milked by hand, meaning that less agitation occurs during the milking process. While the curds are great, Pasture Pride is known for its award-winning juusto cheese. Juusto (pronounced *hoo-stah*, *you-stoy*, or *hoo-stoh*, depending on who you ask) is a buttery, mild, soft bread cheese native to Scandinavia where it is traditionally made with reindeer milk. Juusto is produced when cheesemakers press curds tightly together, then bake the cheese bricks in such a way that caramelizes the sugar on the outside. You can eat it hot or cold; warming it doesn't melt it but does produce a smooth texture. Some people like to eat it as is, others grill it, or you can do as the Scandinavians do and serve it for breakfast with a cup of hot coffee. Pasture Pride has multiple variations of juusto for you to try, including traditional, garlic, bacon, jalapeño, chipotle, Italian, and Guusto (made from goat's milk).

Detour

Not far from Westby along Highway 27 is Organic Valley's distribution center. Organic Valley is the country's biggest farmer-owned organic cooperative, and it receives milk to produce its dairy products from Wisconsin and farmers around the country. The La Farge location has a small retail shop with both Organic Valley products and other natural and organic food and home items.

Pasture Pride Cheese, Cashton

More cheese? Why not. Take a quick detour off Highway 27 to **Old Country Cheese**, a shop that makes its products from 230 Amish milk producers who live nearby and each day bring in one hundred twenty thousand pounds of fresh supplies in milk cans. Old Country makes tons of varieties, including cheddar aged from two to twelve years, flavored cheddars, and a number of fresh curd flavors. Old Country Cheese also has spreads from Pine River, juusto from Pasture Pride, baby swiss, colby jack, colby salami, muenster, and the crowd favorite Bacon Fest, a cheese that combines bacon, onion, and dill pickles.

If you're interested in the farm-to-table movement, double back and head to **Footjoy Farm and Brewing**, where you can't get much more local. All of the grain in each beer Footjoy brews is grown on the owners' Cashton farm. Whether you're enjoying an IPA, brown ale, amber, lager, pilsner, or any one of Footjoy's other craft beers, you'll be tasting the wheat and barley grown just feet from where you're sipping. Same goes for the restaurant, which offers a rotating menu made from seasonal, local ingredients. Most nights pizza is available, but some evenings you'll also have the option of a cheesy sandwich, chili cheese fries, or an organic vegetable platter with house-made dip.

A twenty-minute drive north will land you in Sparta. There, in what used to be a gas station and repair shop dating back to 1939, is **Beer Shop**, a store, tasting room, community gathering spot with outdoor patio, game space, and more. It's not a place for house-brewed craft beer, but it is the perfect location to try an array of beers from around Wisconsin (and the rest of the Midwest too). Beer Shop has twenty-two taps and another sixty or so beers available in cans and bottles, and the bartenders are happy to offer recommendations and help you find exactly what you're looking for. If nonalcoholic options are calling your name, the store has you covered on that, with ciders, pop, and sparkling water, all made in the Midwest. While your tastebuds take a beer tour of the region, you can settle on the patio or sit inside the converted garage and enjoy a board game, listen to baseball, or help put together a puzzle. Once you've found your favorite (yes, Beer Shop does offer flights), you can fill a growler or build your own four- or six-pack and take it to go. Beer Shop has many events each week, including cruise-ins, vinyl nights, yoga, cornhole, and trivia. Each weekly event comes with a beer special as well.

Now, head toward La Crosse, with a quick stop for cheese along the way. Unlike the Mars Cheese Castle, **Le Coulee Cheese Castle** isn't housed in a castle-esque building. Instead, it's tucked into historic downtown West Salem, right off I-90. Don't be fooled by the small storefront; Le Coulee carries dozens of varieties of Wisconsin cheese, plus local gifts and ice

WisconsInsights

Two unique cheese varieties were invented in Wisconsin: brick and colby. The mild, semisoft brick cheese was created in 1877 by John Jossi. Colby cheese was invented less than a decade later, in 1885, by Joseph Steinwand, who named his soft, cheddar-like product after the town in which it was first made.

cream. If you can't decide what to buy, go for the variety round or half-moon and sample a number of excellent Wisconsin cheeses. Pro tip: be sure to fill up on snacks here—the food selection at the breweries in La Crosse is minimal.

Snacks in hand, it's time to brewery-hop through La Crosse. The first breweries in the city came onto the scene in the 1850s, and there were always at least four in operation between 1868 and 1920, with brewing taking the place of the lumber industry as it was on the decline. After Prohibition, this Mississippi River port town was home to the fourth-largest brewery in the United States, G. Heileman, original brewer of Old Style. With easy access to fresh water and transportation hubs, the city's breweries aggressively marketed themselves throughout the region and around the world in the late nineteenth and early twentieth centuries. More recently, however, craft brewers have taken over.

Among them is **Skeleton Crew Brew**, a pirate-themed nanobrewery located in a converted office park and attached to a winery (Lost Island Wine) in Onalaska. Leaning into the name, the flight of four, four-ounce samples is called Walk the Plank. Because it's a relatively small operation, expect to find a different array of craft brews each time you visit. Sometimes the options are heavy on the stouts, porters, and IPAs, and other times it's more easy drinkers, like a red ale, farmhouse ale, or flavored wheat beer. Skeleton Crew also produces collaborations with other La Crosse breweries. One popular example was the French Toast Porter, an 8.5 percent ABV brew with flavors of maple syrup, cinnamon toast cereal, and vanilla. In addition, Skeleton Crew often partners with 608, Turtle Stack, and Pearl Street on promos that will get you unique items and savings if you visit each spot. Ask a bartender for more details. Food-wise, expect to find prepackaged snacks and food trucks, but not a full kitchen menu.

WisconsInsights

Beginning in 2023, Old Style (now owned by Pabst) was again brewed in La Crosse, for the first time in more than two decades.

Now head south toward the campus of the University of Wisconsin–La Crosse (yes, La Crosse is a college town, but that doesn't mean all the beer is mass produced and sold in cubes at the Kwik Trip). Shortly before you get there, you'll come across **Pearl Street Brewery**, located in perhaps one of the most unique restored buildings: an old footwear factory. Today there are sixteen taps, including beers with year-round or seasonal availability and limited release offerings that run the style spectrum. Pearl Street has, for example, Shitty Lyte Beer, a traditional light lager crafted by the brewmaster as an answer to patrons asking, Got anything light?, and the Al Caporter, a porter brewed with roasted barley, caramel, and chocolate malts, then flavored with chocolate and strawberry. If you're not quite sure what you want, go for the flight of sixteen. The brewing area is open to the taproom so you can watch the brewmaster and his crew at work, or check out a tour on the first Saturday of each month. For around ten dollars, you'll get the inside scoop on the brewery, a souvenir pint glass, a free fill, and a coupon for BOGO specials at local bars and restaurants. Or if you really want to go all in, pair your tour with a hotel package that includes accommodations at the Candlewood Suites La Crosse (contact the hotel or check the brewery's website for details). Pro tip: be sure to park in the gravel lot along the row of trees to avoid getting towed (a parking map is available on the brewery's website).

Pit Stop

Where can you find the longest-running Oktoberfest celebration in the Midwest? La Crosse! Since 1961, members of the community and beyond have been coming together each September for beer, brats, music, lederhosen games, parades, a carnival, and more beer. Advance passes are available on OktoberfestUSA.com or at the gate. Be sure to check the schedule on the event website or Facebook page so you don't miss out on Craft Beer Night, a special ticketed event with dozens of participating beer vendors, both Wisconsin and national.

La Crosse's burgeoning craft beer scene includes **608 Brewing Company**, founded by a group of friends who set out to create a product and brewery environment that would welcome everyone, from the craft beer aficionado to the newbie. The offerings at 608 trend toward juicier fruit flavors, and that's true across the IPAs, stouts, sours, and lagers. It also has a small selection of snacks and nonalcoholic beverages.

Pit Stop

If you didn't make it to La Crosse for Oktoberfest, the city has two other beer- and cheese-focused events to check out. Each April, the Between the Bluffs Beer, Wine, and Cheese Festival brings together more than eighty cheese, beer, meat, wine, and food vendors for an afternoon of samples, live music, Hammer-Schlagen, and axe throwing. Tickets can be purchased in advance and start at around fifty-five dollars, which will get you a tasting glass, samples, a Tavern League safe ride home pass (if requested), and a shuttle to and from area hotels. Then, in early December, the city is host to Frothbite—Beer and Bites, an event pairing unique craft beers and other alcoholic beverages with holiday-themed snacks. Tickets start at forty dollars and include beer and snack samples, live music, games, and a souvenir sampling glass.

If you need a quick bite on your way to the next stop (or if you want some brats to take home for later), pop into **Schuby's Neighborhood Butcher**. The shop focuses on high-quality, regionally sourced meats. You'll taste the passion in its deli sandwiches (available both hot and cold and ranging from a traditional ham and cheese to a wagyu pastrami to a banh mi), charcuterie and cheese boards, Wisconsin brats, and fresh cuts of beef, pork, chicken, and lamb. If you're local, you can preorder Schuby's party and butcher boxes, but if you're just passing through, grab a sandwich or board (complete with house-made pickles and other seasonal accompaniments) and pull up a chair at the cozy counter.

La Crosse Bierhaus, La Crosse

When you're looking for more of a sit-down meal with a full menu, try **The Crow**, a gastropub with sandwiches, flatbread pizzas, and appetizers. The restaurant is well-known locally for its unique selection of burgers, which includes one served on donuts, another stuffed between two grilled cheese sandwiches, and yet another smothered in nacho toppings. Two cheesy favorites include the Cheese Curd Burger, piled high with jalapeño cheese curds, and the Mac & Cheese Burger, topped with creamy noodles and bacon. For something to drink, the restaurant has an assortment of craft beers.

WisconsInsights

During Prohibition, some breweries stopped producing beer in favor of making cheese.

Another dining option in the historic downtown area is **La Crosse Bierhaus**, a great place to grab a brat. The atmosphere is a bit kitschy and over-the-top German beer hall–esque, but that doesn't detract from the flavorful original, German, cheese, and Bierhaus brats, all served with a side of your choice. Don't forget to try the white cheddar beer-battered cheese curds. For vegetarians, there's a Beyond Brat on the menu. Come on a Thursday afternoon or evening to enjoy BOGO brats, or on a Saturday for live polka music. If school's in session, get there early to avoid the college crowd, which can get a bit rowdy.

Within a block of both La Crosse Bierhaus and The Crow is **Turtle Stack Brewery**. Its name pays tribute to the turtles that can be seen sunbathing on logs along the channels and tributaries of the Mississippi River valley. It also honors the Dr. Seuss book *Yertle the Turtle*, in which the turtle king continues to stack turtles to build himself a taller throne until one turtle disrupts the stack and frees all the others. Through this story and its name, the brewery wants to support the needs of craft beer enthusiasts seeking to find a more flavorful beer in the growing stack of craft offerings. What does that look like? A selection of nine rotating taps that focus on seasonal specialties and a wide variety to help all patrons find something they like. You might try an IPA, a golden ale or lager, a wheat beer, an Oktoberfest-style brew, or even something darker. The small taproom is decorated with local art available for purchase. The brewery offers some snacks, but is also conveniently located near multiple restaurants (and hotels, in case you want to make La Crosse your base for the night).

CHAPTER 3

Eau Claire and West Central Wisconsin

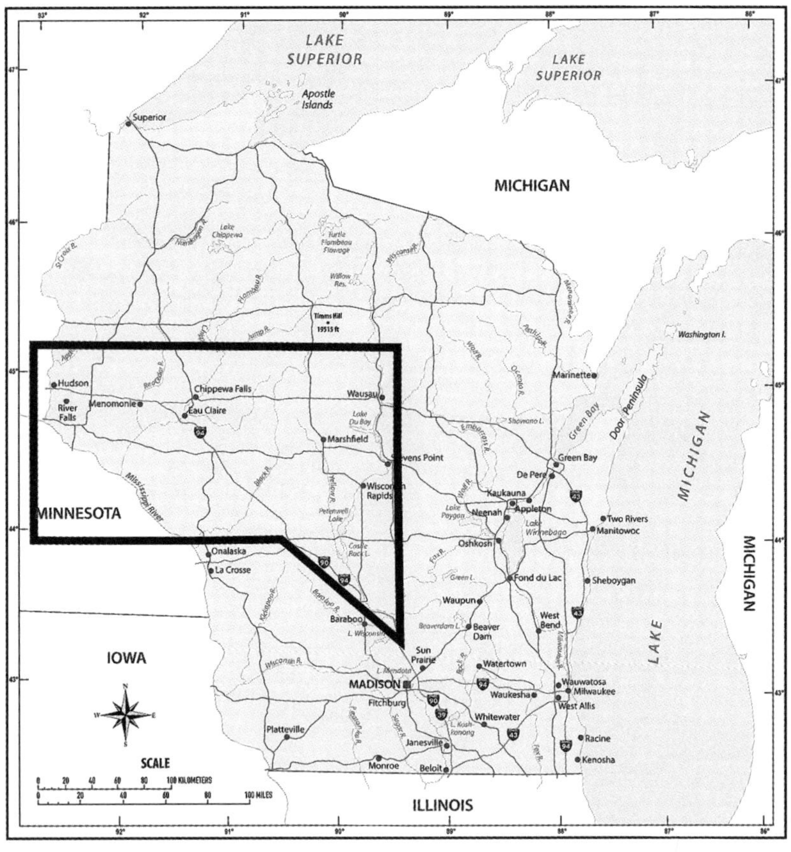

The boxed region indicates the approximate Eau Claire and west central Wisconsin area covered in this chapter.

No matter the season, the people of Wisconsin's central and west central regions are keen to enjoy everything the outdoors has to offer. There's mountain biking in Wausau's Nine Mile Forest, whitewater rafting on the Flambeau River, skiing at Rib Mountain State Park, fishing at Buckhorn State Park, hiking in the Blue Hills—the list goes on. Between these natural wonders are communities with deep ties to the state's cheese and beer history. Colby was invented in Clark County, which also is home to the dairy that supplies fast-food giant Culver's with its cheese curds. One of the nation's oldest breweries, Leinenkugel's, has been in the same spot in Chippewa Falls for more than 150 years. The area's cranberry bogs are the source of many a Wisconsin cheese, beer, and brat infusion. And the craft breweries that have slowly gained a foothold in the region have been responsible for revitalizing downtowns and renovating long-forgotten dilapidated storefronts. No matter what brings you to this part of the state, there's a little something for everyone's tastes and pleasures.

~

Start your visit to this Wisconsin region at **Humbird Cheese Mart** in Tomah. Back in the 1930s, the company operated a cheese factory in nearby Humbird. While the plant has long since closed, Humbird continues to operate two shops, one in Tomah and the other in the Wisconsin Dells, where it sells more than one hundred tons of carefully selected Wisconsin cheese annually. Humbird's bulk cheeses come from twenty-five Wisconsin manufacturers and range from gouda and edam to colby, brick, brie, American, and flavored cheddars. You'll also find cheese in its string, curd, and spreadable forms. Local summer sausages, jams, fudge, and other snacks (including a selection of cranberry products) are on the shelves to help you build the perfect cheese board.

Heading up Highway 173 into Wisconsin Rapids, you'll come across **Aaron's Wines and Steins**. This place is all about the pizza, specifically, the Wisco Cheese Fry. The crust is topped with garlic butter sauce, then covered in a shredded mozzarella blend with provolone and muenster, grated parmesan, and Italian seasoning. If you visit in fall, try the Oktoberfest, a pillowy crust topped with beer cheese sauce, sliced brats, caramelized onions, mozzarella, cheese curds, and stone-ground mustard. As the name suggests, the restaurant also has a selection of beer, some from Wisconsin breweries and some from out of state.

In nearby Plover, a renovated Shopko is home to Artist & Fare, a collection of small local businesses that includes **O'So Brewing**. The taproom itself is a large, open space surrounding a huge multisided bar. There are thirty taps, and each brew is made almost entirely with Wisconsin products—we're talking everything from the grain to the can sleeves to the bottles to the boxes. There are collaboration beers, like the light O'So Graceful, a coffee kölsch, and Perfect Bite, an imperial stout brewed with coffee, vanilla, coconut, and lactose. There's a nitro oatmeal porter and amber ale. There's a lager with jalapeño and an imperial stout aged in rye whiskey barrels. Basically, O'So has it all, plus some beer profiles you've probably never even thought of. If you're hungry, the menu includes pizzas, soft pretzels (with cheese, of course), sandwiches, and a garlic cheese bread.

Just a few minutes away is **Feltz Family Farms**, a dairy with 680 cows now in its fifth generation of family ownership. Since 2017, the farm has operated Feltz's Dairy Store, which has quickly become a family-favorite stop for fresh dairy products (like cheese curds and ice cream) and a peek into the milking barn and cheese plant. Visitors in spring and fall can request a tour of the farm and its robotic milking facility that includes a stop to see the baby calves. The store carries smoked gouda, colby jack, cheese whips, American slices, swiss cheese, aged cheddar, and more.

Next it's time for a trip into Stevens Point. If you need a bite, look no further than **Hilltop Pub & Grill**, where you can have a one-third pound Wisconsin brat, covered in sauerkraut and served on a brat bun or pretzel roll. If you don't like your brat covered in pickled cabbage, Hilltop is happy to add raw or fried onions instead. In addition to fried white cheddar curds, you'll find Mac n' Jack bites made of spicy cubes of macaroni and cheese with bacon, dipped in beer batter then fried and served up with a side of ranch. The full menu also includes sandwiches, burgers, a fish fry, salads, and wraps.

Afterward, stop by the city's namesake brewery. **Stevens Point Brewery**, founded in 1857, is one of the oldest continuously operating breweries in the nation. Today it produces beer and pop under its Point label, hard cider under the Ciderboys name, Tea Runner hard iced tea, and Whole Hog beer. Stevens Point Brewery has a small gift shop with cases, six-packs, and individual cans and bottles of many of its products, along with souvenirs. The brewery offers a thirty-minute tour that includes samples, and an outdoor beer garden opens for tasting in summer.

Head up Division Street until you reach **District 1 Brewing Company**. An old grocery store makes an unassuming brewery, but it's the perfect spot to house a large brewing operation and a huge taproom and still have plenty of space left over for pinball, cornhole, giant Scrabble, and Connect Four. In fact, there's so much to see and do between watching the beer brew, chatting with the bartenders, playing games, and drinking beer, this could be your only stop of the day. From IPAs to stouts to easy drinkers to seltzers (including those mixed to order with a house-made fruit purée), it's hard to choose just one. So better yet, grab a seat, pick a game, and tuck into a flight. If you want to follow the crowd, the most popular beers are the Apple Pie, a smoothie sour; Sundial: Tropics, a fruited sour; Uncle Mike's Great Adventure, a Russian imperial stout; and the Sweeney Todd, an English dark mild. Or tell the bartenders what you like to drink at home (and be honest—they won't judge your taste), and they'll pick the perfect beer for you. There's no food at the taproom, but you're welcome to bring your own or try one of the occasional food trucks.

About twenty minutes west in Rudolph is **Wisconsin Dairy State Cheese Company**. Led by a Master Cheesemaker, the store has a lineup of its own cheeses (and a ton of Wisconsin varieties) you won't want to miss. On your visit, be sure you pick up a bag or two or three of the curds. The store has traditional plain curds, along with many specialty flavors, such as pizza, ranch, and Bloody Mary. It also sells CoJack, cheddars, cheese spreads, camembert, gouda, and so much more. Whether it's in curd, whip, string, block, wheel, wedge, or waxed form, you're likely to find your perfect cheese match. If you need help deciding, the friendly staff is glad to point you in the right direction (and offer plenty of samples). Need something to nibble as you drive? Wisconsin Dairy State Cheese Company has ready-made cheese and meat platters. Want a sweet treat? There's ice cream in a small room just off the cheese shop floor, which you can enjoy while watching the cheesemaking operation through the large windows.

Driving north again, **Mullins Cheese** in Mosinee is the largest family-owned cheese manufacturer and whey processor in the state and has been in operation for more than fifty years. Every day, it receives seven million pounds of milk at its two plants from around seven hundred farms located across Wisconsin, then turns that into 40- and 640-pound blocks of cheese, six days a week. The company's retail store has a large collection of cheese products—curds, cheddar, colby, monterey jack, colby jack, parmesan, romano, asiago, chili gouda—the list goes on—plus whey protein isolate (in multiple flavors and made from the byproduct of the cheese manufacturing process). Mullins also has deep-fried cheese curds made to order, take-and-bake pizzas, local meats, soft-serve ice cream, and more. Not sure what you're looking for? The friendly, knowledgeable staff are always ready to help, and there are plenty of samples to aid your decision-making.

Detour

West of Wausau is the city of Colby, where colby cheese was invented in 1885. Today you can view a historical marker downtown commemorating this Wisconsin original. Created by Joseph Steinwand, the cheese differs from the process used to make cheddar because instead of being molded immediately after the whey is drained from the curd, colby is washed and cooled in cold water, then aged only a few months, giving it a higher moisture content and less sharp flavor. On the site of the original Steinwand factory stands the Colby Cheese Factory, though it is no longer in operation. Each July, the city holds Colby Cheese Days, with a midway, parade, entertainment, and a lot of free colby cheese.

While taking in the beautiful scenery along the Wisconsin River in the town of Mosinee, you'll reach the cozy yet sophisticated **Mosinee Brewing**

Mullins Cheese, Mosinee

Company. Located in a grocery store turned junk store turned brewery, the taproom serves the community everything from blondes, hazy IPAs, and hard seltzers, to milkshake IPAs, pastry stouts, and sours. The tap list rotates frequently, so if you're picky check the website, Untappd, or social media before you visit. But if you're up for whatever, pop in for a flight. If you're local, once you have a favorite, you can order your crowlers and six-packs ahead of time so it's ready to go when you arrive. The brewery offers some snacks and pizza, but you can bring any other food you like or place an order from a local restaurant. Just remember to supply your own plates and utensils, and don't forget to clean up after yourself!

WisconsInsights

Mozzarella and cheddar make up 51 percent of all the cheese Wisconsin produces.

Up Highway 51 is the city of Wausau and its collection of restaurants and breweries. Among them is **Bull Falls Brewery**, born out of an off-the-shelf home-brew kit, gifted to one of the owners in the late 1990s. That was the gateway to a home-brew club, local competitions, a brewing course with the Siebel Institute in Chicago, and the purchase of a former brewery's three-barrel system. That's also around the same time Red Bull (yes, the energy drink maker) took an interest in the fledgling company. After Bull Falls filed a logo with the US Patent and Trademark Office, Austria-based Red Bull reached out, concerned that the brewery's logo could cause potential confusion with its own. Thankfully, it all worked out, and in 2007 the brewery fired up its ten-barrel brew system and crafted an Oktoberfest lager. Today Bull Falls makes stouts, lagers (including a coffee lager), ales, IPAs, porters, pilsners, and many other styles. Some beers have a high ABV, some are low, and some feature locally sourced products. As many as fourteen beers are available on tap at any given time, and if you want to learn more about the operation, check the website for tour dates. The tour comes with a souvenir and a fourteen-ounce beer.

WisconsInsights

Wisconsin is home to the inventor of the Turbo Tap, which is intended to pour draft beer up to four times faster with less waste.

Part restaurant, part brewery, the nearby **Red Eye Brewing Company** is a perfect stop for some cheese magic. Admittedly, you might have a hard time deciding what to get, but don't fret, the friendly servers and bartenders would be more than happy to make some recommendations. You really can't go wrong, and you can be certain you're eating some of the freshest ingredients around, given that Red Eye sources locally as much as possible. That extends to the Red Eye Mac & Cheese Gratin, made with Carr Valley's fontina, Sartori's sarvecchio parmesan, Sassy Cow cream, and Nueske's bacon, then topped with breadcrumbs and baked to perfection. Or go for the local favorite pizzas. Among the choices are the Formaggio with a Wisconsin cheddar cream sauce and house-rolled mozzarella, parmesan, and asiago, and the Locavore, a basil pesto base pizza, covered with fennel sausage, Nueske's bacon, carrot, kale, radish, Sartori's basil olive oil asiago, and microgreens from Whitefeather Organics. There are many more mouthwatering styles to try, including a rotating seasonal pizza from which two dollars of each sale goes toward a charity. If none of that piques your interest, there are plenty of sandwiches, starters, soups, salads, and entrées to try. Compared with some of the other breweries in the state, Red Eye has a smaller tap list, but it still packs a flavor punch. Red Eye has light easy drinkers, sours, ambers, IPAs, and often something dark on tap.

Whitewater Music Hall and Brew Works, less than a mile away, is a community gathering spot. It's where you'll see locals having a coffee, enjoying live music, partaking in the indoor farmers' market, or, of course, drinking a beer. The beer menu is small, with only a handful of house brews available (and sometimes a couple of guest taps). It changes with some frequency, so you'll want to check the website or social media pages before you visit to see what you can snag. The food menu is also limited and rotating, but you'll typically find a large cheese plate with plenty of Wisconsin cheeses, homemade pretzel cheese dogs, plus fancy toasts and hot dogs.

WisconsInsights

The average American consumes 38.1 pounds of cheese each year.

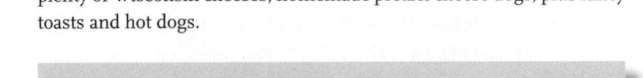

When you're hungry, head up to the next stop, **Clark's Cup N Cone and Cheese Shop** in Merrill. This is a great place for ice cream, but if you're looking for something a bit more substantial, the specialty grilled cheese sandwiches are the answer. Choose from your basic grilled cheese (with white and yellow American cheese, toasted on three pieces of sourdough bread), pizza grilled cheese, smoked cheddar turkey bacon, or popping jalapeño and cream cheese. There is often a sandwich special, too, like a ham, turkey, and tomato with chipotle sauce or ham and cheddar with cream cheese onion spread. If you prefer, the shop has plenty of Wisconsin cheeses, including a wide selection of cheddars, to check out.

Follow the Wisconsin River through Merrill to **Sawmill Brewing Company**, a taproom housed in a 1940s Department of Natural Resources headquarters. In addition to rotating food trucks (check Facebook or Instagram before you visit for information), Sawmill offers Sam's Pizza and charcuterie boards. As for the beer, it's primarily low ABV, easy drinkers, including a blonde ale, wheat ale, kettle sour, and a maple pecan brown ale (brewed with locally sourced maple syrup). When the nights get crisp and the sun sets early, Fridays become Flannel Fridays, when anyone wearing red flannel gets fifty cents off a pint of beer. On weeknights you might see patrons sipping from mason jars while dressed up as Disney characters, surfers, nurses, and construction workers—the regulars take their themed trivia nights seriously.

If you're trekking through the central part of Wisconsin on a Friday or Saturday evening between early April and mid-November, **Stoney Acres Farm** is a nice place to relax, eat, and try a few craft brews. Two nights a

Sawmill Brewing Company, Merrill

week through summer and into fall, this organic farm offers house-made wood-fired pizzas on its lawn. Grab a table or bring your own chair, explore the farm, visit the cows and pigs, or just kick back and enjoy the great outdoors. Pizzas are made using ingredients from the farm, local cheeses, and artisan cheeses from around the state. The menu changes each week, but the farm strives to keep its Facebook and Instagram pages updated with current choices and pizza and pitcher specials. While you're enjoying your pizza, might as well try some of the farm's unfiltered, unpasteurized beer. Stoney Acres offers a cider, light lager, saison, Opetoberfest (depending on the time of year), IPA, and stout. It's small-batch beer, so there might not always be a full selection available. Your kids are more than welcome on the farm, but pets are not.

Detour

Poniatowski, an unincorporated area within Marathon County, is known as "the exact center of the Northwest Hemisphere." Back in the 1960s, a local resident named John Gesicki located the intersection of the ninetieth meridian of longitude and forty-fifth parallel of latitude here, and the US Geological Survey agreed that near the tiny spot Gesicki identified in Poniatowski was the midpoint between the North Pole and the equator. The town put a small park and plaque at the site, and visitors can join the 45–90 Club to commemorate their trip by signing a log at the Wausau/Central Wisconsin Convention & Visitors Bureau. It's worth noting that some scientists have disputed the claim (given that the Earth isn't smooth and round, but rather bulging in some spots and pitted in others). They pinpoint the exact center around ten miles north.

Farther south along Highway 97 is **Blue Heron BrewPub**. This seven-barrel-system brewery is located inside an old dairy processing plant. Parkin Dairy constructed the building and served the community until 1966, after which it was sold and became a storage facility, space for a bar, shops, and even an apartment. In 2004 Blue Heron's owners began to restore the building, and in 2005 the brewery opened its doors. Today Blue Heron is cranking out its signature beers—Honey Blonde, Tiger's Eye (a super-low ABV mild ale), and Loch Ness Scotch Ale, as well as an assortment of seasonal and specialty beers. If you're hungry, try the Ranch Beer Cheese Dip (served with pretzel crisps or soft pretzel bites), fried Nasonville Dairy cheese curds, or the Adult Grilled Cheese, a parmesan crusted sourdough topped with cheddar, swiss, pepper jack, bacon, and whiskey caramelized onions. If those don't meet your needs, there's always the mac and cheese pizza as a fallback plan.

WisconsInsights

Wisconsin is home to more than two hundred breweries, from nationally known mass-produced brands to tiny one-barrel taprooms.

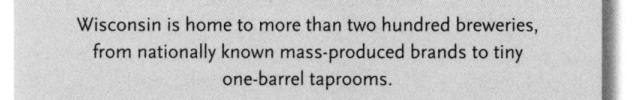

Once you're on I-94, **Sand Creek Brewing Company** is an easy stop to make. Calling itself "one of Wisconsin's largest microbreweries," the company got its start in a dairy farm shed making beer with a hodgepodge of equipment (intended for both brewing and not). But those bootstrap beginnings turned into something incredible: a brewery headed by a brewmaster who has won gold thrice at the World Beer Cup. The site the brewery calls home has an extensive beer history. The Oderbolz Brewing Co. was founded there in 1856, but after a series of tragedies struck the family, the brewery was sold in 1911 to a group of business owners who renamed it Badger Brewing Co. Prohibition spelled the end of Badger, and the building housed a poultry company (before fire destroyed much of it) and later a soft-drink bottling plant. In 1995 it became the home of Pioneer Brewing Co., and in 2004 it was sold to the current owners, who as an extension of the brewpub are also successful contract brewers for labels both within and outside of Wisconsin. Today Sand Creek operates out of what's left of the original 1856 building and stores its beer in the original cellar. Enough about the history. What can you actually drink? Sand Creek brews about a dozen craft beers and hard seltzers, including Wild Ride, an IPA that's a bit spicy, a bit citrusy, and even just a little floral; English Style Special Ale, a mildly hopped brown ale that has a touch of biscuit flavor; and Badger Porter, a creamy, easy drinker (for a porter). Among the most popular brews is Oscar's Chocolate Oatmeal Stout, which has hints of dark chocolate and roasted coffee. If you can't decide, try a flight or ask a bartender for some recommendations (you might even get a full flavor-profile rundown from the owner). If you ask nicely, expect a hefty sample before you pick your drink.

For your next stop, in Osseo, be sure to pay extra close attention to your GPS or you're likely to miss the turnoff for **Northwoods Brewpub and Grill**. Set back from the main road, this Osseo restaurant (with a second location in Cumberland) has a sizable food menu, with even bigger flavor. The squeaky, fresh, beer-battered Lynn Dairy cheese curds are alone worth the drive, but if you pair it with the Bacon Mac & Cheese Burger, you have truly arrived. Travel Wisconsin named it one of the seven most unique burgers in the state, and Visit Eau Claire calls it one of the best burgers in the area, which is a pretty big deal when you consider that Osseo is twenty-five miles south of Eau Claire. A hand-pattied burger cooked to perfection, slathered with creamy macaroni and cheese, then topped with bacon, this sandwich is great for sharing if you want to save room for your next stop (be sure to grab some extra napkins). To go along with your meal, there's a selection of Northwoods' own beers, which include lagers, ales, IPAs, porters, stouts, and a selection of limited release beers. Northwoods has two award winners, Lil' Bandit, an English brown ale, which won the silver medal at the Great American Brewfest, and Floppin' Crappie, an English mild, named the number-one beer at Sturgis Brewfest. The brewpub also has a line of Walter's Beer, a popular brand brewed in Eau Claire from 1874 until 1989.

The cheesemakers of Wisconsin are passionate about their craft (just as passionate as the Wisconsinites eating the cheese), and that shines through at **Eau Galle Cheese** in Durand. Since 1945, this family-owned cheese factory has been producing award-winning parmesan and asiago, along with blue, gouda, havarti, monterey jack, and, most recently, plain and flavored white cheddar curds. Its sweet, nutty, buttery parmesan and

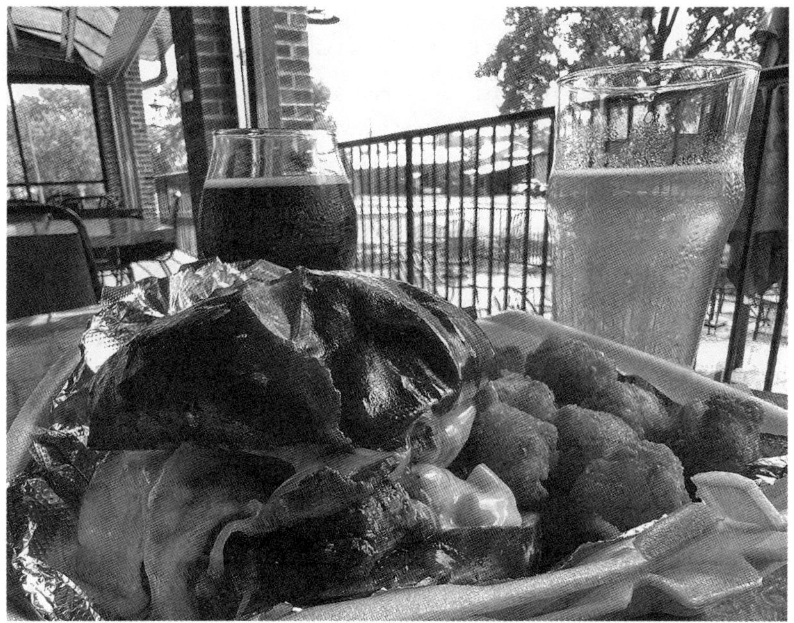

Northwoods Brewpub and Grill, Osseo

other cheese varieties can be found gracing the take-and-bake pizzas too. Stop in for some samples, curds, and maybe even a conversation with the Master Cheesemaker leading the operation. Eau Galle also has local beverages (including beer), brats, and other snacks if you want to take something home. One thing is for certain: you won't be left wanting. Eau Galle produces nineteen million pounds of cheese annually.

Pro tip: If you can't get a take-and-bake pizza from Eau Galle because you don't have a way to keep it cold or cook it, you can buy one at **Durand Brewing Company**, a mere half mile away. While you wait for a fresh pie, try a flight of some of Durand's most popular beers, including Butterfly Scream, an American IPA; Retread Red, an amber ale; or Honey Wheat, an American pale wheat brewed with local organic honey. Among Durand's fourteen taps, you might also find a cream ale, dark stout, kölsch, or blonde ale. If you're from Wisconsin, or you just love games, you'll be delighted to find cribbage boards at every indoor table.

WisconsInsights

In 2012, the Wisconsin State Fair added a Latin American cheese category to its cheese awards for the first time.

From Durand you have about a forty-minute drive to the next stop. Along the way you can ponder whether you want beer or coffee. But good news: there's really no need to decide at **K Point Brewing**, located inside The Coffee Grounds in Eau Claire. Enter through the combo coffee shop/specialty store/restaurant and head toward the back to find the brewery. What's on tap? Blood orange pale ale, an American lager, farmhouse ale, wheat beer, German lager, and a coffee stout brewed with cold press from The Coffee Grounds. The tap list rotates frequently, so you never know what you'll see the day of your visit. Order a beer at the bar and choose a table inside, amid the rich aroma of freshly brewed coffee, or outside. There are games to keep you entertained, and when you get hungry, pop into the store or coffee shop, which serves breakfast and lunch all day.

The next leg of the journey is essentially a craft beer lover and foodie tour in the area of Eau Claire, Wisconsin's seventh-most populous city. It begins in Altoona at **Ombibulous Brewing Company**. Its taproom is a little unassuming as you approach (be sure to choose the right-side door when you enter the vestibule or you'll be at the counter of an internet service provider), but once you're inside, the strip mall fades away and a Prohibition-era speakeasy comes into view. The fireplace is surrounded by couches if you're looking to relax, but upstairs there's shuffleboard and board games. Outdoor seating is available, weather permitting, and you might even stumble into a live performance by a local musician.

WisconsInsights

Wisconsin crafted the world's largest cheese board in 2018. It was thirty-five feet long and seven feet wide, weighed 4,437 pounds, and featured 145 different varieties of cheese.

K Point Brewing, Eau Claire

As for the beer, among the brewery's most popular are Hankey Pankey, a New England hazy IPA; Bee's Knees, a red lager; and Mug Shot, an oatmeal stout. If you're not in the beer mood, Ombibulous also has a selection of house-made seltzers.

Heading back across Highway 53, stop by **The Growler Guys**, a chain restaurant with twelve locations around the country (most of them in the West) but only one Wisconsin outpost. The one in Eau Claire is relatively small, yet it offers a good chance to try multiple Wisconsin beers from breweries you didn't have time to explore. Beer aside, the real reason to come here is for one of the signature menu items: the Cheesecurd-tastrophe. It's a pizza crust piled high with spicy cheese sauce, cheese curds, bacon pieces, mozzarella, and cheddar (plus jalapeños, if you like). Two people can easily share one of the ten-inch offerings. Of course, the restaurant has other options on the menu, including toasted subs, calzones, wings, and sides, like garlic cheese bread and Dank Stix, a cheddar-stuffed breadstick covered in mozzarella sauce.

If you haven't yet gotten your cheese fill, move on to **Eau Claire Cheese & Deli**. This small sandwich shop has a selection of Wisconsin cheeses and some local snacks too. The friendly staff are happy to offer samples before you settle on your purchase. The store, which is open daily, has a robust sandwich lineup (of course, most feature thick slices of Wisconsin cheese), including a BLT, a Reuben, and the Eau Claire special with roast beef, spicy pastrami, hot pepper cheese, lettuce, tomato, onion, and a special sauce on pumpernickel. If the weather is nice, staff fry up fresh cheese curds right outside the shop entrance. A perfect excuse for a summer trip to Eau Claire.

Not far away, in an old furniture showroom overlooking the Chippewa River, stands **Lazy Monk Brewing**, the brainchild of Leos Frank, who came to the United States from the former Czechoslovakia. The taproom brings the charm of an old bier hall, with long wooden benches for seating and doilies and table runners as far as the eye can see. Come in summer and you can also try out the biergarten. On weekends, the family- and dog-friendly bier hall fills up quickly, so get there when it opens to snag a seat and a flight. Given the theme and the owner's background, beers tend to be on the lighter side, and lagers, farmhouse ales,

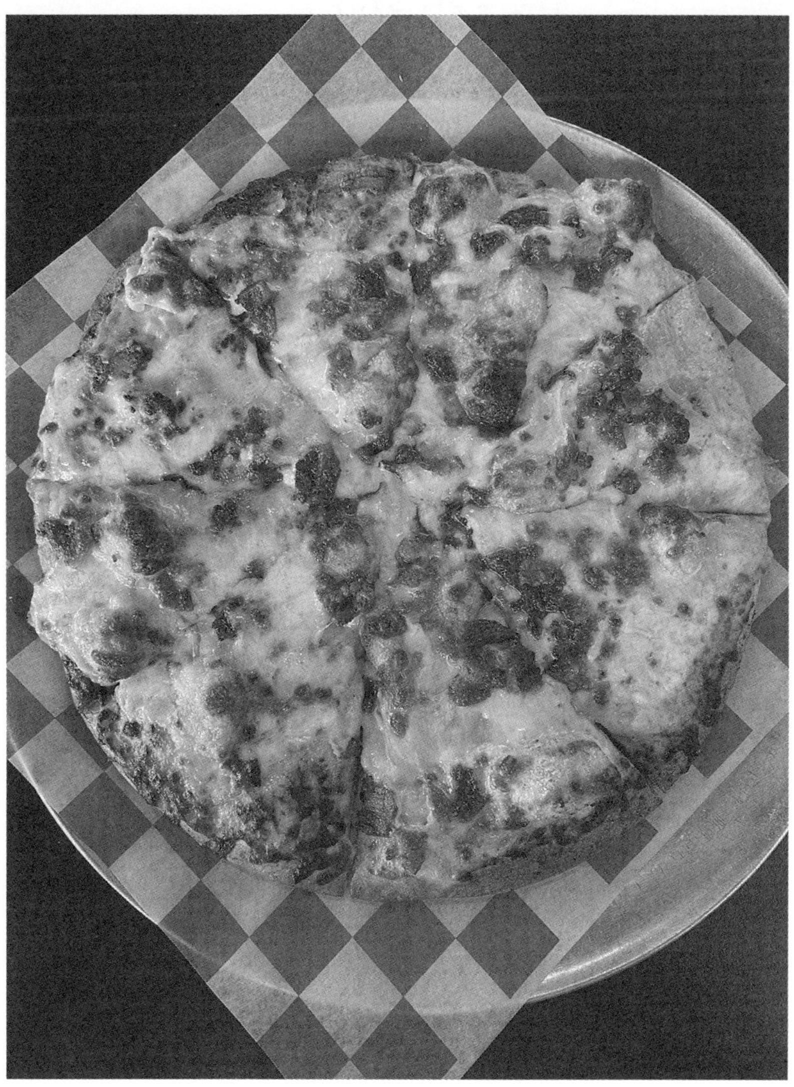

The Growler Guys, Eau Claire

Pit Stop

Throughout the year, Phoenix Park in downtown Eau Claire hosts a farmers' market, bursting with locally produced goods. Among the stalls is St. Isidore's Dairy, a farm located in Osseo that sells cheddar made from the raw milk of its ten Jersey cows, who pasture graze on Wisconsin grasses, wildflowers, and clover. Unlike a traditional cheddar, this is smooth and creamy, with a light color that is a result of the beta-carotene in the cows' diet. The farmers at St. Isidore's complete every step of the cheesemaking process by hand, following early American and European traditions. Hidden Springs Creamery, a relative newcomer, produces farmstead artisan cheese from the milk of its flock of around 350 sheep that graze in the Driftless region and enjoy the personal attention of the so-called Chief Sheep Cuddler. Hidden Springs has a handful of varieties available, some of which have won national and international awards. Among its offerings are Bad Axe, an aged cheese that melts perfectly on a grilled cheese or pizza; Driftless, a spreadable cheese available in flavors like honey lavender; and Bohemian Blue, a dry, crumbly blue cheese produced in cooperation with Hook's Cheese.

and pilsners abound, but you'll also see milk stouts, hoppy IPAs, and dark lagers for balance. As with many of the other Eau Claire breweries, this one doesn't have a kitchen, but you can check out one of the weekend food trucks or bring your own snacks. In keeping with the atmosphere, the first Saturday in December features a Christkindlmarkt, and late September means Oktoberfest. During those days, you can get food at the brewery, including (depending on the day) a brat.

Just up the street is **The Brewing Projekt**, a brewery that almost didn't get off the ground because of the 2013 federal government shutdown that delayed a federal brewer's license. But that's ancient history. Today the brewery has come far enough that the owners say they make so many things they don't even bother to list all the varieties on the website.

Lazy Monk Brewing, Eau Claire

Detour

Whether you're looking for something to commemorate your road trip, a gift to send someone back home, or just need more Wisconsin snacks and beers, make sure you stop by The Local Store. The shop has a little bit of everything—much of it locally made—from apparel to art to home goods to toys to food to drinks, all with some Wisconsin flair.

The Brewing Projekt's lineup changes fairly frequently, so it's worth checking Untappd before you visit if you're looking for something specific. In general, you'll find a number of smoothie-style sours (which are surprisingly thick for a beer), fruited sours, hazy IPAs, milkshake IPAs, and seltzers. If you're into pilsners or light lagers, this probably isn't the stop for you, but it does have a fun atmosphere worth checking out. The brewery is dog friendly (and kid friendly), whether you want to sit inside or outside, and sometimes you'll even see the staff walking around with treats for your four-legged friend. Because it's Wisconsin and the weather is unpredictable, there's a covered porch in addition to rooftop space and a huge indoor area where you can watch the brew operation or play a board game to pass the time.

You could easily overlook a place like **3rd & Vine** on a beer, brat, and cheese road trip, but you'd be missing out. What at first glance seems like a wine store is actually a craft beer and cheese-pairing venue. Although 3rd & Vine doesn't make its own cheese or brew its own beers, it stands ready to help you sample some of what Wisconsin does best. Many of the beers available are from the state, though some are from other parts of the country as well. There are six rotating tap lines and more than 150 beers in the cooler, meaning there's a high chance of finding what you want, even if that thing is a cider or seltzer. Pick your own cheeses from the case or let the staff pair a cheese with your beverage, then sit back and let your worries melt away. Whether you settle at the bar or grab a cozy table, you'll be enveloped in the warmth of friendly conversation all around you.

The Brewing Projekt, Eau Claire

If you head out of Eau Claire and toward Chippewa Falls in the morning, you can enjoy breakfast at **Mom's Kitchen**. The restaurant has your standard eggs, bacon, pancakes, and the like, but for a one-of-a-kind dish, go for the Rodgers "Hail Mary" Omelet. It's a true Wisconsin feast: an omelet stuffed with sliced brats, fried onions, and cheddar and mozzarella cheese, topped with a hollandaise sauce. Pro tip: Mom's Kitchen is closed on Tuesdays and Wednesdays, so plan accordingly.

It would be hard to take a road trip through the Chippewa Falls area without stopping by the **Jacob Leinenkugel Brewing Company**. Sure, you can now find Leinie's brews on the shelves of stores in all fifty states, but there's something fun about actually drinking it where it's been brewed and bottled for more than 150 years. The founder chose the brewery location because it was set higher on a hill than one of its competitors and, clearly, it worked (that or the beer is just really good). Leinie's successfully survived Prohibition by brewing a near beer and a soda

Pit Stop

To encourage visitors and locals to try out the area's breweries, Visit Eau Claire offers a mobile prize-earning pass: the Eau Claire Brew Pass. Simply sign up on your smartphone and you'll immediately receive a text and email with your pass, which you can save to your phone's home screen (there's no app to download). As you visit participating venues, ask the waitstaff for the venue code (or have them enter it for you) and you'll be "checked in" to another location on the crawl. The Brew Pass has more than a dozen possible check-in locations, and your combined visits could earn you a sticker, deck of cards, or T-shirt. Good news: no matter where you came from, the visitor's bureau will ship your prizes for free.

water, and by the end of World War II, it was one of the biggest breweries in the state not in Milwaukee. After expansion and an acquisition, Leinie's was purchased by Miller Brewing Co. in 1988. That purchase allowed Leinie's to expand operations to support booming popularity, as well as its growth into new markets outside of the Midwest. If you can, visit on a weekday to avoid the crowds. But either way, plan to arrive when Leinie's opens so you're sure to get a parking spot. The brewery is smack dab in the middle of a neighborhood, and if the lot at the brewery is full, you'll have to hunt for street parking. Just be kind, stay on

Pit Stop

Join locals and visitors each year in mid-September to celebrate German heritage at the Chippewa Falls Oktoberfest. With more than ten thousand in attendance, this lively event at the Northern Wisconsin State Fairgrounds features music, Glockenspiel performances, keg rolling, dancing, sauerkraut-eating competitions, German food and beer, games, and even a stein-holding contest.

Jacob Leinenkugel Brewing Company, Chippewa Falls

the sidewalks, and avoid trampling the lawns and gardens of the locals. If you like, start your visit with a tour of the brewery (book in advance online). You can choose the standard one-hour tour, a special tour with a member of the Leinenkugel family, or the pilot brewery tour to see Leinie's small-batch system and try some samples. When your tour is complete, head to the Leinie Lodge, shop for some merchandise, and try a flight (tours include four five-ounce samples, but you can also purchase flights without the tour). The lodge typically offers more than fifteen taps, including some available only there, and craft beer mixes. If you're hungry, the lodge sells fresh curds and Usinger's sausage sticks, and food trucks are parked outside on Fridays and Saturdays from May to October, including those selling delicious, juicy brats with a side of fried gouda mac and cheese bites. Pro tip: Check the website before planning your visit to see when the Leinie Lodge is having its half-off happy hour. At $2.50 a pint, you can't beat the price.

Pit Stop

In mid-June, the Leinie Lodge hosts its Summer Kick Off event, featuring food trucks, beer, games, live music, vendors, autographs from Leinenkugel family members, and more. A ticket (twenty dollars in advance or twenty-five dollars at the door) will get you three pints of beer.

After a visit to Leinie's, head east to fill your stomach (and car) with cheese. First up is **Yellowstone Cheese** in Cadott (a town with a sign proclaiming its distinction as "halfway between the Equator and the North Pole"), a relative newcomer to the Wisconsin dairy scene. Since late 2007, the creamery has been using milk from local farms to produce colbys, cheddars, monterey jacks, and cheese curds. In addition to the more straightforward options, Yellowstone—so named because it is along the Yellowstone Trail, the first vehicle route connecting Plymouth Rock to Puget Sound—offers flavored cheeses, such as green olive colby, ranch cheddar, and Yellowstone Crunch, a dessert monterey jack with chocolate, caramel, and walnuts. Fresh curds are available every day except Tuesday (closed Sunday).

Next, head southeast to **LaGrander's Hillside Dairy**. The family running the creamery, now in its third generation, is headed by Wisconsin Master Cheesemakers who each year bring in eight hundred thousand pounds of fresh milk from 140 dairy farms within a fifty-mile radius of Stanley, where the creamery is located. That milk is then turned into twenty-seven million pounds of curds annually, of which seven million pounds go to Culver's to be breaded and fried. In addition to the fresh curds, LaGrander's has colby, cheddar, pepper jack, gouda, and various other cheese varieties to try at the store.

PIT STOP

Each July, Chippewa Falls is home to the Northern Wisconsin State Fair. The event originated in 1897 because northern Wisconsin citizens struggled to get to the Wisconsin State Fair in West Allis. It's definitely smaller than the state fair, but you can still get your fill of beer, brats, and cheese (plus rides, games, farm animals, and grandstand shows). The fair abounds with brat stands and has two beer pavilions (both sponsored by hometown brewery Leinenkugel's). Among the most original of the cheese curd offerings are those at the stand with a giant sign advertising Cheese Curd Tacos. A must-try is the Wisconsin Cheese Curds and Brat Taco, a fried tortilla shell stuffed with brat slices and topped with cheese curds, slaw, and a spicy mayo.

By now, you likely know that Wisconsin is home to some of the best producers of swiss, cheddar, colby, and more. But in the small town of Thorp is some of the freshest gouda outside of the Netherlands—which makes sense, because the owners of **Marieke Gouda** grew up in the Netherlands, emigrated, and imported their cheesemaking equipment from there. All of their gouda is made within five hours of milking (you

Marieke Gouda, Thorp

can watch through the milking parlor windows at the farm across the street from the store), and then aged for at least sixty days rather than being pasteurized or processed. On your visit, tour the farm and milking parlor—you might even catch a glimpse of the cow "fitbits" that help track their digestion, health, and exercise. When you're done, visit Café Dutchess, the creamery restaurant that is open from 8 a.m. to 4 p.m. daily, for some farm fresh food. The lunch and dinner menu includes gouda melts and sandwiches created with Marieke Gouda, or you can sample its wares with the cheese board.

After sampling all things gouda, it's time to head west toward Lake Menomin. With more than a dozen taps, **Zymurgy Brewing Company** is a nice place to try something new. When possible, Zymurgy adds local ingredients (like cranberries and honey) to its brews, and even has a permanent collaboration with Brewery Nønic—a German pilsner called Zeitgeist. Some beers are available year-round, while others are seasonal or limited release. If you need a beer break, Zymurgy has house-made craft pop, hard seltzer, and root beer. The large taproom and patio has established itself as a community gathering space, and on any day of the week, you'll see locals listening to music, playing pool, taking a brewing class, or listening to experts discussing beer-related topics (fittingly, given that *zymurgy* is a branch of chemistry dealing with the study or practice of fermentation).

Less than a mile away, a refurbished train station plays home to **Brewery Nønic** and its eight taps and two cask beers. The flagships are a British bitter, Scottish ale, milk stout, IPA, and German-style pilsner. On top of that, the brewery has a multitude of seasonal beers and specialty items. Brewery Nønic doesn't have a kitchen, but there are food trucks on occasion, in addition to themed events, music, and movie nights. Check out social media for beer selections, hours, and events before you visit.

Just a bit farther up the road is **Lucette Brewing Company**, where the pizza flows as freely as the beer. There's really no way to go wrong sampling some of Wisconsin's finest cheeses here, with at least eight pizzas to choose from, all atop twenty-four-hour fermented dough (the brewery has gluten-sensitive crust alternatives) and smothered in local ingredients. There's also a huge, warm, soft pretzel served with house-made

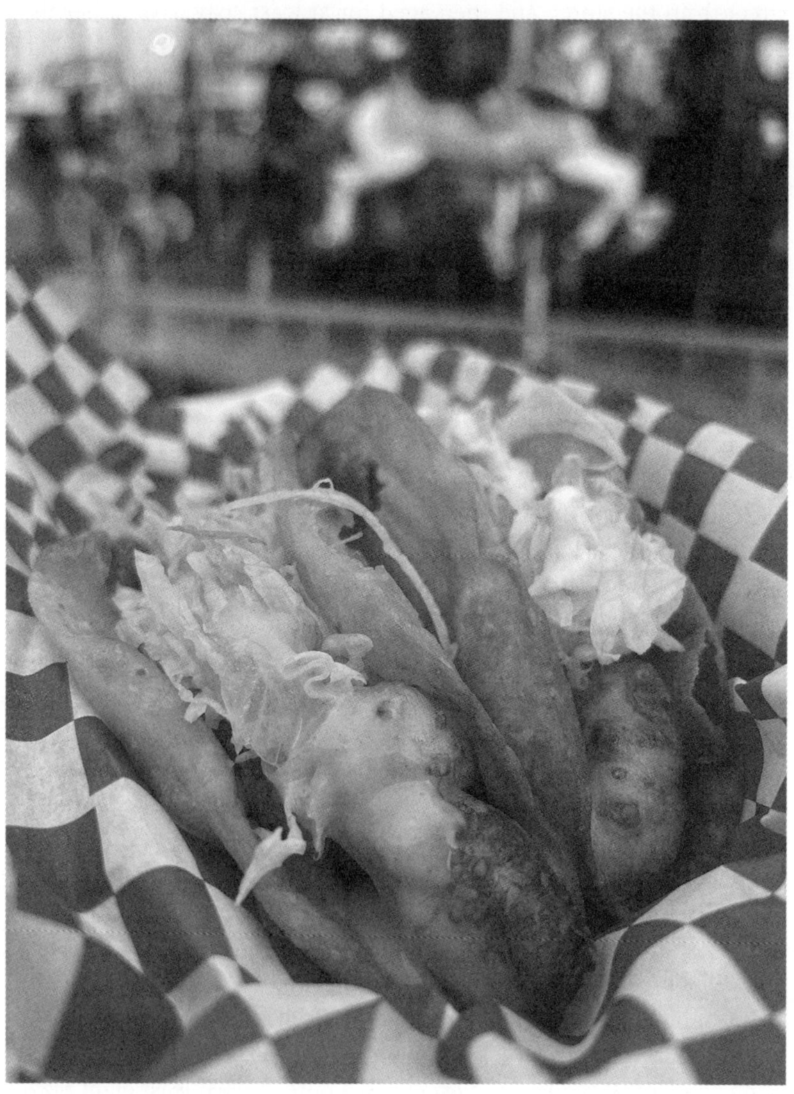

Northern Wisconsin State Fair, Chippewa Falls

bacon beer cheese, bruschetta sticks, and a dish called the OG Cheese, a breadstick with oregano, hand-pulled mozzarella, sea salt, a side of tomato sauce, and the option to add pepperoni. As for the beer—the brewery is happy to recommend pairings for your meal—Lucette has a blonde ale, imperial golden ale, some IPAs, a Munich helles-style lager, a dunkel, and the list goes on. Get it on draft or in cans if you want it to go.

If you still have room for cheese, now is the time to swing into the **Cady Cheese Factory & Store**. The company began as a cooperative in 1908. In the late 1910s, the cheese factory burned down and was rebuilt, only to be almost completely destroyed again in 1990. A new larger cheese factory was erected in its place, and that's what you'll find in Wilson today. This award-winning operation specializes in colby, cheddar (especially aged cheddars), monterey jack, colby jack, and gouda. You can find more than one hundred varieties of Wisconsin cheese in the store, including cheese curds.

Pit Stop

June is Dairy Month, and Ellsworth celebrates it with an annual curd festival. Over two days at the city's East End Park, visitors can expect six thousand pounds of curds for tasting, more than thirty craft beers to try, a curd-eating contest, cinnamon-sugar fried curds, a curd and craft beer–pairing battle featuring local breweries, a car show, entertainment, and more. Admission is free.

If you're still looking for more cheese, head southwest into Ellsworth, the Cheese Curd Capital of Wisconsin, to visit the **Ellsworth Cooperative Creamery** retail store (the company also has a shop in Menomonie). As you've no doubt noticed, many restaurants serve battered Ellsworth curds, and breweries stock them with snacks. Popping by the shop is your chance to try them at their squeakiest. Fresh curds are available every day of the week starting at 11 a.m., and believe it or not, customers will start lining up early just to get the first taste of the one hundred eighty thousand pounds of cheddar curds Ellsworth makes each day. In addition to curds, the store carries dozens of varieties of Ellsworth cheese, like the Antonella artisan cheese collection, a pressed curd, semisoft variety that's infused with natural flavors then aged and rolled in spice. Flavors include pepperoni with marinara, sun-dried tomato and pesto, and salsa with cilantro. Ellsworth block cheese comes in multiple styles, with everything from salami colby to cranberry muenster to caraway monterey jack and more available. The store also sells plenty of snacks, beverages, ice cream, and other local treats to round out your visit.

WisconsInsights

In 1984, Wisconsin's governor proclaimed Ellsworth the Cheese Curd Capital of the state.

Now it's off to River Falls, home to a University of Wisconsin campus, abundant trout fishing in the Kinnickinnic River, and miles and miles of hiking and biking trails through beautiful scenery. You wouldn't be blamed for thinking you're in the wrong spot when you arrive at **The Garage Bikes and Brews**. But if you've stumbled on a group of sweaty, spandex-clad bikers (bicycles, not motorcycles), you're in the right place. On the banks of the Kinnickinnic River (the Kinni or KK for short) is a bike shop and brewery. The brewery has a few of its own brews but, because it's crafted in small batches, the beer sometimes sells out. If that's the case, The Garage Bikes and Brews also has a selection of beers from other Wisconsin breweries. Drink in hand, you can sit on the patio or in the taproom, or just wander around and look at the dazzling array of bikes. Who knows? Maybe you'll decide to get a rental and cruise around River Falls for the afternoon! Just know that The Garage Bikes and Brews has limited hours, especially in winter, so plan accordingly.

If you did end up renting that bike, you can easily reach **Rush River Brewing Company** on the trails (of course, you can get there by car too). The brewery is located in an industrial park that also houses the River Falls Police Department and a Coca-Cola bottling plant. From late spring

The Garage Bikes and Brews, River Falls

to fall, covered outdoor seating is available, but there's plenty of space year-round in the large taproom. There are sixteen rotating taps to choose from, including some that are offered in the taproom only, board games to keep you entertained, and snacks and weekend food trucks to fill your belly. Year-round, a farmers' and makers' market is held weekly at Rush River in the early evening, where you can sample local goods and enjoy some music as well.

WisconsInsights

A total of 95 percent of all Wisconsin dairy farms are family owned.

Heading north, **Pitchfork Brewing Co.** serves up a classic combo: beer and pizza—one-of-a-kind craft pizzas to be exact. The crust is made from spent grain that is then smothered with a unique variety of toppings: pulled chicken with gouda; cream cheese, bacon, chicken, jalapeños, and a blueberry chipotle sauce; smoked roast beef and giardiniera; and more. Pitchfork also has a rotating specialty pizza topped with whatever the chef dreams up. There are other food options, including a giant soft pretzel with a side of pub cheese sauce, stuffed cornbread, loaded nachos, and paninis. As for the beer, Pitchfork is brewing up small batches of everything from brown ales and IPAs to cream ales and hefeweizens, all with locally sourced ingredients whenever possible. Far and away the most popular beer is the French Toast Ale, brewed with cinnamon and maple and served in a cinnamon-and-sugar-rimmed glass. On the second and third Wednesday of each month, a portion of the beer sales is donated to an organization chosen by a staff member (the week's charity is announced on Pitchfork's social media pages and website). Pro tip: Apple Maps tends to direct customers to the wrong (old) location. The address for the brewery is 745 Ryan Drive in Hudson. Best to just manually type it in so you don't miss out.

Only a stone's throw from Minnesota is the Wisconsin outpost of **Hop and Barrel Brewing** (be sure to slow down on Highway 35 or you might

Hop and Barrel Brewing, Hudson

miss it). The taproom is small, but makes up for its size in an abundance of pinball machines and other games. If you buy a beer (and really, why else are you there?), you can take a free tour as long as you book in advance. Hop and Barrel brews all kinds of styles, including the Minnesconsin, a helles lager, meant to honor the company's locations in both states. The brewery doesn't have its own food, but it has menus for local places that offer takeout or delivery and occasionally food trucks. There's a sizable free parking lot next to the brewery, while street parking will cost you a few dollars.

About fifteen minutes away in Somerset, **Bass Lake Cheese Factory** is family owned and operated and has tons of award-winning cheese varieties that you can watch being made through the viewing window. The Master Cheesemaker is certified in six varieties: cheddar, monterey jack, muenster, chèvre, colby, and juustoleipa. Plan your visit so you can enjoy either lunch or dinner at the deli. Choose from deep-fried cheese curds, a cheese sandwich, a grilled cheese served on Texas toast, or any one of its burgers and pizzas.

It's easy to miss **Oliphant Brewing**, but if you take a second to scope it out behind the Liquor Depot, you'll be treated to a taproom with plenty of character. It's certainly the only one included in this book with a wall lined entirely with VHS tapes. That uniqueness extends to the beer selection, in both taste and name. Past beers have included Meat Tubes of Antiquity, an imperial stout; Lumberjack Baes, a hazy IPA with citra, amarillo, and mosaic hops; and Sealed VHS Copy of the Kindness Trap (Coffee Edition), a bourbon barrel-aged imperial stout. The artwork on the cans is as unique as the beer names, but a flight is the best way to go if you want to sample the wide-ranging styles (you can always buy your favorites in cans on the way out). There are tables inside and a couple outside when the weather is nice, but it's best to get there early to nab a seat or visit on a weekday.

Heading east again is **Lift Bridge Brewery**, which, like Hop and Barrel, takes advantage of its border location to have a taproom in both Minnesota and Wisconsin. The New Richmond location is its newest and biggest, and the fairly large space quickly fills up on evenings and weekends. Grab a seat next to the interior windows if you want to watch the brew process in action, or just sit back and enjoy your beer. You might go for a cranberry golden ale, New England hazy IPA, fruity blonde, Baltic porter, or a fall favorite, the Fireside Flannel, a brown ale with notes of hazelnuts, coffee, and chocolate.

WisconsInsights

The village of Centerville came into existence in part because a brewery was established there in 1866 by a former resident of Manitowoc. The town's first cheese factory opened six years later.

Rounding out this portion of the road trip is **MoonRidge Brew Pub**, a quaint mom-and-pop establishment that's also making cheesy spent-grain pizza. Tap beers are named for local sites, for example, Shaws Road, an Irish draft; Below the Dam, an oatmeal stout; and Haymeadow, an Irish blonde ale. The pizzas are made fresh to order, and customers have the option to build their own or pick one of the brewery's specialty pizzas, with flavors like cheeseburger, Reuben, and BBQ smoked sausage. Hours are limited, especially between October and May when MoonRidge is open only Thursday through Saturday. This family-owned operation also closes for weddings, vacations, and some Wisconsin weather, so it's best to check the Facebook page before visiting.

CHAPTER 4

Up North and the Northwoods

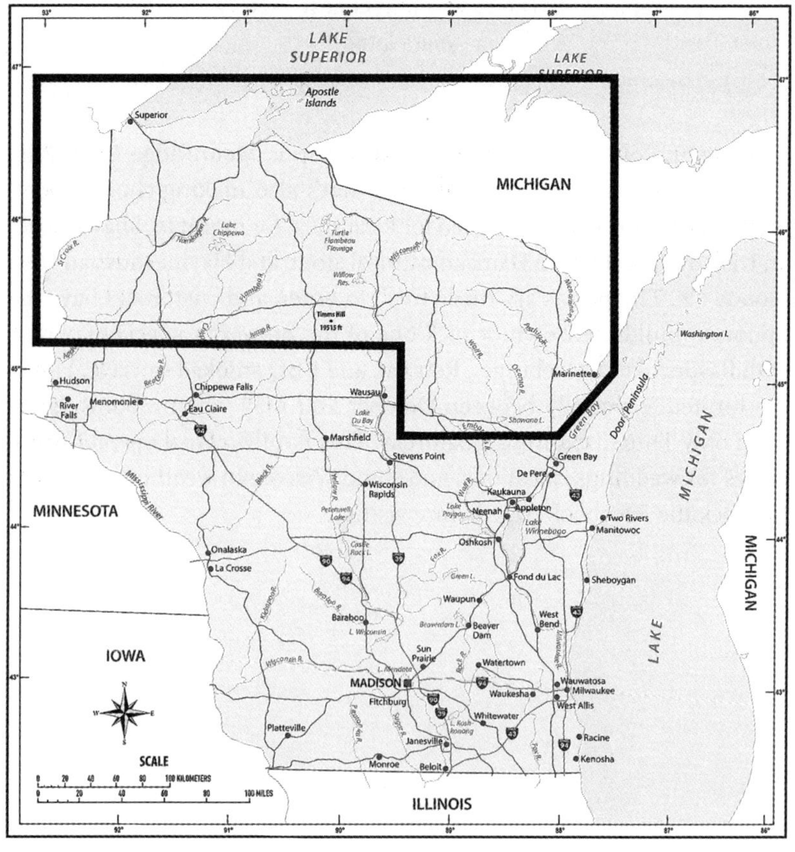

The boxed region indicates the approximate Up North and Northwoods area covered in this chapter.

There's a great debate among Wisconsinites about where "Up North"—the land of pristine lakes, lush forests, and woodsy cabins—actually begins. The answer tends to have something to do with where you grew up, though others argue it's about distinct changes in the landscape or when four-lane roads shrink down to two. Things get more interesting when you pile on the Northwoods, because while the Northwoods is Up North, not all of Up North is the Northwoods. For the purpose of this road trip, we'll define Up North as beginning midway between Highways 8 and 64. Compared to many other parts of the state, northern Wisconsin was never a cheesemaking powerhouse, because it lacks the acres and acres of clear farmland that allow dairy cattle to graze. Instead, from the mid-nineteenth century, this part of the state, and the Northwoods in particular, was for logging (around this time men working in the logging camps started telling tales about Paul Bunyan). Cured meats, like sausages, were especially popular in logging camps, as was drinking (though some expressly prohibited it to prevent unruly behavior). While the logging didn't last long once the forests were depleted (they've since been replenished), hearty food and drinks stuck around, and that's what you'll see today, among vacation homes, the vast Chequamegon-Nicolet National Forest, and miles and miles of sparsely populated forestland.

There are many unique establishments you'll visit on your road trip, and **Sawmill Pizza & Brew Shed** is no exception. It's open only on Sundays from noon to 7 p.m. and only in summer. If you can make it, you'll feel like you're at a backyard cookout. After a scenic drive (during which you may wonder if you're heading the wrong way), park your car in the grass lot and head into the first shed to order a pizza. The flavors are unique. You'll usually find the Spicy Jameese, a chewy wood-fired crust topped with tomato sauce, strawberry jam, sriracha, cheddar, and pepper cheeses, as well as the Pep Fest, with tomato sauce, pepperoni, and CoJack. The other pizzas on the menu are the monthly specials. You might see a BBQ with pulled pork and figs; a chicken, bacon, ranch; or, if you're lucky, the Best Wurst, with brats, sauerkraut, Ellsworth cheese

Sawmill Pizza & Brew Shed, Clear Lake

curds, green onion, and cheddar. Then, head to shed #2 and grab a beer. There's a couple IPAs, a porter, a brown ale, two tart ales, a Belgian witbier, and the Run of the Mill, the brewery's answer to "What's the closest thing you have to [insert Big Beer Brand] Light?" Once you have your drink, pick a seat on one of the porches and wait to hear the dinner bell ring, signaling that your pizza is ready. Stay all day, try all the pies and beers, bring a football to toss, or just listen to some live music.

Whether or not your visit coincides with Sawmill's open hours, there's another spot not too far away to try. In a converted barn in the woods is **Amery Ale Works**, where, as its slogan says, Great People Deserve Good Beer. The food menu is relatively small, though you can't go wrong with Tom's Famous Nachos, tortilla chips topped with beer-smoked brisket or chicken, beer cheese sauce, cheddar cheese, and all the usual nacho fixings. For something a little lighter, you might choose the pretzels with beer cheese, or just go all in and order a fresh, cheesy pizza. Amery Ale

Works doesn't have a ton of its own brews on tap, though it does usually have at least one that is brewed in-house, plus some other Wisconsin guest taps and commercial beers. Take care when parking at the brewery; the entrance (which is well signed) is located between two residential driveways. It's also best to check the website or Facebook page before you visit, because it keeps limited hours.

WisconsInsights

Wisconsin is the only state in the nation to require a cheesemaking license. Today there are upward of twelve hundred licensed cheesemakers who produce more than six hundred varieties of cheese.

Near Woolly Mountain Bike Trails, Gandy Dancer State Trail, and Interstate State Park—summer favorites among the area's hikers, bikers, and paddlers—is **Trap Rock Brewing Company**, a microbrewery focused on producing creative beers out of locally sourced ingredients. On tap Trap Rock has a pilsner, IPA, pastry stout, blonde ale, red ale, maple brown ale, and some rotating seasonal specialties and experimental brews. In summer, the patio accommodates outdoor enthusiasts just starting or wrapping up long treks, friends taking in the beautiful Wisconsin weather, and friendly pooches hoping their owners drop something from the week's food truck. The brewery is family friendly and has pizza available for purchase. On Thursdays, expect trivia night or bingo, and if you're feeling sporty, head out with the running club Thursday evenings. Of course, Trap Rock would still like you to stop by even in winter months, and the large yet cozy interior will warm you up.

Let's say on your journey farther into the Up North area, you need some fish, paper towel, and a hat, and also just happen to be thirsty for a cold beer. You can find all that and more under one roof at **Balsam Lake Brewery and Market**. The shop has everything you need while in town—produce, meat, dairy, snacks, meal kits, spices, and paper products. While there, you can check out the taproom and try a pizza and a house-brewed beer or two. Blondes, West Coast IPAs, and cream ales are available on draft. On Saturdays and Sundays during football season you can sample another Wisconsin specialty at the DIY Bloody Mary bar.

WisconsInsights

In 2023, the average herd size for dairy cattle in Wisconsin was around 215, as compared to more than 1,600 in California, the next largest cheese-producing state.

If you have time, take a detour about thirty minutes east to Cumberland for a stop at **Louie's Finer Meats**. Since 1970, longtime butcher Louis Muench Sr. and his family have been providing high-quality, fresh meats and sausages to the Cumberland community—in fact, any time you visit the shop, you're likely to find at least one member of the Muench family behind the counter. The store carries dozens of flavors of fresh brats you can take home, including those paying homage to the state: the Packer, stuffed with onion, garlic, cheddar cheese, and sauerkraut; the Badger, filled with onion, garlic, mozzarella, and pimento; the Northwoods, with jalapeño, cranberry, cheddar, honey, and maple syrup; and the Wisconsin, full of cranberries, cheddar, honey, and maple syrup. If you're in the area around Labor Day, be sure to check Louie's website or Facebook page for the date and time of Wurstfest, a festival of brats, beer, live music, raffles, free food samples, tastings, and door prizes.

Continuing on this detour, trek a bit farther east to the town of Rice Lake. There, a renovated feed mill turned brewery houses **Agonic Brewing Company**, where craft beers for locals and out-of-towners have been cranked out since mid-2021. One of its most popular brews is the Northerner's Ale, a dark wheat beer that is a take on German dunkelweizen, with a slightly sweet and fruity aroma. If that's not your style, there's a nitro chocolate oatmeal stout, wheat ale, hefeweizen, hopped amber ale, and an IPA, plus a few guest taps. The comfy, wood-adorned taproom hosts themed trivia nights on Thursdays, and a wood-fired pizza truck shows up some weeks to feed patrons. The open days are fairly limited, especially in winter, so be sure to check Agonic's website, Instagram, or Facebook page for details before you visit.

WisconsInsights

Wisconsin produces a billion more pounds of cheese than the next top cheese producer in the nation, California.

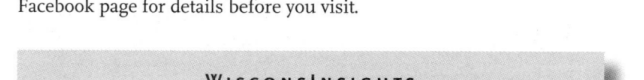

If you made the trek out to Louie's Finer Meats or Agonic, it's another seventy-five minutes northwest to the next stop (or a shorter forty minutes from Balsam Lake Brewery). Either way, if you're looking for an early drink, get yourself to **Brickfield Brewing** in Grantsburg. The family-friendly taproom, with dog-friendly outdoor patio (with fire pit) along Memory Lake, opens at 11 a.m. Monday through Friday and at noon Saturday and Sunday. Brickfield offers many beer styles, from light lagers to fruity and sour beers, medium and dark ales, porters and stouts, and even hoppy IPAs. Nonalcoholic options are also available if drinking before noon just isn't for you. If you get a chance, ask one of the bartenders (or owners) about how the brewery came to be. The short version: The old creamery building constructed in 1919, where the brewery is located, wasn't always meant to house Brickfield. Instead, owners Ben and Nicki Peterson bought it as office space for Nicki's marketing business. But, as people passionate about revitalizing Grantsburg, they felt like it could be more, so they decided to open a microbrewery. Ben is a fifth-generation dairy farmer, and the owners thought they could combine these two passions. The farm grows barley that is custom malted for Brickfield's beers, and the spent grain is fed to the farm's cows. While the brewery doesn't have its own kitchen, it does have a food truck some days, giving you the chance to order burgers and sandwiches made from meat from the family's farm. If you want to get your cheese on, opt for the loaded beer cheese fries, patty melt, or the grown-up grilled cheese topped with onions sautéed in Brickfield's milk stout.

The more you drive around Wisconsin, the easier it becomes to spot delicious cheese from a mile away. In Grantsburg, once you see the silos

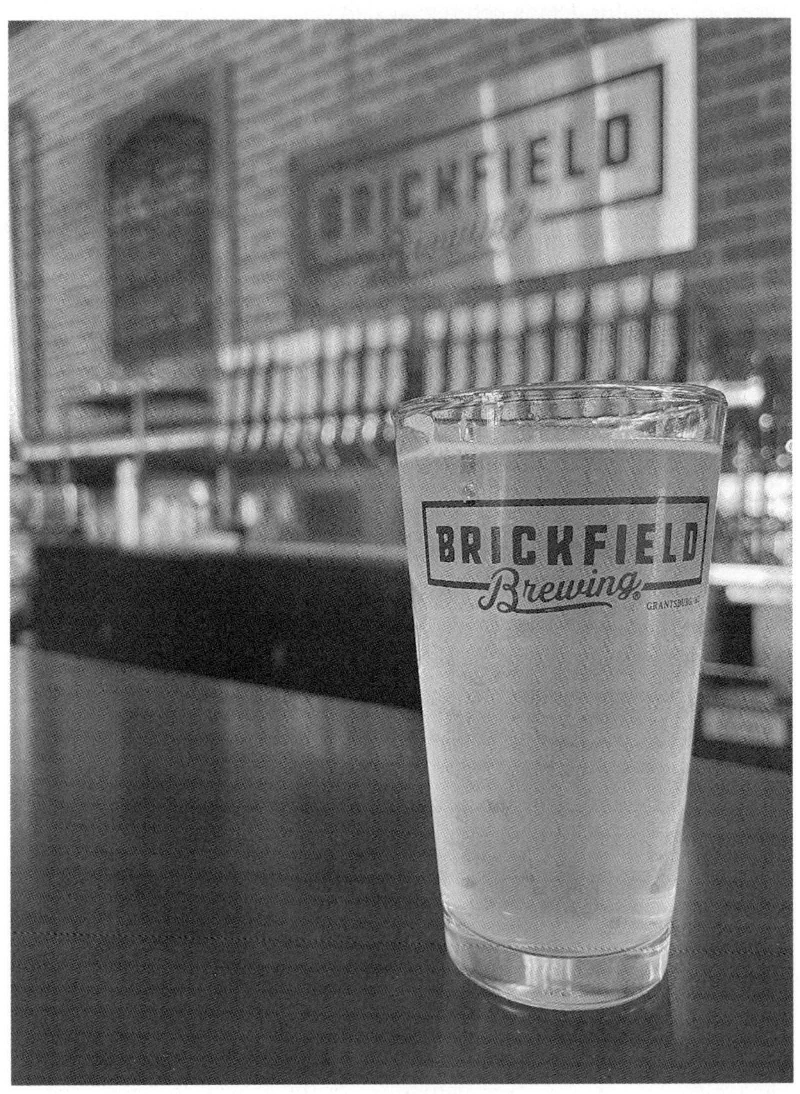

Brickfield Brewing, Grantsburg

you'll know you're close to **Burnett Dairy Cooperative**, a feast for the eyes, nose, and tastebuds. The hundred+-year-old co-op is owned by dozens of Wisconsin and Minnesota farmers and is one of the only remaining full-service agricultural cooperatives producing cheese. With more than one hundred varieties of cheese, plus a bistro cranking out warm sandwiches, soups, and fried cheese curds, it's hard to decide where to start. Since it can be dangerous to shop on an empty stomach, head to the bistro counter first. For breakfast, try an egg sandwich topped with Burnett's award-winning cheeses. If it's after 11 a.m., grilled sandwiches, pizza, soup, and appetizers (did someone say fried cheese curds and macaroni bites?) are ready for you to sink your teeth into. With a full, happy stomach, get browsing. Among the cheese of all sizes, colors, tastes, and forms, you'll find fresh cheese curds, cheese whips, plenty of snacks, and Wisconsin beers to go. Burnett Dairy makes its own string cheese, smoked string cheese, three- and five-cheese shredded blends, and a few other shredded cheese varieties. Under the Wood River Creamery moniker, the Master Cheesemaker crafts small-batch cheddar gruyère in myriad flavors, from black truffle to mango habanero. From the Cady Cheese plant, expect colby, gouda, havarti, swiss, and American, among others. Some of the cheeses are available in tiny one-serving packages if you can't make up your mind.

Farther east, Spooner offers another opportunity for a meal or snack. **Round Man Brewing Co.** bears an old nickname of one of the owner's (Jeff Churchill), but the logo bears a striking resemblance to former British Prime Minister Winston Churchill's physique. Located along Spooner's main thoroughfare, it's the perfect stop during an afternoon of strolling through the area's unique shops. Here you'll encounter more than fourteen taps with its original and signature brews. Among the most popular are the Mud Duck, a sweet milk stout that carries the name of Wisconsinites' less-than-friendly nickname for their Minnesota neighbors; the Hop Holding, a black IPA; and the Ha-Spoonah Colada hazy IPA, with hints of pineapple and coconut (availability is limited, mainly summertime). There's also an extensive menu to choose from, including a giant soft pretzel with beer cheese, poutine, cheese curds, smoked turkey nachos, and a host of sandwiches, soups, salads, and pizza. Seating

Round Man Brewing Co., Spooner

in the taproom and outdoors (weather permitting) is extensive, but the place definitely fills up most days of the week for lunch and dinner.

Detour

If you're looking for a unique way to see the Northwoods, consider visiting the small town of Trego and booking a ticket for the two-hour scenic Wine and Cheese Train. With a small group in a glass-domed car, you'll sample four Wisconsin cheeses and wines while watching the natural landscape ease by.

Continuing north, you'll come across Hayward, a tiny town that hosts two major racing events—one for cross-country skiing and another for biking. More important, there's also the cheesy stuffed pretzels, with a side of beer for good measure, at **Angry Minnow Brewery**, located in a historic 1889 building that housed the offices of the Northern Wisconsin Lumber Company. The dough for the stuffed pretzels is made from the brewery's spent grain, then each one is filled with either gouda, gouda and bacon, or gouda, pickles, and peppers. As for the beer, Angry Minnow makes a handful of its own microbrews, including an oatmeal stout, pale ale, honey wheat ale, light beer, and some seasonals. The brewery has limited hours (the kitchen hours are even fewer), so best to check the Facebook page before you visit to be sure Angry Minnow is open.

WisconsInsights

Twenty-three percent of the dairy farms in the United States are located in Wisconsin, and 90 percent of the milk they produce is turned into cheese.

Full of bread and cheese, it's time to drive up to Wisconsin's northwestern-most tip. Along the way, stop at **Superior Meats**, an award-winning butcher selling more than fifty flavors of fresh and frozen brats, including one that features Burntwood Black ale from Thirsty Pagan (a stop coming up next). Other flavors include cranberry wild rice, Thai curry, pizza, raspberry jalapeño popper, and sweet honey mustard. Superior Meats is open daily, so you have plenty of opportunity to take home a new flavor each time you visit.

Continuing farther north, just across the bridge from Duluth, Minnesota, are two breweries. Visit both if you have the time (they're vastly different in their beer selection), but if you're trying to pick one, it really depends on whether you're hungry.

In addition to craft beer, **Thirsty Pagan Brewing** is known for its house-made pizzas, topped with local ingredients (when possible), that easily pair with some of its brews (ask your server for ideas). Among the most popular offerings are the Derailed Ale, an American pale ale; Burntwood Black, a dark ale; and Lawnchair, a cream ale. Thirsty Pagan also has multiple seasonally available beers to wash down your pizza. The brewery has plenty of interior seating within what was built in 1908 as a passenger depot for the Wisconsin Central Railroad.

Earth Rider Brewery, on the other hand, is more focused on the beer, which is brewed with water from nearby Lake Superior. You can try its creations at the Cedar Lounge, the official Earth Rider tasting venue, which was built in 1912 by the Northern Brewing Company. In fact, Earth Rider was the first brewery to open in Superior after Northern Brewing shut its doors in 1967. The Cedar Lounge has that small-town bar feeling, with a stage for live performances, sports on TV, and random paraphernalia covering the walls. There you can sample Earth Rider's pale ale, helles lager, IPA, stout, pilsner, hazy IPA, blueberry cream ale, and a handful of other beers plus some hard seltzers (if you opt for cans to go, check out the intricate artwork on each, designed by a local artist who makes hand-cut woodblocks). The lounge does have pub pizza and some snacks for purchase, but no full kitchen; food trucks occasionally appear, otherwise you can get delivery. In summer, Earth Rider has a pop-up beer garden at the nearby aquarium.

Leave the industrial area of Superior behind for a scenic drive through the forests of the Northwoods as you head down Highway 2 into Iron River. The tap list at the cozy **Raven's Breath Brewery** is small, but that

Earth Rider Brewery, Superior

doesn't mean it's lacking in flavor. The brewer honed his craft over a quarter century to bring locals something to look forward to Wednesday through Saturday evenings. Among the most popular features of this nanobrewery are the Wailing Loon Black, a stout; Soaring Eagle Golden, a golden ale; Raven's Breath, an American pale ale; and Vulture's Head Red, an amber ale. The brewery is really a mom-and-pop shop, so it's best to check the Facebook page to figure out whether Raven's Breath is open the day you plan to visit.

Not far from Raven's Breath Brewery you can pick up a snack of meat and cheese at **Jim's Meat Market**, an area staple since 1981. The hickory-smoked pepper sticks, with flavors including teriyaki, cheddar, and pepper jack, are a popular local delight, as are the brats (so long as you have a way to keep these fresh sausages cool until you can cook them). Brat flavors include some standard offerings, as well as unique varieties like wild rice, onion garlic, chili cheese, and sauerkraut. Don't forget a bag of cheese curds for the road.

WisconsInsights

While Wisconsin as a whole ranks third in bars per capita, Iron County leads the nation in bars per capita.

A slight detour off Highway 2 will get you to **Benoit Cheese Haus**, a specialty shop selling more than 150 cheese varieties. Since 1973, the store has been operating under its mission statement: Sell Great Cheese at a Great Price. On any day you visit, expect to find everything from the freshest curds to a twenty-year aged cheddar. If you stop by on a Tuesday, Thursday, or Friday, you'll be greeted by fresh curds (assuming you get there before the curds sell out!). Fresh colby is available on Thursdays.

Given that you're now driving primarily through forests and lightly populated areas, you might find yourself doing a bit of backtracking for these next few locations, but they're worth it. **Tetzner Dairy Farm** is an absolute gem of a stop (pro tip: be sure you have cash on hand for this one). As you drive up to the farm, you'll first suspect that you're lost, and then you'll be sure that you're in the wrong place. But trust the process. Find a good spot to park your car (one that doesn't look like it will block farm equipment or the door to the store) and head inside the unassuming shop. The small room you find yourself in has all the fresh dairy you could ask for: milk, ice cream, cheese cubes, cheese curds, ice cream sandwiches, string cheese, and more. What you'll quickly notice, however, is that there's no register or staff. Instead, take an envelope near the door you came in, write on the outside what you purchased and the price, then pop your money into the envelope and place it in the locked box. The cheese you see in the cold cases comes from Anderson Distributors, a company that picks up cheese from factories around the state, while the curds are specifically from Nasonville Dairy in Marshfield. For another protein to snack on, get a bag of beef sticks (or the beef stick–cheese cube mixed bag). Now, even though this is a beer, brat, and cheese road trip, you'd be missing out if you don't try an ice cream sandwich to go with a bag of variety cheese. The ice cream is made once every one to two weeks at the farm, and the sandwiches are made by hand. Choose from vanilla, chocolate, chocolate mint, and cherry.

The coastal town of Bayfield, around twenty minutes north from your last stop, hosts **Adventure Club Brewing**. Admittedly (and the owners would tell you so themselves), it's an über-small craft brewery, but a favorite among locals, which means that sometimes the house taps are, well, tapped out. When that happens, Adventure Club invites another brewery to host a tap takeover and tries to announce it on social media. If you're lucky and in at the right time, you might be treated to Adventure Club's Cider Donut Beer, Wisco Bay cream ale, or the high-ABV Imperial Siberian, a Russian imperial stout that is one of the brewery's best sellers. Just be sure you pick the right door when you arrive—or you'll be buying outdoor gear instead of beer. If it's one of those few months when it isn't bone-chillingly cold in the North, stay for a round on the nine-hole disc golf course.

After backtracking down Highway 13, you'll reach northern Wisconsin's first modern microbrewery and the seventh licensed in the state, **South Shore Brewery**. The outlet has two locations, one in Ashland and one in Washburn. At both spots, you can find its flagship beers, including Nut

Brown Ale with a smooth caramel flavor (winner of the 2002 World Beer Cup silver medal), a chocolate stout, the Northern Lights cream ale, a pilsner brewed with honey, and a pale ale brewed with Wisconsin-grown malts and hops plus some water from Lake Superior. Depending on when you visit, expect some seasonal brews, like an Oktoberfest or the Apple Fest Ale. The Washburn taphouse invites well-behaved dogs to hang out both outside and inside but doesn't have a kitchen of its own (you're welcome to bring in your own food, get delivery, or try a food truck if one is hanging around). The Ashland location is located in the same building as Deep Water Grille and The Alley. The Alley has more traditional bar food (curds, wings, pizza, and the like), but it also has a beer cheese soup brewed with South Shore's Nut Brown Ale, plus a host of mac and cheese options served bubbling hot in a cast-iron skillet. The options at Deep Water Grille are a bit more upscale, but it creatively uses South Shore beers as well, such as in the poutine, which is topped with chicken braised in the Nut Brown Ale and the beer cheese soup. The good news is that you don't have to hop from place to place to get some food and drinks. They all operate out of the same space, so you can order and relax.

WisconsInsights

Wisconsin has more than one hundred cheese factories.

It's a long trip to the next spot (some seventy-five miles), but **Some Nerve Brewing Company** will help you feel like you've truly arrived in the Northwoods. The cozy taproom abuts the forest, the large picture window behind the bar gives a great view of Wisconsin's four seasons, and the deer and bird feeders mean you might see some local wildlife. There's no kitchen, so plan to eat elsewhere or bring in your own food (maybe some of that cheese from Tetzner Dairy), or help yourself to the free popcorn. Some Nerve has four beers available year-round: Cream Abdul-Jabbar, a cream ale; Gobsmacked, a British oatmeal stout; Geronimo Jackson, an IPA; and Tim McCracken, an Irish red ale. As for the rest of the lineup, it depends on what the brewer wants to make. The brewery is constantly producing new beers, such as ginger-cranberry blonde ale (made with local cranberries), a chocolate and peanut butter porter, or a cherry milkshake sour. Some Nerve's website has the most up-to-date tap list so you can plan your visit on what sounds good.

Cutting your way southeast through the forests and past lakes along Highway 51 will take you to the Snowmobile Capital of the World and Hockey Capital of Wisconsin, Eagle River. **Tribute Brewing Company** uses its beers to honor the town it calls home. For example, there's 28 Lake Lager, named after the world's largest chain of freshwater lakes; Old Eagle Porter, after the first steamboat that navigated the Eagle River; and Summerwind IPA, whose namesake is the eerie ruins of a mansion of the same name on the shore of West Bay Lake. The name of one of its most popular beers, Blueberry Train Wheat Ale, honors the trains that used to take blueberries into Chicago in the early 1900s, while Motor Toboggan is a coffee stout named after a vehicle meant to travel over snow designed and tested nearby in the 1920s. In addition to these flagships and favorites, plenty of others are on tap, including limited brews and seasonal offerings. The hours are somewhat sporadic, so be sure to check the website before you visit to confirm that Tribute is open.

When you're back in your car, head west, past the dozens of campgrounds that dot the state parks and natural areas. Before you reach Minocqua, around sixteen taps are ready to greet you at **Rocky Reef Brewing Company**, the number-one thing to do in Woodruff, according to TripAdvisor. What can you expect? Ping-pong, friendly conversation, dogs, live music, food trucks, plenty of patio seating, and a giant taproom when the weather gets too Wisconsin-y. The beer menu really does run the gamut, with plenty of fruity sours, a few IPAs, multiple dark ales, and some light, easy drinkers. Among patron favorites are the Musky Bite, a West Coast IPA; The Outhouse, a brown ale; Staycation, a blonde ale; and Juicer McGavin, a New England IPA.

Minocqua is located on a small peninsula in a lake of the same name. It's a water-sports heaven, and in summer months its streets are packed with locals and out-of-towners. Small shops and restaurants litter the map, and among them is **The Cheese Board of Wisconsin**. While that might sound like the name of an official agency that grades and rates cheese, it's actually a store full of friendly staff and a great many Wisconsin cheeses (plus meats, fudge, and specialty foods that could complete any cheese board). Locals know it's the place to go when you need cheese spread—flavors include garden vegetable, sharp cheddar, and cheddar with bacon. But the curds, flavored stiltons, aged cheddars, salami loaf, and muenster with walnuts also have a discerning audience.

Minocqua's downtown offers **Otto's Beer & Brat Garden**. This pub has an old-world European feel and a large beer garden. The star, as the name implies, is the brat, made in Sheboygan for the restaurant. You can get it a couple different ways. Otto's Famous Bratwurst is flattened with the casing removed, charbroiled, and served on a soft bun with a side of sauerkraut. The Spatenbrat is simmered in beer and charbroiled before being placed on a bun and served with sauerkraut. The flavor of the brat shines through no matter how you order it, and pairs especially well with a beer cheese soup and a beer (Otto's doesn't brew its own, but has plenty to try). Be sure to check Otto's Facebook page before you visit to avoid any off-season closures.

Thirty more minutes of driving will put you in the home of the Hodag, a folkloric creature born out of lumberjack campfire tales that has been described as a combination of a frog, elephant, and dinosaur, complete with a speared tail and long claws. The city is also home to **Rhinelander Brewing Company**. Rhinelander Brewery was founded in the late 1800s and made a name for itself with its Shorty bottle, a seven-ounce serving. The company lasted until 1967, when it closed its doors and sold the rights to its beer to the Joseph Huber Brewing Company (now Minhas). Enter Jyoti Auluck, a Canadian-born beer enthusiast, who purchased Rhinelander's brand name and all its assets in 2009 with the aim of reintroducing the Shorty. After brewing in various locations around the state, Auluck settled on bringing the product back to Rhinelander. Today you can hunt a Hodag, then settle into the Rhinelander Brewing Company taproom for a Shorty or any one of its other beers, like a double IPA, traditional ale, stout, or light lager. There's no food at the brewery, though they have plenty of popcorn to keep you happy until you get to your next stop.

Big Daddy's, Rhinelander

The last stop on the Up North portion of this road trip comes courtesy of **Big Daddy's** in Rhinelander for two reasons: cheese and brats. At this hole-in-the-wall bar, start with the Wisconsin Roll, an eggroll wrapper stuffed with brats, mozzarella cheese, onions, dill pickle relish, and sauerkraut. They're sold by the roll, and if you're with someone, be sure to get two or you'll be fighting over who gets the bigger half. Then, for your main course, order the Wisconsin Cliché Burger, topped with a brat patty, cheese curds, American cheese, and drizzled with a beer cheese sauce. Patience is key here: everything is made to order, which pays dividends in big flavor, and the bartenders are happy to keep you entertained while you wait.

CHAPTER 5

Green Bay and Northeastern Wisconsin

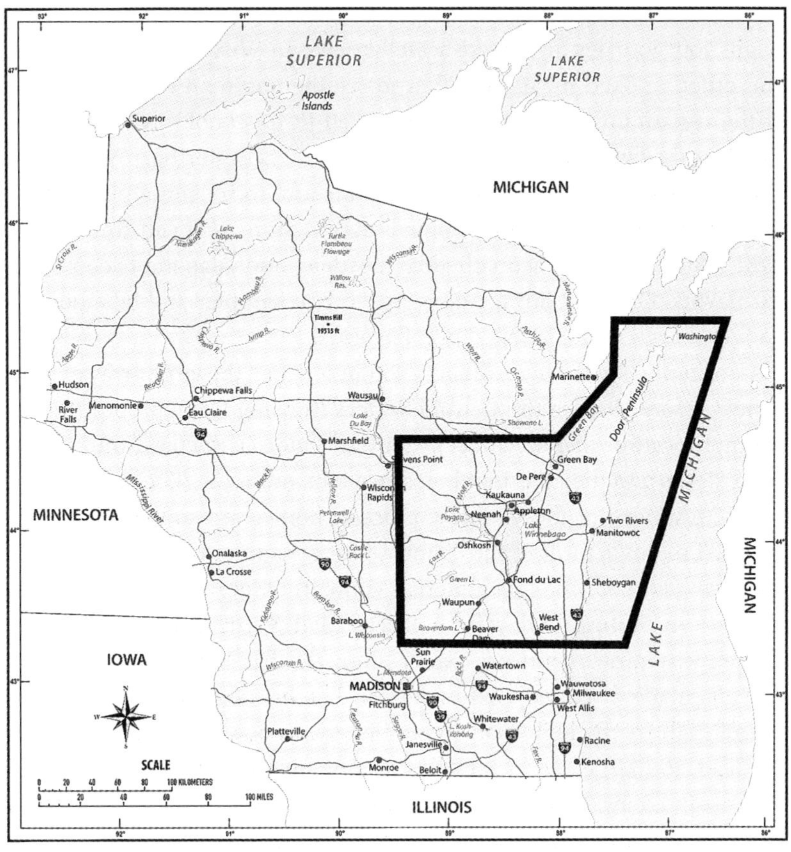

The boxed region indicates the approximate Green Bay and northeastern Wisconsin area covered in this chapter.

This portion of your Wisconsin culinary adventure takes you to some of the state's most iconic spots, namely, Green Bay (home of the Packers), Sheboygan (home of the brat), and Door County (home of the summer vacation). Much like the southern half of the state, the northeast corner of Wisconsin attracted large numbers of European immigrants who used the regional climate and their know-how of cheese, sausage, and beer production to craft the foods and libations that made Wisconsin famous.

~

Begin your journey at **Nueske's**, well-known in Wisconsin for its bacon and other smoked meats (you'll even see the name on menus of some of the restaurants and brewpubs featured in this book). And why not? The Nueske family has been selling its products in northern Wisconsin since the 1930s. While in Wittenberg, be sure to try some of Nueske's other applewood-smoked delights: brats. In store, you can find a standard brat, as well as bacon cheddar, cheddar, and jalapeño bacon cheddar flavors. Or go all out for the smoked brat sampler and take home a pound of each of the smoked brat flavors.

Continuing south into Amherst, you might spot the large array of solar panels before you see the **Central Waters Brewing Co.** taproom (there's another location in Milwaukee). Central Waters is focused on being a good steward to the land that helps make its products. The solar panels keep the water hot for the brew process, bottles are sourced from the greenest manufacturer in the country, post-consumer recycled cardboard packaging is used, and raw materials come from local vendors whenever possible (including barley from Briess Malt & Ingredients Company, located just ninety minutes away). Even the bar top in the sampling space is made from recycled materials. The brewery's environmentally friendly efforts made it Wisconsin's first green-powered brewery. As for the beer, the large menu includes a honey blonde ale made with real Wisconsin honey; Mudpuppy Porter, a chocolatey, malty porter; and HHG Pale Ale, an American pale ale inspired by Wisconsin rockers Horseshoes & Hand Grenades. Food trucks are around during the warmer months, but you're otherwise welcome to bring your own food or get something delivered. Free brewery tours are offered on Saturday afternoons. Patio seating opens early at the brewery each day, but the indoor taproom seats aren't available until afternoon.

WisconsInsights

The Milwaukee Brewers High-A minor league baseball affiliate, the Wisconsin Timber Rattlers, have played as the Wisconsin Brats, complete with jerseys meant to mimic lederhosen, to celebrate the sausage's place in Wisconsin life.

A mere twenty minutes away is the town of Waupaca, home to **H. H. Hinder Brewing Co.** The taproom opened there specifically because the owner set out to find a city in Wisconsin that had never had a brewery and told his friends its name would be the opposite of Hooters (then refined the name a bit at the suggestion of his wife). They've gone all in on the theme, and the atmosphere reflects the owner's brand of humor. There's the Café Keister coffee stout, Butt Lite lager, Uncle Heine white IPA, and the GladAss porter. The menu rotates and features standard bar fare (cheese curds, pretzel bites, chicken tenders, and pizza), as well as lumpia, Filipino eggrolls with flavors like five-cheese mac, Philly cheese, Korean beef, chicken enchiladas, and Nashville hot chicken and cheesy mac.

It's just a short drive to **Weyauwega Star Dairy**, a cheese producer known for its Italian cheeses, such as parmesan, asiago, and romano (though Weyauwega makes plenty of other varieties too). Owner Jim Knaus comes from a long line of cheesemakers and has used his skills to craft some tasty cheeses while having a little fun along the way. The company was listed in the Guinness Book of World Records in 1995 for having the world's longest string cheese. Coming in at 1.5 miles long, it was carried through the company's namesake town of Weyauwega on people's shoulders. The dairy farmers who supply the milk for Weyauwega's cheese all work within a fifty-mile radius of the factory, ensuring only the freshest milk is used to make its products. At its small storefront, in addition to the Italian cheeses, all of which are aged a minimum of ten months, you'll find an aged sharp cheddar, aged brick cheese, processed American cheese, baby swiss, blue cheese, cheddar cheese curds (of various flavors), yellow cheddar, cheese spread, colby, marbled cheese, farmers cheese, feta, and more. The store also has other grab-and-go products, including meats, beer, snacks, and drinks.

Nearby, **Rio Lobo** bills itself as a winery, but it also brews craft beer and makes some charcuterie platters out of local cheeses. If pizza is more your style, check the website before your visit to see if it's on the menu that day. Rio Lobo makes its dough and sauce from scratch, and many of the toppings come from its family farm. The most popular beer on tap at Rio Lobo is the Wolf Blood, a dark red lager, followed by the El Toro Rojo red lager and Black Boar dark lager.

In the small town of Fremont, the 8 a.m. tour at **Union Star Cheese Factory** is well worth waking up for. This tiny place has been cranking out artisanal cheeses since 1906. It has an interesting backstory that involves dairy farmer Henry Metzig getting upset with the creation of the Babcock test, a method for determining the fat content in milk, which labeled his product as "low fat." So what's a Wisconsinite to do? Start a cheese factory, of course. Henry's daughter, Edna, would go on to become one of the first women in the state to earn a cheesemaker license and work in a factory setting. The Union Star name has continued to live on, and today Edna's great-niece and great-nephew own the place. All made from 100 percent local milk, Union Star's cheese includes provolone, mozzarella, marble, monterey jack, salami colby, farmhouse cheddar, flavored and aged cheddars, swiss, feta, brick, flavored muenster, havarti, farmers cheese, gouda, and what Union Star calls Curds in a Cloud Muenster, a traditional muenster with curds added to the mold to produce a unique-looking block cheese that's almost too neat to eat (almost). Two stars of the show here are the cheese curds and cheese whips.

The constant rotation of beers is what draws Omro locals to **Omega Brewing Experience**. The husband-and-wife team running this small brewery along the Fox River keep around twelve beers on tap (impressive, considering they're classified as a nanobrewery) and make anything from a rye barrel-aged Scottish ale to an imperial double IPA to an American porter to a farmhouse ale to a barley wine brewed with cherries from Door County. Expect a new lineup every time you visit.

Come for the craft beer, stay for the wood-fired pizza at **Knuth Brewing Company** in Ripon. The owner and brewmaster got his start with a home-brewing kit he received from his father-in-law. That small-batch know-how has carried over to the brewery, which has a constantly evolving selection of ales, stouts, IPAs, hefeweizens, lagers, and pilsners. As for the pizza, it's all cooked in the hand-built pizza oven and starts with scratch-made dough before being topped with sauce and freshly shredded mozzarella. Build your own or go for one of the specialties, like the Thai chicken peanut, pesto chicken, or The Meats, loaded with sausage, pepperoni, bacon, and ham. Not for you? How about the Wisconsin meat and cheese board or mozzarella and parmesan cheese sticks? There are also plenty of sandwiches and salads to try, including the Brown Bag Special, a sandwich topped with Wisconsin cheddar, Dusseldorf mustard, sliced pickles, and oven-roasted ham.

Not far east, downtown Fond du Lac is dotted with small local restaurants, and among them is **18 Hands Ale Haus** on East Division Street. Located in part of a former livery stable that dates back to the 1880s, the pub is a showcase of German-style bier hall flavors, from the homemade pretzels to the warm potato salad to the lineup of wursts. You can enjoy a brat here multiple ways: on a pretzel bun topped with sauerkraut, German mustard, and raw onions; as a flight with a side of pickled red onions; on top of a thin pretzel crust, smothered in beer cheese, gruyère, sweet onion sauce, and German mustard drizzle; as part of a pretzel kabob; or as a nacho topping on a pile of kettle chips with beer cheese, sauerkraut, and gruyère. The restaurant always has eighteen beers on tap, including some from Germany and a handful of Wisconsin brands.

Driving up Highway 45 along the shores of Lake Winnebago, you'll arrive in Wisconsin's ninth-largest city, Oshkosh. If you like your beer on the fruitier side, then the city's **Fifth Ward Brewing Company**, which took its name from the nearby Fifth Ward Brewery that operated in the 1800s, is a must-stop. This small taproom has around twenty rotating offerings, and while there's a good selection of malty, hoppy, and light beers, many of them trend toward the sweeter side, for example, the popular Raspberry Pie Frootenanny, a fruited sour, or the Sconnie Surfboard, a dry-hopped pineapple sour. Choose a seat at the bar, a high table, or outside in the beer garden. A comedy showcase is held the first Friday of each month, and there are live music acts regularly.

WisconsInsights

More than thirteen festivals in Wisconsin are dedicated to cheese.

On the other side of the river that bisects Oshkosh is the **Fox River Brewing Company** (another location is at the Fox River Mall in Appleton). Sited along the waterfront, patrons can choose from indoor seating or a private riverside dome. Fox River's signature beers include the Blü Bobber blueberry ale, Red Bobber raspberry ale, White Bobber pineapple wheat ale, Reel It In IPA, Fox Light blonde ale, and Marble Eye, a malt-forward ale with hints of caramel, toffee, and coffee. The restaurant also boasts a large menu, full of pub classics and wild game specialties, like the elk and brisket burger, BLT made with venison bacon, and an elk, beef, and pork meatloaf. On Packer game days, you might see the Tailgater Pizza on the menu, with Johnsonville beer brats, sauerkraut, caramelized onions, and a signature sauce.

Continuing up Highway 45, you'll arrive at **Bare Bones Brewery**, a taproom whose theme was inspired by the owner's rescue pit bulls. The brewery's motto is Fear No Beer, and the aim is to familiarize visitors with various types of craft beers and inspire them to try styles they may have been skeptical to sample in the past. Bare Bones keeps a handful of house beers on tap, including its popular Dog Daze IPA and Amber Ale. This is definitely a place where everybody knows everybody, but the bartenders are happy to welcome and chat with visitors too. If you're interested, the brewery rents electric bikes for use on the nearby Wiouwash Trail that wends its way through Winnebago, Outagamie, Waupaca, and Shawano Counties.

The nearby **Lion's Tail Brewing Co.** now has two locations, one in Neenah and one in Wauwatosa, and it cranks out thirty or more new beers every year. That means each time you visit, you're likely to see something new on the tap list. Lion's Tail has cream ales and IPAs, sours and lagers, and stouts and porters. Neither location has a full kitchen, but depending on the day of the week, you might be able to catch a food truck (or even a food bus), or you can order delivery (events and food trucks are listed on a calendar on the brewery's website). Fun fact: the brewery once offered a Custom Pale Ale that customers were able to dry-hop themselves on a French coffee press at the bar.

From Neenah, head northeast into Appleton and pull off when you see the giant red barn and blue silo east of the highway. Inside **Lamers Dairy**—which has been family owned and operated since 1913—there's a wonderland of milk and dairy products. All of the milk Lamers uses and sells comes from family farms within a thirty-mile radius of the store. In fact, the milk it bottles and sells—which has won six first-place awards at the World Dairy Expo Championship Dairy Product Contest—is usually ready for sale within hours of pickup. It's about as fresh as you can get without heading to the farm yourself. The shop also has plenty of cheese to choose from, both that crafted for Lamers and other Wisconsin brands, along with snacks, gift items, and ice cream.

If lunch or dinner is on your mind, plan to get to **Appleton Beer Factory** early because it fills up fast, and be sure to come hungry. The brewery is located in a former auto supply building, and most of the chairs and tables inside were built from found materials in the shop and apartments above. The food menu is packed full of soups and salads, sandwiches, pizzas, tacos, burgers, and plenty of appetizers. Among the sandwiches and appetizers are both jalapeño and plain brats (served in baskets of one or two), plus the Brats & Bites Basket, with two cheesy jalapeño brats and pretzel bites topped with shredded cheddar, beer cheese sauce, bacon, more jalapeños, and green onions. There's also the crowd favorite Ouisconsin Poutine, a plate of homemade pub fries topped with Wisconsin cheese curds, beef gravy, mozzarella, green onions, and—if you're feeling adventurous—a sliced brat. Appleton Beer Factory has about a dozen taps, most of which are house craft beers plus a couple guest taps. Among the on-site brewed beers are a cucumber lager, blood orange IPA, chocolate coffee stout, chai black ale, apple and cranberry golden ale, and a barrel-aged apricot wheat sour.

Pit Stop

Each October, Appleton's State Street shuts down and the local breweries take over for Fox Valley LagerFest, organized by McFleshman's Brewing Company. A ticket will get you all the lager you can drink from twenty different breweries, a commemorative glass, and the chance to win raffle prizes. Some of the participating breweries also offer transportation from their establishments to the festival, if you'd rather not drive.

Just up the street, **Hop Yard Ale Works** serves up pizza and pints on the patio whether the air is warm or chilly (of course, you can always grab a seat in the taproom where Hop Yard also has live music and karaoke). The handcrafted, wood-fired pizzas are a local favorite and come with your standard toppings, but also some imaginative creations, like the 30 Point Buck, smothered with red sauce, mozzarella, venison sausage, diced jalapeño, a mushroom red wine reduction, and cheese curd crumbles. For the beer, expect to find a wide variety (from both Hop Yard and other Wisconsin breweries). Hop Yard brews ales, hard seltzers, sessions, and IPAs. Among its most popular is the Fentons Irish Red, a malt-forward beer with a touch of caramel flavor.

A quick drive to **The Meat Block** in Greenville offers you the chance to sample brats made by Phil Schmidt, a graduate of the University of Wisconsin–Madison Master Meat Crafter Program. Phil has been winning awards for his brats since 1989. Visit the shop to take home some of his brat links and patties, with flavors ranging from macaroni and cheese to bacon cheeseburger to double beer (or have the best of both worlds with the Ultimate Tailgate Bratwurst, a double beer brat stuffed with colby cheese).

Appleton Beer Factory, Appleton

Pit Stop

Just outside of Appleton each June is the Little Chute Great Wisconsin Cheese Festival. For three days in Doyle Park, residents gather for a family-friendly celebration of all things cheese. Attendees enjoy cheese samples, cheese carving, gourmet mac and cheese booths, catch-the-curd and curd-eating contests, the cheddar chase walk/run, music, rides, and the crowning of the cheese king and queen.

Heading north to Shawano, stop next at **Stubborn Brothers Brewery**. Hopefully by the time you arrive, you've worked up an appetite. From appetizers and flatbreads to soups, burgers, wraps, and sandwiches, there are many cheese-forward offerings to enjoy. For example, you might like the beer-battered Renard's white cheddar curds or the beer mac and cheese topped with bacon crumbles. Or perhaps the beer cheese soup or the grilled cheese with bacon, grilled apples, and bacon jam on homemade bread is more your style. As for the beer, Stubborn Brothers is a small-batch brewer, so the offerings rotate regularly. Everything available follows a farm-to-table mentality with locally sourced malts and hops. In the past, some of Stubborn Brothers' most popular beers have been a fruited sour flavored like a passionfruit daiquiri, a peanut butter porter, a lambic cherry sour, and a hazy IPA with citra hops.

Follow Highway 22 northeast past Shawano Lake toward Oconto Falls, where, in 1973, Wayne R. Hintz and his family purchased a small cheese factory. The **Springside Cheese** operation pulled in milk from sixty local dairy farmers and churned out 1,700 pounds of cheddar every day. Less than ten years later, Springside was making 4,000 pounds of cheese per day, and by 1995, that number grew to 15,500 pounds. While the aged cheddars and cheddar curds are among the best sellers, this award-winning cheese company has expanded its production to a number of other styles, including monterey jack (available in various flavors, like chicken soup and apple cinnamon), smoked mozzarella string cheese, and an original creation called Krakow, a buttery, semisoft cheese, perfect for melting. The Wisconsin shop (Springside also has a location in Colorado) is open Monday, Wednesday, Friday, and Saturday.

Nearby, in the tiny town of Lena (fewer than six hundred people), is **Kugel's Cheese Mart**. This family-owned business has been serving cheese to the surrounding community since 1952. Kugel's most popular products are a six-year aged cheddar, string cheese, and, of course, fresh cheese curds. But you'll also find cheese spreads, baby swiss and aged swiss, colby, gorgonzola, monterey jack, buffalo-wing jack, mild cheddar, and more. Kugel's carries many other Wisconsin cheeses and a handful of imports. If you can't choose, the knowledgeable, friendly staff will be glad to work with you to find exactly what you need for your next snack or recipe creation.

If you're looking for a place to try multiple Wisconsin beers at the same location, head straight down Highway 141 to **Station 1 Brewing Company**. This relatively new spot in a renovated Suamico fire station has quickly brought its brewery up to full functionality. Station 1 offers a number of styles, including ales, stouts, porters, and IPAs. They also carry beers from breweries in Green Bay, Milwaukee, Door County, and many of the other best beer towns in the state. Enjoy them inside the taproom or on the patio around the cozy fire pit. Trivia happens on Tuesdays (check the Facebook page for the topic), and live music is on-site most Thursdays and Saturdays.

In Green Bay's northern suburbs is **Ahnapee Brewery**, a revival of a brewery of the same name that produced beer from the 1860s into the 1880s in what is now Algoma. In 2013, the brewery was reimagined and opened two doors down from the original location, in a building formerly owned by Carnival Guernsey Dairy. Then in 2020, the brewery decided to open a second location in Suamico. The brewery has sixteen of its own craft brews on hand, both small-batch experimental varieties and staples. The year-round offerings include Little Soldier, an American amber ale; Hail Mary Helles, a helles lager; Two Stall, a chocolate milk stout named after the original taproom that was located in a two-stall garage; and Cherry Mechanic, a gluten-free cherry ale. Seasonally, Ahnapee has IPAs, golden ales, blonde ales, sours, strong ales, and myriad other styles. Unlike many Wisconsin breweries, it typically offers a few gluten-free beer options. While Ahnapee Brewery has been distributing within Wisconsin since 2016, some of its limited-release beers are available only at the taproom.

If you get hungry while you're at Ahnapee, you can order from **888 Cheese & Co.**, a gourmet grilled cheese restaurant that will deliver. It has a wide variety of perfectly melted sandwiches, from your classic grilled cheese to one served up on jalapeño cornbread, another topped with mac and cheese, a chicken-and-waffle grilled cheese, and one with goat cheese, crispy kale, garlic-roasted mushrooms, and portabella mushrooms. Or go for the B.R.A.T., tomato focaccia bread topped with bacon, ranch, avocado, roast turkey, and monterey jack.

Much like Milwaukee, Green Bay abounds with options for visiting brewpubs, breweries, creameries, and restaurants. **Titletown Brewing Co.**'s brewery, taproom, and rooftop are housed in the former Larson Canning Company buildings that were erected between 1908 and 1922 (you can't miss the smokestack as you arrive). Titletown brews five beers with year-round availability: Green19, an IPA; Johnny "Blood" Red, an Irish red ale; Tundra Tropics, a hazy IPA; Gridiron Glory, a lager; and 400 Honey, a blonde ale. Everything else on tap is either a seasonal beer or a limited release. Every day except Tuesday, Primal Eats serves food at Titletown, with a small menu that includes three signature baked mac and cheeses: plain, brisket, and pulled pork. The brewery has tacos on Tuesdays and a limited menu including nachos, soup, and grilled cheese available daily.

Not too far away, **Copper State Brewing Co.**'s mission statement is "Connecting people. Creating experiences. Crafting great beer," which are all on display in the restaurant and beer garden (and coffee shop, if that's what you need). When it comes to cheese-oriented foods, Copper State is doing it right, from the gooey cheese curds to loaded beer cheese fries to the King of Grilled Cheese, with herbed garlic cream cheese, provolone, gouda, and havarti. What comes on the side of that sandwich? A heaping scoop of beer mac and cheese. The brewpub has eighteen taps with a selection of its house beers. Among their most popular varieties have been Uphill Both Ways, an imperial stout; Five:

Double Oaked Imperial Stout; and Cupid Schmupid, a fruited sour. The restaurant and brewery also have plenty of hop-forward and easy-drinking options.

It's now time to head toward the Frozen Tundra. Inside Lambeau Field is **1919 Kitchen & Tap**, so unless you have a ticket to a Packers game, plan to visit on a non–game day (only ticketed fans are allowed in when there's a game). On the menu, select from parmesan-breaded cheese curds, a Wisconsin cheese board, beer cheese bisque, a beer brat, and the beer cheese mac skillet, topped with a pretzel crumble and to which you can add a sliced brat. Of course, there's beer on the menu, and you'll see multiple Wisconsin brands represented, including Noble Roots, Titletown, Capital Brewery, and Leinenkugel's, plus some domestic and imported bottles.

Hinterland Brewery began in an old cheese factory under its corporate name Green Bay Brewing Co. and eventually grew into the massive brewpub it is today, located in a renovated meatpacking warehouse right near Lambeau Field. The beer hall has many offerings, some of which are brewed with Wisconsin products, like the WisCransin kettle sour and the For Fruits Sake kettle-soured wheat ale, made with Wisconsin cranberries and Door County cherries, respectively. Hinterland also serves plenty of popular styles, like a kölsch, Berliner weisse, saison, grand cru, imperial stout, hazy IPA, maple bock, coffee stout, and more. The food menu relies on whatever is freshest and in season so it's constantly rotating, but you can count on small plates, sandwiches, pizzas, and entrées. On the brewery's second floor is the test kitchen, open on select weekends throughout the year and specializing in experimental dishes. If you can snag it, the chef's table overlooks Lambeau Field. It's best to visit on a non–game day or when there's no big event at the stadium, otherwise it can be difficult to get a seat.

Also in the shadow of Lambeau Field sits **Kroll's West**, a burger joint that, because this is Wisconsin, also makes a juicy brat. For more than eighty years, Kroll's has been perfecting its craft and serving the Green Bay community, Packers players, politicians, and everyone else. The brat is served butterflied on a hard roll and slathered in mustard, pickles, and

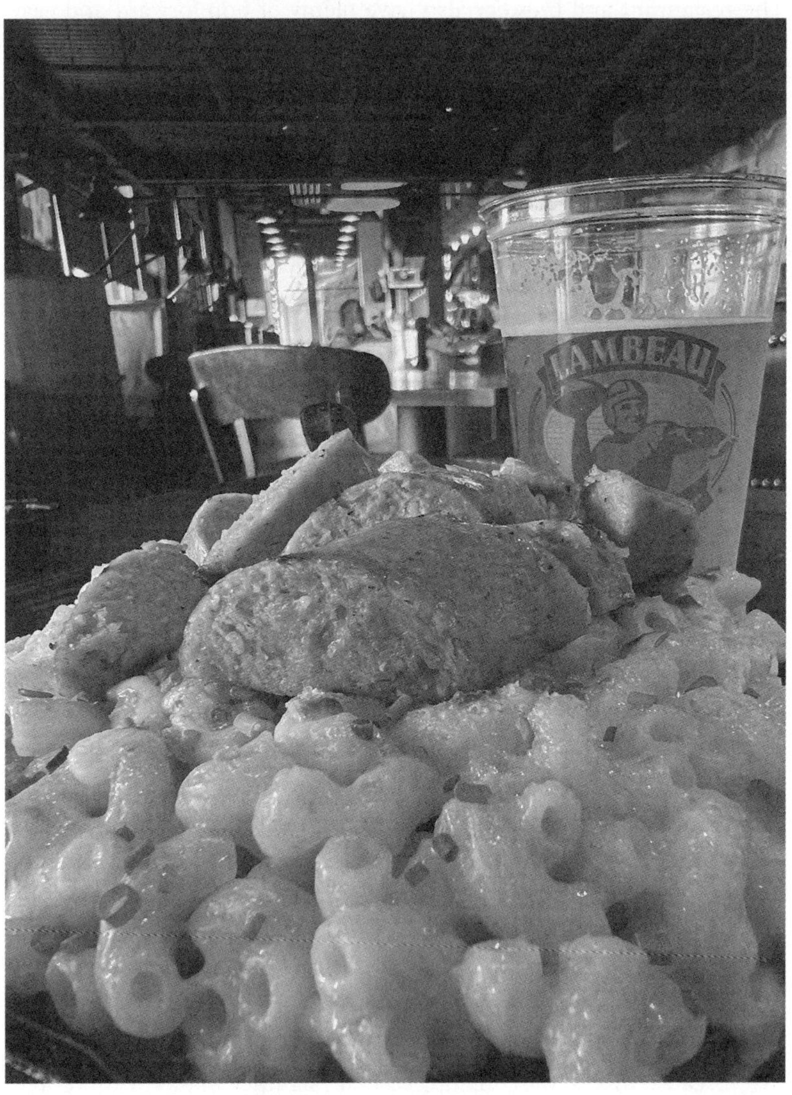

1919 Kitchen & Tap, Green Bay

onions (you can get it with sauerkraut if you like). What makes the best side is up to you, but the fried cheese curds, jack mac cheese bites, and broccoli cheddar poppers definitely pair well with the brat.

Detour

If you're looking for another spot to sample Wisconsin's state pastry, look no further than Uncle Mike's Bake Shoppe. Its sea salt caramel pecan kringle was named best in North America, and the bakery has plenty of other varieties, including cream cheese, strawberry cream, and caramel apple, plus seasonal styles like pumpkin cream cheese, s'mores, caramel fudge cake, and brandy old-fashioned. There are four locations to choose from: De Pere, Green Bay, Suamico, and Appleton.

Your last stop on the west side of the Fox River is at **Badger State Brewing Company**'s taproom and beer garden, which are a showcase of Wisconsin craft brewing and a tribute to sustainability. Badger State has two dozen beer offerings, plus hard seltzers and hard cider. The brewery's owners sought to pay homage to what makes Wisconsin a great place to live, work, and play in everything they offer their patrons. On tap you'll notice "the regulars," an array of IPAs, beermosas, pale ales, the BRW-SKI lager, fruit ales, red ales, a wheat beer, and a coffee stout. Seasonal and specialty beers are also in the lineup, such as Udder Tuggers cream ale, the Porte Des Morts maple porter, and Brunchfest Coffee Stout. If you want to get really wild, visit on a Packers game day (just don't plan to park in Badger State's lot). On the sustainability side, Badger State purchases 100 percent of its power from Midwest wind farms. The owners are also big into collaborating with other local breweries, and you'll often see some of these beers on tap, including the Locals Only! line, which has produced everything from a key lime gose to a cookies-and-cream stout.

On the other side of the river, **Zambaldi Beer** has a warm, friendly, communal environment. It's a perfect place to bring the family to hang out, while also being a great spot to spend time with friends. The large indoor space is suited for Green Bay winters and gives you a view into the brewery. Plus, who can resist the old-school cafeteria-style chairs? Beer-wise, the most popular include the Mulled Cherry Air, a spiced beer made with Door County cherries; Maple Brown Ale; Detention Dunkel, a Munich lager; Udderly Smoooth milk stout; and Put Me In Kölsch. When it comes to food, Zambaldi has some snacks, including a giant pretzel, a cheese and sausage board, local custard, popcorn, and chips. You can also order from the pizza shop next door (Gallagher's). The taproom has events throughout the month, including family-friendly Sunday Fundays, with face painting, balloon artists, and an ice cream truck. A fun fact about the company: its name combines the owners' last names (Zander and Malcom) and the hairstyle of two of the three owners.

Pit Stop

If you happen to be in Brown County in June, July, September, or October, check out the county's historical society and get the schedule for its Beer Baron Cemetery Walks. The guided tour takes place at Woodlawn Cemetery and gives guests the chance to learn about the pioneering beer barons in the county and their place in state brewing history. Tickets are required, and each purchase comes with a coupon book full of savings at local breweries.

Stillmank Brewing Company's founder has a traditional Wisconsin beer story (of this century, that is). After growing up in-state, Brad Stillmank fled to Colorado, graduated from college, worked at a Colorado brewery, got his brewers certificates from the University of California at Davis, became one of the nation's first Certified Cicerones (a trademarked designation bestowed on those with proven experience selecting and serving beer), and then decided to move back to Wisconsin after marrying the love of his life. In 2011, Brad started contract brewing Stillmank's flagship beer, Wisco Disco, an amber ale, at Milwaukee Brewing

Company. With popularity booming, three years later he was able to purchase an old Builders Supply warehouse in Green Bay and set up shop. Today the taproom has expanded well beyond Wisco Disco and also brews a rye wine ale, doppelbock, kölsch, IPAs, fruit beers, wheat beers, porters, and its own hard seltzers and ciders. The taproom is open Wednesday through Sunday.

The tiny **Noble Roots Brewing Company** in Green Bay is making up for its small size with bold beer flavors. The brews are available mainly in the taproom (though Noble Roots does have a small regional distribution) and come in ten- and nineteen-ounce pours, plus flights and growlers. Noble Roots crafts IPAs, ales (of the amber, brown, blonde, Belgian, and cream variety), stouts, goses, Belgian dubbels, and Belgian tripels. One of its most popular offerings is Blueberry Cream, a classic Wisconsin cream ale with just a touch of blueberry flavor.

Detour

If you'd like to learn a bit more about northeast Wisconsin's history and culture, check out Heritage Hill State Historical Park. This living history park in Green Bay offers an account of the area from the 1600s to the present. Among the buildings on the fifty-four-acre property is a cheese factory, originally built in 1894 in Kewaunee County and relocated to the park in 1994.

Twenty minutes south in De Pere, **Scray Cheese** has been bringing handcrafted cheddar, edam, fontina, and gouda to the Green Bay area since 1924. The Scray family emigrated from Belgium in 1849, and two generations later, Edward Scray decided to open up a small factory where he could process milk delivered by horse and buggy from local farms. Edward's son Edgar took over in 1948 and used the newest dairy technologies to create award-winning cheeses. He managed to keep the company alive amid creamery closures and consolidations that saw Brown County's cheese-factory ranks shrink from the hundreds to only two in 1982, when Edgar's son James took the reins. James has continued to

Noble Roots Brewing Company, Green Bay

grow the company. He was even behind the decision to begin producing fontina, which has proved to be among Scray's most popular varieties. When you visit the shop today, you can watch the cheesemaking and packaging process through the shop's large windows, and if you visit Monday, Tuesday, Thursday, or Saturday, you'll be treated to some fresh curds that will roll straight off the line and into your shopping bag. Or simply hit the drive-through window and choose from more than one hundred different cheese varieties, the vast majority of which come from Wisconsin.

Right off Highway 32 inside LedgeStone Vineyards is **Gnarly Cedar Brewery**, a microbrewery situated on a beautiful piece of property. If you're wondering how the brewery got its name, look to the cliffsides behind the building. There, you'll see Wisconsin's oldest tree, estimated to be more than thirteen hundred years old. The vineyard and farmland surrounding the winery/brewery combo are perfect for relaxing in summer, listening to live music by the fire in fall, or even snowshoeing in winter. On tap, expect standard favorites, like a red ale, IPAs, porters, stouts, and pilsners, as well as some unique flavors that incorporate grapes into the production. For example, the Sauvignon Blanc Gose is brewed with sauvignon blanc grape juice made at the winery, and the farmhouse ale is fermented with Marquette grapes.

Your drive next takes you thirty minutes northeast to **Krohn Dairy**, which has been fashioning cheese for more than 125 years. Whether you're looking for fresh warm curds, a breakfast sandwich, a homemade pizza (including a biscuits-and-gravy breakfast pizza), or your new favorite cheese flavor, the friendly staff at Krohn's are happy to help. And, they're glad to give you a sample of the cheese you're considering before you buy it, just to make sure it's the right snack for you—good news, because with more than one hundred styles of Wisconsin cheese, it can be difficult to narrow down. A few important hints for shopping at Krohn's: curds are fresh on Monday and Friday mornings, string cheese is made Monday and Wednesday afternoons, and fresh cheddar is made on Mondays and Fridays. Curd flavors include BBQ, buffalo, garlic, Louisiana cajun, Northwoods pepper, pizza, taco, Carolina gold, and six pepper blend. In-store you'll also find plenty of bread cheese, colby, swiss, flavored and aged cheddars, feta, provolone, jack, and many other unique varieties, including a maple vanilla cheese fudge. Plus, there are plenty of cheese spreads from Ron's, Laack's, Pine River, Simon's, Vern's, and Malcore's.

Just ten minutes north, **Ron's Wisconsin Cheese** first opened in 1976, carrying a range of cheese products. The Luxemburg store is a bit different today, however. In 2014, the Pagel family (owner of Pagel's Ponderosa Dairy) purchased Ron's Cheese and launched a cheese line of its own. Now the shop sells various flavors of cheese spread, fresh cheese curds (on Monday and Thursday), homemade pizzas, the Ponderosa cheese line, and many other cheese products. Ron's cheese spreads remain a Wisconsin institution, and there are plenty of flavors to tempt your tastebuds, including herb and spice, bacon cheese, cheddar garlic, wine, horseradish, zesty beer, and more.

Thumb Knuckle Brewing Company is definitely not what you expect from its exterior. But, as the saying goes, don't judge a book by its cover. You'll be treated to beers brewed by someone so committed to the craft that he studied in Germany to become a brewmaster and even completed an eighteen-month internship in Bavaria. What does that kind of experience bring to Wisconsin? Porters, IPAs, wheat beers, and lagers, all served up in a cozy, wood-paneled taproom alongside pizzas made for the brewery by Ron's Wisconsin Cheese. As for the name? If you look at Wisconsin as a hand, the brewery is located in—you guessed it—the thumb's knuckle.

It's now time to head into Wisconsin's vacationland. Start your trek into Door County at **Renard's Cheese** for some handcrafted snacks to keep you full on the drive. Take your time trying the samples before you pick your favorites. The specialties are flavored and aged cheddars, including a Wisconsin beer cheddar, maple syrup cheddar, and a cherry white cheddar. But if that's not for you, there are plenty of other varieties, from both Renard's own stock and other Wisconsin cheesemakers. If you want something a bit more substantial, within Renard's is Melt Bistro, which uses Renard's cheeses in its sandwiches, paninis, pizzas, and macaroni and cheese. If you really want the full Door County experience, check out the Door County Cherry Melt on the breakfast menu, a sweetened cream cheese and sourdough sandwich that is dipped in french toast batter, then grilled and topped with Door County cherries, almonds, and whipped cream.

WisconsInsights

More than seventy individual varieties of cheese are produced by cheesemakers in Door County.

Just south of the bridge that will take you across Sturgeon Bay is one of **Bridge Up Brewing Company**'s two locations (the other is at the Door County Cherry Hut). The Sturgeon Bay location is open year-round, and the other is open seasonally from May to October. Its flagship beers are available most of the year and include Knee-High cream ale, Roofed Goat Red American red ale, 1851 Zwickel lager, Harbors & Bays IPA, Escarpment citra pale ale, and Stubborn Sturgeon hazy IPA. Depending on when you visit, you can also find some experimental offerings and guest taps. If you opt for the Cherry Hut location, there is plenty of outdoor seating and, naturally, some cornhole for your enjoyment.

On the other side of the bridge is **Starboard Brewing Company**, Door County's first nanobrewery. The small-batch system means you'll consistently see different craft beers, from Oktoberfests in fall to ales in summer and everything in between. Starboard broadcasts its latest releases on Facebook, and if you get hungry, you can pair your beers with Starboard's current Wisconsin cheese offerings.

No matter the season, **Wisconsin Cheese Masters** in Egg Harbor is ready to educate you on the highest quality cheeses Wisconsin has to offer and let you sample to your heart's content. The staff will even give you beer, wine, and chocolate pairing ideas once you've selected your favorites. The company started as a mail order business, so the good news is that if you find some cheeses you can't live without, Wisconsin Cheese Masters will gladly ship them anywhere within the United States (season depending). Even better, if you really want to learn more about Wisconsin cheese and continue your sampling journey, sign up for a three-, six-, or nine-month cheese club subscription, which comes complete with three half-pounds of Wisconsin cheese in each box.

One Barrel Brewing Company in Egg Harbor is kid and dog friendly with a huge outdoor beer garden and a pizza company located inside the taproom, making it a great spot to swing by while you're in the area. The draft offerings include year-round favorites Commuter, a kölsch; Ninja Dust, a juicy IPA; and Up North, a Wisconsin lager. Then there are the special releases, seasonal releases, and multiple rotating IPAs that the brewmaster crafts with the freshest hops currently available (hard ciders and seltzers are also on offer). As for the food, Pizza Bros is located on-site and serves craft wood-fired pizzas. Pizza Bros has some standard fare, including an all-meat pepperoni, sausage, ham, and bacon pie; daily specials, like the creamy mac and cheese pizza; and build your own offerings. While you enjoy your beer or wait on your pizza, the taproom has plenty of board games plus some old-school Nintendos to keep you entertained. Outside, there's cornhole, yard games, and live music (weather permitting).

WisconsInsights

In 2001, Uplands Cheese Company's Pleasant Ridge Reserve won the biggest international cheese competition in its first year in production. Each year, cheese connoisseurs await the release of this aged, alpine-style cheese, which is only produced May through October.

A mere three minutes away is **Door Artisan Cheese Company**, a shop known for its world champion cave-aged English-style Top Hat Cheddar. The owner is a second-generation cheesemaker and has earned the coveted Master Cheesemaker certification. In addition to the cheddar, other styles you can find in the shop include a wine-soaked asiago, a beer-washed gouda, and Dorianna, a Door County original cave-aged cheese with a sweet nutty flavor. The staff can offer samples or point you in the direction of a cheese you'll enjoy based on your favorite flavor profiles.

One Barrel Brewing Company, Egg Harbor

Pit Stop

In mid-June, Baileys Harbor hosts the Door County Beer Festival, where you can choose from more than 150 beers brewed in Door County and elsewhere in Wisconsin and the Midwest while listening to live music and trying out the food vendors. Tickets are fifty-five dollars and must be purchased in advance.

The laid-back atmosphere at Sister Bay's **Peach Barn Farmhouse and Brewery** would have you coming back time and time again, even if it weren't for the beers. The craft lineup is constantly changing, but you're likely to see a couple of IPAs, a farmhouse ale, or a witbier. Many of the options are brewed with peaches grown by the establishment (you can even order peaches for pickup, or, if the season is right, you might be offered a peach to enjoy with your beer). Pro tip: visit at night to enjoy the beautifully lit outdoor seating area and fire pit.

Similar to other shops and restaurants in the area, the nearby **Door County Creamery** has limited hours and is closed in the winter. But a visit to the shop is well worth planning your trip around. The small store has home goods, plenty of Wisconsin cheeses, and its own varieties, including farmhouse, feta, and chèvre in an array of flavors (cherry, truffle, wild ramp, everything bagel, smoked whitefish, the list goes on), plus curds, and some Wisconsin beers and other assorted wines and beverages. If you're willing to wait—and there's plenty to explore right near the creamery—order one of its cheesy sandwiches. The Hot Honey & Chèvre with baked truffle goat cheese, hot honey sauce, crispy onions, arugula, fresh basil, and baby pepperoni on a crusty batard does not disappoint, but really, none of the sandwiches do. If a sweet treat is calling your name, try out the goat's milk gelato, made daily and available in assorted flavors. Door County Creamery is a great stop whether you want lunch or fixings for a picnic or late-night snack.

Should you decide to take the ferry to Washington Island in summer, be sure to visit the **Washington Island Biergarten**, located at the island's

Detour

Door County is beautiful, no matter what time of year you visit, so it's worth the drive almost all the way to the tip of the peninsula to reach Island Orchard Cider. This company grows its own apples at an orchard on Washington Island just northeast of the peninsula, then turns that into ciders that run the gamut from über-sweet ice cider to dry, oak-aged bruts. Like any brewery, the best way to take in the offerings from this cidery is with a flight. Pair it with a fresh hunk of Marieke Gouda's raw milk gouda and some local crackers and meats, and you'll have the perfect little tasting plate. Before you make the drive out, see its website for seasonal hours.

golf resort. Here you'll find beers and ciders from Door County and Wisconsin vendors, games, food, and a fire pit. The menu includes fried cheese curds, a soft pretzel served with beer cheese, a Wisconsin cheese and charcuterie board, and a brat poached in pilsner and served on a pretzel roll.

As you've no doubt learned while driving around Wisconsin's thumb, Door County is a vacation mecca for Wisconsinites and out-of-state visitors, well-known for its beautiful landscape, quaint towns, and recreational activities. But for decades, it did not have its own production brewery to capitalize on summer tourism. That changed in 2013 when **Door County Brewing Co.** was founded. After contract brewing, Door County Brewing was able to bring its operation in-house and opened its doors to the public in 2014. Year-round at Door County Brewing Co. you can try its Vacationland juicy IPA, League Night lager, Little Sister witbier, Pallet Jack Cruiser session IPA, and Polka King porter, each named for a feature near and dear to Door County. There are also some seasonal beers, and you can find all of the beer experiments at its other company, **Hacienda Beer Co.**, with locations in Baileys Harbor and Milwaukee. If you're feeling a bit peckish, head to Door County Brewing Co.'s food venture just next door to the taproom for a BBQ nacho box with kettle chips covered in mac and cheese, BBQ pork or chicken, baked beans, diced onion, and BBQ sauce. Or skip the chips and go for the big bowl of mac and cheese covered with BBQ chicken or pork. And, of course, you should always try the brat. At this restaurant, that means a smoked brat topped with spicy mustard, chopped onions, and BBQ sauce on a pretzel roll.

Detour

If you venture to Island Orchard Cider, continue north along the Door County Coastal Byway, an official National Scenic Byway. The sixty-six-mile loop will provide some breathtaking views of the Niagara Escarpment's landscape, including Lake Michigan's shores, limestone cliffs, and lush forests that have deep golden and red hues in fall.

The nearly hundred-mile drive from Door County's northern point down to the next stop is a good time to try out the cheeses you picked up and enjoy the views of Lake Michigan. Once you arrive in Manitowoc, head straight to **Pine River Dairy**. Even if you don't know the name, you've probably seen its cheese spreads in a grocery store somewhere in the United States. The family behind this spreadable delight—the Olms—has been in the cheesemaking business for six generations, ever since the sons of a Civil War veteran decided to start dairy production. The company's manufacturing facility in Manitowoc has a retail store attached, which carries a plethora of cheese spreads, but also more than 250 varieties of cheese, ranging from muenster and gouda to Italian and swiss to colby and brick. Pine River has cheese in block form, string form, curd form, and even powdered form.

Due west is **Rowland's Calumet Brewing Co.**, which has a long history in Chilton and is located in a historic building that was once home to the city's first fire department and, later, city hall. Bob and Bonita Rowland bought the building—then being used as a tavern—in 1983 and renamed it Roll-In. To bring in more business, Bob decided to give brewing a try, after reading about the growing popularity of brewpubs. By 1990, the first beer was on tap and Rowland's was bragging that it was located in the smallest city in the country with a brewery. Today the brewery crafts around thirty-five different beers per year, about one dozen of which are on tap at any time. Among the most popular are the Detention Ale (a wheat beer) and the Jack Daniels Barrel-Aged Imperial Stout. The brewery makes its own root beer too.

WisconsInsights

Chilton is home to Briess Malt & Ingredients Company, a leading producer of specialty malts and ingredients for the nation's brewing, distilling, and food sectors. It's been in business since 1876, and for a time, Rowland's Calumet Brewing Co. operated a pilot brewery for Briess.

A visit to **LaClare Creamery** near Lake Winnebago isn't just a quick pit stop for cheese, though it can be. More often, it's an hours-long family-friendly adventure that includes a self-guided tour of the creamery, a visit to the goat silo and barn, an event with baby goats (if your timing is right—be sure to check the website before you go), lunch at the café, and, finally, some cheese shopping. In the café, you can take some pointers from the menu on how to use LaClare's many cheese offerings, from a turkey chèvre sandwich with cranberry aioli to a gourmet grilled cheese with two house-made cheeses to french toast topped with blueberry vanilla chèvre. The cheeses you see on the café menu and more can be found in the shop. Perhaps you'll be tempted to take home a truffle goat cheese, aged cheddar goat cheese, or mozzarella goat cheese. Or maybe Evalon, a gouda-style goat cheese, will tempt your tastebuds once you learn that it made LaClare's head cheesemaker, Katie Hedrich Fuhrmann, the youngest person ever (and only the second woman) to win the US Championship Cheese Contest award. No matter what you pick, you're certain to get some of the highest quality goat's milk cheese around. In fact, LaClare makes some of the country's only completely domestically produced goat cheese. LaClare keeps the process as local as possible, sourcing its goat's milk from dairies within a fifteen-mile radius of the creamery. Why is that important? Less transportation means less agitation, which keeps the proteins from breaking down, resulting in a better flavor.

Henning's Cheese has been producing cheese since 1914, and today is known for making giant wheels of cheese that weigh thousands of pounds. In fact, it's the last cheese company in the United States producing wheels larger than seventy-five pounds. During a visit to the shop, you can watch cheese being made, taste samples, and walk through the cheese museum, which showcases equipment and other cheesemaking memorabilia. Head there Monday through Friday if you want fresh, warm curds.

Pit Stop

Wisconsin Micro Brewers Beer Fest is hosted by Rowland's each May at the Calumet County Fairgrounds. Around thirty Wisconsin breweries participate and provide samples of more than one hundred microbrews. Tickets can be purchased in advance at Rowland's.

Elkhart Lake draws huge crowds most of the year, whether they're coming for water sports, Road America, or a long weekend visiting the local shops and restaurants. While you're in town, head to the former feed mill that is now home to **SwitchGear Brewing Co.** With more than a dozen beers on tap, you're sure to find something to enjoy. Local favorites include the Pontoon Pounder, an American pale wheat; the 43×88, an imperial double stout; and the Last Resort, a bourbon barrel-aged red ale. If you're bringing friends or family, you can challenge them to shuffleboard, darts, pinball, Ringo, or board and card games. Pro tip: if you visit on a fall Friday, be sure to come in your flannel and your first beer is half off (or buy one of the SwitchGear flannels, and get your first beer free).

WisconsInsights

Plymouth brands itself the Cheese Capital of the World, and an estimated 10 to 15 percent of all of the cheese consumed in the United States is processed and sold from companies within the city limits. Major industry players, including Sartori, Sargento, and Masters Gallery, all call Plymouth home.

Ten minutes down Highway 67 and you'll arrive at **Plymouth Brewing Company**, a production brewery. Although it focuses more on brewing, packing, and distributing beer, it also has a small taproom where you can sample its craft brews. These include the Sconsin farmhouse ale, Nutt Hill pistachio nut brown ale, Galaxy Cloud juicy IPA, and the Stone Blue blueberry ale. You're welcome to bring your own food and snacks (Plymouth doesn't have any to offer), and because the focus is production, the taproom hours are limited, so be sure to check the website before you visit.

Detour

While you're in Plymouth, be sure to visit Antoinette the Cow, a twenty-foot-tall fiberglass Holstein built in 1977 to celebrate the city's centennial and honor the area's dairy-producing legacy.

If you're hungry in Plymouth, head to **PJ Campbell's at the Depot** for an American twist on German specialties. On the appetizer menu is the Beer & Brat Dip, made with PJ's amber ale, aged cheddar, brats, and sauerkraut, and served with pretzel crostinis for dipping. Among the dinner plates is a sausage platter with various wursts, including a brat, served on a bed of sauerkraut. Locals also love the Three Cheese Mac & Cheese, a penne pasta topped with a creamy sauce and cheddar jack, parmesan, and cheddar cheeses, then baked until golden brown.

Pit Stop

If you want to check out one of the quirkiest New Year's Eve celebrations, stop in Plymouth on December 31 for the big cheese drop. Each year, a massive wedge of Sartori's BellaVitano Gold is lowered at 10 p.m., followed by live music and a champagne toast at midnight.

Since you're on a beer, brat, and cheese trip, you can't skip a stop at the brat mecca, **Johnsonville**, the Sheboygan Falls company that helped put Wisconsin brats on the map. Visit the huge Johnsonville campus, which includes a large store that's open to the public near an art deco piece that spells out BRAT. It has items any brat lover would enjoy, from actual brats and Johnsonville branded apparel, to tools for cooking brats, cornhole boards, and more. The store also carries products from Wisconsin-based manufacturers, like Uncle Mike's kringles, Baron's gelato, and Vern's cheese.

Detour

Plymouth is home to the Cheese Counter and Dairy Heritage Center, a facility for educating the public about Wisconsin's cheesemaking prowess through interactive displays and samples of the state's finest artisan cheeses. In addition to cheese-themed merchandise and cold cases with wedges for purchase, the center has a lunch counter with specialty grilled cheese sandwiches, paninis, mac and cheese, and more.

While it doesn't have them ready to eat, Sheboygan's **Miesfeld's Triangle Market** is one of the city's (and state's) go-to stores for award-winning brats. The butchers have been perfecting their craft since 1941, and today the store sells more than twenty-five types of fresh and frozen brat flavors, including garlic, Cajun, nacho cheese, mac and cheese, and beer,

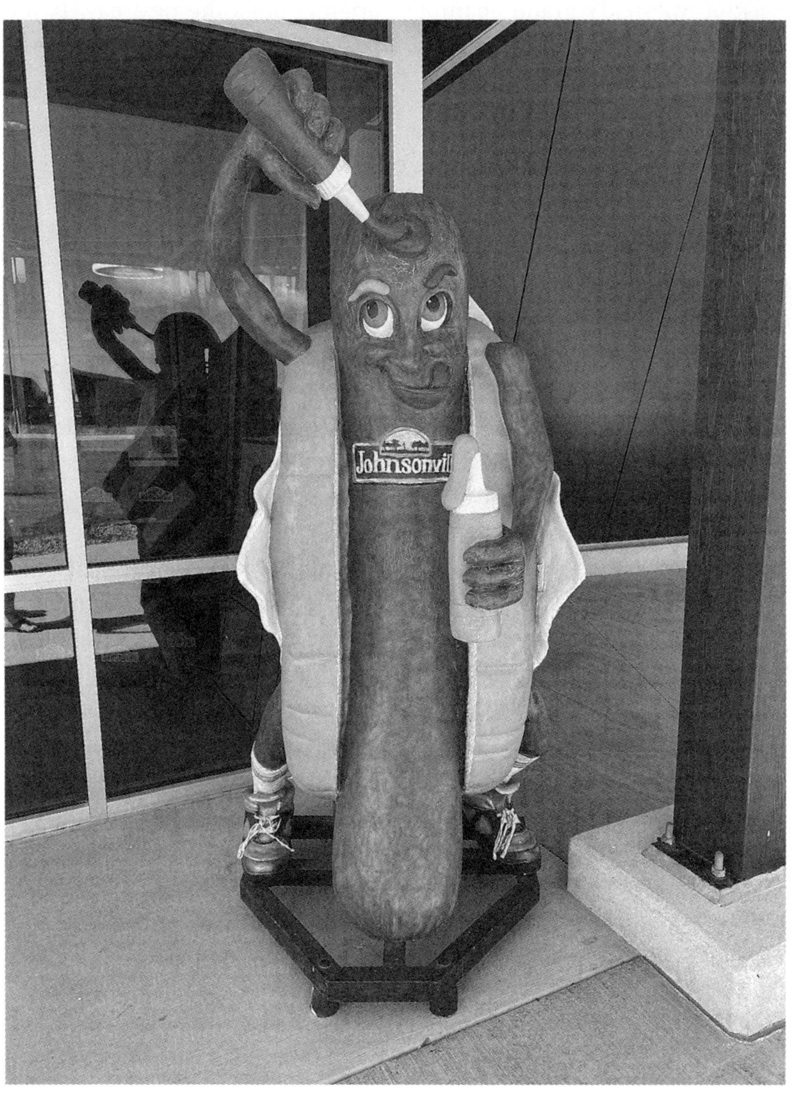

Johnsonville, Sheboygan Falls

butter, and onions. When the Packers win, you can save 25 percent on a pack of Miesfeld's grand champion original brats the next day. If you can't take brats to go, Miesfeld's also has Wisconsin cheeses and snacks to pick from.

Detour

To learn a bit more about the early days of cheesemaking in Wisconsin, visit the 1867 Bodenstab Cheese Factory on the grounds of the Sheboygan County Historical Society and Museum, where you can view artifacts and equipment used to process cheese in the mid-nineteenth century. Pro tip: the museum is open only from February 1 to October 31, and then for special holiday hours from the day after Thanksgiving to December 30.

Just a few minutes down Highway 42, in a large industrial space that once housed a Coca-Cola bottling plant, is **3 Sheeps Brewing Company**, which started with a home-brewing kit and became a packaging brewery. The latter was located in a sock factory and allowed the company to produce only three hundred gallons at a time, so 3 Sheeps relocated to its current spot. The spacious taproom you see today is filled with picnic tables and bar seating and has a casual vibe that is both family and dog friendly. In summer, choose sun or shade as you challenge your friends to a round of bocce. Twenty-five taps at 3 Sheeps feature both year-round beers and those that you can get only in the taproom. The brewery is known for its barrel-aged beers and hard seltzer, but it also has IPAs, pale ales, lagers, ambers, and stouts to enjoy, plus seasonal favorites like Oktoberfest.

Old World Creamery in Sheboygan is part of a fourth generation family-owned company, and since 1912 that family has been producing various products, including cheese and butter, all crafted with milk from local family-owned dairy farms. In the small shop, located at the front of the butter plant, you can buy many of the company's products, along with other food and gift items from Wisconsin.

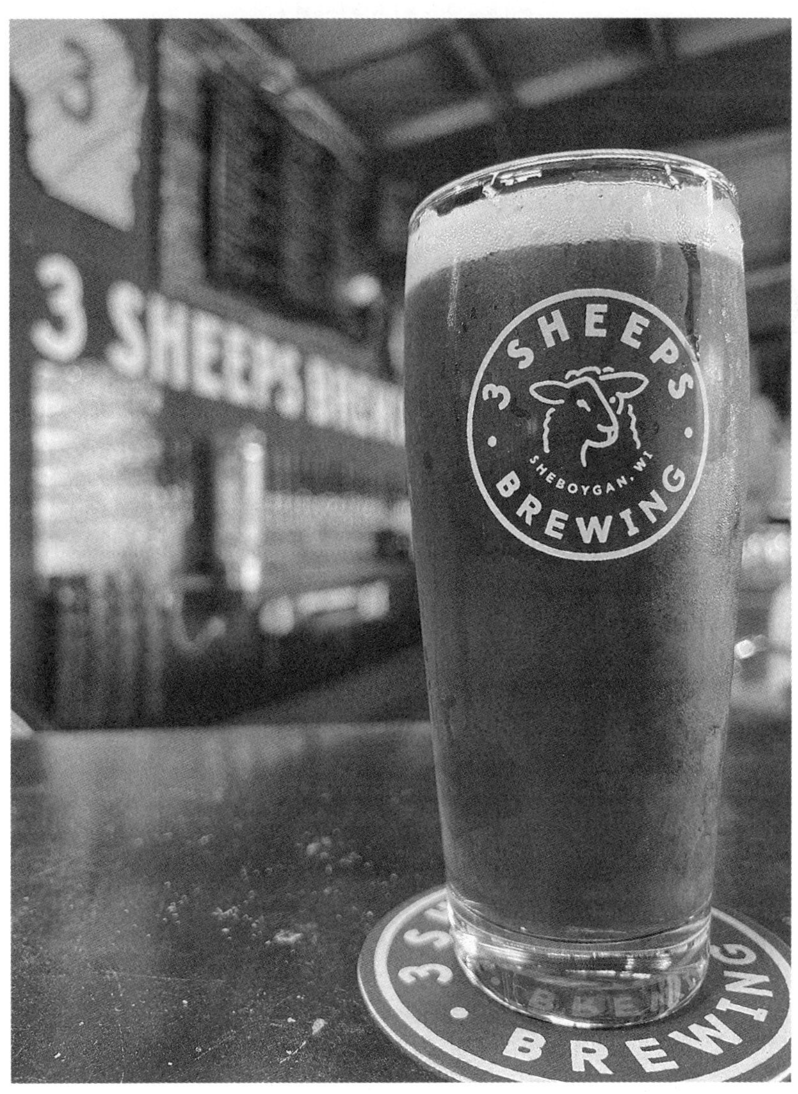

3 Sheeps Brewing Company, Sheboygan

WisconsInsights

Hankscraft AJS Tap Handles, in Random Lake, is the largest US manufacturer of tap handles, and it was responsible for making many iconic designs you'll see on your road trip, including the New Glarus Spotted Cow handle.

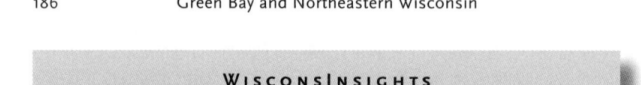

A few minutes away you can sample a more modern take on brat preparation at **Sheboygan Pasty Company**. Located in the back of Ranieri's Four of a Kind Bar & Grill, this tiny shop serves up fresh and frozen pasties, a flaky savory pie that originated in England among mining communities and was brought to the United States by immigrants. The owners who make the pasties each day were introduced to the food by their grandparents, who were born and raised in Michigan's Upper Peninsula. On the menu, there's the Sheboygan, a flaky pastry crust stuffed with brats, potato, onion, and cheddar cheese. The shop has plenty of other flavors as well, such as those with beef or Italian sausage. Pro tip: order ahead on the website (maybe while you're at 3 Sheeps) and pick up a piping hot pasty in a flash.

As you now know, when in Sheboygan, have a brat. There's no better place to do that than **Al & Al's Steinhaus**. This classic German restaurant serves a single or a double brat the traditional Sheboygan way, with sides of fries, onion peels, cheese nuggets, salad, or homemade chips. On the dinner menu, you can choose the Bavarian Mac n' Cheese, a spaetzle covered in homemade cheese sauce and topped with a brat or ham. Al & Al's also has plenty of sausage plates if you don't want to go the handheld brat route. You can be certain that you're getting German authenticity here: the family that owns the restaurant began immigrating to the United States from Germany in the 1950s.

If you can make it happen, on your way out of Sheboygan you'll want to stop by **Gibbsville Cheese Co.** on a Wednesday after 2 p.m. That's when the curds are off the production line and onto the shelves. You can even watch them make and package the cheese, if you're interested. But no matter which day or time you come, the factory store sells various cheeses, including—if you dare—"mystery cheese." Family-owned Gibbsville has been producing the cheesy good stuff for more than sixty-five years, so you know you're getting a quality product each time you visit.

WisconsInsights

Thanks to innovation, dairy farmers today use 90 percent less land per gallon than they used to.

Twenty miles down Interstate 43, check out **Inventors Brewpub**. The building in which the taproom and restaurant are housed has a lengthy Wisconsin beer-making history. In 1847, one year before Wisconsin became a state, Lakeside Brewery opened on the site, which later turned into the Port Washington Brewing Company and then Old Port Brewing Company (with its slogan, The Beer That Made Milwaukee Furious). Old Port operated until 1947, and, eventually, in 2017 Inventors Brewpub opened its doors in what remained of the historic buildings. There are plenty of house-brewed beers to choose from, of which the most popular are Ozaukee Wheat hefeweizen, chocolatey SS Porter, and Tesla's Coil double IPA. The brewpub also has a full food menu, including burgers, wraps, sandwiches, and poutines, like the Wisconsin Brat Poutine, topped with beer cheese, brats, and deep-fried cheese curds.

Another eleven miles southwest and you're at **Frannie's Market**, a specialty food store where you can buy various local products, from jams and syrups to tea and crackers. Perhaps most important, this is the place to pick up some of Wisconsin's finest artisan cheeses, including goat cheese produced by Blakesville Creamery in nearby Port Washington. One of its most popular varieties is its fresh chèvre, a perfect accompaniment to your next sweet or savory dish. This bright, soft cheese took home an award at the 2022 American Cheese Society competition, and you'll see why the moment you spread it on a cracker or a sweet bread. Select some local meats, cheeses, and snacks for a DIY charcuterie board, and if you can't decide what to pick, ask the owner Sarah for her recommendations.

A mere five minutes up the road you'll reach **The Fermentorium**'s headquarters in Cedarburg (or if you don't have the time now, try them the next time you're in Wauwatosa). The tasting room has twenty-four taps, but is perhaps best known for its Juice Packets IPA, an unfiltered beer with fresh citrus and piney notes, available year-round. The beertenders say it's even popular among the non-IPA crowd. Whether or not IPAs are your thing, there's a lot to like here, from a lemony hefeweizen to a malty banana dunkelweizen to a crisp Mexican lager and even a hazelnut coffee IPA. The brewery also has some upscale bar food, including totchos, mac and cheese bites, Mexican corn bites, a soft pretzel with cheese and a house-made beer mustard, and some creative hot dogs. Notably, The Fermentorium is interested in getting all of its staff excited about its products, and offers what it calls the Pilot Series, which gives any employee the chance to try brewing a ten-gallon batch that (assuming it turns out) ends up on tap. In fact, Juice Packets IPA was an employee brew.

Pit Stop

Ozaukee County has multiple beer gardens and beer-tasting events every summer. These include the Port Washington beer garden each Saturday from July through mid-October, the Grafton Beer on the Bridge tasting event, and the Cedarburg Art Museum's Thursday and Saturday beer garden from June through early October. Additionally, each August, the Saukville Chamber of Commerce hosts Bags and Brews, a beer garden and cornhole tournament with live music and food vendors.

If you're looking for some brats to take home, don't miss the unique selection at **Ney's Natural Premium Meats and Sweets**. There aren't many other places in the state making more than two dozen types of homemade brats with flavors including Bloody Mary, cheesy baked potato, chicken cordon bleu, dill pickle, nacho supreme, pineapple and teriyaki, and the pizza-esque tomato basil. Be sure to check the Facebook page before you visit for a listing of the weekly sandwich and soup specials. If you're lucky, you might catch a brat fry, fresh fried cheese curds, or even the Wisconsin beer cheese and brat soup.

Rounding out your time in this part of Wisconsin, stop at **Foxtown Brewing** in Mequon. In the mid-1800s, the building housed the Opitz Zimmerman Brewery. The current owners undertook extensive renovations to both the main building and the two levels of lager caves that sit below it. Monday through Friday you can take a tour of the original beer caves to learn more about Mequon's brewing history. Each tour comes with a souvenir taster glass and two free taster beers. Whether or not you come for the tour, you can enjoy a drink and a bite in the taproom. The brewery has two dozen taps, offering everything from IPAs and wheat beers, to Belgian quadrupels, red ales, and fruited sours. The food menu includes wraps, salads, burgers, sandwiches, and dinner entrées, including its popular Brisket Mac, a cavatappi pasta topped with smoked brisket, beer cheese sauce, maple bacon BeerBQ, and pico de gallo.

Final Thoughts

There are more restaurants, creameries, brewpubs, taprooms, butcher shops, and the like than could ever be included in an easy-to-use guide that can fit in your glovebox. And, of course, new ones open every day, while others close. As mentioned in the introduction, this guide is meant to serve as a highlight reel to all that Wisconsin has to offer in the realm of beer, brats, and cheese. If you're hungry for more, keep up with the guide and the changes happening in the state—and dig into the history behind the state's beer, brats, and cheese—on Instagram (@somelikeitbrat) or at hkerrigan.com. If you have recommendations, questions, comments, tips, or anything else to share, feel free to reach out on social media or at heather@riverhorsecomms.com. Happy road-tripping!

Appendix

An alphabetical listing of all establishments in boldface in the main text follows (note: establishments beginning with *The* have been alphabetized under the second word in the name). In addition to the address and phone, each listing includes, if available and regularly updated, a website, Facebook page, and Instagram handle. Many of the locations included in the book regularly post specials, tap lists, events, and updated hours on their social media pages, and some also maintain their tap lists on the Untappd app.

18 Hands Ale Haus
18 E. Division St., Fond du Lac
920-933-3610
www.18handswi.com
facebook.com/18handswi
@18handsalehaus

1919 Kitchen & Tap
1265 Lombardi Ave., Green Bay
920-965-6970
www.1919kitchenandtap.com
facebook.com/1919KitchenandTap

3 Sheeps Brewing Company
1837 North Ave., Sheboygan
920-395-3583
https://3sheepsbrewing.com
facebook.com/3sheeps
@3sheepsbrewing

3rd & Vine
1929 Third St., Eau Claire
715-514-1997
www.3rdandvine.com
facebook.com/3rdandvine
@3rdandvineec

3rd Street Market Hall
275 W. Wisconsin Ave., Milwaukee
414-249-5062
https://3rdstmarkethall.com
facebook.com/3rdstreetmarkethall/
@3rdstmarkethall

608 Brewing Co.
83 Copeland Ave., La Crosse
608-519-9686
www.608brewingcompany.com
facebook.com/608brewingcompany
@608brewco

888 Cheese & Co.
1582 Lineville Rd., Suamico
920-455-0097
www.888cheeseandco.com
facebook.com/profile.php?id=100073260084713
@888.cheese.and.co

Aaron's Wines and Steins
160 First St. N., Wisconsin Rapids
715-423-4763
facebook.com/AaronsWinesandSteins/

Adventure Club Brewing
35265 S. County Road J, Bayfield
715-779-1010
https://adventureclubbrewing.com
facebook.com/adventureclubbrewing

Agonic Brewing Company
17c E. Messenger St., Rice Lake
715-434-2739
www.agonicbrewing.com
facebook.com/agonicbrewing
@agonicbrewing

Ahnapee Brewery
1824 Parkfield Court, Suamico
920-785-0895
www.ahnapeebrewery.com
facebook.com/AhnapeeGB
@ahnapeegb

Al & Al's Steinhaus
1502 S. Twelfth St., Sheboygan
920-452-5530
www.alnals.com
facebook.com/profile.php?id=100049475265176

AL. Ringling Brewing Co.
623 Broadway St., Baraboo
608-448-4013
https://alringlingbrewing.com
facebook.com/alringlingbrewingco
@alringlingbrewingco

Alp and Dell Cheese Store
657 Second St., Monroe
608-328-3355
https://alpanddellcheese.com
facebook.com/AlpandDellCheeseStore/

ALT Brew
1808 Wright St., Madison
608-352-3373
www.altbrew.com
facebook.com/altbrew
@altbrew

Amery Ale Works
588 115th St., Amery
715-268-5226
www.ameryaleworks.com
facebook.com/ameryaleworks/
@ameryaleworks

Amorphic Beer
3700 N. Fratney St., Milwaukee
414-485-6705
www.amorphicbeer.com
facebook.com/amorphicbeer
@amorphicbeer

Angry Minnow Brewery
10440 Florida Ave., Hayward
715-934-3055
https://angryminnow.com
facebook.com/AngryMinnowBrewPub

Appleton Beer Factory
603 W. College Ave., Appleton
920-364-9931
www.appletonbeerfactory.com
facebook.com/appletonbeerfactory/
@appletonbeerfactory

Arena Cheese
300 US Hwy. 14, Arena
608-753-2501
www.arenacheese.com
facebook.com/p/Arena-Cheese-Inc-100057883740371/

Asgard Axe and Tap
714 Oak St., Wisconsin Dells
608-432-3505
www.asgardaxethrow.com
facebook.com/asgardaxe
@asgardaxeandtap

Badger State Brewing Company
990 Tony Canadeo Run, Green Bay
920-634-5687
www.badgerstatebrewing.com
facebook.com/BadgerStateBrewing/
@badgerstatebrewing

Balsam Lake Brewery and Market
101 First Ave. E., Balsam Lake
715-405-3669
www.balsamlakebrewery.com
facebook.com/BalsamLakeBreweryMarket
@balsamlakebrewerymarket

Bare Bones Brewery
4362 County Road S, Oshkosh
920-744-8045
https://barebonesbrewery.us
facebook.com/barebonesbrew/
@barebonesbrewery

Bass Lake Cheese Factory
598 Valley View Trail, Somerset
715-247-5585
https://blcheese.com
facebook.com/CheezyRiders/

Baumgartner's Cheese Store & Tavern
1023 Sixteenth Ave., Monroe
608-325-6157
www.baumgartnercheese.com
facebook.com/profile.php?id=100064797993660

Becher Meats
2079 S. Sixty-Ninth St., West Allis
414-543-4230
www.bechermeats.com
facebook.com/bechermeats/?ref=bookmarks
@bechermeats

Beer Shop
200 W. Wisconsin St., Sparta
608-487-9800
www.beershopsparta.com
facebook.com/beershopsparta/
@beer_shop_sparta

Benoit Cheese Haus
23920 County Road F, Benoit
715-746-2561
www.benoitcheese.com
facebook.com/benoitcheese/

Bevy Brewery & Winery
805 Business Park Rd., Wisconsin Dells
262-419-2389
www.bevy.llc
facebook.com/bevy.wi
@bevy.wi

Big Daddy's
21 W. Davenport St., Rhinelander
715-362-3444
www.bigdaddysbar.com
facebook.com/BigDaddysRhinelander/

Big Head Brewing Co.
6204 W. State St., Wauwatosa
414-257-9782
https://bigheadbrewingco.com
facebook.com/bigheadbrewing

Black Husky Brewing
909 E. Locust St., Milwaukee
414-763-4141
https://blackhuskybrewing.com
facebook.com/profile.php?id=100063536051677
@blackhuskybrews

Black Rose Blending Co.
1602 Gilson St., Madison
608-284-7377
www.blackroseblendingco.com
facebook.com/blackroseblendingco
@blackroseblendingco

Blue Heron BrewPub
108 W. Ninth St., Marshfield
715-389-1868
https://blueheronbrewpub.com
facebook.com/blue.brewpub/

Brat House Grill
49 Wisconsin Dells Pkwy. S., Lake Delton
608-254-8508
www.brathousedells.com
facebook.com/brathouse.grill/

Brat Stop
12304 Seventy-Fifth St., Kenosha
262-857-2011
https://bratstop.com
facebook.com/bratstop
@bratstop

Brewery Nønic
621 Fourth St. W., Menomonie
715-578-9078
www.brewerynonic.com
facebook.com/brewerynonic
@brewery_nonic

Brewfinity Brewing Company
N58W39800 Industrial Rd., Ste. D, Oconomowoc
262-456-2843
www.brewfinitybrewing.com
facebook.com/Brewfinity

Brewing Projekt, The
1807 N. Oxford Ave., Eau Claire
715-214-3728
www.thebrewingprojekt.com
facebook.com/thebrewingprojekt/
@thebrewingprojekt

Brickfield Brewing
130 W. Olson Dr., Grantsburg
715-463-1900
https://brickfieldbrewing.com
facebook.com/BrickfieldBrewing/
@brickfieldbrewing

Bridge Up Brewing Company
129 N. Madison Ave., Sturgeon Bay
920-743-2300
https://bridgeupbrewing.com
facebook.com/bridgeupbrewing
@bridgeupbrewing

Broken Bat Brewing Co.
135 E. Pittsburgh Ave., Milwaukee
414-316-9197
https://brokenbatbrewery.com
facebook.com/BrokenBatBrewing Company/
@brokenbatbrew

Bull Falls Brewery
901 E. Thomas St., Wausau
715-842-2337
https://bullfallsbrewery.com
facebook.com/bullfallsbrewery

Bullquarian Brewhouse
1128 Seventeenth Ave., Monroe
608-426-6720
facebook.com/Bullquarianbrewhouse/

Bunzel's Meat Market
9015 W. Burleigh St., Milwaukee
414-873-7960
https://bunzels.com
facebook.com/Bunzels/
@bunzelmeats

Burnett Dairy Cooperative
11631 State Hwy. 70, Grantsburg
715-689-2059
www.burnettdairy.com
facebook.com/burnettdairy
@burnettdairy

Cady Cheese Factory & Store
126 State Hwy. 128, Wilson
715-772-4218 ext. 4
www.cadycheese.com
facebook.com/burnettdairycady/

Capital Brewery
7734 Terrace Ave., Middleton
608-836-7100
www.capitalbrewery.com
facebook.com/CapBrew/
@capitalbrewery

Carr Valley Cheese
1675 Lincoln Ave., Fennimore
608-820-8818
https://carrvalleycheese.com/
facebook.com/carrvalleycheese
@carrvalley

Cedar Grove Cheese
E5904 Mill Rd., Plain
608-546-5284
https://cedargrovecheese.com
facebook.com/cedargrovecheese

Central Waters Brewing Co.
351 Allen St., Amherst
715-824-2739
https://centralwaters.com
facebook.com/CWBrewing/
@centralwaters

Century Pub & Eatery
5511 Sixth Ave., Kenosha
262-764-6501
facebook.com/centurypubandeatery/

Cercis Brewing Company
140 N. Dickason Blvd., Columbus
920-350-0500
www.cercisbrewingco.com
facebook.com/cercisbrewing/

Chalet Cheese Cooperative
N4858 County Road N, Monroe
608-325-4343
https://chaletcheesecoop.com
facebook.com/ChaletCheeseCoop

Cheese Board of Wisconsin, The
8524 US Hwy. 51 N., Minocqua
715-356-7225
www.thecheeseboard.com

Cheese Store and More, The
185 E. Madison St., Hillsboro
608-489-2651
https://thecheesestoreandmore.com

Cheesers LoKal Market
183 E. Main St., Stoughton
608-873-1777
www.cheesers.com
facebook.com/Cheesers
@cheeserslm

CheezHEAD Brewing
414 Pleasant St., Beloit
608-312-2081
www.cheezheadbrewing.com
facebook.com/CheezHeadbrewing/

City Lights Brewing Co.
2200 W. Mount Vernon Ave., Milwaukee
414-279-7004
https://citylightsbrewing.com
facebook.com/citylightsbrewing
@citylightsbrewing

City Service Brewing
404 Main St., Darlington
608-482-5212
https://cityservicebrewing.wixsite.com/cityservicebrewing
facebook.com/cityservicebrewing/

Clark's Cup N Cone and Cheese Shop
2802 E. Main St., Merrill
715-536-9799
www.clarkscheeseshop.com
facebook.com/clarkscupnconeandcheeseshop/

Commerce Street Brewery & Hotel
23 Commerce St., Mineral Point
608-987-3298
www.commercehotel.com
facebook.com/CommerceHotel/
@commercehotel

Company Brewing
735 E. Center St., Milwaukee
414-930-0909
www.companybrewing.com
facebook.com/CompanyBrewing/
@companybrewing

Copper State Brewing Co.
313 Dousman St., Green Bay
920-489-8575
www.copperstate.beer
facebook.com/copperstatebrewing/
@copperstatebrewing

Crow, The
100 Third St. S., La Crosse
608-519-5400
www.thecrowlacrosse.com
facebook.com/OldCrowLaCrosse/
@thecrowlacrosse

Decatur Dairy
W1668 County Road F, Brodhead
608-897-8661
https://decaturdairy.com
facebook.com/decaturdairy/

Delafield Brewhaus
3832 Hillside Dr., Delafield
262-646-7821
www.delafieldbrewhaus.com
facebook.com/delafieldbrewhaus

Delta Beer Lab
167 E. Badger Rd., Madison
608-640-4500
www.delta.beer
facebook.com/deltabeerlab
@delta.beer

District 1 Brewing Company
200 N. Division St., Ste. G, Stevens Point
715-544-6707
www.district1brewing.com
facebook.com/D1Brewing/
@d1brewing

Door Artisan Cheese Company
8103 State Hwy. 42 N., Egg Harbor
920-868-1444
www.doorartisancheese.com
facebook.com/DoorArtisanCheese/
@doorartisancheese

Door County Brewing Co.
8099 State Hwy. 57, Baileys Harbor
920-239-8181
www.doorcountybrewingco.com
facebook.com/DoorCountyBrewingCo
@doorcountybrewingco

Door County Creamery
10653 N. Bay Shore Dr., Sister Bay
920-854-3388
https://doorcountycreamery.com
facebook.com/DoorCountyCreamery/

Driftless Café
118 W. Court St., Viroqua
608-637-7778
https://driftlesscafe.com
facebook.com/profile.php?id=100064418630685
@driftlesscafe

Durand Brewing Company
N6649 State Hwy. 25, Durand
715-283-4040
https://durandbrewingcompany.com
facebook.com/durandbrewingco

Eagle Park Brewing and Distilling Company
823 E. Hamilton St., Milwaukee
414-585-0123
www.eagleparkbrewing.com
facebook.com/EPbeer/
@eagleparkbrewing

Earth Rider Brewery
1617 N. Third St., Superior
715-394-7391
https://earthrider.beer
facebook.com/EarthRiderBeer/
@earthriderbeer

East Troy Brewery
2905 Main St., East Troy
262-642-2670
https://etbrew.com
facebook.com/ETBrew/
@easttroybrewery

Eau Claire Cheese & Deli
1636 Harding Ave., Eau Claire
715-834-2000
www.ecdeli.com
facebook.com/profile.php?id=100063601612531

Eau Galle Cheese
N6765 State Hwy. 25, Durand
715-283-4211
www.eaugallecheese.com
facebook.com/EauGalleCheese/

Edge-O-Dells Bar & Restaurant
N555 US Hwys. 12 & 16, Wisconsin Dells
608-254-6144
www.edgeodells.com/bar-restaurant/
facebook.com/edgeodells
@edgeodells

Ellsworth Cooperative Creamery
232 N. Wallace St., Ellsworth
715-273-4311 ext. 225
www.ellsworthcheese.com
@ellsworthcreamery

Feltz Family Farms
5796 Porter Dr., Stevens Point
715-344-1293
https://feltzsdairystore.com
facebook.com/FeltzFamilyFarmsandDairyStore

Fermentorium, The
7481 State Hwy. 60, Cedarburg
262-421-8593
https://thefermentorium.com
facebook.com/TheFermentorium/
@thefermentorium

Fifth Ward Brewing Company
1009 S. Main St., Oshkosh
920-479-1876
https://fifthwardbrewing.com
facebook.com/FifthWardBrewing
@fifthwardbrewing

Footjoy Farm and Brewing
407 Central Dr., Cashton
608-654-5662
facebook.com/Footjoybrewing/
@footjoyfarmandbrewing

Fort Mulligan's Grill Pub
214 W. Blackhawk Ave., Prairie du Chien
608-326-0639
www.fortmulligans.com
facebook.com/p/Fort-Mulligans-100057491017597/

Forward Craft & Coffee
2166 Atwood Ave., Madison
608-467-6325
https://forwardcraft.com
facebook.com/ForwardCraftandCoffee/
@forwardcraftandcoffee

Fox River Brewing Company
1501 Arboretum Dr., Oshkosh
920-232-2337
www.foxriverbrewing.com
facebook.com/FoxRiverBrewingCompany
@frbcompany

Foxtown Brewing
6411 W. Mequon Rd., Mequon
262-292-5700
https://foxtownbrewing.com
facebook.com/FoxtownBrewingWI
@foxtownbrewingwi

Franksville Craft Beer Garden
9614 Northwestern Ave., Franksville
262-930-8530
https://hopheadscraftbeer.com/beer-garden
facebook.com/franksvillecraftbeer/
@franksvillecraftbeer

Frannie's Market
W61 N486 Washington Ave., Cedarburg
262-271-1848
https://franniesmarket.com
facebook.com/Frannies.Market/
@frannies.market

Fromagination
12 S. Carroll St., Madison
608-255-2430
https://fromagination.com
facebook.com/Fromagination
@fromagination

Full Mile Beer Company & Kitchen
132 Market St., Ste. 100, Sun Prairie
608-318-2074
www.fullmilebeercompany.com
facebook.com/fullmilebeerco/
@fullmilebeerco

G5 Brewing Company
1895 Gateway Blvd., Beloit
608-368-7492
www.g5brewing.net
facebook.com/G5Brewing
@g5brewco

Garage Bikes and Brews, The
109 W. Cedar St., River Falls
715-629-7086
https://garagebikesbrews.com
facebook.com/garagebikesbrews
@garagebikesbrews

Gathering Place Brewing Company
811 E. Vienna Ave., Milwaukee
414-635-0569
www.gatheringplacebrewing.com
facebook.com/gatheringplacebrewing
@gatheringplacebrewing

Giant Jones Brewing
931 E. Main St., Ste. 9, Madison
608-620-5172
https://giantjones.com
facebook.com/giantjonesbeer/
@giantjonesbrewing

Gibbsville Cheese Co.
W2663 County Road OO, Sheboygan Falls
920-564-3242
https://gibbsvillecheese.com
facebook.com/gibbsvillecheese/

Glarner Stube
518 First St., New Glarus
608-527-2216
facebook.com/glarnerstube

Gnarly Cedar Brewery
6381 State Hwy. 57, Greenleaf
920-532-4384
www.gnarlycedar.com
facebook.com/GnarlyCedarBrewery/
@gnarlycedarbrewery_wi

Good City Brewing
11200 W. Burleigh St., Wauwatosa
414-539-4343
www.goodcitybrewing.com
facebook.com/GoodCityBrewing
@goodcitybrewing

Gravity Box Brewing Company
134 E. State St., Mauston
608-747-2337
www.gravityboxbrewing.com
facebook.com/gravityboxbrewingco
@gravityboxbrewingcompany

Green Grocer
24 W. Geneva St., Williams Bay
262-245-9077
https://greengrocergenevalake.com
facebook.com/GreenGrocerWB/

Growler Guys, The
2832 London Rd., Eau Claire
715-514-5140
https://thegrowlerguys.com/locations/eau-claire-wisconsin/
facebook.com/TheGrowlerGuysEauClaire/

Grumpy Troll Brew Pub
105 S. Second St., Mt. Horeb
608-437-2739
https://thegrumpytroll.com
facebook.com/grumpytrollbrew/
@grumpytrollbrew

Hacienda Beer Co.
8099 State Hwy. 57, Baileys Harbor
920-239-8181
www.haciendabeerco.com/home
facebook.com/haciendabeerco
@haciendabeerco

Henning's Cheese
20201 Point Creek Rd., Kiel
920-894-3032
https://henningscheese.com
facebook.com/henningscheese/

H. H. Hinder Brewing Co.
804 Churchill St., Waupaca
715-942-8018
https://hinderbrewingco.com
facebook.com/HHHinder/

Hill Valley Cheese Bar & Shop
510 and 512 Broad St., Lake Geneva
262-684-9524
https://hillvalleydairy.com
facebook.com/HillValleyDairy/
@hillvalleydairy

Hillsboro Brewing Company
206 E. Madison St., Hillsboro
608-489-7486
www.hillsborobrewingcompany.com
facebook.com/HillsboroBrewingCompany/
@hillsborobrewingcompany

Hilltop Pub & Grill
4917 Main St., Stevens Point
715-341-3037
https://hilltoppubandgrill.com
facebook.com/hilltoppubandgrill
@hilltoppubandgrill

Hinterland Brewery
1001 Lombardi Ave., Green Bay
920-438-8050
https://hinterlandbeer.com
facebook.com/HinterlandBrewery/
@hinterlandbeer

Hometown Sausage Kitchen
W1184 County Road L, East Troy
262-642-3264
www.hometownsausagekitchen.com
facebook.com/hometownsausage/
@hometownsausage

Hop and Barrel Brewing
310 Second St., Hudson
715-808-8390
www.hopandbarrelbrewing.com/hudson-wi
facebook.com/hopandbarrelbrewing/
@hopandbarrel

Hop Yard Ale Works
512 W. Northland Ave., Appleton
https://hopyardaleworks.com
facebook.com/hopyardaleworks/
@hopyardaleworks

Humbird Cheese Mart
2010 Eaton Ave., Tomah
608-372-6069
www.humbirdcheese.com
facebook.com/humbirdcheese/

Indeed Brewing Company
530 S. Second St., Milwaukee
414-216-9007
www.indeedbrewing.com
facebook.com/indeedmilwaukee/
@indeedmilwaukee

Inventors Brewpub
435 N. Lake St., Port Washington
262-284-4690
www.inventorsbrewpub.com
facebook.com/inventorsbrewpub/
@inventorsbrewpub

Jacob Leinenkugel Brewing Company
124 E. Elm St., Chippewa Falls
888-534-6437
www.leinie.com
facebook.com/Leinenkugels
@leinenkugels

Jim's Meat Market
68455 District St., Iron River
715-372-8566
https://jimsmeat.com
facebook.com/profile.php?id=100057853605817

Johnsonville
N6877 Rio Rd., Sheboygan Falls
920-453-5678
www.johnsonvillemarketplace.com

K Point Brewing
4212 Southtowne Dr., Eau Claire
715-834-1733
www.thecoffeegrounds.com/k-point-brewing
facebook.com/kpointbeers/
@kpointbrewing

Karben4
3698 Kinsman Blvd., Madison
608-241-4812
https://karben4.com
facebook.com/Karben4/
@karben4brewing

Kenosha Brewing Company
4017 Eightieth St., Kenosha
262-694-9494
www.kenoshabrewingcompany.com
facebook.com/profile.php?id=100086503782672
@kenoshabrewingco

Knuth Brewing Company
230 Watson St., Ripon
920-748-5188
https://knuthbrewingcompany.com
facebook.com/knuthbrewingcompany
@knuthbrewingcompany

Kraemer Wisconsin Cheese
1173 N. Fourth St., Watertown
920-261-6363
https://kraemerwisconsincheese.com
facebook.com/profile.php?id=100057156502416

Krohn Dairy
N2915 County Road AB, Luxemburg
920-845-2901
www.krohncheese.com
facebook.com/awardwinningcheese

Kroll's West
1990 S. Ridge Rd., Green Bay
920-497-1111
www.krollswest.com
facebook.com/p/Krolls-West-Restaurant-100063673775704/

Kugel's Cheese Mart
3111 N. Rosera St., Lena
920-829-5537
https://kugelscheese.com

La Crosse Bierhaus
128 Third St. S., La Crosse
608-519-5217
http://www.lacrossebierhaus.com
facebook.com/LAXBierhaus/

LaClare Creamery
W2994 County Road HH, Malone
920-670-0051
http://www.laclarefamilycreamery.com
facebook.com/laclarecreamery/
@laclarecreamery

LaGrander's Hillside Dairy
W11299 Broek Rd., Stanley
715-644-2275
https://lagranderscheese.com
facebook.com/profile.php?id=100041322351780

Lakefront Brewery
1872 N. Commerce St., Milwaukee
414-372-8800
https://lakefrontbrewery.com
facebook.com/lakefront/
@lakefrontbrewery

Lamers Dairy
N410 Speel School Rd., Appleton
920-830-0980
https://lamersdairyinc.com

Landmark Creamery
6895 Paoli Rd., Paoli
608-848-1162
https://landmarkcreamery.com
facebook.com/landmarkcreamery/
@landmark_creamery

Lazy Monk Brewing
97 W. Madison St., Eau Claire
715-271-0848
www.lazymonkbrewing.com
facebook.com/profile.php?id=100063787050805

Le Coulee Cheese Castle
112 S. Leonard St., West Salem
608-786-2811
https://lecouleecheese.net
facebook.com/p/Le-Coulee-Cheese-Castle-100057418669291/

Lift Bridge Brewery
1280 Madison Ave., New Richmond
888-430-2337
www.liftbridgebrewery.com
facebook.com/LiftBridgeNew Richmond/
@liftbridgenewrichmond

Lion's Tail Brewing Co.
116 S. Commercial St., Neenah
920-215-6443
https://lionstailbrewing.com
facebook.com/LionsTailBrewing/
@lionstailbrew

Littleport Brewing Company
214 Third St, Racine
262-629-6976
https://littleport-brewing.com
facebook.com/LittleportBrew/
@littleportbrewing

Lone Girl Brewing Company, The
114 E. Main St., Ste. 101, Waunakee
608-850-7175
https://thelonegirl.com
@lonegirlbrewing

Louie's Finer Meats
2025 Superior Ave., Cumberland
715-822-4728
www.louiesfinermeats.com
facebook.com/louiesmeats/
@louiesmeats

Low Daily
700 N. Pine St., Burlington
262-758-6002
www.lowdailybeer.com
facebook.com/lowdailybeer
@lowdailybeer

Lucette Brewing Company
910 Hudson Rd., Menomonie
715-231-6836
www.lucettebrewing.com
facebook.com/LucetteBrewing Company
@lucettebrewing

Marieke Gouda
200 W. Liberty Dr., Thorp
715-669-5230
www.mariekegouda.com
facebook.com/MariekeGouda
@mariekegouda

Market Square Cheese
1150 Wisconsin Dells Pkwy. S., Lake Delton
608-254-8388
www.marketsquarecheese.com

Mars Cheese Castle
2800 W. Frontage Rd., Kenosha
855-352-6277
www.marscheese.com
facebook.com/MarsCheese/
@marscheesecastle

Meat Block, The
N1739 Lily of the Valley Dr., Greenville
920-757-6622
https://themeatblock.com
facebook.com/profile.php?id=100063684214518
@meatblock

Meister Cheese
1050 E. Industrial Dr., Muscoda
608-739-3134
www.meistercheese.com
facebook.com/meistercheese

Mel's Micro
21733 US Hwy. 14, Richland Center
608-647-1116
www.melsmicro.com
facebook.com/melsmicro/

Miesfeld's Triangle Market
4811 Venture Dr., Sheboygan
920-565-6328
https://miesfelds.com
facebook.com/MiesfeldsTriangleMarket

Milwaukee Brat House
1013 N. Old World Third St., Milwaukee
414-273-8709
https://downtown.milwaukeebrathouse.com
facebook.com/milwaukeebrathouse/
@mkebrathouse

Minhas Craft Brewery
1208 Fourteenth Ave., Monroe
608-328-9120
http://minhasbrewery.com/minhas-craft-brewery-wisconsin
facebook.com/MinhasCraftBrewery/

Mom's Kitchen
3035 N. Hastings Way, Eau Claire
715-838-8994
https://momskitchenec.com
facebook.com/momskitcheneauclaire/
@moms_kitchen_eau_claire

MoonRidge Brew Pub
501 Bridge St., Cornell
715-239-1341
www.moonridgebrewery.com
facebook.com/profile.php?id=100063769681138
@moon.ridgebrewingcompany

Mosinee Brewing Company
401 Fourth St., Mosinee
715-693-2739
www.mosineebrewing.com
facebook.com/MosineeBrewing/
@mosineebrewingcompany

Mousehouse Cheesehaus
4494 Lake Circle, Windsor
608-846-4455
www.mousehousecheese.com
facebook.com/mousehousecheese/

Mullins Cheese
203843 County Road DB, Mosinee
715-693-3205
www.mullinscheese.com
facebook.com/mullinscheese/
@mullinscheese

New Glarus Brewing Company
2400 State Hwy. 69, New Glarus
608-527-5850
https://newglarusbrewing.com
facebook.com/newglarusbrewing
@newglarusbrewing

Ney's Natural Premium Meats and Sweets
310 E. Washington St., Slinger
262-297-1400
www.neysbigsky.com
facebook.com/neyspremium/
@neyspremium

Noble Rind Cheese Company
110 W. Court St., Viroqua
608-638-2743
www.noblerind.com
facebook.com/NobleRind
@noblerind

Noble Roots Brewing Company
2790 University Ave., Green Bay
920-489-2874
www.noblerootsbrewing.com/home
facebook.com/NobleRootsBrewing/
@noblerootsbrewing

Nordic Creamery
202 W. Old Towne Rd., Westby
608-634-3276
www.nordiccreamery.com
facebook.com/NordicCreamery/

Northwoods Brewpub and Grill
50819 West St., Osseo
715-597-1828
https://northwoodsbrewpub.com

Nueske's
1390 E. Grand Ave., Wittenberg
715-253-4059
www.nueskes.com
facebook.com/nueskesmeats/
@nueskes

O'So Brewing
1800 Plover Rd., Plover
715-254-2163
www.osobrewing.com
facebook.com/OsoBrewingCompany/
@oso_brewing

Octopi
1131 Uniek Dr., Waunakee
608-218-5917
https://drinkoctopi.com
facebook.com/DrinkOctopi
@drinkoctopi

Old Country Cheese
S502 County Road D, Cashton
608-654-5411
www.oldcountrycheese.com

Old World Creamery
1606 Erie Ave., Sheboygan
920-593-9999
www.owcreamery.com

Oliphant Brewing
350 Main St., Ste. 2, Somerset
651-705-6070
https://oliphantbrewing.com
facebook.com/oliphantbrewing/
@oliphantbrewing

Ombibulous Brewing Company
1419 Winchester Way, Ste. 8, Altoona
715-318-7179
facebook.com/OmbibulousBrewing/

Omega Brewing Experience
115 E. Main St., Omro
facebook.com/p/Omega-Brewing-Experience-100063586692791/

One Barrel Brewing Company
4633 Market St., Egg Harbor
920-868-5262
www.onebarrelbrewing.com
facebook.com/obbcdc/

Ooga Brewing Company
301 S. Spring St., Beaver Dam
920-306-5100
www.oogabrewing.com
facebook.com/OOGABrewingCompany/

Ope! Brewing Co.
6751 W. National Ave., West Allis
414-509-6700
www.opebrewingco.com
facebook.com/OpeBrewingCo/
@opebrewingco

Otto's Beer & Brat Garden
509 Oneida St., Minocqua
715-356-6134
facebook.com/p/Ottos-Beer-Brat-Garden-61551218001070/

Outpost Natural Foods
7000 W. State St., Wauwatosa
414-778-2012
www.outpost.coop
facebook.com/outpostnaturalfoods
@outpostnaturalfoods

Pasture Pride Cheese
111 Eagle Dr., Cashton
608-654-7444
www.pasturepridecheese.com
facebook.com/PasturePrideCheese/
@pasturepride

Peach Barn Farmhouse and Brewery
2450 S. Bay Shore Dr., Sister Bay
https://peachbarnbrewing.com
facebook.com/peachbarnbrewing
@peachbarnbrewing

Pearl Street Brewery
1401 St. Andrew St., La Crosse
608-784-4832
https://pearlstreetbrewery.com
facebook.com/pearlstreetbrewery

Petrifying Springs Biergarten
5555 Seventh St., Pavilion 1, Kenosha
www.petrifyingspringsbiergarten.com
facebook.com/petsbiergarten

Pine River Dairy
10115 English Lake Rd., Manitowoc
920-758-2233
https://pineriverdairy.com
facebook.com/PineRiverDairy/

Pitchfork Brewing Co.
745 Ryan Dr., Hudson
715-245-3675
www.pitchforkbrewing.com
facebook.com/PitchforkBrewing
@pitchforkbrew

PJ Campbell's at the Depot
114 Depot Rd., Plymouth
920-893-8600
www.pjcampbellsatthedepot.com

Plymouth Brewing Company
222 E. Mill St., Plymouth
920-400-1722
www.plymouthbrewingcompany.com

Potosi Brewery
209 S. Main St., Potosi
608-763-4002
www.potosibrewery.com
facebook.com/PotosiBrewingCo/
@potosibrewingco

PUBLIC Craft Brewing Co.
628 Fifty-Eighth St., Kenosha
262-652-2739
https://publiccraftbrewing.com
facebook.com/PublicCraftBrewing/
@publicbrewing

R'Noggin Brewing Company
6521 120th Ave., Kenosha
262-960-1298
https://rnoggin.com
facebook.com/rnogginbrewing/
@rnogginbrewing

Raised Grain Brewing Company
1725 Dolphin Dr., Waukesha
262-505-5942
www.raisedgrainbrewing.com
facebook.com/raisedgrainbrewing/
@raisedgrainbrewingco

Raven's Breath Brewery
68295 S. Main St., Iron River
715-372-4359
www.ravensbreathbrewery.com
facebook.com/profile.php?id=
100057281116370

Red Eye Brewing Company
612 Washington St., Wausau
715-843-7334
www.redeyebrewing.com
facebook.com/RedEyeBrewing

Reef Point Brew House
2 Christopher Columbus Causeway,
Racine
262-898-7333
www.reefpointbrewhouse.com
facebook.com/Reefpointbrewhouse
@reefpointbrewhouse

Renard's Cheese
2189 County Road DK, Sturgeon Bay
920-825-7272
www.renardscheese.com
facebook.com/renardscheese
@renardscheese

Rhinelander Brewing Company
43 S. Brown St., Rhinelander
715-550-2337
https://rhinelanderbrewingco.mybig
commerce.com
facebook.com/RhinelanderBrewery/

Rio Lobo
E6485 County Road F, Weyauwega
920-505-0302
www.riolobollc.com
facebook.com/riolobowinery/
@riolobollc

Rock County Brewing Company
10 N. Parker Dr., Ste. 16, Janesville
608-531-8120
www.rockcountybrewingco.com
facebook.com/rockcountybrewing/
@rockcountybrewing

Rocky Reef Brewing Company
1101 First Ave., Woodruff
715-439-4055
www.rockyreefbrewing.com
facebook.com/rrbrewco
@rockyreefbrewing

Ron's Wisconsin Cheese
124 Main St., Luxemburg
920-845-5330
https://ronscheese.com
facebook.com/RonsWisconsinCheese/

Round Man Brewing Co.
234 Walnut St., Spooner
715-939-1800
www.roundmanbrewing.com
facebook.com/roundmanbrewing
@roundmanbrewing

Rowland's Calumet Brewing Co.
25 N. Madison St., Chilton
920-849-2534
www.rowlandsbrewery.com
facebook.com/profile.php?id=
100063466601954

Runaway Micropub & Nanobrewery, The
109 E. Chestnut St., Burlington
262-806-7048
www.runawayburlington.com
facebook.com/runawayburlington
@runawayburlington

Rush River Brewing Company
990 Antler Ct., River Falls
715-426-2054
http://rushriverbeer.com
facebook.com/rushriverbrewing/
@rushriverbrewery

Rustic Road Brewing Company
5706 Sixth Ave., Kenosha
262-320-7623
www.rusticbrewing.com
facebook.com/rusticroadbrewery
@rusticroadbrewingcompany

Sand Creek Brewing Company
320 Pierce St., Black River Falls
715-284-7553
www.sandcreekbrewing.com
@sandcreekbrewery

Sassy Cow Creamery
W4192 Bristol Rd., Columbus
608-837-7766
https://sassycowcreamery.com/
facebook.com/SassyCowCreamery/
@sassycowcreamery

Sawmill Brewing Company
1110 E. Tenth St., Merrill
715-722-0230
https://sawmillbrewing.net
facebook.com/Sawmillbrewing/
@sawmillbrew

Sawmill Pizza & Brew Shed
805 Thirtieth Ave., Clear Lake
facebook.com/sawmillpizzabrewshed/
@sawmillpizzabrewshed

Schuby's Neighborhood Butcher
321 State St., La Crosse
608-615-1076
www.schubys.com
facebook.com/schubys
@schubys

Schurman's Wisconsin Cheese
233 N. Iowa St., Dodgeville
608-935-5741
www.schurmanscheese.com

Scray Cheese
2082 Old Martin Rd., De Pere
920-347-0303
https://scraycheese.com
facebook.com/p/Scray-Cheese-100057168561893/

Sheboygan Pasty Company
811 Indiana Ave., Sheboygan
920-395-2132
https://sheboyganpasty.com
facebook.com/profile.php?id=100064243684039

Shullsburg Creamery
208 W. Water St., Shullsburg
888-331-1193
https://shullsburgcreamery.com
facebook.com/shullsburgcheesestoreandgiftshop/
@shullsburgcreamery

Skeleton Crew Brew
570 Theater Rd., Onalaska
715-570-9463
www.skeletoncrewbrew.com
facebook.com/skeletoncrewbrew
@skeletoncrewbrew

Some Nerve Brewing Company
5586 US Hwy. 51, Manitowish Waters
608-576-6040
www.somenervebrewing.com
facebook.com/SomeNerveBrewing/
@somenervebrewing

South Shore Brewery
808 Main St. W., Ashland
715-682-9199
www.southshorebrewery.com
facebook.com/southshorebrewery/
@southshorebrewery

Sprecher Brewing Co.
701 W. Glendale Ave., Glendale
414-967-0411
https://sprecherbrewery.com
facebook.com/sprecherbrewing/?rf=104105796291283
@sprecherbrewery

Springside Cheese
7989 Arndt Rd., Oconto Falls
920-829-6395
https://springsidecheese.com
facebook.com/SpringsideCheese
@springsidecheese

Starboard Brewing Company
151 N. Third Ave., Sturgeon Bay
920-818-1062
https://starboardbrewing.com
facebook.com/starboardbrewing/

Starkweather Brewing Company
2439 Atwood Ave., Madison
608-467-6949
https://starkweatherbrewing.com
facebook.com/StarkweatherBrewingCompany/
@starkweatherbrewing

State Street Brats
603 State St., Madison
608-255-5544
https://statestreetbrats.com
facebook.com/StateStreetBrats/
@statestreetbrats

Station 1 Brewing Company
1745 Riverside Dr., Suamico
920-393-1004
www.station1brewing.com
facebook.com/station1brewing
@station1brewingcompany

SteelTank Brewing Co.
1225 Robruck Dr., Oconomowoc
262-569-6000
https://steeltankbrewing.com
facebook.com/SteelTankBrewing/
@steeltankbrewingco

Stevens Point Brewery
2617 Water St., Stevens Point
715-344-9310
www.pointbeer.com
@pointbrewery

Stillmank Brewing Company
215 N. Henry St., Green Bay
920-785-2337
https://stillmankbrewing.com
facebook.com/StillmankBeerCompany
@stillmankbrewing

Stoney Acres Farm
245728 Baldwin Creek Rd., Athens
715-432-6285
https://stoneyacres.farm
facebook.com/stoneyacresfarmandpizza/

Stubborn Brothers Brewery
220 S. Main St., Shawano
715-201-0859
www.stubbornbros.com
facebook.com/StubbornBrothersBrewery
@stubbornbeer

Sunshine Brewing Company
121 S. Main St., Lake Mills
920-320-9735
https://sunshinebrewco.com
facebook.com/sunshinebrewco
@sunshinebrewco

Superior Meats
6301 Tower Ave., Superior
715-394-4431
www.superior-meats.com
facebook.com/superiormeats54880/

SwitchGear Brewing Co.
44D Gottfried St., Elkhart Lake
920-781-5120
www.switchgearbrewing.com
facebook.com/switchgearbrewing
@switchgearbrewingco

Tetzner Dairy Farm
30455 Nevers Rd., Washburn
715-373-2330
http://tetznerdairy.com
facebook.com/TetznersDairy

Third Space Brewing
1505 W. St. Paul Ave., Milwaukee
414-909-2337
https://thirdspacebrewing.com
facebook.com/thirdspacebrewing/
@thirdspacebrewing

Thirsty Pagan Brewing
1615 Winter St., Superior
715-394-2500
www.thirstypaganbrewing.com
facebook.com/ThirstyPaganBrewing/
@thirstypagan

Thumb Knuckle Brewing Company
E0208 State Hwy. 54, Luxemburg
www.thumbknuckle.beer
facebook.com/ThumbKnuckleBrewingCo

Titletown Brewing Co.
320 N. Broadway, Green Bay
920-437-2337
www.titletownbrewing.com
facebook.com/titletownbrewingco
@titletownbrewingco

Topsy Turvy Brewery
727 Geneva St., Lake Geneva
262-812-8323
www.topsyturvybrewery.com
facebook.com/topsyturvybrewery/
@topsyturvybrewery

Trap Rock Brewing Company
520 S. Blanding Woods Rd., St. Croix Falls
715-483-1338
http://traprockbrewing.com
facebook.com/traprockbrewing/
@traprockbrewing

Tribute Brewing Company
1106 Bluebird Rd., Eagle River
715-480-2337
https://tributebrewing.com

Tumbled Rock Brewery & Kitchen
S5718 State Hwy. 136 & County Road DL, Baraboo
608-448-4340
https://tumbledrock.com
facebook.com/tumbledrock/
@tumbled.rock.brewery.kitchen

Turtle Stack Brewery
125 Second St. S., La Crosse
608-519-2284
https://turtlestackbrewery.com
facebook.com/turtlestackbrewery/
@turtlestackbrewery

Tyranena Brewing Company
1025 Owen St., Lake Mills
920-648-8699
https://tyranena.com
facebook.com/tyranena/
@tyranena

Udder Brothers' Creamery
1100 Elm St., Boscobel
608-391-3120
www.udderbrotherscreamery.com
facebook.com/udderbrotherscreamery/
@udderbrothers

Union Star Cheese Factory
7742 County Road II, Fremont
920-836-2804
www.unionstarcheese.com
facebook.com/UnionStarCheese

Vennture Brew Co.
5519 W. North Ave., Milwaukee
414-856-4321
https://vennturebrewco.square.site
facebook.com/VenntureBrewCo
@vennturebrewco

Viking Brew Pub
211 E. Main St., Stoughton
608-719-5041
https://vikingbrew.pub
@vikingbrewpub

Village Cheese Shop, The
1430 Underwood Ave., Wauwatosa
414-488-2099
www.villagecheesetosa.com
facebook.com/TVCSTosa/
@tosacheese

Washington Island Biergarten
1885 Michigan Rd., Washington Island
920-847-2017

West Allis Cheese and Sausage Shop
6832 W. Becher St., West Allis
414-543-4230
www.westallischeese.com
@westallischeese

Westby Cooperative Creamery
206 S. Main St., Westby
608-634-3181
www.westbycreamery.com
facebook.com/WestbyCreameryFanPage/
@westbycoopcreamery

Weyauwega Star Dairy
109 N. Mill St., Weyauwega
920-867-2870
https://stardairy.com
facebook.com/WeyauwegaStarDairy/

Whitewater Music Hall and Brew Works
130 First St., Wausau
715-298-3202
www.whitewatermusichall.com
facebook.com/whitewatermusichall
@whitewatermusichall

Widmer's Cheese Cellars
214 W. Henni St., Theresa
920-488-2503
www.widmerscheese.com
facebook.com/WidmersCheese/
@widmerscheese

Wisconsin Cheese Masters
4692 Rainbow Ridge Ct., Egg Harbor
920-868-4320
www.wisconsincheesemasters.com
facebook.com/Wisconsincheese masters/

Wisconsin Dairy State Cheese Company
6860 State Hwy. 34, Rudolph
715-435-3144

Wisconsin River Meats
N5340 County Road HH, Mauston
608-847-7413
www.wisconsinrivermeats.com
facebook.com/wisconsinrivermeats/
@wisconsinrivermeats

Wizard Works Brewing
231 E. Buffalo St., Lower Level, Milwaukee
414-477-0222
https://wizardworksbrewing.com
facebook.com/wizardworksbrewing
@wizard_works_brewing

Working Draft Beer Company
1129 E. Wilson St., Madison
608-709-5600
www.workingdraftbeer.com
facebook.com/workingdraftbeer/
@workingdraftbeer

Yellowstone Cheese
24105 County Road MM, Cadott
715-289-3800
https://yellowstonecheese.com

Young Blood Beer Company
112 King St., Madison
608-630-9028
www.youngbloodbeerco.com
facebook.com/youngbloodbeer company
@youngbloodbeerco

Zambaldi Beer
1649 S. Webster Ave., Allouez
920-455-0473
www.zambaldi.com
facebook.com/ZambaldiBeer/
@zambaldi_beer

Zymurgy Brewing Company
624 Main St. E., Menomonie
715-578-9026
www.zymurgybrew.com
@zymurgybrewing

Bibliography

Adams, Barry. "Wisconsin Cheese Production Reigns." *AgriView*, May 10, 2023. https://agupdate.com/agriview/news/business/wisconsin-cheese-production-reigns/article_1043da12-7b07-503c-b256-68a88996cc3b.html.

Allen, Terese. "The Stuff of History: Sausage in Wisconsin." *Edible Madison*, December 13, 2013. https://ediblemadison.com/stories/the-stuff-of-history-sausage-in-wisconsin.

Anderson, Andrea. "Tapped in Random Lake: Company Brings Art to Tap Handles." *Wisconsin Public Radio*, May 15, 2019. https://wisconsinlife.org/story/tapped-in-random-lake-company-brings-art-to-tap-handles/.

Apple, R. W., Jr. "The Meat That Made Sheboygan Famous." *New York Times*, June 5, 2002.

Apps, Jerry. *Cheese: The Making of a Wisconsin Tradition*. Madison: University of Wisconsin Press, 2020.

Behling, Andrea. "The Wisconsin Bratwurst Is Encased in Tradition: Our Wisconsinite Penchant for Brats Is Untouchable." *Madison Magazine*, April 21, 2016. https://www.channel3000.com/madison-magazine/dining-and-drink/the-wisconsin-bratwurst-is-encased-in-tradition/article_9e600e45-4880-5f69-a98d-fbb769ec52c2.html.

"Beverages: Bubbling Battle of the Brewers." *Time*, August 18, 1975. https://content.time.com/time/subscriber/article/0,33009,917760-1,00.html.

Brewers Association. "Brewers Association Releases Annual Craft Brewing Industry Production Report and Top 50 Producing Craft Brewing Companies for 2022." April 18, 2023. https://www.brewersassociation.org/press-releases/brewers-association-releases-annual-craft-brewing-industry-production-report-and-top-50-producing-craft-brewing-companies-for-2022/.

Brewers Association. "Wisconsin's Craft Beer Sales & Production Statistics, 2022." 2022. https://www.brewersassociation.org/statistics-and-data/state-craft-beer-stats/?state=WI.

Busch, Jason. "Craft Beer: A Local Love Story." *In Business*, October 2, 2019. https://www.ibmadison.com/craft-beer-a-local-love-story/.

Chua, Meghan. "Brushing Up on Brats, a Staple of Wisconsin Culture." *Sun Prairie Star*, August 2, 2017. https://www.hngnews.com/sun_prairie_star/community/brushing-up-on-brats-a-staple-of-wisconsin-culture/article_66c5a8d4-7610-11e7-bd0e-537cddf948f6.html.

Cisar, Katjusa. "Queso without Borders: 'Hispanic Style' in America's Dairyland." *Culture*, January 18, 2020. https://culturecheesemag.com/stories/queso-without-borders-hispanic-style-in-americas-dairyland/.

Curd, Dan. "Wisconsin's History of Brats, Beer and Beyond: The German Influence on Customs, Culture and Food." *Madison Magazine*, January 10, 2018. https://www.channel3000.com/madison-magazine/dining-and-drink/wisconsin-s-history-of-brats-beer-and-beyond/article_af367d89-5e88-57aa-b86b-75f7ea969bc7.html.

Dairy Farmers of Wisconsin. https://www.wisconsindairy.org.

Dairy Farmers of Wisconsin. "Wisconsin Cheese Shines as America's Most Awarded at American Cheese Society Competition." July 24, 2023. https://www.wisconsindairy.org/our-story/press-releases/detail?url=wisconsin-cheese-shines-at-acs-competition.

Dippel, Beth. "Bratwurst Phenomenon in Sheboygan Born Out of Neighborhood Meat Markets." *Sheboygan Beacon*, October 8, 2019, https://sheboyganbeacon.com/2019/10/08/bratwurst-phenomenon-in-sheboygan-born-out-of-neighborhood-meat-markets/.

Dippel, Beth. "History Column: The Sausage That Made Sheboygan Famous." *Sheboygan Press*, August 1, 2014. https://www.sheboyganpress.com/story/news/local/2014/08/01/history-column-sausage-made-sheboygan-famous/13498299/.

Eig, Jonathan, and Bryan Gruley. "For This Inventor, the Perfect Beer Is All about the Tap: Mr. Younkle Creates Device." *Wall Street Journal*, July 14, 2005. https://www.wsj.com/articles/SB112130747570985459.

Flanigan, Kathy. "Almost All of the Country's Bars Have Beer Tap Handles Made in This Small Wisconsin Factory." *Milwaukee Journal Sentinel*, March 14, 2019. https://www.jsonline.com/story/life/food/2019/03/14/random-lakes-hanks craft-ajs-countrys-leading-maker-tap-handles/2919356002/.

Higgins, Daniel. "Crowlers Go Tap-to-Can with Craft Beer." *Green Bay Press Gazette*, December 13, 2016. https://www.greenbaypressgazette.com/story/entertainment/nightlife/beer/2016/12/13/crowlers-go-tap--can-craft-beer/90516018/.

Hildebrandt, Dirk. "They Brought Their Beer: German Brewing on the Wisconsin Frontier." *Wisconsin Magazine of History* 102, no. 1 (Autumn 2018): 14–27. https://www.jstor.org/stable/26541153.

Hillibish, Jim. "The Bratwurst Has Deep History, German Roots." Wicked Local, August 2, 2012. https://www.wickedlocal.com/story/bulletin-tab/2012/08/02/jim-hillibish-bratwurst-has-deep/65128785007/.

Hoverson, Doug. *The Drink That Made Wisconsin Famous: Beer and Brewing in the Badger State*. Minneapolis: University of Minnesota Press, 2019.

Hoverson, Doug. "The Most Important Beers in Wisconsin Brewing History: A 12-Pack of Leaders & Legends." *Growler Magazine*, February 24, 2020.

Hurt, Jeanette. *The Cheeses of Wisconsin: A Culinary Travel Guide*. Woodstock, Vt.: Countryman Press, 2008.

International Dairy Foods Association. "History of Cheese." Accessed March 2, 2022. https://www.idfa.org/history-of-cheese.

Jahnke, Pam. "Wisconsin's Rich Ag History." *Mid-West Farm Report*, July 27, 2018. https://www.midwestfarmreport.com/2018/07/27/wisonsins-rich-ag-history/.

Johnsonville. www.johnsonville.com.

Johnsonville. "Our Story." Accessed December 14, 2023. https://johnsonville.com/our-story/.

Kapler, Joseph, Jr. "On Wisconsin Icons: When You Say 'Wisconsin,' What Do You Say?" *Wisconsin Magazine of History* 85, no. 3 (Spring 2022): 18–31. https://content.wisconsinhistory.org/digital/collection/wmh/id/43274.

Keith, Jim. "Brats: Tales of the Northwest Territory." *Herald-Times*, July 5, 2019. https://www.heraldtimesonline.com/story/lifestyle/home-garden/2019/07/05/brats/46654015/.

Kierzek, Kristine M. "America's Dairyland Finding New Markets with Hispanic Cheeses." *Milwaukee Journal Sentinel*, September 10, 2013. https://archive.jsonline.com/features/food/americas-dairyland-finding-new-markets-with-hispanic-cheeses-b99906642z1-223176191.html.

La Crosse County Convention and Visitors Bureau. "The 'Driftless' Region History." February 21, 2022. https://explorelacrosse.com/the-driftless-region-history/.

McDonald, Andy. "Here's Proof That Nobody Eats and Drinks Better Than Wisconsin." *Huffington Post*, June 20, 2014. https://www.huffpost.com/entry/wisconsin-best-food-beer_n_5429225.

Milewski, Todd D. "Data: Only 2 States Have More Bars Than Wisconsin." *Wisconsin State Journal*, May 8, 2013. https://madison.com/news/local/data-only-2-states-have-more-bars-than-wisconsin/html_1a7a0e58-b732-11e2-99a0-001a4bcf887a.html.

National Agricultural Statistics Service. "Dairy Products—2022 Summary." US Department of Agriculture. April 2023. https://downloads.usda.library.cornell.edu/usda-esmis/files/jm214p131/h415qq48q/9g54zx77c/daryan23.pdf.

National Agricultural Statistics Service. "2023 Wisconsin Agricultural Statistics." US Department of Agriculture. October 2023. https://www.nass.usda.gov/Statistics_by_State/Wisconsin/Publications/Annual_Statistical_Bulletin/2023AgStats_WI.pdf/.

National Agricultural Statistics Service. "Wisconsin Ag News—Specialty Cheese." US Department of Agriculture. May 5, 2022. https://www.nass.usda.gov/Statistics_by_State/Wisconsin/Publications/Dairy/2022/WI-SpecialtyCheese-05-22.pdf.

National Historic Cheesemaking Center. https://nationalhistoriccheesemakingcenter.org.

National Historic Cheesemaking Center. "History of Cheese." Accessed December 14, 2023. https://nationalhistoriccheesemakingcenter.org/history-of-cheese/.

National Hot Dog and Sausage Council. "Hot Dog Facts, Figures and Folklore." 2019. https://www.hot-dog.org/sites/default/files/pdf/Hotdog-Facts-Figures-Folklore-Brochure.pdf.

Oncken, John. "Immerse Yourself in the History of Cheese in Green County." *Wisconsin State Farmer*, June 14, 2022. https://www.wisfarmer.com/story/opinion/columnists/2022/06/14/there-plenty-cheese-please-green-county/7550466001/.

Oncken, John. "The Sadness and Joys of Wisconsin Cheese." *Wisconsin State Farmer*, June 23, 2021. https://www.wisfarmer.com/story/opinion/columnists/2021/06/23/sadness-and-joys-wisconsin-cheese/7719007002/.

Price, Anna. "Just Brew It: A Brief Legislative History about Homebrewing in the United States – Part 1." *In Custodia Legis*, February 2, 2023. https://blogs.loc.gov/law/2023/02/just-brew-it-a-brief-legislative-history-about-homebrewing-in-the-united-states-part-1/.

Price, Walter V. "Cheese Manufacture." *Journal of Dairy Science* 39, no. 6 (June 1956): 824–32, doi: https://doi.org/10.3168/jds.S0022-0302(56)91208-5.

Rueckert, Noreen. *1914–2014 Green County Cheese Days: A Pictorial History of the First 100 Years*. Monroe, WI: Green County Cheese Days, Inc., 2014.

School Library Education Cooperative. "Cheesemaking." University of Wisconsin System. Accessed March 2, 2022. https://uwsslec.libguides.com/c.php?g=187091&p=1234610.

Seyler, Lainey. "Un-Brie-Lievable but True, Dairy Farmers of Wisconsin Has the Guinness World Record for the Largest Cheeseboard." *Milwaukee Journal Sentinel*, August 2, 2018. https://www.jsonline.com/story/life/food/2018/08/02/wisconsin-has-guinness-world-record-largest-cheeseboard/889104002/.

Sheboygan County Historical Research Center with Richard A. Stoelb. *The Sausage That Made Sheboygan Famous: The Rise of the Bratwurst.* CreateSpace Independent Publishing Platform, 2016.

Shepard, Robin. "The Wisconsin Brewing Industry since Repeal." *Journal of the Brewery History Society* 153 (2013): 26–47. http://www.breweryhistory.com/journal/archive/153/Wisconsin.pdf.

Stack, Martin H. "A Concise History of America's Brewing Industry." Economic History Association. Accessed March 2, 2022. https://eh.net/encyclopedia/a-concise-history-of-americas-brewing-industry/.

Travel Wisconsin. "The 10 Cheesiest Facts about Wisconsin Cheese." *Milwaukee Journal Sentinel,* May 12, 2019. https://www.jsonline.com/story/sponsor-story/travel-wisconsin/2019/05/12/10-cheesiest-facts-wisconsin-cheese/1134309001/.

UW–Madison Digital Libraries Collection. Manitowoc County Images. Accessed December 1, 2023. https://images.library.wisc.edu/WI/EFacs/MTWCImages/manGlimpses/reference/wi.manglimpses.i0010.pdf.

Visit Sheboygan. "Sheboygan Brat Oath." Accessed December 4, 2023. https://visitsheboygan.com/soundboard/.

Whitman-Salkin, Sarah. "Cranberries, a Thanksgiving Staple, Were a Native American Superfood." *National Geographic,* November 29, 2013. https://www.nationalgeographic.com/science/article/131127-cranberries-thanksgiving-native-americans-indians-food-history.

Wills, Warren. "The State of American Craft Beer—Wisconsin." *American Craft Beer,* January 12, 2018. https://www.americancraftbeer.com/state-american-craft-beer-wisconsin/.

Wilson, Reid. "Bars vs. Grocery Stores: Mapping America's Beer Belly." *Washington Post,* June 3, 2014. https://www.washingtonpost.com/blogs/govbeat/wp/2014/06/03/bars-vs-grocery-stores-mapping-americas-beer-belly/.

Wisconsin Cheese. www.wisconsincheese.com.

Wisconsin Department of Agriculture, Trade and Consumer Protection. "Wisconsin Agricultural Statistics." Last updated May 8, 2023. https://datcp.wi.gov/Pages/Publications/WIAgStatistics.aspx.

Wisconsin Historical Society. www.wisconsinhistory.org.

Wisconsin Historical Society. "Cheesemaking in Wisconsin." Accessed December 1, 2023. https://www.wisconsinhistory.org/Records/Article/CS1896.

Wisconsin Historical Society. "Cranberry Farming in Wisconsin." Accessed December 1, 2023. https://www.wisconsinhistory.org/Records/Article/CS3858.

Wisconsin Historical Society. "Dairy Farming in Wisconsin: How Wisconsin Became the Dairy State." Accessed December 1, 2023. https://www.wisconsinhistory.org/Records/Article/CS1744.

Wisconsin Historical Society. "Farming and Rural Life." Accessed December 1, 2023. https://www.wisconsinhistory.org/turningpoints/tp-061/?action=more_essay.

Wisconsin Historical Society. "The Rise of Dairy Farming." Accessed December 1, 2023. https://www.wisconsinhistory.org/turningpoints/tp-028/?action=more_essay.

Wisconsin State Legislature. SJR20: Enrolled Joint Resolution. 1997. https://docs.legis.wisconsin.gov/1997/related/enrolled/sjr20.

Zaferos, Barbara. "Largest Wisconsin Breweries." *Milwaukee Business Journal*, April 14, 2023. https://www.bizjournals.com/milwaukee/subscriber-only/2023/04/14/largest-wisconsin-breweries.html.

Index

Orphan Train Riders

A Brief History of the Orphan Train Era (1854–1929)

with

Entrance Records from the American Female Guardian Society's Home for the Friendless in New York

Volume One

Tom Riley

HERITAGE BOOKS
2014

HERITAGE BOOKS
AN IMPRINT OF HERITAGE BOOKS, INC.

Books, CDs, and more—Worldwide

For our listing of thousands of titles see our website
at
www.HeritageBooks.com

Published 2014 by
HERITAGE BOOKS, INC.
Publishing Division
5810 Ruatan Street
Berwyn Heights, Md. 20740

Heritage Books by the author:

Orphan Train Riders: A Brief History of the Orphan Trail Era (1854–1929) with Entrance Records from the American Female Guardian Society's Home for the Friendless in New York
Volume One

Orphan Train Riders: Entrance Records from the American Female Guardian Society's Home for the Friendless in New York
Volume Two

International Standard Book Numbers
Paperbound: 978-0-7884-3169-2
Clothbound: 978-0-7884-6064-7

DEDICATION

This book is dedicated to the memory of all the children who rode the rails across America and to the goodhearted souls who took them in and gave them a better life. The Orphan Train Era (1854-1929) was the largest mass migration of children across this country. Over a quarter of a million children were transported by rail across America. Many went on to achieve the American dream and some fell by the wayside, victims of intolerance, cruelty and the absence of love. It is also dedicated to the unsung, heroic work of women, many who were members of Christian temperance societies. In the absence of a social safety net these women offered shelter and more to the homeless.

CONTENTS

PREFACE

This book was written as I was searching for information on Happy Valley School in Pomona, New York. I was asked if I would like to go through several boxes of uncataloged records left to the Rockland County Historical Society by the childcare agency that had occupied the site where Happy Valley once stood. As I perused the records I realized they held a treasure trove of Americana comprising orphanage entrance book entries and volume after volume of the periodical *Advocate for Moral Reform* published by the American Female Guardian Society. This magazine had a nationwide readership and recruited families as hosts for the Orphan Train riders. The American Female Guardian Society established the Home for the Friendless, which took in thousands of destitute (not necessarily orphaned) women and girls, and later, boys.

Having discovered the AFGS records, I became inexorably pulled into the stories of these homeless children. Happy Valley School had been a home for thousands of neglected boys and girls in the metropolitan New York area from 1911 to 1972. My three brothers and my sister and I called it home. I imagine what orphan train riders felt was somewhat similar to what I experienced as a homeless child about to be placed in a school that was to be my home for ten years. It shaped my character and saved our lives.

Briefly, the Happy Valley School connection with the AFGS goes like this: the AFGS merged with Greer Woodycrest Youth Services in 1965. In 1972 Happy Valley School began merger talks with Woodycrest Youth Services and became known as Crystal Run School. After another merger in 1977 the school became known as Greer Woodycrest Children's Services. In 1991 it was purchased and turned into a golf course.

On Sunday, July 19, 1992, a very special gathering took place. People from many states and the greater New York area drove onto the ground of the Crystal Run School in Pomona, New York for an alumni gathering that was the culmination of a labor of love. Haya Khoury, a New York City corporate lawyer and a Happy Valley School alumni had arranged the affair with the help of countless others so that a

fitting goodbye could be said to a special place in time, the Happy Valley of our youth. In three months workers would be shaping the grounds into a new golf course.

As each car rode onto the ground, cries of recognition would go up and embraces and jokes revived long ago memories of the way we were. The transformation from homeless and neglected children had been complete. Now bankers, carpenters, designers, teachers, laborers, photographers, builders, postal workers and a lawyer talked animatedly about the days they shared as children. They gazed into each other's eyes searchingly for the child they remembered. Some had held up well to the years while others showed on their faces the struggle it took to be where they were today. All accepted each other with spontaneity and generosity. The Ashcrofts, Carneys, Khourys, Greys, Grippers, Fiorellis, Rileys, Reineckes, Wenzes and Towles and many other alumni families found warmth, nostalgia and joy in the company of each other.

We can never know how difficult it was to be an abandoned or neglected child in the late nineteenth or early twentieth century. A close-knit family suddenly splintered by the death of a breadwinner; a loss of a job, addiction to alcohol, medical problems, imprisonment of a spouse or eviction from a tenement caused severe dislocation and nowhere to turn, as social safety nets were non-existent.

Today, in fifteen states across America, Orphan Train riders and their families meet and hold three-day gatherings recalling those days of their youth. They held fast to the promise of America: that anyone can rise above his harsh and humble beginnings to become all he can, if he is willing to work hard enough to reach his dreams.

The search for roots is universal. I hope this book will aid others in putting branches on the family tree.

ACKNOWLEDGMENTS

Meaningful art results from collaboration among many individuals. I would like to thank Mary Ellen Johnson for encouraging me to tell the story of the orphan train riders and for making available the index of names found in the Books of Surrender. The unnamed volunteers of the Orphan Train Heritage Society of America who put in hundreds of hours computerizing the historical information found in those boxes deserve my deepest gratitude.

I would like to thank Connie DiPasquale for "A Partial List of Institutions That Orphan Train Children Came From" that was listed on "The Orphan Trains of Kansas" website. I thank Gary F. Wills, one of America's finest journalists for use of material from a newspaper article on "Salvage Archeology in Lower Manhattan." I thank *Newsweek* for the use of information in the May 14, 1951 edition on the Five Points House of Industry. I thank Vic Remer, Archivist of the Children's Aid Society in Manhattan for the use of a photograph and a short biography of Charles Loring Brace. I thank Holly Canham of The Orleans County Genealogical Society. She hosted the largest Orphan Train Re-enactment ever to take place in America. Over five hundred people showed up at the Medina Train Museum and Railroad Station to take a two-hour train ride, to which I was invited to be the main speaker. I would like to thank Art Smith, Bill Oser, Bud Canham, Beth Plumley, Barbara Bacon and Fred Werner for making it a memorable event. I would like to thank Virginia Kropf, ace reporter for the *Daily News* for her kind support. And thanks to the Rockland County Historical Society for granting permission to publish these lists.

Most of all I would like to thank my wife for her patience and support while writing this book. She has been my friend and companion for 33 years. I love you dearly. To Professor Gina Riley and soon to be Dr. Bernadette Riley, I can't tell you how fortunate I feel to have you as my daughters. And to Peter Riley, my grandson, I can't wait to read your book on geology some day.

If this book motivates you to learn more about the Orphan Trains you can contact the Orphan Train Heritage Society of America, Inc. in Concordia, Kansas, by emailing OTHSA@msn.com, or by contacting the Orleans County Genealogical Society in Albion, New York by emailing Holliscan@aol.com. If you are interested in other books by Tom Riley, email him at CARYER99@cs.com. Tom Riley is the author of the following books:

We Deliver
The Stuyvesant Connection
Johnny Eden
Peter's Book on Stamp Collecting For Kids
Happy Valley School: A History and Remembrance
Tales for Children

ABOUT THE AUTHOR

Tom Riley joined the Air Force at the age of 17. He was sent to photo school at Lowery Air Force Base in Aurora, Colorado. Upon completion of photographic training he received Secret Clearance and worked at Edwards Air Force Base in California doing mechanical photography on advanced weapons systems, the X-15, and nuclear weapons. He was among the first 5,000 men sent to support the Vietnam War. He was stationed in the Philippines where he worked in aerial reconnaissance. He lives in New City, New York.

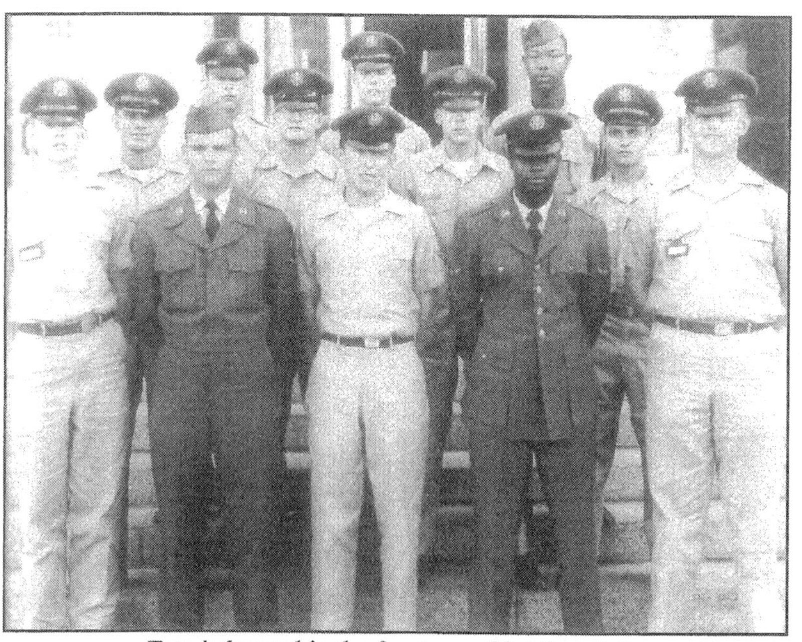

Tom is located in the front row, third from left.

CHAPTER 1

THE ORPHAN TRAIN ERA MOVES INTO AMERICAN CONSCIOUSNESS

In America during a seventy-five-year period (1854-1929) over 200,000 homeless children were relocated by means of what were known as "orphan trains." Placing children to live with people other than their parents has gone on from the beginning of time. Known by various names, placing-out has come to be called "foster care" today. The Orphan Train Riders were America's first documented foster children.

During my research on the formation of Happy Valley School I began to understand how life was in the teeming ghettos of New York City in the 1800's. Happy Valley School was an outgrowth of the work of the Five Points House of Industry, a private charitable foundation organized in the 1850's to relieve the terrible conditions of an area in New York City known as the Five Points District.

People poured into New York City from rural farms. Boatloads of immigrants crowded the docks and swarms of peddlers hawked their wares in the city. The cacophony of languages was sweet music to the shrewd, enterprising denizens of lower Manhattan. Jobs were plentiful and acted as magnets to the poor. A man with grit, determination and imagination could succeed beyond his wildest dreams. The mansions lining Fifth Avenue acted as a beacon to able-bodied, aggressive men (and some women, too) whose vision and determination shaped our country to the powerhouse it is today.

This dynamic city had its dark side. Alcoholism, disease, poverty, and ruthlessness in pursuit of money scoured the underbelly of an economic giant. Street Arabs (the name given to homeless children) wandered the streets of the city in search of meager scraps of food and shelter. They engaged in gambling, drugs, prostitution, theft, and murder. Gangs roamed the streets of lower Manhattan. The Five Points area of lower Manhattan, long regarded as the toughest section in New York City, was recently featured in a major motion

picture, "The Gangs of New York" starring Leonardo DiCaprio.

"How did they live in Five Points?" asked Gary F. Wills, one of America's best journalists, in his article, "Salvage Archaeology in Lower Manhattan." (*Washington Post,* Dec. 29, 1991) The answer was, "Nastily, brutishly and often briefly. When after the 1832 cholera epidemic, the Mayor ordered the streets scraped of animal and human filth, a lady who lived all her life there exclaimed, 'I never knew the streets were paved with stones.' In the 1849 epidemic, pigs rooting in the streets were, a report said, 'contaminated by the contact with children.' It was said that in death the victims continued the tenement system, buried six tiers deep."

Wills goes on to describe the conditions uncovered by "salvage archaeology" at a construction site in lower Manhattan. "Most Five Points buildings, the rubble from which is now 15 to 20 feet below street level, contained a saloon. The police raided one in which 42 people were crammed in one small room, in the corner of which on a pile of dirty straw lay a woman just delivered of a child. Famous gangs like the Plug Uglies, Dead Rabbits and the Roach Guard fueled the riots of July 1863. They began as draft riots, became race riots then turned to pillaging the rich."

Another view of the terrible conditions that existed in the Five Points District was expressed in an article in the May 14, 1951 edition of *Newsweek*. The article was entitled "Five Points to Happiness" and is reprinted below:

"When in 1850, the members of the Ladies Home Missionary Society of the Methodist Episcopal Church in New York discovered that the Rev. Lewis Pease had not preached a sermon in two days, they severed their connection with him. His mission stood near 'Murderers Alley,' in lower Manhattan in an area known as the Five Points. Charles Dickens once described this section as an appalling 'world of vice and misery...men, women and boys slink off to sleep, forcing dislodged rats to move away in quest of better lodgings.'

"Mr. Pease believed in a neighborhood with 270 saloons and several times that many dance halls and bawdy houses, preaching the Gospel was not enough. The following year he established the Five Points House of Industry along with a Ladies Auxiliary of the Methodist Episcopal Church. Its goal was to educate and find work for residents of the most dismal slum in America. Since then 45,000 children have been helped by that institution.

"In 1863 draft riots occurred when many newly minted Americans, mostly Irish, rebelled against the notion that the rich could buy their way out of military service in the Civil War. This inequity caused the ranks of the military to be filled with legions of poor, immigrant, able-bodied young men who in many cases became cannon fodder in the killing fields of the Civil War.

"Over two thousand New Yorkers were killed when the draft riots turned ugly. In a recruiting station in lower Manhattan, draftees set fires and went on a rampage. Stores, factories and dwellings were burned to the ground. Gangs like the Plug Uglies and the Roach Guard added fuel to the fires and innocent city dwellers were slaughtered in the performance of their daily routines. The riots grew from being draft riots, to race riots and then the pillaging of the rich. Federal troops were dispatched and finally put down the insurrection after much house-to-house fighting and hand-to-hand combat. When the last burning tinder was put out, the body count showed that over two thousand New Yorkers had been slain. It was the worst riot ever to take place in an America city. It increased the number of orphaned children wandering the streets of New York City."

It was in this social environment that children's welfare societies were founded and the placing out of children on "orphan trains" began. The earliest known group of women who gathered with the clergy to discuss the plight of the homeless females who were forced to enter a life of prostitution and degradation due to their friendless condition in large cities was the American Female Guardian Society. Untimely deaths of parents, sickness and addiction to alcohol and drugs left thousands of orphaned children. The complete absence of social services and access to medical care that we know today caused a huge influx of people cast into the streets because of non-payment of rent or death of a household figure. The situation screamed out for a remedy.

The AFGS published a bi-monthly periodical originally entitled *The Advocate for Moral Reform and Family Guardian.* This extraordinary periodical was published for over a century and the work done by the American Female Guardian Society deserves acclaim. For over a century this organization took in the friendless and the homeless and found permanent homes throughout America for children as young as one year old and up to eighteen years old.

They created the Home for the Friendless, initially accepting only females, but this changed to accepting boys also, after a few years of operation. They opened boarding schools and operated twelve industrial schools throughout the country, many in large cities where boys and girls could learn technical skills in order to earn a living. Hundreds of thousands of young children were saved from a life of poverty and destitution by the efforts of this society whose only income came from donations and sales of the *Advocate*.

They were for all intents a temperance society. Their moral outrage against the evils of alcohol was often shrill and Victorian in tone. Early issues of the *Advocate* strongly condemned the havoc and abuse caused by alcohol consumption and asked people to reform their lives and take pledges to abstain from drinking.

When the orphan train era began, the AFGS required indigent parents to sign a legal release form to care for the children. Through the *Advocate* church groups across the heartland of America responded and took in these waifs, orphaned and abandoned children. They settled in communities across America and were in most cases adopted or indentured.

Letter after letter to the AFGS from these children or their guardians scattered throughout America attest to the good work done by this organization and how grateful the children were for the AFGS intervention in hopeless situations. In some cases the children wrote inquiring about their natural parents. The AFGS succeeded in rare cases in reuniting children with their natural families; most had simply abandoned their children.

The "orphan train era" was the brainchild of a Connecticut minister, Charles Loring Brace (see Chapter 2). Appalled at the misery of orphaned and abandoned children living in deplorable conditions on the streets of New York City, he founded the Children's Aid Society. The Children's Aid Society used a contract when placing children with families throughout America and advertised extensively in the *Advocate* since it was church-affiliated and had a nationwide readership. The New York Foundling Hospital headed by the Sisters of Charity used a legal indenture form rather than a contract. Both legal documents listed the requirements to be met for the child's welfare and for family's guidelines.

The New England Home For Little Wanderers in Boston placed children on orphan trains, as did the New York

Juvenile Asylum. For a time, the Chicago Home Society placed children using the orphan train method. Guardians (agents, nurses, and caretakers) traveled with a group of children until the destinations were reached. In cases where children were placed under the indenture system, the receiving "parents" were notified in advance of the arrival date and time. Upon arrival, they claimed the child, signed the papers and took the child with them.

Under the contract system, flyers were sent out in advance telling folks the train would be coming on a specific date and the children could be seen at a pre-determined site. Those who were not chosen got back on the train and traveled to the next stop. Many of these placements made in haste did not work out well and the child was returned to the Children's Aid Society.

The Home for the Friendless and the social work being done there inspired other citizens (mostly women) to try and make a difference. Acting out of a deep religious faith, these women slowly began to transform the ghettos of New York City into a more caring environment. Settlement houses meeting the needs of the citizens of the Lower East Side were established and aided Jewish immigrants in their assimilation into American society. In 1854 the Ladies Auxiliary of the Methodist Episcopal Missionary Society bought an old brewery and turned it into the Five Points House of Industry. The social work done there aided hundreds of thousands of men, women and children in the ghettos of the Five Points area.

Charles Loring Brace (Courtesy of the Children's Aid Society)

CHAPTER 2

CHILDREN'S WELFARE PHILANTHROPISTS: Charles Loring Brace and Edwin Gould

CHARLES LORING BRACE, 1826-1890
Founder of the Children's Aid Society

During the mid-1800s when enormous numbers of immigrants flooded New York City, thousands of poor and homeless children roamed the city streets. Having worked in the notorious Five Points Mission, this young minister was appointed the first secretary of the newly formed Children's Aid Society. For thirty-seven years, from 1853 until the time of his death, he was a tireless and passionate defender of children. He created services to meet the needs of poor homeless, sick and disabled children and served as an advocate of children's rights at a time when they were considered chattels.

He helped more than 100,000 youngsters get foster and adoptive homes with families in forty-eight states, the District of Columbia, Canada and the West Indies. He set up industrial schools and lodging houses for boys and girls. Warm, nutritious meals and shoes and clothing were provided. Medical help, summer vacations, sanatoria and convalescent care were offered, as well as schooling for "crippled children." Sanctuary was provided for African American children during the draft riots in 1863, the Padrone system was eliminated (the indenturing of children sold in Italy by their parents for labor in America). The Society received a medal and citation for this achievement. Mr. Brace established New York's first free kindergarten, was instrumental in the enactment of compulsory education legislation and in an article in *The Independent* in July 1862 he urged acceptance of women in medical colleges.

Brace helped change society's views of children and its expectations of them. He felt the family, not institutions, was the best environment for a child's growth and development to

his or her full potential because families provided essential love and security and preserved important values and traditions. It was estimated at his death in 1890 that he had touched the lives of more than 300,000 people.

That legacy of love and devotion continues today as the Society serves over 150,000 persons each year in an expanded network of interrelated services based in thirty-eight locations. One of the oldest and largest proprietary, non-sectarian, child and family welfare organizations in America, it provides foster care and adoption, medical and dental care, preventive and emergency services, summer and winter camping, work with the disabled, arts, education and job training as well as technical assistance programs for others seeking to replicate or adapt its specialized services in teen pregnancy prevention and community school services.

EDWIN GOULD:
A Titan Of Philanthropy To Children

Edwin Gould, son of Jay Gould, a notorious railroad magnate, was born on February 25, 1866 in a mansion in New York City. The second of six Gould children, he enjoyed his family's great wealth. His father, a titan of Wall Street, was a loving parent who took pleasure in his family. The boy spent long, happy summers at estates on Long Island and Tarrytown, New York. He swam in the river, sailed near the Tappan Zee and canoed for hours on the Hudson River. This love of nature was to remain with him all his life.

Edwin attended Columbia University. He was not an outstanding scholar but he enjoyed rowing and was on the Columbia University crew team. His father's annoyance at his failure to complete college led Edwin to set himself up as an independent broker and speculator. In less than a year he earned a million dollars and established himself as a reputable investor. His father's confidence in him was re-established and he was invited to join the family firm. When his father died, Edwin's fortune was estimated at 20 million dollars, eight of which he had made himself since leaving Columbia University.

He had always been a generous man but a specific incident would change his life forever. The unexpected death of his son, Edwin Jr. at age 23, in a hunting accident in 1917 caused Edwin to dedicate the remaining fifteen years of his

life to the disadvantaged, homeless children. His dedication to enhance the quality of life of children by the thousands both in America and abroad was to give him great peace of mind and much happiness for the remaining years of his life.

The scope of his philanthropic activities is simply amazing. His enjoyment of nature and the happiness of children caused him to set up summer camps throughout the United States. It is estimated that he personally paid for up to a million camper days for children. At Happy Valley Colony he built and donated two camp buildings and established a large camping program for hundreds of disadvantaged children. He continually made generous donations of time and energy to Happy Valley throughout his lifetime. In 1931 he took over the Boarding Home program from the Trustees of the Five Points House of Industry so the trustees could devote their financial resources to the Pomona residence. The stock market crash of 1929 had severely depleted resources available to Happy Valley.

The Edwin Gould Foundation for Children was set up by special act of the New York State Legislature to centralize his many philanthropic activities. When he died in 1933 over ninety charitable institutions were beneficiaries of his will. He is especially remembered for starting up Lakeside School, formerly The Messiah Home for Children in Spring Valley, New York. Lakeside School is still in full operation under the name of the Edwin Gould Academy due to Mr. Gould's foresight in establishing a foundation that gave broad scope to its trustees to act in any manner that benefited the welfare of children in New York State and in the U.S. The funds from the Edwin Gould Foundation continue to support the works of the Edwin Gould Academy and many other endeavors.

Not to be forgotten was his early commitment to the care of disadvantaged black children in New York City. He established the Booker T. Washington Home School on Boston Road in the Bronx and paid for all of its operation out of his own expense. Eventually it was merged into the Edwin Gould Foundation For Children and his commitment to cultural diversity continues to this day. Mr. Gould is also remembered for his concerns for quality medical care for children and the establishment of scholarships for disadvantaged children.

CHAPTER 3

INSTITUTIONS AND THE SURRENDER OF CHILDREN

A Partial List Of New York Area Institutions That Sent Orphan Train Children Out West

The following is a partial list of New York area institutions that provided "orphans" to be sent west on the Orphan Trains to new homes. If you have an ancestor who spent time in one of these homes and ended up in Kansas, it is likely that he was an Orphan Train Rider. (Courtesy of Connie DiPasquale)

Angel Guardian Home
Association for Befriending Children & Young Girls
Association for Benefit of Colored Orphans
Baby Fold
Baptist Children's Home of Long Island
Bedford Maternity, Inc.
Bellevue Hospital
Bensonhurst Maternity
Berachah Orphanage
Berkshire Farm for Boys
Berwind Maternity Clinic
Beth Israel Hospital
Bethany Samaritan Society
Bethlehem Lutheran Children's Home
Booth Memorial Hospital
Borough Park Maternity Hospital
Brace Memorial Newsboys House
Bronx Maternity Hospital
Brooklyn Benevolent Society
Brooklyn Hebrew Orphan Asylum
Brooklyn Home for Children
Brooklyn Hospital
Brooklyn Industrial School
Brooklyn Maternity Hospital

Brooklyn Nursery & Infants Hospital
Brookwood Child Care
Catholic Child Care Society
Catholic Committee for Refugees
Catholic Guardian Society
Catholic Home Bureau
Child Welfare League of America
Children's Aid Society
Children's Haven
Children's Village, Inc.
Church Mission of Help
Colored Orphan Asylum
Convent of Mercy
Dana House
Door of Hope
Duval College for Infant Children
Edenwald School for Boys
Erlanger Home
Euphrasian Residence
Family Reception Center
Fellowship House for Boys
Ferguson House
Five Point House of Industry
Florence Crittendon League
Goodhue Home
Grace Hospital
Graham Windham Services
Greer-Woodycrest Children's Services
Guardian Angel Home
Guild of the Infant Savior
Hale House for Infants, Inc.
Half-Orphan Asylum
Harman Home for Children
Heartsease Home
Hebrew Orphan Asylum
Hebrew Sheltering Guardian Society
Holy Angels' School
Home for Destitute Children
Home for Destitute Children of Seamen
Home for Friendless Women and Children
Hopewell Society of Brooklyn
House of the Good Shepherd
House of Mercy
House of Refuge

Howard Mission & Home for Little Wanderers
Infant Asylum
Infants' Home of Brooklyn
Institution of Mercy
Jewish Board of Guardians
Jewish Protectory & Aid Society
Kallman Home for Children
Little Flower Children's Services
Maternity Center Association
McCloskey School & Home
McMahon Memorial Shelter
Mercy Orphanage
Messiah Home for Children
Methodist Child Welfare Society
Misericordia Hospital
Morrisania City Hospital
Other Theodore's Memorial Girls' Home
Mothers & Babies Hospital
Mount Sinai Hospital
New York Foundling Hospital
New York Home for Friendless Boys
New York House of Refuge
New York Juvenile Asylum
New York Society for Prevention of Cruelty to Children
Ninth St. Day Nursery & Orphans' Home
Orphan Asylum Society of the City of Brooklyn
Orphan House
Ottilie Home for Children

* * * * *

Examples transcribed from ***Surrender of Children From Aug 1, 1849, through April 21, 1859, Parents Guardians' Book***

New York, July 1, 1850
I George N. Levison do hereby give up to the AFG Soc my four children, Virginia Levison aged 13, Charles Levison aged 10, Francis Morton Levison aged 8 & Anna May Levison aged 6. Their mother also giving her consent.
Signed George N. Levison, Withrop Probanco, Z. P. Weed

This is to certify that I, Bridget Keyes, now a resident of New Orleans, State of Louisiana, having some time since left my child Patrick Keyes in the care of the American Female Guardian Society in the city & state of New York & finding myself unable to support the said infant he being about eight years of age & his father dead. I do hereby surrender & commit him to the care & control of the Managers of the above named Society to be provided for agreeably to their Charter given by the State of New York.
Signed in the presence of Charles C. Berry
New Orleans June 19, 1851
Mrs. B. Keyes

This may certify, That I have this day March 20th, 1849, received into my family Emma Burns from the Managers of the Home For The Friendless and that I hereby engage to train this child with a view to her present and future well being: to regard Her interests, mental, moral and physical, and so to educate her in these respects that she may become a blessing to herself and to others.

Ann Amelia Elliott
Note on side: Emma was returned this 4th day of Nov. 1861 by Mrs. Elliott as she could do easily without her.

This may certify, That I have this day May 22nd received into my family Mary Jane Harvey from the Managers of the Home For The Friendless and that I hereby engage to train this child with a view to her present and future well being: to regard her interests, mental moral and physical, and so to educate her in these respects that she may become a blessing to herself and to others.

Phoebe C. Brant

Children's Aid Society,

105 EAST 22D STREET, NEW YORK

The Society reserves the right to remove the child previous to legal adoption if at any time the circumstances of the home become such as in the judgment of the Agent are injurious to the child's future prospects.

Children are not allowed to correspond with any friends or relatives without obtaining permission to do so from the Society.

NAME OF CHILD: Edward Hoyt (born ~~May~~ Nov 1st 1902 AGE: 8 yrs

TO LIVE WITH FAMILY OF: J. Irving Spence

TOWN: Valley Falls COUNTY: STATE: Kan

DATED, Jan 13 191[illegible] J. W. Swan[illegible] PLACING AGENT

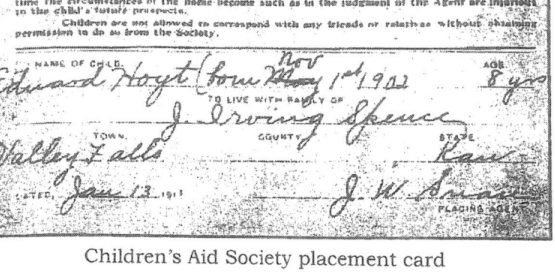

Children's Aid Society placement card

A Record Of Two Children Sent Out For Placement On The Orphan Train, Taken From The Files Of The American Female Guardian Society

August 1872 – John Mannigan was surrendered to the AFGS by the Society for the Prevention of Cruelty to Children. He was found on a corner of a street almost destitute of clothes on a bitter cold night. This boy was a most pitiable object, and it took months to heal the flesh wounds made by the burrowing of vermin. Once well he is a very bright boy. No inquiries were ever made for him.

September 1877 – Taken by Mr. Fry of the Children's Aid Society ona train to find a home with Mr. Nad Mrs. Ranson in Red Oak, Iowa.

July 1879 – John is now with Mr. And Mrs. James of Greenwood, Nebraska who write that they think much of John, he's a real good boy but not without faults. Particulars desired and sent.

June 1880 – Letter received from Mrs. James reporting on John favorably and they hope his habits improve.

August 1881 – Letter of inquiry sent.

October 1881 – John is now with Minnie Garrison in Lancaster, Nebraska and is now called Glenn Garrison. "Glenn is well and goes to school. We think a lot of him. And could not keep house without him."

June 1883 – Letter of inquiry sent.

October 1883 – John is well, loved and cared for as our own child.

February 1886 – Mrs. Garrison reports favorably.

May 1888 – Letter of inquiry sent.

December 1889 – Mr. Rolste writes for particulars of John's history for him.

—Of Age—No need to write further.

* * *

June 1869 – Mary Remick is brought to AFGH with sister and brother by her mother to live there for three weeks, as the mother is ill. The mother dies three weeks later. The father is a drinking man who shamefully neglects his children.

February 1878 – Mary is sent to live with Mrs. McDonald in Stark County, Illinois.

April 1880 – Mary is well and is attending school.

April 1883 – Mary sends a letter. "I am well and have a sweet home."

July 1885 – Letter of inquiry sent.

September 1885 – Mary is doing well, complains of sore knees. Is taking music lessons and makes beautiful quilts.

—Of Age – Mary is married.

October 1893 – Mary calls and inquires about family history. She is trying to prove her relationship to a Remick who died 110 years earlier and was connected to the fur trade with Jacob Astor. He died and left his estate to all blood relatives. The estate is being held until the heirs can prove their identity.

Art Smith, an orphan train rider who was sent to Iowa. On the right is Holly Canham, the founder of the first New York State Orphan Train Museum and on the left is her mother. *(Photo courtesy of Orleans County Genealogical Society.)*

CHAPTER 4

THE 2004 MEDINA, NEW YORK ORPHAN TRAIN REENACTMENT

The Orleans County Genealogical Society Holds The Largest Orphan Train Reenactment At The Medina Railroad Museum

Over five hundred people gathered at the Medina, New York Railroad Station and Museum on April 17, 2004 to participate in what Mary Ellen Johnson, the founder of the Orphan Train Heritage Society, called the largest Orphan Train Reenactment ever to take place in America. Children dressed in period costumes presented an onboard reenactment to a thrilled audience. Whistle and bells clanged as Tom Riley narrated the two-hour ride. The ride included a cast of hundreds as Bill Oser, 82, an original Orphan Train rider, sang "Some Enchanted Evening" and regaled the riders with his humor.

Children broke into song with rave reviews. The ride owes its success to Holly Canham of OCGS. It was such a success two separate rides had to be planned. People came from as far as Colorado to take the ride. Holly worked hard to make it the wonderful success it was and now people want to make it an annual event. On board were Art Smith, 82, who was sent to Iowa, Beth Plumley and Barbara Bacon who were sent to Medina as children and Bill Oser who was sent to Michigan.

Mary Ellen Johnson sat back and was amazed at the event. As founder of the Orphan Train Heritage Society she is seeing her dream come true. Americans are becoming aware of the 250,000 children who participated in the Orphan Train era (1854-1929). It was the largest mass relocation of children in American history. All the events a child went through were reenacted on the train ride. Television, radio and print reporters recorded all the action. People waiting for the train had an opportunity to stroll through a world-class railroad museum.

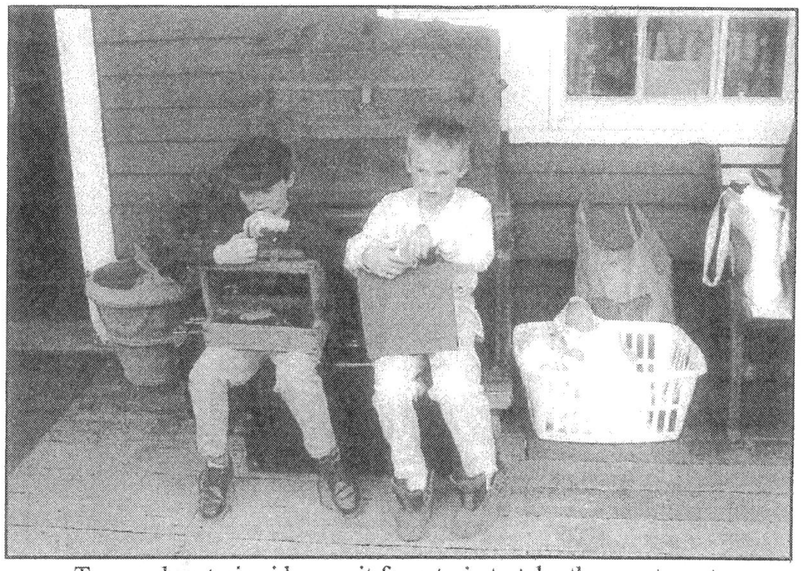

Two orphan train riders wait for a train to take them out west.
(Photo courtesy of Orleans County Genealogical Society.)

The orphans sell apples before the train arrives.
(Photo courtesy of Orleans County Genealogical Society.)

A homeless child waits at the Medina station with a Teddy bear for comfort.
(Photo courtesy of Orleans County Genealogical Society.)

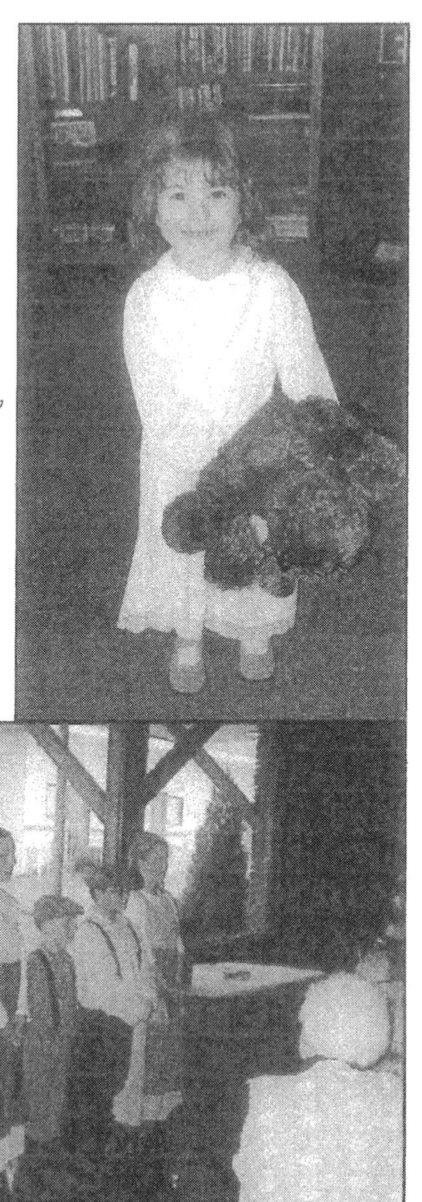

A school play about the orphan train riders was voted best in the nation and the audience enjoyed it at the dinner held after the train rides.
(Photo courtesy of Orleans County Genealogical Society.)

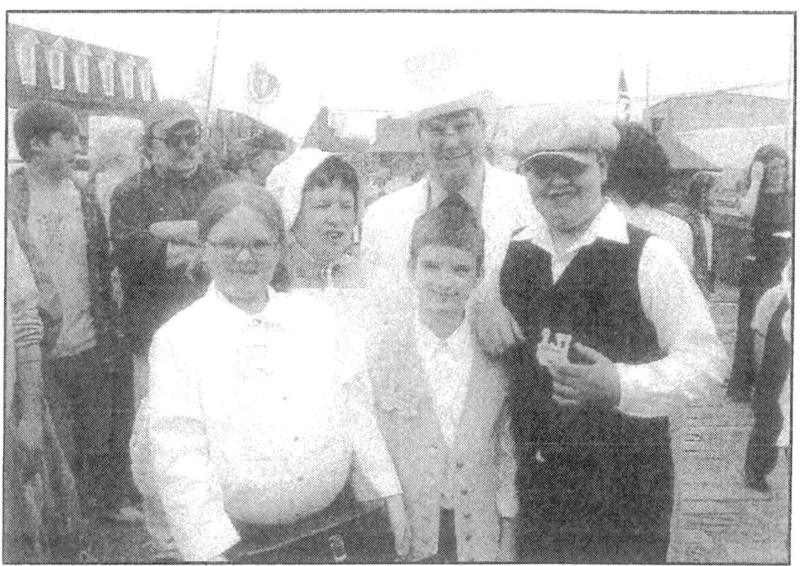

A respected gentleman poses with the three children he "adopted."
(Photo courtesy of Orleans County Genealogical Society.)

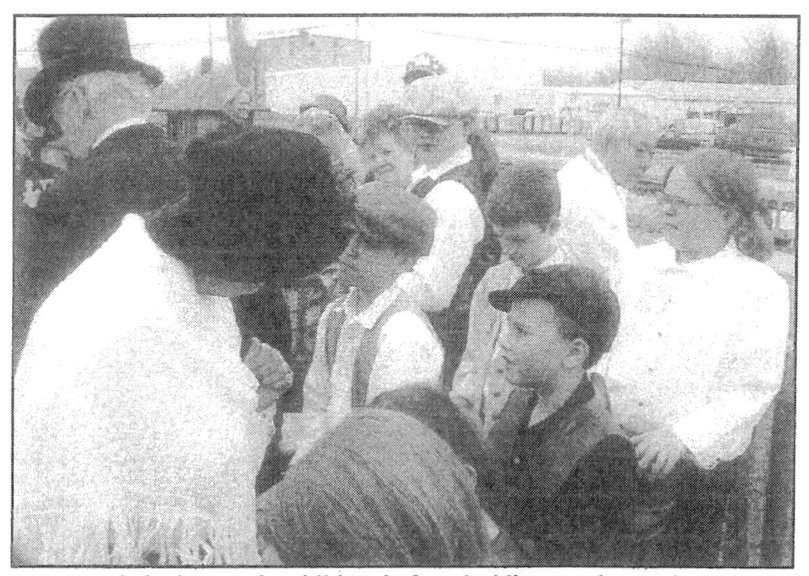

People look over the children before deciding to take one home.
(Photo courtesy of Orleans County Genealogical Society.)

Mary Ellen Johnson, the founder of the Orphan Train Heritage Society, waits for the train and talks with one of the "caretakers" for the children. *(Photo courtesy of Orleans County Genealogical Society.)*

Beth Plumley and Barbara Bacon were sent to Medina as children on an orphan train. *(Photo courtesy of Orleans County Genealogical Society.)*

Mrs. Comstock lines the children up at the Medina Station as they anxioiusly wait to be chosen for their new homes.
(Photo courtesy of Orleans County Genealogical Society.)

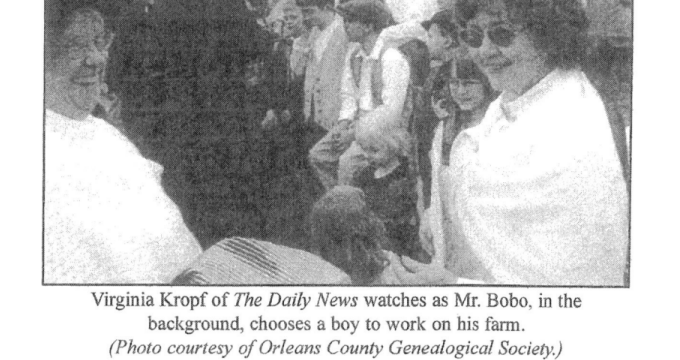

Virginia Kropf of *The Daily News* watches as Mr. Bobo, in the background, chooses a boy to work on his farm.
(Photo courtesy of Orleans County Genealogical Society.)

Bill Oser, 82, was sent to Michigan as a child. He is being interviewed as TV, radio, and print media covered the Great Train Ride.
(Photo courtesy of Orleans County Genealogical Society.)

The world-class Medina Railroad Museum is a stop not to be missed.
(Photo courtesy of Orleans County Genealogical Society.)

Two orphans waiting for their train.
(Photo courtesy of Orleans County Genealogical Society.)

These boys are a little anxious and hope they find a good home out west.
(Photo courtesy of Orleans County Genealogical Society.)

CHAPTER 5

BOOKS OF SURRENDER AND ENTRANCE RECORDS FROM THE HOME FOR THE FRIENDLESS

The following pages were indexed by volunteers of the Orphan Train Heritage Society of America, founded by Mary Ellen Johnson of Springdale, Arkansas. A schoolteacher holding several jobs, she became fascinated by the stories of some local residents who had been Orphan Train Riders. Her fascination grew into an obsession. It was to find and locate Orphan Train Riders throughout America so that this historical phenomenon would receive the attention it deserves. She founded a research center and museum that serves as a resource point for anything related to the orphan trains. People began to piece together their family trees, and soon took pride in their forbears who pulled themselves up by their own bootstraps with the help of complete strangers across America. Two Orphan Train Riders became governors and at least five served in Congress. Their stories are uniquely American in the sense that any man or woman can rise above deprivation, illness, prejudice, exploitation and fear and become part of the great mosaic that is America. Through sheer hard work, drudgery, creativity, character and vision these Orphan Train Riders overcame early obstacles to success.

Former President Ronald Reagan was fond of telling a story about a farmer who was trying to sell an old barn along with 60 acres. The first interested buyer surveyed the land and was quite impressed. He accompanied the farmer to take a look at the big, old barn. The buyer opened the big old doors and was quickly overcome by the stink and fumes emanating from manure that filled the barn. He quickly retreated to his car and drove off.

The second buyer was a farmer who lived down the road a piece. He drove up on a tractor and visualized the property as expanding his own empire. He came to the big, old, red barn and opened the doors with his callused hands. He

immediately gasped for fresh air and took a second look. The barn was filled with horse manure as far as the hayloft. He ran to his tractor and sped off down the gravel road to his farm.

The third interested buyer drove up from the city with his eight-year-old son. He wanted a place of peace and quiet. A place where his wife could indulge her interest in gardening and flowers and where he could maybe buy some horses, learn to ride and teach his son. Impressed with the land he too accompanied the old farmer to the big, old, red, rusting barn. The old farmer swung open the doors. The fumes almost overcame the farmer and the city man. They were bent over, trying to catch their breath.

"Son, we gotta get outta here, fast," said the city man.

His son, though was jumping up and down with sheer joy.

"Poppy, Poppy," he yelled, "there's got to be a pony in there somewhere."

Most of the Orphan Train Riders found that pony and became good citizens. It is estimated that two million Americans are descended from Orphan Train Riders.

Meaning Of Notes And References Listed In Children's Court Cases

Where the term "John Doe" is listed as a name for a child it means they were never able to learn the name of the child; for example, "he was found in a basket on the front steps of St. Mary's Church without any identification."

The abbreviation S.P.C.C. means Society for the Prevention of Cruelty to Children

"Free Cases" means no public entity or institution would pay for care of the child so the Children's Aid Society would undertake payment for care of the child.

"Public Charge" means a public entity or institution or government agency would pay for care of the child.

"FC to PC" meant that the child's care went from a Free Case to a Public Charge.

Court Case numbers and letters describe the Case #, the court where the case was heard and often the volume # of the Book of Surrender in which the case was listed.

Due to the prevailing attitudes of the time many African-American children were boarded out with other African-American families. The Children's Aid Society or governmental agencies would provide payment for their care.

These records were converted from database tables into regular text in order to fit these pages. The columns of the original databases are indicated by commas; thus, several commas in a row indicate blank columns in the database.

The books were not named; hence, this book retains the labels assigned by the compilers.

AMERICAN FEMALE GUARDIAN SOCIETY
HOME FOR THE FRIENDLESS
ENTRANCE BOOK 1

Arnold, Annie, , 1876, father: Charles Arnold, 73, 8.531
Arnold, Carrie, , 1876, father: Charles Arnold, 74, 8.532
Arnold, Charlie, , 1876, father: Charles Arnold, 75, 8.533
Arnold, Frederick, , 1876, father: Charles Arnold, 76, 8.534
Arnold, Louisa, , 1876, father: Charles Arnold, 72, 8.530
Barry, John, 1871, 1877, mother: Ellen Barry, 164, 8.617
Barry, Kate, 1869, 1877, mother: Ellen Barry, 163, 8.616
Beatty, Bessie, 1877, 1877, mother: Maria Beatty; father deceased, 154, 8.612
Beatty, Joseph, 1876, 1877, Parents: Edward and Margaret Beatty, 223, 9.35
Bedell, Susie, 1871, 1877, father: William Bedell, 128, 8.585
Bellemore, Annie, 1868, 1876, Parents: Joseph (deceased) and Eliza Bellemore, 3, 8.463
Bellemore, Eddie, 1867, 1876, Parents: Joseph (deceased) and Eliza Bellemore, 2, 8.462
Bellemore, Lizzie, 1872, 1876, Parents: Joseph (deceased) and Eliza Bellemore, 3, 8.464
Bendleben, Adolph, 1873, 1876, father: Adolph Bendleben, 11, 8.471
Bendleton, Marietta, 1868, 1876, Parents: Adolph and Anna Bendleton, 16, 8.472
Bennett, Agnes, 1874, 1876, Parents: James and Eliza Bennett, 1, 8.444
Bentz, George, 1872, 1877, , 94, 8.547
Bertels, Amelia, 1874, 1877, Parents: Anton and Antonia Bertels, 137, 8.594
Bertels, Anna, 1872, 1877, Parents: Anton and Antonia Bertels, 138, 8.595
Besier, Julia, 1872, 1876, Parents: John and Charlotte Besier, 5, 8.466
Besier, Lottie, 1870, 1876, Parents: John and Charlotte Besier, 4, 8.465
Birdsall, Daniel, 1872, 1877, Parents: Read and Adelia Birdsall, 83, 8.540
Birdsall, Janes, 1868, 1877, Parents: Read and Adelia Birdsall, 82, 8.539
Birdsell, Ella, , 1877, Parents: Arba and Adelia Birdsell, 187, 9.2
Blackburn, Birdie, 1876, 1876, Parents: Charles Henton and Bertha Blackburn, 31, 8.492
Boehles, Anna, 1866, 1876, Parents: Peter and Christina Boehles, 34, 8.496

Boehles, Julia, 1865, 1876, Parents: Peter and Christina Boehles, 33, 8.495

Boehles, Mary, 1870, 1876, Parents: Peter and Christina Boehles, 35, 8.497

Boltz, Ida, 1872, 1876, Parents: Lewis and Agatha Boltz, 42,

Brines, Frederick, 1871, 1877, Parents: John and Eliza Brines, 170,

Brines, James, 1870, 1877, Parents: John and Eliza Brines, 169,

Brines, Jeanie, 1874, 1877, Parents: John and Eliza Brines, 167,

Brines, John, 1868, 1877, Parents: John and Eliza Brines, 168,

Brines, Katie, 1867, 1877, Parents: John and Eliza Brines, 166,

Brooks, George, 1876, 1876, Parents: Peter and Bridget Brooks, 28, 8.489

Brown, Daniel, 1875, 1877, "Deserted by mother, Mary Kelly, at 6 weeks old", 162, 8.618

Brown, Gracie, 1876, 1876, Parents: George and Jennie Brown, 8, 8.474

Bruce, Florence, 1871, 1877, Parents: James and Helen Bruce, 141, 8.598

Brumund, Johanna, 1876, 1877, mother: Johanna Brumund, 149, 8.605

Burns, Catharine, 1877, 1877, mother: Mary Burns; no father reported, 243, 9.45

Calender, Alice, 1866, 1877, parents unknown, 147, 8.604

Canfield, Sadie, 1871, 1877, mother: Catharine Canfield; father unknown, 222, 9.34

Carlson, Mary, 1874, 1876, parents unknown, 21, 8.481

Carroll, Frances, 1865, 1876, mother: Jane Carroll, 57, 8.516

Casy, Mary, 1874, 1876, parents unknown, 19, 8.479

Cauley, John, 1870, 1877, parents unknown, 156, 8.609

Clark, Nellie, 1877, 1877, mother only 16 yrs old; father unknown, 148, 8.601

Claybrielle, Lizzie, 1864, 1877, Parents: Thomas and Catherine Claybrielle, 92, 8.548

Claybrielle, Thomas, , 1877, Parents: Thomas and Catherine Claybrielle, 93, 8.549

Clute, Charles, 1875, 1876, Parents: Charles Clute and Mary Smith, 9, 8.475

Cole , James, 1868, 1877, Parents: William (deceased) and Eliza Cole, 202, 9.17

Coleman, Cassie, 1868, 1877, Parents: John and Mary Jane Coleman, 161, 8.615

Coleman, Emma, 1866, 1877, Parents: John and Mary Jane Coleman, 160, 8.614

Coley, Lilly, 1876, 1876, Parents: John and Ellen Coley, 22, 8.482

Collum, John, 1869, 1877, left by father at home, 157, 8.610

Condon, Elizabeth, 1877, 1877, Parents: John and Margaret Grey, 244, 9.46

Coovish, Mary, 1873, 1877, mother: Rosanna Coovish, 129, 8.586

Coutant, George, 1876, 1877, Parents: William and Julia (deceased) Coutant, 95, 8.547
Coutant, Jacob, 1871, 1876, father: William Coutant, 80, 8.538
Coutant, Julia, 1874, 1876, father: William Coutant, 79, 8.537
Coutant, Sophia, 1867, 1876, father: William Coutant, 78, 8.536
Coutant, Susan, 1865, 1876, father: William Coutant, 77, 8.535
Cox, Emma, 1876, 1876, Parents: Dr. Seth Close and Emma Cox, 38, 8.499
Crane, Fanny, 1876, 1877, Parents: George and Maria Crane, 102, 8.556
Crane, Lizzie, 1876, 1876, parents unknown, 54, 8.513
Deshay, Phebe, 1876, 1876, mother: Mary Ann Deshay, 39, 8.500
Dew, Bertha, 1871, 1877, mother: Bertha Dew, 214, 9.29
Dew , Annie, 1867, 1877, mother: Bertha Dew, 213, 9.28
DeWitt, Dora, 1875, 1877, mother left the child and went with a strange man, 186, 8.632
Dillon, Elizabeth, 1870, 1877, , 134, 8.592
Dillon, Patrick, 1873, 1877, , 135, 8.593
Dolan, Ezeta, 1877, 1877, parents unknown, 171, 8.620
Donigan, Rebecca, 1876, 1877, surrendered by grandmother: Rebecca Abrahams, 152, 8.608
Donovan, Ellen, 1876, 1877, Parents: William and Ellen Donovan, 208, 9.23
Donovan, John, 1872, 1877, Parents: William and Ellen Donovan, 207, 9.22
Donovan, William, 1874, 1877, Parents: William and Ellen Donovan, 208, 9.23
Downing, Bernard, 1871, 1877, parents unknown, 235, 9.37
Downing, Franklin, 1874, 1877, mother: Oliza Downing; father unknown, 113, 8.566
Downs, Flaurence, 1874, 1876, Parents: James Herbard and Eliza Downs, 29, 8.491
Drake, Grace, 1876, 1876, father: Charles Drake, 26, 8.487
Drake, Susan, 1876, 1876, father: Charles Drake, 25, 8.486
Dunn, Lottie, 1868, 1877, Parents: George and Angeline (deceased) Dunn, 85, 8.542
Elliott, Bertie, 1874, 1877, Parents: Thomas and Hellen Elliott, 177, 8.627
Ellis, Frederick, 1869, 1877, parents are acrobats, 191, 9.7
Ellis, Harry, 1867, 1877, parents are acrobats, 190, 9.6
Emrich, John, 1867, 1877, father: William Emrich, 206, 9.21
Emrich, Lena, 1877, 1877, father: William Emrich, 204, 9.19
Emrich, Mary, 1877, 1877, father: William Emrich, 203, 9.18
Emrich, Matilda, 1877, 1877, father: William Emrich, 205, 9.20
Ferry, Mary, 1876, 1877, Parents: James and Susan Ferry, 96, 8.551
Fields, Ethel, 1876, 1876, Parents: Mr. and Mrs. Lowdon, 37, 8.498
Fitzsimmons, Lizzie, 1869, 1877, mother: Ella Fitzsimmons, 212, 9.24

Flannigan, John, 1872, 1877, , 188, 9.4
Flannigan, Willie, 1874, 1876, parents unknown, 15, 8.476
Flynn, Joseph, 1872, 1877, parents unknown, 189, 9.5
Forest, Susan, 1876, 1876, Parents: John and Mary Forest, 45, 8.501
Frances, Clara, 1877, 1877, mother: Ms. Francis; father unknown, 143, 8.599
Gibson, Maggie, 1873, 1876, parents unknown, 18, 8.478
Giff, Mary, 1876, 1877, Parents: John and Fannie Giff, 108, 8.563
Gockman, Minnie, 1877, 1877, Parents: Samuel and Catharine Gockman, 122, 8.578
Goodrich, Eddie, 1874, 1877, , 126, 8.579
Gordon, Frank, 1876, 1876, father: Thomas Osman, 7, never received
Gottchalk, Frances, 1876, 1876, Parents: Frank Gottchalk and Mary Honeyman, 6, 8.467
Gough, Mary, 1874, 1876, Parents: Michael and Katy Gough, 70, 8.528
Gray, Jamie, 1874, 1877, Parents: Patrick and Ellen Gray, 104, 8.558
Gray, Mamie, 1873, 1877, Parents: Patrick and Ellen Gray, 103, 8.557
Green, Elizabeth, 1867, 1877, Parents: George and Margaret Green, 200, 9.15
Halloran, Michael, 1872, 1877, , 140, 8.597
Harrington, Charlie, 1877, 1877, mother: Cordelia Harrington, 144, 8.600
Hart, Catharine, 1873, 1876, Parents: Peter and Mildred Hart, 60, 8.519
Hart, Rosena, 1867, 1876, Parents: Peter and Mildred Hart, 59, 8.518
Harvey, Katy, 1869, 1876, surrendered by mother, 69, 8.527
Harvey, Thomas, 1871, 1876, Parents: John and Maria Harvey, 68, 8.526
Heitz, Rachel, 1863, 1877, , 119, 8.574
Herwig, Rosa, 1874, 1877, mother: Katy Herwig, 182, 8.629
Hoeffle, Jacob, 1871, 1876, father: Fred Hoeffle, 56, 8.515
Hoeffle, Katrina, , 1876, father: Fred Hoeffle, 55, 8.514
Hohenthal, Dora, 1869, 1877, mother: Mrs. Charlotte Hohenthal; father deceased, 145, 8.602
Hohenthal, Tillie, 1871, 1877, mother: Mrs. Charlotte Hohenthal; father deceased, 146, 8.603
Hoyt, Robert, 1877, 1877, , 201, deceased
Huber, Charlie, 1871, 1877, Parents: Henry and Elizabeth Huber, 197, 9.11
Huber, Louisa, 1870, 1877, Parents: Henry and Elizabeth Huber, 196, 9.12
Huber, Sophia, 1873, 1877, Parents: Henry and Elizabeth Huber, 198, 9.13

Hulbig, Tillie, 1865, 1877, , 195, 9.3
Hutchinson, Emma, 1876, 1877, Parents: August and Rosa Hutchinson, 105, 8.559
Jackson, Alice, 1867, 1877, , 178, 8.626
Johnson, Nellie, 1870, 1877, mother: Nettie Johnson, 237, 9.39
Jones, William, 1877, 1877, Parents: Thomas and Sarah Jones, 211, 9.27
Kebel, John, 1874, 1877, mother: Lizzie Kebel; father deceased, 220, 9.32
Keefe, Emma, 1868, 1876, Parents: Jeremiah and Lucy Keefe, 36,
Kehoe, David, 1869, 1877, Parents: Michael (stepfather) and Eliza Quinn, 88, 8.544
Kehoe, Maggie, 1865, 1877, Parents: Michael (stepfather) and Eliza Quinn, 88, 8.543
Kepler, Caroline, 1867, 1877, Parents: George and Caroline (deceased) Kepler, 175, 8.624
Kinsley, Rachel, 1875, 1876, Parents: Wesley and Mary Ann Kinsley, 65, 8.521
Kipp, Guy, 1876, 1877, Parents: Frederic and Eliza Kipp, 101, 8.555
Kruger, Carrie, 1874, 1877, Parents: August and Wilhelmena Kruger, 159, returned to mother
Kruger, Wilhelmena, 1872, 1877, Parents: August and Wilhelmena Kruger, 158, returned to mother
Kubeske, Johannah, 1876, 1876, Parents: John and Lena Kubeske, 71, 8.529
Kuister, Amanda, , 1877, , 107, "8.561, 8.562"
Lamson, Ada, , 1876, , 66, 8.517
Lang, Johanna, , 1876, Parents: John and Sophia Lang, 63, 8.523
Lang, Margaret, , 1876, Parents: John and Sophia Lang, 64, 8.524
Lang, Rosa, , 1876, Parents: John and Sophia Lang, 62, 8.522
Lee, John, 1874, 1877, mother: Jane Lee, 131, 8.588
Leggatt, Isabella, 1872, 1876, Parents: Samuel and Jane Leggett, 47, 8.507
Leggatt, James, 1868, 1876, Parents: Samuel and Jane Leggett, 46, 8.506
Leggatt, Robert, 1874, 1876, Parents: Samuel and Jane Leggett, 48, 8.508
Leggett, Jane, 1876, 1876, Parents: Samuel and Jane Leggett, 23, 8.483
Lehman, Emma, 1877, 1877, Parents: Jacob and Rosa Lehman, 127, 8.584
Lent, Estella, 1872, 1877, , 239, 9.41
Lougnet, Eddie, 1868, 1876, Parents: Louis (deceased) Lougnet and Emily Rattean, 44, 8.505
Lougnet, Maxine, 1864, 1876, Parents: Louis (deceased) Lougnet and Emily Rattean, 43, 8.504
Lovett, Harry, 1876, 1877, Parents: Thomas and Katie Lovett, 115, 8.570
Magner, Lizzie, 1876, 1876, parents unknown, 53, 8.512

May, Mary, 1877, 1877, parents not yet known, 150, 8.606

McBride, John, 1874, 1877, mother deceased; father's whereabouts unknown, 174, 8.623

McCleren, Ellen, 1867, 1877, father: James McCleren, 215,

McCleren, Fannie, 1872, 1877, father: James McCleren, 217,

McCleren, Mary, 1869, 1877, father: James McCleren, 216,

McGinn, Joseph, 1873, 1876, Parents: Joseph and Susan McGinn, 61, returned to mother

McGinnis, Catharine, 1877, 1877, mother: Catharine McGinnis, 236, 9.38

McKennea, James, 1865, 1876, orphan, 10, 8.473

McKenney, Andrew, 1873, 1877, Parents: Andrew and Annie McKenney, 91, returned to mother

McKenney, James, 1871, 1877, Parents: Andrew and Annie McKenney, 90, returned to mother

McKenney, Loretta, 1869, 1877, Parents: Andrew and Annie McKenney, 89, never received

Melmore, Mary, 1873, 1877, mother: Lizzie Melmore committed for habitual intoxic., 240, 9.42

Millar, Carrie, 1874, 1876, Parents: Theo and Carrie Millar, 27, 8.485

Mitchel, Hattie, 1867, 1877, Parents: John and Jane Mitchel, 84, 8.541

Mitchell, Mary, 1870, 1877, Parents: David and Sarah Jane Mitchell, 165, 8.619

Moore, Charlie, 1875, 1876, Parents: Hugh McGill and Jessie Moore, 50, 8.509

Moore, Katie, 1877, 1877, Parents: Mr. Marshall and Katie Moore, 184, 8.631

Moran, Anna, 1877, 1877, Parents: James and Margaret Moran, 218, 9.30

Munn, Agnes, , 1877, Parents: Armstrong and Margaret Munn, 180,

Munn, Walter, , 1877, Parents: Armstrong and Margaret Munn, 181, never received

Murray, Agnes, 1869, 1877, "mother: Rose Casey, father: ??? Murray", 121, 8.575

Murray, Margaret, 1875, 1877, Parents: David and Eliza Murray, 153, 8.611

Murray, Mary, 1866, 1877, orphan, 125, 8.167

Neotia, Lottie, 1877, 1877, Parents: Charlie Bowten and Mary Sprague, 123, 8.582

O'Connell, Margaret, 1866, 1877, Parents: Patrick and Margaret (deceased) O'Connell, 172, 8.621

Oliver, Mary, 1874, 1877, Parents: Abram Oliver and Maggie O'Brien, 87, 8.545

Ponson, Lewis, 1876, 1877, Parents: Lewis and Mary Ponson, 106, 8.560

Ponson, Margaretta, 1874, 1877, Parents: Lewis and Mary Ponson, 155, 8.613

Rademaker, Charles, , 1877, both parents deceased; father murdered, 242, 9.44

Regan, Mary, 1877, 1877, father: Martin Regan; mother deceased, 183, 9.1

Reynolds, Augusta, 1875, 1877, mother: Mrs. Lizzie Reynolds; father has deserted them, 151, 8.607

Reynolds, Emma, 1876, 1877, mother: Josephine Reynolds, 124, 8.583

Richards, Charles, 1876, 1877, Parents: William and Minnie Richards, 114, 8.567

Richter, Frederick, 1873, 1877, Parents: Frederick and Katy Richter, 100, 8.554

Richter, Lizzie, 1871, 1877, Parents: Frederick and Katy Richter, 99, 8.553

Richter, Louisa, 1866, 1877, Parents: Frederick and Katy Richter, 118, 8.573

Richter, Louisa, 1866, 1877, Parents: Frederick and Katy Richter, 120, 8.573

Richter, Maggie, 1877, 1877, Parents: Frederick and Katy Richter, 98, 8.552

Riley, Ellen, , 1877, mother: Julia Riley, 142,

Riley, Rose, 1865, 1877, mother: Kate Riley, 185, 8.630

Ritzer, Henry, 1872, 1877, parents living but unknown, 224, 9.36

Rivers, Charlie, 1873, 1877, , 238, 9.40

Robinson, Sarah, 1869, 1877, Parents: James and Susannah Robinson, 194, 9.9

Robinson, Willie, 1870, 1877, Parents: James and Susannah Robinson, 193, 9.8

Ryan, Annie, 1874, 1876, parents unknown, 20, 8.480

Saules, Charles, 1875, 1877, father: Horatio Saules, 192, 9.1

Schenk, Hattie, 1866, 1877, Parents: Charles and Louisa Schenk, 117, 8.569

Schenk, Minnie, 1863, 1877, Parents: Charles and Louisa Schenk, 116, 8.568

Segenhorn, Augusta, 1869, 1877, mother: Johanna Segenhorn; father deceased, 209, 9.25

Seymour, Emma, 1867, 1877, father: William Seymour, 109, 8.563 1/2

Seymour, George, 1875, 1877, father: William Seymour, 112, 8.565

Seymour, John, 1871, 1877, father: William Seymour, 111, 8.564

Seymour, Mary, , 1877, Parents: William and Mary Seymour, 133, 8.590

Seymour, William, 1869, 1877, father: William Seymour, 110, 8.563 3/4

Sheerer, John, 1874, 1876, Parents: Peter and Adelphine Sheerer, 40, 8.502

Sheerer, Mary, 1876, 1876, Parents: Peter and Adelphine Sheerer, 41, 8.503

Simmerman, Lena, 1871, 1877, Parents: Fred Newhart and Rosa Simmerman, 139, 8.596

St. Clair, Ella, , 1876, , 17, 8.477

String, Louisa, 1864, 1877, Parents: George and Anna String, 219, 9.31

Swartz, James, 1868, 1877, Parents: James and Kate Swartz, 179, 8.628

Taylor, Catherine, 1861, 1877, surrendered by Mr. George Kellock, 97, 8.184

Taylor, Edward, 1874, 1877, mother: Mary Taylor, 132, 8.589

Thompson, Maggie, 1876, 1876, mother: Maggie Thompson, 67, 8.525

Twibell, William, 1871, 1877, Parents: William and Alice Twibell, 241, 9.43

Upton, Nellie, 1875, 1876, mother: Margaret Upton (deceased), 32, 8.494

Valentine, William, 1867, 1877, Parents: Henry and Mary Valentine, 199, 9.14

Wagner, Lilly, 1877, 1877, mother: Mary Wagner; no legal father, 176, 8.625

Walker, Mary, 1866, 1877, , 210, 9.26

Walters, Samuel, 1876, 1876, Parents: Samuel Walters and Maggie O'Neil, 30, 8.490

Warren, Nettie, 1876, 1876, mother: Annie Warren, 49, returned to mother

Watson, Addie, 1864, 1876, Parents: Edgar and May Watson, 12, 8.468

Watson, Margaret, 1873, 1876, Parents: Edgar and May Watson, 14, 8.470

Watson, William, 1871, 1876, Parents: Edgar and May Watson, 13, 8.469

Webb, Charlie, , 1876, mother: Julia Webb, 58, 8.520

Whitman, Henry, 1871, 1877, father: Henry Whitman, 136, 8.591

Whitter, Elnora, 1870, 1877, father: James Whitter, 221, 9.33

Wilson, Mary, 1876, 1876, Parents: Mr. and Mrs. Wilson, 52, 8.511

Wolfe, Charles, 1875, 1876, parents unknown, 51, 8.510

Woods, Penn, 1874, 1877, Parents: Janus and Sarah Woods, 130, 8.587

Woods, Susie, 1864, 1877, , 173, 8.622

Woolworth, Freddie, 1876, 1877, Parents: Herman and Amelia Woolworth, 86, never received

Young, Hannah, 1876, 1876, mother: Sarah Fishback, 24, 8.484

AMERICAN FEMALE GUARDIAN SOCIETY
HOME FOR THE FRIENDLESS
VOLUME 11

Abdaliau, Fabel, , 1897, parents: Dr. Nahabed and Haygreti Abdaliau (father shot), 128

Abdaliau, Takouki, , 1897, father was member of Broadway Tabernacle-Divinity School CT 1879, 128

Adams, Dora, , 1896, , 54

Adams, Frank, , 1896, parents: Anton F. and Lena Adams (deceased), 54

Adams, Kate, , 1896, , 54

Adams, Lena, , 1896, "father, German mother, American", 54

Aguado, Ernest, 1896, 1899, "parents: Charles (Mexican) and Elizabeth (German) one child, Alphonso", 242

Aguardo, Alphonso, 1893, 1896, "parents: Charles and Elizabeth, baby boy not surrendered", 89

Ahbend, Robert, 1892, 1897, parents: Herman and Annie both of German origin, 132

Albert, Annie, 1889, 1896, "two sisters not surrendered Emma, 13 and Mollie, 14", 74

Albert, Charles, 1886, 1896, parents: Charles and Amelia Albert, 74

Albert, Mary, 1892, 1896, "parents: Charles and Amelia Albert sister, Emma, 13", 85

Albert, Rose, 1889, 1896, parents from Sweden, 74

Aldridge, Carrie, 1887, 1896, parents: Carrie and Charles Aldridge (deceased), 48

Aldridge, William, 1889, 1896, "a sister, Jenny, not surrendered at this time", 48

Allen, John D., 1889, 1896, parents: Kate and Henry Allen father deserted family, 109

Allen, Rachel, 1888, 1899, parents: Sarah and Peter (father dead), 247

Anderson, Gertrude, 1888, 1899, "mother: Mary Fastrow Anderson, father deceased", 227

Anderson, Isabella, 1893, 1898, "fathers residence, 200 E. 93rd St.", 190

Anderson, James, 1890, 1898, mother sent to Seton Hospital with consumption, 190

Anderson, Jessie, 1889, 1898, parents: Robert and Jessie Anderson, 190

Anderson, Robert, 1892, 1898, "all children born in Scotland, as well as parents", 190

Anderson, Torvo, 1897, 1900, parents: Karl and Johanna, 260

Anderson, Tyyne, 1898, 1900, mother is in a Harlem Hosp., 260

Andrean, Louisa, 1885, 1895, father deceased/mother was a midwife, 17

Anglade, Charles, 1893, 1899, parents: Augustine and Charles Eugene (both died 1899), 220

Barber, James, 1886, 1896, parents;Margaret and James Barber 2 other children, 44

Barber, Willie, 1889, 1896, father insane (Northhampton Mass. Asylum mother had tumor, 44

Bauer, Christina, 1886, 1898, parents: Adolf and Minnie (father died 1896), 188

Bauer, George, 1893, 1898, "grandmother, Mrs. W. Boehm #1696 2nd Ave., aunt, Miss A. Kaift, 211 E. 31st St.", 189

Bauer, Louisa G., 1893, 1899, parents: Wilhemenia and Adolf (father dead) siblings-Christina and George, 221

Bennett, Edward, 1888, 1897, "parents: Agnes and John, Newport, RI", 136

Blaise, Mamie, 1891, 1897, parents: Lena and Alexander, 140

Blaise, Mamie, 1891, 1897, parents: Lena and Alexander Blaise Catholic in faith-eye trouble, 155

Blome, Annie, 1893, 1896, father died in 1895, 96

Blome, Emma, 1889, 1896, parents: Amelia and Louis Blome 2 other children, 96

Bock, Mary, 1889, 1895, parents of German origin, 21

Bock, Minnie, 1883, 1895, parents: Louisa and Adam Bock (dead) mother in poor health, 21

Bocoffer, Mabel, 1890, 1896, father deserted family 6 months ago, 86

Bocoffer, Rose, 1888, 1896, parents: Rose and John Bocoffer, 86

Bosler, Edward, 1896, 1899, "parents: Clara and Albert, father deserted family, Rosanna 5yrs. Still home", 237

Boyd, Annie, 1888, 1895, , 23

Boyd, Joseph, 1890, 1895, , 23

Boyd, Martha, , 1896, mother going to Infant Asylum to be confined-illegitimate child, 117

Boyd, Mary, 1884, 1895, parents: Julia and William Boyd (deceased), 23

Boyd, Mary, 1887, 1896, parents: Julia and William Boyd (dead), 117

Boyd, Sadie, , 1896, two siblings already confined-Annie and Joseph, 117

Brady, Katie, 1896, 1899, "parents: Mary and Phillip, sister Lizzie already committed", 255

Brady, Lizzie, 1892, 1897, "parents: Many and Philip Brady, baby girl, 18 months still home", 141

Breaseu, Charles, 1888, 1898, "parents: Carles and Eliza (mother died April 20, 1898)", 200

Breaseu, Elsa, 1894, 1898, father lived at 512 E. 16th St., 200

Breaseu, Emma, 1891, 1898, parents from Germany, 200

Breaseu, Henry, 1896, 1898, , 200

Bridge, Annie, 1895, 1898, "parents: Katie and Julius, both from Switzerland, baby boy still at home", 213

Brinkman, Annie, 1891, 1898, "parents: Herman and Eliza (Lina), Johanna, Minnie, and Cecilia siblings)", 203

Brugger, Fred, 1894, 1896, "father in Geranan Hospital, mother in Bellvue Hospital", 55

Brugger, Martha, 1891, 1896, parents: Fred and Mary Brugger, 55

Bullwinkle, Richard, 1888, 1898, no known relatives, 193

Burns, Frances, 1893, 1896, parents: Lizzie and Frank Burns (deceased), 38

Bussell, Bessie, 1896, 1899, "parents: Richard and Antoinette, 2 other children already there", 246

Bussell, Philip, 1893, 1898, "sister, Bessie, 2yrs., boarding with Mrs. Jacob Miller", 197

Bussell, Richard, 1891, 1898, "parents: Richard and Antoinette, mother died", 197

Bussell, Victor, 1894, 1898, "grandmother, Mrs. MR Carlon, Temple Grove, NY", 197

Candler, Allen, 1891, 1897, , 139

Candler, Arthur, 1888, 1897, "Mrs. Maria Wilson, grandmother, surrendered the children", 139

Candler, Ethel, 1884, 1897, parents: Sarah (dead) and George father remarried, 139

Cardell, Antonio, 1891, 1896, "another sibling listed as ""Baby"" not surrendered", 40

Cardell, John, 1889, 1896, parents: Lena and Conrad Cardell father deserted family, 40

Childs, Albert, 1892, 1897, mother: Annie, 127

Chippendale, Julie, 1894, 1900, parents: Mary and Walter, 274

Chirlstein, Mamie, 1892, 1897, parents: Lena and Julins (Russian) , 162

Chirlstein, Pincus, 1895, 1897, "father deserted family, mother attempted suicide, Mt. Sinii", 162

Christopher, Charles, 1892, 1897, "Lena, 3 yr old sister still of the home", 147

Christopher, Frances, 1889, 1897, , 147

Christopher, Henry, 1887, 1897, parents: Maggie and Henry father doesn't support family, 147

Clerc, Eddie, 1890, 1895, parents: Jennie and Emil Clerc, 8

Clerc, Emil, 1892, 1895, "siblings: Lillie, Jennie, and Lewis (not surrendered)", 8

Clerc, Jane, 1888, 1896, parents: Jennie and Emil Clerc, 81

Clerc, Louis, 1893, 1896, "deserted by father committed brother Eddie, Nov. 11, '95", 81

Clutt, Charles, 1888, 1895, vagrancy, 7

Clutt, Emma, 1891, 1895, vagrancy, 7

Cochrane, Agnes, 1894, 1897, parents: Annie and Joseph Wright taken temporarily, 121

Collins, Cyril, 1893, 1900, , 267

Collins, John G., 1891, 1900, "Uncle, William Collins paid board", 267
Collins, William R., 1889, 1900, parents: John and Margaret (mother just died), 267
Costello, Grace, , 1896, , 31
Costello, Loretta, , 1896, parents: Ellen and Frank father deserted the family, 31
Crate, Arthur, 1895, 1898, mother was to have operation, 184
Crate, Percy, 1894, 1898, parents: Percy and Amelia-taken temp., 184
Crawford, Albert, , 1898, "Father doesn't know about the children and isn't to know where they are.", 181
Crawford, Viola, , 1898, parents: Minnie and Thomas, 181
Currie, Florence, 1888, 1899, parents: Ralph (whereabouts unknown) and Sarah (dead), 222
Daumann, Margaret, , 1896, sent to Island Hospital soon after arrival for scabies, 36
DeVries, Anne, 1893, 1900, "parents: John and Johanna, mother deserted family", 262
DeVries, Mary, 1895, 1900, parents from Holland, 262
Diede, Henry Jr., 1888, 1897, parents: Henry and Emily Diede (deceased) from London, 129
Dodderer, Raymond, 1896, 1899, parents: Emma Dodderer and Dwight Reeves completely surrendered, 245
Doe, Jane, 1896, 1900, "brought by officers, no particulars", 257
Doe, Jane , 1893, 1895, Jane Doe # 8, 5
Doe, John, 1893, 1895, John Doe # 22, 6
Doe, John, 1893, 1896, John Doe # 25 vagrancy, 66
Doe, John, 1894, 1897, John Doe # 28, 126
Doe, John, 1892, 1897, John Doe #30, 169
Dolanny, Ethel, , 1896, mother: Eliza Dolanny father dead, 39
Dolanny, Gracie, , 1896, "Mother is a member of the Salvation Army. Neglects her children", 39
Doran, Eliza, 1893, 1897, parents: Thomas and Dora(mother insane on Blackwell Isl. Father in prison), 167
Doyle, Katie, 1885, 1897, parents Nellie and Teddy Doyle (mother died), 148
Driscoll, Arthur, 1897, 1899, , 251
Driscoll, Lucy, 1894, 1899, parents: Daniell (Irish) and Rose (English), 251
Driscoll, William, 1896, 1899, parents live at 536 W. 55th St., 251
Driver, George, 1895, 1899, parents: Anna (ill) and Frances, 224
Duggan, Charles, 1888, 1897, parents: John and Lizzie Duggan (father in jail for drunkenness), 166
Duggan, Lizzie, 1892, 1897, two sisters not committed: Madeline and Mamie, 166
Dunworth, Ruth, 1893, 1896, parents: Vina and Thomas Dunworth, 37

Durenmatt, John, 1896, 1900, parents: Paul (Swiss) and Josephine (French), 256
Egau, Christopher, 1888, 1896, parents: Thomas and Kate Egau, 58
Egau, Helen, 1891, 1896, "father unemployed, mother sick with bronchitis", 58
Farrilla, Bennie, 1887, 1896, "Louis Farilli, brother kept contact", 91
Fazhriaseu, Leopold Randolph, 1895, 1899, "parents: Anna Fazhriaseu and Leopold True, mother ill", 219
Ford, John, , 1895, another brother not surrendered-15 years old, 19
Ford, Julia, , 1895, parents: Jeremiah and Hanna Ford, 19
Ford, Theresa, , 1895, parents born in Ireland, 19
Foster, Cassimir, 1896, 1897, parents: Kate Goodtear and Fred Ansore, 125
Friedman, Rebecca, , 1896, father: Adolf Freidman vagrancy, 34
Fuegel, Anna, 1889, 1896, parents: Sophie and Carl Fuegel, 82
Fuegel, Lizzie, 1890, 1896, "father is on Wards Island. Is out of his mind.", 82
Fuegel, Maggie, 1892, 1896, 3 other children not surrendered, 82
Fuhrer, William L., 1895, 1899, "parents: Emilia K. and Peter (dead) 3 children in the Home for the Homeless, Jersey City", 254
Fuller, Alice, 1888, 1898, "parents: George and Annie, mother died 5 yrs. Ago", 211
Gaflau, Sadie, 1890, 1896, parents: John and Ida Gaflau mother died in 1891, 35
Gildersleeve, Edith, 1892, 1898, parents: Martha and John mother ill, 201
Girard, Minnie, 1893, 1896, "father: Alexander Girard, mother: deceased", 64
Godwin, Ethelberl, , 1896, parents: Katherine (mulatto) and Richard (white) Godwin, 102
Godwin, Kathleen, 1893, 1897, parents: Kathleen and Richard Godwin-taken temp., 152
Grant, Harold, 1896, 1899, parents: Sarah Grant and Lyndon Abels, 229
Green, Elizabeth, 1892, 1898, parents: Henry and Elizabeth both from London, 183
Gregor, Emilia, 1884, 1895, parents: Freda and Adolf Gregor, 15
Gregor, Julia, 1888, 1895, , 15
Gregor, Willie, 1886, 1895, , 15
Gribbin, Arthur, 1893, 1897, "parents: Rose and John (drowned) Emma and John, siblings at St. Joseph Asylum", 137
Griffin, Florence, 1885, 1896, parents: Fanny and John Griffin mother going to the Convalescent Home, 56
Hagel, Otto, 1894, 1898, "mother insane from drinking, baby girl, 5 months. Still at home", 212
Hagel, William, 1892, 1898, parents: Otto and Lizzie mother at Ward's Island, 212

Hance, George, 1888, 1896, , 94
Hance, John, 1890, 1896, parents: Mary and George Hance died Feb. '96), 94
Hansen, Harry, 1893, 1898, "parents: Charles and Hannah, father deserted family", 207
Hanson, Charles, 1895, 1898, "4 more children, parents from Norway", 207
Hargeu, Stanley, 1888, 1896, parents: Fannie and Thomas Hargeu, 99
Hargeu, Thomas, 1894, 1896, taken temp. mother near confinment, 99
Harris, Margaret, 1888, 1895, father deserted family, parents: Jessie and William Harris, 20
Hartman, John, 1889, 1896, "parents: Mary and John Hartman father died, consumption", 98
Hartman, Maud, 1894, 1896, , 98
Heinman, Charles, 1895, 1898, "parents: Henry and Annie, father insane on Ward's Island", 192
Hensel, Annetta, 1886, 1897, parents: Charles and Julia (dead), 133
Hensel, Carrie, 1887, 1897, "another sibling, Fred, 17 months, still at the home", 133
Hensel, John, 1892, 1897, "father from Germany, mother from Pennsylvania", 133
Hergesheimer, Albert, 1896, 1900, parents: Isabel and Thomas father deserted family, 272
Hilgner, Joseph, 1894, 1900, "Parents: Emma and Oscar, family divorced", 261
Hill, Laura, 1889, 1896, parents: Andrew and Carrie Hill, vagrancy, 108
Hoffman, Louis, 1894, 1896, "Came from the Island", 50
Houffe, Annie, 1888, 1895, father deserted family, 14
Houffe, Lillian, 1892, 1895, parents: Magdalena and Felix Houffe one brother and one sister (not surrendered), 14
Howe, Otto Jr., 1896, 1899, parents: Otto and Ida (German), 218
Hoye, Alvina, 1894, 1896, , 116
Hoye, Howard, 1892, 1896, , 116
Hoye, Richard, 1891, 1896, parents: Caroline and Richard Hoye father deserted, 116
Hugaboom, Jennie, 1890, 1895, mother going into hospital, 10
Hugaboom, Mary Frances, 1888, 1895, 2 other children (not surrendered), 10
Hughes, Annie, 1887, 1897, both parents deceased mother: Elizabeth died in St. Lukes Hospital, 153
Hughes, Ethel, 1886, 1896, parents: Gearge and Abby Hughes (deceased) vagrancy, 84
Jacoberger, Edward, 1892, 1895, parents: Emma and Adolf Jacoberger, 13
Jacobson, Eddie, 1893, 1900, , 277
Jacobson, Elizabeth, 1896, 1900, , 277

Jacobson, Gertrude, 1892, 1900, parents: Joseph and Mary (mother died), 277

James, Josephine E., 1884, 1896, "Sent to us un the 'Wright Trust'", 51

Jarvis, Montagu, 1889, 1897, parents: Frank and Mary Jane Jarvis (mother dead), 124

Jaubert, Henrietta, 1887, 1896, father: Louis Jaubert (child surrendered in 1891-paid for board), 118

Johnson, Helen M., 1895, 1900, mother: Matilda not a proper gaurdian, 264

Johnston, Lillie, 1894, 1900, "parents: Mary (English) and Richard (Irish), no work", 275

Johnston, Percy, 1896, 1900, "a sister, Cecilia, almost 2yrs., still at home", 275

Jones, Fannie, 1886, 1896, , 72

Jones, Harriet, 1885, 1896, parents: Kate and Louis Jones, father is sick and has no work, 72

Kaercher, Lillie, 1888, 1897, parents: Mary and Phillip Kaercher-one sister and two brothers, 123

Keeu, Freda, 1889, 1897, parents: Annie and Albert Keeu father living with another woman, 120

Keeu, Helena, 1890, 1897, "another sister, Annie, 14, not surrendered", 120

Kelber, Charles, 1894, 1900, "parents: Louise and Frederick (father died) 2 siblings, Wm. And Louise at home", 265

Kelber, Fredik, 1890, 1899, "parents: Louise and Frederick, father sick in Bellevue Hosp.", 231

Kelber, Minnie, 1892, 1899, parents were German, 231

Kemmert, Martha, 1892, 1896, "mother is at Wards Island. Is insane", 27

Kemmert, Otto, 1890, 1896, parents: Albert and Antonia Kemmert, 27

Kerill, Katie, 1889, 1897, parents: Mary and William, 143

Kerill, Maggie, 1891, 1897, father in Bellevue Hospital for swollen glands of the legs, 143

Kerns, Ella, 1891, 1896, father unemployed, 26

Kerns, Lizzie, 1887, 1896, parents: Emma and John Kerns, 26

Kerr, Kate, 1888, 1896, parents: Kate and Hugh Kerr father wasn't supporting family, 70

Keruskof, Charles, 1890, 1897, "parents: Carrie and Wm., mother insane, father no work", 174

Keruskof, Henry, 1895, 1897, 2 other children at home, 174

Khourie, Rose, 1886, 1896, father: John Kourie, 104

Kiesel, William, 1889, 1895, father was deceased and mother was in prison, 12

Kilton, Eveline, , 1900, mother: Mary, "mother an immoral woman-improper guardianship", 263

Kimmel, May, 1897, 1899, "parents: Sadie and Samuel (father imprisoned) sister Mollie, 7wks", 250

Kimmerle, Edward, 1891, 1897, parents: Emma and Louis K. father deserted his family, 149
Knudson, John, 1891, 1896, parents: Kate and John Knudson mother ill, 67
Knudson, Thomas, 1894, 1896, "baby Kate, a sister at 51st St.", 67
Koch, Clara, 1890, 1896, parents: William and Martha Koch, 83
Koch, Elsa, 1892, 1896, mother was ill with consumption-St. Joseph Hospital, 83
Koch, Lulu, 1893, 1896, "4th sister, Annie, 13 months, not committed", 83
Koennecke, Kate, 1882, 1896, parents: William and Ann Koennecke (both deceased about 6yrs., 77
Kruger, Irene, 1891, 1899, parents: Charles (German) and Rose (Am. Catholic) both dead, 223
Kuhlman, Freddie, 1894, 1897, parents: Frank and Annie (2 brothers already admitted), 138
Kuhlmau, Rousseau, 1889, 1897, parents: Annie and Frederick (father died), 135
Kuhlmau, Siegfried, 1890, 1897, "another boy, 3 yrs., still in the home", 135
Kurth, Herman, 1889, 1896, , 100
Kurth, William, 1890, 1896, parents: Emilie and Herman Kurth (deceased) 2 children, 95
Lacy, Charles, 1896, 1899, "parents: Erie and Minnie, mother ill, Albert, 7mo. Still home", 238
Lanzit, Viola, 1887, 1898, "parents: Julia and Joseph, mother is being confined", 186
Lauro, Frances, 1885, 1897, parents: Rachel and Louis father injured and can't work much, 145
Lauro, George, 1890, 1897, "7 children, one baby still of the home", 145
Lauro, Lawrence, 1892, 1897, parents from Italy, 145
Lawrence, Clarence, 1893, 1899, parents: Isaac and Lillian, 253
Lawrence, Lester, 1895, 1899, "father sent to Hosp., mother an opium eater-neglects children", 253
Lawson, Frances, 1895, 1897, "mother: Margaret ("about to be confined") father in Presbyterian Hosp.", 160
Lebree, Ellen, , 1898, "parents: Samual and Mary, father deserted family", 205
Lynch, Edith, 1894, 1897, "parents: Minnie and Garrett Lynch mother died, father deserted", 161
Mack, Albert, 1894, 1897, "found on street, brought by officer", 163
Maloney, Florence, 1888, 1898, "parents: Annie and Amos, parents deserted child when a yr. Old", 194
Maloof, Adele, 1891, 1898, "parents: Abraham and Hannah, all born in Syria", 210
Marnell, Annie, 1896, 1899, "parents: Annie and Henry, father left sister Kate, not admitted too young", 244

Marshall, Catherine, 1892, 1896, parents: John and Catherine Marshall father deserted, 53
Marshall, Gabrielle, 1890, 1896, had 12 year old brother in Juvenile Asylum, 53
Martin, Jennie, 1890, 1898, "parents: John and Ellen, baby, 5 months still home", 208
Martin, John, 1895, 1898, resided at 359 W. 39th St., 208
Martin, Mary, 1894, 1898, parents were Irish, 208
Mathers, Frank, 1893, 1896, parents: Charles and Minnie Mathers, wife is in NYIA with baby, 78
Mathieus, Juliette, 1898, 1900, parents: Fanny and Ernest (both from France), 269
Maynard, Mabel, 1883, 1895, "Brought by Officer King from Society", 1
McCarthy, Mary, 1896, 1898, "parents: George and Ella, no work", 199
McGaggart, Lizzie, 1888, 1896, father; John, 59
McGaggart, Marcella, 1892, 1896, , 59
McIlveen, Flora, 1897, 1900, parents: Lilian and Joseph, 268
McIlveen, William, 1898, 1900, mother from Ireland, 268
McMullan, Charlotte, 1888, 1900, parents: Margaret and William (father dead) brought by officer found with colored people named Brookes, 258
McShane, Granville, 1896, 1899, parents: Rose and Thomas-taken temp. father dying, 228
Medley, Susan, 1895, 1900, "parents: Mary and Henry, three other children", 276
Melville, Ethel , 1894, 1896, mother: Minnie (imprisoned) father: dead, 114
Messner, Christian, 1891, 1896, parents: Catherine and Christian Messner 3 other children, 60
Messner, Frank, 1892, 1896, father died, 60
Metzer, Antomdle, 1889, 1897, parents: Josephine and John, 142
Metzer, John, 1892, 1897, "mother had leg amputated, father injured", 142
Metzer, Matilda, 1890, 1897, both parents in Trinity Hospital, 142
Meyer, Edna, 1891, 1898, parents: Charles and Mary (dying of consumption), 196
Meyer, Geraldine, 1894, 1898, , 196
Meyer, Herman, 1891, 1896, one child at home-1 yr. old, parents born in Germany, 106
Meyer, Lillie, 1888, 1896, mother: Lizzie, husband deserted wife, 106
Mill, Fanny, 1897, 1900, parents: Maggie and Samual, father deserted family, 271
Monahau, Thomas D., 1894, 1896, parents: Helen and Patrick Monahau, 73
Monahau, Thomas Dixore, 1894, 1896, parents: Helen and Patrick Monahau, 28

Montague, Florence, 1893, 1897, "parents: Julia and Joseph, father deserted family", 179
Montague, Julia, 1895, 1897, "Gertrude, 13 yrs. Still at home", 179
Moore, Isabelle, , 1897, parents: Jerome and Charlotte Moore-father invalid, 146
Moore, John, 1893, 1897, "sisters, Eleanor, 12yrs., and Nannie, 2 1/2yrs. Still home", 178
Moore, Lillie, 1890, 1897, "no work for father, parents were Irish", 178
Moore, Margaret, 1887, 1897, parents: Elizabeth and Samuel-taken temp., 178
Morrison, Ellen, 1892, 1896, , 61
Morrison, Flora, 1890, 1896, parents: Charlotte and John Morrison, 61
Morrison, John, 1891, 1896, , 61
Muller, Adam, 1890, 1896, mother on Wards Island-declared insane, 119
Munro, Beatrice, 1891, 1899, parents: James and Alice now divorced, 226
Murphy, Jeremiah, 1890, 1890, , 22
Murphy, John, 1886, 1895, parents: Jeremiah and Josephine Murphy, 22
Murphy, Ruth, 1893, 1895, , 22
Nass, Albert, 1890, 1896, father: Theodore, 71
Nass, Frederick, 1889, 1896, mother died 2 1/2 years prior, 71
Nass, Julius, 1893, 1896, parents of German origins, 71
O'Connor, William C., 1889, 1897, parents: Mary and William H. 2 other girls not admitted, 130
Ohlweiler, Emily, , 1896, parents: Charles and Mary Ohlweiler father deserted family, 32
Ohlweiler, Nicholas, , 1896, , 32
Owens, Bessie, 1894, 1898, parents: John and Emma, 198
Owens, Georgie, 1896, 1898, "grandmother Mary Berriman, 201 W. 80th St.", 198
Parr, Harry F., 1896, 1899, "parents: William and Florence father deserted family, Vincent 6 months", 239
Paul, Frederick, 1893, 1899, "parents: Annie and Frederic, father deserted family Harold, 4 yrs.", 243
Perdelwitz, Edgar, 1883, 1897, father sick and in Bellevue Hospital of German origin, 156-158
Perdelwitz, Selma, 1886, 1897, parents: Lillie and Edgar Perdelwitz, 156-158
Perry, Albert C., 1895, 1900, both were of English in origin, 279
Pfaff, Alice Clara, 1894, 1899, parents: William A. and Alvine (both German) father blind, 236
Phillips, Mary, 1889, 1896, parents: Samual and Matilda Phillips (father dead), 30
Ploch, Christina, 1886, 1898, parents: Charles and Pauline Ploch (both dead), 33

Portmau, Mary, 1887, 1896, parents: Anna and Joseph Portmau father doesn't support family, 115
Possenreid, Annie, 1894, 1896, "sister, Katie, 7 yrs. Not surrendered", 110
Possenreid, George, 1892, 1896, parents: Annie and Gerritt Possenreid father died of pneumonia, 110
Quigley, Albert, 1890, 1898, parents: William and Elizabeth, 191
Quigley, Laura, 1894, 1898, "father is a good man. The home is broken up.", 191
Quigley, Lester, 1891, 1898, mother was dying in St. Luke's Hosp. Of consumption of the spine, 191
Rahaim, George, 1888, 1896, "All children born in Farzeen, Mt. Lebanon, Syria", 105
Rahaim, Peter, 1892, 1896, "taken temporarily", 105
Rahaim, Tom, 1886, 1896, both parents deceased father: Abdalla R., 105
Rainbird, Ethel, 1893, 1897, parents: Maggie and Robert Rainbird, 122
Rathke, Ernest, 1891, 1896, "Own mother dead-step mother abusive", 43
Rathke, Ernest, 1891, 1897, "previously committed Vol. 4, pg. 226", 159
Rathke, Lizzie, 1889, 1896, parents: Ernest and Marie Roberts, 43
Rathke, Lizzie, 1888, 1897, parents: Ernest and Marie R. (mother dead) step mother abusive, 159
Reilly, Agnes, , 1898, parents: Frank and Hannah, 195
Reilly, Fannie, , 1898, "Catholic, mother ill", 195
Reilly, Irene, , 1898, , 195
Reilly, Mary, , 1898, mother at Columbus Hosp. 226 E. 20th St., 195
Reilly, Winnifred, , 1898, mothers real address was 221 W. 62nd St., 195
Reubli, Fred, 1890, 1895, parents born in Switzerland, 18
Reubli, Rosina, 1888, 1895, parents: Emil and Rosina Reubli, 18
Rice, Ralph, 1891, 1897, parents: Robert and Ida Rice mother left family 4 times, 154
Rich, Harry, 1895, 1897, "a baby, 6 months old, not committed", 170
Rich, Charles, 1893, 1897, "parents: Abraham and Maggie Rich, mother deserted family", 170
Richards, Kenny, 1893, 1896, parents: Rosa and Henry Richards, 68
Riess, August, 1889, 1896, parents: Bertha and step father Leo Riess mother died, 112
Roos, Hazel, 1887, 1896, "Dismissed Sept. 24. Paid $30.00", 76
Roos, Mabel, 1885, 1896, parents: Clarence and Mollie Roos, 76
Rosenlicht, Annie, 1889, 1897, parents: Christina and John (both died), 177

Rosenlicht, Martha, 1894, 1897, “committed by a step-mother, parents of German origin”, 177

Roseu, Julia, , 1897, “Jewish-” not counted. . .sent back Sept. 14 ‘97”, 172

Roseu, Julia, , 1897, , 176

Roseu, Moses, , 1897, two other children at home, 172

Roseu, Rosie, , 1897, “children were in NY Infant Asylum, transferred by State Board”, 176

Ross, Lizzie, 1891, 1899, “father: Alexander, mother dead, father is a drunk”, 225

Saebold, Alice, 1861?, 1897, parents: Lena and Leonard father deserted family, 151

Saebold, Frieda, 1888, 1897, parents: Lena and John (father died 1892), 150

Schmidt, Ernest, 1894, 1898, parents: Herman and Lena father deserted family, 206

Schmidt, Walter, 1895, 1898, mother lived at 344 Pleasant Ave. , 206

Schnabel, Bertha, 1891, 1897, parents from Germany, 131

Schnabel, Lizzie, 1889, 1897, parents: Mary and John (dead), 131

Schwitzer, Annie, 1888, 1896, parents: Thomas and Anna Schwitzer (died of consumption) sister Minnie , 62

Scrobliss, Elfreda, 1881, 1896, parents: Emma and Martin Scrobliss (German), 103

Sealer, Mary, 1893, 1899, “parents: Mary and Henry, three other children”, 252

Seeger, Dorothy N., 1896, 1898, parents: Wm (German) and Dorothy (Swiss), 215

Sellers, Elizabeth, 1892, 1896, parents: Nellie and Frank Sellers (deceased) Lizzie Hemmer had care of her, 107

Semming, Amelia, 1894, 1896, father is on Wards Island, 87

Semming, Sophia, 1893, 1896, parents: Pauline and Robert Semming, 87

Shaw, Emma, 1888, 1896, parents: Sydney and Nellie Shaw father deserted family, 80

Shaw, Mollie, 1890, 1896, brother or sister listed as Marion, 80

Shrug, Charlotte, 1892, 1898, “parents: Philip and Louisa, sister Lizzie 8yrs, not admitted”, 214

Silfuerburg, Alma, 1885, 1896, parents: Catherine and Eric Silfuerburg (both deceased), 113

Skogland, Dagmar, 1891, 1899, parents: John and Christina (mother died), 240

Skogland, Ethel, 1896, 1899, 5 children still home, 240

Smith, Bertha, 1895, 1898, “father was German, mother was English”, 204

Smith, Elsa, 1893, 1898, parents: Charles and Emily, 204

Smith, Emma, 1894, 1898, “father in Navy, gone to war”, 204

Sonneborn, Adolphine, 1898, 1895, parents: Ida and Hilton Sonneborn, 25

Sonneborn, Hilton, 1890, 1895, mother confined father unemployed, 25

Stanley, Annie, 1890, 1897, , 144

Stanley, Lizzie, 1886, 1897, parents: Robert and Lizzie (deceased), 144

Stein, Willard, 1891, 1895, "parents: Mary and Willard Stein-taken until January 10, 1896", 24

Steinmetz, Madeline, 1896, 1899, parents: Christina and John abandoned by parents to Nellie Twokig, 230

Stern, Lavina, 1894, 1899, "parents: William and Tilly, two brothers, William and Arthur", 233

Stork, Lillie, 1892, 1895, , 4

Stork, Minnie, 1889, 1895, , 4

Stuhm, Carrie, 1893, 1896, both parents born in Germany, 75

Stuhm, Ellie, 1890, 1896, parents: Bertha and Andrew Stuhm father died in 1893, 75

Stuhm, Sophia, 1891, 1896, "2 sisters not surrendered Annie, 19 and Becky, 12", 75

Sullivan, May, 1896, 1899, parents: Annie and Jeremiah (father died), 249

Summers, Lilly, 1887, 1896, parents: Mary and Edward Summers, 57

Summers, Mary, 1890, 1896, , 57

Sutton, Harry, 1883, 1896, parents: Eleanor and Frederick Thomas Sutton (deceased), 52

Swallow, Florence, 1890, 1898, parents: Jane and William father deserted family 3yrs. Ago, 180

Swallow, Mabel, 1895, 1898, "mother from Wales, father from England", 180

Swift, George, 1892, 1898, , 209

Swift, Renie, 1889, 1898, "parents: William and Alice, Catholic", 209

Tabib, Aziz, 1893, 1896, parents: Mary and Sarkik Tabib-taken temporarily, 93

Talbot, Marion, 1897, 1900, parents: Theresa and Edward (father died 2 yrs ago), 278

Thomson, Woodward, 1891, 1896, parents: Sarah and Frank Thomson (deceased), 29

Thorndike, Marguerite, 1892, 1900, parents: Hannah and James E. father died, 273

Tommasini, Santina, 1893, 1896, parents: Maria and Santina from Itlay`, 41

Tontjeau, Grace, , 1896, one brother not surrendered, 79

Tontjeau, Robert, , 1896, "children taken temporarily-father is a Reverend", 79

Tontjeau, Susie, , 1896, parents: L. Vartau M. and Lucie V. Tontjeau, 79

Tracy, Joseph, 1897, 1899, Catholic, 248

Tracy, Thomas, 1895, 1899, "parents: Delia and James taken temp., father ill", 248

Trautor, Mabel, 1893, 1896, parents: William and Louisa Trautor, 17 month sibling, 46

Treu, Laura, 1891, 1896, “a son, Edward, 2 yrs, not surrendered”, 90

Treu, Louisa, 1889, 1896, parents: Edward and Wilhemina (dead) father unemployed, 90

Turk, Edward, 1892, 1896, parents: Julius and Matilda Turk father unemployed, 47

VanWickleu, John, 1893, 1896, parents: Anna and John L. VanWickleu father deserted, 101

Vautrim, Alfred, 1890, 1895, parents: Victor and Octava Vautrim (deceased), 9

Vautrim, Octava, 1892, 1895, of French origin, 9

Veighler, Susan, 1895, 1899, “no known family, found in a hallway in Greenwich St.”, 217

Volker, Frances, 1891, 1897, “parents: Henry and Prudence, father blind, 5 Pts House of Industry”, 175

Wade, Lulu, 1885, 1898, “parents: Estelle and Robert, mother in Bellevue, 5 other siblings”, 187

Wagner, Ella, 1894, 1900, “parents: Frank and Hannah, deserted by parents”, 259

Wagner, Emma, 1892, 1900, parents: Anna and Conrad (mother ill), 270

Wagner, Harry, 1898, 1900, “sister, 3 months, on Ward’s Island”, 259

Walker, Frank, 1890, 1896, parents: Mary and Daniel Walker (died 1893), 92

Wallace, Ada, , 1898, “(mother died) see pg. 182, brother and sister”, 185

Wallace, Grace, 1894, 1897, mother from Germany, 168

Wallace, James, 1892, 1897, parents: Mary and Frances father at King’s Park Insane Asylum, 168

Wallace, John, , 1898, “parents: Maggie and John, mother died and father drank”, 182

Wallace, Lizzie, , 1898, “sent by Rev. Mr. Forbes of 30th St. Church, went there to S.S.”, 182

Wallace, William, 1897, 1899, “mother: Bertha E. Strange, child given for adoption”, 232

Wallace, William Edward, 1892, 1896, parents: Mary and William Wallace father deserted family, 111

Walsh, Joseph, 1893, 1896, parents: Margaret and Thomas Walsh (died 1894), 42

Wanner, Emma, 1894, 1897, “12 yr. Old sister, Annie, not committed, German in origin”, 171

Wanner, Ernest, 1892, 1897, “parents: Christina and Ernest, father died 1896”, 171

Ward, Charles, 1893, 1896, parents: Frank and Mary Ward abandoned with a Kate Kearney, 63

Watts, Agnes, 1887, 1895, , 3

Watts, James, 1889, 1895, , 3
Watts, Jeannette, 1891, 1895, , 3
Watts, Rubina, 1886, 1895, father and mother born in Scotland, 3
Webb, Fella, 1888, 1899, parents: Fred and Emily, 234
Webb, Fred, 1894, 1899, father lived at 633 E. 183rd St., 234
Webb, John R., 1897, 1899, "parents: Fred and Emily, mother ill gone to Ward's Island", 241
Webb, Lola, 1890, 1899, "mother was ill, gone to Ward's Island", 234
Webb, Sybil, 1892, 1899, "father from England, mother from Canada", 234
Webb, William, 1895, 1899, , 234
Wehlbyrg, Alice Louisa, 1895, 1898, parents: Lillian and John father died 1896, 216
Weidling, Archer, 1890, 1896, taken temp. for mother to have operation, 88
Weidling, Archer, 1890, 1897, "were there previously, Aug. 1896, pg. 88", 157
Weidling, Lester, 1888, 1896, parents: Charles G. and Ida Weidling, 88
Weidling, Lester, 1888, 1897, parents: Charles and Ida Weidling taken temp., 157
Weithe (Braun), Emma, 1887, 1896, mother: Annie Weithe, 65
Weschler, Becky, 1892, 1896, parents: Dora and Jacob Weschler father deserted family, 69
White, Alberta, 1891, 1897, unmarried mother: Sophia Grufe committed suicide, 164
Williams, Edward, 1892, 1899, "parents: Cora and Charles Linnekiu, trouble in family", 235
Williams, Florence, 1894, 1897, parents: Robert and Mary Williams father deserted family-no home, 165
Wilson, Frances, 1893, 1895, mother was living at 100 W. 89th St., 16
Wilson, Frances, 1892, 1897, "Bertram, 7months, still at home", 173
Wilson, Hazel, 1893, 1895, "Brought by Officer King", 2
Wilson, Ida, 1888, 1895, parents: Charles and Frances Wilson, 16
Wilson, Ida, 1888, 1897, "parents: Frances and Charles, destitute", 173
Wolf, Elsie, 1882, 1895, born in Germany, 11
Woods, Ella, 1893, 1898, "mother, Irish, father from Australia", 202
Woods, Thomas, 1890, 1898, "parents: Lizzie and Henry, father to Cuba in the Army", 202
Worre, Lauretta, 1883, 1896, "mother: Hannah Worre "has conjunctivitis trachmatosa", 45

AMERICAN FEMALE GUARDIAN SOCIETY
HOME FOR THE FRIENDLESS
VOLUME 12

Ahlf, Chrissie, 1898, 1902, parents: Theodore and Barbara 2 siblings already admitted, 106
Ahlf, Dora, , 1902, "sister, Chrissie not surrendered", 96
Ahlf, Theodore, 1897, 1902, parents: Theodore (dead) and Barbara, 96
Ahrens, Adaline, 1893, 1903, , 216
Ahrens, Blanche, 1897, 1903, , 216
Ahrens, Dorothy, 1898, 1903, , 216
Ahrens, Henry, 1892, 1903, parents: Adaline (ill) and Henry C. (dead) , 216
Albrecht, Bertha, 1898, 1903, joined 3 siblings admitted in 1902, 182
Albrecht, Freddie, 1891, 1902, parents: Fred K. and Mary, 167
Albrecht, Henry, 1896, 1902, , 167
Albrecht, Susie, 1892, 1902, both parents from Germany, 167
Albrecht, Willie, 1894, 1902, mother died Oct. 1902, 167
Allen, John H., 1897, 1903, , 241
Allen, Walter, 1900, 1903, , 241
Allen, William E., 1895, 1903, parents: George and Elizabeth (mother died May 1903), 241
Alling, Charles, 1893, 1902, "parents: John and Jane 3 siblings (John, Lillian, and Wm.) not in home", 104
Amebec, Yvonne, 1896, 1903, parents: Marie and Marcisse of France, 211
Anderson, Dorothy, 1896, 1901, parents: Olivia and August father disappeared, 79
Anderson, Ethel, 1897, 1901, both parents from Sweden, 79
Annabee, Lucieu?, 1899, 1903, parents: Marie and Narcisse from France, 217
Augelo, Rafael, 1893, 1902, parents: Paul and Rosa (mother died 7yrs. prior), 166
Beers, Emma M., 1899, 1903, parents: Emily and Charles father gone to Colorado, 168
Benson, Eva, 1897, 1902, parents: John (dead) and Christina (ill) both from Sweden, 99
Benson, John, 1898, 1902, , 99
Biele, Frank, 1897, 1903, the boys were taken for 2wks. While mother went to the country, 210
Biele, Harry, 1894, 1903, parents: Theodore (dead) and Clara (ill), 210
Blomquist, Carl Arthur, 1898, 1903, , 235
Blomquist, Gertrude E., 1896, 1903, , 235

Blomquist, Ida C., 1892, 1903, parents: Charles and Mary Swedish, 235

Bobbe, Christopher, 1896, 1900, parents: Ella and Claus (father died), 21

Boeckman, Bertha Smith, 1896, 1903, "father from Germany, mother from England", 170

Boeckman, Clara, 1897, 1901, "parents: Emily and Carl brother, Ernest 8 months still home", 59

Boeckman, Elsie Smith, 1893, 1903, parents: Emily and Charles father murdered mother, 170

Bogland, Fritz, 1897, 1903, parents: Anna and Christian (father died 1899) Swedish, 249

Brimeu, Edgar, 1895, 1901, , 55

Brimeu, John, 1896, 1901, parents: Fred K. and Elizabeth (mother died Easter Sunday), 55

Bruce, William, 1899, 1903, parents: Jennie (Irish) and William (English) father died, 181

Brunner, Margaret, 1892, 1902, parents: Fred K. and Margaret, 118

Brunner, Robert, , 1902, brother Fred K. not surrendered, 118

Bunhardi, Conrad, 1897, 1903, "1 sister, Annie 4 yrs. Living with an uncle", 229

Bunhardi, William, 1895, 1903, parents: Wm. And Mary (mother died Aug 1902) father hurt, 229

Burnham, William George, 1895, 1901, parents: Cornelia and Newell father deserted family, 46

Burtt, Mary E., 1896, 1902, parents: George W. and Minerva M. (mother is intemperate), 128

Cadieux, George, 1896, 1903, parents: Clarence and Madeline mother is intemperate, 205

Casson, Robert, 1897, 1901, "parents: Robert and Mabel one brother David, not admitted", 48

Chambers, Clara, 1893, 1902, parents: Randolph and Elizabeth (deceased) Children's Fold, 141

Chaminade, Arlene, 1894, 1903, "brother, Leon, not surrendered", 198

Chaminade, Vera, 1891, 1903, parents: Katherine and Augustus, 198

Christian, Ormond, 1893, 1903, "mother from Ireland, father from NY State", 195

Christian, William, 1891, 1903, parents: Maggie and Wm., 195

Clark, Alex K., 1893, 1902, parents: Catherine and John (father died July 1901), 97

Clark, Samual, 1895, 1902, other siblings Manice and Mary not surrendered, 97

Cummings, John, 1896, 1900, grandmother resides at 176 Madison St., 19

Cummings, Robert, 1894, 1900, "Margaret Hurley. Grandmother, brought children ", 19

Cummings, William, 1891, 1900, parents: Margaret (ill) and Robert (dead), 19

Davis, Charles L., 1896, 1903, parents: Florence and William Henry (father died 1900), 188

Davis, Dorothy M., 1900, 1903, siblings not admitted-Mildred and Sybill, 188

Davis, Hubert V., 1898, 1903, both parents were from England, 188

Davis, Mildred, 1893, 1903, parents: Florence and Wm. Henry (father died), 202

Davis, Sybil, , 1903, other siblings already at Home, 202

Diringer, Annie, 1898, 1902, , 109

Diringer, Charles, 1896, 1902, , 109

Diringer, Louisa, 1895, 1902, mother from Mass. And father from Germany, 109

Diringer, Richard, 1894, 1902, parents: Mary and Charles (father died), 109

Dodge, Jennie, 1896, 1901, parents: Edward and Pearl (father died), 93

Doe, Jane, 1898, 1900, " Jane Doe #12- "no proof of guardianship", 20

Doe, John, 1896, 1900, John Doe #47 found on street, 18

Donnelly, Frank, 1897, 1901, "Marine Hospital at Staten Island", 77

Donnelly, Jennie, 1894, 1901, "parents: Jennie and Wm. Sister Mary, 13yrs", 77

Donnelly, John, 1895, 1902, parents: John and Lillie (mother dead), 114

Donnelly, Minnie, 1897, 1902, , 114

Dowling, Lawrence, 1897, 1900, parents: Frances and John (Catholic) father doesn't support family, 4

Downey, John, 1894, 1900, "baby, 15 months still of the home", 13

Downey, Walter, 1896, 1900, father lived at 414 W. 49th St., 13

Downey, William, 1882, 1900, parents: John P. and Margaret (mother was intemperate), 13

Dreukerd, Johanna, 1897, 1901, parents: Frank and Margaretta, 74

Dublan, Ignacio, 1895, 1903, parents: Jane and Ignacio father was Mexican, 186

Dublan, John, 1898, 1903, "siblings not admitted-Carman, 11 and Beatrice, 10", 186

Dumont, Rene, 1897, 1903, "mother: Juliette 'immoral' brought by officer from Socy. PCC", 215

Emerson, Eleanor Henrietta, 1897, 1901, parents: John and Bridget (mother died), 70

Emsou, Charles, 1898, 1900, parents: Charles and Isabelle (died June 10), 27

Erikson, Mary, 1890, 1903, parents: Fannie and Andrew from Finland-brought by Socy. PCC, 203

Farnum, James, 1898, 1901, both parents from Ireland, 65

Farnum, John, 1897, 1901, parents: Margaret and James father deserted family, 65

Fauner, May, 1892, 1903, parents: Jacob (dead) and Martha (ill) siblings-Harry and Victoria, 207
Fecker, Conrad, 1896, 1900, , 11
Fenton, John, 1900, 1903, parents: Mary and Joseph not proper guardianship, 222
Fenton, May, 1894, 1903, , 223
Ferguson, George, 1893, 1903, parents: Margaret and Thomas (father is a drunk), 226
Ferguson, Maggie, 1894, 1903, "mother from Scotland, father from Ireland", 226
Ferguson, Willie, 1896, 1903, , 226
Finn, George, 1892, 1902, George previously committed-dismissed to mother 1897, 131
Finn, William, 1894, 1902, parents: Bertha and George father deserted family, 131
Fisher, Edith, 1888, 1900, , 10
Fisher, Mary, 1891, 1901, parents: Albert and Mary (mother died), 57
Fisher, Wlater, 1895, 1901, both parents from Switzerland, 57
FitzPatrick, Eddie, 1896, 1901, parents: Mary and Patrick (Irish) father away in England, 66
Foell, Helena, 1895, 1901, parents: Theodore (Germany) and Louisa (Denmark), 92
Forbes, Maxwell, 1897, 1903, parents: Charles and Alta father intemperate, 230
Forbes, Maxwell H., 1897, 1903, parents: Alta and Charles (father intemperate), 179
Forbes, Stanley, 1898, 1903, "brother Harlow, 10yrs. Not committed", 179
Forbes, Stanley, 1898, 1903, "brother, Harlow, 11yrs. Not surrendered", 230
Foru, Herman, 1900, 1902, "parents: Mary and Herman, sister Mabel in Home", 117
Foru, Mabel B., 1895, 1902, parents: Mary and Herman (father died 1900) brother Herman 2yrs., 98
Foster, Jennie, 1896, 1901, "sister, Florence, 4mo. Still of the home", 88
Foster, May, 1894, 1901, parents: James and Jennie father out of work, 88
Foulau, Pauline, 1896, 1903, parents: Charles Blomquist (stepfather) and Mary, 237
Frank, Herbert, 1895, 1902, parents: Charles and Annie, 113
Frost, George, 1900, 1903, siblings not surrendered-Chester and Mildred, 185
Frost, Herbert, 1898, 1903, parents: George W. and Clara E. (mother deserted family), 185
Fuhrer, Isabelle, 1891, 1901, parents: Peter and Amelia (father deceased), 71

Garabadiau, Jacob, , 1900, parents: Kirkon Garabadiau and Julia Salem (mother dead), 44

Gesner, Frank, 1895, 1902, , 154

Gesner, Peter, 1890, 1902, parents: Marian and Peter D. Children's Fold to Juv. Asylum, 154

Gesner, William, 1893, 1902, "3 other siblings-Howard, Marian, and Florence not admitted", 154

Giavin, Frederick J., 1891, 1903, parents: James P. and Ada (mother died) English, 178

Glick, Anna, 1893, 1903, parents: Bertha (ill) and Max (dead), 221

Golden, Daniel, 1893, 1903, parents: Carrie and James (father died) 3 siblings, 248

Golden, Edna, 1898, 1903, parents: Carrie and James Henry (father dead), 200

Golden, Martha, 1892, 1902, parents: James and Caroline (father dead) Children's Fold, 138

Gray, Robert, 1899, 1902, parents: Kate and Thomas (father died), 148

Green, Grant, 1893, 1903, siblings-Catherine and Joel,

Green, John, 1890, 1903, parents: Joe and Grant father doesn't support family, 191

Green, Margaret, 1892, 1902, parents: Tillie and Sydney (father died) mother sick with malaria, 105

Guckenbichl, Irene, 1898, 1902, parents: Peter and Bertha (mother died over a yr. Before), 125

Guckenbichl, Peter, 1894, 1902, "sister, Mary, 13yrs., not surrendered", 125

Gundlack, Dora, 1898, 1903, , 171

Gundlack, George, 1894, 1903, parents: Wm. And Dora mother deserted family, 171

Gundlack, William, 1900, 1903, , 171

Hartman, Carrie, 1892, 1903, parents: Jacob and Sophie (both dead) German, 227

Hayden, Helen, 1894, 1901, parents: Annie and Edward both from Ireland baby (7mo) at home, 84

Heath, Mazie, 1893, 1902, parents: Edward (died insane) and Mary (ill), 100

Heide, Frank, 1895, 1900, surrendered after the death of their mother in 1898, 1

Heide, Grace, 1892, 1900, "sister to Viola, Frank and Mabel (pg. 1)", 16

Heide, Mabel, 1897, 1900, father lived at 63 Delaney St., 1

Heide, Viola, 1894, 1900, "parents: Frank and Nellie sister, Ella, 11yrs., not surrendered", 1

Hennedy, Beulah, 1898, 1901, parents: Frances and SL Kennedy, 61

Herbert, Oscar, 1897, 1900, parents: William H. and Lena mother deserted family, 40

Hoffman, Howard, 1896, 1901, parents: Maggie and Lewis father suicidal and abusive, 52

Hogarty, Mary, 1890, 1900, "mother Mary from Ireland-2 sisters, 1 married, 2 intemperate brothers", 41

Hollenbeck, Russell, 1896, 1900, illegitimate child of Agnes Hollenbeck, 37

Holmes, Townley, 1897, 1902, parents: Grace and James H. (dead), 150

Hornbacker, Arthur, 1897, 1900, , 6

Hornbacker, Howard, 1899, 1902, parents: Adolf and Matilda 4 siblings already in Home, 102

Hornbacker, John, 1893, 1900, "sibling: Amelia and Howard, not surrendered", 6

Hornbacker, Mabel, 1895, 1900, their uncle surrendered them-he lived at 406 2nd Ave., 6

Hornbacker, Mamie, 1891, 1900, parents: Adolf and Matilda (mother deceased), 6

Howell, Florence, 1897, 1900, parents: Carrie and George father deserted family, 34

Howell, John, 1898, 1901, parents: Carrie and George father in the army. Mother at service, 51

Hubenthal, Otto, 1895, 1903, parents: Eliza and Elias (mother ill) German, 233

Jackson, Ethel M., 1893, 1903, no proof of gaurdianship, 204

Jensen, Carlowe, 1894, 1900, "siblings: boy, 12, girls 14 and 16", 32

Jensen, Katie, 1891, 1900, parents: Mariqu and Peter (father intemperate), 32

Johnston, Blanche, 1895, 1901, parents: Mary and Samual (father in jail) baby 14mo. Home, 69

Kampf, Henry, 1900, 1902, parents: Antonia and Henry (paralyzed in Hosp.) German, 130

Keating, Louisa, 1893, 1902, parents: Lillie and Patrick (father died 1901), 123

Kelly, Mayfield, 1897, 1901, "parents: Lulu and C. Holman, daughter Bessie, 8mo., home", 62

Kersten, Katie, 1893, 1901, parents: August and Katie (both died) both from Germany, 90

Kingsland, Edna, 1896, 1902, "brother, Walter, not committed", 149

Kingsland, Emma, 1897, 1902, brought by Bureau of Dependent Children, 149

Kingsland, Harry, 1892, 1902, parents: Alice and Frank, 149

Kirschner, George, , 1902, parents: Charles and Arjunda (mother insane) all from Russia, 155

Knaff (Knapp?), Madeline, 1898, 1901, parents: Ida and Eugene mother abandoned family, 75

Knight, Irene, 1894, 1900, parents: Lottie C. and Ira father deserted family, 7

Knight, Irene, 1894, 1903, "parents: Lottie C, and Ida taken temp.", 194
Knight, Lawrence, 1895, 1900, parents born in Mass., 7
Kuhlmaier, Anthonie, 1895, 1901, "father from Germany, mother from Prussia", 82
Kuhlmaier, Pauline, 1894, 1901, parents: Henry (died Apr. 1901) and Mary (died June 1901), 82
LaFarge, Randolph, 1896, 1903, 2 sisters-Bessie and Lottie, 213
LaFarge, Whillett, 1894, 1903, parents: Randolph L. and Elizabeth (mother died), 213
Laird, Gertrude, 1899, 1903, parents: Frederick and Marie father doesn't support family, 251
Lamplugh, Dorothy, 1896, 1903, parents: Anna Wheatly and Benjammine Lamplugh, 225
Lamplugh, Robert, 1899, 1903, "Ruth, 9yrs. and John 2 yrs. not surrendered", 225
Lamplugh, Willie, 1897, 1903, father is ill and mother must support herself, 225
Langmichael, Tillie, 1892, 1900, "parents: Wm. and Tillie from Germany, mother died, brother Albert", 5
Law, Gwendolin, 1896, 1902, "mother: Margaret Law "mother in an immoral woman-is now in jail", 127
Lods, Emile, 1899, 1901, , 85
Lods, Emily, 1898, 1901, , 85
Lorrain, Hilda, 1899, 1903, "alias: Hilda Graham" brought by Socy. PCC", 208
Lovett, James, 1898, 1902, "Father was brought up in the Sheltering Arms", 122
Lovett, Robert, 1900, 1903, mother died May 1902-James and Thomas Lovett in Home, 218
Lovett, Thomas, 1896, 1902, parents: Thomas and Catherine mother died, 122
Lum, George Albert, 1896, 1902, parents: Albert Clark and Jennie (mother died 1902), 121
Lunney, Amelia, 1890, 1902, "parents: John and Emma (mother died) 2 brothers, 18 and 20", 115
Lunney, Walter, 1892, 1902, , 115
Magnusson, John, , 1900, parents: John and Christina a 325 Brook Ave., 8
Marcoe, Edmund J., 1898, 1900, unmarried parents: Mary Marcoe and John P. Kana, 42
Marcotte, Margaret, 1898, 1901, "mother is with EF Lang Tammersville, NY (June 12, 01)", 87
Marcotte, Ruth, 1894, 1901, parents: Bella and Oscar (father dead), 87
Matthaus, Olga, 1892, 1901, parents: Emil and Annie (father died) mother headed back to Sweden, 81
McArthur, John, 1895, 1901, Scottish, 50

McAusland, Margaret, 1896, 1900, parents: Charles and Mary father deserted family, 3
McCracken, Maggie, 1893, 1903, "brought by Socy. PCC-brother, 13 yrs. still there", 219
McCracken, Mary, 1890, 1903, parents: Harry and Josephine not proper guardianship, 219
McGowan, Mary Frances, 1897, 1902, parents: Harry (dead) and Winifred (ill) brother Harry, 107
McGrath, Eileeu, 1896, 1901, parents: Annie and Richard father went insane and wouldn't support family, 67
McIlveau, Flora, 1897, 1900, parents: Lilian and Joseph previously admitted April 1900, 31
McIlveau, William, 1898, 1900, "dismissed to mother, 265 W. 38th St. March 20, 1901", 31
McKay, Harry, 1895, 1902, , 112
McKay, James, 1894, 1902, parents: Mary (Ireland) and John (NYC), 112
McKenna, Margaret, 1897, 1900, parents: Elizabeth and James, 23
McKenna, Margaret, 1897, 1900, found in a saloon with mother (Elizabeth) who had been in a fight, 39
McKeon, Lizzie, 1894, 1901, , 91
McKeon, Maggie, 1889, 1901, parents: Michael and Emma, 91
McKeon, Mary, 1892, 1901, , 91
McKeon, Nellie, 1897, 1901, , 91
McKeou, Lizzie, 1894, 1900, , 38
McKeou, Maggie, 1889, 1900, parents: Emma and Michael, 38
McKeou, Mary, 1892, 1900, , 38
McKeou, Nellie, 1897, 1900, , 38
McNeil, Andrew, 1891, 1901, parents: John and Christina, 94
McNeil, William, 1897, 1901, "brother, James, called in Nov. 1902", 94
Melville, Charles, 1895, 1902, parents: Hilda and Charles sister Hulda not surrendered, 108
Mertens, Erna, 1891, 1903, father dead-for temp. vacation for mother, 242
Messner, Louis, 1898, 1900, "sister, Elsie, already there", 26
Miller, Bessie, 1891, 1900, parents: Elizabeth and John, 35
Miller, Edith, 1894, 1902, parents: John and Katherine improper guardianship, 160
Miller, Joseph, 1899, 1902, "parents: Maggie (dead) and George sister Lottie, 5yrs", 136
Miller, Mary, 1893, 1902, parents: Peter and Rose (father died) 2 other children-Bertha and James, 157
Miller, Minnie, 1898, 1903, parents: Vigo Miller and Murial Ehrickson, 244
Miller, Pauline M., 1893, 1903, parents: Theresa and Arthur father deserted family, 199
Miller, Willie, 1897, 1903, parents: Annie and Charles father doesn't support family, 224

Mills, Roger, 1893, 1902, parents: Angelina and Joaquin (mother died 8 yrs. ago), 151
Mirou, Amelia, 1899, 1903, no proper guardianship sent by officer from Socy. PCC, 174
Mobert, Elsie, 1891, 1900, parents: Max and Adelaide (mother died), 36
Mobert, Freda, 1893, 1900, parents of German decent, 36
Mobert, Helen, 1896, 1900, father resides at 314 W. 39th St., 36
Moercher, August, 1894, 1900, parents: Ernest and Blanche (mother confined in hospital), 14
Moercher, Elenora, 1898, 1900, "father from Germany, mother from England", 14
Moessner, Elsie, 1893, 1900, parents: Louisa and Louis father died 1898 both from Austria, 9
Monahau, Patrice, 1897, 1901, parents: Statia and Michael 6 other children, 78
Monahau, William, 1898, 1901, parents: Helen and Patrick both parents deserted child to grandmother, 56
Montrose, Leora, 1890, 1902, , 110
Moore, Harry, 1897, 1900, "parents: Katherine and Harry, mother his a sick baby", 29
Morau, Margaret, 1893, 1900, "parents: Mary and Derius (father dead) "Dis. to mother Oct. 25", 22
Morningstar, Kathleen, 1897, 1902, parents: Lizzie and Wm. (father died), 153
Morris, Agnes, 1897, 1901, parents: Agnes and Wm. father died and family is very poor, 89
Muller, Harry, 1898, 1902, parents: John O. and Marie of Denmark, 103
Neidhardt, Alex, 1899, 1903, parents: Annie and Christopher (father died 1898), 193
Neubauer, George, 1900, 1903, parents: Michael and Hannah father deserted family, 245
Norris, Mamie, 1890, 1902, parents: James H. and Kate brought by Socy. PCC for petit larceny, 119
Olds, Doris C., 1892, 1902, "parents: JB and Minnie, has 2 brothers not committed", 133
Palm, Lizzie, 1896, 1901, brought by officer from Socy. PCC, 63
Patterson, Bessie, 1897, 1902, parents: George and Agnes (mother intemperate), 158
Patterson, Helen, 1894, 1901, parents: Helen and Henry (father deceased), 68
Patterson, Robert, 1899, 1902, both parents are Scotch, 158
Patterson, William, 1900, 1902, , 158
Paul, Harold, 1896, 1900, "parents: Annie and William, brother Fred K. already there", 24
Pavellac, Barbara, 1898, 1902, parents from Bohemia, 162
Pavellac, Bertha, 1900, 1902, "siblings still of the home-Annie, Mary and Josie", 162

Pavellac, William, 1897, 1902, parents: Wm. and Barbara (mother died Sept 1902), 162

Peacock, Esther L., 1894, 1903, parents: Hugh and Enelsie (mother in jail), 234

Pearce, Eva, 1890, 1902, mother: Mary Pearce Children's Fold, 146

Perry, Calvin, , 1902, , 129

Perry, Helen G., 1897, 1902, parents: Wm. and Marian E. (mother died), 144

Perry, Marian E., 1891, 1902, parents: Wm. B. and Marian E. (mother died), 129

Peter, Arthur, 1896, 1903, parents: Peter and Josephine parents dead-brought by sister, 184

Pollard, Archibald, 1899, 1900, both parents from England, 33

Pollard, Daisy, 1894, 1900, parents: Frederick and Louisa (mother deceased), 33

Pornlesou, Hazel, , 1903, "brother, Herbert, 14yrs. Not admitted", 176

Pornlesou, Mabel, 1892, 1903, father: Raymond A. mother deserted family, 176

Pornlesou, Ross, , 1903, both parents from NJ, 176

Prockel, Edward, , 1902, brought by woman from Randall's Island, 164

Prother?, Harold, 1899, 1901, parents: Eugene (died) and Jennie illegitimate child, 58

Purcell, Charles, 1893, 1901, "parents: Ellen and Peter "Dis. To mother 1908", 53

Purcell, Charles, 1893, 1901, parents: Ellen and Peter mother had consumption, 76

Purcell, Josephine, 1897, 1901, parents both from Ireland and Catholic, 53

Purcell, Josephine, 1897, 1901, was here before, 76

Radisch, Elsie, 1892, 1902, parents: August and Henrietta (father dead) Children's Fold, 137

Reavy, Sally, 1893, 1902, parents: Alexander and Jeannette Children's Fold, 143

Redmond, Charles Henry, 1895, 1903, parents: Charles and Emily-2 children already in Home, 228

Redmond, Geoffrey, 1898, 1903, parents: Charles and Emily, 173

Redmond, Josephine, 1894, 1902, parents: Charles and Emily father deserted family Childrens Fold, 142

Ridge, Hazel, 1900, 1903, parents: Maud and Cecil father deserted family, 183

Riedell, Ethel, 1897, 1903, parents: Belle and Julius (father died), 209

Riedell, Gladys, 1898, 1903, , 209

Rohde, Frances, 1895, 1903, "3 brothers-Harry (6), Frank (8), Alfred (10), and 1 sister-Irene (4)", 247

Rohde, Meta, 1893, 1903, parents: Charles and Emma (father died in 1901), 247

Rosenfeld, Ernest, 1896, 1903, "parents: Edna and Adolph (mother died, father deserted)", 250

Ruff, Willie, 1895, 1902, parents: Mary and Christian (died) both from Germany, 111

Ruhl, Joseph, , 1902, parents: Martin and Ida (mother died 1901) sister-Mary deaf and dumb, 165

Schamm, Annie, 1898, 1902, , 132

Schamm, Lottie, , 1902, , 132

Schamm, Mary, 1896, 1902, "4 other children, John, David, Paul, and Wm. Not committed", 132

Schamm, Minnie, 1893, 1902, parents: Amelia and John (father died May 1902), 132

Schaulin, Herman, 1900, 1902, mother is insane and on Ward's Island, 152

Schaulin, Katie , 1896, 1902, parents: Emil (Swiss) and Lena (German), 152

Schriver, Annie, 1894, 1901, mother is insane and on Ward's Island, 83

Schriver, Emma, 1891, 1901, parents: Frederick and Mary both from Germany, 83

Schriver, Francis, 1899, 1901, , 83

Schriver, Freddie, 1896, 1901, father resided at 946 Columbus Ave., 83

Schultz, Louisa, 1894, 1900, , 12

Seabring, Cecilia, 1889, 1903, parents: Mary and Louis (father died) brought by Socy. PCC, 212

Seamau, Lillian, 1900, 1902, , 156

Seamau, Marguerite, 1898, 1902, parents: Lillian and George (mother is going to confinement), 156

Sharp, Bessie, 1898, 1903, parents: Edward and Mary, 201

Sharp, Florence, 1900, 1903, mother is intemperate-brought by Socy. PCC, 201

Shecler, Daniel, 1895, 1903, parents: George and Mary (mother died July 1902), 220

Shecler, Douglass, 1899, 1903, , 220

Shecler, George, 1897, 1903, , 220

Shofflin, Minnie, , 1901, notation about a Martha Rosenlicht, 72

Simon, Elroy, 1894, 1903, parents: Henry (deserted family) and Ruth (dead), 180

Simon, Idylene, 1895, 1903, "sisters-Madel, Gladys, and Alice not surrendered", 180

Skinner, Matilda, 1893, 1902, parents: Charlotte and James, 124

Smith, Bessie, 1899, 1903, parents: Katherine and Harry (father sick), 190

Smith, Edwin, 1895, 1901, Aunt Mary Carroll, 54

Smith, Gladys, 1896, 1902, parents: Lizzie and John father deserted family, 126

Smith, Harry, 1893, 1901, parents: Nora and Michael father doesn't support family, 54

Smith, John, 1899, 1902, parents: Fannie and Frank brought by officer, 120

Smith, Millicent, 1891, 1900, "parents: Josephine and Melville (father dead) sister, May, 11", 30

Smith, Robert, 1900, 1902, , 126

Smith, Virginia, 1899, 1902, 7mo. old baby not surrendered, 126

Smith, William, 1894, 1903, parents: Thomas and Ada (both dead), 189

Soffcke, George, 1897, 1901, parents: Celia and George, 49

Stein, Lavinia, 1893, 1902, parents: Wm. and Helen Children's Fold, 140

Steinmetz, Charles A., 1900, 1903, "wife is intemperate and immoral", 197

Steinmetz, William A., 1898, 1903, parents: Augustus and Jennie in process of divorce, 197

Stewert, Grace E., 1895, 1903, parents: Thomas C. and Martha (mother died Jan. 1903), 236

Stewert, Hazel F., 1898, 1903, parents both from Rhode Island, 236

Suffe, Adolf, 1893, 1903, parents: Adolf and Ella child ran away next day, 175

Sutton, Marvin Curtis, 1897, 1900, parents: Alice and Clarence, 43

Szucs, Helen, 1898, 1901, "unmarried mother, Frances Szucs from Hungary", 60

Tellman, Lars E., 1892, 1902, parents: Hedwig and Carl (father died) Swedish, 134

Tellman, Margaret, 1897, 1903, parents: Hedwig and Carl, 177

Thacher, Persis, 1894, 1902, no proper gaurdianship, 147

Thompson, James, 1896, 1902, parents: Robert and Kate (dead) improper guardianship, 161

Tingley, Spencer, 1896, 1900, "parents: Albert and Harriet father deserted family, mother had consumption", 15

Torello, Michaelina, 1895, 1901, parents: Baptiste and Theresa from Italy, 64

Torello, Prenzia, 1896, 1901, "brother, Maurice, of the home, 2 yrs.", 64

Traband, Gerald, 1899, 1903, "3 brothers-18, 16, 13 and 1 sister-11", 246

Traband, Luke, 1896, 1903, parents: Carrie and Louis (neither parent is well), 246

True., Willie, 1897, 1902, parents: Katie and Harry (father died 1899) siblings-Katie and Henry, 163

Ulrich, Lizzie, 1894, 1903, father: August mother dead, 192

Underhill, Elliott, 1893, 1902, parents: May and Alfred father doesn't support family, 116

Underhill, Ernest, 1895, 1902, , 116

Vaas, Eddie, 1891, 1902, parents: Anthony and Regina (mother died Feb. 1902), 101

Vaas, Julia, 1895, 1902, both parents from Germany, 101

Vaas, William, 1897, 1902, Catholic, 101

Valley, Jennie, 1893, 1902, parents: Walter and Jane (father dead) Children's Fold, 139
Valley, Stella, 1894, 1901, parents: Jane and Walter (father insane) 3 other children, 73
Vessella, Maria, 1900, 1903, parents: Amalia and Eurica (father dead) Italian, 240
Vogt, Oscar, 1897, 1902, parents: Annie and John (father died 1900) German, 135
Vogt, Oscar, 1897, 1903, parents: Annie and John (father died 1900) German, 252
Walker, Ethel, 1895, 1900, parents: Gertrude and Howard (father deceased), 2
Warlow, Charlie, 1897, 1900, parents: Clara and Allen father doesn't support family, 17
Washburn, Edward, 1896, 1902, parents: Arthur and Margaret (mother died 1901), 159
Washburn, Howard, 1898, 1902, 2 sisters still of the home, 159
Webb, John, 1897, 1900, parents: Fred (sick) and Emily (insane) brought for 2nd time, 45
Weickle, Adam, , 1903, parents: Adam and Madeline mother going into hospital, 196
Weickle, Edward, , 1903, , 196
Weickle, Geroge, , 1903, both parents from Germany, 196
Weiss, Louisa, 1890, 1901, parents: Bertha and Adam both from Germany, 86
Whitney, Seymour Judson, 1893, 1903, parents: Martina and Charles Wesley (father died 7yrs prior), 231
Wiener, Florence, 1892, 1903, parents: Annie and Victor (mother died July 1891), 239
Wiener, Victor, 1897, 1903, siblings-Edith 14yrs. and Violet 3 yrs. not admitted, 239
Will, Lillie, 1897, 1903, parents: Andrew and Augusta (both died), 206
Willard, Russell, 1898, 1901, parents: Edward and Louisa (mother died Dec. 1901), 95
Willard, Wallace, 1898, 1901, "twin to brother Russell-other siblings Louisa, Harry, and Edward", 95
Williams, Edith, 1892, 1903, parents: Ella and Edward (mother died 9 yrs. prior), 169
Williams, Ella, 1893, 1903, 3 other children at home, 169
Williams, Harry, 1899, 1903, , 243
Williams, Melvin, 1897, 1903, parents: Lottie and Henry, 243
Wilsey, Henry Tunisou, 1897, 1900, parents: Willard and Mary Tunisou Wilsey (mother neglectful), 28
Wood, Isabelle, 1895, 1902, parents: Isabelle and Lester (father died), 145
Wood, Mabel, 1889, 1903, parents: Mildred and Abraham improper guardianship, 172

Worley, Arthur, 1896, 1903, parents: Thomas and Isabelle (mother died Jan 1900), 187

Wright, Tillie, 1894, 1900, parents: Henry (German) and Annie (Irish) brother Harry, 25

Wychoff, Anna, 1897, 1903, parents: Catherine and Richard father doesn't support family, 238

Young, Henry, 1894, 1903, parents: Annie and Frederick father is in Manhattan Hosp., 232

Young, John, 1897, 1903, parents: Annie and Wm. James, 214

Young, Margaret, 1899, 1903, "brother, George 17mo. not surrendered", 214

Young, William, 1896, 1903, 4 other children, 232

AMERICAN FEMALE GUARDIAN SOCIETY
HOME FOR THE FRIENDLESS
ENTRANCE BOOK 13

Last Name, First name, , , , Page, Book, Ref.

Acker, Lulu, 1887, 1893, Parents: Henry and Harriet Acker, 2, Ent. Bk. 13, crt. 3.343

Acker, Willie, 1889, 1893, Parents: Henry and Harriet Acker, 2, Ent. Bk. 13, crt. 3.344

Albert, Louis, 1892, 1895, Parents: Isaac and Sarah Albert, 218, Ent. Bk. 13, crt. 4.127

Andre, Henry, 1887, 1894, brought by an officer, 167, Ent. Bk. 13, crt. 4.85

Arvonen, Arna, 1892, 1895, Parents: Victor and Arna Avonen, 282, Ent. Bk. 13, crt. 4.180

Arvonen, Warne, 1890, 1895, Parents: Victor and Arna Avonen, 282, Ent. Bk. 13, crt. 4.180

Aschenbach, Arthur, 1890, 1895, father leaving for Germany; mother deceased, 208, Ent. Bk. 13, temporary

Assmuss, Anna, 1881, 1895, father is in California; mother is deceased, 203, Ent. Bk. 13, crt. 4.116

Assmuss, Carl, 1888, 1895, , 291, Ent. Bk. 13, temporary

Assmuss, Elizabeth, 1886, 1895, father is in California; mother is deceased, 203, Ent. Bk. 13, crt. 4.116

Assmuss, Emma, 1885, 1895, father is in California; mother is deceased, 203, Ent. Bk. 13, crt. 4.116

Assmuss, Martha, 1887, 1895, , 291, Ent. Bk. 13, temporary

Banks, Edward, 1888, 1894, Parents: Edward and Maggie Banks, 174, Ent. Bk. 13, crt. 4.90

Banks, Winifred, 1891, 1894, Parents: Edward and Maggie Banks, 174, Ent. Bk. 13, crt. 4.90

Bannister, Lillie, 1892, 1894, Parents: William and Lillie Bannister, 146, Ent. Bk. 13, crt. 4.66

Barrat, Dolly, 1888, 1895, Parents: Robert (deceased) and Dora Barrat, 285, Ent. Bk. 13, crt. 4.183

Barrat, Robert, 1889, 1895, Parents: Robert (deceased) and Dora Barrat, 285, Ent. Bk. 13, crt. 4.183

Battersly, Elizabeth, 1885, 1893, Parents: William and Margaret Battersly, 62, Ent. Bk. 13, crt. 4.2

Battersly, Isabella, 1882, 1893, Parents: William and Margaret Battersly, 62, Ent. Bk. 13, crt. 4.2

Battersly, Minnie, 1891, 1894, Parents: William and Margaret Battersly, 83, Ent. Bk. 13, crt. 4.16

Battersly, William, 1888, 1893, Parents: William and Margaret Battersly, 62, Ent. Bk. 13, crt. 4.2

Bayer, Rudolph, 1890, 1894, father: William Bayer, 153, Ent. Bk. 13, crt. 4.72

Bayer, William, 1888, 1894, father: William Bayer, 153, Ent. Bk. 13, crt. 4.72

Beauman, Thomas, 1891, 1894, Parents: William and Virginia Beauman, 166, Ent. Bk. 13, crt. 4.84

Becker, Bertha, , 1895, Parents: Christopher and Katie (deceased) Becker, 230, Ent. Bk. 13, crt. 4.136

Becker, Louisa, , 1895, Parents: Christopher and Katie (deceased) Becker, 230, Ent. Bk. 13, crt. 4.136

Beckman, Morris, 1892, 1895, Parents: Jake and Jennie Beckman, 288, Ent. Bk. 13, crt. 4.186

Behrens, Henry, 1884, 1894, Parents: Paul and Fannie Behrens (both deceased), 184, Ent. Bk. 13, perm. 11.231

Bennett, Anita, 1881, 1893, Parents: Caleb (deceased) and Harriet Bennett, 55, Ent. Bk. 13, crt. 3.453

Bennett, Hattie, 1886, 1893, Parents: Caleb and Harriet Bennett, 117, Ent. Bk. 13, crt. 4.42

Bennett, Sarah, 1889, 1893, Parents: Caleb (deceased) and Harriet Bennett, 55, Ent. Bk. 13, crt. 3.453

Benson, Lillie, 1889, 1895, father cannot be found; mother in Bellevue Hospital, 194, Ent. Bk. 13, crt. 4.107

Bentel, Amelia, 1890, 1894, father deceased; mother unfit to care for children, 132, Ent. Bk. 13, crt. 4.54

Bentel, George, 1887, 1894, father deceased; mother unfit to care for children, 132, Ent. Bk. 13, crt. 4.54

Berger, Jacob, 1888, 1895, Parents: John and Dora Berger, 228, Ent. Bk. 13, crt. 4.135

Berger, Mary, 1890, 1895, Parents: John and Dora Berger, 228, Ent. Bk. 13, crt. 4.135

Berger, Morris, 1892, 1895, Parents: John and Dora Berger, 228, Ent. Bk. 13, crt. 4.135

Bigelow, Gordon, 1891, 1894, Parents: Thomas and Rachel Bigelow, 180, Ent. Bk. 13, crt. 4.95

Blockees, Benjamin, 1893, 1895, parents unknown, 278, Ent. Bk. 13, crt. 4.176

Blum, Edward, 1890, 1895, father deserted the family a year ago; surrendered by mom, 196, Ent. Bk. 13, crt. 4.109

Blum, John, 1889, 1895, father deserted the family a year ago; surrendered by mom, 196, Ent. Bk. 13, crt. 4.109

Bock, Annie, 1892, 1895, Parents: Adam (deceased) and Louisa Bock, 243, Ent. Bk. 13, crt. 4.146

Bock, Julia, 1881, 1893, Parents: Adam and Louisa Bock, 51, Ent. Bk. 13, crt. 3.446

Bock, Mary, 1889, 1893, Parents: Adam and Louisa Bock, 51, Ent. Bk. 13, crt. 3.447

Bock, Minnie, 1883, 1893, Parents: Adam and Louisa Bock, 51, Ent. Bk. 13, crt. 3.446

Boehle, Arthur, 1889, 1895, Parents: William and Selma Boehle, 222, Ent. Bk. 13, crt. 4.130

Boehle, Oscar, 1891, 1895, Parents: William and Selma Boehle, 222, Ent. Bk. 13, crt. 4.130

Boehmkay, Hyman, 1890, 1894, mother: Sarah, 169, Ent. Bk. 13, crt. 4.86

Bogart, Effie, 1886, 1894, Parents: James and Lillie (deceased) Bogart, 145, Ent. Bk. 13, crt. 4.65

Bogart, Ida, 1884, 1894, Parents: James and Lillie (deceased) Bogart, 145, Ent. Bk. 13, crt. 4.65

Bonziano, Philip, 1890, 1894, father: Michelangelo Bonziano, 81, Ent. Bk. 13, crt. 4.14

Bretthauer, Alvina, 1885, 1894, Parents: Henry and Lena Bretthauer, 176, Ent. Bk. 13, crt. 4.92

Bretthauer, Louisa, 1888, 1894, Parents: Henry and Lena Bretthauer, 176, Ent. Bk. 13, crt. 4.92

Brinker, Franklin, 1891, 1895, Parents: Bernard and Mary Ellen Brinker, 209, Ent. Bk. 13, crt. 4.121

Brinker, Lillian, 1890, 1895, Parents: Bernard and Mary Ellen Brinker, 209, Ent. Bk. 13, crt. 4.121

Briskin, Morris, , 1894, Parents: Mike and Rachel Briskin, 179, Ent. Bk. 13, crt. 4.94

Brower, Frank, 1888, 1894, Parents: Charles and Mary Brower, 175, Ent. Bk. 13, crt. 4.91

Brower, Ruby, 1892, 1894, Parents: Charles and Marguerite Brower (both deceased), 171, Ent. Bk. 13, perm. 11.171

Brown, George, 1891, 1894, Parents: George Beltzly and Margaret Brown, 128, Ent. Bk. 13, crt. 4.50

Brummerhof, Elizabeth, 1889, 1894, Parents: Henry and Elizabeth Brummerhof, 158, Ent. Bk. 13, crt. 4.77

Brummerhof, Otto, 1890, 1894, Parents: Henry and Elizabeth Brummerhof, 158, Ent. Bk. 13, crt. 4.77

Callatz, Eugene, 1890, 1895, mother: Wanda Callatz, 226, Ent. Bk. 13, crt. 4.133

Carley, John, 1892, 1894, Parents: Thomas and Elizabeth Carley, 90, Ent. Bk. 13, crt. 4.20

Carpenter, Mabel, 1890, 1895, Parents: William and Kate Carpenter, 198, Ent. Bk. 13, crt. 4.111

Carter, Gertrude, 1887, 1895, Parents: William and Josephine Carter, 254, Ent. Bk. 13, crt. 4.152

Carter, Richard, 1892, 1895, Parents: William and Josephine Carter, 254, Ent. Bk. 13, crt. 4.152

Carter, Willie, 1890, 1895, Parents: William and Josephine Carter, 254, Ent. Bk. 13, crt. 4.152

Charles, Ethel, 1887, 1895, mother dead; stepmother abusive; father intemperate, 286, Ent. Bk. 13, crt. 4.184

Chatterton, Emma, 1892, 1895, Parents: William (deceased) and Carrie Chatterton, 256, Ent. Bk. 13, crt. 4.156

Chatterton, Lizzie, 1889, 1895, Parents: William (deceased) and Carrie Chatterton, 256, Ent. Bk. 13, crt. 4.156

Childs, Harry, 1888, 1895, Parents: Martin and Margaret Childs, 224, Ent. Bk. 13, crt. 4.132

Childs, Lizzie, 1886, 1895, Parents: Martin and Margaret Childs, 224, Ent. Bk. 13, crt. 4.132

Childs, Raymond, 1890, 1895, Parents: Martin and Margaret Childs, 224, Ent. Bk. 13, crt. 4.132

Christie, Frederick, 1891, 1894, Parents: Charles and Clara Christie, 185, Ent. Bk. 13, temporary

Clancy, John, 1887, 1895, Parents: Maurice and Elizabeth (deceased) Clancy, 251, Ent. Bk. 13, crt. 4.152

Clancy, Mary, 1892, 1895, Parents: Maurice and Elizabeth (deceased) Clancy, 251, Ent. Bk. 13, crt. 4.152

Clancy, Thomas, 1885, 1895, Parents: Maurice and Elizabeth (deceased) Clancy, 251, Ent. Bk. 13, crt. 4.152

Clark, Agnes, 1892, 1893, Parents: Samuel and Mary Clark, 25, Ent. Bk. 13, perm. 11.155

Clark, Ethel, , 1895, mother: Bessie Clark, 253, Ent. Bk. 13, crt. 4.154

Clark, Hilda, 1886, 1893, Parents: Josiah and Clara Clark, 33, Ent. Bk. 13, crt. 3.404

Clark, Jessie, 1890, 1893, Parents: Josiah and Clara Clark, 33, Ent. Bk. 13, crt. 3.404

Clark, Lillian, 1889, 1893, Parents: Samuel and Mary Clark, 24, Ent. Bk. 13, crt. 3.378

Coleman, George, 1888, 1894, father: James, 113, Ent. Bk. 13, crt. 3.40

Coleman, Rebecca, 1886, 1894, father: James, 113, Ent. Bk. 13, crt. 3.40

Coleman, William, 1890, 1894, father: James, 113, Ent. Bk. 13, crt. 3.40

Conlon, Lizzie, 1889, 1895, Parents: John and Sarah Conlon, 289, Ent. Bk. 13, crt. 4.187

Conlon, Sadie, 1888, 1895, Parents: John and Sarah Conlon, 289, Ent. Bk. 13, crt. 4.187

Cook, Annie, 1883, 1894, Parents: Daniel and Annie (stepmother) Cook, 125, Ent. Bk. 13, crt. 4.48

Cornelison, Annie, 1892, 1895, father: George Cornelison; mother deceased, 290, Ent. Bk. 13, perm. 11.243

Cornelison, George, 1890, 1895, father: George Cornelison; mother deceased, 290, Ent. Bk. 13, perm. 11.242

Cornelison, Katie, 1889, 1895, father: George Cornelison; mother deceased, 290, Ent. Bk. 13, perm. 11.241

Curry, Harold, 1892, 1895, Parents: Hugh and Lillian Curry, 240, Ent. Bk. 13, temporary

Daken, William, 1891, 1893, Parents: John and Joan Daken, 63, Ent. Bk. 13, crt. 4.3

Darvas, George, 1892, 1894, , 178, Ent. Bk. 13, temporary

Dean, Edward, 1892, 1895, Parents: William and Ellen (deceased) Dean, 242, Ent. Bk. 13, crt. 4.145

Dean, Margaret, 1891, 1895, Parents: William and Ellen (deceased) Dean, 242, Ent. Bk. 13, crt. 4.145

Devenny, Sarah, 1887, 1893, Parents: Charles and Lydia Devenny, 66, Ent. Bk. 13, crt. 4.5

Diercks, Johanna, 1885, 1894, Parents: Frederick and Sarah Diercks, 79, Ent. Bk. 13, crt. 4.13

Diercks, Susanna, 1883, 1894, Parents: Frederick and Sarah Diercks, 79, Ent. Bk. 13, crt. 4.13

Dietz, Philip, 1891, 1893, Parents: Philip and Rosa Dietz, 73, Ent. Bk. 13, crt. 4.10

Dietz, Sarah, 1887, 1893, Parents: Philip and Rosa Dietz, 73, Ent. Bk. 13, crt. 4.10

Dobbins, Esther, 1889, 1893, Parents: George and Agnes Dobbins, 11, Ent. Bk. 13, temporary

Dobbins, Rose, 1887, 1893, Parents: George and Agnes Dobbins, 11, Ent. Bk. 13, temporary

Doe, "John, No. 18", 1892, 1894, parents unknown, 143, Ent. Bk. 13, crt. 4.63

Doe, "John, No. 19", 1891, 1894, brought by an officer, 151, Ent. Bk. 13,

Donahue, Mary, 1885, 1893, Parents: Daniel and Jane Donahue, 27, Ent. Bk. 13, crt. 3.386

Donahue, Samuel, 1887, 1893, Parents: Daniel and Jane Donahue, 27, Ent. Bk. 13, crt. 3.387

Dougherty, Ethel, 1892, 1895, Parents: Giben and Mary Dougherty, 210, Ent. Bk. 13, temporary

Dougherty, Kathie, 1892, 1894, Parents: John and Carrie Dougherty, 88, Ent. Bk. 13, temporary

Drews, Elsie, 1890, 1894, mother deceased, 104, Ent. Bk. 13, crt. 4.33

Druckman, Ellie, 1885, 1893, mother: Yetta Druckman, 68, Ent. Bk. 13, crt. 4.6

Druckman, Flora, 1888, 1893, mother: Yetta Druckman, 68, Ent. Bk. 13, crt. 4.6

Eggen, Emil, 1888, 1894, mother: Julia Eggen, 109, Ent. Bk. 13, crt. 4.35

Eggen, Martha, 1886, 1894, mother: Julia Eggen, 109, Ent. Bk. 13, crt. 4.35

Eiben, Stella, 1890, 1893, Parents: Eibe and Julia Eiben; mother is prostitute, 56, Ent. Bk. 13, crt. 3.455

Eiben, Tillie, 1884, 1893, Parents: Eibe and Julia Eiben; mother is prostitute, 56, Ent. Bk. 13, crt. 3.454

Emery, Bessie, 1889, 1895, mother: Maggie Emery; father deceased, 212, Ent. Bk. 13, crt. 4.123

Eusign, Rubnia, 1891, 1895, brought by Officer Wakefield, 268, Ent. Bk. 13, crt. 4.167

Fagan, Annie, 1894, 1894, surrendered due to illness of mother, 102, Ent. Bk. 13, crt. 4.31

Fagan, Frances, 1886, 1894, surrendered due to illness of mother, 102, Ent. Bk. 13, crt. 4.31

Fagan, Walter, 1889, 1894, surrendered due to illness of mother, 102, Ent. Bk. 13, crt. 4.31

Fehn, Louis, 1885, 1894, Parents: Louis (deceased) and Christine Fehn, 191, Ent. Bk. 13, crt. 4.104

Fischer, Gertrude, 1890, 1894, Parents: Charles and Katie Fisher, 124, Ent. Bk. 13, crt. 4.47

Fischer, Lillie, 1892, 1894, Parents: Charles and Katie Fisher, 124, Ent. Bk. 13, crt. 4.47

Fisher, Edna, 1887, 1893, Parents: Edward and Mary Fisher, 26, Ent. Bk. 13, crt. 3.381

Fisher, Harry, 1884, 1893, Parents: Edward and Mary Fisher, 26, Ent. Bk. 13, crt. 3.380

Fitzpatrick, Joseph, 1892, 1894, Parents: Patrick and Mary Fitzpatrick, 105, Ent. Bk. 13, crt. 4.34

Flanagan, Sarah, 1885, 1894, surrendered by her aunt, 107, Ent. Bk. 13, crt. 4.37

Flecker, Mary, , 1893, Parents: John and Mary Flecker (deceased), 39, Ent. Bk. 13, crt.

Flemming, Archibald, 1878, 1894, Parents: James and Annie Flemming, 188, Ent. Bk. 13, crt. 4.102

Flood, James, 1892, 1895, Parents: Ambrose and Elizabeth Flood, 215, Ent. Bk. 13, crt. 4.125

Flynn, John, 1892, 1895, mother: Mary Flynn; father deceased, 221, Ent. Bk. 13, crt. 4.129

Flynn, Julia, 1886, 1895, mother: Mary Flynn; father deceased, 221, Ent. Bk. 13, crt. 4.129

Forst, Fred, 1892, 1895, Parents: Michael and Annie (deceased) Forst, 232, Ent. Bk. 13, crt. 4.138

Franklin, Julia, 1885, 1894, Parents: Philip and Julia (deceased) Franklin, 135, Ent. Bk. 13, crt. 4.56

Frenay, Bella, 1884, 1893, sent to Institution of Mercy, 45, Ent. Bk. 13,

Frenay, Mary, 1886, 1893, sent to Institution of Mercy, 45, Ent. Bk. 13,

French, Henry, 1889, 1893, parents unknown, 32, Ent. Bk. 13, crt. 3.403

Gardner, James, 1888, 1893, Parents: James and Maggie; in city prison, 41, Ent. Bk. 13, crt. 3.419

Gardner, Lizzie, 1890, 1893, Parents: James and Maggie; in city prison, 41, Ent. Bk. 13, crt. 3.420

Gardner, Minnie, 1885, 1893, Parents: James and Maggie; in city prison, 41, Ent. Bk. 13, crt. 3.419

Garrett, Martha, 1887, 1893, Parents: Albert Mott and Bessie Garrett, 63, Ent. Bk. 13, crt.

Gerrard, John, 1890, 1895, father: Alex Gerrard; mother deceased, 267, Ent. Bk. 13, crt. 4.166

Girard, John, 1889, 1893, mother deceased, 52, Ent. Bk. 13, crt. 3.450

Goebel, Elsie, 1885, 1895, Parents: August (deceased) and Frances Goebel, 271, Ent. Bk. 13, crt. 4.169

Goebel, Florence, 1887, 1895, Parents: August (deceased) and Frances Goebel, 271, Ent. Bk. 13, crt. 4.169

Goebel, Richard, 1889, 1895, Parents: August (deceased) and Frances Goebel, 271, Ent. Bk. 13, crt. 4.169

Goldberg, Fanny, 1891, 1894, Parents: Isidore (deceased) and Sarah Goldberg, 163, Ent. Bk. 13, crt. 4.81

Golde, William, 1886, 1895, both parents deceased, 192, Ent. Bk. 13, crt. 4.105

Goodfried, Maurice, 1889, 1893, Parents: Solomon and Sophia Goodfried, 65, Ent. Bk. 13, crt. 4.3

Graff, Kate, 1892, 1895, father dead; mother intemperate, 287, Ent. Bk. 13, crt. 4.185

Greenberg, Charles, 1889, 1894, , 159, Ent. Bk. 13, crt. 4.76

Gretzinger, Annie, 1886, 1894, Parents: William (deceased) and Amelia Gretzinger, 161, Ent. Bk. 13, crt. 4.79

Gretzinger, Willie, 1889, 1894, Parents: William (deceased) and Amelia Gretzinger, 161, Ent. Bk. 13, crt. 4.79

Gudehuss, Emma, 1890, 1893, Parents: Carl and Anna Gudehuss, 30, Ent. Bk. 13, crt. 3.394

Gudehuss, May, 1888, 1893, Parents: Carl and Anna Gudehuss, 30, Ent. Bk. 13, crt. 3.393

Gunther, Emma, 1887, 1894, Parents: Otto and Martha Gunther, 99, Ent. Bk. 13, crt. 4.28

Gunther, Frederick, 1890, 1893, Parents: Frederick and Louisa Gunther (deceased), 50, Ent. Bk. 13, crt. 3.444

Gunther, Henry, 1889, 1894, Parents: Otto and Martha Gunther, 99, Ent. Bk. 13, crt. 4.28

Haggerty, Abbie, 1881, 1894, , 156, Ent. Bk. 13, temporary

Halpern, Rose, 1884, 1894, Parents: Henry and Rachel Halpern, 131, Ent. Bk. 13, crt. 4.53

Hanschin, Annie, 1882, 1893, Parents: Theodore and Mary Hanschin, 29, Ent. Bk. 13, crt. 3.391

Hanschin, Mary, 1886, 1893, Parents: Theodore and Mary Hanschin, 29, Ent. Bk. 13, crt. 3.392

Harris, Julia, 1887, 1895, Parents: William (deceased) and Jane Harris, 248, Ent. Bk. 13, crt. 4.149

Hatfield, William, , 1894, mother deceased, 141, Ent. Bk. 13, crt. 4.61

Heckel, Christopher, 1890, 1893, Parents: Godfrey and Catherine Heckel, 54, Ent. Bk. 13, crt. 3.452

Heckel, Emma, 1883, 1893, Parents: Godfrey and Catherine Heckel, 54, Ent. Bk. 13, crt. 3.452

Heinrich, Annie, 1885, 1895, Parents: Charles and Annie Heinrich, 216, Ent. Bk. 13, temporary

Heinrich, Charlie, 1888, 1895, Parents: Charles and Annie Heinrich, 216, Ent. Bk. 13, temporary

Heinrich, Freddie, 1884, 1895, Parents: Charles and Annie Heinrich, 216, Ent. Bk. 13, temporary

Heinrich, Richard, 1890, 1895, Parents: Charles and Annie Heinrich, 216, Ent. Bk. 13, temporary

Helene, Siegre, 1887, 1893, Parents: August and Sophie Helene, 1, Ent. Bk. 13, crt. 3.342

Helfrich, Charles, , 1894, Parents: Charles and Katie Helfrich, 94, Ent. Bk. 13, crt. 4.23

Helfrich, Katie, , 1894, Parents: Charles and Katie Helfrich, 94, Ent. Bk. 13, crt. 4.23

Helfrich, Louisa, , 1894, Parents: Charles and Katie Helfrich, 94, Ent. Bk. 13, crt. 4.23

Henn, Gertrude, 1890, 1895, father's whereabouts unknown; mother in hospital, 206, Ent. Bk. 13, crt. 4.119

Hermann, Sophie, , 1895, Parents: Theodore and Freda Hermann, 273, Ent. Bk. 13, crt. 4.171

Herwig, Frieda, 1891, 1895, parents unknown, 246, Ent. Bk. 13, crt. 4.148

Hewig, Peter, 1889, 1895, both parents deceased, 211, Ent. Bk. 13, crt. 4.122

Heyman, Annie, 1892, 1894, mother: Sarah Heyman; father's whereabouts unknown, 110, Ent. Bk. 13, crt. 4.38

Heyman, Harry, 1890, 1894, mother: Sarah Heyman; father's whereabouts unknown, 110, Ent. Bk. 13, crt. 4.38

Higgins, Jennie, 1888, 1894, Parents: Daniel and Theresa Higgins, 78, Ent. Bk. 13, temporary

Hoefner, Bertha, 1882, 1894, Parents: William and Rita Hoefner (both deceased), 77, Ent. Bk. 13, crt. 4.12

Hoefner, Clara, 1885, 1894, Parents: William and Rita Hoefner (both deceased), 77, Ent. Bk. 13, crt. 4.12

Hoff, Nicholas, 1885, 1893, Parents: George and Gertrude Hoff (both deceased), 67, Ent. Bk. 13, perm. 11.171

Hookway, Edna, 1890, 1894, Parents: Thomas and Martha Hookway, 144, Ent. Bk. 13, crt. 4.64

Hope, John, 1890, 1893, mother: Harriet Davis (25 years old; unmarried), 31, Ent. Bk. 13, crt. 3.396

Housechild, John, 1891, 1893, parents unknown, 22, Ent. Bk. 13, crt. 3.373

Houston, Laura, 1889, 1895, Parents: Frank and Kate (stepmother) Houston, 205, Ent. Bk. 13, crt. 4.118

Houston, Thomas, 1887, 1895, Parents: Frank and Kate (stepmother) Houston, 205, Ent. Bk. 13, crt. 4.118

Hughes, Charles, 1883, 1894, Parents: John and Margaret Hughes, 111, Ent. Bk. 13, temporary

Ible, Joseph, 1892, 1895, Parents: Samuel and Eva (deceased) Ible, 235, Ent. Bk. 13, crt. 4.141

Igle, Tillie, 1880, 1893, surrendered by mother, 5, Ent. Bk. 13, temporary

Ingles, Kate, 1890, 1894, Parents: David and Jennie Inglis, 157, Ent. Bk. 13, crt. 4.75

Innes, William, 1887, 1895, Parents: George and Annie Innes, 229, Ent. Bk. 13, temporary

Jesseman, Florence, 1889, 1894, Parents: Henry and Mary Jesseman, 186, Ent. Bk. 13, crt. 4.99

Jesseman, Harry, 1887, 1894, Parents: Henry and Mary Jesseman, 186, Ent. Bk. 13, crt. 4.99

Jesseman, Walter, 1891, 1894, Parents: Henry and Mary Jesseman, 186, Ent. Bk. 13, crt. 4.99

Johnson, John, 1891, 1894, Parents: John and Lena Johnson, 155, Ent. Bk. 13, crt. 4.74

Johnston, Theodore, 1891, 1893, Parents: Theodore and Rebecca Johnston, 36, Ent. Bk. 13, perm. 11.162

Jones, Albert, 1892, 1895, Parents: William and Mary Jones, 258, Ent. Bk. 13, crt. 4.158

Jones, Margaret, 1888, 1895, Parents: Thomas and Annie Jones (deceased), 281, Ent. Bk. 13, crt. 4.179

Jones, Thomas, 1890, 1895, Parents: Thomas and Annie Jones (deceased), 281, Ent. Bk. 13, crt. 4.179

Jones, Willie, 1889, 1895, Parents: William and Mary Jones, 258, Ent. Bk. 13, crt. 4.158

Kanapal, Samuel, 1888, 1893, parents unknown, 40, Ent. Bk. 13, crt. 3.418

Kawppus, Lena, 1892, 1894, Parents: Joseph and Anna Kawppus, 170, Ent. Bk. 13, crt. 4.87

Kawppus, William, 1889, 1894, Parents: Joseph and Anna Kawppus, 170, Ent. Bk. 13, crt. 4.87

Kelly, Lillian, 1891, 1894, mother: Elizabeth, 187, Ent. Bk. 13, crt. 4.100

Kelly, Winifred, 1894, 1894, mother: Elizabeth, 187, Ent. Bk. 13, crt. 4.100

Kimmel, Charles, 1888, 1893, Parents: Albert and Minnie Kimmel, 43, Ent. Bk. 13, crt. 3.427

Kimmel, Minnie, 1886, 1893, Parents: Albert and Minnie Kimmel, 43, Ent. Bk. 13, crt. 3.427

Kinnicutt, Harry, 1891, 1893, Parents: William and Mary Kinnicutt, 13, Ent. Bk. 13, crt. 3.355

Klink, Jacob, 1890, 1895, Parents: Solomon and Betsey Klink, 233, Ent. Bk. 13, crt. 4.139

Klink, Samuel, 1892, 1895, Parents: Solomon and Betsey Klink, 233, Ent. Bk. 13, crt. 4.139

Knab, Johanna, 1887, 1893, Parents: Joseph and Lizzie Knab, 46, Ent. Bk. 13, crt. 3.432

Knab, Josephine, 1881, 1893, Parents: Joseph and Lizzie Knab, 46, Ent. Bk. 13, crt. 3.432

Knab, Philip, 1890, 1893, Parents: Joseph and Lizzie Knab, 46, Ent. Bk. 13, crt. 3.433

Knopple, August, 1890, 1893, Parents: Charley and Mary Knopple, 58, Ent. Bk. 13, crt. 3.460

Knopple, Herman, 1886, 1893, Parents: Charley and Mary Knopple, 58, Ent. Bk. 13, crt. 3.460

Knudson, Alma, 1889, 1895, brought by Officer Dietrich of the S.P.C.C., 279, Ent. Bk. 13, crt. 4.177

Krebs, Antoinette, 1889, 1895, mother: Mary Krebs, 280, Ent. Bk. 13, crt. 4.178

Krebs, Rudolph, 1892, 1895, mother: Mary Krebs, 280, Ent. Bk. 13, crt. 4.178

Krueger, Theoodre, , 1893, Parents: Louis and Emma Krueger, 28, Ent. Bk. 13, crt. 3.388

Krueger, Theresa, , 1893, Parents: Louis and Emma Krueger, 28, Ent. Bk. 13, crt. 3.389

Krulis, Louis, 1891, 1893, mother: Marie Krulis, 15, Ent. Bk. 13, crt. 3.361

Kruse, Annie, 1884, 1893, Parents: Cord and Eva Kruse, 69, Ent. Bk. 13, crt. 4.7

Kruse, Lizzie, 1886, 1893, Parents: Cord and Eva Kruse, 60, Ent. Bk. 13, crt. 3.466

Labreque, Claudine, 1891, 1894, Parents: Isidor and Madge Labreque, 162, Ent. Bk. 13, crt. 4.80

Labreque, Vibert, 1889, 1894, Parents: Isidor and Madge Labreque, 162, Ent. Bk. 13, crt. 4.80

Laird, George, 1890, 1895, Parents: William and Elizabeth Laird, 239, Ent. Bk. 13, crt. 4.144

Laird, Harry, 1886, 1895, Parents: William and Elizabeth Laird, 239, Ent. Bk. 13, crt. 4.144

Lang, Clara, 1888, 1894, Parents: Frederick (deceased) and Helen Lang, 172, Ent. Bk. 13, crt. 3.88

Lang, Harry, , 1894, mother: Minnie Lang, 85, Ent. Bk. 13, crt. 4.16

Lang, Helen, 1891, 1894, Parents: Frederick (deceased) and Helen Lang, 172, Ent. Bk. 13, crt. 3.88

Lawrence, Ella, 1887, 1893, Parents: Alexander and Alvaretta Lawrence, 70, Ent. Bk. 13, perm. 11.174

Leonard, Emma, 1886, 1894, Parents: William (deceased) and Emma Leonard, 106, Ent. Bk. 13, crt. 4.36

Leonard, Peter, 1889, 1894, Parents: William (deceased) and Emma Leonard, 106, Ent. Bk. 13, crt. 4.36

Leonard, William, 1887, 1894, Parents: William (deceased) and Emma Leonard, 106, Ent. Bk. 13, crt. 4.36

Lieberman, David, 1891, 1894, brought by an officer, 136, Ent. Bk. 13, crt. 4.56

Lind, Myrtle, 1891, 1895, Parents: Adolph and Maud Lind, 264, Ent. Bk. 13, temporary

Litt, Fred, 1883, 1894, both parents deceased, 114, Ent. Bk. 13, temporary

Little, Robert, 1890, 1895, parents unknown, 225, Ent. Bk. 13, crt. 4.133

Lowry, Irwin, 1889, 1894, Parents: Leo and Alice Lowry, 127, Ent. Bk. 13, temporary

Ludin, Bertha, 1889, 1895, Parents: Charles (deceased) and Lena Ludin, 200, Ent. Bk. 13, crt. 4.113

Ludin, Caroline, 1887, 1895, Parents: Charles (deceased) and Lena Ludin, 200, Ent. Bk. 13, crt. 4.113

Lund, John, 1889, 1894, father: John, 183, Ent. Bk. 13, crt. 4.98

Lundine, Edward, 1893, 1895, Parents: Jeremiah and Dorothy Lundine, 252, Ent. Bk. 13, temporary

Luther, Elan, 1884, 1893, mother: Sarah, 53, Ent. Bk. 13, crt. 3.448

Luther, Ike, 1887, 1893, mother: Sarah, 53, Ent. Bk. 13, crt. 3.448

Luther, Pauline, 1888, 1893, mother: Sarah, 53, Ent. Bk. 13, crt. 3.449

Maas, Mary, 1892, 1895, mother: Mary, 236, Ent. Bk. 13, crt. 4.137

Maas, Willie, 1890, 1895, mother: Mary, 236, Ent. Bk. 13, crt. 4.137

Maroney, Edward, 1884, 1894, Parents: Edward and Mary Maroney, 91, Ent. Bk. 13, crt. 4.21

Martin, Harry, 1890, 1894, Parents: Harry and Eva Martin, 165, Ent. Bk. 13, crt. 4.83

Martin, John, 1887, 1894, Parents: Harry and Eva Martin, 165, Ent. Bk. 13, crt. 4.83

McAlees, Annie, 1887, 1893, Parents: Bernard and Annie McAlees, 59, Ent. Bk. 13, crt. 3.462

McAlees, Mary, 1890, 1893, Parents: Bernard and Annie McAlees, 59, Ent. Bk. 13, crt. 3.462

McCarthy, Emma, 1885, 1894, Parents: Fred and Lena McCarthy, 154, Ent. Bk. 13, crt. 4.73

McGowan, John, 1885, 1894, Parents: Martin (deceased) and Kate McGowan, 181, Ent. Bk. 13, crt. 4.96

McGowan, Joseph, 1887, 1894, Parents: Martin (deceased) and Kate McGowan, 181, Ent. Bk. 13, crt. 4.96

McGregor, Edith, 1887, 1893, Parents: William and Josephine McGregor, 37, Ent. Bk. 13, crt. 3.412

McGregor, Robert, 1889, 1894, Parents: William and Josephine McGregor, 95, Ent. Bk. 13, crt. 4.24

McVeigh, Ethel, 1891, 1894, Parents: William and Selma McVeigh, 148, Ent. Bk. 13, crt. 3.68

McVeigh, William, 1889, 1894, Parents: William and Selma McVeigh, 148, Ent. Bk. 13, crt. 3.68

Meehan, Maggie, 1891, 1894, Parents: John and Maggie Meehan, 142, Ent. Bk. 13, crt. 4.62

Meehan, Manne, 1889, 1894, Parents: John and Maggie Meehan, 142, Ent. Bk. 13, crt. 4.62

Meehan, Patrick, 1887, 1894, Parents: John and Maggie Meehan, 142, Ent. Bk. 13, crt. 4.62

Metz, Christina, 1886, 1894, Parents: John and Augusta Metz, 121, Ent. Bk. 13, crt. 3.43

Meyer, Charley, 1884, 1894, Parents: Julius and Dorothy Meyer, 118, Ent. Bk. 13, temporary

Meyer, Charley, 1884, 1894, Parents: Julius and Dorothy Meyer, 134, Ent. Bk. 13, crt. 4.55

Meyer, David, 1891, 1894, mother: Mary Meyer; father deceased, 96, Ent. Bk. 13, crt. 4.25

Meyer, Edwin, 1889, 1893, Parents: Charles and Augusta Meyer, 21, Ent. Bk. 13, crt. 3.374

Meyer, Max, 1889, 1894, mother: Mary Meyer; father deceased, 96, Ent. Bk. 13, crt. 4.25

Meyer, Nettie, 1886, 1894, Parents: Julius and Dorothy Meyer, 118, Ent. Bk. 13, temporary

Meyer, Nettie, 1886, 1894, Parents: Julius and Dorothy Meyer, 134, Ent. Bk. 13, crt. 4.55

Meyer, William, 1891, 1893, Parents: Charles and Augusta Meyer, 21, Ent. Bk. 13, crt. 3.374

Michael, Kate, 1892, 1894, father: Herman, 173, Ent. Bk. 13, crt. 3.89

Michael, Lizzie, 1889, 1894, father: Herman, 173, Ent. Bk. 13, crt. 3.89

Midler, Izzie, 1892, 1894, Parents: Samuel and Ida Midler; father has deserted them, 147, Ent. Bk. 13, crt. 4.67

Miller, Emilia, 1892, 1895, Parents: Joseph and Ann Amelia Miller, 202, Ent. Bk. 13, crt. 4.115

Miller, Ida, 1889, 1894, Parents: John and Nellie Miller, 89, Ent. Bk. 13, crt. 4.19

Miller, John, 1887, 1894, Parents: John and Nellie Miller, 89, Ent. Bk. 13, crt. 4.19

Miller, Joseph, 1893, 1895, Parents: Joseph and Ann Amelia Miller, 202, Ent. Bk. 13, crt. 4.115

Millner, Flora, 1892, 1894, Parents: Edward (deceased) and Lizzie Millner, 139, Ent. Bk. 13, crt. 4.59

Mohr, August, 1886, 1893, Parents: Carl and Barbara Mohr; both deceased, 47, Ent. Bk. 13, crt. 3.434

Mohr, Jennie, 1888, 1893, Parents: Carl and Barbara Mohr; both deceased, 47, Ent. Bk. 13, crt. 3.435

Mohr, Kate, 1885, 1894, Parents: John and Catherine (deceased) Mohr, 140, Ent. Bk. 13, crt. 4.60

Mohr, Lizzie, 1883, 1894, Parents: John and Margaret Mohr, 137, Ent. Bk. 13, crt. 4.57

Moll, Antoinette, 1886, 1893, Parents: John and Sarah Moll, 35, Ent. Bk. 13, crt. 3.410

Moll, Florence, 1889, 1893, Parents: John and Sarah Moll, 35, Ent. Bk. 13, crt. 3.411

Moll, John, 1884, 1893, Parents: John and Sarah Moll, 35, Ent. Bk. 13, crt. 3.410

Morrison, Flora, 1890, 1893, Parents: John and Charlotte Morrison, 10, Ent. Bk. 13, crt. 3.353

Morrison, John H., 1891, 1893, Parents: John and Charlotte Morrison, 10, Ent. Bk. 13, crt. 3.353

Munn, Agnes, 1885, 1894, Parents: Walter and Elizabeth Munn, 87, Ent. Bk. 13, temporary

Munn, Mary, 1887, 1894, Parents: Walter and Elizabeth Munn, 87, Ent. Bk. 13, temporary

Munn, Walter, 1884, 1894, Parents: Walter and Elizabeth Munn, 87, Ent. Bk. 13, temporary

Murray, Irene, 1890, 1895, Parents: William and Sarah (deceased) Murray, 199, Ent. Bk. 13, crt. 4.112

Murray, Maggie, 1882, 1894, Parents: William and Sarah (deceased) Murray, 116, Ent. Bk. 13, crt. 4.41

Murray, Tessie, 1885, 1893, Parents: William and Sarah (deceased) Murray, 116, Ent. Bk. 13, crt. 4.41

Nixon, Grace, 1889, 1893, Parents: Thomas and Louisa Nixon, 9, Ent. Bk. 13, crt. 3.352

Nixon, William, 1884, 1893, Parents: Thomas and Louisa Nixon, 9, Ent. Bk. 13, crt. 3.352

Nolan, Joseph, 1889, 1894, Parents: John (deceased) and Hattie Nolan, 123, Ent. Bk. 13, crt. 4.46

Northrop, Ethel, 1892, 1895, Parents: Charles and Lillie Northrop, 231, Ent. Bk. 13, temporary

Northrop, Hattie, 1890, 1895, Parents: Charles and Lillie Northrop, 231, Ent. Bk. 13, temporary

O'Brien, Maude, 1884, 1893, Parents: Mike and Martha O'Brien, 14, Ent. Bk. 13, crt. 3.359

Ochner, Frederick, 1887, 1895, Parents: William (deceased) and Louisa Ochner, 207, Ent. Bk. 13, crt. 4.120

Ochner, Rosie, 1890, 1895, Parents: William (deceased) and Louisa Ochner, 207, Ent. Bk. 13, crt. 4.120

Oesterling, Charles, 1890, 1893, both parents deceased, 7, Ent. Bk. 13, crt. 3.350

Oesterling, Dora, 1887, 1893, both parents deceased, 7, Ent. Bk. 13, crt. 3.349

Oesterling, Kate, 1885, 1893, both parents deceased, 7, Ent. Bk. 13, crt. 3.349

Oesterling, Max, 1888, 1893, both parents deceased, 7, Ent. Bk. 13, crt. 3.350

Oesterling, William, 1889, 1893, both parents deceased, 7, Ent. Bk. 13, crt. 3.350

Olsen, Thomas, 1888, 1894, Parents: John and Lena Johnson, 155, Ent. Bk. 13, crt. 4.74

O'Neil, Jessie, 1887, 1895, Parents: John and Lottie O'Neil, 217, Ent. Bk. 13, crt. 4.126

O'Neil, Lottie, 1888, 1895, Parents: John and Lottie O'Neil, 217, Ent. Bk. 13, crt. 4.126

O'Neil, Ruth, 1892, 1895, Parents: John and Lottie O'Neil, 217, Ent. Bk. 13, crt. 4.126

Ottenbacher, Fanny, 1883, 1894, Parents: Gottlieb and Pauline Ottenbacher (both deceased), 138, Ent. Bk. 13, crt. 4.58

Pandjiris, Fanny, 1878, 1893, Parents: Nicholas (deceased) and Sarah Pandjiris, 72, Ent. Bk. 13, crt. 4.9

Peeling, Ida, 1885, 1895, Parents: Benjamin and Martha Peeling, 261, Ent. Bk. 13, crt. 4.161

Perkins, Elmer, 1885, 1894, Parents: Andrew and Isabella Perkins (both deceased), 84, Ent. Bk. 13, crt. 4.17

Peters, Herman, 1881, 1895, Parents: Herman and Lena Peters, 265, Ent. Bk. 13, crt. 4.164

Peters, Lena, 1880, 1895, Parents: Herman and Lena Peters, 265, Ent. Bk. 13, crt. 4.164

Phelps, Eva, 1885, 1894, Parents: Herbert and Mary Phelps, 129, Ent. Bk. 13, crt. 4.52

Post, Carrie, 1883, 1893, Parents: George and Caroline Post, 8, Ent. Bk. 13, crt. 3.351

Post, Martha, 1887, 1893, Parents: George and Caroline Post, 8, Ent. Bk. 13, crt. 3.351

Powell, William, 1889, 1894, mother: Sarah, 160, Ent. Bk. 13, crt. 4.78

Radish, Elsie, 1892, 1894, parents: Henriquez, 126, Ent. Bk. 13, crt. 4.49

Radish, Minnie, 1887, 1894, parents: Henriquez, 126, Ent. Bk. 13, crt. 4.49

Readman, Francis, 1890, 1894, Parents: Benjamin (deceased) and Ellen Readman, 130, Ent. Bk. 13, crt. 4.51

Readman, Mamie, 1891, 1894, Parents: Benjamin (deceased) and Ellen Readman, 130, Ent. Bk. 13, crt. 4.51

Rettig, Rachel, 1891, 1895, Parents: Solomon and Lauretta Rettig, 220, Ent. Bk. 13, crt. 4.128

Reynolds, Stella, 1890, 1894, Parents: Arthur and Ann Reynolds, 86, Ent. Bk. 13, crt. 4.18

Reynolds, Stella, 1891, 1894, Parents: Elias and Annie (deceased) Reynolds, 133, Ent. Bk. 13, perm. 11.227

Rice, Charles, 1888, 1894, Parents: Stephen and Catherine Rice, 190, Ent. Bk. 13, crt. 4.103

Rice, Louis, 1889, 1894, Parents: Stephen and Catherine Rice, 190, Ent. Bk. 13, crt. 4.103

Rice, Thomas, 1886, 1894, Parents: Stephen and Catherine Rice, 190, Ent. Bk. 13, crt. 4.103

Richter, Emma, 1887, 1893, father: Otto Richter, 34, Ent. Bk. 13, crt. 3.407

Rickert, Agnes, 1887, 1894, Parents: Henry (deceased) and Ida Rickert, 150, Ent. Bk. 13, crt. 4.70

Rickert, Elsie, 1888, 1894, Parents: Henry (deceased) and Ida Rickert, 150, Ent. Bk. 13, crt. 4.70

Rickert, Henry, 1891, 1894, Parents: Henry (deceased) and Ida Rickert, 150, Ent. Bk. 13, crt. 4.70

Rider, Jennie, 1886, 1893, parents unknown, 57, Ent. Bk. 13, crt. 3.459

Robb, Jessie, 1883, 1894, Parents: Steward and Lizzie Robb, 152, Ent. Bk. 13, crt. 4.69

Robb, Maggie, 1891, 1894, Parents: Steward and Lizzie Robb, 149, Ent. Bk. 13, crt. 4.69

Rodriguez, Celina, 1883, 1894, Parents: Rufino and Joaquina Rodriguez, 82, Ent. Bk. 13, crt. 4.15

Rodriguez, Joseph, 1884, 1894, Parents: Rufino and Joaquina Rodriguez, 82, Ent. Bk. 13, crt. 4.15

Rodriguez, Manuel, 1886, 1894, Parents: Rufino and Joaquina Rodriguez, 82, Ent. Bk. 13, crt. 4.15

Rodriguez, Toby, 1888, 1894, Parents: Rufino and Joaquina Rodriguez, 103, Ent. Bk. 13, crt. 4.32

Rodriguez, Trina, 1889, 1894, Parents: Rufino and Joaquina Rodriguez, 103, Ent. Bk. 13, crt. 4.32

Rogers, James, 1890, 1895, father: George Rogers, 274, Ent. Bk. 13, crt. 4.173

Rohde, Helen, 1882, 1893, Parents: William and Augusta Rohde, 4, Ent. Bk. 13, crt. 3.347

Rohde, Willie, 1891, 1893, Parents: William and Augusta Rohde, 4, Ent. Bk. 13, crt. 3.347

Romano, Rosina, 1889, 1895, Parents: Dionisio and Isabella Romano, 245, Ent. Bk. 13, crt. 4.148

Russell, Ethel, 1889, 1893, Parents: Frank and Mary Russell, 44, Ent. Bk. 13, crt. 3.431

Russell, Molly, 1888, 1893, Parents: Frank and Mary Russell, 44, Ent. Bk. 13, crt. 3.430

Ryan, Andrew, , 1895, mother: Theresa, 262, Ent. Bk. 13, crt. 4.162

Ryan, Nora, 1888, 1894, vagrancy; father convicted for assaulting child, 168, Ent. Bk. 13, crt. 4.85

Ryan, Norah, , 1895, mother: Theresa, 262, Ent. Bk. 13, crt. 4.162

Sauret, Julia, 1883, 1895, Parents: Auguste (deceased) and Josephine Sauret, 284, Ent. Bk. 13, crt. 4.182

Sauret, Renee, 1885, 1895, Parents: Auguste (deceased) and Josephine Sauret, 284, Ent. Bk. 13, crt. 4.182

Schaumburg, Willie, 1890, 1895, mother: Maggie, 213, Ent. Bk. 13, temporary

Schmidt, Charles, 1891, 1895, Parents: Frederick and Catherine Schmidt, 272, Ent. Bk. 13, crt. 4.172

Schmidt, Katie, 1884, 1895, Parents: Frederick and Catherine Schmidt, 272, Ent. Bk. 13, crt. 4.172

Schmitt, William, 1882, 1895, Parents: John and Louisa Schmitt, 204, Ent. Bk. 13, crt. 4.117

Schneider, John, 1890, 1895, mother: Dora Schneider; father deceased, 195, Ent. Bk. 13, crt. 4.108

Schneider, Louis, 1891, 1895, mother: Dora Schneider; father deceased, 195, Ent. Bk. 13, crt. 4.108

Schweizer, Albert, 1887, 1895, Parents: Emil and Amelia Schweizer, 276, Ent. Bk. 13, crt. 4.174

Schweizer, John, 1892, 1895, Parents: Emil and Amelia Schweizer, 276, Ent. Bk. 13, crt. 4.174

Schweppe, Annie, 1890, 1893, Parents: John and Mary Schweppe, 74, Ent. Bk. 13, crt. 4.11

Schweppe, Annie, 1889, 1895, Parents: John and Mary (deceased) Schweppe, 269, Ent. Bk. 13, crt. 4.168

Seamount, Charles, 1890, 1895, Parents: Charles and Mary Seamount; father has left, 193, Ent. Bk. 13, crt. 4.106

Shearer, Annie, 1888, 1893, Parents: Mr. Koch and Annie Shearer (deceased), 6, Ent. Bk. 13, crt. 3.348

Shunk, Edward, 1892, 1895, mother: Mary; father has deserted the family, 238, Ent. Bk. 13, crt. 4.142

Shunk, Florence, 1891, 1895, mother: Mary; father has deserted the family, 238, Ent. Bk. 13, crt. 4.142

Sigler, Grace, 1887, 1895, Parents: George and Katherine (deceased) Sigler, 257, Ent. Bk. 13, crt. 4.157

Sigler, Katy, 1889, 1895, Parents: George and Katherine (deceased) Sigler, 257, Ent. Bk. 13, crt. 4.157

Silverhorn, George, 1889, 1893, Parents: Christian and Mary Silverhorn, 42, Ent. Bk. 13, crt. 3.423

Simonia, Clementine, 1890, 1893, mother: Eliza Simonia, 17, Ent. Bk. 13, crt. 3.366

Simonia, Marie, 1889, 1893, mother: Eliza Simonia, 17, Ent. Bk. 13, crt. 3.366

Sinclair, Adaline, 1887, 1893, Parents: Joseph and Pauline Sinclair, 12, Ent. Bk. 13, crt. 3.354

Sinclair, Katie, 1886, 1893, Parents: Joseph and Pauline Sinclair, 12, Ent. Bk. 13, crt. 3.354

Singer, Carrie, 1891, 1895, Parents: Casper and Emma Singer, 197, Ent. Bk. 13, crt. 4.110

Singer, Joseph, 1887, 1895, Parents: Casper and Emma Singer, 197, Ent. Bk. 13, crt. 4.110

Singer, William, 1890, 1895, Parents: Casper and Emma Singer, 197, Ent. Bk. 13, crt. 4.110

Smith, Annie, 1892, 1895, Parents: Charles and Lena (deceased) Smith, 244, Ent. Bk. 13, crt. 4.147

Smith, James, 1889, 1895, Parents: Frank and Annie Smith, 259, Ent. Bk. 13, crt. 4.159

Smith, Mamie, 1888, 1895, Parents: Frank and Annie Smith, 259, Ent. Bk. 13, crt. 4.159

Smith, Margaret E., 1882, 1894, father: John Smith, 97, Ent. Bk. 13, crt. 4.26

Solomon, Mabel, 1881, 1893, father: John A. Solomon, 18, Ent. Bk. 13, temporary

Solomon, Mary, 1882, 1883, father: John A. Solomon, 18, Ent. Bk. 13, temporary

Sorley, Harold, 1890, 1894, Parents: Charles and Ethel Sorley, 93, Ent. Bk. 13, crt. 3.22

Spence, Alfred, 1889, 1893, Parents: Alfred and Mary Spence; both intemperate, 48, Ent. Bk. 13, crt. 3.437

Spence, William, 1887, 1893, Parents: Alfred and Mary Spence; both intemperate, 48, Ent. Bk. 13, crt. 3.437

Stedman, Gordon, 1891, 1894, Parents: Carl and Mary (deceased) Stedman, 76, Ent. Bk. 13, temporary

Stedman, Harry, 1889, 1894, Parents: Carl and Mary (deceased) Stedman, 76, Ent. Bk. 13, temporary

Steinman, Matilda, 1888, 1894, Parents: Robert (deceased) and Mary Steinman, 115, Ent. Bk. 13, temporary

Steinman, Matilda, 1888, 1895, mother: Mary Steinman; in hospital with consumption, 227, Ent. Bk. 13, crt. 4.134

Steinman, Sophie, 1886, 1894, Parents: Robert (deceased) and Mary Steinman, 115, Ent. Bk. 13, temporary

Steinman, Sophie, 1886, 1895, mother: Mary Steinman; in hospital with consumption, 227, Ent. Bk. 13, crt. 4.134

Stephens, Edward, 1891, 1894, Parents: Harry and Annie Stephens, 112, Ent. Bk. 13, crt. 4.39

Stevens, Thomas, 1892, 1895, Parents: George and Jennie (deceased) Stevens, 214, Ent. Bk. 13, crt. 4.124

Stevenson, Archie, , 1894, Parents: William and Julia Stevenson, 164, Ent. Bk. 13, crt. 4.82

Stevenson, Charles, , 1894, Parents: William and Julia Stevenson, 164, Ent. Bk. 13, crt. 4.82

Stevenson, Harry, , 1894, Parents: William and Julia Stevenson, 164, Ent. Bk. 13, crt. 4.82

Stevenson, Lizzie, , 1894, Parents: William and Julia Stevenson, 164, Ent. Bk. 13, crt. 4.82

Stevenson, William, , 1894, Parents: William and Julia Stevenson, 164, Ent. Bk. 13, crt. 4.82

Stiner, Curtis, 1892, 1895, Parents: Morris and Jennie Stiner, 201, Ent. Bk. 13, crt. 4.114

Stream, Charles, 1888, 1895, Parents: Alexander and Johanna (deceased) Stream, 260, Ent. Bk. 13, crt. 4.160

Sturm, Caroline, 1890, 1893, parents unknown, 61, Ent. Bk. 13, crt. 3.467

Sturm, Charles, 1889, 1893, mother: Anna Sturm, 16, Ent. Bk. 13, crt. 3.365

Taber, Harriet, 1888, 1894, Parents: George and Jennie Taber, 122, Ent. Bk. 13, crt. 4.35

Thompson, Christina, 1891, 1895, Parents: James and Margaret Thompson, 277, Ent. Bk. 13, crt. 4.175

Thompson, Florence, 1884, 1893, Parents: Charles and Kate Thompson, 38, Ent. Bk. 13, crt. 3.413

Thompson, Rachael, 1889, 1895, Parents: James and Margaret Thompson, 277, Ent. Bk. 13, crt. 4.175

Thomson, Culver, 1889, 1895, Parents: Frank (deceased) and Sarah Thomson, 237, Ent. Bk. 13, crt. 4.143

Thomson, McCauley, 1886, 1895, Parents: Frank (deceased) and Sarah Thomson, 237, Ent. Bk. 13, crt. 4.143

Thomson, Woodward, 1891, 1895, Parents: Frank (deceased) and Sarah Thomson, 250, Ent. Bk. 13, crt. 4.151

Ulmer, Jacob, 1892, 1894, Parents: Joseph and Carrie Ulmer, 120, Ent. Bk. 13, crt. 3.44

Ulmer, Martha, 1890, 1894, Parents: Joseph and Carrie Ulmer, 120, Ent. Bk. 13, crt. 3.44

Umback, Zika, 1889, 1894, parents cannot be found, 177, Ent. Bk. 13, crt. 4.93

Valardo, Angelo, 1890, 1894, father deceased; mother dying in Bellevue Hospital, 189, Ent. Bk. 13, temporary

Vogan, Eliza, 1882, 1894, Parents: John and Katharine Vogan, 182, Ent. Bk. 13, crt. 4.97

Vogan, George, 1889, 1894, Parents: John and Katharine Vogan, 182, Ent. Bk. 13, crt. 4.97

Vohdin, Bella, 1891, 1893, Parents: Philip and Lena Vohdin (deceased), 3, Ent. Bk. 13, crt. 3.346

Vohdin, Charlotte, 1889, 1893, Parents: Philip and Lena Vohdin (deceased), 3, Ent. Bk. 13, crt. 3.346

Vohdin, Nellie, 1885, 1893, Parents: Philip and Lena Vohdin (deceased), 20, Ent. Bk. 13, crt. 3.368

Vohdin, Philip, 1887, 1893, Parents: Philip and Lena Vohdin (deceased), 3, Ent. Bk. 13, crt. 3.345

Volker, Henrietta, 1883, 1895, Parents: Henry and Prudence Volker, 249, Ent. Bk. 13, crt. 4.150

Walters, May, , 1894, mother: Emma, 108, Ent. Bk. 13, crt. 4.37

Ward, Ralph, 1888, 1894, been at Wards Island, 92, Ent. Bk. 13, crt. 4.20

Weisberg, Israel, 1888, 1893, Parents: Morris and Sarah Weisberg, 49, Ent. Bk. 13, crt. 3.439

White, Joseph, 1889, 1893, parents unknown, 23, Ent. Bk. 13, crt. 3.376

Wilhelm, Kate, 1890, 1894, Parents: Henry and Louisa Wilhelm, 100, Ent. Bk. 13, crt. 4.29

Williams, Edith, 1891, 1894, Parents: Edward and Ella (deceased) Williams, 119, Ent. Bk. 13, crt. 3.43

Williams, Jessie, 1888, 1894, Parents: Edward and Ella (deceased) Williams, 119, Ent. Bk. 13, crt. 3.43

Williamson, Ellen, 1890, 1895, Parents: Leslie and Ellen Williamson, 255, Ent. Bk. 13, crt. 4.155

Williamson, John, 1892, 1895, Parents: Leslie and Ellen Williamson, 255, Ent. Bk. 13, crt. 4.155

Williamson, Thomas, 1889, 1895, Parents: Leslie and Ellen Williamson, 255, Ent. Bk. 13, crt. 4.155

Wilson, Anna, 1886, 1893, Parents: Charles and Alberta Wilson, 64, Ent. Bk. 13, crt. 4.4

Wilson, Eda, 1888, 1893, Parents: Charles and Alberta Wilson, 64, Ent. Bk. 13, crt. 4.4

Wilson, Karl, 1890, 1893, Parents: Charles and Alberta Wilson, 64, Ent. Bk. 13, crt. 4.4

Wiseman, Lillie, 1885, 1895, Parents: William and Martha Wiseman, 247, Ent. Bk. 13, temporary

Witt, Louisa, 1892, 1895, , 263, Ent. Bk. 13, crt. 4.163

Witt, Mary, 1890, 1895, , 263, Ent. Bk. 13, crt. 4.163

Wood, Roderick, 1886, 1894, Parents: John (deceased) and Rose Wood, 80, Ent. Bk. 13, crt. 4.14

Wooddell, Mamie, 1884, 1893, Parents: Simon and Eleanor Wooddell (both deceased), 71, Ent. Bk. 13, crt. 4.8

Woods, Agnes, 1885, 1895, mother: Mary Woods; in Bellevue Hospital, 266, Ent. Bk. 13, crt. 4.165

Woods, May, 1891, 1895, mother: Mary Woods; in Bellevue Hospital, 266, Ent. Bk. 13, crt. 4.165

Worl, Marie, 1888, 1893, Parents: William (deceased) and Charlotte Worl, 75, Ent. Bk. 13, temporary

Worl, Oakes, 1890, 1893, Parents: William (deceased) and Charlotte Worl, 75, Ent. Bk. 13, temporary

Wurch, Alphonse, 1890, 1895, Parents: Paul and Mary Wurch, 223, Ent. Bk. 13, crt. 4.131

Wurch, Olymphia, 1892, 1895, Parents: Paul and Mary Wurch, 223, Ent. Bk. 13, crt. 4.131

Yobs, Annie, , 1895, Parents: Frederick and Augusta Yobs, 234, Ent. Bk. 13, crt. 4.140

Yobs, Lizzie, , 1895, Parents: Frederick and Augusta Yobs, 234, Ent. Bk. 13, crt. 4.140

Young, Elizabeth, 1894, 1895, Parents: John and Mary Young, 219, Ent. Bk. 13, perm. 11.235

Young, Eugene, 1890, 1893, Parents: William and Annie Young, 19, Ent. Bk. 13, crt. 3.370

Young, Eugene, 1890, 1894, Parents: William and Annie Young, 98, Ent. Bk. 13, crt. 4.27

Young, Ruth, 1884, 1895, Parents: Robert Young and Emma Bent, 241, Ent. Bk. 13, temporary

Zimmerman, Arthur, 1888, 1894, Parents: Otto and Bernardino Zimmerman, 101, Ent. Bk. 13, temp. crt. Case

Zimmerman, Oliver, 1890, 1894, Parents: Otto and Bernardino Zimmerman, 101, Ent. Bk. 13, temp. crt. Case

Zimmerman, Walter, 1891, 1894, Parents: Otto and Bernardino Zimmerman, 101, Ent. Bk. 13, temp. crt. Case

Zinn, George, 1892, 1895, Parents: George and Bertha Zinn, 283, Ent. Bk. 13, crt. 4.181

Zinn, Mamie, 1890, 1895, Parents: George and Bertha Zinn, 283, Ent. Bk. 13, crt. 4.181

Zoller, Bertha, 1891, 1895, mother deceased, 275, Ent. Bk. 13, crt. 4.170

Zoller, Frederick, 1885, 1895, mother deceased, 275, Ent. Bk. 13, crt. 4.170

Zoller, Minnie, 1886, 1895, mother deceased, 275, Ent. Bk. 13, crt. 4.170

AMERICAN FEMALE GUARDIAN SOCIETY
HOME FOR THE FRIENDLESS
BOOK 16

Last Name, First Name, Admitted Date, Age/Yrs., Age/Mos., Recorded Date, Notes

Abdallian, Queenie, "Mar. 1, 1897", , , August 1899 Tempy. & Home Book 16
Abdallian, Queenie, "Mar. 1, 1897", , , July 1899 Tempy. & Home Book 16,
Abdallian, Queenie, "Mar. 1, 1897", , , June 1899 Tempy & Home Book 16,
Abdallian, Queenie, "Mar. 1, 1897", , , Oct. 1899 Tempy & Home Book 16, "Dis. To mother Oct. 27, 1899"
Abdallian, Queenie, "Mar. 1, 1897", , , Sept. 1899 Temp. & Home Book 16,
Abdallian, Queenie, "Mar. 1, 1897", 8, 2, May 1899 Home & Tempy. Book 16,
Aguado, Alphonso, "Nov. 14, 1898", , , Apr. 1900 Court Book 16
Aguado, Alphonso, "Nov. 14, 1898", , , August 1899 Court Book 16
Aguado, Alphonso, "Nov. 14, 1898", , , Dec. 1899 Court Book 16,
Aguado, Alphonso, "Nov. 14, 1898", , , Feb. 1900 Court Book 16,
Aguado, Alphonso, "Nov. 14, 1898", , , Jan. 1900 Court Book 16
Aguado, Alphonso, "Nov. 14, 1898", , , July 1899 Court Book 16
Aguado, Alphonso, "Nov. 14, 1898", , , June 1899 Court Book 16,
Aguado, Alphonso, "Nov. 14, 1898", , , June 1900 Court Book 16
Aguado, Alphonso, "Nov. 14, 1898", , , Mar. 1900 Court Book 16
Aguado, Alphonso, "Nov. 14, 1898", , , May 1900 Court Book 16
Aguado, Alphonso, "Nov. 14, 1898", , , Nov. 1899 Court Book 16
Aguado, Alphonso, "Nov. 14, 1898", , , Oct. 1899 Court Book 16
Aguado, Alphonso, "Nov. 14, 1898", , , Sept. 1899 Court Book 16
Aguado, Alphonso, "Nov. 14, 1898", 5, 8, May 1899 Court - Boys Book 16,
Aguado, Ernest, "Sept. 15, 1899", , , Dec. 1899 Nursery Court Book 16
Aguado, Ernest, "Sept. 15, 1899", , , Feb. 1900 Tempy & Home Book 16,
Aguado, Ernest, "Sept. 21, 1899", , , Nov. 1899 Tempy & Home Book 16,
Aguado, Ernest, "Sept. 21, 1899", , , Nov. 1899 Tempy & Home Book 16,
Aguado, Ernest, "Sept. 21, 1899", 3, 6, Sept. 1899 Tempy. & Home Book 16,
Aguardo, Ernest, "Sept. 15, 1899"

Aguardo, Ernest, “Sept. 15, 1899”, , , Apr. 1900 Tempy & Home Book 16,
Aguardo, Ernest, “Sept. 15, 1899”, , , Feb. 1900 Tempy & Home Book 16, Board paid $6.00
Aguardo, Ernest, “Sept. 15, 1899”, , , Jan. 1900 Tempy & Home Book 16,
Aguardo, Ernest, “Sept. 15, 1899”, , , June 1900 Tempy & Home Book 16, Board paid
Aguardo, Ernest, “Sept. 15, 1899”, , , Mar. 1900 Tempy & House Book 16,
Aguardo, Ernest, “Sept. 15, 1899”, , , May 1900 Tempy & Home Book 16,
Aguardo, Ernest, “Sept. 21, 1899”, , , Dec. 1899 Tempy & Home Book 16,
Aguardo, Ernest, “Sept. 21, 1899”, , , Nov. 1899 Tempy & Home Book 16,
Aguardo, Ernest, “Sept. 21, 1899”, 3, 7, Oct. 1899 Tempy & Home Book 16, Board paid
Allen, Rachel, “Oct. 6, 1899”
Allen, Rachel, “Oct. 6, 1899”, , , Apr. 1900 Tempy & Home Book 16,
Allen, Rachel, “Oct. 6, 1899”, , , Feb. 1900 Tempy & Home Book 16,
Allen, Rachel, “Oct. 6, 1899”, , , Jan. 1900 Tempy & Home Book 16,
Allen, Rachel, “Oct. 6, 1899”, , , June 1900 Tempy & Home Book 16,
Allen, Rachel, “Oct. 6, 1899”, , , Mar. 1900 Tempy & House Book 16,
Allen, Rachel, “Oct. 6, 1899”, , , May 1900 Tempy & Home Book 16,
Allen, Rachel, “Oct. 9, 1899”, , , Dec. 1899 Tempy & Home Book 16,
Allen, Rachel, “Oct. 9, 1899”, , , Nov. 1899 Tempy & Home Book 16,
Allen, Rachel, “Oct. 9, 1899”, 11, 7, Oct. 1899 Tempy & Home Book 16,
Anderson, Gertrude, “Apr. 24, 1899”, , , June 1899 Tempy & Home Book 16, “Dis. To mother June 27, 1899”
Anderson, Gertrude, “Apr. 24, 1899”, 11, 1, May 1899 Home & Tempy. Book 16,
Anderson, Torvo, “Feb. 1, 1900”, 3, , Feb. 1900 Nursery Court Book 16, “Dis. To father Feb. 20, 1900”
Anderson, Tygne, “Feb. 1, 1900”, 2, , Feb. 1900 Nursery Court Book 16, “Dis. To father Feb. 20, 1900”
Anglade, Charles, “Apr. 1, 1899”, , , August 1899 Tempy. & Home Book 16
Anglade, Charles, “Apr. 1, 1899”, , , July 1899 Tempy. & Home Book 16,
Anglade, Charles, “Apr. 1, 1899”, , , June 1899 Tempy & Home Book 16,
Anglade, Charles, “Apr. 1, 1899”, , , Oct. 1899 Tempy & Home Book 16, “Dis. To sister Oct. 28, 1899”
Anglade, Charles, “Apr. 1, 1899”, , , Sept. 1899 Temp. & Home Book 16

Anglade, Charles, "Apr. 1, 1899", 6, 3, May 1899 Home & Tempy. Book 16, hosp.
Bauer, Christina, "Feb. 25, 1898", , , Apr. 1900 Court Book 16,
Bauer, Christina, "Feb. 25, 1898", , , August 1899 Court Book 16
Bauer, Christina, "Feb. 25, 1898", , , Dec. 1899 Court Book 16
Bauer, Christina, "Feb. 25, 1898", , , Feb. 1900 Court Book 16,
Bauer, Christina, "Feb. 25, 1898", , , Jan. 1900 Court Book 16,
Bauer, Christina, "Feb. 25, 1898", , , July 1899 Court Book 16,
Bauer, Christina, "Feb. 25, 1898", , , June 1899 Court Book 16,
Bauer, Christina, "Feb. 25, 1898", , , June 1900 Court Book 16,
Bauer, Christina, "Feb. 25, 1898", , , Mar. 1900 Court Book 16,
Bauer, Christina, "Feb. 25, 1898", , , May 1900 Court Book 16
Bauer, Christina, "Feb. 25, 1898", , , Nov. 1899 Court Book 16,
Bauer, Christina, "Feb. 25, 1898", , , Oct. 1899 Court Book 16
Bauer, Christina, "Feb. 25, 1898", , , Sept. 1899 Court Book 16,
Bauer, Christina, "Feb. 25, 1898", 13, 3, May 1899 Court - Girls Book 16,
Bauer, George, "Jan. 26, 1898", , , Apr. 1900 Court Book 16
Bauer, George, "Jan. 26, 1898", , , August 1899 Court Book 16
Bauer, George, "Jan. 26, 1898", , , Dec. 1899 Court Book 16,
Bauer, George, "Jan. 26, 1898", , , Feb. 1900 Court Book 16
Bauer, George, "Jan. 26, 1898", , , Jan. 1900 Court Book 16
Bauer, George, "Jan. 26, 1898", , , July 1899 Court Book 16
Bauer, George, "Jan. 26, 1898", , , June 1899 Court Book 16,
Bauer, George, "Jan. 26, 1898", , , June 1900 Court Book 16
Bauer, George, "Jan. 26, 1898", , , Mar. 1900 Court Book 16
Bauer, George, "Jan. 26, 1898", , , May 1900 Court Book 16
Bauer, George, "Jan. 26, 1898", , , Nov. 1899 Court Book 16
Bauer, George, "Jan. 26, 1898", , , Oct. 1899 Court Book 16
Bauer, George, "Jan. 26, 1898", , , Sept. 1899 Court Book 16
Bauer, George, "Jan. 26, 1898", 6, 8, May 1899 Court - Boys Book 16,
Bauer, Louisa, "Apr. 5, 1899", , , August 1899 Tempy. & Home Book 16
Bauer, Louisa, "Apr. 5, 1899", , , Dec. 1899 Tempy & Home Book 16,
Bauer, Louisa, "Apr. 5, 1899", , , July 1899 Tempy. & Home Book 16, Board Paid
Bauer, Louisa, "Apr. 5, 1899", , , June 1899 Tempy & Home Book 16, Board paid June 1899
Bauer, Louisa, "Apr. 5, 1899", , , Nov. 1899 Tempy & Home Book 16,
Bauer, Louisa, "Apr. 5, 1899", , , Oct. 1899 Tempy & Home Book 16, Board paid
Bauer, Louisa, "Apr. 5, 1899", , , Sept. 1899 Temp. & Home Book 16
Bauer, Louisa, "Apr. 5, 1899", 5, 6, May 1899 Home & Tempy. Book 16,
Bauer, Louisa, "Mar. 11, 1899", , , ,

Bauer, Louisa, "Mar. 11, 1899", , , Apr. 1900 Tempy & Home Book 16, Board

Bauer, Louisa, "Mar. 11, 1899", , , Feb. 1900 Tempy & Home Book 16, Board paid $5.00

Bauer, Louisa, "Mar. 11, 1899", , , Jan. 1900 Tempy & Home Book 16, board paid $5.00

Bauer, Louisa, "Mar. 11, 1899", , , June 1900 Tempy & Home Book 16, Trans. To Court list Board paid

Bauer, Louisa, "Mar. 11, 1899", , , Mar. 1900 Tempy & House Book 16,

Bauer, Louisa, "Mar. 11, 1899", , , May 1900 Tempy & Home Book 16,

Benson, Lillie, "Jan. 4, 1895", , , Apr. 1900 Court Book 16,

Benson, Lillie, "Jan. 4, 1895", , , August 1899 Court Book 16

Benson, Lillie, "Jan. 4, 1895", , , Dec. 1899 Court Book 16

Benson, Lillie, "Jan. 4, 1895", , , Feb. 1900 Court Book 16

Benson, Lillie, "Jan. 4, 1895", , , Jan. 1900 Court Book 16,

Benson, Lillie, "Jan. 4, 1895", , , July 1899 Court Book 16

Benson, Lillie, "Jan. 4, 1895", , , June 1899 Court Book 16,

Benson, Lillie, "Jan. 4, 1895", , , June 1900 Court Book 16,

Benson, Lillie, "Jan. 4, 1895", , , Mar. 1900 Court Book 16,

Benson, Lillie, "Jan. 4, 1895", , , May 1900 Court Book 16,

Benson, Lillie, "Jan. 4, 1895", , , Nov. 1899 Court Book 16,

Benson, Lillie, "Jan. 4, 1895", , , Oct. 1899 Court Book 16,

Benson, Lillie, "Jan. 4, 1895", , , Sept. 1899 Court Book 16

Benson, Lillie, "Jan. 4, 1895", 10, 4, May 1899 Court - Girls Book 16,

Blaise, Mamie, "Mar. 11, 1899", , , August 1899 Tempy. & Home Book 16

Blaise, Mamie, "Mar. 11, 1899", , , Dec. 1899 Tempy & Home Book 16, "Dis. To mother Dec. 15, 1899"

Blaise, Mamie, "Mar. 11, 1899", , , July 1899 Tempy. & Home Book 16, Board Paid

Blaise, Mamie, "Mar. 11, 1899", , , June 1899 Tempy & Home Book 16,

Blaise, Mamie, "Mar. 11, 1899", , , Nov. 1899 Tempy & Home Book 16,

Blaise, Mamie, "Mar. 11, 1899", , , Oct. 1899 Tempy & Home Book 16, Board paid

Blaise, Mamie, "Mar. 11, 1899", , , Sept. 1899 Temp. & Home Book 16

Blaise, Mamie, "Mar. 11, 1899", 8, 2, May 1899 Home & Tempy. Book 16,

Blome, Annie, "Oct. 26, 1896", , , August 1899 Court Nursery Book 16

Blome, Annie, "Oct. 26, 1896", , , July 1899 Court - Nursery Book 16

Blome, Annie, "Oct. 26, 1896", , , June 1899 Court Book 16

Blome, Annie, "Oct. 26, 1896", , , Sept. 1899 Court-Nursery Book 16, "Dis. To mother Sept. 26, 1899"
Blome, Annie, "Oct. 26, 1896", 5, 11, May 1899 Court - Nursery Book 16,
Blome, Emma, "July 26, 1898", , , August 1899 Court Book 16
Blome, Emma, "July 26, 1898", , , July 1899 Court Book 16,
Blome, Emma, "July 26, 1898", , , June 1899 Court Book 16,
Blome, Emma, "July 26, 1898", , , Sept. 1899 Court Book 16, "Dis. To mother Sept. 8, 1899"
Blome, Emma, "July 26, 1898", 10, , May 1899 Court - Girls Book 16,
Bock, Annie, "July 23, 1895", , , Apr. 1900 Nursery Court Book 16
Bock, Annie, "July 23, 1895", , , August 1899 Court Nursery Book 16
Bock, Annie, "July 23, 1895", , , Dec. 1899 Nursery Court Book 16,
Bock, Annie, "July 23, 1895", , , Feb. 1900 Nursery Court Book 16,
Bock, Annie, "July 23, 1895", , , Jan. 1900 Nursery Court Book 16
Bock, Annie, "July 23, 1895", , , July 1899 Court - Nursery Book 16
Bock, Annie, "July 23, 1895", , , June 1899 Court Book 16,
Bock, Annie, "July 23, 1895", , , June 1900 Nursery Court Book 16,
Bock, Annie, "July 23, 1895", , , Mar. 1900 Nursery Court Book 16
Bock, Annie, "July 23, 1895", , , May 1900 Nursery Court Book 16,
Bock, Annie, "July 23, 1895", , , Nov. 1899 Nursery Court Book 16
Bock, Annie, "July 23, 1895", , , Oct. 1899 Court - Nursery Book 16,
Bock, Annie, "July 23, 1895", , , Sept. 1899 Court-Nursery Book 16
Bock, Annie, "July 23, 1895", 7, 4, May 1899 Court - Nursery Book 16,
Bock, Mary, "Dec. 16, 1895", , , Apr. 1900 Nursery Court Book 16
Bock, Mary, "Dec. 16, 1895", , , August 1899 Court Nursery Book 16
Bock, Mary, "Dec. 16, 1895", , , Dec. 1899 Nursery Court Book 16,
Bock, Mary, "Dec. 16, 1895", , , Feb. 1900 Nursery Court Book 16,
Bock, Mary, "Dec. 16, 1895", , , Jan. 1900 Nursery Court Book 16
Bock, Mary, "Dec. 16, 1895", , , July 1899 Court - Nursery Book 16
Bock, Mary, "Dec. 16, 1895", , , June 1899 Court Book 16,
Bock, Mary, "Dec. 16, 1895", , , June 1900 Nursery Court Book 16,
Bock, Mary, "Dec. 16, 1895", , , Mar. 1900 Nursery Court Book 16
Bock, Mary, "Dec. 16, 1895", , , May 1900 Nursery Court Book 16,
Bock, Mary, "Dec. 16, 1895", , , Nov. 1899 Nursery Court Book 16
Bock, Mary, "Dec. 16, 1895", , , Oct. 1899 Court - Nursery Book 16,
Bock, Mary, "Dec. 16, 1895", , , Sept. 1899 Court-Nursery Book 16
Bock, Mary, "Dec. 16, 1895", 9, 1, May 1899 Court - Nursery Book 16,
Boslen, Edward, "Sept. 11, 1899", 3, 7, Sept. 1899 Tempy. & Home Book 16,
Bosler, Edward, "Aug. 21, 1899", , , ,
Bosler, Edward, "Aug. 21, 1899", , , Apr. 1900 Tempy & Home Book 16, Board

Bosler, Edward, "Aug. 21, 1899", , , Feb. 1900 Tempy & Home Book 16, Board paid $4.00
Bosler, Edward, "Aug. 21, 1899", , , Jan. 1900 Tempy & Home Book 16,
Bosler, Edward, "Aug. 21, 1899", , , June 1900 Tempy & Home Book 16, Board paid
Bosler, Edward, "Aug. 21, 1899", , , Mar. 1900 Tempy & House Book 16,
Bosler, Edward, "Aug. 21, 1899", , , May 1900 Tempy & Home Book 16,
Bosler, Edward, "Nov. 22, 1899", , , Dec. 1899 Nursery Court Book 16
Bosler, Edward, "Sept. 11, 1899", , , Dec. 1899 Tempy & Home Book 16,
Bosler, Edward, "Sept. 11, 1899", , , Nov. 1899 Tempy & Home Book 16,
Bosler, Edward, "Sept. 11, 1899", , , Nov. 1899 Tempy & Home Book 16,
Bosler, Edward, "Sept. 11, 1899", , , Nov. 1899 Tempy & Home Book 16
Bosler, Edward, "Sept. 11, 1899", , , Oct. 1899 Tempy & Home Book 16,
Brady, Katie, "Dec. 29, 1899"
Brady, Katie, "Dec. 29, 1899", , , Apr. 1900 Tempy & Home Book 16, Board
Brady, Katie, "Dec. 29, 1899", , , Feb. 1900 Tempy & Home Book 16, Board paid $5.00
Brady, Katie, "Dec. 29, 1899", , , Jan. 1900 Tempy & Home Book 16,
Brady, Katie, "Dec. 29, 1899", , , June 1900 Tempy & Home Book 16, board paid
Brady, Katie, "Dec. 29, 1899", , , Mar. 1900 Tempy & House Book 16,
Brady, Katie, "Dec. 29, 1899", , , May 1900 Tempy & Home Book 16,
Brady, Katie, "Dec. 29, 1899", 3, 10, Dec. 1899 Tempy & Home Book 16
Brady, Lizzie, "Dec. 14, 1898", , , Apr. 1900 Nursery Court Book 16
Brady, Lizzie, "Dec. 14, 1898", , , Dec. 1899 Nursery Court Book 16,
Brady, Lizzie, "Dec. 14, 1898", , , Feb. 1900 Nursery Court Book 16,
Brady, Lizzie, "Dec. 14, 1898", , , Jan. 1900 Nursery Court Book 16
Brady, Lizzie, "Dec. 14, 1898", , , June 1900 Nursery Court Book 16
Brady, Lizzie, "Dec. 14, 1898", , , Mar. 1900 Nursery Court Book 16
Brady, Lizzie, "Dec. 14, 1898", , , May 1900 Nursery Court Book 16
Brady, Lizzie, "Dec. 18, 1898", , , August 1899 Court Nursery Book 16
Brady, Lizzie, "Dec. 18, 1898", , , July 1899 Court - Nursery Book 16
Brady, Lizzie, "Dec. 18, 1898", , , June 1899 Court - Nursery Book 16

Brady, Lizzie, "Dec. 18, 1898", , , Nov. 1899 Nursery Court Book 16
Brady, Lizzie, "Dec. 18, 1898", , , Oct. 1899 Court - Nursery Book 16,
Brady, Lizzie, "Dec. 18, 1898", , , Sept. 1899 Court-Nursery Book 16
Brady, Lizzie, "Dec. 18, 1898", 6, 11, May 1899 Court - Nursery Book 16,
Breasen, Elia, "May 2, 1898", , , Apr. 1900 Nursery Court Book 16,
Breasen, Elia, "May 2, 1898", , , August 1899 Court Nursery Book 16
Breasen, Elia, "May 2, 1898", , , Dec. 1899 Nursery Court Book 16,
Breasen, Elia, "May 2, 1898", , , Feb. 1900 Nursery Court Book 16
Breasen, Elia, "May 2, 1898", , , Jan. 1900 Nursery Court Book 16,
Breasen, Elia, "May 2, 1898", , , July 1899 Court - Nursery Book 16
Breasen, Elia, "May 2, 1898", , , June 1899 Court - Nursery Book 16
Breasen, Elia, "May 2, 1898", , , June 1900 Nursery Court Book 16,
Breasen, Elia, "May 2, 1898", , , Mar. 1900 Nursery Court Book 16
Breasen, Elia, "May 2, 1898", , , May 1900 Nursery Court Book 16
Breasen, Elia, "May 2, 1898", , , Nov. 1899 Nursery Court Book 16
Breasen, Elia, "May 2, 1898", , , Oct. 1899 Court - Nursery Book 16,
Breasen, Elia, "May 2, 1898", , , Sept. 1899 Court-Nursery Book 16,
Breasen, Elia, "May 2, 1898", 5, , May 1899 Court - Nursery Book 16,
Breasen, Harry, , , , Apr. 1900 Nursery Court Book 16,
Breasen, Harry, , , , June 1900 Nursery Court Book 16,
Breason, Emma, "May 2, 1898", , , Apr. 1900 Court Book 16,
Breason, Emma, "May 2, 1898", , , August 1899 Court Book 16
Breason, Emma, "May 2, 1898", , , Dec. 1899 Court Book 16
Breason, Emma, "May 2, 1898", , , Feb. 1900 Court Book 16,
Breason, Emma, "May 2, 1898", , , Jan. 1900 Court Book 16,
Breason, Emma, "May 2, 1898", , , July 1899 Court Book 16,
Breason, Emma, "May 2, 1898", , , June 1899 Court Book 16,
Breason, Emma, "May 2, 1898", , , June 1900 Court Book 16,
Breason, Emma, "May 2, 1898", , , Mar. 1900 Court Book 16
Breason, Emma, "May 2, 1898", , , May 1900 Court Book 16
Breason, Emma, "May 2, 1898", , , Nov. 1899 Court Book 16
Breason, Emma, "May 2, 1898", , , Oct. 1899 Court Book 16
Breason, Emma, "May 2, 1898", , , Sept. 1899 Court Book 16,
Breason, Emma, "May 2, 1898", 8, , May 1899 Court - Girls Book 16,
Breason, Harry, , , , May 1900 Nursery Court Book 16
Breason, Harry, "Apr. 25, 1898", 3, 1, June 1899 Court - Nursery Book 16
Breason, Harry, "May 2, 1898", , , August 1899 Court Nursery Book 16
Breason, Harry, "May 2, 1898", , , Nov. 1899 Nursery Court Book 16
Breason, Harry, "May 2, 1898", , , Oct. 1899 Court - Nursery Book 16,

Breason, Harry, “May 2, 1898”, , , Sept. 1899 Court-Nursery Book 16

Breason, Harry, “May 2, 1898”, 3, 2, July 1899 Court - Nursery Book 16

Breason, Harry, “May 5, 1899”, , , Dec. 1899 Nursery Court Book 16

Breason, Harry, “May 5, 1899”, , , Jan. 1900 Nursery Court Book 16

Bussell, Bessie, “Oct. 7, 1899”, , , Nov. 1899 Tempy & Home Book 16, “Sent to Mrs. Slagle Nov. 2, 1899”

Bussell, Bessie, “Oct. 7, 1899”, 2, 11, Oct. 1899 Tempy & Home Book 16, Board paid

Bussell, Philip, “Apr. 16, 1900”

Bussell, Philip, “Apr. 16, 1900”, , , June 1900 Tempy & Home Book 16, board paid

Bussell, Philip, “Apr. 16, 1900”, , , May 1900 Tempy & Home Book 16,

Bussell, Philip, “Apr. 16, 1900”, 6, 9, Apr. 1900 Tempy & Home Book 16, Board

Bussell, Richard, “Apr. 8, 1898”, , , August 1899 Tempy. & Home Book 16

Bussell, Richard, “Apr. 8, 1898”, , , Dec. 1899 Tempy & Home Book 16,

Bussell, Richard, “Apr. 8, 1898”, , , July 1899 Tempy. & Home Book 16, Board Paid

Bussell, Richard, “Apr. 8, 1898”, , , June 1899 Tempy & Home Book 16, Board paid June 1899

Bussell, Richard, “Apr. 8, 1898”, , , Nov. 1899 Tempy & Home Book 16,

Bussell, Richard, “Apr. 8, 1898”, , , Oct. 1899 Tempy & Home Book 16, Board paid $5.00

Bussell, Richard, “Apr. 8, 1898”, , , Sept. 1899 Temp. & Home Book 16,

Bussell, Richard, “Apr. 8, 1898”, 8, 3, May 1899 Home & Tempy. Book 16,

Bussell, Richard, “Aug. 12, 1897”, , , ,

Bussell, Richard, “Aug. 12, 1897”, , , Apr. 1900 Tempy & Home Book 16, Board

Bussell, Richard, “Aug. 12, 1897”, , , Feb. 1900 Tempy & Home Book 16, Board paid $5.00

Bussell, Richard, “Aug. 12, 1897”, , , Jan. 1900 Tempy & Home Book 16, board paid $5.00

Bussell, Richard, “Aug. 12, 1897”, , , June 1900 Tempy & Home Book 16, Board paid

Bussell, Richard, “Aug. 12, 1897”, , , Mar. 1900 Tempy & House Book 16,

Bussell, Richard, “Aug. 12, 1897”, , , May 1900 Tempy & Home Book 16, Time remaining 197

Bussell, Victor, “Dec. 14, 1898”, , , August 1899 Tempy. & Home Book 16

Bussell, Victor, "Dec. 14, 1898", , , Dec. 1899 Tempy & Home Book 16,
Bussell, Victor, "Dec. 14, 1898", , , July 1899 Tempy. & Home Book 16, Board Paid
Bussell, Victor, "Dec. 14, 1898", , , June 1899 Tempy & Home Book 16, Board paid June 1899
Bussell, Victor, "Dec. 14, 1898", , , Nov. 1899 Tempy & Home Book 16,
Bussell, Victor, "Dec. 14, 1898", , , Oct. 1899 Tempy & Home Book 16, Board paid $5.00
Bussell, Victor, "Dec. 14, 1898", , , Sept. 1899 Temp. & Home Book 16,
Bussell, Victor, "Dec. 14, 1898", 4, 6, May 1899 Home & Tempy. Book 16,
Bussell, Victor, "July 20, 1898", , , ,
Bussell, Victor, "July 20, 1898", , , Apr. 1900 Tempy & Home Book 16, Board
Bussell, Victor, "July 20, 1898", , , Feb. 1900 Tempy & Home Book 16, Board paid $5.00
Bussell, Victor, "July 20, 1898", , , Jan. 1900 Tempy & Home Book 16, board paid $5.00
Bussell, Victor, "July 20, 1898", , , June 1900 Tempy & Home Book 16, Board paid
Bussell, Victor, "July 20, 1898", , , Mar. 1900 Tempy & House Book 16,
Bussell, Victor, "July 20, 1898", , , May 1900 Tempy & Home Book 16,
Cardell, Antonio, "Feb. 28, 1896", , , Apr. 1900 Court Book 16
Cardell, Antonio, "Feb. 28, 1896", , , August 1899 Court Book 16
Cardell, Antonio, "Feb. 28, 1896", , , Dec. 1899 Court Book 16,
Cardell, Antonio, "Feb. 28, 1896", , , Feb. 1900 Court Book 16,
Cardell, Antonio, "Feb. 28, 1896", , , Jan. 1900 Court Book 16
Cardell, Antonio, "Feb. 28, 1896", , , July 1899 Court Book 16
Cardell, Antonio, "Feb. 28, 1896", , , June 1899 Court Book 16,
Cardell, Antonio, "Feb. 28, 1896", , , June 1900 Court Book 16,
Cardell, Antonio, "Feb. 28, 1896", , , Mar. 1900 Court Book 16,
Cardell, Antonio, "Feb. 28, 1896", , , May 1900 Court Book 16,
Cardell, Antonio, "Feb. 28, 1896", , , Nov. 1899 Court Book 16
Cardell, Antonio, "Feb. 28, 1896", , , Oct. 1899 Court Book 16
Cardell, Antonio, "Feb. 28, 1896", , , Sept. 1899 Court Book 16
Cardell, Antonio, "Feb. 28, 1896", 8, 1, May 1899 Court - Boys Book 16,
Cardell, John, "Feb. 28, 1896", , , Apr. 1900 Court Book 16
Cardell, John, "Feb. 28, 1896", , , August 1899 Court Book 16
Cardell, John, "Feb. 28, 1896", , , Dec. 1899 Court Book 16,
Cardell, John, "Feb. 28, 1896", , , Feb. 1900 Court Book 16,
Cardell, John, "Feb. 28, 1896", , , Jan. 1900 Court Book 16
Cardell, John, "Feb. 28, 1896", , , July 1899 Court Book 16
Cardell, John, "Feb. 28, 1896", , , June 1899 Court Book 16,

Cardell, John, "Feb. 28, 1896", , , June 1900 Court Book 16,
Cardell, John, "Feb. 28, 1896", , , Mar. 1900 Court Book 16,
Cardell, John, "Feb. 28, 1896", , , May 1900 Court Book 16,
Cardell, John, "Feb. 28, 1896", , , Nov. 1899 Court Book 16
Cardell, John, "Feb. 28, 1896", , , Oct. 1899 Court Book 16
Cardell, John, "Feb. 28, 1896", , , Sept. 1899 Court Book 16
Cardell, John, "Feb. 28, 1896", 10, 1, May 1899 Court - Boys Book 16,
Childs, Albert, "Feb. 27, 1897", , , Apr. 1900 Court Book 16
Childs, Albert, "Feb. 27, 1897", , , August 1899 Court Book 16
Childs, Albert, "Feb. 27, 1897", , , Dec. 1899 Court Book 16,
Childs, Albert, "Feb. 27, 1897", , , Feb. 1900 Court Book 16
Childs, Albert, "Feb. 27, 1897", , , Jan. 1900 Court Book 16
Childs, Albert, "Feb. 27, 1897", , , July 1899 Court Book 16
Childs, Albert, "Feb. 27, 1897", , , June 1899 Court Book 16,
Childs, Albert, "Feb. 27, 1897", , , June 1900 Court Book 16,
Childs, Albert, "Feb. 27, 1897", , , Mar. 1900 Court Book 16
Childs, Albert, "Feb. 27, 1897", , , May 1900 Court Book 16
Childs, Albert, "Feb. 27, 1897", , , Nov. 1899 Court Book 16
Childs, Albert, "Feb. 27, 1897", , , Oct. 1899 Court Book 16
Childs, Albert, "Feb. 27, 1897", , , Sept. 1899 Court Book 16
Childs, Albert, "Feb. 27, 1897", 7, 2, May 1899 Court - Boys Book 16,
Chippendale, Julie, "Apr. 30, 1900"
Chippendale, Julie, "Apr. 30, 1900", , , May 1900 Tempy & Home Book 16, "Dis. To mother May 28, 1900"
Chippendale, Julie, "Apr. 30, 1900", 5, 9, Apr. 1900 Tempy & Home Book 16, Board
Clerc, Eddie, "Nov. 11, 1895", , , Apr. 1900 Court Book 16
Clerc, Eddie, "Nov. 11, 1895", , , August 1899 Court Book 16
Clerc, Eddie, "Nov. 11, 1895", , , Dec. 1899 Court Book 16,
Clerc, Eddie, "Nov. 11, 1895", , , Feb. 1900 Court Book 16,
Clerc, Eddie, "Nov. 11, 1895", , , Jan. 1900 Court Book 16
Clerc, Eddie, "Nov. 11, 1895", , , July 1899 Court Book 16
Clerc, Eddie, "Nov. 11, 1895", , , June 1899 Court Book 16,
Clerc, Eddie, "Nov. 11, 1895", , , June 1900 Court Book 16,
Clerc, Eddie, "Nov. 11, 1895", , , Mar. 1900 Court Book 16,
Clerc, Eddie, "Nov. 11, 1895", , , May 1900 Court Book 16,
Clerc, Eddie, "Nov. 11, 1895", , , Nov. 1899 Court Book 16
Clerc, Eddie, "Nov. 11, 1895", , , Oct. 1899 Court Book 16
Clerc, Eddie, "Nov. 11, 1895", , , Sept. 1899 Court Book 16
Clerc, Eddie, "Nov. 11, 1895", 8, 5, May 1899 Court - Boys Book 16,
Clerc, Jennie, "Nov. 14, 1898", , , Apr. 1900 Court Book 16
Clerc, Jennie, "Nov. 14, 1898", , , August 1899 Court Book 16
Clerc, Jennie, "Nov. 14, 1898", , , Dec. 1899 Court Book 16
Clerc, Jennie, "Nov. 14, 1898", , , Feb. 1900 Court Book 16,
Clerc, Jennie, "Nov. 14, 1898", , , Jan. 1900 Court Book 16,
Clerc, Jennie, "Nov. 14, 1898", , , July 1899 Court Book 16
Clerc, Jennie, "Nov. 14, 1898", , , June 1899 Court Book 16,

Clerc, Jennie, "Nov. 14, 1898", , , June 1900 Court Book 16,
Clerc, Jennie, "Nov. 14, 1898", , , Mar. 1900 Court Book 16
Clerc, Jennie, "Nov. 14, 1898", , , May 1900 Court Book 16
Clerc, Jennie, "Nov. 14, 1898", , , Nov. 1899 Court Book 16
Clerc, Jennie, "Nov. 14, 1898", , , Oct. 1899 Court Book 16
Clerc, Jennie, "Nov. 14, 1898", , , Sept. 1899 Court Book 16,
Clerc, Jennie, "Nov. 14, 1898", 10, 9, May 1899 Court - Girls Book 16,
Clerc, Louis, "Dec. 7, 1898", , , Apr. 1900 Court Book 16
Clerc, Louis, "Dec. 7, 1898", , , August 1899 Court Book 16
Clerc, Louis, "Dec. 7, 1898", , , Dec. 1899 Court Book 16,
Clerc, Louis, "Dec. 7, 1898", , , Feb. 1900 Court Book 16,
Clerc, Louis, "Dec. 7, 1898", , , Jan. 1900 Court Book 16
Clerc, Louis, "Dec. 7, 1898", , , July 1899 Court Book 16
Clerc, Louis, "Dec. 7, 1898", , , June 1899 Court Book 16,
Clerc, Louis, "Dec. 7, 1898", , , June 1900 Court Book 16
Clerc, Louis, "Dec. 7, 1898", , , Mar. 1900 Court Book 16
Clerc, Louis, "Dec. 7, 1898", , , May 1900 Court Book 16,
Clerc, Louis, "Dec. 7, 1898", , , Nov. 1899 Court Book 16
Clerc, Louis, "Dec. 7, 1898", , , Oct. 1899 Court Book 16,
Clerc, Louis, "Dec. 7, 1898", , , Sept. 1899 Court Book 16
Clerc, Louis, "Dec. 7, 1898", 5, 9, May 1899 Court - Boys Book 16,
Collins, Cyril B., "Mar. 20, 1900", , , Apr. 1900 Tempy & Home Book 16, "Dis to uncle (board) Apr. 9, 1900"
Collins, Cyril B., "Mar. 20, 1900", 6, 9, Mar. 1900 Tempy & House Book 16,
Collins, John G., "Mar. 20, 1900", , , Apr. 1900 Tempy & Home Book 16, "Dis to uncle (board) Apr. 9, 1900"
Collins, John G., "Mar. 20, 1900", 8, 6, Mar. 1900 Tempy & House Book 16,
Collins, William R., "Mar. 20, 1900", , , Apr. 1900 Tempy & Home Book 16, "Dis to uncle (board) Apr. 9, 1900"
Collins, William R., "Mar. 20, 1900", 10, 3, Mar. 1900 Tempy & House Book 16,
Currie, Florence, "Apr. 6, 1898", , , Apr. 1900 Court Book 16
Currie, Florence, "Apr. 6, 1898", , , August 1899 Court Book 16
Currie, Florence, "Apr. 6, 1898", , , Dec. 1899 Court Book 16
Currie, Florence, "Apr. 6, 1898", , , Feb. 1900 Court Book 16,
Currie, Florence, "Apr. 6, 1898", , , Jan. 1900 Court Book 16,
Currie, Florence, "Apr. 6, 1898", , , July 1899 Court Book 16
Currie, Florence, "Apr. 6, 1898", , , June 1899 Court Book 16,
Currie, Florence, "Apr. 6, 1898", , , June 1900 Court Book 16,
Currie, Florence, "Apr. 6, 1898", , , Mar. 1900 Court Book 16
Currie, Florence, "Apr. 6, 1898", , , May 1900 Court Book 16
Currie, Florence, "Apr. 6, 1898", , , Nov. 1899 Court Book 16
Currie, Florence, "Apr. 6, 1898", , , Oct. 1899 Court Book 16
Currie, Florence, "Apr. 6, 1898", , , Sept. 1899 Court Book 16
Currie, Florence, "Apr. 6, 1898", 10, 1, May 1899 Court - Girls Book 16,

Curry, Harold, "May 16, 1895", , , August 1899 Tempy. & Home Book 16
Curry, Harold, "May 16, 1895", , , July 1899 Tempy. & Home Book 16, Board Paid
Curry, Harold, "May 16, 1895", , , Sept. 1899 Temp. & Home Book 16, Dis. To Mother Sept. 12
Curry, Harold, "May 16, 1895", 6, 7, May 1899 Home & Tempy. Book 16,
Curry, Harold, "May 16, 1895", 6, 8, June 1899 Tempy & Home Book 16, Board paid June 1899
Dauman, Margaret, "Aug. 4, 1898", , , Dec. 1899 Nursery Court Book 16,
Dauman, Margaret, "Aug. 4, 1898", , , Jan. 1900 Nursery Court Book 16, "Dis. To home out of state Jan. 11, 1900"
Dauman, Margaret, "Nov. 14, 1898", , , August 1899 Court Nursery Book 16
Dauman, Margaret, "Nov. 14, 1898", , , July 1899 Court - Nursery Book 16
Dauman, Margaret, "Nov. 14, 1898", , , June 1899 Court - Nursery Book 16
Dauman, Margaret, "Nov. 14, 1898", , , Nov. 1899 Nursery Court Book 16
Dauman, Margaret, "Nov. 14, 1898", , , Oct. 1899 Court - Nursery Book 16,
Dauman, Margaret, "Nov. 14, 1898", , , Sept. 1899 Court-Nursery Book 16
Dauman, Margaret, "Nov. 14, 1898", 6, 7, May 1899 Court - Nursery Book 16, H.
DeVries, Anna, "Feb. 5, 1900", , , Mar. 1900 Tempy & House Book 16, "Dis. To father Mar. 5, 1900"
DeVries, Anna, "Feb. 5, 1900", 6, 2, Feb. 1900 Tempy & Home Book 16, Board paid $6.00
DeVries, Mary, "Feb. 5, 1900", , , Mar. 1900 Tempy & House Book 16, "Dis. To father Mar. 5, 1900"
DeVries, Mary, "Feb. 5, 1900", 4, 5, Feb. 1900 Tempy & Home Book 16, Board paid $6.00
Diede, Henry, "Mar. 13, 1897", , , Apr. 1900 Court Book 16
Diede, Henry, "Mar. 13, 1897", , , August 1899 Court Book 16
Diede, Henry, "Mar. 13, 1897", , , Dec. 1899 Court Book 16,
Diede, Henry, "Mar. 13, 1897", , , Feb. 1900 Court Book 16
Diede, Henry, "Mar. 13, 1897", , , Jan. 1900 Court Book 16
Diede, Henry, "Mar. 13, 1897", , , July 1899 Court Book 16
Diede, Henry, "Mar. 13, 1897", , , June 1899 Court Book 16,
Diede, Henry, "Mar. 13, 1897", , , June 1900 Court Book 16
Diede, Henry, "Mar. 13, 1897", , , Mar. 1900 Court Book 16
Diede, Henry, "Mar. 13, 1897", , , May 1900 Court Book 16
Diede, Henry, "Mar. 13, 1897", , , Nov. 1899 Court Book 16
Diede, Henry, "Mar. 13, 1897", , , Oct. 1899 Court Book 16
Diede, Henry, "Mar. 13, 1897", , , Sept. 1899 Court Book 16

Diede, Henry, “Mar. 13, 1897”, 10, 11, May 1899 Court - Boys Book 16,
Dodderer, Raymond, “Oct. 6, 1899”, , , Dec. 1899 Tempy & Home Book 16,
Dodderer, Raymond, “Oct. 6, 1899”, , , Nov. 1899 Tempy & Home Book 16,
Dodderer, Raymond, “Oct. 6, 1899”, 3, 6, Oct. 1899 Tempy & Home Book 16,
Dodderer, Raymond, “Sept. 25, 1899”
Dodderer, Raymond, “Sept. 25, 1899”, , , Apr. 1900 Tempy & Home Book 16,
Dodderer, Raymond, “Sept. 25, 1899”, , , Feb. 1900 Tempy & Home Book 16,
Dodderer, Raymond, “Sept. 25, 1899”, , , Jan. 1900 Tempy & Home Book 16,
Dodderer, Raymond, “Sept. 25, 1899”, , , June 1900 Tempy & Home Book 16,
Dodderer, Raymond, “Sept. 25, 1899”, , , Mar. 1900 Tempy & House Book 16,
Dodderer, Raymond, “Sept. 25, 1899”, , , May 1900 Tempy & Home Book 16,
Doe, Jane, “Jan. 16, 1900”, , , Apr. 1900 Nursery Court Book 16
Doe, Jane, “Jan. 16, 1900”, , , Feb. 1900 Nursery Court Book 16,
Doe, Jane, “Jan. 16, 1900”, , , June 1900 Nursery Court Book 16
Doe, Jane, “Jan. 16, 1900”, , , Mar. 1900 Nursery Court Book 16,
Doe, Jane, “Jan. 16, 1900”, , , May 1900 Nursery Court Book 16,
Doe, Jane, “Jan. 16, 1900”, 4, , Jan. 1900 Nursery Court Book 16
Doe, John #22, “Nov. 8, 1895”, , , August 1899 Court Nursery Book 16
Doe, John #22, “Nov. 8, 1895”, , , Dec. 1899 Nursery Court Book 16, “Dis. To home in state Dec. 2, 1899”
Doe, John #22, “Nov. 8, 1895”, , , July 1899 Court - Nursery Book 16
Doe, John #22, “Nov. 8, 1895”, , , June 1899 Court Book 16,
Doe, John #22, “Nov. 8, 1895”, , , Nov. 1899 Nursery Court Book 16
Doe, John #22, “Nov. 8, 1895”, , , Oct. 1899 Court - Nursery Book 16,
Doe, John #22, “Nov. 8, 1895”, , , Sept. 1899 Court-Nursery Book 16
Doe, John #22, “Nov. 8, 1895”, 5, 5, May 1899 Court - Nursery Book 16,
Doe, John #25, “Feb. 26, 1897”, , , August 1899 Court Book 16
Doe, John #25, “Feb. 26, 1897”, , , Dec. 1899 Court Book 16, “sent West Dec. 5, 1899”
Doe, John #25, “Feb. 26, 1897”, , , July 1899 Court Book 16
Doe, John #25, “Feb. 26, 1897”, , , June 1899 Court Book 16, H.
Doe, John #25, “Feb. 26, 1897”, , , Nov. 1899 Court Book 16
Doe, John #25, “Feb. 26, 1897”, , , Oct. 1899 Court Book 16
Doe, John #25, “Feb. 26, 1897”, , , Sept. 1899 Court Book 16

Doe, John #25, "Feb. 26, 1897", 5, 11, May 1899 Court - Boys Book 16, H.
Doe, John #30, "Aug. 18, 1897", , , August 1899 Court Book 16
Doe, John #30, "Aug. 18, 1897", , , Dec. 1899 Court Book 16, "sent West Dec. 5, 1899"
Doe, John #30, "Aug. 18, 1897", , , July 1899 Court Book 16
Doe, John #30, "Aug. 18, 1897", , , June 1899 Court Book 16,
Doe, John #30, "Aug. 18, 1897", , , Nov. 1899 Court Book 16
Doe, John #30, "Aug. 18, 1897", , , Oct. 1899 Court Book 16
Doe, John #30, "Aug. 18, 1897", , , Sept. 1899 Court Book 16
Doe, John #30, "Aug. 18, 1897", 6, 8, May 1899 Court - Boys Book 16,
Dolanny, Edith, "Feb. 25, 1896", , , Apr. 1900 Court Book 16,
Dolanny, Edith, "Feb. 25, 1896", , , August 1899 Court Book 16
Dolanny, Edith, "Feb. 25, 1896", , , Dec. 1899 Court Book 16
Dolanny, Edith, "Feb. 25, 1896", , , Feb. 1900 Court Book 16
Dolanny, Edith, "Feb. 25, 1896", , , Jan. 1900 Court Book 16
Dolanny, Edith, "Feb. 25, 1896", , , July 1899 Court Book 16
Dolanny, Edith, "Feb. 25, 1896", , , June 1899 Court Book 16,
Dolanny, Edith, "Feb. 25, 1896", , , June 1900 Court Book 16,
Dolanny, Edith, "Feb. 25, 1896", , , Mar. 1900 Court Book 16,
Dolanny, Edith, "Feb. 25, 1896", , , May 1900 Court Book 16,
Dolanny, Edith, "Feb. 25, 1896", , , Nov. 1899 Court Book 16,
Dolanny, Edith, "Feb. 25, 1896", , , Oct. 1899 Court Book 16,
Dolanny, Edith, "Feb. 25, 1896", , , Sept. 1899 Court Book 16
Dolanny, Edith, "Feb. 25, 1896", 12, 1, May 1899 Court - Girls Book 16,
Dolanny, Grace, "June 19, 1896", , , Apr. 1900 Court Book 16,
Dolanny, Grace, "June 19, 1896", , , August 1899 Court Book 16
Dolanny, Grace, "June 19, 1896", , , Dec. 1899 Court Book 16
Dolanny, Grace, "June 19, 1896", , , Feb. 1900 Court Book 16
Dolanny, Grace, "June 19, 1896", , , Jan. 1900 Court Book 16
Dolanny, Grace, "June 19, 1896", , , July 1899 Court Book 16
Dolanny, Grace, "June 19, 1896", , , June 1899 Court Book 16,
Dolanny, Grace, "June 19, 1896", , , June 1900 Court Book 16,
Dolanny, Grace, "June 19, 1896", , , Mar. 1900 Court Book 16,
Dolanny, Grace, "June 19, 1896", , , May 1900 Court Book 16,
Dolanny, Grace, "June 19, 1896", , , Nov. 1899 Court Book 16,
Dolanny, Grace, "June 19, 1896", , , Oct. 1899 Court Book 16
Dolanny, Grace, "June 19, 1896", , , Sept. 1899 Court Book 16,
Dolanny, Grace, "June 19, 1896", 10, , May 1899 Court - Girls Book 16,
Doran, Eliza, "Aug. 11, 1897", , , Apr. 1900 Nursery Court Book 16,
Doran, Eliza, "Aug. 11, 1897", , , August 1899 Court Nursery Book 16
Doran, Eliza, "Aug. 11, 1897", , , Dec. 1899 Nursery Court Book 16,
Doran, Eliza, "Aug. 11, 1897", , , Feb. 1900 Nursery Court Book 16
Doran, Eliza, "Aug. 11, 1897", , , Jan. 1900 Nursery Court Book 16,

Doran, Eliza, "Aug. 11, 1897", , , July 1899 Court - Nursery Book 16
Doran, Eliza, "Aug. 11, 1897", , , June 1899 Court - Nursery Book 16
Doran, Eliza, "Aug. 11, 1897", , , June 1900 Nursery Court Book 16,
Doran, Eliza, "Aug. 11, 1897", , , Mar. 1900 Nursery Court Book 16
Doran, Eliza, "Aug. 11, 1897", , , May 1900 Nursery Court Book 16
Doran, Eliza, "Aug. 11, 1897", , , Nov. 1899 Nursery Court Book 16
Doran, Eliza, "Aug. 11, 1897", , , Oct. 1899 Court - Nursery Book 16,
Doran, Eliza, "Aug. 11, 1897", , , Sept. 1899 Court-Nursery Book 16,
Doran, Eliza, "Aug. 11, 1897", 5, 9, May 1899 Court - Nursery Book 16,
Dowling, Lawrence, "June 15, 1900", 3, 2, June 1900 Tempy & Home Book 16, Board paid
Drews, Elsie, "Jan. 18, 1895", , , August 1899 Court Nursery Book 16
Drews, Elsie, "Jan. 18, 1895", , , July 1899 Court - Nursery Book 16
Drews, Elsie, "Jan. 18, 1895", , , June 1899 Court Book 16, H.
Drews, Elsie, "Jan. 18, 1895", , , Oct. 1899 Court - Nursery Book 16, "Dis. To home in state Oct. 11, 1899"
Drews, Elsie, "Jan. 18, 1895", , , Sept. 1899 Court-Nursery Book 16
Drews, Elsie, "Jan. 18, 1895", 9, , May 1899 Court - Nursery Book 16, H.
Driscoll, Arthur, "Nov. 18, 1899", , , Dec. 1899 Tempy & Home Book 16, transferred to Court list
Driscoll, Arthur, "Nov. 18, 1899", 2, 1, Nov. 1899 Tempy & Home Book 16,
Driscoll, Arthur, "Nov. 20, 1899", , , Dec. 1899 Nursery Court Book 16
Driscoll, Arthur, "Nov. 20, 1899", , , Feb. 1900 Nursery Court Book 16, "Dis. To parents Feb. 23, 1900"
Driscoll, Arthur, "Nov. 20, 1899", , , Jan. 1900 Nursery Court Book 16
Driscoll, Lucy, "Nov. 18, 1899", , , Dec. 1899 Tempy & Home Book 16, transferred to Court list
Driscoll, Lucy, "Nov. 18, 1899", 5, 3, Nov. 1899 Tempy & Home Book 16,
Driscoll, Lucy, "Nov. 20, 1899", , , Feb. 1900 Court Book 16, "Dis. To parents Feb. 23, 1900"
Driscoll, Lucy, "Nov. 20, 1899", , , Jan. 1900 Court Book 16
Driscoll, Lucy, "Nov. 20, 1899", , , Mar. 1900 Court Book 16,
Driscoll, Lucy, "Nov. 20, 1899", 5, 4, Dec. 1899 Court Book 16
Driscoll, William, "Nov. 18, 1899", , , Dec. 1899 Tempy & Home Book 16, transferred to Court list
Driscoll, William, "Nov. 18, 1899", 3, 3, Nov. 1899 Tempy & Home Book 16,

Driscoll, William, "Nov. 20, 1899", , , Feb. 1900 Court Book 16, "Dis. To parents Feb. 23, 1900"
Driscoll, William, "Nov. 20, 1899", , , Jan. 1900 Court Book 16
Driscoll, William, "Nov. 20, 1899", 3, 4, Dec. 1899 Court Book 16,
Fuegel, Anna, "July 23, 1896", , , Apr. 1900 Court Book 16,
Fuegel, Anna, "July 23, 1896", , , August 1899 Court Book 16
Fuegel, Anna, "July 23, 1896", , , Dec. 1899 Court Book 16
Fuegel, Anna, "July 23, 1896", , , Feb. 1900 Court Book 16
Fuegel, Anna, "July 23, 1896", , , Jan. 1900 Court Book 16
Fuegel, Anna, "July 23, 1896", , , July 1899 Court Book 16
Fuegel, Anna, "July 23, 1896", , , June 1899 Court Book 16,
Fuegel, Anna, "July 23, 1896", , , June 1900 Court Book 16, "Dis. To mother June 27, 1900"
Fuegel, Anna, "July 23, 1896", , , Mar. 1900 Court Book 16,
Fuegel, Anna, "July 23, 1896", , , May 1900 Court Book 16,
Fuegel, Anna, "July 23, 1896", , , Nov. 1899 Court Book 16,
Fuegel, Anna, "July 23, 1896", , , Oct. 1899 Court Book 16
Fuegel, Anna, "July 23, 1896", , , Sept. 1899 Court Book 16,
Fuegel, Anna, "July 23, 1896", 9, 9, May 1899 Court - Girls Book 16,
Fuegel, Lizzie, "July 23, 1896", , , Apr. 1900 Nursery Court Book 16,
Fuegel, Lizzie, "July 23, 1896", , , August 1899 Court Nursery Book 16
Fuegel, Lizzie, "July 23, 1896", , , Dec. 1899 Nursery Court Book 16,
Fuegel, Lizzie, "July 23, 1896", , , Feb. 1900 Nursery Court Book 16
Fuegel, Lizzie, "July 23, 1896", , , Jan. 1900 Nursery Court Book 16,
Fuegel, Lizzie, "July 23, 1896", , , July 1899 Court - Nursery Book 16
Fuegel, Lizzie, "July 23, 1896", , , June 1899 Court Book 16
Fuegel, Lizzie, "July 23, 1896", , , June 1900 Nursery Court Book 16,
Fuegel, Lizzie, "July 23, 1896", , , Mar. 1900 Nursery Court Book 16
Fuegel, Lizzie, "July 23, 1896", , , May 1900 Nursery Court Book 16,
Fuegel, Lizzie, "July 23, 1896", , , Nov. 1899 Nursery Court Book 16
Fuegel, Lizzie, "July 23, 1896", , , Oct. 1899 Court - Nursery Book 16,
Fuegel, Lizzie, "July 23, 1896", , , Sept. 1899 Court-Nursery Book 16,
Fuegel, Lizzie, "July 23, 1896", 7, 9, May 1899 Court - Nursery Book 16,
Fuegel, Maggie, "July 11, 1896", , , Apr. 1900 Nursery Court Book 16,
Fuegel, Maggie, "July 11, 1896", , , August 1899 Court Nursery Book 16
Fuegel, Maggie, "July 11, 1896", , , Dec. 1899 Nursery Court Book 16,

Fuegel, Maggie, “July 11, 1896”, , , Feb. 1900 Nursery Court Book 16
Fuegel, Maggie, “July 11, 1896”, , , Jan. 1900 Nursery Court Book 16,
Fuegel, Maggie, “July 11, 1896”, , , July 1899 Court - Nursery Book 16
Fuegel, Maggie, “July 11, 1896”, , , June 1899 Court Book 16
Fuegel, Maggie, “July 11, 1896”, , , June 1900 Nursery Court Book 16,
Fuegel, Maggie, “July 11, 1896”, , , Mar. 1900 Nursery Court Book 16
Fuegel, Maggie, “July 11, 1896”, , , May 1900 Nursery Court Book 16,
Fuegel, Maggie, “July 11, 1896”, , , Nov. 1899 Nursery Court Book 16
Fuegel, Maggie, “July 11, 1896”, , , Oct. 1899 Court - Nursery Book 16,
Fuegel, Maggie, “July 11, 1896”, , , Sept. 1899 Court-Nursery Book 16,
Fuegel, Maggie, “July 11, 1896”, 5, 9, May 1899 Court - Nursery Book 16,
Fuhrer, William, “Jan. 3, 1900”
Fuhrer, William, “Jan. 3, 1900”, , , Apr. 1900 Tempy & Home Book 16,
Fuhrer, William, “Jan. 3, 1900”, , , Feb. 1900 Tempy & Home Book 16,
Fuhrer, William, “Jan. 3, 1900”, , , June 1900 Tempy & Home Book 16, board paid
Fuhrer, William, “Jan. 3, 1900”, , , Mar. 1900 Tempy & House Book 16,
Fuhrer, William, “Jan. 3, 1900”, , , May 1900 Tempy & Home Book 16,
Fuhrer, William, “Jan. 3, 1900”, 4, 6, Jan. 1900 Tempy & Home Book 16,
Fuller, Alice, “July 7, 1898”, , , Apr. 1900 Court Book 16,
Fuller, Alice, “July 7, 1898”, , , August 1899 Court Book 16
Fuller, Alice, “July 7, 1898”, , , Dec. 1899 Court Book 16
Fuller, Alice, “July 7, 1898”, , , Feb. 1900 Court Book 16,
Fuller, Alice, “July 7, 1898”, , , Jan. 1900 Court Book 16,
Fuller, Alice, “July 7, 1898”, , , July 1899 Court Book 16,
Fuller, Alice, “July 7, 1898”, , , June 1899 Court Book 16,
Fuller, Alice, “July 7, 1898”, , , June 1900 Court Book 16,
Fuller, Alice, “July 7, 1898”, , , Mar. 1900 Court Book 16
Fuller, Alice, “July 7, 1898”, , , May 1900 Court Book 16
Fuller, Alice, “July 7, 1898”, , , Nov. 1899 Court Book 16
Fuller, Alice, “July 7, 1898”, , , Oct. 1899 Court Book 16
Fuller, Alice, “July 7, 1898”, , , Sept. 1899 Court Book 16,
Fuller, Alice, “July 7, 1898”, 10, 10, May 1899 Court - Girls Book 16,

Garrett, Martha, “Aug. 1, 1898”, , , August 1899 Court Book 16
Garrett, Martha, “Aug. 1, 1898”, , , Dec. 1899 Court Book 16
Garrett, Martha, “Aug. 1, 1898”, , , Jan. 1900 Court Book 16, “To home out of state Jan. 26, 1900”
Garrett, Martha, “Aug. 1, 1898”, , , July 1899 Court Book 16
Garrett, Martha, “Aug. 1, 1898”, , , June 1899 Court Book 16, H.
Garrett, Martha, “Aug. 1, 1898”, , , Nov. 1899 Court Book 16
Garrett, Martha, “Aug. 1, 1898”, , , Oct. 1899 Court Book 16
Garrett, Martha, “Aug. 1, 1898”, , , Sept. 1899 Court Book 16,
Garrett, Martha, “Aug. 1, 1898”, 11, 6, May 1899 Court - Girls Book 16, H.
Girard, Minnie, “May 22, 1896”, , , Apr. 1900 Nursery Court Book 16, “Dis. To Soc. P.C.C. Apr. 25, 1900”
Girard, Minnie, “May 22, 1896”, , , August 1899 Court Nursery Book 16
Girard, Minnie, “May 22, 1896”, , , Dec. 1899 Nursery Court Book 16,
Girard, Minnie, “May 22, 1896”, , , Feb. 1900 Nursery Court Book 16,
Girard, Minnie, “May 22, 1896”, , , Jan. 1900 Nursery Court Book 16
Girard, Minnie, “May 22, 1896”, , , July 1899 Court - Nursery Book 16
Girard, Minnie, “May 22, 1896”, , , June 1899 Court Book 16
Girard, Minnie, “May 22, 1896”, , , Mar. 1900 Nursery Court Book 16
Girard, Minnie, “May 22, 1896”, , , Nov. 1899 Nursery Court Book 16
Girard, Minnie, “May 22, 1896”, , , Oct. 1899 Court - Nursery Book 16,
Girard, Minnie, “May 22, 1896”, , , Sept. 1899 Court-Nursery Book 16,
Girard, Minnie, “May 22, 1896”, 5, 11, May 1899 Court - Nursery Book 16,
Godwin, Ethelbert, “Sept. 15, 1897”, , , August 1899 Outside Book 16, Island Hospital
Godwin, Ethelbert, “Sept. 15, 1897”, , , July 1899 Outside Book 16
Godwin, Ethelbert, “Sept. 15, 1897”, , , June 1899 Outside Book 16,
Godwin, Ethelbert, “Sept. 15, 1897”, , , Nov. 1899 Outside Book 16, Island Hospital
Godwin, Ethelbert, “Sept. 15, 1897”, , , Oct. 1899 Outside Book 16,
Godwin, Ethelbert, “Sept. 15, 1897”, , , Sept. 1899 Outside Book 16,
Godwin, Ethelbert, “Sept. 15, 1897”, 7, 6, May 1899 Outside Book 16,
Godwin, Ethelbert, “Sept. 25, 1899”, , , Dec. 1899 Nursery Court Book 16, “Island Hosp. Sent to mother Dec. 4, 1899”
Grant, Harold, “Mar. 11, 1899”, , , Apr. 1900 Nursery Court Book 16

Grant, Harold, "Mar. 11, 1899", , , Dec. 1899 Nursery Court Book 16
Grant, Harold, "Mar. 11, 1899", , , Feb. 1900 Nursery Court Book 16,
Grant, Harold, "Mar. 11, 1899", , , Jan. 1900 Nursery Court Book 16
Grant, Harold, "Mar. 11, 1899", , , June 1900 Nursery Court Book 16
Grant, Harold, "Mar. 11, 1899", , , Mar. 1900 Nursery Court Book 16,
Grant, Harold, "Mar. 11, 1899", , , May 1900 Nursery Court Book 16,
Grant, Harold, "May 5, 1899", , , August 1899 Court Nursery Book 16,
Grant, Harold, "May 5, 1899", , , July 1899 Court - Nursery Book 16
Grant, Harold, "May 5, 1899", , , June 1899 Court - Nursery Book 16
Grant, Harold, "May 5, 1899", , , Nov. 1899 Nursery Court Book 16
Grant, Harold, "May 5, 1899", , , Oct. 1899 Court - Nursery Book 16,
Grant, Harold, "May 5, 1899", , , Sept. 1899 Court-Nursery Book 16
Grant, Harold, "May 5, 1899", 2, 9, May 1899 Court - Nursery Book 16,
Hagel, Otto, "Dec. 3, 1898", , , August 1899 Court Nursery Book 16
Hagel, Otto, "Dec. 3, 1898", , , July 1899 Court - Nursery Book 16
Hagel, Otto, "Dec. 3, 1898", , , June 1899 Court - Nursery Book 16
Hagel, Otto, "Dec. 3, 1898", , , Nov. 1899 Nursery Court Book 16
Hagel, Otto, "Dec. 3, 1898", , , Oct. 1899 Court - Nursery Book 16, "Dis. To father Oct. 12, 1899"
Hagel, Otto, "Dec. 3, 1898", , , Sept. 1899 Court-Nursery Book 16
Hagel, Otto, "Dec. 3, 1898", 3, 10, May 1899 Court - Nursery Book 16,
Hagel, William, "June 3, 1898", , , August 1899 Court Nursery Book 16
Hagel, William, "June 3, 1898", , , July 1899 Court - Nursery Book 16
Hagel, William, "June 3, 1898", , , June 1899 Court - Nursery Book 16
Hagel, William, "June 3, 1898", , , Oct. 1899 Court - Nursery Book 16, "Dis. To father Oct. 12, 1899"
Hagel, William, "June 3, 1898", , , Sept. 1899 Court-Nursery Book 16
Hagel, William, "June 3, 1898", 5, 10, May 1899 Court - Nursery Book 16,
Hartman, John, "Nov. 5, 1896", , , Apr. 1900 Court Book 16
Hartman, John, "Nov. 5, 1896", , , August 1899 Court Book 16
Hartman, John, "Nov. 5, 1896", , , Dec. 1899 Court Book 16,
Hartman, John, "Nov. 5, 1896", , , Feb. 1900 Court Book 16
Hartman, John, "Nov. 5, 1896", , , Jan. 1900 Court Book 16

Hartman, John, "Nov. 5, 1896", , , July 1899 Court Book 16
Hartman, John, "Nov. 5, 1896", , , June 1899 Court Book 16,
Hartman, John, "Nov. 5, 1896", , , June 1900 Court Book 16,
Hartman, John, "Nov. 5, 1896", , , Mar. 1900 Court Book 16,
Hartman, John, "Nov. 5, 1896", , , May 1900 Court Book 16
Hartman, John, "Nov. 5, 1896", , , Nov. 1899 Court Book 16
Hartman, John, "Nov. 5, 1896", , , Oct. 1899 Court Book 16
Hartman, John, "Nov. 5, 1896", , , Sept. 1899 Court Book 16
Hartman, John, "Nov. 5, 1896", 8, 6, May 1899 Court - Boys Book 16,
Heide, Frank, "June 4, 1900", 4, 9, June 1900 Tempy & Home Book 16,
Heide, Mabel, "June 4, 1900", 3, 3, June 1900 Tempy & Home Book 16,
Heide, Viola, "June 4, 1900", 6, 5, June 1900 Tempy & Home Book 16,
Heilgner, Joseph, "Feb. 5, 1900", , , Apr. 1900 Nursery Court Book 16,
Heilgner, Joseph, "Feb. 5, 1900", , , June 1900 Nursery Court Book 16,
Heilgner, Joseph, "Feb. 5, 1900", , , May 1900 Nursery Court Book 16,
Heilgner, Joseph, "Feb. 5, 1900", 6, 2, Mar. 1900 Nursery Court Book 16,
Henn, Gertrude, "Jan. 28, 1895", , , June 1899 Court Book 16, "Dis. To mother June 30, 1899"
Henn, Gertrude, "Jan. 28, 1895", 9, 4, May 1899 Court - Girls Book 16, H.
Hergsheimer, Albert, "Apr. 20, 1900"
Hergsheimer, Albert, "Apr. 20, 1900", , , June 1900 Tempy & Home Book 16,
Hergsheimer, Albert, "Apr. 20, 1900", , , May 1900 Tempy & Home Book 16,
Hergsheimer, Albert, "Apr. 20, 1900", 3, 7, Apr. 1900 Tempy & Home Book 16, Board
Hill, Laura, "Aug. 26, 1898", , , Apr. 1900 Court Book 16,
Hill, Laura, "Aug. 26, 1898", , , August 1899 Court Book 16
Hill, Laura, "Aug. 26, 1898", , , Dec. 1899 Court Book 16
Hill, Laura, "Aug. 26, 1898", , , Feb. 1900 Court Book 16,
Hill, Laura, "Aug. 26, 1898", , , Jan. 1900 Court Book 16,
Hill, Laura, "Aug. 26, 1898", , , July 1899 Court Book 16
Hill, Laura, "Aug. 26, 1898", , , June 1899 Court Book 16,
Hill, Laura, "Aug. 26, 1898", , , June 1900 Court Book 16,
Hill, Laura, "Aug. 26, 1898", , , Mar. 1900 Court Book 16
Hill, Laura, "Aug. 26, 1898", , , May 1900 Court Book 16
Hill, Laura, "Aug. 26, 1898", , , Nov. 1899 Court Book 16
Hill, Laura, "Aug. 26, 1898", , , Oct. 1899 Court Book 16
Hill, Laura, "Aug. 26, 1898", , , Sept. 1899 Court Book 16,

Hill, Laura, “Aug. 26, 1898”, 9, 5, May 1899 Court - Girls Book 16, surname may have been Hill

Hoffman, Rosanna, “Nov. 13, 1899”, , , Dec. 1899 Tempy & Home Book 16,

Hoffman, Rosanna, “Nov. 13, 1899”, 12, 8, Nov. 1899 Tempy & Home Book 16,

Hoffman, Rosanna, “Oct. 11, 1899”, , , Feb. 1900 Tempy & Home Book 16, “To home out of state Feb. 5, 1900”

Hoffman, Rosanna, “Oct. 11, 1899”, , , Jan. 1900 Tempy & Home Book 16,

Hornbacker, Arthur, “June 27, 1900”, 3, 4, June 1900 Tempy & Home Book 16,

Hornbacker, John, “June 27, 1900”, 7, 5, June 1900 Tempy & Home Book 16,

Hornbacker, Mabel, “June 27, 1900”, 5, 1, June 1900 Tempy & Home Book 16,

Hornbacker, Mamie, “June 27, 1900”, 9, 2, June 1900 Tempy & Home Book 16,

“Howe, Jr.”, Otto, “Mar. 21, 1899”, , , August 1899 Court Nursery Book 16,

“Howe, Jr.”, Otto, “Mar. 21, 1899”, , , July 1899 Court - Nursery Book 16

“Howe, Jr.”, Otto, “Mar. 21, 1899”, , , June 1899 Court - Nursery Book 16

“Howe, Jr.”, Otto, “Mar. 21, 1899”, , , Oct. 1899 Court - Nursery Book 16, “Dis. To mother Oct. 2, 1899”

“Howe, Jr.”, Otto, “Mar. 21, 1899”, , , Sept. 1899 Court-Nursery Book 16

“Howe, Jr.”, Otto, “Mar. 21, 1899”, 3, 2, May 1899 Court - Nursery Book 16,

Ible (?), Joseph, “Apr. 6, 1899”, , , Apr. 1900 Court Book 16

Ible (?), Joseph, “Apr. 6, 1899”, , , August 1899 Court Book 16

Ible (?), Joseph, “Apr. 6, 1899”, , , Dec. 1899 Court Book 16,

Ible (?), Joseph, “Apr. 6, 1899”, , , Feb. 1900 Court Book 16,

Ible (?), Joseph, “Apr. 6, 1899”, , , Jan. 1900 Court Book 16

Ible (?), Joseph, “Apr. 6, 1899”, , , July 1899 Court Book 16

Ible (?), Joseph, “Apr. 6, 1899”, , , June 1900 Court Book 16

Ible (?), Joseph, “Apr. 6, 1899”, , , Mar. 1900 Court Book 16

Ible (?), Joseph, “Apr. 6, 1899”, , , May 1900 Court Book 16,

Ible (?), Joseph, “Apr. 6, 1899”, , , Nov. 1899 Court Book 16

Ible (?), Joseph, “Apr. 6, 1899”, , , Oct. 1899 Court Book 16,

Ible (?), Joseph, “Apr. 6, 1899”, , , Sept. 1899 Court Book 16

Ible (?), Joseph, “Apr. 6, 1899”, 6, 11, May 1899 Court - Boys Book 16, H.

Ible , Joseph, “Apr. 6, 1899”, , , June 1899 Court Book 16,

Jacobson, Eddie, “May 29, 1900”

Jacobson, Eddie, “May 29, 1900”, , , June 1900 Tempy & Home Book 16,

Jacobson, Eddie, "May 29, 1900", 5, 5, May 1900 Tempy & Home Book 16,
Jacobson, Elizabeth, "May 29, 1900"
Jacobson, Elizabeth, "May 29, 1900", , , June 1900 Tempy & Home Book 16,
Jacobson, Elizabeth, "May 29, 1900", 4, 3, May 1900 Tempy & Home Book 16,
Jacobson, Gertrude, "May 29, 1900"
Jacobson, Gertrude, "May 29, 1900", , , June 1900 Tempy & Home Book 16,
Jacobson, Gertrude, "May 29, 1900", 8, 2, May 1900 Tempy & Home Book 16,
James, Josephine, "Nov. 18, 1899"
James, Josephine, "Nov. 18, 1899", , , Apr. 1900 Tempy & Home Book 16, "To home out of state Apr. 14, 1900"
James, Josephine, "Nov. 18, 1899", , , Feb. 1900 Tempy & Home Book 16,
James, Josephine, "Nov. 18, 1899", , , Jan. 1900 Tempy & Home Book 16,
James, Josephine, "Nov. 18, 1899", , , Mar. 1900 Tempy & House Book 16,
James, Josephine, "Nov. 18, 1899", , , May 1900 Tempy & Home Book 16,
James, Josephine, "Nov. 21, 1899", , , Dec. 1899 Tempy & Home Book 16,
James, Josephine, "Nov. 21, 1899", 14, 3, Nov. 1899 Tempy & Home Book 16,
Johnson, Helen M., "Feb. 24, 1900", , , Apr. 1900 Nursery Court Book 16,
Johnson, Helen M., "Feb. 24, 1900", , , June 1900 Nursery Court Book 16, trans. To Board list
Johnson, Helen M., "Feb. 24, 1900", , , Mar. 1900 Nursery Court Book 16,
Johnson, Helen M., "Feb. 24, 1900", , , May 1900 Nursery Court Book 16,
Johnson, Helen M., "Feb. 24, 1900", 6, , Feb. 1900 Nursery Court Book 16,
Johnston, Lillie, "May 11, 1900"
Johnston, Lillie, "May 11, 1900", , , June 1900 Tempy & Home Book 16,
Johnston, Lillie, "May 11, 1900", 6, 1, May 1900 Tempy & Home Book 16,
Johnston, Percy, "May 11, 1900"
Johnston, Percy, "May 11, 1900", , , June 1900 Tempy & Home Book 16,
Johnston, Percy, "May 11, 1900", 3, 11, May 1900 Tempy & Home Book 16,
Keen, Freda, "Jan. 2, 1897", , , August 1899 Court Book 16
Keen, Freda, "Jan. 2, 1897", , , Dec. 1899 Court Book 16

Keen, Freda, "Jan. 2, 1897", , , Feb. 1900 Court Book 16
Keen, Freda, "Jan. 2, 1897", , , Jan. 1900 Court Book 16
Keen, Freda, "Jan. 2, 1897", , , July 1899 Court Book 16
Keen, Freda, "Jan. 2, 1897", , , June 1899 Court Book 16,
Keen, Freda, "Jan. 2, 1897", , , Mar. 1900 Court Book 16, "Dis. To mother Mar. 9, 1900"
Keen, Freda, "Jan. 2, 1897", , , Nov. 1899 Court Book 16,
Keen, Freda, "Jan. 2, 1897", , , Oct. 1899 Court Book 16
Keen, Freda, "Jan. 2, 1897", , , Sept. 1899 Court Book 16,
Keen, Freda, "Jan. 2, 1897", 10, 2, May 1899 Court - Girls Book 16,
Keen, Helena, "Jan. 2, 1897", , , August 1899 Court Book 16
Keen, Helena, "Jan. 2, 1897", , , Dec. 1899 Court Book 16
Keen, Helena, "Jan. 2, 1897", , , Feb. 1900 Court Book 16
Keen, Helena, "Jan. 2, 1897", , , Jan. 1900 Court Book 16
Keen, Helena, "Jan. 2, 1897", , , July 1899 Court Book 16
Keen, Helena, "Jan. 2, 1897", , , June 1899 Court Book 16,
Keen, Helena, "Jan. 2, 1897", , , Mar. 1900 Court Book 16, "Dis. To mother Mar. 9, 1900"
Keen, Helena, "Jan. 2, 1897", , , Nov. 1899 Court Book 16,
Keen, Helena, "Jan. 2, 1897", , , Oct. 1899 Court Book 16
Keen, Helena, "Jan. 2, 1897", , , Sept. 1899 Court Book 16,
Keen, Helena, "Jan. 2, 1897", 8, 10, May 1899 Court - Girls Book 16,
Kelber, Charles, "Mar. 6, 1900", , , Apr. 1900 Court Book 16
Kelber, Charles, "Mar. 6, 1900", , , June 1900 Court Book 16,
Kelber, Charles, "Mar. 6, 1900", , , May 1900 Court Book 16,
Kelber, Charles, "Mar. 6, 1900", 5, 11, Mar. 1900 Court Book 16
Kelber, Frederick, "May 15, 1899", , , Apr. 1900 Court Book 16
Kelber, Frederick, "May 15, 1899", , , August 1899 Court Book 16
Kelber, Frederick, "May 15, 1899", , , Dec. 1899 Court Book 16,
Kelber, Frederick, "May 15, 1899", , , Feb. 1900 Court Book 16,
Kelber, Frederick, "May 15, 1899", , , Jan. 1900 Court Book 16
Kelber, Frederick, "May 15, 1899", , , July 1899 Court Book 16
Kelber, Frederick, "May 15, 1899", , , June 1899 Court Book 16,
Kelber, Frederick, "May 15, 1899", , , June 1900 Court Book 16
Kelber, Frederick, "May 15, 1899", , , Mar. 1900 Court Book 16
Kelber, Frederick, "May 15, 1899", , , May 1900 Court Book 16,
Kelber, Frederick, "May 15, 1899", , , Nov. 1899 Court Book 16
Kelber, Frederick, "May 15, 1899", , , Oct. 1899 Court Book 16,
Kelber, Frederick, "May 15, 1899", , , Sept. 1899 Court Book 16
Kelber, Frederick, "May 15, 1899", 8, , May 1899 Court - Boys Book 16,
Kelber, Minnie, "May 15, 1898", , , Apr. 1900 Court Book 16
Kelber, Minnie, "May 15, 1898", , , August 1899 Court Book 16
Kelber, Minnie, "May 15, 1898", , , Dec. 1899 Court Book 16
Kelber, Minnie, "May 15, 1898", , , Feb. 1900 Court Book 16,
Kelber, Minnie, "May 15, 1898", , , Jan. 1900 Court Book 16,
Kelber, Minnie, "May 15, 1898", , , July 1899 Court Book 16
Kelber, Minnie, "May 15, 1898", , , June 1899 Court Book 16,

Kelber, Minnie, "May 15, 1898", , , June 1900 Court Book 16,
Kelber, Minnie, "May 15, 1898", , , Mar. 1900 Court Book 16
Kelber, Minnie, "May 15, 1898", , , May 1900 Court Book 16
Kelber, Minnie, "May 15, 1898", , , Nov. 1899 Court Book 16
Kelber, Minnie, "May 15, 1898", , , Oct. 1899 Court Book 16
Kelber, Minnie, "May 15, 1898", , , Sept. 1899 Court Book 16
Kelber, Minnie, "May 15, 1898", 6, , May 1899 Court - Girls Book 16,
Kiesel, Willie, "Nov. 20, 1895", , , Apr. 1900 Court Book 16
Kiesel, Willie, "Nov. 20, 1895", , , August 1899 Court Book 16
Kiesel, Willie, "Nov. 20, 1895", , , Dec. 1899 Court Book 16,
Kiesel, Willie, "Nov. 20, 1895", , , Feb. 1900 Court Book 16,
Kiesel, Willie, "Nov. 20, 1895", , , Jan. 1900 Court Book 16
Kiesel, Willie, "Nov. 20, 1895", , , July 1899 Court Book 16
Kiesel, Willie, "Nov. 20, 1895", , , June 1899 Court Book 16,
Kiesel, Willie, "Nov. 20, 1895", , , June 1900 Court Book 16,
Kiesel, Willie, "Nov. 20, 1895", , , Mar. 1900 Court Book 16,
Kiesel, Willie, "Nov. 20, 1895", , , May 1900 Court Book 16,
Kiesel, Willie, "Nov. 20, 1895", , , Nov. 1899 Court Book 16
Kiesel, Willie, "Nov. 20, 1895", , , Oct. 1899 Court Book 16
Kiesel, Willie, "Nov. 20, 1895", , , Sept. 1899 Court Book 16
Kiesel, Willie, "Nov. 20, 1895", 9, 6, May 1899 Court - Boys Book 16,
Kilton, Eveline, "Feb. 14, 1900", , , Apr. 1900 Court Book 16
Kilton, Eveline, "Feb. 14, 1900", , , June 1900 Court Book 16,
Kilton, Eveline, "Feb. 14, 1900", , , May 1900 Court Book 16,
Kilton, Eveline, "Feb. 14, 1900", 4, 1, Mar. 1900 Court Book 16,
Kimmel, Max, "Nov. 16, 1899", 2, 7, Nov. 1899 Nursery Court Book 16
Kimmel, Max, "Sept. 20, 1899", , , Apr. 1900 Nursery Court Book 16
Kimmel, Max, "Sept. 20, 1899", , , Dec. 1899 Nursery Court Book 16
Kimmel, Max, "Sept. 20, 1899", , , Feb. 1900 Nursery Court Book 16,
Kimmel, Max, "Sept. 20, 1899", , , Jan. 1900 Nursery Court Book 16
Kimmel, Max, "Sept. 20, 1899", , , June 1900 Nursery Court Book 16
Kimmel, Max, "Sept. 20, 1899", , , Mar. 1900 Nursery Court Book 16,
Kimmel, Max, "Sept. 20, 1899", , , May 1900 Nursery Court Book 16,
Kimmerle, Edward, "June 22, 1897", , , Apr. 1900 Court Book 16
Kimmerle, Edward, "June 22, 1897", , , August 1899 Court Book 16
Kimmerle, Edward, "June 22, 1897", , , Dec. 1899 Court Book 16,
Kimmerle, Edward, "June 22, 1897", , , Feb. 1900 Court Book 16
Kimmerle, Edward, "June 22, 1897", , , Jan. 1900 Court Book 16
Kimmerle, Edward, "June 22, 1897", , , July 1899 Court Book 16
Kimmerle, Edward, "June 22, 1897", , , June 1899 Court Book 16,
Kimmerle, Edward, "June 22, 1897", , , June 1900 Court Book 16
Kimmerle, Edward, "June 22, 1897", , , Mar. 1900 Court Book 16

Kimmerle, Edward, "June 22, 1897", , , May 1900 Court Book 16
Kimmerle, Edward, "June 22, 1897", , , Nov. 1899 Court Book 16
Kimmerle, Edward, "June 22, 1897", , , Oct. 1899 Court Book 16
Kimmerle, Edward, "June 22, 1897", , , Sept. 1899 Court Book 16
Kimmerle, Edward, "June 22, 1897", 7, 5, May 1899 Court - Boys Book 16,
Knight, Irene, "June 30, 1900", 6, 4, June 1900 Tempy & Home Book 16,
Knight, Lawrence, "June 30, 1900", 5, 2, June 1900 Nursery Court Book 16,
Kruger, Irene, "Apr. 12, 1899", , , August 1899 Tempy. & Home Book 16
Kruger, Irene, "Apr. 12, 1899", , , June 1899 Tempy & Home Book 16, "Dis. To aunt June 26, 1899"
Kruger, Irene, "Apr. 12, 1899", 8, 3, May 1899 Home & Tempy. Book 16,
Kruskop, Charles, "Jan. 14, 1898", , , Apr. 1900 Court Book 16
Kruskop, Charles, "Jan. 14, 1898", , , August 1899 Court Book 16
Kruskop, Charles, "Jan. 14, 1898", , , Dec. 1899 Court Book 16,
Kruskop, Charles, "Jan. 14, 1898", , , Feb. 1900 Court Book 16
Kruskop, Charles, "Jan. 14, 1898", , , Jan. 1900 Court Book 16
Kruskop, Charles, "Jan. 14, 1898", , , July 1899 Court Book 16
Kruskop, Charles, "Jan. 14, 1898", , , June 1899 Court Book 16,
Kruskop, Charles, "Jan. 14, 1898", , , June 1900 Court Book 16
Kruskop, Charles, "Jan. 14, 1898", , , Mar. 1900 Court Book 16
Kruskop, Charles, "Jan. 14, 1898", , , May 1900 Court Book 16
Kruskop, Charles, "Jan. 14, 1898", , , Nov. 1899 Court Book 16
Kruskop, Charles, "Jan. 14, 1898", , , Oct. 1899 Court Book 16
Kruskop, Charles, "Jan. 14, 1898", , , Sept. 1899 Court Book 16
Kruskop, Charles, "Jan. 14, 1898", 8, 8, May 1899 Court - Boys Book 16,
Kruskop, Henry, "Dec. 10, 1898", , , August 1899 Court Nursery Book 16
Kruskop, Henry, "Dec. 10, 1898", , , July 1899 Court - Nursery Book 16
Kruskop, Henry, "Dec. 10, 1898", , , June 1899 Court - Nursery Book 16
Kruskop, Henry, "Dec. 10, 1898", , , Nov. 1899 Nursery Court Book 16
Kruskop, Henry, "Dec. 10, 1898", , , Oct. 1899 Court - Nursery Book 16,
Kruskop, Henry, "Dec. 10, 1898", , , Sept. 1899 Court-Nursery Book 16
Kruskop, Henry, "Dec. 10, 1898", 3, 8, May 1899 Court - Nursery Book 16,
Kruskop, Henry, "Nov. 25, 1898", , , Apr. 1900 Nursery Court Book 16
Kruskop, Henry, "Nov. 25, 1898", , , Dec. 1899 Nursery Court Book 16,

Kruskop, Henry, "Nov. 25, 1898", , , Feb. 1900 Nursery Court Book 16,
Kruskop, Henry, "Nov. 25, 1898", , , Jan. 1900 Nursery Court Book 16
Kruskop, Henry, "Nov. 25, 1898", , , June 1900 Nursery Court Book 16
Kruskop, Henry, "Nov. 25, 1898", , , Mar. 1900 Nursery Court Book 16
Kruskop, Henry, "Nov. 25, 1898", , , May 1900 Nursery Court Book 16
Kuhlman, Rousseau, "May 15, 1899", , , August 1899 Court Book 16
Kuhlman, Rousseau, "May 15, 1899", , , Dec. 1899 Court Book 16,
Kuhlman, Rousseau, "May 15, 1899", , , Feb. 1900 Court Book 16, "Died Feb. 25, 1900"
Kuhlman, Rousseau, "May 15, 1899", , , Jan. 1900 Court Book 16
Kuhlman, Rousseau, "May 15, 1899", , , July 1899 Court Book 16
Kuhlman, Rousseau, "May 15, 1899", , , June 1899 Court Book 16,
Kuhlman, Rousseau, "May 15, 1899", , , Nov. 1899 Court Book 16
Kuhlman, Rousseau, "May 15, 1899", , , Oct. 1899 Court Book 16,
Kuhlman, Rousseau, "May 15, 1899", , , Sept. 1899 Court Book 16
Kuhlman, Rousseau, "May 15, 1899", 9, 8, May 1899 Court - Boys Book 16,
Kuhlman, Siegfried, "Mar. 21, 1897", , , Apr. 1900 Court Book 16
Kuhlman, Siegfried, "Mar. 21, 1897", , , August 1899 Court Book 16
Kuhlman, Siegfried, "Mar. 21, 1897", , , Dec. 1899 Court Book 16,
Kuhlman, Siegfried, "Mar. 21, 1897", , , Feb. 1900 Court Book 16
Kuhlman, Siegfried, "Mar. 21, 1897", , , Jan. 1900 Court Book 16
Kuhlman, Siegfried, "Mar. 21, 1897", , , July 1899 Court Book 16
Kuhlman, Siegfried, "Mar. 21, 1897", , , June 1899 Court Book 16,
Kuhlman, Siegfried, "Mar. 21, 1897", , , June 1900 Court Book 16
Kuhlman, Siegfried, "Mar. 21, 1897", , , Mar. 1900 Court Book 16
Kuhlman, Siegfried, "Mar. 21, 1897", , , May 1900 Court Book 16
Kuhlman, Siegfried, "Mar. 21, 1897", , , Nov. 1899 Court Book 16
Kuhlman, Siegfried, "Mar. 21, 1897", , , Oct. 1899 Court Book 16
Kuhlman, Siegfried, "Mar. 21, 1897", , , Sept. 1899 Court Book 16
Kuhlman, Siegfried, "Mar. 21, 1897", 8, 5, May 1899 Court - Boys Book 16,
Kummert, Martha, "Apr. 30, 1898", , , Apr. 1900 Court Book 16,
Kummert, Martha, "Apr. 30, 1898", , , August 1899 Court Book 16
Kummert, Martha, "Apr. 30, 1898", , , Dec. 1899 Court Book 16
Kummert, Martha, "Apr. 30, 1898", , , Feb. 1900 Court Book 16,
Kummert, Martha, "Apr. 30, 1898", , , Jan. 1900 Court Book 16,
Kummert, Martha, "Apr. 30, 1898", , , July 1899 Court Book 16,
Kummert, Martha, "Apr. 30, 1898", , , June 1899 Court Book 16,
Kummert, Martha, "Apr. 30, 1898", , , June 1900 Court Book 16,
Kummert, Martha, "Apr. 30, 1898", , , Mar. 1900 Court Book 16
Kummert, Martha, "Apr. 30, 1898", , , May 1900 Court Book 16
Kummert, Martha, "Apr. 30, 1898", , , Nov. 1899 Court Book 16,

Kummert, Martha, "Apr. 30, 1898", , , Oct. 1899 Court Book 16
Kummert, Martha, "Apr. 30, 1898", , , Sept. 1899 Court Book 16,
Kummert, Martha, "Apr. 30, 1898", 7, 1, May 1899 Court - Girls Book 16,
Kummert, Otto, "Jan. 31, 1896", , , Apr. 1900 Court Book 16
Kummert, Otto, "Jan. 31, 1896", , , August 1899 Court Book 16
Kummert, Otto, "Jan. 31, 1896", , , Dec. 1899 Court Book 16,
Kummert, Otto, "Jan. 31, 1896", , , Feb. 1900 Court Book 16,
Kummert, Otto, "Jan. 31, 1896", , , Jan. 1900 Court Book 16
Kummert, Otto, "Jan. 31, 1896", , , July 1899 Court Book 16
Kummert, Otto, "Jan. 31, 1896", , , June 1899 Court Book 16,
Kummert, Otto, "Jan. 31, 1896", , , June 1900 Court Book 16,
Kummert, Otto, "Jan. 31, 1896", , , Mar. 1900 Court Book 16,
Kummert, Otto, "Jan. 31, 1896", , , May 1900 Court Book 16,
Kummert, Otto, "Jan. 31, 1896", , , Nov. 1899 Court Book 16
Kummert, Otto, "Jan. 31, 1896", , , Oct. 1899 Court Book 16
Kummert, Otto, "Jan. 31, 1896", , , Sept. 1899 Court Book 16
Kummert, Otto, "Jan. 31, 1896", 8, 11, May 1899 Court - Boys Book 16,
Lacy, Charles Milton, "Sept. 11, 1899", , , Dec. 1899 Nursery Court Book 16
Lacy, Charles Milton, "Sept. 11, 1899", , , Feb. 1900 Tempy & Home Book 16, "Dis. To mother Feb. 1, 1900"
Lacy, Charles Milton, "Sept. 11, 1899", , , Jan. 1900 Tempy & Home Book 16,
Lacy, Charles Milton, "Sept. 13, 1899", , , Dec. 1899 Tempy & Home Book 16,
Lacy, Charles Milton, "Sept. 13, 1899", , , Nov. 1899 Tempy & Home Book 16,
Lacy, Charles Milton, "Sept. 13, 1899", , , Nov. 1899 Tempy & Home Book 16,
Lacy, Charles Milton, "Sept. 13, 1899", , , Nov. 1899 Tempy & Home Book 16
Lacy, Charles Milton, "Sept. 13, 1899", 3, 7, Sept. 1899 Tempy. & Home Book 16,
Lacy, Charles Milton, "Sept. 13, 1899", 3, 8, Oct. 1899 Tempy & Home Book 16, Board paid
Langmichel, Tillie, "June 19, 1900", 7, 9, June 1900 Tempy & Home Book 16,
Lawrence, Clarence, "Dec. 19, 1899", , , Jan. 1900 Tempy & Home Book 16, "Dis. To mother Jan. 5, 1900"
Lawrence, Clarence, "Dec. 19, 1899", 5, , Dec. 1899 Tempy & Home Book 16
Lawrence, Lester, "Dec. 19, 1899", 4, 2, Dec. 1899 Tempy & Home Book 16
Lawrence, Lester, "Nov. 21, 1899", , , Jan. 1900 Tempy & Home Book 16, "Dis. To mother Jan. 5, 1900"
Lebree, Ellen, "June 3, 1898", , , Apr. 1900 Nursery Court Book 16, "Dis. To mother Apr. 5, 1900"

Lebree, Ellen, "June 3, 1898", , , August 1899 Court Nursery Book 16

Lebree, Ellen, "June 3, 1898", , , Dec. 1899 Nursery Court Book 16,

Lebree, Ellen, "June 3, 1898", , , Feb. 1900 Nursery Court Book 16

Lebree, Ellen, "June 3, 1898", , , Jan. 1900 Nursery Court Book 16,

Lebree, Ellen, "June 3, 1898", , , July 1899 Court - Nursery Book 16

Lebree, Ellen, "June 3, 1898", , , June 1899 Court - Nursery Book 16

Lebree, Ellen, "June 3, 1898", , , Mar. 1900 Nursery Court Book 16

Lebree, Ellen, "June 3, 1898", , , Nov. 1899 Nursery Court Book 16

Lebree, Ellen, "June 3, 1898", , , Oct. 1899 Court - Nursery Book 16,

Lebree, Ellen, "June 3, 1898", , , Sept. 1899 Court-Nursery Book 16

Lebree, Ellen, "June 3, 1898", 4, 5, May 1899 Court - Nursery Book 16,

Lynch, Edith, "Sept. 15, 1897", , , Apr. 1900 Nursery Court Book 16,

Lynch, Edith, "Sept. 15, 1897", , , Dec. 1899 Nursery Court Book 16,

Lynch, Edith, "Sept. 15, 1897", , , Feb. 1900 Nursery Court Book 16, ?? Feb. 21 (maybe died?)

Lynch, Edith, "Sept. 15, 1897", , , Jan. 1900 Outside Book 16, Island Hospital

Lynch, Edith, "Sept. 15, 1897", , , June 1900 Nursery Court Book 16,

Lynch, Edith, "Sept. 15, 1897", , , Mar. 1900 Nursery Court Book 16,

Lynch, Edith, "Sept. 15, 1897", , , May 1900 Nursery Court Book 16,

Lynch, Edith, "Sept. 8, 1897", , , August 1899 Outside Book 16, Island Hospital

Lynch, Edith, "Sept. 8, 1897", , , July 1899 Outside Book 16

Lynch, Edith, "Sept. 8, 1897", , , June 1899 Outside Book 16,

Lynch, Edith, "Sept. 8, 1897", , , Nov. 1899 Outside Book 16, Island Hospital

Lynch, Edith, "Sept. 8, 1897", , , Oct. 1899 Outside Book 16,

Lynch, Edith, "Sept. 8, 1897", , , Sept. 1899 Outside Book 16,

Lynch, Edith, "Sept. 8, 1897", 4, 9, May 1899 Outside Book 16,

Maas, Mary, "May 1, 1895", , , Apr. 1900 Nursery Court Book 16

Maas, Mary, "May 1, 1895", , , August 1899 Court Nursery Book 16

Maas, Mary, "May 1, 1895", , , Dec. 1899 Nursery Court Book 16,

Maas, Mary, "May 1, 1895", , , Feb. 1900 Nursery Court Book 16,

Maas, Mary, "May 1, 1895", , , Jan. 1900 Nursery Court Book 16

Maas, Mary, "May 1, 1895", , , July 1899 Court - Nursery Book 16

Maas, Mary, "May 1, 1895", , , June 1899 Court Book 16,

Maas, Mary, "May 1, 1895", , , June 1900 Nursery Court Book 16, "Dis. To mother June 12, 1900"

Maas, Mary, "May 1, 1895", , , May 1900 Nursery Court Book 16,

Maas, Mary, "May 1, 1895", , , Nov. 1899 Nursery Court Book 16

Maas, Mary, “May 1, 1895”, , , Oct. 1899 Court - Nursery Book 16,
Maas, Mary, “May 1, 1895”, , , Sept. 1899 Court-Nursery Book 16
Maas, Mary, “May 1, 1895”, 6, 11, May 1899 Court - Nursery Book 16,
Maas, Mary, “May 1, 1895”, 7, 9, Mar. 1900 Nursery Court Book 16
Maas, Willie, “May 1, 1895”, , , Apr. 1900 Court Book 16
Maas, Willie, “May 1, 1895”, , , August 1899 Court Book 16
Maas, Willie, “May 1, 1895”, , , Dec. 1899 Court Book 16,
Maas, Willie, “May 1, 1895”, , , Feb. 1900 Court Book 16,
Maas, Willie, “May 1, 1895”, , , Jan. 1900 Court Book 16
Maas, Willie, “May 1, 1895”, , , July 1899 Court Book 16
Maas, Willie, “May 1, 1895”, , , June 1899 Court Book 16,
Maas, Willie, “May 1, 1895”, , , June 1900 Court Book 16, “Dis. To mother June 12, 1900”
Maas, Willie, “May 1, 1895”, , , Mar. 1900 Court Book 16,
Maas, Willie, “May 1, 1895”, , , May 1900 Court Book 16,
Maas, Willie, “May 1, 1895”, , , Nov. 1899 Court Book 16
Maas, Willie, “May 1, 1895”, , , Oct. 1899 Court Book 16
Maas, Willie, “May 1, 1895”, , , Sept. 1899 Court Book 16
Maas, Willie, “May 1, 1895”, 9, , May 1899 Court - Boys Book 16,
Mack, Albert, “Aug. 3, 1897”, , , August 1899 Court Nursery Book 16
Mack, Albert, “Aug. 3, 1897”, , , Dec. 1899 Nursery Court Book 16, Sent west Dec. 5
Mack, Albert, “Aug. 3, 1897”, , , July 1899 Court - Nursery Book 16
Mack, Albert, “Aug. 3, 1897”, , , June 1899 Court Book 16
Mack, Albert, “Aug. 3, 1897”, , , Nov. 1899 Nursery Court Book 16
Mack, Albert, “Aug. 3, 1897”, , , Oct. 1899 Court - Nursery Book 16,
Mack, Albert, “Aug. 3, 1897”, , , Sept. 1899 Court-Nursery Book 16,
Mack, Albert, “Aug. 3, 1897”, 4, 8, May 1899 Court - Nursery Book 16,
Magnusson, John, “June 28, 1900”, 4, , June 1900 Nursery Court Book 16,
Maloney, Florence, “July 5, 1898”, , , Apr. 1900 Court Book 16,
Maloney, Florence, “July 5, 1898”, , , August 1899 Court Book 16
Maloney, Florence, “July 5, 1898”, , , Dec. 1899 Court Book 16
Maloney, Florence, “July 5, 1898”, , , Feb. 1900 Court Book 16,
Maloney, Florence, “July 5, 1898”, , , Jan. 1900 Court Book 16,
Maloney, Florence, “July 5, 1898”, , , July 1899 Court Book 16
Maloney, Florence, “July 5, 1898”, , , June 1899 Court Book 16,
Maloney, Florence, “July 5, 1898”, , , June 1900 Court Book 16, “To home in state June 26, 1900”
Maloney, Florence, “July 5, 1898”, , , Mar. 1900 Court Book 16
Maloney, Florence, “July 5, 1898”, , , May 1900 Court Book 16
Maloney, Florence, “July 5, 1898”, , , Nov. 1899 Court Book 16
Maloney, Florence, “July 5, 1898”, , , Oct. 1899 Court Book 16
Maloney, Florence, “July 5, 1898”, , , Sept. 1899 Court Book 16,
Maloney, Florence, “July 5, 1898”, 10, 10, May 1899 Court - Girls Book 16,

Marnell, Annie, “oct. 3, 1899”, 3, 9, Oct. 1899 Court - Nursery Book 16, “Dis. To mother Oct. 23, 1899”
McAusland, Margaret, “June 13, 1900”, 3, 7, June 1900 Tempy & Home Book 16,
McIlveen, Flora, “Apr. 4, 1900”
McIlveen, Flora, “Apr. 4, 1900”, , , June 1900 Tempy & Home Book 16, board paid
McIlveen, Flora, “Apr. 4, 1900”, , , May 1900 Tempy & Home Book 16,
McIlveen, Flora, “Apr. 4, 1900”, 3, , Apr. 1900 Tempy & Home Book 16, Board
McIlveen, William, “Apr. 4, 1900”
McIlveen, William, “Apr. 4, 1900”, , , June 1900 Tempy & Home Book 16, board paid
McIlveen, William, “Apr. 4, 1900”, , , May 1900 Tempy & Home Book 16,
McIlveen, William, “Apr. 4, 1900”, 1, 8, Apr. 1900 Tempy & Home Book 16, Board
McMillan, Charlotte, “Jan. 19, 1900”, , , Apr. 1900 Court Book 16
McMillan, Charlotte, “Jan. 19, 1900”, , , Feb. 1900 Court Book 16,
McMillan, Charlotte, “Jan. 19, 1900”, , , June 1900 Court Book 16,
McMillan, Charlotte, “Jan. 19, 1900”, , , Mar. 1900 Court Book 16,
McMillan, Charlotte, “Jan. 19, 1900”, , , May 1900 Court Book 16,
McMillan, Charlotte, “Jan. 19, 1900”, 11, , Jan. 1900 Court Book 16
McShayne, Granville, “May 3, 1899”, 2, 10, May 1899 Home & Tempy. Book 16,
McTaggart, Lizzie, “Apr. 29, 1896”, , , Apr. 1900 Court Book 16, “Dis. To mother Apr. 3, 1900”
McTaggart, Lizzie, “Apr. 29, 1896”, , , August 1899 Court Book 16
McTaggart, Lizzie, “Apr. 29, 1896”, , , Dec. 1899 Court Book 16
McTaggart, Lizzie, “Apr. 29, 1896”, , , Feb. 1900 Court Book 16
McTaggart, Lizzie, “Apr. 29, 1896”, , , Jan. 1900 Court Book 16
McTaggart, Lizzie, “Apr. 29, 1896”, , , July 1899 Court Book 16
McTaggart, Lizzie, “Apr. 29, 1896”, , , June 1899 Court Book 16,
McTaggart, Lizzie, “Apr. 29, 1896”, , , Mar. 1900 Court Book 16,
McTaggart, Lizzie, “Apr. 29, 1896”, , , Nov. 1899 Court Book 16,
McTaggart, Lizzie, “Apr. 29, 1896”, , , Oct. 1899 Court Book 16,
McTaggart, Lizzie, “Apr. 29, 1896”, , , Sept. 1899 Court Book 16,
McTaggart, Lizzie, “Apr. 29, 1896”, 11, , May 1899 Court - Girls Book 16,
McTaggart, Marcella, “Apr. 29, 1896”, , , Apr. 1900 Court Book 16,
McTaggart, Marcella, “Apr. 29, 1896”, , , August 1899 Court Book 16
McTaggart, Marcella, “Apr. 29, 1896”, , , Dec. 1899 Court Book 16
McTaggart, Marcella, “Apr. 29, 1896”, , , Feb. 1900 Court Book 16
McTaggart, Marcella, “Apr. 29, 1896”, , , Jan. 1900 Court Book 16
McTaggart, Marcella, “Apr. 29, 1896”, , , July 1899 Court Book 16
McTaggart, Marcella, “Apr. 29, 1896”, , , June 1899 Court Book 16,
McTaggart, Marcella, “Apr. 29, 1896”, , , Mar. 1900 Court Book 16,

McTaggart, Marcella, "Apr. 29, 1896", , , Nov. 1899 Court Book 16,
McTaggart, Marcella, "Apr. 29, 1896", , , Oct. 1899 Court Book 16
McTaggart, Marcella, "Apr. 29, 1896", , , Sept. 1899 Court Book 16,
McTaggart, Marcella, "Apr. 29, 1896", 7, , May 1899 Court - Girls Book 16,
McVeigh, Ethel, "July 7, 1894", , , Apr. 1900 Court Book 16,
McVeigh, Ethel, "July 7, 1894", , , August 1899 Court Book 16
McVeigh, Ethel, "July 7, 1894", , , Dec. 1899 Court Book 16
McVeigh, Ethel, "July 7, 1894", , , Feb. 1900 Court Book 16,
McVeigh, Ethel, "July 7, 1894", , , Jan. 1900 Court Book 16,
McVeigh, Ethel, "July 7, 1894", , , July 1899 Court Book 16,
McVeigh, Ethel, "July 7, 1894", , , June 1899 Court Book 16,
McVeigh, Ethel, "July 7, 1894", , , June 1900 Court Book 16,
McVeigh, Ethel, "July 7, 1894", , , Mar. 1900 Court Book 16,
McVeigh, Ethel, "July 7, 1894", , , May 1900 Court Book 16,
McVeigh, Ethel, "July 7, 1894", , , Nov. 1899 Court Book 16,
McVeigh, Ethel, "July 7, 1894", , , Oct. 1899 Court Book 16,
McVeigh, Ethel, "July 7, 1894", , , Sept. 1899 Court Book 16
McVeigh, Ethel, "July 7, 1894", 7, 9, May 1899 Court - Girls Book 16, H.
Medley, Jessie, "May 28, 1900"
Medley, Jessie, "May 28, 1900", , , June 1900 Tempy & Home Book 16,
Medley, Jessie, "May 28, 1900", 5, , May 1900 Tempy & Home Book 16,
Melville, Ethel, "Mar. 20, 1897", , , Apr. 1900 Nursery Court Book 16,
Melville, Ethel, "Mar. 20, 1897", , , August 1899 Court Nursery Book 16
Melville, Ethel, "Mar. 20, 1897", , , Dec. 1899 Nursery Court Book 16,
Melville, Ethel, "Mar. 20, 1897", , , Feb. 1900 Nursery Court Book 16
Melville, Ethel, "Mar. 20, 1897", , , Jan. 1900 Nursery Court Book 16,
Melville, Ethel, "Mar. 20, 1897", , , July 1899 Court - Nursery Book 16
Melville, Ethel, "Mar. 20, 1897", , , June 1899 Court Book 16
Melville, Ethel, "Mar. 20, 1897", , , June 1900 Nursery Court Book 16,
Melville, Ethel, "Mar. 20, 1897", , , Mar. 1900 Nursery Court Book 16
Melville, Ethel, "Mar. 20, 1897", , , May 1900 Nursery Court Book 16,
Melville, Ethel, "Mar. 20, 1897", , , Nov. 1899 Nursery Court Book 16
Melville, Ethel, "Mar. 20, 1897", , , Oct. 1899 Court - Nursery Book 16,

Melville, Ethel, "Mar. 20, 1897", , , Sept. 1899 Court-Nursery Book 16,

Melville, Ethel, "Mar. 20, 1897", 4, 4, May 1899 Court - Nursery Book 16,

Messner, Christian, "Apr. 29, 1896", , , Apr. 1900 Court Book 16

Messner, Christian, "Apr. 29, 1896", , , August 1899 Court Book 16

Messner, Christian, "Apr. 29, 1896", , , Dec. 1899 Court Book 16,

Messner, Christian, "Apr. 29, 1896", , , Feb. 1900 Court Book 16

Messner, Christian, "Apr. 29, 1896", , , Jan. 1900 Court Book 16

Messner, Christian, "Apr. 29, 1896", , , July 1899 Court Book 16

Messner, Christian, "Apr. 29, 1896", , , June 1899 Court Book 16,

Messner, Christian, "Apr. 29, 1896", , , Mar. 1900 Court Book 16,

Messner, Christian, "Apr. 29, 1896", , , May 1900 Court Book 16, "Dis. To mother May 14, 1900"

Messner, Christian, "Apr. 29, 1896", , , Nov. 1899 Court Book 16

Messner, Christian, "Apr. 29, 1896", , , Oct. 1899 Court Book 16

Messner, Christian, "Apr. 29, 1896", , , Sept. 1899 Court Book 16

Messner, Christian, "Apr. 29, 1896", 7, 1, May 1899 Court - Boys Book 16,

Messner, Frank, "Apr. 29, 1896", , , Apr. 1900 Court Book 16

Messner, Frank, "Apr. 29, 1896", , , August 1899 Court Book 16

Messner, Frank, "Apr. 29, 1896", , , Dec. 1899 Court Book 16,

Messner, Frank, "Apr. 29, 1896", , , Feb. 1900 Court Book 16

Messner, Frank, "Apr. 29, 1896", , , Jan. 1900 Court Book 16

Messner, Frank, "Apr. 29, 1896", , , July 1899 Court Book 16

Messner, Frank, "Apr. 29, 1896", , , June 1899 Court Book 16,

Messner, Frank, "Apr. 29, 1896", , , Mar. 1900 Court Book 16,

Messner, Frank, "Apr. 29, 1896", , , May 1900 Court Book 16, "Dis. To mother May 14, 1900"

Messner, Frank, "Apr. 29, 1896", , , Nov. 1899 Court Book 16

Messner, Frank, "Apr. 29, 1896", , , Oct. 1899 Court Book 16

Messner, Frank, "Apr. 29, 1896", , , Sept. 1899 Court Book 16

Messner, Frank, "Apr. 29, 1896", 6, , May 1899 Court - Boys Book 16,

Meyer, Geraldine, "Dec. 14, 1898", , , August 1899 Tempy. & Home Book 16

Meyer, Geraldine, "Dec. 14, 1898", , , Dec. 1899 Tempy & Home Book 16,

Meyer, Geraldine, "Dec. 14, 1898", , , Feb. 1900 Tempy & Home Book 16, "Dis to father Feb. 6, 1900"

Meyer, Geraldine, "Dec. 14, 1898", , , Jan. 1900 Tempy & Home Book 16,

Meyer, Geraldine, "Dec. 14, 1898", , , July 1899 Tempy. & Home Book 16,

Meyer, Geraldine, "Dec. 14, 1898", , , June 1899 Tempy & Home Book 16,

Meyer, Geraldine, "Dec. 14, 1898", , , Nov. 1899 Tempy & Home Book 16,

Meyer, Geraldine, "Dec. 14, 1898", , , Oct. 1899 Tempy & Home Book 16,

Meyer, Geraldine, "Dec. 14, 1898", , , Sept. 1899 Temp. & Home Book 16,

Meyer, Geraldine, "Dec. 14, 1898", 5, , May 1899 Home & Tempy. Book 16,

Mills, Fanny, "Apr. 16, 1900"

Mills, Fanny, "Apr. 16, 1900", , , June 1900 Tempy & Home Book 16, board paid

Mills, Fanny, "Apr. 16, 1900", , , May 1900 Tempy & Home Book 16,

Mills, Fanny, "Apr. 16, 1900", 2, 8, Apr. 1900 Tempy & Home Book 16, Board

Montague, Florence, "Mar. 11, 1899", , , Apr. 1900 Nursery Court Book 16

Montague, Florence, "Mar. 11, 1899", , , August 1899 Court Nursery Book 16,

Montague, Florence, "Mar. 11, 1899", , , Dec. 1899 Nursery Court Book 16

Montague, Florence, "Mar. 11, 1899", , , Feb. 1900 Nursery Court Book 16,

Montague, Florence, "Mar. 11, 1899", , , Jan. 1900 Nursery Court Book 16

Montague, Florence, "Mar. 11, 1899", , , July 1899 Court - Nursery Book 16

Montague, Florence, "Mar. 11, 1899", , , June 1899 Court - Nursery Book 16

Montague, Florence, "Mar. 11, 1899", , , June 1900 Nursery Court Book 16

Montague, Florence, "Mar. 11, 1899", , , Mar. 1900 Nursery Court Book 16

Montague, Florence, "Mar. 11, 1899", , , May 1900 Nursery Court Book 16

Montague, Florence, "Mar. 11, 1899", , , Nov. 1899 Nursery Court Book 16

Montague, Florence, "Mar. 11, 1899", , , Oct. 1899 Court - Nursery Book 16,

Montague, Florence, "Mar. 11, 1899", , , Sept. 1899 Court-Nursery Book 16

Montague, Florence, "Mar. 11, 1899", 5, 10, May 1899 Court - Nursery Book 16,

Montague, Julia, "Dec. 17, 1897", , , Apr. 1900 Nursery Court Book 16,

Montague, Julia, "Dec. 17, 1897", , , August 1899 Court Nursery Book 16

Montague, Julia, "Dec. 17, 1897", , , Dec. 1899 Nursery Court Book 16,

Montague, Julia, "Dec. 17, 1897", , , Feb. 1900 Nursery Court Book 16

Montague, Julia, "Dec. 17, 1897", , , Jan. 1900 Nursery Court Book 16,
Montague, Julia, "Dec. 17, 1897", , , July 1899 Court - Nursery Book 16
Montague, Julia, "Dec. 17, 1897", , , June 1899 Court - Nursery Book 16
Montague, Julia, "Dec. 17, 1897", , , June 1900 Nursery Court Book 16,
Montague, Julia, "Dec. 17, 1897", , , Mar. 1900 Nursery Court Book 16
Montague, Julia, "Dec. 17, 1897", , , May 1900 Nursery Court Book 16
Montague, Julia, "Dec. 17, 1897", , , Nov. 1899 Nursery Court Book 16
Montague, Julia, "Dec. 17, 1897", , , Oct. 1899 Court - Nursery Book 16,
Montague, Julia, "Dec. 17, 1897", , , Sept. 1899 Court-Nursery Book 16,
Montague, Julia, "Dec. 17, 1897", 3, 11, May 1899 Court - Nursery Book 16,
Morrison, Ellen, "Apr. 21, 1896", , , Apr. 1900 Nursery Court Book 16
Morrison, Ellen, "Apr. 21, 1896", , , August 1899 Court Nursery Book 16
Morrison, Ellen, "Apr. 21, 1896", , , Dec. 1899 Nursery Court Book 16,
Morrison, Ellen, "Apr. 21, 1896", , , Feb. 1900 Nursery Court Book 16,
Morrison, Ellen, "Apr. 21, 1896", , , Jan. 1900 Nursery Court Book 16
Morrison, Ellen, "Apr. 21, 1896", , , July 1899 Court - Nursery Book 16
Morrison, Ellen, "Apr. 21, 1896", , , June 1899 Court Book 16,
Morrison, Ellen, "Apr. 21, 1896", , , Mar. 1900 Nursery Court Book 16
Morrison, Ellen, "Apr. 21, 1896", , , May 1900 Nursery Court Book 16, "Dis. To mother May 29, 1900"
Morrison, Ellen, "Apr. 21, 1896", , , Nov. 1899 Nursery Court Book 16
Morrison, Ellen, "Apr. 21, 1896", , , Oct. 1899 Court - Nursery Book 16,
Morrison, Ellen, "Apr. 21, 1896", , , Sept. 1899 Court-Nursery Book 16
Morrison, Ellen, "Apr. 21, 1896", 6, , May 1899 Court - Nursery Book 16,
Morrison, Flora, "Apr. 24, 1896", , , Apr. 1900 Court Book 16,
Morrison, Flora, "Apr. 24, 1896", , , August 1899 Court Book 16
Morrison, Flora, "Apr. 24, 1896", , , Dec. 1899 Court Book 16
Morrison, Flora, "Apr. 24, 1896", , , Feb. 1900 Court Book 16

Morrison, Flora, “Apr. 24, 1896”, , , Jan. 1900 Court Book 16
Morrison, Flora, “Apr. 24, 1896”, , , July 1899 Court Book 16
Morrison, Flora, “Apr. 24, 1896”, , , June 1899 Court Book 16,
Morrison, Flora, “Apr. 24, 1896”, , , Mar. 1900 Court Book 16,
Morrison, Flora, “Apr. 24, 1896”, , , May 1900 Court Book 16, “Dis. To mother may 29, 1900”
Morrison, Flora, “Apr. 24, 1896”, , , Nov. 1899 Court Book 16,
Morrison, Flora, “Apr. 24, 1896”, , , Oct. 1899 Court Book 16,
Morrison, Flora, “Apr. 24, 1896”, , , Sept. 1899 Court Book 16,
Morrison, Flora, “Apr. 24, 1896”, 9, , May 1899 Court - Girls Book 16,
Muller, Adam, “Dec. 29, 1896”, , , Apr. 1900 Court Book 16
Muller, Adam, “Dec. 29, 1896”, , , August 1899 Court Book 16
Muller, Adam, “Dec. 29, 1896”, , , Dec. 1899 Court Book 16,
Muller, Adam, “Dec. 29, 1896”, , , Feb. 1900 Court Book 16
Muller, Adam, “Dec. 29, 1896”, , , Jan. 1900 Court Book 16
Muller, Adam, “Dec. 29, 1896”, , , July 1899 Court Book 16
Muller, Adam, “Dec. 29, 1896”, , , June 1899 Court Book 16, H.
Muller, Adam, “Dec. 29, 1896”, , , June 1900 Court Book 16,
Muller, Adam, “Dec. 29, 1896”, , , Mar. 1900 Court Book 16
Muller, Adam, “Dec. 29, 1896”, , , May 1900 Court Book 16
Muller, Adam, “Dec. 29, 1896”, , , Nov. 1899 Court Book 16
Muller, Adam, “Dec. 29, 1896”, , , Oct. 1899 Court Book 16
Muller, Adam, “Dec. 29, 1896”, , , Sept. 1899 Court Book 16
Muller, Adam, “Dec. 29, 1896”, 8, 4, May 1899 Court - Boys Book 16, H.
Munro, Beatrice, “Apr. 19, 1899”, , , August 1899 Tempy. & Home Book 16
Munro, Beatrice, “Apr. 19, 1899”, , , Dec. 1899 Tempy & Home Book 16, “Dis. To father Dec. 25, 1899”
Munro, Beatrice, “Apr. 19, 1899”, , , July 1899 Tempy. & Home Book 16, Board Paid
Munro, Beatrice, “Apr. 19, 1899”, , , June 1899 Tempy & Home Book 16,
Munro, Beatrice, “Apr. 19, 1899”, , , Nov. 1899 Tempy & Home Book 16,
Munro, Beatrice, “Apr. 19, 1899”, , , Oct. 1899 Tempy & Home Book 16, Board paid
Munro, Beatrice, “Apr. 19, 1899”, , , Sept. 1899 Temp. & Home Book 16
Munro, Beatrice, “Apr. 19, 1899”, 8, , May 1899 Home & Tempy. Book 16,
Murray, Maggie, “Sept. 28, 1897”, , , Apr. 1900 Court Book 16,
Murray, Maggie, “Sept. 28, 1897”, , , August 1899 Court Book 16
Murray, Maggie, “Sept. 28, 1897”, , , Dec. 1899 Court Book 16
Murray, Maggie, “Sept. 28, 1897”, , , Feb. 1900 Court Book 16
Murray, Maggie, “Sept. 28, 1897”, , , Jan. 1900 Court Book 16
Murray, Maggie, “Sept. 28, 1897”, , , July 1899 Court Book 16,
Murray, Maggie, “Sept. 28, 1897”, , , June 1899 Court Book 16, H.

Murray, Maggie, "Sept. 28, 1897", , , Mar. 1900 Court Book 16,
Murray, Maggie, "Sept. 28, 1897", , , May 1900 Court Book 16, "Out June 1, 1900"
Murray, Maggie, "Sept. 28, 1897", , , Nov. 1899 Court Book 16,
Murray, Maggie, "Sept. 28, 1897", , , Oct. 1899 Court Book 16
Murray, Maggie, "Sept. 28, 1897", , , Sept. 1899 Court Book 16,
Murray, Maggie, "Sept. 28, 1897", 17, , May 1899 Court - Girls Book 16,
Parr, Harry F., "Sept. 13, 1899", , , ,
Parr, Harry F., "Sept. 13, 1899", , , Apr. 1900 Tempy & Home Book 16,
Parr, Harry F., "Sept. 13, 1899", , , Dec. 1899 Nursery Court Book 16
Parr, Harry F., "Sept. 13, 1899", , , Feb. 1900 Tempy & Home Book 16, Board paid $5.00
Parr, Harry F., "Sept. 13, 1899", , , Jan. 1900 Tempy & Home Book 16,
Parr, Harry F., "Sept. 13, 1899", , , Mar. 1900 Tempy & House Book 16,
Parr, Harry F., "Sept. 13, 1899", , , May 1900 Tempy & Home Book 16, "sent to Laura Franklin Hosp. May 7, 1900"
Parr, Harry F., "Sept. 15, 1899", , , Dec. 1899 Tempy & Home Book 16,
Parr, Harry F., "Sept. 15, 1899", , , Nov. 1899 Tempy & Home Book 16,
Parr, Harry F., "Sept. 15, 1899", , , Nov. 1899 Tempy & Home Book 16,
Parr, Harry F., "Sept. 15, 1899", , , Nov. 1899 Tempy & Home Book 16
Parr, Harry F., "Sept. 15, 1899", 2, 10, Sept. 1899 Tempy. & Home Book 16,
Parr, Harry F., "Sept. 15, 1899", 2, 11, Oct. 1899 Tempy & Home Book 16, Board paid
Paul, Fred, "Oct. 2, 1899", , , Apr. 1900 Court Book 16
Paul, Fred, "Oct. 2, 1899", , , June 1900 Court Book 16
Paul, Fred, "Oct. 2, 1899", , , May 1900 Court Book 16,
Paul, Fred, "Oct. 2, 1899", 6, 3, Mar. 1900 Court Book 16
Paul, Frederick, "Oct. 2, 1899", , , Dec. 1899 Court Book 16,
Paul, Frederick, "Oct. 2, 1899", , , Feb. 1900 Court Book 16,
Paul, Frederick, "Oct. 2, 1899", , , Jan. 1900 Court Book 16
Paul, Frederick, "Oct. 2, 1899", , , Nov. 1899 Court Book 16
Paul, Frederick, "Oct. 2, 1899", 5, 10, Oct. 1899 Court Book 16,
Perdelwitz, Edgar, "Jan. 18, 1898", , , Apr. 1900 Court Book 16
Perdelwitz, Edgar, "Jan. 18, 1898", , , August 1899 Court Book 16
Perdelwitz, Edgar, "Jan. 18, 1898", , , Dec. 1899 Court Book 16,
Perdelwitz, Edgar, "Jan. 18, 1898", , , Feb. 1900 Court Book 16
Perdelwitz, Edgar, "Jan. 18, 1898", , , Jan. 1900 Court Book 16
Perdelwitz, Edgar, "Jan. 18, 1898", , , July 1899 Court Book 16
Perdelwitz, Edgar, "Jan. 18, 1898", , , June 1899 Court Book 16,

Perdelwitz, Edgar, "Jan. 18, 1898", , , June 1900 Court Book 16
Perdelwitz, Edgar, "Jan. 18, 1898", , , Mar. 1900 Court Book 16
Perdelwitz, Edgar, "Jan. 18, 1898", , , May 1900 Court Book 16
Perdelwitz, Edgar, "Jan. 18, 1898", , , Nov. 1899 Court Book 16
Perdelwitz, Edgar, "Jan. 18, 1898", , , Oct. 1899 Court Book 16
Perdelwitz, Edgar, "Jan. 18, 1898", , , Sept. 1899 Court Book 16
Perdelwitz, Edgar, "Jan. 18, 1898", 5, 9, May 1899 Court - Boys Book 16,
Perdelwitz, Selma, "Apr. 11, 1898", , , Apr. 1900 Court Book 16,
Perdelwitz, Selma, "Apr. 11, 1898", , , August 1899 Court Book 16
Perdelwitz, Selma, "Apr. 11, 1898", , , Dec. 1899 Court Book 16
Perdelwitz, Selma, "Apr. 11, 1898", , , Feb. 1900 Court Book 16,
Perdelwitz, Selma, "Apr. 11, 1898", , , Jan. 1900 Court Book 16,
Perdelwitz, Selma, "Apr. 11, 1898", , , July 1899 Court Book 16,
Perdelwitz, Selma, "Apr. 11, 1898", , , June 1899 Court Book 16,
Perdelwitz, Selma, "Apr. 11, 1898", , , June 1900 Court Book 16,
Perdelwitz, Selma, "Apr. 11, 1898", , , Mar. 1900 Court Book 16
Perdelwitz, Selma, "Apr. 11, 1898", , , May 1900 Court Book 16
Perdelwitz, Selma, "Apr. 11, 1898", , , Nov. 1899 Court Book 16,
Perdelwitz, Selma, "Apr. 11, 1898", , , Oct. 1899 Court Book 16
Perdelwitz, Selma, "Apr. 11, 1898", , , Sept. 1899 Court Book 16,
Perdelwitz, Selma, "Apr. 11, 1898", 12, 11, May 1899 Court - Girls Book 16,
Perry, Albert C., "May 31, 1900"
Perry, Albert C., "May 31, 1900", , , June 1900 Tempy & Home Book 16,
Perry, Albert C., "May 31, 1900", 4, 8, May 1900 Tempy & Home Book 16,
Pfaff, Alice, "Aug. 21, 1899", , , Dec. 1899 Tempy & Home Book 16,
Pfaff, Alice, "Aug. 21, 1899", , , Nov. 1899 Tempy & Home Book 16,
Pfaff, Alice, "Aug. 21, 1899", , , Oct. 1899 Tempy & Home Book 16,
Pfaff, Alice, "Aug. 21, 1899", , , Sept. 1899 Temp. & Home Book 16
Pfaff, Alice, "Aug. 21, 1899", 4, 8, August 1899 Tempy. & Home Book 16
Pfaff, Alice, "July 15, 1899", , , ,
Pfaff, Alice, "July 15, 1899", , , Apr. 1900 Tempy & Home Book 16,
Pfaff, Alice, "July 15, 1899", , , Feb. 1900 Tempy & Home Book 16,
Pfaff, Alice, "July 15, 1899", , , Jan. 1900 Tempy & Home Book 16,
Pfaff, Alice, "July 15, 1899", , , Mar. 1900 Tempy & House Book 16,
Pfaff, Alice, "July 15, 1899", , , May 1900 Tempy & Home Book 16, "Dis. To mother May 28, 1900"
Pfaff, Clara, "Aug. 21, 1899", , , ,
Pfaff, Clara, "Aug. 21, 1899", , , Apr. 1900 Tempy & Home Book 16,
Pfaff, Clara, "Aug. 21, 1899", , , Dec. 1899 Tempy & Home Book 16,
Pfaff, Clara, "Aug. 21, 1899", , , Feb. 1900 Tempy & Home Book 16,
Pfaff, Clara, "Aug. 21, 1899", , , Jan. 1900 Tempy & Home Book 16,
Pfaff, Clara, "Aug. 21, 1899", , , Mar. 1900 Tempy & House Book 16,
Pfaff, Clara, "Aug. 21, 1899", , , May 1900 Tempy & Home Book 16, "Dis. To mother May 28, 1900"

Pfaff, Clara, "Aug. 21, 1899", , , Nov. 1899 Tempy & Home Book 16,
Pfaff, Clara, "Aug. 21, 1899", , , Oct. 1899 Tempy & Home Book 16,
Pfaff, Clara, "Aug. 21, 1899", , , Sept. 1899 Temp. & Home Book 16
Pfaff, Clara, "Aug. 21, 1899", 4, 8, August 1899 Tempy. & Home Book 16
Porter, Carlotta, "Apr. 8, 1898", , , Feb. 1900 Tempy & Home Book 16,
Porter, Carlotta, "Apr. 8, 1898", , , Jan. 1900 Tempy & Home Book 16,
Porter, Carlotta, "Apr. 8, 1898", , , Mar. 1900 Tempy & House Book 16, "To home in state Mar. 9, 1900"
Porter, Carlotta, "July 20, 1898", , , August 1899 Tempy. & Home Book 16
Porter, Carlotta, "July 20, 1898", , , Dec. 1899 Tempy & Home Book 16,
Porter, Carlotta, "July 20, 1898", , , July 1899 Tempy. & Home Book 16,
Porter, Carlotta, "July 20, 1898", , , June 1899 Tempy & Home Book 16,
Porter, Carlotta, "July 20, 1898", , , Nov. 1899 Tempy & Home Book 16,
Porter, Carlotta, "July 20, 1898", , , Oct. 1899 Tempy & Home Book 16,
Porter, Carlotta, "July 20, 1898", , , Sept. 1899 Temp. & Home Book 16,
Porter, Carlotta, "July 20, 1898", 8, 11, May 1899 Home & Tempy. Book 16, H.
Possenried, Annie, "Nov. 14, 1898", , , Apr. 1900 Nursery Court Book 16
Possenried, Annie, "Nov. 14, 1898", , , Dec. 1899 Nursery Court Book 16,
Possenried, Annie, "Nov. 14, 1898", , , Feb. 1900 Nursery Court Book 16
Possenried, Annie, "Nov. 14, 1898", , , Jan. 1900 Nursery Court Book 16
Possenried, Annie, "Nov. 14, 1898", , , June 1900 Nursery Court Book 16
Possenried, Annie, "Nov. 14, 1898", , , Mar. 1900 Nursery Court Book 16
Possenried, Annie, "Nov. 14, 1898", , , May 1900 Nursery Court Book 16
Possenried, Annie, "Nov. 25, 1898", , , August 1899 Court Nursery Book 16
Possenried, Annie, "Nov. 25, 1898", , , July 1899 Court - Nursery Book 16
Possenried, Annie, "Nov. 25, 1898", , , Nov. 1899 Nursery Court Book 16
Possenried, Annie, "Nov. 25, 1898", , , Oct. 1899 Court - Nursery Book 16,

Possenried, Annie, "Nov. 25, 1898", , , Sept. 1899 Court-Nursery Book 16

Possenried, Annie, "Nov. 25, 1898", 5, 1, May 1899 Court - Nursery Book 16,

Possenried, George, "Dec. 8, 1896", 6, 11, May 1899 Court - Boys Book 16,

Posseuried, Annie, "Nov. 25, 1898", , , June 1899 Court - Nursery Book 16

Posseuried, George, "Dec. 8, 1896", , , Apr. 1900 Court Book 16

Posseuried, George, "Dec. 8, 1896", , , August 1899 Court Book 16

Posseuried, George, "Dec. 8, 1896", , , Dec. 1899 Court Book 16,

Posseuried, George, "Dec. 8, 1896", , , Feb. 1900 Court Book 16

Posseuried, George, "Dec. 8, 1896", , , Jan. 1900 Court Book 16

Posseuried, George, "Dec. 8, 1896", , , July 1899 Court Book 16

Posseuried, George, "Dec. 8, 1896", , , June 1899 Court Book 16,

Posseuried, George, "Dec. 8, 1896", , , June 1900 Court Book 16,

Posseuried, George, "Dec. 8, 1896", , , Mar. 1900 Court Book 16

Posseuried, George, "Dec. 8, 1896", , , May 1900 Court Book 16

Posseuried, George, "Dec. 8, 1896", , , Nov. 1899 Court Book 16

Posseuried, George, "Dec. 8, 1896", , , Oct. 1899 Court Book 16

Posseuried, George, "Dec. 8, 1896", , , Sept. 1899 Court Book 16

Quigley, Albert, "Mar. 3, 1898", , , Apr. 1900 Court Book 16

Quigley, Albert, "Mar. 3, 1898", , , August 1899 Court Book 16

Quigley, Albert, "Mar. 3, 1898", , , Dec. 1899 Court Book 16,

Quigley, Albert, "Mar. 3, 1898", , , Feb. 1900 Court Book 16,

Quigley, Albert, "Mar. 3, 1898", , , Jan. 1900 Court Book 16

Quigley, Albert, "Mar. 3, 1898", , , July 1899 Court Book 16

Quigley, Albert, "Mar. 3, 1898", , , June 1899 Court Book 16,

Quigley, Albert, "Mar. 3, 1898", , , June 1900 Court Book 16

Quigley, Albert, "Mar. 3, 1898", , , Mar. 1900 Court Book 16

Quigley, Albert, "Mar. 3, 1898", , , May 1900 Court Book 16

Quigley, Albert, "Mar. 3, 1898", , , Nov. 1899 Court Book 16

Quigley, Albert, "Mar. 3, 1898", , , Oct. 1899 Court Book 16

Quigley, Albert, "Mar. 3, 1898", , , Sept. 1899 Court Book 16

Quigley, Albert, "Mar. 3, 1898", 8, 7, May 1899 Court - Boys Book 16,

Quigley, Laura, "Mar. 3, 1898", , , August 1899 Court Nursery Book 16

Quigley, Laura, "Mar. 3, 1898", , , Dec. 1899 Nursery Court Book 16, "Dis. To father Dec. 18, 1899"

Quigley, Laura, "Mar. 3, 1898", , , July 1899 Court - Nursery Book 16

Quigley, Laura, "Mar. 3, 1898", , , June 1899 Court - Nursery Book 16

Quigley, Laura, "Mar. 3, 1898", , , Nov. 1899 Nursery Court Book 16

Quigley, Laura, "Mar. 3, 1898", , , Oct. 1899 Court - Nursery Book 16,

Quigley, Laura, "Mar. 3, 1898", , , Sept. 1899 Court-Nursery Book 16,

Quigley, Laura, "Mar. 3, 1898", 4, 8, May 1899 Court - Nursery Book 16,
Quigley, Lester, "Mar. 3, 1898", , , Apr. 1900 Court Book 16
Quigley, Lester, "Mar. 3, 1898", , , August 1899 Court Book 16
Quigley, Lester, "Mar. 3, 1898", , , Dec. 1899 Court Book 16,
Quigley, Lester, "Mar. 3, 1898", , , Feb. 1900 Court Book 16,
Quigley, Lester, "Mar. 3, 1898", , , Jan. 1900 Court Book 16
Quigley, Lester, "Mar. 3, 1898", , , July 1899 Court Book 16
Quigley, Lester, "Mar. 3, 1898", , , June 1899 Court Book 16,
Quigley, Lester, "Mar. 3, 1898", , , June 1900 Court Book 16
Quigley, Lester, "Mar. 3, 1898", , , Mar. 1900 Court Book 16
Quigley, Lester, "Mar. 3, 1898", , , May 1900 Court Book 16
Quigley, Lester, "Mar. 3, 1898", , , Nov. 1899 Court Book 16
Quigley, Lester, "Mar. 3, 1898", , , Oct. 1899 Court Book 16
Quigley, Lester, "Mar. 3, 1898", , , Sept. 1899 Court Book 16
Quigley, Lester, "Mar. 3, 1898", 7, 7, May 1899 Court - Boys Book 16,
Reitch, Lena, "July 30, 1898", , , August 1899 Court Book 16
Reitch, Lena, "July 30, 1898", , , Dec. 1899 Court Book 16
Reitch, Lena, "July 30, 1898", , , Feb. 1900 Court Book 16, "To Consumptive Home feb. 24, 1900"
Reitch, Lena, "July 30, 1898", , , Jan. 1900 Court Book 16,
Reitch, Lena, "July 30, 1898", , , July 1899 Court Book 16
Reitch, Lena, "July 30, 1898", , , June 1899 Court Book 16, H.
Reitch, Lena, "July 30, 1898", , , Nov. 1899 Court Book 16
Reitch, Lena, "July 30, 1898", , , Oct. 1899 Court Book 16
Reitch, Lena, "July 30, 1898", , , Sept. 1899 Court Book 16,
Reitch, Lena, "July 30, 1898", 11, 10, May 1899 Court - Girls Book 16, H.
Reynolds, Stella, "Mar. 10, 1894", , , August 1899 Court Book 16
Reynolds, Stella, "Mar. 10, 1894", , , Dec. 1899 Court Book 16
Reynolds, Stella, "Mar. 10, 1894", , , Feb. 1900 Court Book 16,
Reynolds, Stella, "Mar. 10, 1894", , , Jan. 1900 Court Book 16,
Reynolds, Stella, "Mar. 10, 1894", , , July 1899 Court Book 16,
Reynolds, Stella, "Mar. 10, 1894", , , June 1899 Court Book 16,
Reynolds, Stella, "Mar. 10, 1894", , , Mar. 1900 Court Book 16, "To home in state Mar. 5, 1900"
Reynolds, Stella, "Mar. 10, 1894", , , Nov. 1899 Court Book 16,
Reynolds, Stella, "Mar. 10, 1894", , , Oct. 1899 Court Book 16,
Reynolds, Stella, "Mar. 10, 1894", , , Sept. 1899 Court Book 16
Reynolds, Stella, "Mar. 10, 1894", 9, 2, May 1899 Court - Girls Book 16, H.
Rich, Charles, "Sept. 3, 1897", , , Apr. 1900 Court Book 16
Rich, Charles, "Sept. 3, 1897", , , August 1899 Court Book 16
Rich, Charles, "Sept. 3, 1897", , , Dec. 1899 Court Book 16,
Rich, Charles, "Sept. 3, 1897", , , Feb. 1900 Court Book 16
Rich, Charles, "Sept. 3, 1897", , , Jan. 1900 Court Book 16
Rich, Charles, "Sept. 3, 1897", , , July 1899 Court Book 16
Rich, Charles, "Sept. 3, 1897", , , June 1899 Court Book 16,

Rich, Charles, "Sept. 3, 1897", , , June 1900 Court Book 16
Rich, Charles, "Sept. 3, 1897", , , Mar. 1900 Court Book 16
Rich, Charles, "Sept. 3, 1897", , , May 1900 Court Book 16
Rich, Charles, "Sept. 3, 1897", , , Nov. 1899 Court Book 16
Rich, Charles, "Sept. 3, 1897", , , Oct. 1899 Court Book 16
Rich, Charles, "Sept. 3, 1897", , , Sept. 1899 Court Book 16
Rich, Charles, "Sept. 3, 1897", 5, 9, May 1899 Court - Boys Book 16,
Rich, Harry, "Apr. 25, 1898", , , August 1899 Court Nursery Book 16
Rich, Harry, "Apr. 25, 1898", , , Dec. 1899 Nursery Court Book 16,
Rich, Harry, "Apr. 25, 1898", , , Jan. 1900 Nursery Court Book 16, "To home in state Jan. 31, 1900"
Rich, Harry, "Apr. 25, 1898", , , July 1899 Court - Nursery Book 16
Rich, Harry, "Apr. 25, 1898", , , June 1899 Court - Nursery Book 16
Rich, Harry, "Apr. 25, 1898", , , Nov. 1899 Nursery Court Book 16
Rich, Harry, "Apr. 25, 1898", , , Oct. 1899 Court - Nursery Book 16,
Rich, Harry, "Apr. 25, 1898", , , Sept. 1899 Court-Nursery Book 16,
Rich, Harry, "Apr. 25, 1898", 5, , May 1899 Court - Nursery Book 16,
Rosen, Julia, "Nov. 5, 1897", , , Apr. 1900 Nursery Court Book 16,
Rosen, Julia, "Nov. 5, 1897", , , August 1899 Court Nursery Book 16
Rosen, Julia, "Nov. 5, 1897", , , Dec. 1899 Nursery Court Book 16,
Rosen, Julia, "Nov. 5, 1897", , , Feb. 1900 Nursery Court Book 16
Rosen, Julia, "Nov. 5, 1897", , , Jan. 1900 Nursery Court Book 16,
Rosen, Julia, "Nov. 5, 1897", , , July 1899 Court - Nursery Book 16
Rosen, Julia, "Nov. 5, 1897", , , June 1899 Court - Nursery Book 16
Rosen, Julia, "Nov. 5, 1897", , , June 1900 Nursery Court Book 16,
Rosen, Julia, "Nov. 5, 1897", , , Mar. 1900 Nursery Court Book 16
Rosen, Julia, "Nov. 5, 1897", , , May 1900 Nursery Court Book 16
Rosen, Julia, "Nov. 5, 1897", , , Nov. 1899 Nursery Court Book 16
Rosen, Julia, "Nov. 5, 1897", , , Oct. 1899 Court - Nursery Book 16,
Rosen, Julia, "Nov. 5, 1897", , , Sept. 1899 Court-Nursery Book 16,
Rosen, Julia, "Nov. 5, 1897", 6, 6, May 1899 Court - Nursery Book 16,
Rosen, Rosie, "Nov. 5, 1897", , , Apr. 1900 Nursery Court Book 16,
Rosen, Rosie, "Nov. 5, 1897", , , August 1899 Court Nursery Book 16
Rosen, Rosie, "Nov. 5, 1897", , , Dec. 1899 Nursery Court Book 16,
Rosen, Rosie, "Nov. 5, 1897", , , Feb. 1900 Nursery Court Book 16
Rosen, Rosie, "Nov. 5, 1897", , , Jan. 1900 Nursery Court Book 16,
Rosen, Rosie, "Nov. 5, 1897", , , July 1899 Court - Nursery Book 16
Rosen, Rosie, "Nov. 5, 1897", , , June 1899 Court - Nursery Book 16
Rosen, Rosie, "Nov. 5, 1897", , , June 1900 Nursery Court Book 16,
Rosen, Rosie, "Nov. 5, 1897", , , Mar. 1900 Nursery Court Book 16
Rosen, Rosie, "Nov. 5, 1897", , , May 1900 Nursery Court Book 16
Rosen, Rosie, "Nov. 5, 1897", , , Nov. 1899 Nursery Court Book 16
Rosen, Rosie, "Nov. 5, 1897", , , Oct. 1899 Court - Nursery Book 16,
Rosen, Rosie, "Nov. 5, 1897", , , Sept. 1899 Court-Nursery Book 16,

Rosen, Rosie, "Nov. 5, 1897", 6, 6, May 1899 Court - Nursery Book 16,

Rosenlicht, Annie, "Dec. 13, 1897", , , Apr. 1900 Court Book 16,

Rosenlicht, Annie, "Dec. 13, 1897", , , August 1899 Court Book 16

Rosenlicht, Annie, "Dec. 13, 1897", , , Dec. 1899 Court Book 16

Rosenlicht, Annie, "Dec. 13, 1897", , , Feb. 1900 Court Book 16,

Rosenlicht, Annie, "Dec. 13, 1897", , , Jan. 1900 Court Book 16,

Rosenlicht, Annie, "Dec. 13, 1897", , , July 1899 Court Book 16,

Rosenlicht, Annie, "Dec. 13, 1897", , , June 1899 Court Book 16,

Rosenlicht, Annie, "Dec. 13, 1897", , , June 1900 Court Book 16,

Rosenlicht, Annie, "Dec. 13, 1897", , , Mar. 1900 Court Book 16

Rosenlicht, Annie, "Dec. 13, 1897", , , May 1900 Court Book 16

Rosenlicht, Annie, "Dec. 13, 1897", , , Nov. 1899 Court Book 16,

Rosenlicht, Annie, "Dec. 13, 1897", , , Oct. 1899 Court Book 16

Rosenlicht, Annie, "Dec. 13, 1897", , , Sept. 1899 Court Book 16,

Rosenlicht, Annie, "Dec. 13, 1897", 9, 6, May 1899 Court - Girls Book 16,

Rosenlicht, Martha, "Dec. 18, 1898", , , Apr. 1900 Nursery Court Book 16

Rosenlicht, Martha, "Dec. 18, 1898", , , Dec. 1899 Nursery Court Book 16

Rosenlicht, Martha, "Dec. 18, 1898", , , Feb. 1900 Nursery Court Book 16,

Rosenlicht, Martha, "Dec. 18, 1898", , , Jan. 1900 Nursery Court Book 16

Rosenlicht, Martha, "Dec. 18, 1898", , , June 1900 Nursery Court Book 16

Rosenlicht, Martha, "Dec. 18, 1898", , , Mar. 1900 Nursery Court Book 16

Rosenlicht, Martha, "Dec. 18, 1898", , , May 1900 Nursery Court Book 16

Rosenlicht, Martha, "Mar. 11, 1899", , , August 1899 Court Nursery Book 16

Rosenlicht, Martha, "Mar. 11, 1899", , , July 1899 Court - Nursery Book 16

Rosenlicht, Martha, "Mar. 11, 1899", , , June 1899 Court - Nursery Book 16

Rosenlicht, Martha, "Mar. 11, 1899", , , Nov. 1899 Nursery Court Book 16

Rosenlicht, Martha, "Mar. 11, 1899", , , Oct. 1899 Court - Nursery Book 16,

Rosenlicht, Martha, "Mar. 11, 1899", , , Sept. 1899 Court-Nursery Book 16

Rosenlicht, Martha, "Mar. 11, 1899", 5, 3, May 1899 Court - Nursery Book 16,

Ross, Lizzie, "Apr. 18, 1898", , , Apr. 1900 Court Book 16

Ross, Lizzie, "Apr. 18, 1898", , , August 1899 Court Book 16

Ross, Lizzie, "Apr. 18, 1898", , , Dec. 1899 Court Book 16

Ross, Lizzie, "Apr. 18, 1898", , , Feb. 1900 Court Book 16,

Ross, Lizzie, "Apr. 18, 1898", , , Jan. 1900 Court Book 16,
Ross, Lizzie, "Apr. 18, 1898", , , July 1899 Court Book 16
Ross, Lizzie, "Apr. 18, 1898", , , June 1899 Court Book 16,
Ross, Lizzie, "Apr. 18, 1898", , , June 1900 Court Book 16,
Ross, Lizzie, "Apr. 18, 1898", , , Mar. 1900 Court Book 16
Ross, Lizzie, "Apr. 18, 1898", , , May 1900 Court Book 16
Ross, Lizzie, "Apr. 18, 1898", , , Nov. 1899 Court Book 16
Ross, Lizzie, "Apr. 18, 1898", , , Oct. 1899 Court Book 16
Ross, Lizzie, "Apr. 18, 1898", , , Sept. 1899 Court Book 16
Ross, Lizzie, "Apr. 18, 1898", 8, 1, May 1899 Court - Girls Book 16,
Schmidt, Ernest, , , , Dec. 1899 Nursery Court Book 16,
Schmidt, Ernest, , , , Jan. 1900 Nursery Court Book 16,
Schmidt, Ernest, "June 3, 1898", , , Apr. 1900 Nursery Court Book 16,
Schmidt, Ernest, "June 3, 1898", , , August 1899 Court Nursery Book 16
Schmidt, Ernest, "June 3, 1898", , , Feb. 1900 Nursery Court Book 16
Schmidt, Ernest, "June 3, 1898", , , July 1899 Court - Nursery Book 16
Schmidt, Ernest, "June 3, 1898", , , June 1899 Court - Nursery Book 16
Schmidt, Ernest, "June 3, 1898", , , June 1900 Nursery Court Book 16
Schmidt, Ernest, "June 3, 1898", , , Mar. 1900 Nursery Court Book 16
Schmidt, Ernest, "June 3, 1898", , , May 1900 Nursery Court Book 16
Schmidt, Ernest, "June 3, 1898", , , Nov. 1899 Nursery Court Book 16
Schmidt, Ernest, "June 3, 1898", , , Oct. 1899 Court - Nursery Book 16,
Schmidt, Ernest, "June 3, 1898", , , Sept. 1899 Court-Nursery Book 16,
Schmidt, Ernest, "June 3, 1898", 4, 11, May 1899 Court - Nursery Book 16,
Schmidt, Walter, "June 3, 1898", , , Apr. 1900 Nursery Court Book 16,
Schmidt, Walter, "June 3, 1898", , , August 1899 Court Nursery Book 16
Schmidt, Walter, "June 3, 1898", , , Dec. 1899 Nursery Court Book 16,
Schmidt, Walter, "June 3, 1898", , , Feb. 1900 Nursery Court Book 16
Schmidt, Walter, "June 3, 1898", , , Jan. 1900 Nursery Court Book 16,
Schmidt, Walter, "June 3, 1898", , , July 1899 Court - Nursery Book 16

Schmidt, Walter, "June 3, 1898", , , June 1899 Court - Nursery Book 16
Schmidt, Walter, "June 3, 1898", , , June 1900 Nursery Court Book 16
Schmidt, Walter, "June 3, 1898", , , Mar. 1900 Nursery Court Book 16
Schmidt, Walter, "June 3, 1898", , , May 1900 Nursery Court Book 16
Schmidt, Walter, "June 3, 1898", , , Nov. 1899 Nursery Court Book 16
Schmidt, Walter, "June 3, 1898", , , Oct. 1899 Court - Nursery Book 16,
Schmidt, Walter, "June 3, 1898", , , Sept. 1899 Court-Nursery Book 16
Schmidt, Walter, "June 3, 1898", 3, 7, May 1899 Court - Nursery Book 16,
Schnabel, Bertha, "Jan. 14, 1897", , , Apr. 1900 Court Book 16,
Schnabel, Bertha, "Jan. 14, 1897", , , August 1899 Court Book 16
Schnabel, Bertha, "Jan. 14, 1897", , , Dec. 1899 Court Book 16
Schnabel, Bertha, "Jan. 14, 1897", , , Feb. 1900 Court Book 16
Schnabel, Bertha, "Jan. 14, 1897", , , Jan. 1900 Court Book 16
Schnabel, Bertha, "Jan. 14, 1897", , , July 1899 Court Book 16
Schnabel, Bertha, "Jan. 14, 1897", , , June 1899 Court Book 16,
Schnabel, Bertha, "Jan. 14, 1897", , , June 1900 Court Book 16,
Schnabel, Bertha, "Jan. 14, 1897", , , Mar. 1900 Court Book 16,
Schnabel, Bertha, "Jan. 14, 1897", , , May 1900 Court Book 16,
Schnabel, Bertha, "Jan. 14, 1897", , , Nov. 1899 Court Book 16,
Schnabel, Bertha, "Jan. 14, 1897", , , Oct. 1899 Court Book 16
Schnabel, Bertha, "Jan. 14, 1897", , , Sept. 1899 Court Book 16,
Schnabel, Bertha, "Jan. 14, 1897", 6, 11, May 1899 Court - Girls Book 16,
Schnabel, Lizzie, "Jan. 14, 1897", , , Apr. 1900 Court Book 16, "Dis. To mother Apr. 3, 1900"
Schnabel, Lizzie, "Jan. 14, 1897", , , August 1899 Court Book 16
Schnabel, Lizzie, "Jan. 14, 1897", , , Dec. 1899 Court Book 16
Schnabel, Lizzie, "Jan. 14, 1897", , , Feb. 1900 Court Book 16
Schnabel, Lizzie, "Jan. 14, 1897", , , Jan. 1900 Court Book 16
Schnabel, Lizzie, "Jan. 14, 1897", , , July 1899 Court Book 16
Schnabel, Lizzie, "Jan. 14, 1897", , , June 1899 Court Book 16,
Schnabel, Lizzie, "Jan. 14, 1897", , , June 1900 Court Book 16,
Schnabel, Lizzie, "Jan. 14, 1897", , , Mar. 1900 Court Book 16,
Schnabel, Lizzie, "Jan. 14, 1897", , , May 1900 Court Book 16,
Schnabel, Lizzie, "Jan. 14, 1897", , , Nov. 1899 Court Book 16,
Schnabel, Lizzie, "Jan. 14, 1897", , , Oct. 1899 Court Book 16
Schnabel, Lizzie, "Jan. 14, 1897", , , Sept. 1899 Court Book 16,
Schnabel, Lizzie, "Jan. 14, 1897", 9, 11, May 1899 Court - Girls Book 16,
Schneider, John, "Jan. 5, 1895", , , Apr. 1900 Court Book 16
Schneider, John, "Jan. 5, 1895", , , August 1899 Court Book 16

Schneider, John, "Jan. 5, 1895", , , Dec. 1899 Court Book 16
Schneider, John, "Jan. 5, 1895", , , Feb. 1900 Court Book 16,
Schneider, John, "Jan. 5, 1895", , , Jan. 1900 Court Book 16
Schneider, John, "Jan. 5, 1895", , , July 1899 Court Book 16
Schneider, John, "Jan. 5, 1895", , , June 1899 Court Book 16,
Schneider, John, "Jan. 5, 1895", , , June 1900 Court Book 16,
Schneider, John, "Jan. 5, 1895", , , Mar. 1900 Court Book 16,
Schneider, John, "Jan. 5, 1895", , , May 1900 Court Book 16,
Schneider, John, "Jan. 5, 1895", , , Nov. 1899 Court Book 16
Schneider, John, "Jan. 5, 1895", , , Oct. 1899 Court Book 16
Schneider, John, "Jan. 5, 1895", , , Sept. 1899 Court Book 16
Schneider, John, "Jan. 5, 1895", 9, 11, May 1899 Court - Boys Book 16,
Schneider, Louis, "Jan. 5, 1895", , , Apr. 1900 Court Book 16
Schneider, Louis, "Jan. 5, 1895", , , August 1899 Court Book 16
Schneider, Louis, "Jan. 5, 1895", , , Dec. 1899 Court Book 16
Schneider, Louis, "Jan. 5, 1895", , , Feb. 1900 Court Book 16,
Schneider, Louis, "Jan. 5, 1895", , , Jan. 1900 Court Book 16
Schneider, Louis, "Jan. 5, 1895", , , July 1899 Court Book 16
Schneider, Louis, "Jan. 5, 1895", , , June 1899 Court Book 16,
Schneider, Louis, "Jan. 5, 1895", , , June 1900 Court Book 16,
Schneider, Louis, "Jan. 5, 1895", , , Mar. 1900 Court Book 16,
Schneider, Louis, "Jan. 5, 1895", , , May 1900 Court Book 16,
Schneider, Louis, "Jan. 5, 1895", , , Nov. 1899 Court Book 16
Schneider, Louis, "Jan. 5, 1895", , , Oct. 1899 Court Book 16
Schneider, Louis, "Jan. 5, 1895", , , Sept. 1899 Court Book 16
Schneider, Louis, "Jan. 5, 1895", 8, 3, May 1899 Court - Boys Book 16,
Schweppe, Annie, "Aug. 13, 1895", , , August 1899 Court Book 16
Schweppe, Annie, "Aug. 13, 1895", , , Dec. 1899 Court Book 16
Schweppe, Annie, "Aug. 13, 1895", , , Jan. 1900 Court Book 16, "To home in state Jan. 31, 1900"
Schweppe, Annie, "Aug. 13, 1895", , , July 1899 Court Book 16
Schweppe, Annie, "Aug. 13, 1895", , , June 1899 Court Book 16,
Schweppe, Annie, "Aug. 13, 1895", , , Nov. 1899 Court Book 16,
Schweppe, Annie, "Aug. 13, 1895", , , Oct. 1899 Court Book 16,
Schweppe, Annie, "Aug. 13, 1895", , , Sept. 1899 Court Book 16
Schweppe, Annie, "Aug. 13, 1895", 9, 9, May 1899 Court - Girls Book 16, H.
Schweppe, Annie, "June 27, 1900", 9, 11, June 1900 Court Book 16,
Seabold, Alice, "June 22, 1897", , , Apr. 1900 Court Book 16,
Seabold, Alice, "June 22, 1897", , , August 1899 Court Book 16
Seabold, Alice, "June 22, 1897", , , Dec. 1899 Court Book 16
Seabold, Alice, "June 22, 1897", , , Feb. 1900 Court Book 16
Seabold, Alice, "June 22, 1897", , , Jan. 1900 Court Book 16
Seabold, Alice, "June 22, 1897", , , July 1899 Court Book 16,
Seabold, Alice, "June 22, 1897", , , June 1899 Court Book 16,

Seabold, Alice, "June 22, 1897", , , June 1900 Court Book 16, "Dis. To mother June 27, 1900"
Seabold, Alice, "June 22, 1897", , , Mar. 1900 Court Book 16,
Seabold, Alice, "June 22, 1897", , , May 1900 Court Book 16,
Seabold, Alice, "June 22, 1897", , , Nov. 1899 Court Book 16,
Seabold, Alice, "June 22, 1897", , , Oct. 1899 Court Book 16
Seabold, Alice, "June 22, 1897", , , Sept. 1899 Court Book 16,
Seabold, Alice, "June 22, 1897", 8, 7, May 1899 Court - Girls Book 16,
Seabold, Freda, "June 22, 1897", , , August 1899 Court Book 16
Seabold, Freda, "June 22, 1897", , , Dec. 1899 Court Book 16
Seabold, Freda, "June 22, 1897", , , Feb. 1900 Court Book 16
Seabold, Freda, "June 22, 1897", , , Jan. 1900 Court Book 16
Seabold, Freda, "June 22, 1897", , , July 1899 Court Book 16,
Seabold, Freda, "June 22, 1897", , , June 1899 Court Book 16,
Seabold, Freda, "June 22, 1897", , , Mar. 1900 Court Book 16, "To home in state Mar. 23, 1900"
Seabold, Freda, "June 22, 1897", , , Nov. 1899 Court Book 16,
Seabold, Freda, "June 22, 1897", , , Oct. 1899 Court Book 16
Seabold, Freda, "June 22, 1897", , , Sept. 1899 Court Book 16,
Seabold, Freda, "June 22, 1897", 10, 7, May 1899 Court - Girls Book 16,
Sealer, Mary, "Nov. 16, 1899", , , Apr. 1900 Nursery Court Book 16
Sealer, Mary, "Nov. 16, 1899", , , Dec. 1899 Nursery Court Book 16
Sealer, Mary, "Nov. 16, 1899", , , Feb. 1900 Nursery Court Book 16,
Sealer, Mary, "Nov. 16, 1899", , , Jan. 1900 Nursery Court Book 16
Sealer, Mary, "Nov. 16, 1899", , , June 1900 Nursery Court Book 16
Sealer, Mary, "Nov. 16, 1899", , , Mar. 1900 Nursery Court Book 16,
Sealer, Mary, "Nov. 16, 1899", , , May 1900 Nursery Court Book 16,
Sealer, Mary, "Nov. 22, 1899", 6, 1, Nov. 1899 Nursery Court Book 16
Silverberg, Alma, "May 7, 1900", , , June 1900 Court Book 16, Dis. June 2 to Jewish Asylum
Silverberg, Alma, "May 7, 1900", 14, 6, May 1900 Court Book 16,
Silverberg, Alma, "Nov. 1, 1898", , , August 1899 Court Book 16
Silverberg, Alma, "Nov. 1, 1898", , , Dec. 1899 Court Book 16
Silverberg, Alma, "Nov. 1, 1898", , , Feb. 1900 Court Book 16, "Dis. To home in state Feb. 6, 1900"
Silverberg, Alma, "Nov. 1, 1898", , , Jan. 1900 Court Book 16,
Silverberg, Alma, "Nov. 1, 1898", , , July 1899 Court Book 16
Silverberg, Alma, "Nov. 1, 1898", , , June 1899 Court Book 16, H.
Silverberg, Alma, "Nov. 1, 1898", , , Nov. 1899 Court Book 16
Silverberg, Alma, "Nov. 1, 1898", , , Oct. 1899 Court Book 16
Silverberg, Alma, "Nov. 1, 1898", , , Sept. 1899 Court Book 16,
Silverberg, Alma, "Nov. 1, 1898", 13, 6, May 1899 Court - Girls Book 16, H.
Skogland, Dagmar, "Sept. 20, 1899", , , Apr. 1900 Court Book 16
Skogland, Dagmar, "Sept. 20, 1899", , , Dec. 1899 Court Book 16
Skogland, Dagmar, "Sept. 20, 1899", , , Feb. 1900 Court Book 16,

Skogland, Dagmar, "Sept. 20, 1899", , , Jan. 1900 Court Book 16
Skogland, Dagmar, "Sept. 20, 1899", , , Mar. 1900 Court Book 16
Skogland, Dagmar, "Sept. 20, 1899", , , May 1900 Court Book 16, "Dis. To father May 11, 1900"
Skogland, Dagmar, "Sept. 20, 1899", , , Nov. 1899 Court Book 16
Skogland, Dagmar, "Sept. 20, 1899", , , Oct. 1899 Court Book 16
Skogland, Dagmar, "Sept. 20, 1899", 7, 11, Sept. 1899 Court Book 16
Skogland, Ethel, "July 3, 1899", , , Apr. 1900 Nursery Court Book 16
Skogland, Ethel, "July 3, 1899", , , Dec. 1899 Nursery Court Book 16
Skogland, Ethel, "July 3, 1899", , , Feb. 1900 Nursery Court Book 16,
Skogland, Ethel, "July 3, 1899", , , Jan. 1900 Nursery Court Book 16
Skogland, Ethel, "July 3, 1899", , , Mar. 1900 Nursery Court Book 16,
Skogland, Ethel, "July 3, 1899", , , May 1900 Nursery Court Book 16, "Dis. To father May 11, 1900"
Skogland, Ethel, "Sept. 20, 1899", , , Nov. 1899 Nursery Court Book 16
Skogland, Ethel, "Sept. 20, 1899", , , Oct. 1899 Court - Nursery Book 16,
Skogland, Ethel, "Sept. 20, 1899", 3, 4, Sept. 1899 Court-Nursery Book 16,
Smith, Bertha, "July 29, 1898", , , August 1899 Court Nursery Book 16
Smith, Bertha, "July 29, 1898", , , July 1899 Court - Nursery Book 16
Smith, Bertha, "July 29, 1898", , , June 1899 Court - Nursery Book 16
Smith, Bertha, "July 29, 1898", , , Nov. 1899 Nursery Court Book 16
Smith, Bertha, "July 29, 1898", , , Oct. 1899 Court - Nursery Book 16,
Smith, Bertha, "July 29, 1898", , , Sept. 1899 Court-Nursery Book 16
Smith, Bertha, "July 29, 1898", 3, 4, May 1899 Court - Nursery Book 16, Hosp.
Smith, Bertha, "June 3, 1898", , , Apr. 1900 Nursery Court Book 16,
Smith, Bertha, "June 3, 1898", , , Dec. 1899 Nursery Court Book 16,
Smith, Bertha, "June 3, 1898", , , Feb. 1900 Nursery Court Book 16
Smith, Bertha, "June 3, 1898", , , Jan. 1900 Nursery Court Book 16,
Smith, Bertha, "June 3, 1898", , , June 1900 Nursery Court Book 16

Smith, Bertha, "June 3, 1898", , , Mar. 1900 Nursery Court Book 16
Smith, Bertha, "June 3, 1898", , , May 1900 Nursery Court Book 16
Smith, Elsa, "Aug. 4, 1898", , , August 1899 Court Nursery Book 16
Smith, Elsa, "Aug. 4, 1898", , , July 1899 Court - Nursery Book 16
Smith, Elsa, "Aug. 4, 1898", , , June 1899 Court - Nursery Book 16
Smith, Elsa, "Aug. 4, 1898", , , Nov. 1899 Nursery Court Book 16
Smith, Elsa, "Aug. 4, 1898", , , Oct. 1899 Court - Nursery Book 16,
Smith, Elsa, "Aug. 4, 1898", , , Sept. 1899 Court-Nursery Book 16
Smith, Elsa, "Aug. 4, 1898", 5, 11, May 1899 Court - Nursery Book 16,
Smith, Elsa, "July 29, 1898", , , Apr. 1900 Nursery Court Book 16
Smith, Elsa, "July 29, 1898", , , Dec. 1899 Nursery Court Book 16,
Smith, Elsa, "July 29, 1898", , , Feb. 1900 Nursery Court Book 16
Smith, Elsa, "July 29, 1898", , , Jan. 1900 Nursery Court Book 16,
Smith, Elsa, "July 29, 1898", , , June 1900 Nursery Court Book 16
Smith, Elsa, "July 29, 1898", , , Mar. 1900 Nursery Court Book 16
Smith, Elsa, "July 29, 1898", , , May 1900 Nursery Court Book 16
Stanley, Agnes, "Feb. 6, 1900", 12, 5, Feb. 1900 Court Book 16, "To home out of state Feb. 23, 1900"
Stanley, Annie, "June 4, 1897", , , August 1899 Court Book 16
Stanley, Annie, "June 4, 1897", , , July 1899 Court Book 16
Stanley, Annie, "June 4, 1897", , , June 1899 Court Book 16, H.
Stanley, Annie, "June 4, 1897", , , Sept. 1899 Court Book 16, "To home in state Sept. 15, 1899"
Stanley, Annie, "June 4, 1897", 11, 11, May 1899 Court - Girls Book 16,
Stanley, Lizzie, "June 4, 1897", , , August 1899 Court Book 16
Stanley, Lizzie, "June 4, 1897", , , July 1899 Court Book 16
Stanley, Lizzie, "June 4, 1897", , , June 1899 Court Book 16, H.
Stanley, Lizzie, "June 4, 1897", , , Sept. 1899 Court Book 16, "To home out of state Sept. 25, 1899"
Stanley, Lizzie, "June 4, 1897", 12, 11, May 1899 Court - Girls Book 16, H.
Stein, Lavina, "July 11, 1899", , , Dec. 1899 Nursery Court Book 16
Stein, Lavina, "July 11, 1899", , , Feb. 1900 Nursery Court Book 16, "Dis. To father Feb. 12, 1900"
Stein, Lavina, "July 11, 1899", , , Jan. 1900 Nursery Court Book 16
Stein, Lavina, "July 3, 1898", 5, 1, August 1899 Court Nursery Book 16,
Stein, Lavina, "July 3, 1899", , , Nov. 1899 Nursery Court Book 16
Stein, Lavina, "July 3, 1899", , , Oct. 1899 Court - Nursery Book 16,
Stein, Lavina, "July 3, 1899", 5, 2, Sept. 1899 Court-Nursery Book 16,
Steinmetz, Madeline , "Apr. 5, 1899", , , Apr. 1900 Tempy & Home Book 16, "Dis. To home out of state Apr. 4, 1900"
Steinmetz, Madeline , "Apr. 5, 1899", , , Feb. 1900 Tempy & Home Book 16,
Steinmetz, Madeline , "Apr. 5, 1899", , , Jan. 1900 Tempy & Home Book 16,

Steinmetz, Madeline , "Apr. 5, 1899", , , Mar. 1900 Tempy & House Book 16,

Steinmetz, Madeline , "May 5, 1899", , , Dec. 1899 Tempy & Home Book 16,

Steinmetz, Madeline , "May 5, 1899", , , Nov. 1899 Tempy & Home Book 16,

Steinmetz, Madeline , "May 5, 1899", , , Oct. 1899 Tempy & Home Book 16,

Steinmetz, Madeline , "May 5, 1899", 2, 11, August 1899 Tempy. & Home Book 16

Steinmetz, Madeline, "May 5, 1899", , , Sept. 1899 Temp. & Home Book 16

Steinmetz, Madeline, "May 5, 1899", 2, ,

Steinmetz, Madeline, "May 5, 1899", 2, 6, May 1899 Court - Nursery Book 16, Put on Home list

Stiner, Curtis, "Jan. 17, 1895", , , Apr. 1900 Court Book 16

Stiner, Curtis, "Jan. 17, 1895", , , August 1899 Court Book 16

Stiner, Curtis, "Jan. 17, 1895", , , Dec. 1899 Court Book 16

Stiner, Curtis, "Jan. 17, 1895", , , Feb. 1900 Court Book 16,

Stiner, Curtis, "Jan. 17, 1895", , , Jan. 1900 Court Book 16

Stiner, Curtis, "Jan. 17, 1895", , , July 1899 Court Book 16

Stiner, Curtis, "Jan. 17, 1895", , , June 1899 Court Book 16,

Stiner, Curtis, "Jan. 17, 1895", , , June 1900 Court Book 16,

Stiner, Curtis, "Jan. 17, 1895", , , Mar. 1900 Court Book 16,

Stiner, Curtis, "Jan. 17, 1895", , , May 1900 Court Book 16,

Stiner, Curtis, "Jan. 17, 1895", , , Nov. 1899 Court Book 16

Stiner, Curtis, "Jan. 17, 1895", , , Oct. 1899 Court Book 16

Stiner, Curtis, "Jan. 17, 1895", , , Sept. 1899 Court Book 16

Stiner, Curtis, "Jan. 17, 1895", 7, 2, May 1899 Court - Boys Book 16,

Stuhm, Carrie, "Feb. 24, 1897", , , Apr. 1900 Nursery Court Book 16,

Stuhm, Carrie, "Feb. 24, 1897", , , August 1899 Court Nursery Book 16

Stuhm, Carrie, "Feb. 24, 1897", , , Dec. 1899 Nursery Court Book 16,

Stuhm, Carrie, "Feb. 24, 1897", , , Feb. 1900 Nursery Court Book 16

Stuhm, Carrie, "Feb. 24, 1897", , , Jan. 1900 Nursery Court Book 16,

Stuhm, Carrie, "Feb. 24, 1897", , , July 1899 Court - Nursery Book 16

Stuhm, Carrie, "Feb. 24, 1897", , , June 1899 Court Book 16

Stuhm, Carrie, "Feb. 24, 1897", , , June 1900 Nursery Court Book 16,

Stuhm, Carrie, "Feb. 24, 1897", , , Mar. 1900 Nursery Court Book 16

Stuhm, Carrie, "Feb. 24, 1897", , , May 1900 Nursery Court Book 16,

Stuhm, Carrie, "Feb. 24, 1897", , , Nov. 1899 Nursery Court Book 16

Stuhm, Carrie, "Feb. 24, 1897", , , Oct. 1899 Court - Nursery Book 16,

Stuhm, Carrie, "Feb. 24, 1897", , , Sept. 1899 Court-Nursery Book 16,

Stuhm, Carrie, "Feb. 24, 1897", 5, 4, May 1899 Court - Nursery Book 16,

Stuhm, Ellie, "July 21, 1898", , , Apr. 1900 Court Book 16,

Stuhm, Ellie, "July 21, 1898", , , August 1899 Court Book 16

Stuhm, Ellie, "July 21, 1898", , , Dec. 1899 Court Book 16

Stuhm, Ellie, "July 21, 1898", , , Feb. 1900 Court Book 16,

Stuhm, Ellie, "July 21, 1898", , , Jan. 1900 Court Book 16,

Stuhm, Ellie, "July 21, 1898", , , July 1899 Court Book 16,

Stuhm, Ellie, "July 21, 1898", , , June 1899 Court Book 16,

Stuhm, Ellie, "July 21, 1898", , , June 1900 Court Book 16,

Stuhm, Ellie, "July 21, 1898", , , Mar. 1900 Court Book 16

Stuhm, Ellie, "July 21, 1898", , , May 1900 Court Book 16

Stuhm, Ellie, "July 21, 1898", , , Nov. 1899 Court Book 16

Stuhm, Ellie, "July 21, 1898", , , Oct. 1899 Court Book 16

Stuhm, Ellie, "July 21, 1898", , , Sept. 1899 Court Book 16,

Stuhm, Ellie, "July 21, 1898", 10, 11, May 1899 Court - Girls Book 16,

Stuhm, Sophia, "June 30, 1896", , , Apr. 1900 Nursery Court Book 16,

Stuhm, Sophia, "June 30, 1896", , , August 1899 Court Nursery Book 16

Stuhm, Sophia, "June 30, 1896", , , Dec. 1899 Nursery Court Book 16,

Stuhm, Sophia, "June 30, 1896", , , Feb. 1900 Nursery Court Book 16

Stuhm, Sophia, "June 30, 1896", , , Jan. 1900 Nursery Court Book 16

Stuhm, Sophia, "June 30, 1896", , , July 1899 Court - Nursery Book 16

Stuhm, Sophia, "June 30, 1896", , , June 1899 Court Book 16

Stuhm, Sophia, "June 30, 1896", , , June 1900 Nursery Court Book 16,

Stuhm, Sophia, "June 30, 1896", , , Mar. 1900 Nursery Court Book 16

Stuhm, Sophia, "June 30, 1896", , , May 1900 Nursery Court Book 16,

Stuhm, Sophia, "June 30, 1896", , , Nov. 1899 Nursery Court Book 16

Stuhm, Sophia, "June 30, 1896", , , Oct. 1899 Court - Nursery Book 16,

Stuhm, Sophia, "June 30, 1896", , , Sept. 1899 Court-Nursery Book 16,

Stuhm, Sophia, "June 30, 1896", 7, 5, May 1899 Court - Nursery Book 16,

Sullivan, May, "Oct. 19, 1899", , , Nov. 1899 Tempy & Home Book 16, "Dis. To mother Nov. 22, 1899"

Sullivan, May, "Oct. 19, 1899", 3, 6, Oct. 1899 Tempy & Home Book 16,

Summers, Lilly, "Apr. 21, 1896", 11, , May 1899 Court - Girls Book 16, Dis. To Mother

Summers, Mary, "Apr. 21, 1896", , , July 1899 Court - Nursery Book 16

Summers, Mary, "Apr. 21, 1896", 9, , May 1899 Court - Nursery Book 16, Dis. To mother May 15

Swallow, Florence, "Jan. 8, 1898", , , August 1899 Court Book 16

Swallow, Florence, "Jan. 8, 1898", , , July 1899 Court Book 16,

Swallow, Florence, "Jan. 8, 1898", , , June 1899 Court Book 16,

Swallow, Florence, "Jan. 8, 1898", , , Nov. 1899 Court Book 16, "Dis. To mother Nov. 16, 1899"

Swallow, Florence, "Jan. 8, 1898", , , Oct. 1899 Court Book 16

Swallow, Florence, "Jan. 8, 1898", , , Sept. 1899 Court Book 16,

Swallow, Florence, "Jan. 8, 1898", 9, , May 1899 Court - Girls Book 16,

Talbot, Marion, "May 29, 1900"

Talbot, Marion, "May 29, 1900", , , June 1900 Tempy & Home Book 16,

Talbot, Marion, "May 29, 1900", 3, 4, May 1900 Tempy & Home Book 16,

Thorndike, Marguerite, "Apr. 27, 1900"

Thorndike, Marguerite, "Apr. 27, 1900", , , June 1900 Tempy & Home Book 16,

Thorndike, Marguerite, "Apr. 27, 1900", , , May 1900 Tempy & Home Book 16,

Thorndike, Marguerite, "Apr. 27, 1900", 7, 7, Apr. 1900 Tempy & Home Book 16,

Tracy, Joseph, "Oct. 11, 1899", , , Dec. 1899 Tempy & Home Book 16, "Dis. To mother Dec. 15, 1899"

Tracy, Joseph, "Oct. 11, 1899", , , Nov. 1899 Tempy & Home Book 16,

Tracy, Joseph, "Oct. 11, 1899", 2, 2, Oct. 1899 Tempy & Home Book 16,

Tracy, Thomas, "Oct. 11, 1899", , , Dec. 1899 Tempy & Home Book 16, "Dis. To mother Dec. 15, 1899"

Tracy, Thomas, "Oct. 11, 1899", , , Nov. 1899 Tempy & Home Book 16,

Tracy, Thomas, "Oct. 11, 1899", 4, 10, Oct. 1899 Tempy & Home Book 16,

Van Wicklen, John, "Nov. 12, 1896", , , Apr. 1900 Court Book 16

Van Wicklen, John, "Nov. 12, 1896", , , August 1899 Court Book 16

Van Wicklen, John, "Nov. 12, 1896", , , Dec. 1899 Court Book 16,

Van Wicklen, John, "Nov. 12, 1896", , , Feb. 1900 Court Book 16

Van Wicklen, John, "Nov. 12, 1896", , , Jan. 1900 Court Book 16
Van Wicklen, John, "Nov. 12, 1896", , , July 1899 Court Book 16
Van Wicklen, John, "Nov. 12, 1896", , , June 1899 Court Book 16,
Van Wicklen, John, "Nov. 12, 1896", , , June 1900 Court Book 16,
Van Wicklen, John, "Nov. 12, 1896", , , Mar. 1900 Court Book 16
Van Wicklen, John, "Nov. 12, 1896", , , May 1900 Court Book 16
Van Wicklen, John, "Nov. 12, 1896", , , Nov. 1899 Court Book 16
Van Wicklen, John, "Nov. 12, 1896", , , Oct. 1899 Court Book 16
Van Wicklen, John, "Nov. 12, 1896", , , Sept. 1899 Court Book 16
Van Wicklen, John, "Nov. 12, 1896", 5, 5, May 1899 Court - Boys Book 16,
Vogan, Eliza, "Nov. 19, 1894", , , Apr. 1900 Court Book 16,
Vogan, Eliza, "Nov. 19, 1894", , , August 1899 Court Book 16
Vogan, Eliza, "Nov. 19, 1894", , , Dec. 1899 Court Book 16
Vogan, Eliza, "Nov. 19, 1894", , , Feb. 1900 Court Book 16,
Vogan, Eliza, "Nov. 19, 1894", , , Jan. 1900 Court Book 16,
Vogan, Eliza, "Nov. 19, 1894", , , July 1899 Court Book 16
Vogan, Eliza, "Nov. 19, 1894", , , June 1899 Court Book 16,
Vogan, Eliza, "Nov. 19, 1894", , , June 1900 Court Book 16,
Vogan, Eliza, "Nov. 19, 1894", , , Mar. 1900 Court Book 16,
Vogan, Eliza, "Nov. 19, 1894", , , May 1900 Court Book 16,
Vogan, Eliza, "Nov. 19, 1894", , , Nov. 1899 Court Book 16,
Vogan, Eliza, "Nov. 19, 1894", , , Oct. 1899 Court Book 16,
Vogan, Eliza, "Nov. 19, 1894", , , Sept. 1899 Court Book 16
Vogan, Eliza, "Nov. 19, 1894", 16, 9, May 1899 Court - Girls Book 16,
Volker, Frances, "Oct. 19, 1897", , , Apr. 1900 Court Book 16,
Volker, Frances, "Oct. 19, 1897", , , August 1899 Court Book 16
Volker, Frances, "Oct. 19, 1897", , , Dec. 1899 Court Book 16
Volker, Frances, "Oct. 19, 1897", , , Feb. 1900 Court Book 16,
Volker, Frances, "Oct. 19, 1897", , , Jan. 1900 Court Book 16
Volker, Frances, "Oct. 19, 1897", , , July 1899 Court Book 16,
Volker, Frances, "Oct. 19, 1897", , , June 1899 Court Book 16,
Volker, Frances, "Oct. 19, 1897", , , June 1900 Court Book 16,
Volker, Frances, "Oct. 19, 1897", , , Mar. 1900 Court Book 16,
Volker, Frances, "Oct. 19, 1897", , , May 1900 Court Book 16
Volker, Frances, "Oct. 19, 1897", , , Nov. 1899 Court Book 16,
Volker, Frances, "Oct. 19, 1897", , , Oct. 1899 Court Book 16
Volker, Frances, "Oct. 19, 1897", , , Sept. 1899 Court Book 16,
Volker, Frances, "Oct. 19, 1897", 7, 11, May 1899 Court - Girls Book 16,
Volker, Henrietta, "Dec. 20, 1895", , , Apr. 1900 Nursery Court Book 16
Volker, Henrietta, "Dec. 20, 1895", , , August 1899 Court Nursery Book 16
Volker, Henrietta, "Dec. 20, 1895", , , Dec. 1899 Nursery Court Book 16,
Volker, Henrietta, "Dec. 20, 1895", , , Feb. 1900 Nursery Court Book 16,

Volker, Henrietta, "Dec. 20, 1895", , , Jan. 1900 Nursery Court Book 16

Volker, Henrietta, "Dec. 20, 1895", , , July 1899 Court - Nursery Book 16

Volker, Henrietta, "Dec. 20, 1895", , , June 1899 Court Book 16,

Volker, Henrietta, "Dec. 20, 1895", , , June 1900 Nursery Court Book 16,

Volker, Henrietta, "Dec. 20, 1895", , , Mar. 1900 Nursery Court Book 16

Volker, Henrietta, "Dec. 20, 1895", , , May 1900 Nursery Court Book 16,

Volker, Henrietta, "Dec. 20, 1895", , , Nov. 1899 Nursery Court Book 16

Volker, Henrietta, "Dec. 20, 1895", , , Oct. 1899 Court - Nursery Book 16,

Volker, Henrietta, "Dec. 20, 1895", , , Sept. 1899 Court-Nursery Book 16

Volker, Henrietta, "Dec. 20, 1895", 6, 3, May 1899 Court - Nursery Book 16,

Wagner, Ella, "Jan. 26, 1900", , , Apr. 1900 Nursery Court Book 16

Wagner, Ella, "Jan. 26, 1900", , , Feb. 1900 Nursery Court Book 16,

Wagner, Ella, "Jan. 26, 1900", , , June 1900 Nursery Court Book 16,

Wagner, Ella, "Jan. 26, 1900", , , Mar. 1900 Nursery Court Book 16,

Wagner, Ella, "Jan. 26, 1900", , , May 1900 Nursery Court Book 16,

Wagner, Ella, "Jan. 26, 1900", 6, , Jan. 1900 Nursery Court Book 16,

Wagner, Emma, "Apr. 16, 1900"

Wagner, Emma, "Apr. 16, 1900", , , June 1900 Tempy & Home Book 16, "Dis to mother June 2, 1900"

Wagner, Emma, "Apr. 16, 1900", , , May 1900 Tempy & Home Book 16,

Wagner, Emma, "Apr. 16, 1900", 7, 11, Apr. 1900 Tempy & Home Book 16, Board

Wagner, Harry, "Jan. 26, 1900", , , Apr. 1900 Nursery Court Book 16

Wagner, Harry, "Jan. 26, 1900", , , Feb. 1900 Nursery Court Book 16,

Wagner, Harry, "Jan. 26, 1900", , , June 1900 Nursery Court Book 16,

Wagner, Harry, "Jan. 26, 1900", , , Mar. 1900 Nursery Court Book 16,

Wagner, Harry, "Jan. 26, 1900", , , May 1900 Nursery Court Book 16,

Wagner, Harry, "Jan. 26, 1900", 2, , Jan. 1900 Nursery Court Book 16,

Walker, Ethel, "June 6, 1900", 4, 7, June 1900 Tempy & Home Book 16,

Walker, Frank, "Aug. 12, 1897", , , August 1899 Outside Book 16, Island Hospital
Walker, Frank, "Aug. 12, 1897", , , July 1899 Outside Book 16
Walker, Frank, "Aug. 12, 1897", , , June 1899 Outside Book 16,
Walker, Frank, "Aug. 12, 1897", , , Nov. 1899 Outside Book 16, Island Hospital
Walker, Frank, "Aug. 12, 1897", , , Oct. 1899 Outside Book 16,
Walker, Frank, "Aug. 12, 1897", , , Sept. 1899 Outside Book 16,
Walker, Frank, "Aug. 12, 1897", 8, 7, May 1899 Outside Book 16,
Walker, Frank, "Sept. 8, 1897", , , Apr. 1900 Nursery Court Book 16,
Walker, Frank, "Sept. 8, 1897", , , Dec. 1899 Nursery Court Book 16,
Walker, Frank, "Sept. 8, 1897", , , Feb. 1900 Nursery Court Book 16, island Hospital
Walker, Frank, "Sept. 8, 1897", , , Jan. 1900 Outside Book 16, Island Hospital
Walker, Frank, "Sept. 8, 1897", , , June 1900 Nursery Court Book 16,
Walker, Frank, "Sept. 8, 1897", , , Mar. 1900 Nursery Court Book 16, "Dis. To public charities Mar. 7, 1900"
Wallace, James, "Dec. 21, 1898", , , Apr. 1900 Court Book 16
Wallace, James, "Dec. 21, 1898", , , August 1899 Court Book 16
Wallace, James, "Dec. 21, 1898", , , Dec. 1899 Court Book 16,
Wallace, James, "Dec. 21, 1898", , , Feb. 1900 Court Book 16,
Wallace, James, "Dec. 21, 1898", , , Jan. 1900 Court Book 16
Wallace, James, "Dec. 21, 1898", , , July 1899 Court Book 16
Wallace, James, "Dec. 21, 1898", , , June 1899 Court Book 16,
Wallace, James, "Dec. 21, 1898", , , June 1900 Court Book 16
Wallace, James, "Dec. 21, 1898", , , Mar. 1900 Court Book 16
Wallace, James, "Dec. 21, 1898", , , May 1900 Court Book 16,
Wallace, James, "Dec. 21, 1898", , , Nov. 1899 Court Book 16
Wallace, James, "Dec. 21, 1898", , , Oct. 1899 Court Book 16,
Wallace, James, "Dec. 21, 1898", , , Sept. 1899 Court Book 16
Wallace, James, "Dec. 21, 1898", 6, 10, May 1899 Court - Boys Book 16,
Wallace, Lizzie, "Feb. 5, 1898", , , June 1899 Court Book 16, "Dis. To father June 29, 1899"
Wallace, Lizzie, "Feb. 5, 1898", 8, 3, May 1899 Court - Girls Book 16,
Wallace, William, "Oct. 20, 1899", , , Dec. 1899 Tempy & Home Book 16,
Wallace, William, "Oct. 20, 1899", , , Nov. 1899 Tempy & Home Book 16,
Wallace, William, "Oct. 20, 1899", 1, 10, Oct. 1899 Tempy & Home Book 16,
Wallace, William, "Oct. 9, 1899", , , Jan. 1900 Tempy & Home Book 16, "To home in state Jan. 30, 1900"
Walsh, Joseph, "Feb. 28, 1896", , , August 1899 Court Book 16

Walsh, Joseph, "Feb. 28, 1896", , , Dec. 1899 Court Book 16,
Walsh, Joseph, "Feb. 28, 1896", , , Feb. 1900 Court Book 16
Walsh, Joseph, "Feb. 28, 1896", , , Jan. 1900 Court Book 16
Walsh, Joseph, "Feb. 28, 1896", , , July 1899 Court Book 16
Walsh, Joseph, "Feb. 28, 1896", , , June 1899 Court Book 16,
Walsh, Joseph, "Feb. 28, 1896", , , Mar. 1900 Court Book 16, Sent to Island Hospital
Walsh, Joseph, "Feb. 28, 1896", , , Nov. 1899 Court Book 16
Walsh, Joseph, "Feb. 28, 1896", , , Oct. 1899 Court Book 16
Walsh, Joseph, "Feb. 28, 1896", , , Sept. 1899 Court Book 16
Walsh, Joseph, "Feb. 28, 1896", 6, 2, May 1899 Court - Boys Book 16,
Wanner, Emma, "Dec. 10, 1898", , , Apr. 1900 Nursery Court Book 16
Wanner, Emma, "Dec. 10, 1898", , , Dec. 1899 Nursery Court Book 16,
Wanner, Emma, "Dec. 10, 1898", , , Feb. 1900 Nursery Court Book 16,
Wanner, Emma, "Dec. 10, 1898", , , Jan. 1900 Nursery Court Book 16
Wanner, Emma, "Dec. 10, 1898", , , June 1900 Nursery Court Book 16
Wanner, Emma, "Dec. 10, 1898", , , Mar. 1900 Nursery Court Book 16
Wanner, Emma, "Dec. 10, 1898", , , May 1900 Nursery Court Book 16
Wanner, Emma, "Dec. 14, 1898", , , August 1899 Court Nursery Book 16
Wanner, Emma, "Dec. 14, 1898", , , July 1899 Court - Nursery Book 16
Wanner, Emma, "Dec. 14, 1898", , , June 1899 Court - Nursery Book 16
Wanner, Emma, "Dec. 14, 1898", , , Nov. 1899 Nursery Court Book 16
Wanner, Emma, "Dec. 14, 1898", , , Oct. 1899 Court - Nursery Book 16,
Wanner, Emma, "Dec. 14, 1898", , , Sept. 1899 Court-Nursery Book 16
Wanner, Emma, "Dec. 14, 1898", 4, 7, May 1899 Court - Nursery Book 16,
Wanner, Ernest, "Sept. 7, 1897", , , Apr. 1900 Court Book 16
Wanner, Ernest, "Sept. 7, 1897", , , August 1899 Court Book 16
Wanner, Ernest, "Sept. 7, 1897", , , Dec. 1899 Court Book 16,
Wanner, Ernest, "Sept. 7, 1897", , , Feb. 1900 Court Book 16
Wanner, Ernest, "Sept. 7, 1897", , , Jan. 1900 Court Book 16
Wanner, Ernest, "Sept. 7, 1897", , , July 1899 Court Book 16
Wanner, Ernest, "Sept. 7, 1897", , , June 1899 Court Book 16,
Wanner, Ernest, "Sept. 7, 1897", , , June 1900 Court Book 16
Wanner, Ernest, "Sept. 7, 1897", , , Mar. 1900 Court Book 16

Wanner, Ernest, "Sept. 7, 1897", , , May 1900 Court Book 16
Wanner, Ernest, "Sept. 7, 1897", , , Nov. 1899 Court Book 16
Wanner, Ernest, "Sept. 7, 1897", , , Oct. 1899 Court Book 16
Wanner, Ernest, "Sept. 7, 1897", , , Sept. 1899 Court Book 16
Wanner, Ernest, "Sept. 7, 1897", 6, 7, May 1899 Court - Boys Book 16,
Webb, Ernest, "Sept. 25, 1899", 2, 1, Oct. 1899 Tempy & Home Book 16, Board paid
Webb, Fred K., "July 11, 1898", 4, 1, August 1899 Court Nursery Book 16,
Webb, Fred K., "July 11, 1899", , , Nov. 1899 Nursery Court Book 16
Webb, Fred K., "July 11, 1899", , , Oct. 1899 Court - Nursery Book 16,
Webb, Fred K., "July 11, 1899", , , Sept. 1899 Court-Nursery Book 16,
Webb, Fred K., "July 11, 1899", 4, , July 1899 Court - Nursery Book 16
Webb, Fred K., "May 2, 1898", , , Apr. 1900 Nursery Court Book 16
Webb, Fred K., "May 2, 1898", , , Dec. 1899 Nursery Court Book 16
Webb, Fred K., "May 2, 1898", , , Feb. 1900 Nursery Court Book 16,
Webb, Fred K., "May 2, 1898", , , Jan. 1900 Nursery Court Book 16
Webb, Fred K., "May 2, 1898", , , June 1900 Nursery Court Book 16
Webb, Fred K., "May 2, 1898", , , Mar. 1900 Nursery Court Book 16,
Webb, Fred K., "May 2, 1898", , , May 1900 Nursery Court Book 16,
Webb, John R., "Sept. 21, 1899"
Webb, John R., "Sept. 21, 1899", , , Apr. 1900 Tempy & Home Book 16,
Webb, John R., "Sept. 21, 1899", , , Dec. 1899 Nursery Court Book 16
Webb, John R., "Sept. 21, 1899", , , Feb. 1900 Nursery Court Book 16,
Webb, John R., "Sept. 21, 1899", , , Feb. 1900 Tempy & Home Book 16,
Webb, John R., "Sept. 21, 1899", , , Feb. 1900 Tempy & Home Book 16, Board paid $5.00
Webb, John R., "Sept. 21, 1899", , , Jan. 1900 Tempy & Home Book 16,
Webb, John R., "Sept. 21, 1899", , , June 1900 Tempy & Home Book 16, Board paid
Webb, John R., "Sept. 21, 1899", , , Mar. 1900 Tempy & House Book 16,
Webb, John R., "Sept. 21, 1899", , , May 1900 Tempy & Home Book 16,
Webb, John R., "Sept. 25, 1899", , , Dec. 1899 Tempy & Home Book 16,
Webb, John R., "Sept. 25, 1899", , , Nov. 1899 Tempy & Home Book 16,

Webb, John R., "Sept. 25, 1899", , , Nov. 1899 Tempy & Home Book 16,
Webb, John R., "Sept. 25, 1899", , , Nov. 1899 Tempy & Home Book 16,
Webb, John R., "Sept. 25, 1899", 2, , Sept. 1899 Tempy. & Home Book 16,
Webb, Lola, , , , Sept. 1899 Court Book 16
Webb, Lola, "July 11, 1899", , , Apr. 1900 Court Book 16
Webb, Lola, "July 11, 1899", , , August 1899 Court Book 16
Webb, Lola, "July 11, 1899", , , Dec. 1899 Court Book 16
Webb, Lola, "July 11, 1899", , , Feb. 1900 Court Book 16,
Webb, Lola, "July 11, 1899", , , Jan. 1900 Court Book 16
Webb, Lola, "July 11, 1899", , , June 1900 Court Book 16,
Webb, Lola, "July 11, 1899", , , Mar. 1900 Court Book 16
Webb, Lola, "July 11, 1899", , , May 1900 Court Book 16
Webb, Lola, "July 11, 1899", , , Nov. 1899 Court Book 16
Webb, Lola, "July 11, 1899", , , Oct. 1899 Court Book 16
Webb, Lola, "July 11, 1899", 9, , July 1899 Court - Nursery Book 16
Webb, Sybil, "July 11, 1898", 6, 1, August 1899 Court Nursery Book 16,
Webb, Sybil, "July 11, 1899", , , Apr. 1900 Court Book 16
Webb, Sybil, "July 11, 1899", , , Dec. 1899 Court Book 16
Webb, Sybil, "July 11, 1899", , , Feb. 1900 Court Book 16,
Webb, Sybil, "July 11, 1899", , , Jan. 1900 Court Book 16
Webb, Sybil, "July 11, 1899", , , June 1900 Court Book 16,
Webb, Sybil, "July 11, 1899", , , Mar. 1900 Court Book 16
Webb, Sybil, "July 11, 1899", , , May 1900 Court Book 16,
Webb, Sybil, "July 11, 1899", , , Nov. 1899 Court Book 16
Webb, Sybil, "July 11, 1899", , , Oct. 1899 Court Book 16
Webb, Sybil, "July 11, 1899", , , Sept. 1899 Court-Nursery Book 16,
Webb, Sybil, "July 11, 1899", 6, , July 1899 Court - Nursery Book 16
Webb, William, "July 11, 1898", 3, 1, August 1899 Court Nursery Book 16,
Webb, William, "July 11, 1899", , , Apr. 1900 Nursery Court Book 16
Webb, William, "July 11, 1899", , , Dec. 1899 Nursery Court Book 16
Webb, William, "July 11, 1899", , , Feb. 1900 Nursery Court Book 16,
Webb, William, "July 11, 1899", , , Jan. 1900 Nursery Court Book 16
Webb, William, "July 11, 1899", , , June 1900 Nursery Court Book 16
Webb, William, "July 11, 1899", , , Mar. 1900 Nursery Court Book 16,
Webb, William, "July 11, 1899", , , May 1900 Nursery Court Book 16,

Webb, William, "July 11, 1899", , , Nov. 1899 Nursery Court Book 16

Webb, William, "July 11, 1899", , , Oct. 1899 Court - Nursery Book 16,

Webb, William, "July 11, 1899", , , Sept. 1899 Court-Nursery Book 16,

Webb, William, "July 11, 1899", 3, , July 1899 Court - Nursery Book 16

Webb, Zella, , , , Sept. 1899 Court Book 16

Webb, Zella, "July 11, 1899", , , Apr. 1900 Court Book 16

Webb, Zella, "July 11, 1899", , , August 1899 Court Book 16

Webb, Zella, "July 11, 1899", , , Dec. 1899 Court Book 16

Webb, Zella, "July 11, 1899", , , Feb. 1900 Court Book 16,

Webb, Zella, "July 11, 1899", , , Jan. 1900 Court Book 16

Webb, Zella, "July 11, 1899", , , June 1900 Court Book 16,

Webb, Zella, "July 11, 1899", , , Mar. 1900 Court Book 16

Webb, Zella, "July 11, 1899", , , May 1900 Court Book 16

Webb, Zella, "July 11, 1899", , , Nov. 1899 Court Book 16

Webb, Zella, "July 11, 1899", , , Oct. 1899 Court Book 16

Webb, Zella, "July 11, 1899", 11, 10, July 1899 Tempy. & Home Book 16

Wehlberg, Alice, "Feb. 1, 1900", , , June 1900 Nursery Court Book 16,

Wehlberg, Alice, "Feb. 1, 1900", , , May 1900 Nursery Court Book 16,

Wehlberg, Alice, "Feb. 1, 1900", 4, 9, Apr. 1900 Nursery Court Book 16,

Wehlburg, Alice, "Dec. 14, 1898", , , Feb. 1900 Tempy & Home Book 16, Trans. To court nursery list Feb. 1st

Wehlburg, Alice, "Dec. 14, 1898", , , Jan. 1900 Tempy & Home Book 16,

Wehlburg, Alice, "Dec. 16, 1898", , , August 1899 Tempy. & Home Book 16

Wehlburg, Alice, "Dec. 16, 1898", , , Dec. 1899 Tempy & Home Book 16,

Wehlburg, Alice, "Dec. 16, 1898", , , July 1899 Tempy. & Home Book 16,

Wehlburg, Alice, "Dec. 16, 1898", , , June 1899 Tempy & Home Book 16,

Wehlburg, Alice, "Dec. 16, 1898", , , Nov. 1899 Tempy & Home Book 16,

Wehlburg, Alice, "Dec. 16, 1898", , , Oct. 1899 Tempy & Home Book 16,

Wehlburg, Alice, "Dec. 16, 1898", , , Sept. 1899 Temp. & Home Book 16

Wehlburg, Alice, "Dec. 16, 1898", 3, 10, May 1899 Home & Tempy. Book 16,

White, Alberta, "Aug. 6, 1897", , , July 1899 Court Book 16, "Sent to Syracuse, Ny July 3"

White, Alberta, "Aug. 6, 1897", , , June 1899 Court Book 16,
White, Alberta, "Aug. 6, 1897", 7, 9, May 1899 Court - Girls Book 16,
Williams, Edward , "Apr. 19, 1899", , , Feb. 1900 Tempy & Home Book 16, "To home out of state Feb. 7, 1900"
Williams, Edward , "Apr. 19, 1899", , , Jan. 1900 Tempy & Home Book 16,
Williams, Edward , "July 15, 1899", , , Dec. 1899 Tempy & Home Book 16,
Williams, Edward , "July 15, 1899", , , Nov. 1899 Tempy & Home Book 16,
Williams, Edward , "July 15, 1899", , , Oct. 1899 Tempy & Home Book 16,
Williams, Edward, "July 15, 1899", 7, 7, August 1899 Tempy. & Home Book 16
Williams, Edward, "July 15, 1899", , , Sept. 1899 Temp. & Home Book 16
Wilson, Frances, "Sept. 15, 1897", , , Apr. 1900 Court Book 16,
Wilson, Frances, "Sept. 15, 1897", , , August 1899 Court Book 16
Wilson, Frances, "Sept. 15, 1897", , , Dec. 1899 Court Book 16
Wilson, Frances, "Sept. 15, 1897", , , Feb. 1900 Court Book 16
Wilson, Frances, "Sept. 15, 1897", , , Jan. 1900 Court Book 16
Wilson, Frances, "Sept. 15, 1897", , , July 1899 Court Book 16,
Wilson, Frances, "Sept. 15, 1897", , , June 1899 Court Book 16,
Wilson, Frances, "Sept. 15, 1897", , , June 1900 Court Book 16,
Wilson, Frances, "Sept. 15, 1897", , , Mar. 1900 Court Book 16,
Wilson, Frances, "Sept. 15, 1897", , , May 1900 Court Book 16,
Wilson, Frances, "Sept. 15, 1897", , , Nov. 1899 Court Book 16,
Wilson, Frances, "Sept. 15, 1897", , , Oct. 1899 Court Book 16
Wilson, Frances, "Sept. 15, 1897", , , Sept. 1899 Court Book 16,
Wilson, Frances, "Sept. 15, 1897", 7, 3, May 1899 Court - Girls Book 16,
Wilson, Ida, "Sept. 15, 1897", , , Apr. 1900 Court Book 16,
Wilson, Ida, "Sept. 15, 1897", , , August 1899 Court Book 16
Wilson, Ida, "Sept. 15, 1897", , , Dec. 1899 Court Book 16
Wilson, Ida, "Sept. 15, 1897", , , Feb. 1900 Court Book 16
Wilson, Ida, "Sept. 15, 1897", , , Jan. 1900 Court Book 16
Wilson, Ida, "Sept. 15, 1897", , , July 1899 Court Book 16,
Wilson, Ida, "Sept. 15, 1897", , , June 1899 Court Book 16,
Wilson, Ida, "Sept. 15, 1897", , , June 1900 Court Book 16,
Wilson, Ida, "Sept. 15, 1897", , , Mar. 1900 Court Book 16,
Wilson, Ida, "Sept. 15, 1897", , , May 1900 Court Book 16,
Wilson, Ida, "Sept. 15, 1897", , , Nov. 1899 Court Book 16,
Wilson, Ida, "Sept. 15, 1897", , , Oct. 1899 Court Book 16
Wilson, Ida, "Sept. 15, 1897", , , Sept. 1899 Court Book 16,
Wilson, Ida, "Sept. 15, 1897", 10, 10, May 1899 Court - Girls Book 16,
Woods, Thomas, "May 6, 1898", 9, 3, May 1899 Court - Boys Book 16, Dis. To mother May 10

Worre, Loretta, “Mar. 30, 1896”, , , August 1899 Court Book 16

Worre, Loretta, “Mar. 30, 1896”, , , July 1899 Court Book 16

Worre, Loretta, “Mar. 30, 1896”, , , June 1899 Court Book 16,

Worre, Loretta, “Mar. 30, 1896”, , , Oct. 1899 Court Book 16, “Dis. To mother Oct. 3, 1899”

Worre, Loretta, “Mar. 30, 1896”, , , Sept. 1899 Court Book 16

Worre, Loretta, “Mar. 30, 1896”, 14, 2, May 1899 Court - Girls Book 16,

AMERICAN FEMALE GUARDIAN SOCIETY
HOME FOR THE FRIENDLESS
VOLUME 51

Last Name, First Name, Birth, Data, Parents, Page, Status, Notes

Abill, Lillie, 1872, 1883, Parents: Thomas and Julia Parker Abill, 3, Court 2.13, "Mother insane, father deserted"

Abill, Mamie, 1874, 1883, Parents: Thomas and Julia Parker Abill, 3, Court 2.14, "Mother insane, father deserted"

Badiker, Charlotte, 1876, 1883, mother: Sophia Badiker; father deceased, 79, crt: 2.72

Badiker, Lizzetta, , 1883, mother: Sophia Badiker; father deceased, 79, crt: 2.73

Baker, Jane, 1883, 1883, father: Robert Baker; mother deceased, 110, ref: 10.108

Bean, Fredericka, 1878, 1883, no record of parents, 58, crt: ?

Benson, Emma P., 1873, 1883, Parents: Frederick and Sophie Benson, 49, crt: 2.47

Benson, Frederick, 1875, 1883, Parents: Frederick and Sophie Benson, 49, crt: 2.48

Beverly, Mary, 1881, 1883, Parents: William and Grace Beverly, 114, crt: 2.90

Beverly, Willie, 1879, 1883, Parents: William and Grace Beverly, 114, crt: 2.89

Bice, John Walter, 1881, 1883, Parents; Walter Bice and Annie Jones, 5, ref: 10.59, m.b.32

Boltz, Ida, 1873, 1883, mother: Mrs. Fannie Bernhardt, 64, crt: 2.59

Bradley, Howard Osgood, 1877, 1883, Parents: George and Margaret Bradley, 4, ref: 10.66, f.b.26 1/2

Breen, Caroline, 1871, 1883, Parents: John and Isabell Breen, 115, temporary

Breen, Isabell, 1873, 1883, Parents: John and Isabell Breen, 115, temporary

Briscoe, Mary Ann, 1878, 1883, Parents: Thomas and Mary Ann Briscoe, 85, crt: 2.77

Briscoe, William, 1876, 1883, Parents: Thomas and Mary Ann Briscoe, 85, crt: 2.76

Brown, Mary Ann, , 1883, , 23, Court 2.27

Brucker, Ernestina, 1879, 1883, Parents: Frederick and Magdalena Brucker, 47, crt: 2.41

Brucker, Frederick, 1878, 1883, Parents: Frederick and Magdalena Brucker, 47, crt: 2.40

Buprecht, Ernst, 1876, 1883, Parents: John and Teresa Buprecht, 9, temporary

Buprecht, Hugo, 1878, 1883, Parents: John and Teresa Buprecht, 9, temporary

Burke, Lulu, 1881, 1883, Parents: Robert Burke and Susannah Frameless, 56, crt: 2.55

Burns, Annie, 1882, 1883, Parents: Thomas and Margaret Burns, 7, temporary

Bush, Herman, 1881, 1883, , 26, ref: 10.62, f.b. 27 1/2

Canton, Willie, 1880, 1883, , 32, Court 2.35

Carney, Charlotte, 1877, 1883, Parents: Thomas and Mary Agnes Carney, 102, ref: ?

Carney, Edna, 1873, 1883, Parents: Thomas and Mary Agnes Carney, 102, ref: ?

Cellas, Pillade, 1879, 1883, Parents: Pillade and Concetta Benelli, 73, crt: 2.68

Christy, Maggie, 1875, 1883, , 33, ref: 10.68, f.b. 29

Courter, Annie, 1875, 1883, Parents: Abram and Catherine Courter, 28, ref: 10.64, f.b. 28

Cunningham, Bessie, 1878, 1883, Parents: James and Julia Cunningham, 82, temporary

Dalton, Abbie, 1879, 1883, Parents: Charles and Mabel Dalton, 50, temporary

Davis, John, 1878, 1883, both parents deceased, 86, ref: 10.81

Dearden, Mary, 1880, 1883, Parents: John and Mary Dearden, 57, crt: 2.56

Dietes, Amelia, 1878, 1883, Parents: Hillmer Koerner and Elizabeth Dietes, 6, Court 2.16, Both parents deceased

Dietes, Sonn (?), 1872, 1883, Parents: Hillmer Koerner and Elizabeth Dietes, 6, Court 2.15, Both parents deceased

Dismore, Caroline, 1876, 1883, Parents: Charles and Elizabeth Dismore, 104, temporary

Dismore, Frederick, 1874, 1883, Parents: Charles and Elizabeth Dismore, 104, temporary

Doderer, Emma P., 1879, 1883, Parents: John and Dora Doderer, 60, crt: 2.58

Doeshimn(?), George Y., 1876, 1883, Parents: Valentine and Mary Doeshimn, 8, temporary

Douglass, George, 1879, 1883, Parents: George and Mary Douglass, 44, ref: 10.74

Ehle, Annie, 1879, 1883, no record of parents, 108, crt: 2.88

Evans, Annie, 1880, 1883, Parents: Frederick and Fredericka Evans, 91, ref: 10.86

Evans, May, 1876, 1883, Parents: John and Carrie Evans, 72, crt: 2.67

Farrell, Thomas, 1883, 1883, mother: Bridget Farrell, 107, ref: 10.106

Finacia (?), Christina, , 1883, Parents: Alphonse and Henrietta Finacia, 35, temporary

Finacia (?), Constantia, , 1883, Parents: Alphonse and Henrietta Finacia, 35, temporary

Forsyth, Walter, 1876, 1883, Parents: John and Emma Shaw (foster parents), 2, ref: 10.58, f.b. 26

Frameless, Gertrude, 1873, 1883, Parents: Theodore Pianea and Susannah Frameless, 56, crt: 2.54

Freise, August, 1879, 1883, Parents: August and Louisa Freise, 55, crt: 2.53

Freise, Willie, 1878, 1883, Parents: August and Louisa Freise, 55, crt: 2.52

Gillespie, Katie, 1879, 1883, left in hospital nursery by her mother, 109, ref: 10.107

Goodman, Harry, 1877, 1883, Parents: Charles and Louisa Goodman, 99, temporary

Graff, Caroline, 1880, 1883, Parents: Daniel and Mary Graff, 67, crt: 2.64

Graff, Louisa, 1878, 1883, Parents: Daniel and Mary Graff, 67, crt: 2.63

Gray, William, 1881, 1883, Parents: Charles and Jennie Gray, 51, ref: 10.79

Hall, Eva, 1872, 1883, Parents: Henry A. and Elizabeth Hall, 10, ref: 10.65

Hall, Jessie, 1879, 1883, father: George Hall, 106, temporary

Harding, James, 1878, 1883, no record of parents, 113, ref: 10.112

Hassbacker, Maude, , , , ,

Hayes, Joseph, 1879, 1883, Parents: J.W. and Olivia Hayes, 42, temporary

Henning, Margaret, 1877, 1883, Parents: Richard and Theresa Henning, 37, temporary

Henning, Richard, 1876, 1883, Parents: Richard and Theresa Henning, 37, temporary

Herbek, Bertha, 1878, 1883, Parents: Augustus and Mary Herbek, 62, temporary

Herbek, Mamie, 1880, 1883, Parents: Augustus and Mary Herbek, 62, temporary

Herbst, William, 1876, 1883, no record of parents, 70, crt: 2.65

Hockenyos, Adolph, 1878, 1883, Parents: August and Helena Hockenyos, 15, Court 2.22

Hockenyos, August, 1874, 1883, Parents: August and Helena Hockenyos, 15, Court 2.20

Hockenyos, Emma, 1880, 1883, Parents: August and Helena Hockenyos, 16, Court 2.21

Horrold, Frederick, 1874, 1883, Parents: J. John and Louise Horrold, 89, ref: 10.84

Horrold, Henry, 1879, 1883, Parents: J. John and Louise Horrold, 89, ref: 10.85

Hough, Eugene, 1875, 1883, Parents: Edwin and Belle Hough, 36, temporary

Hurselbee, Albert, 1876, 1883, father: William Hurselbee; mother ill, 74, temporary

Hurselbee, Sarah, 1881, 1883, father: William Hurselbee; mother ill, 74, temporary

Hurselbee, William, 1878, 1883, father: William Hurselbee; mother ill, 74, temporary

Jansen, Anna, 1882, 1883, mother: Anna Jansen; unmarried, 117, temporary

Jordan, Annie, 1873, 1883, Parents: Charles and Fannie Jordan, 43, temporary

Jordan, Segira, 1878, 1883, Parents: Charles and Fannie Jordan, 43, temporary

Kahe, Bertha, 1875, 1883, Parents: Joseph and Annie Kahe, 94, crt: 2.81

Kahe, Clara, 1880, 1883, Parents: Joseph and Annie Kahe, 94, crt: 2.82

Karmann, Annie, 1877, 1883, Parents: John and Margaret Karmann, 101, crt: 2.85

Karmann, Lizzie, 1879, 1883, Parents: John and Margaret Karmann, 101, crt: 2.86

Kennedy, Mamie, 1876, 1883, Mother: Alice Kennedy, 21, temporary

Kinney, Hattie, 1871, 1883, no record of parents, 54, crt: ?

Kruntz, August, 1878, 1883, Parents: William and Mary Kruntz, 29, Court 2.32

Kruntz, Maria, 1874, 1883, Parents: William and Mary Kruntz, 29, Court 2.31

Krutz, Leopold, 1880, 1883, Mother: Mary Krutz, 22, ref: 10.122, f.b. 27

Krutz, Theodore, 1876, 1883, Mother: Mary Krutz, 22, ref: 10.121, f.b. 27

Kuntze, Julia, , 1883, Parents: William and Mary Kuntze, 97, temporary

Lebkuchener, Anthony, 1879, 1883, Parents: Jacob and Minnie Lebkuchener, 78, crt: 2.70

Lebkuchener, Charles, 1881, 1883, Parents: Jacob and Minnie Lebkuchener, 78, crt: 2.71

Letts, Mary Adelaide, 1876, 1883, Parents: Charles and Lily E. Letts, 20, temporary

Lipp, George, 1879, 1883, Parents: John and Mary Lipp, 46, ref: 10.78

Lipp, John, 1876, 1883, Parents: John and Mary Lipp, 46, ref: 10.77

Lipp, Mary, 1874, 1883, Parents: John and Mary Lipp, 46, ref: 10.76

Lupton, Florence Sadie, 1880, 1883, Parents: Henry and Florence Lupton, 26, Court 2.30

Lupton, Victoria Mary, 1877, 1883, Parents: Henry and Florence Lupton, 27, Court 2.29

Lynch, Emily, 1874, 1883, Parents: John and H. Lynch, 19, Court 2.25

Lynch, John, 1879, 1883, Parents: John and H. Lynch, 19, Court 2.26

Mann, William, 1878, 1883, Brother: John, 12, temporary

McCormack, Thomas, 1879, 1883, Parents: Albert and Maggie McCormack, 88, crt: 2.78

McLeod, Lily, 1883, 1883, mother: Margaret McLeod; unmarried, 111, ref: 10.109

Mead, Mary, 1800, 1883, Parents: Leri and Mary Mead, 63, ref: 10.80

Melville, Charles, 1881, 1883, Parents: Charles and Mary Melville, 41, crt: 2.39

Melville, John, 1877, 1883, Parents: Charles and Mary Melville, 41, crt: 2.38

Mezgar, Philip, 1873, 1883, Parents: John and Mary Mezgar, 30, Court 2.33

Mezgar, Walter, 1880, 1883, Parents: John and Mary Mezgar, 30, Court 2.34

Michaelis, Emelia, 1873, 1883, parents unknown; improperly adopted, 92, crt: 2.79

Mills, Annie, 1877, 1883, no record of parents, 98, crt: 2.84

Montagriff, Charlie, 1878, 1883, Parents: Frank and Anna Montagriff, 25, , not received due to running ear

Moran, Kate, 1870, 1883, no record of parents, 66, temporary

Murphy, Lizzie, 1877, 1883, Parents: John and Margaret Murphy, 34, temporary

Newcomb, George, 1879, 1883, Parents: George and Jane Newcomb, 81, crt: 2.74

Nexsen, Sarah, 1875, 1883, Parents: Sheffield and Felicie Nexsen, 105, crt: 2.87

Nichols, Laura, 1880, 1883, Parents: Arthur and Ella Nichols, 100, ref: 10.89

Peltz, Lena, 1880, 1883, "mother: Lena Peltz, deceased", 93, crt: 2.80

Poland, George, 1877, 1883, Parents: Peter and Anne Poland, 53, crt: 2.51

Portas, Harry, 1883, 1883, Parents: Simon Portas and Susie Macomb, 116, ref: 10.116

Renck, Marian, 1878, 1883, Parents: William and Eugenia Renck, 96, crt: 2.83

Ribero, Manuel, 1881, 1883, Parents: Manuel and Mary Ribero, 31, ref: 10.67, f.b. 28 1/2

Richards, Benjamin Franklin, , 1883, Mother: Priscilla Richards father dead, 13, Court 2.18

Richards, Frederick Humphrey, , 1883, Mother: Priscilla Richards father dead, 14, Court 2.19, ref: 10.183

Richards, Mary, , 1883, Mother: Priscilla Richards father dead, 13, Court 2.17

Schavel, Emma, 1876, 1883, Parents: Michael and Mary Schavel, 65, crt: 2.60

Schavel, John, 1880, 1883, Parents: Michael and Mary Schavel, 65, crt: 2.62

Schavel, Katie, 1878, 1883, Parents: Michael and Mary Schavel, 65, crt: 2.61

Shaw, Watler, 1876, 1883, Parents: John and Emma Shaw (foster parents), 2, ref: 10.58, f.b.28 see Forsyth also

Simis, Walter, , 1883, Parents: Samuel and Josephine Simis, 45, ref: 10.75

Sloat, Eddie, 1877, 1883, Parents: John and Sarah Sloat, 90, temporary

Smidt, Josephine, 1879, 1883, Parents: Christian and Josephine Smidt, 59, temporary

Smidt, Julia, 1873, 1883, father surrendered her; mother deceased, 68, temporary

Smith, Albert, 1877, 1883, father: Herman Smith, 75, temporary

Smith, Clara, 1876, 1883, father: Herman Smith, 77, ref: 10.113

Smitt, Martha, 1883, 1883, mother: Annie Smitt; father unknown, 103, ref: 10.105

Starr, Katie, 1877, 1883, Parents: Frank and Annie Starr, 1, Court 2.11, "father died July 27, 1882"

Starr, Mary, 1879, 1883, Parents: Frank and Annie Starr, 1, Court 2.12, "father died July 27, 1882"

Stevens, Katie, 1868, 1883, Parents: John and Sarah Stevens, 84, ref: 10.83

Sweeney, Annie, 1880, 1883, parents: John and Mary Sweeney, 18, ref: 10.61, m.b.34

Taylor, Daisy, 1879, 1883, Parents: Fred and Alice Taylor, 40, crt: 2.37

Taylor, Frederick, 1878, 1883, Parents: Fred and Alice Taylor, 40, crt: 2.36

Thomas, Susan G., 1874, 1883, mother: Jane Thomas Owens, 39, ref: 10.69

Travis, Jennette, 1871, 1883, Parents: William and Matilda Travis, 87, temporary

Ulrich, Eddie, , 1883, Parents: George and Minnie Ulrich, 24, Court 2.28, ref: 10.62 m.b. 35

Vogeney, John, 1877, 1883, Parents: John and Paulina Vogeney, 52, crt: 2.49

Vogeney, William, 1879, 1883, Parents: John and Paulina Vogeney, 52, crt: 2.50

Walter, John, 1877, 1883, Parents: William and Annie Walters, 76, crt: 2.69

Ward, George, 1881, 1883, Parents: Richard and Mary Ward, 69, temporary

Ward, Katy, 1877, 1883, Parents: Richard and Mary Ward, 69, temporary

Watson, Charlotte, 1879, 1883, Parents: William and Jessie Watson, 48, crt: 2.45

Watson, William, 1881, 1883, Parents: William and Jessie Watson, 48, crt: 2.46

Wheeler, Mary, 1880, 1883, no record of parents, 83, ref: 10.82

White, William, 1868, 1883, Mother: Maggie White, 11, ref: 10.60, m.b.33 Illegitimate

Whiteman, Amanda, 1877, 1883, Parents: David and Henrietta Whiteman, 61, temporary

Whiteman, George, 1880, 1883, Parents: David and Henrietta Whiteman, 71, crt: 2.66

Wilson, Annie, 1877, 1883, , 17, Court 2.23

Wilson, Elizabeth, 1873, 1883, Parents: Richard and Elizabeth Wilson, 112, ref: 10.111

Wilson, Frank, 1878, 1883, , 17, Court 2.24

Wilson, Fred, 1878, 1883, left by his foster mother, 95, ref: 10.87

Woods, Hugh, 1879, 1883, Parents: Patrick and Mary Woods, 80, temporary

Woods, John, 1876, 1883, Parents: Patrick and Mary Woods, 38, temporary

AMERICAN FEMALE GUARDIAN SOCIETY
HOME FOR THE FRIENDLESS
INDENTURES

Last Name, First Name, Date, Age, Taken by, Town, St. Reference, Notes

Abbey, Ellen Gertrude, , , , , , Indenture Papers 1854, "See Lawson, Melissa"

Ackerman, Charlotte, "Feb. 6, 1875", , "Bristol, J. Dewey", Warren Co., PA, Binder

Allchin, Lottie, "June 16, 1865", 1, "Truax, Perry", Toledo (Lucas Co.), OH, Indenture Papers 1858, "Released Jan. 3, 1866 & given his time"

Allen, Freely Martha, "June 18, 1882", 4, "Denneston, Mirabel", South Elizabeth, NJ, Indenture Papers 1882, Adopted

Allen, George Boyd, "Apr. 11, 1865", 5, "Sherman, J. M.", Galesburgh (Knox Co.), IL, Indenture Papers 1858, Adopted

Allen, Sarah, "Jan. 7, 1871", 1, "Moreau, Leon", New York City (New York Co.), NY, Indenture Papers 1865-1866, Adopted

Allinger, Lizzie Shepherd, "Mar. 27, 1882", 12, "Degarimo, James", Newark Valley, NY, Indenture Papers 1870-1871, Adopted

Allison, Sarah, "July 15, 1858", 5, "Parks, Thomas", Greenport (Suffolk Co.), NY, Indenture Papers 1854, Bound out

Amidon, Sarah, "Nov. 16, 1857", 4, "Kirk, william H.", Philadelphia, PA, Indenture Papers 1882, Adopted/AFGS Book 9.400

Anderson, Annetta Marion, "July 11, 1882", 12, "Smith, Henry", Port Monmouth, NJ, Indenture Papers 1857, "Cancelled June 13, 1863 by R. P. Penfield"

Anderson, Edith, "Mar. 1, 1882", 6, "Lampman, Willis", Schnectady, NY, Indenture Papers 1865-1866, Adopted

Anderson, Isabella, "Mar. 1, 1898", 4, , , , Indenture Papers 1853, Out-Door Poor to AFGS #5059

Anderson, James, "Mar. 1, 1898", 7, , , , Indenture Papers 1853, Out-Door Poor to AFGS #5057

Anderson, Jessie, "Mar. 1, 1898", 8, , , , Indenture Papers 1853, Out-Door Poor to AFGS #5056

Anderson, John, "Sept. 6, 1871", 7, , , , Indenture Papers 1870-1871, "Surrendered by mother, Hannah Anderson"

Anderson, Robert, "Mar. 1, 1898", 5.5, , , , Indenture Papers 1853, Out-Door Poor to AFGS #5058

Anderson, Torvo, "Jan. 20, 1900", 3, , , , Commitments 1898-1900, "City Magistrates' Court, 5th District AFGS #6028"

Anderson, Tynne, "Jan. 20, 1900", 2, , , , Commitments 1898-1900, "City Magistrates' Court, 5th District AFGS #6029"

Anderson, William, "Apr. 8, 18875", , "Bartlett, John Henry", Hoboken, NJ, Binder

Apley, Henry, "May 22, 1866", 5, "Dillingham, George", Lisbon (St. Lawrence Co.), NY, Indenture Papers 1882, Adopted/AFGS Book 9.563

Appel, Rosa, "June 13, 1882", 11, "Brown, Fred", Newark , NJ, Indenture Papers 1870-1871, Adopted

Armour, Maggie, "June 14, 1882", 11, "Rundell, George L.", Greenville, NY, Indenture Papers 1865-1866, Adopted

Armstrong, John, "Dec. 12, 1865", 3, "Dana, Wm. B.", Englewood, NJ, Indenture Papers 1858, "Completed Dec. 31, 1863"

Armstrong, Matilda, "Apr. 11, 1865", 1, "Cowles, Robert", Wallingford (New Haven Co.), CT, Indenture Papers 1870-1871, Adopted

Astor, Martha, "July 10, 1854", 3, "Earl, James G.", Red Bank (Monmouth Co.), NJ, Indenture Papers 1854, Bound out

Baker, John, "June 8, 1871", 2 mo., , , , Indenture Papers 1870-1871, "Surrendered by mother, Mrs. Ellen Baker"

Bannister, Amelia E., "July 13, 1854", 3, "St. John, Stephen", New York City (New York Co.), NY, Indenture Papers 1870-1871, Adopted

Barnes, Freddy Albert, , , , , , Indenture Papers 1857, See Isaac Stanley

Barr, Amanda , "Aug. 1, 1854", 9, "Van Evcron, John", Canaan 4 Corners (Columbia Co.), NY, Indenture Papers 1857, Bound out

Bartlett, Mary Almira, "Nov. 16, 1857", 13, "Drake, charles M.", Milton (Rock Co.), WI, Indenture Papers 1882, Adopted/AFGS Book 9.57

Barton, James M., "July 24, 1854", 5, "Thompson, Armor", Trivoli (Peoria Co.), IL, Indenture Papers 1858, Adopted

Barton, Oscar W., "July 21, 1854", 9, "Vanderveer, David J.", Freehold (Monmouth Co.), NJ, Indenture Papers 1857, Bound out

Bauer, Christina, "Feb. 25, 1898", 12, , , , Indenture Papers 1853, Out-Door Poor to AFGS #5054

Bauer, George, "Feb. 25, 1898", 5.5, , , , Indenture Papers 1853, Out-Door Poor to AFGS #5055

Bauer, Louisa, "July. 1, 1900", 7, , , , Commitments 1898-1900, Out-Door Poor/AFGS #6037

Baumamm(?), Samuel, "July 1, 1854", 9, "Colt, Neron", Sockport (Niagara Co.), NY, Indenture Papers 1870-1871, Adopted

Beach, James, "Dec. 31, 1874", , "Beveridge, Lyford", Elwood, NJ, Binder

Bedell, Elizabeth, "Nov. 8, 1875", , "Marsh, Charles", New Milford, CT, Binder

Bedell, Harriet, "Sept. 6, 1871", 1 mo., , , , Indenture Papers 1870-1871, "Surrendered/Died Nov. 24, 1871"

Beebe, Cornelia Wakeman, , , , , , Indenture Papers 1854, "See Osborn, Sarah Louisa"

Beebe, William, , , , , , Indenture Papers 1854, "See Lloyd, John"
Bennett, Joseph, Aug. 1858, 6, "Smith, Joel", Beekman Town (Clinton Co.), NY, Indenture Papers 1858, "Completed March 26, 1863"
Berry, Alida, "Feb. 3, 1858", 2, "Wood, James M.", Belfort (Alleghany Co.), NY, Indenture Papers 1857, Adopted
Berry, Eliza, Oct. 1865, 12, "Phelps, Samuel", Salem (Knox Co.), IL, Indenture Papers 1882, Adopted/AFGS Book 9.591
Berry, William Henry, "Feb. 3, 1858", 8, "Spencer, John", Depansville (Jefferson Co.), NY, Indenture Papers 1882, Apprenticed/AFGS Book 9.612
Beyer, Henry, "July 10, 1871", 4 mo., , , , Indenture Papers 1870-1871, "Surrendered by mother, Annie Beyer"
Biggs, Hiraim, "Mar. 15, 1866", 14, "Potter, Joseph", East Brunswick, NJ, Indenture Papers 1857, "Letter of Mar. 18, 1867 sent to him Feb. 20, 1924"
Bird, Frederick, "Sept. 24, 1898", 2, , , , Indenture Papers 1853, City Magistrates Court 7th District AFGS #5099
Blair, Charles, "Sept. 15, 1866", 9, "Clark, James O.", Palmyra (Wayne Co.), NY, Indenture Papers 1858, "Completed March 20, 1863"
Blair, Wilhelmina, "Sept. 15, 1866", 6, "Clark, James O.", Palmyra (Wayne Co.), NY, Indenture Papers 1854, Indentured
Blakemore, William, "Mar. 4, 1862", 2, "Sherman, James", Bethel (Fairfield Co.), CT, Indenture Papers 1865-1866, Adopted
Blakley, Josephine, "Mar. 31, 1871", 12, "White, Harrison", Wellsville (Alleghany Co.), NY, Indenture Papers 1857, Adopted
Boyd, Margaret, "June 26, 1866", 9, "Sarle, John", Jersey City, NJ, Indenture Papers 1870-1871, Adopted
Boyle, Catherine, "June 3, 1861", 2, "Peake, John L.", Hudson (Columbia Co.), NY, Indenture Papers 1858, "Completed May 20, 1862"
Boyle, Jennie, "Feb. 17, 1870", 4, "Morris, George", Niles City (Berrien Co.), MI, Indenture Papers 1857, Adopted
Brady, Anna, "May 11, 1866", 12, "Harrington, Mrs. C.E.", Non Pariel (Knox Cco.), OH, Indenture Papers 1882, Adopted/AFGS Book 9.610
Brady, George, "Aug. 16, 1871", , , , , Indenture Papers 1870-1871, "Surrendered by mother, Maria Brady"
Brady, Sarah, "May 31, 1870", 9, "Hopping, Samuel", Middletown (Monmouth Co.), NJ, Indenture Papers 1882, Adopted/AFGS Book 9.244
Brady, Sarah, "July 7, 1866", 9, "Hopping, Samuel", Middletown (Monmouth Co.), NJ, Indenture Papers 1882, Adopted/AFGS Book 9.491
Brannan, Clara, "Mar. 26, 1863", 9, "Barnes, Cordelia", East Hampton (Suffolk Co.), NY, Indenture Papers 1865-1866, Adopted

Breasen, Charles, "Mar. 28, 1899", , , , , Indenture Papers 1853, "Com. #5074 sent to Juvenile Asylum Mar. 28, 1899"

Breasen, Elsa, "May 2, 1898", 4, , , , Indenture Papers 1853, Out-Door Poor to AFGS #5076

Breasen, Emma , "May 2, 1898", 7, , , , Indenture Papers 1853, Out-Door Poor to AFGS #5075

Breasen, Henry, "May 2, 1898", 2, , , , Indenture Papers 1853, Out-Door Poor to AFGS #5077

Brennan, Catherine, "Sept. 25, 1871", 8, "Bowen, A.", Loami(?)(Sangamon Co.), IL, Indenture Papers 1854, Adopted

Brennan, Catherine, "Apr. 21, 1871", 8, "Bowen, Mr. & Mrs.", Loami (Sangamon Co.), IL, Indenture Papers 1882, Adopted/AFGS Book 9.378

Briddge, Annie, "July 11, 1898", 2, , , , Indenture Papers 1853, "City Magistrates' Court, 7th District #5097"

Brieston, Elizabeth, "Feb. 12, 1866", 12, "Clark, Betsy", Fredonia (Chautuqua Co.), NY, Indenture Papers 1858, "Completed March 26, 1863"

Brinkman, Annie, "May 31, 1898", 7, , , , Indenture Papers 1853, Admit to Home for the Friendless #5080

Brinkman, Minnie, "May 31, 1898", 4, , , , Indenture Papers 1853, Not left

Brower, John, "May 10, 1853", 11, "Rich, James A.", Stamford, NY, Indenture Papers 1882, Adopted/AFGS Book 9.539

Brower, Maria, "July 18, 1854", 10, "Fort, George", New Egypt (Ocean Co.), NJ, Indenture Papers 1865-1866, Bound out

Brown, Emma , , , , , , Indenture Papers 1854, "See Power, Bridget"

Brown, Frances Emma, "Apr. 21, 1866", 5, "Adams, William", Patterson, NJ, Indenture Papers 1882, Adopted/AFGS Book 9.498

Brown, George McKee, "June 16, 1865", 11, "Evans, titus", Green Point (Kings Co.), NY, Indenture Papers 1865-1866, Bound out

Brown, Maria, "Feb. 13, 1865", 10, "Condit, Edgar", Condit (Deleware Co.), OH, Indenture Papers 1858, "Completed June 10, 1862"

Brown, Minnie, "June 11, 1860", 4 mo., "Finkle, Milton", New York City (New York Co.), NY, Indenture Papers 1858, "Com. May 21, 1863 (Mr. Jones in Greenpoint,NY)"

Brown, Robert Alexander, "Mar. 28, 1863", 6, "Agens, James H.", Orange (Essex Co.), NJ, Indenture Papers 1854, "Indenture cancelled Nov. 9, 1863"

Bruce, Bentley, "Apr. 1, 1874", , "King, Henry", New York City (New York Co.), NY, Binder

Bryan, Kate Hall, "Dec. 20, 1882", 4, "Andrews, Stephen", Osborn Hollow, NY, Indenture Papers 1882, Adopted/AFGS Book 9.426

Bullwinkle, Richard, "Mar. 25, 1898", 10, , , , Indenture Papers 1853, Out-Door Poor to AFGS #5064

Burke, Eliza, "Nov. 16, 1857", 10, "Brokaw, David", Oberlin (Loraine Co.), OH, Indenture Papers 1857, Adopted

Burris, Mary, "Jan. 2, 1882", 11 mo., "Hayhurst, John", New York City (New York Co.), NY, Indenture Papers 1857, Adopted

Butler, Henry, "Dec. 6, 1862", 10, "Hammond, Moses", Warsaw (Hancock Co.), IL, Indenture Papers 1854, Bound out

Butler, Jane Louisa, "Dec. 5, 1862", 11, "Hammond, Moses", Warsaw (Hancock Co.), IL, Indenture Papers 1854, Bound out

Campbell, Ellen, "May 29, 1874", , McMonagle, Summercliff, PA, Binder

Campbell, Kate, "June 21, 1854", 3, "Fenner, James", Liverpool (Onondago Co.), NY, Indenture Papers 1865-1866, Adopted

Canning, Eliza Jane, "Aug. 1, 1854", 10, "Carpenter, Philemon", New Rochelle (Westchester Co.), NY, Indenture Papers 1882, Adopted/AFGS Book 9.492

Carlton, Robert, "Aug. 21, 1854", 9, "Lord, Joseph L.", Syme (N. London Co.), CT, Indenture Papers 1870-1871, Adopted

Carpenter, Mary Evalina, "July 7, 1866", 10, "Pauli, James", Stromsburg (Monroe Co.), PA, Indenture Papers 1870-1871, Adopted

Castor, Henry, "Aug. 25, 1871", , , , , Indenture Papers 1870-1871, "Surrendered by mother, Mary Castor"

Caulson, Caroline, "Nov. 3, 1871", 1 mo., , , , Indenture Papers 1870-1871, "Surrendered by mother, Emma Caulson"

Chamberlin, Geo. Washington, "Sept. 14, 1882", 6, "Putnam, Orlando", Dover (Kent Co.), DE, Indenture Papers 1870-1871, Adopted (?)

Chambers, James, "Mar. 18, 1862", 5, "Marvin, P. F.", Andover (Ashtabula Co.), OH, Indenture Papers 1882, Adopted/AFGS Book 9.503

Charters, Mary, "Dec. 13, 1861", 2, "Roberts, John Ruel", Stockbridge (Berkshire Co.), MA, Indenture Papers 1882, Adopted/AFGS Book 9.340

Churchill, Caroline, "Sept. 15, 1866", 3, "Thompson, Mr. & Mrs.", , Rahway, NY, Indenture Papers 1854, Bound out

Clark, Harry, "June 16, 1865", 5, "Palmer, H.", Sparrow Bush (Orange Co.), NY, Indenture Papers 1865-1866, Bound out

Clark, Latimer, "Mar. 2, 1882", 9 mo., "Ernest, Axel", New York City (New York Co.), NY, Indenture Papers 1854, Bound out

Clerey, Susanna, "Aug. 5, 1854", 14, "Coe, Norris", Winchester Centre (Litchfield Co.), CT, Indenture Papers 1882, Apprenticed/AFGS Book 8.164

Clery, Alice, "Oct. 20, 1874", , "Merriman, Dwight", Jacksontown (Licking Co.), MI, Binder

Coler, Caroline, "Nov. 16, 1857", 8, "Hill, Dr. Caleb", Lockport, NY, Indenture Papers 1858, "Completed Sept. 4, 1862"

Collins, Ann, "Aug. 1, 1854", 12, "Davis, John H.", Freehold (Monmouth Co.), NJ, Indenture Papers 1858, "Completed May 21, 1863"

Collins, Fannie, "Dec. 14, 1858", 2, "Barnes, J. B.", Cleveland (Cuyahoga Co.), OH, Indenture Papers 1854, Bound out

Collins, Julia Frances, "June 14, 1875", , Parmenter, Washington, DC, Binder

Conklin, Ida Elizabeth, "Apr. 11, 1865", 4, "Pratt, William", Binghampton (Broome Co.), NY, Indenture Papers 1870-1871, Adopted

Conlin, Ellen, "May 29, 1874", , McMonagle, Summercliff, PA, Binder

Conway, Mary E., "Nov. 16, 1857", 15, "Johnston, Martin", Six-Mile-Run (Somerset Co.), NJ, Indenture Papers 1882, Apprenticed/AFGS Book 9.231

Coombs, Ella, "Apr. 18, 1866", 11, "Browne, John", Freehold (Monmouth Co.), NJ, Indenture Papers 1858, Bound out

Corburier, William Edwin, , , , , , Indenture Papers 1857, See James H. Delaney

Cornell, Amanda, "Aug. 4, 1882", 1, "Burleson, Robert B.", Cambridge, NY, Indenture Papers 1857, Adopted

Cornell, Caroline C., "Jan. 16, 1857", 15, "Thompson, Samuel", Quincy (Adams Co.), IL, Indenture Papers 1858, Adopted

Cosgrove, Wm. (colored), "July 18, 1871", 1, , , , Indenture Papers 1870-1871, Surrendered by Letitia Lutter (mother deserted)

Coskelly, Richard, "May 1, 1863", 9, "Ranney, Alfred", Townsend (Windham Co.), VT, Indenture Papers 1857, Adopted

Cotron, Orville, "Nov. 9, 1863", 7, "Hutton, Michael", Jamestown (Chautuqua Co.), NY, Indenture Papers 1854, Bound out

Cowen, Fannie, "Dec. 14, 1858", 1, "Brown, James", Mecca (Trumball Co.), OH, Indenture Papers 1870-1871, Adopted

Crawford, Albert, "Feb. 2, 1898", 3, , , , Indenture Papers 1853, Out-Door Poor to AFGS #5047

Crawford, Alice, "Dec. 30, 1862", 6, "Fay, Catherine", Moss Run (Washington Co.), OH, Indenture Papers 1854, Bound out

Crawford, Jessie, "Dec.7, 1871", 1 mo., "Finch, Dr. Joseph", New York City (New York Co.), NY, Indenture Papers 1870-1871, Adopted

Crawford, Jessie, "Sept. 6, 1871", 2 mo., , , , Indenture Papers 1870-1871, "Surrendered by mother, Jessie Crawford"

Crawford, Viola, "Feb. 2, 1898", 5.5, , , , Indenture Papers 1853, Out-Door Poor to AFGS #5046

Cronmuller, Caroline, "Apr. 17, 1863", 6, "Fuller, Lyman", Java Village (Wyoming Co.), NY, Indenture Papers 1882, Adopted/AFGS Book 9.538

Crosley, John, "July 19, 1858", 10, "Stein, David", Roseville (Warren Co.), IL, Indenture Papers 1858, Bound out

Crow, Mary Catherine, "June 16, 1871", 4, , , , Indenture Papers 1870-1871, "Cond. Surrender by mother, Catherine Crow"

Crow, Thomas, "June 16, 1871", 7, , , , Indenture Papers 1870-1871, "Cond. Surrender by mother, Catherine Crow"

Crump, Ida Simpson, "Aug. 21, 1871", 2, , , , Indenture Papers 1870-1871, Surrendered by Mrs. Euphemia Coon (abandoned)

Cullum, Sarah E., "Aug. 1, 1857", 8, "Ticknor, Norman", Jewett (Green co.), NY, Indenture Papers 1865-1866, Adopted

Cummings, John, "Sept. 18, 1900", 4, , , , Commitments 1898-1900, "City Magistrates' Court, 3rd District AFGS #6045"

Cummings, Robert, "Sept. 18, 1900", 6, , , , Commitments 1898-1900, "City Magistrates' Court, 3rd District AFGS #6044"

Cummings, William, "Sept. 18, 1900", 9, , , , Commitments 1898-1900, "City Magistrates' Court, 3rd District AFGS #6043"

Currie, Florence, "Apr. 6, 1899", 10, , , , Commitments 1898-1900, Commitment #6003

Curry, Nettie, "Mar. 29, 1875", , "Lewis, A. A.", Friendship, NY, Binder

Daly, Grace, "Aug. 25, 1871", , , , , Indenture Papers 1870-1871, "Surrendered by mother, Augusta Daly"

Darrell, Charlotte, "June 10, 1854", 16, "White, Roderick", Simsbury (Hartford Co.), CT, Indenture Papers 1865-1866, Adopted

Davenport, Henrietta, "Dec. 14, 1857", 10, "Kerr, Lucia", Elmwood (Peoria Co.), IL, Indenture Papers 1858, Bound out

Davis, Mary Ann, "Aug. 15, 1854", 11, "Jones, Mrs. Harriet", Jefferson (Scoharie Co.), NY, Indenture Papers 1853, Adopted

Davis, Sarah Ann, "Oct. 2, 1854", 9, "Cunningham, Wm.", Schenectady (Schenectady Co.), NY, Indenture Papers 1882, Adopted/AFGS Book 9.600

Day, Ethel Sarah, "Oct. 10, 1871", 8 mo., , , , Indenture Papers 1870-1871, "Surrendered by mother, Hannah Elizabeth Day"

De Grace, Emma Jane, "Oct. 24, 1871", 20 mo., , , , Indenture Papers 1870-1871, "Surrendered by mother, Mrs. Anna Maria De Grace"

Dean, Effie, "Oct. 24, 1871", 5 mo., , , , Indenture Papers 1870-1871, "Surrendered by mother, Emma Dyer"

Decker, Benjamin, "Jan. 11, 1871", , "Shuster, Edmund", Bridgeport, CT, Indenture Papers 1853, farmer/Bound out

Delaney, James H., "July 10, 1857", 4 mo., "Corburier, Edwin P.", Williamsburgh (Kings Co.) L.I., NY, Indenture Papers 1857, Bound out

Devereaux, Ada, "Nov. 15, 1871", 2 mo., , , , Indenture Papers 1870-1871, "Surrendered by mother, Mrs. Sarah Devereaux"

Devoe, James, "July 7, 1871", 6, , , , Indenture Papers 1870-1871, Surrendered by Mrs. Margaret J. Moffet (orphaned)

Digby, Harriet Hillman, "Sept. 6, 1871", 3 wks., , , , Indenture Papers 1870-1871, "Surrendered by mother, Harriett Hillman"

Divine, Mary A., "Nov. 17, 1858", 12, "Booth, Samuel", Stratford (Fairfield Co.), CT, Indenture Papers 1865-1866, Adopted

Divine, William, "Oct. 12, 1858", 9, "Shaw, Matthew", Terre Haute (Henderson Co.), IL, Indenture Papers 1882, Apprenticed/AFGS Book 9.418

Doe #11, John, "Jan. 16, 1900", 4, , , , Commitments 1898-1900, "City Magistrates' Court, 2nd District AFGS #6024"

Doe #12, Jane, "Sept. 22, 1900", 2, , , , Commitments 1898-1900, Commitment #6046

Doe #42, John, "Sept. 18, 1900", 4, , , , Commitments 1898-1900, Commitment #6042

Doherty, Ellen, "Feb. 24, 1874", , "Bassett, George", New Bedford, MA, Binder

Donelson, Frederick, "Aug. 8, 1882", 4, "Seguin, Rev. Peter", New York City (New York Co.), NY, Indenture Papers 1870-1871, Bound out

Donnelly, Elizabeth, "July 24, 1854", 3, "Wheeler, George", Mericoville (Oswego Co.), NY, Indenture Papers 1857, Bound out

Donoho, Richard, "Feb. 24, 1857", 2, "Clark, Allen", East hampton (Middlesex Co.), CT, Indenture Papers 1858, Adopted

Dougherty, Albert, "Aug. 5, 1854", 3, "Logan, Thomas S.", Southampton (Burlington Co.), NJ, Indenture Papers 1865-1866, Adopted

Dougherty, Lilly, "Apr. 21, 1866", 4, "Willard, Elias", Holland Patent (Oneida Co.), NY, Indenture Papers 1854, Adopted

Dougherty, Sarah, "June 7, 1854", 15, "Garretson, Reynear", Round Brook (Somerset Co.), NJ, Indenture Papers 1858, Adopted

Douglas, George, "Oct. 5, 1858", 13, "Butler, Lysander", Oberlin (Lorain Co.), OH, Indenture Papers 1858, Bound out

Downey, John, "July. 16, 1900", 6, , , , Commitments 1898-1900, "City Magistrates' Court, 7th District AFGS #6040"

Downey, Walter, "July. 16, 1900", 4, , , , Commitments 1898-1900, "City Magistrates' Court, 7th District AFGS #6041"

Downey, William, "July. 16, 1900", 8, , , , Commitments 1898-1900, "City Magistrates' Court, 7th District AFGS #6039"

Driscoll, Arthur, "Nov. 20, 1899", 2, , , , Commitments 1898-1900, Out-Door Poor to AFGS #6023

Driscoll, Lucy, "Nov. 20, 1899", 5, , , , Commitments 1898-1900, Out-Door Poor to AFGS #6021

Driscoll, Willie, "Nov. 20, 1899", 3, , , , Commitments 1898-1900, Out-Door Poor to AFGS #6022

Duffy, Catherine, "Aug. 5, 1857", 8, "Gilbert, Isaac", Derby, CT, Indenture Papers 1870-1871, Adopted

Duffy, James French, "June 22, 1858", 6, "Covey, Stephen", Southold (Suffolk Co.) L.I., NY, Indenture Papers 1857, Cancelled by order of Ex C...(?)

Duffy, Rosanna, "Aug. 5, 1857", 10, "Gilbert, Isaac", Derby, CT, Indenture Papers 1853, Brick Mason/Adopted & name changed

Earon, Sarah, "July 19, 1854", 11, "Bissell, Edward", Toledo (Lucas Co.), OH, Indenture Papers 1865-1866, Adopted

Eason, William, "Aug. 1, 1853", 10, "Bissell, Edward", Toledo, OH, Indenture Papers 1858, "Completed March 26, 1863"

Eaton, Francis John, "May 30, 1857", 15, "Fisher, Rev. Caleb", Andover (Essex Co.), MA, Indenture Papers 1865-1866, Adopted

Edsell, Richard, "July 7, 1875", , "Ruliffson, Rev.", New York City (New York Co.), NY, Binder

Egan, George, "Oct. 1, 1859", 5, "Lyman, James", Alleghany City (Alleghany Co.), PA, Indenture Papers 1854, Adopted

Ellwood, John Henry, "Apr. 18, 1866", 8, "Ketchum, Thomas", Farmingdale, NJ, Indenture Papers 1858, "Completed May 21, 1863"

Emson, "Charles, Jr.", "Oct. 15, 1900", 2, , , , Commitments 1898-1900, "City Magistrates' Court, 7th District AFGS #6048"

Fahey, Ellen, "Sept. 20, 1871", , , , , Indenture Papers 1870-1871, "Surrendered by mother,"

Farlow, Martha Jane, "Apr. 10, 1857", 14, "Thompson, Daniel", Poughkeepsie, NY, Indenture Papers 1858, Adopted

Farlow, William Robert, "Apr. 10, 1857", 3, "Thompson, Daniel", Poughkeepsie (Dutchess Co.), NY, Indenture Papers 1857, Adopted

Farr, Wilhelmina, "Sept. 15, 1866", 12, "Hawkins, Jonathan", Montgomery P.O. (Orange Co.), NY, Indenture Papers 1865-1866, Bound out

Farrell, Agnes Louise, "Nov. 15, 1882", 9, "Berger, John C.", Somerville (Somerset Co.), NJ, Indenture Papers 1858, Adopted

Faulkner, Ada, "Dec. 7, 1871", 1, "Stevens, Mr. & Mrs.", New York City (New York Co.), NY, Indenture Papers 1870-1871, Adopted

Faulkner, Ada, "Oct. 26, 1871", 1, , , , Indenture Papers 1870-1871, Surrendered by Catherine Bilbrough (deserted)

Fay, Hannah, "Jan. 31, 1854", 8, "Livermore, Wm. S.", Independence (Alleghany Co.), NY, Indenture Papers 1854, Adopted

Fay, Thomas, "Jan. 31, 1854", 7, "Livermore, Wm. S.", Independence (Alleghany Co.), NY, Indenture Papers 1858, Adopted

Fentz, Sallie, "June 14, 1882", 9, "Hoffman, M. A.", Claverack, NY, Indenture Papers 1882, Adopted/AFGS Book 9.291

Finley, Catherine F., "July 13, 1854", 11, "Gear, Samuel", Meniden (New Haven Co.), CT, Indenture Papers 1854, Bound out

Fischer, Elizabeth, "Aug. 24, 1858", 2, "St. John, Nathaniel", Oberlin (Lorain Co.), OH, Indenture Papers 1854, Bound out

Fischer, George, "Sept. 21, 1871", 10, "Reid, Joseph", Colts Neck, NJ, Indenture Papers 1870-1871, Adopted

Fitzgibbon, Catherine, "July 18, 1854", 7, "Tichenor, Isaac", Canandaigua (Ontario Co.), NY, Indenture Papers 1858, "Completed Dec. 31, 1863"

Flint, Wm. Ward, "June 21, 1854", 2, "Murray, Daniel N.", Tonawanda (Erie Co.), NY, Indenture Papers 1858, Bound out

Fowler, Sarah, "Sept. 14, 1870", 8, "Goodwin, James", Maspeth(?)(Queens Co.) L.I., NY, Indenture Papers 1858, "Completed Oct. 1, 1863"

Frazee, Athenia, "Jan. 16, 1857", 9, "Tracy, Alexander", Lenox (Warren Co.), IL, Indenture Papers 1857, Bound out

Freeman, Alice Alberti, "Apr. 29, 1870", 2, "Knope, Charles", Jersey City, NJ, Indenture Papers 1882, Adopted/AFGS Book 9.492

French, Annie, "Aug. 9, 1882", 13, "Phelps, Henry C.", South Greece (Monroe Co.), NY, Indenture Papers 1870-1871, Adopted

Fuller, Alice, "July 5, 1898", 10, , , , Indenture Papers 1853, "#5094 Discharged May 8, 1902"

Fullerton, Mary F., "Jan. 28, 1860", 13, "Hook, Silas", Kahway (Union Co.), NJ, Indenture Papers 1870-1871, Adopted

Gallagher, Anna, "June 13, 1882", 3, "Bray, William", Birmingham, CT, Indenture Papers 1857, Adopted

Galloway, John Thomas, "July 24, 1854", 6, "Gurtin, Anson", Mexico (Oswego Co.), NY, Indenture Papers 1865-1866, Adopted

Geipenger, Antoinette, "Feb. 7, 1870", 5, "Dey, John", New York City (New York Co.), NY, Indenture Papers 1865-1866, Bound out

Genter, Margaret, "July 11, 1882", 11, "Feierabend, Fred", Bridgeport, CT, Indenture Papers 1882, Adopted/AFGS Book 9.339

Gessner, Frank, "June 1, 1899", 4, , , , Commitments 1898-1900, Out-Door Poor to AFGS #7011

Golden, James, "Mar. 29, 1902", 4, , , , Commitments 1898-1900, Trans. NYJA to AFGS/Shepherd's Fold

Golden, Martha, "Mar. 7, 1900", 8, , , , Commitments 1898-1900, Out-Door Poor/Shepherd's Fold/AFGS #6098

Goode, Charles, "July 22, 1871", , , , , Indenture Papers 1870-1871, "Cond. surrendered by mother, Annie Goode"

Gordon, James, "Jan. 18, 1875", , "Palmer, H. W.", Port Jervis, NJ, Binder

Gorman, Lily, "Apr. 11, 1865", 8, "Biggs, Harrison", Groton (Tompkins Co.), NY, Indenture Papers 1854, Surname could be Darnell

Gormandez, Augustine, "Dec. 8, 1853", 12, "Wheeler, Joshua", Colchester (New London Co.), CT, Indenture Papers 1857, Bound out

Goudy, Ida, "Mar. 31, 1871", 1, "Shafer, Richard", Columbia (Northampton Co.), NJ, Indenture Papers 1858, Adopted

Goudy, Ida, "Mar. 31, 1871", 1, "Shafer, Richard", Columbia (Warren Cco.), NJ, Indenture Papers 1865-1866, Bound out

Graham, Mary A., "Oct. 13, 1858", 3, "Bird, Alden S.", Shelby (Orleans Co.), NY, Indenture Papers 1854, Bound out

Granger, George Earley, "Feb. 3, 1858", 12, "Mighells, albert", Lockport (Niagara Co.), NY, Indenture Papers 1857, Adopted

Grant, Harold, "May 5, 1899", 2, , , , Commitments 1898-1900, Out-Door Poor to AFGS #6005

Green, Elizabeth, "Feb. 5, 1898", 5, , , , Indenture Papers 1853, Out-Door Poor to AFGS #5050

Greenwood, Robert, "Aug. 14, 1882", 4, "Linden, Joseph", Milltown, NJ, Indenture Papers 1854, Adopted

Guerne, Mary Augusta, "Dec. 13, 1865", 11, "Smith, Wm. Henry", Greenport (Suffolk Co.) L. I., NY, Indenture Papers 1857, Adopted

Gunther, John Hamilton, "June 19, 1871", 2 wks., , , , Indenture Papers 1870-1871, "Surrendered by mother, Ann Maria Gunther"

Gurtin, John Wm. Elisha, , , , , , Indenture Papers 1854, See Galloway

Hagel, Otto, "July 8, 1898", 3, , , , Indenture Papers 1853, City Magistrates Court 7th District AFGS #5096

Hagel, William, "July 8, 1898", 5, , , , Indenture Papers 1853, City Magistrates Court 7th District AFGS #5095

Hall, Adaline, "Apr. 22, 1875", , "Wood, Frances", North Walton, NY, Binder

Hall, Alexander, "Sept. 14, 1882", 7, "Sason, Orrin", Windom, MN, Indenture Papers 1882, Adopted/AFGS Book 9.224

Hall, Latin, "Apr. 20, 1875", , "Wood, Frances", North Walton, NY, Binder

Hall, Lizzie, "Nov. 17, 1882", 11, "Park, Thomas L.", White Plains, NY, Indenture Papers 1858, Bound out

Hall, Mary, "June 22, 1858", 2, "Hayes, Albert", Lyndenville (Ashtabula Co.), OH, Indenture Papers 1882, Adopted/AFGS Book 9.644

Hamilton, George, "July 7, 1866", 16, "Blackman, Nahur", Verona (Oneida Co.), NY, Indenture Papers 1854, Adopted

Hamilton, Martha Ann, "Mar. 26, 1853", 12, "Compton, Anthony", Millington, NJ, Indenture Papers 1865-1866, Adopted

Hamilton, William, "Nov. 16, 1857", 3, "Ball, W.C.", New York City (New York Co.), NY, Indenture Papers 1865-1866, Apprenticed

Hamilton, William, "June 19, 1857", 3, "Ball, Williamson c.", New York City (New York Co.), NY, Indenture Papers 1865-1866, Apprenticed

Hamm, Caroline, "Apr. 21, 1871", 6 mo., "Lewis, James C.", New York City (New York Co.), NY, Indenture Papers 1865-1866, Adopted

Hamman, Elizabeth Ellen, "Sept. 1, 1854", 15, "Mather, Henry C.", Millers Place (Suffolk Co.), NY, Indenture Papers 1854, Adopted

Hamman, Mary Jane, "July 10, 1854", 9, "Miller, Thomas A.", Gonningford (Litchfield Co.), CT, Indenture Papers 1865-1866, Adopted

Hammond, Lilly, "Apr. 21, 1866", 6, "Hall, Murray", Preston (Chenango Co.), NY, Indenture Papers 1854, Bound out

Hanks, Edmund, "Mar. 20, 1875", , "Evans, George", Indianapolis, IN, Binder

Hanley, Bridget, "Nov. 23, 1858", 15, "Cook, George", Lindenwood (Ogle Co.), IL, Indenture Papers 1853, Merchant-Taylor/Bound out

Hannahs, Henekin Harry, , , , , , Indenture Papers 1853, "See Joice, James"

Hanney, Magdalena, "July 10, 1854", 11, "Voorhees, Isaac", Six Mile run (Somerset Co.), NJ, Indenture Papers 1854, Bound out

Hannon, Edward, "Mar. 8, 1882", 2, "Osgood, Edmund L.", Strittman Valley, IL, Indenture Papers 1854, Suffolk Co. on Long Island

Hansell, Thomas Martin, "July 18, 1854", 10, "Bailey, Luther", Jewett (Green Cco.), NY, Indenture Papers 1858, Passed to Home for Little Wanderers @no consent

Hansen, Charlie, "June 3, 1898", 2, , , , Indenture Papers 1853, Out-Door Poor to AFGS #5088

Hansen, Harry, "June 3, 1898", 4, , , , Indenture Papers 1853, Out-Door Poor to AFGS #5087

Harder, Amy, "June 13, 1882", 7, "Dermott, William B.", Flemington, NJ, Indenture Papers 1865-1866, Adopted (Book 6.510-513)

Harlem, Alice, "Sept. 15, 1858", 3, "Bushnell, J. E.", Chicago (Cook Co.), IL, Indenture Papers 1858, Bound out

Harris, Samuel, "Aug. 1, 1854", 11, "Reynolds, James", Whitlockville (Westchester Co.), NY, Indenture Papers 1882, Apprenticed/AFGS Book 9.148

Hart, Henry, "Jan. 3, 1875", , Smith-Cline, Limsville, PA, Binder

Hatshaw, John, "Nov. 16, 1857", 8, "Cole, Russel", Oberlin (Lorain Co.), OH, Indenture Papers 1882, Adopted/AFGS Book 9.529

Hayes, Arthur, "June 22, 1882", 5, "Hayes, Emerson", Harrington (?), CT, Indenture Papers 1858, Adopted

Haynes, Charles L., "Sept. 12, 1871", 2 wks., , , , Indenture Papers 1870-1871, "Surrendered by mother, Carrie L. Haynes"

Hearn, Johanna, "Feb. 27, 1874", , "Day, George", Stephentown, NY, Binder

Heiman, Charles, "Mar. 18, 1898", 2, , , , Indenture Papers 1853, Out-Door Poor to AFGS #5063

Hemingway, Christhophilas, "June 22, 1858", 11, "Ingraham, Daniel", Windham (Green Co.), NY, Indenture Papers 1882, Adopted/AFGS Book 9.528

Henderson, Mary Emma, "Feb. 3, 1858", 6, "Peck, Samuel", Gorham (Ontario Co.), NY, Indenture Papers 1882, Adopted/AFGS Book 9.553

Hesse, Charles, "Mar. 1, 1882", 5, "Martian, Felix", Brooklyn (Long Island), NY, Indenture Papers 1858, "Completed Dec. 31, 1863"

Hessy, Royena, "June 21, 1854", 11, "Morehouse, Israel", Livingston (Essex Co.), NJ, Indenture Papers 1854, Adopted

Hilgner, Joseph, "Feb. 5, 1900", 6, , , , Commitments 1898-1900, Commitment #6030

Hill, Frederic, "Dec. 8, 1863", 2, "Beardsley, J. G.", Java Village (Wyoming Co.), NY, Indenture Papers 1882, Adopted/AFGS Book 9.312

Hillman, Margaret, "Feb. 3, 1858", 12, "McIlvaine, John D.", Albany (Whiteside Co.), IL, Indenture Papers 1858, "Completed May 21, 1863"

Hope, Annie, "July 21, 1854", 2, "Howard, Aden", Madison (Madison Co.), NY, Indenture Papers 1870-1871, Adopted

Horan, Ellen, "Dec. 5, 1862", 7, "Vedder, Nicholas", Utica (Oneida Co.), NY, Indenture Papers 1865-1866, Adopted

Horan, Ellen, "Dec. 5, 1862", 7, "Vedder, Nicholas", Utica (Oneida Co.), NY, Indenture Papers 1853, Farmer/Bound out

Horncastle, Susan M., "Apr. 11, 1866", 16, "Thurston, George", Lakeland (Suffolk Co.) Long Island, NY, Indenture Papers 1858, Adopted

Horton, Elva, "Aug. 8, 1882", 14, "Austin, J. O.", Unionville (Orange Co.), NY, Indenture Papers 1857, Bound out

Houson, Melissa, "Mar. 27, 1866", 6, "Cochrane, William", "Flatbush, Long Island", NY, Indenture Papers 1857, Adopted

Howard, Margaret, "July 12, 1858", 8, "Watson, George", Roseville (Warren Co.), IL, Indenture Papers 1854, Adopted

Howard, Mary, , , , , , Indenture Papers 1854, "See Hope, Annie"

Howard, Mary Elizabeth, "Feb. 26, 1875", , "Draper, Frank", New York City (New York Co.), Ny, Binder

Howe, "Otto, Jr.", "Mar. 21, 1899", 3, , , , Commitments 1898-1900, Commitment #6001

Hoyle, Julia, "Oct. 8, 1853", 8, "Stowe, John H., Jr.", Westfield, MA, Indenture Papers 1854, Adopted

Hoyle, Margaret, "Sept. 15, 1853", 4, "Cleveland, Stafford", Penn Yan (Yates Co.), NY, Indenture Papers 1857, Bound out

Hufernes, Caroline, "July 7, 1866", 1, "Gibbud, Israel", Nangatuck (New Haven Co.), CT, Indenture Papers 1882, Adopted/AFGS Book 9.557

Hughes, Minnie, "Nov. 9, 1882", 8, "Davison, John", Hopeville, NJ, Indenture Papers 1853, Bound out

Hully, Agnes, "Mar. 29, 1898", 8, , , , Indenture Papers 1853, Out-Door Poor to AFGS #5068

Hully, Fannie, "Mar. 29, 1898", 6, , , , Indenture Papers 1853, Out-Door Poor to AFGS #5069

Hully, Irene, "Mar. 29, 1898", 3.5, , , , Indenture Papers 1853, Out-Door Poor to AFGS #5070

Hully, Mary, "Mar. 29, 1898", 11, , , , Indenture Papers 1853, b. Boston/Out-Door Poor to AFGS #5066

Hully, Winifred, "Mar. 29, 1898", 9, , , , Indenture Papers 1853, "b. Dayton, OH/Out-Door Poor to AFGS #5067"

Igel, Barbara, "May 30, 1857", 12, "Kilton, John", Boston, MA, Indenture Papers 1865-1866, Adopted

Igel, Charles Christian, "Aug. 24, 1858", 7, "Clark, William", Monmouth (Warren Co.), IL, Indenture Papers 1858, Ran away

Innes(?), Jessie, "Apr. 14, 1870", 8, "Henry, James", Yonkers, NY, Indenture Papers 1882, Adoption/AFGS Book 9.252

Innes(?), Victoria Virginia, "Apr. 21, 1871", 7, "Kingsley, James", Westbrook (Middlesex Co.), CT, Indenture Papers 1853, Merchant/Adopted

Irwin, Hannah Adelaide, "Sept. 15, 1866", 7, "Jarvis, Wm.", Yorkville (New York Co.), NY, Indenture Papers 1854, Adopted

Isaacs, Margaret Augusta, “Nov. 16, 1857”, 4, “Gifford, Miss Harriet”, Elgin (Kane Cco.), IL, Indenture Papers 1865-1866, Adopted

Jackson, Alice Rosena, “Dec. 31, 1874”, , “Weingartenier, Frank”, Middletown, CT, Binder

Jayne, Susan, “Nov. 24, 1871”, 1, “Austin, Seth”, New York City (New York Co.), NY, Indenture Papers 1857, Bound out

Johnson, Helen May, “Feb. 24, 1900”, 6, , , , Commitments 1898-1900, Out-Door Poor to AFGS #6033

Johnson, Mary J., “Oct. 18, 1871”, 2 mo., , , , Indenture Papers 1870-1871, “Surrendered by mother, Sarah Isabella McClelland”

Johnson, Susan, “Jan. 14, 1857”, 7, “Reynolds, Henry”, Portland (Chautuqua Co.), NY, Indenture Papers 1858, “Completed April 7, 1862”

Johnson, William, “July 20, 1871”, 5 wks., , , , Indenture Papers 1870-1871, “Surrendered by mother, Mrs. Mary Johnson”

Joice, James, “Jan. 21, 1853”, 6, “Hannahs, Robert”, Newark (Essex Co.), NJ, Indenture Papers 1865-1866, Adopted

Jones, Abigal Jane, “May 20, 1854”, 7, “Ladd, Rev. James S.”, New York City (New York Co.), NY, Indenture Papers 1870-1871, Adopted

Jones, Thomas, “Sept. 8, 1875”, , , Middletown, NY, Binder

Kaehart, Louisa, “Aug. 1, 1854”, 9, “Quick, Ralph”, Ewing (Mercer Co.), NJ, Indenture Papers 1870-1871, Adopted

Kalber, Charles, “Mar. 2, 1900”, 5, , , , Commitments 1898-1900, Out-Door Poor/AFGS #6034

Kane, Elizabeth, “Nov. 11, 1870”, 10, “Murry, David”, Schnectady, NY, Indenture Papers 1854, Adopted

Kane, Katie, “Dec. 7, 1871”, , , , , Indenture Papers 1870-1871, “Surrendered by mother, Charlotte Kane Steele”

Kattry, Margaret, “Nov. 16, 1858”, 8, “Rounds, Lester”, Eureka (Winebago Co.), WI, Indenture Papers 1857, Name changed to Jennie Thompson

Kearman, Ann Eliza, “Dec. 21, 1857”, 12, “Talcott, Henry”, Rockton (Winnebago Co.), IL, Indenture Papers 1858, Adopted

Kelber, Frederick, “May 15, 1899”, 8, , , , Commitments 1898-1900, Out-Door Poor to AFGS #6007

Kelber, Minnie, “May 15, 1899”, 6, , , , Commitments 1898-1900, Out-Door Poor to AFGS #6008

Kelly, Annie, “July 24, 1871”, 4, , , , Indenture Papers 1870-1871, Surrendered by Sarah West (abandoned for 2 years)

Kelly, Clara Teresa, “Nov. 15, 1871”, 5, , , , Indenture Papers 1870-1871, “Cond. surrender by mother, Jane Kelly Stewart”

Kelly, James Oscar, “Nov. 15, 1871”, 7, , , , Indenture Papers 1870-1871, “Cond. surrender by mother, Jane Kelly Stewart”

Kenmore, Elizabeth, “Aug. 5, 1854”, 2, “Fisk, Ephraim”, Java (Wyoming Co.), NY, Indenture Papers 1854, Bound out

Kepler, Caroline, "Apr. 21, 1866", 13, "Price, C. D.", New York City (New York Co.), NY, Indenture Papers 1854, Adopted by Ladd's who lived at 381 8th Ave.

Keyser, Catherine, "Apr. 23, 1874", , "Hopper, Wm.", "Brooklyn, Long Island", NY, Binder

Kilton, Eveline, "Feb. 8, 1900", 4, , , , Commitments 1898-1900, Commitment #6032

Kimmel, Max, "Nov. 16, 1899", 10, , , , Commitments 1898-1900, "City Magistrates' Court, 3rd District AFGS #6019"

Knight, Lawrence, "June. 30, 1900", 5, , , , Commitments 1898-1900, Out-Door Poor to AFGS #6036

Kronenwitt, Lina, "June 21, 1854", 10, "Gulick, Jacob", Kingston (Middlesex Co.), NJ, Indenture Papers 1882, Adopted/AFGS Book 9.476

Lalley, John, "Nov. 16, 1858", 8, "Atwater, Edwin", Coventryville (Chenango Co.), NY, Indenture Papers 1853, Adopted (handwritten agreement)

Lambert, Josephine, "Sept. 10, 1866", 1, "Hanford, Peter", Unionville (Orange Co.), NY, Indenture Papers 1857, Bound out

Lambert, Lizzie, "June 12, 1882", 2, "Center, Sheldon", Center White Creek, NY, Indenture Papers 1854, Adopted

Land, Ann V., "July 18, 1854", 13, "Cannon, Samuel", New Richmond (Crawford Co.), PA, Indenture Papers 1865-1866, Bound out

Lanzit, Viola, "Feb. 16, 1898", 11, , , , Indenture Papers 1853, Out-Door Poor to AFGS #5052

Lautenbahn, Margaret, "Mar. 25, 1874", , "King, Andrew", "Jamesport, Long Island", NY, Binder

Lawrence, Maria, "July 7, 1866", 1, "Van Otto, Carman", New Rochelle (Westchester Co.), NY, Indenture Papers 1858, Bound out

Lawson, Melissa, "July 24, 1854", 6, "Abbey, Henry S.", Akron (Summit Co.), OH, Indenture Papers 1858, "Completed May 20, 1862"

Lebree, Ellen, "June 1, 1898", 3, , , , Indenture Papers 1853, "#5081 Discharged Apr. 7, 1900"

Lecounte, Charles, "Aug. 10, 1866", 7, "Cooley, Eli", South Deerfield (franklin Cco.), MA, Indenture Papers 1858, "Completed Dec. 31, 1863"

Lee, Sarah Rebecca, "Nov. 7, 1863", 3, "Peabody, George", Eastport (Washington Co.), ME, Indenture Papers 1854, Adopted

Lelbar, George, "Aug. 29, 1871", 4 wks., , , , Indenture Papers 1870-1871, "Surrendered by mother, Christina Lelbar"

Lexington, Julia, "Mar. 25, 1875", , "Dunton, B. F.", Oneida, NY, Binder

Lloyd, John, "Sept. 9, 1854", 9, "Beebe, Wm. H.", Petersburgh (Dinwiddie Co.), VA, Indenture Papers 1858, Mar. 1863 trans. to family in same house on trial

Logan, Rosanna, "Aug. 4, 1854", 8, "Shelton, George E.", Black Rock (Fairfield Co.), CT, Indenture Papers 1857, "Enlisted without notice in 1863, void indenture"

Logan, Rosanna, "Nov. 9, 1863", , , , , Indenture Papers 1854, "Mrs. Gregory, Main St., Bridgeport, CT took Rosanna"

Loney, Isabella, "July 21, 1871", , , , , Indenture Papers 1870-1871, "Surrendered by mother, Janet Loney"

Loud, Mary Emma, "Mar. 1, 1853", 15, "Tyler, Mr. J.J.", Austerlitz (Columbia Co.), NY, Indenture Papers 1858, Bound out

Lynch, John Carroll, "Nov. 21, 1871", 5 wks., , , , Indenture Papers 1870-1871, "Surrendered by mother, Margaret Lynch"

Lynch, Richard, "Sept. 22, 1860", 11, "Rice, Elijah", Wallingford (New Haven Co.), CT, Indenture Papers 1854, "Bound out to Mr. Palmer, shoe manufacturer"

Maddox, Sarah, "Nov. 29, 1860", 11, "Shaw, Amos", Freehold (Monmouth Co.), NJ, Indenture Papers 1854, Bound out

Magnusson, John, "June. 28, 1900", 4, , , , Commitments 1898-1900, "City Magistrates' Court, 6th District AFGS #6035"

Maloney, Florence , "Mar. 26, 1898", 9, , , , Indenture Papers 1853, "City Magistrates' Court, 7th District #5065"

Marnell, Annie, "Oct. 3, 1899", 4, , , , Commitments 1898-1900, "City Magistrates' Court, 7th District AFGS #6018"

Marren, John Edward, "July 25, 1871", , , , , Indenture Papers 1870-1871, "Surrendered by mother, Julia Marren"

Marshall, John, "Aug. 9, 1882", 9, "Reichers, Richard", New York City (New York Co.), NY, Indenture Papers 1865-1866, Adopted

Martin, Bessie, "Feb. 6, 1875", , "Curtis, Edward", Wellsville, NY, Binder

Martin, Geo. Robertson, "July 13, 1871", , , , , Indenture Papers 1870-1871, "Surrender cancelled July 14, 1871"

Martin, Jennie, "July 5, 1898", 5, , , , Indenture Papers 1853, Out-Door Poor to AFGS #5091

Martin, John, "July 5, 1898", 2, , , , Indenture Papers 1853, Out-Door Poor to AFGS #5093

Martin, Mary, "July 5, 1898", 4, , , , Indenture Papers 1853, Out-Door Poor to AFGS #5092

Martin, Willie, Dec. 1871, , , , , Indenture Papers 1870-1871, Releasing Society from all claims to him

Marvin, Marietta, "Feb. 3, 1854", 9, "Palmer, James", North Castle (Westchester Co.), NY, Indenture Papers 1854, Bound out

Mastin, Annie, "Jan. 19, 1870", 1, "Smith, Anton & Mary", New York City (New York Co.), NY, Indenture Papers 1865-1866, Adopted

Mattel, Annie, "Mar. 1, 1882", 9, "Gibbud, Israel", Pinion City, CT, Indenture Papers 1865-1866, Adopted

Matthews, Mary, "July 10, 1866", 5, "Delemater, Israel", Kingston (Ulster Co.), NY, Indenture Papers 1870-1871, Adopted

McAdam, Bella Jane, "Nov. 10, 1871", 4 wks., , , , Indenture Papers 1870-1871, "Surrendered by mother, Margaret McAdam"

McArthur, Lizzie, "Apr. 21, 1866", 5, "Kissam, J. R.", Newark , NJ, Indenture Papers 1882, Adopted/AFGS Book 9.401

McArthur, Lizzie, "Apr. 21, 1866", 5, "Kissam, J. R.", Newark , NJ, Indenture Papers 1865-1866, Adopted

McBride, Francis, "May 30, 1857", 12, "Green, Lewis", North East (Erie Co.), PA, Indenture Papers 1858, "Completed May 21, 1863"

McBride, Mary, "May 30, 1857", 10, "Green, Lewis", North East (Erie Co.), PA, Indenture Papers 1858, Adopted

McCabe, David, "Jan. 25, 1866", 9, "Bradley, Mr. & Mrs.", Easton (Fairfield Co.), CT, Indenture Papers 1858, Adopted

McCabe, David, "Jan. 25, 1866", 9, "Bradley, Mr. & Mrs.", Easton (Fairfield Co.), CT, Indenture Papers 1858, Adopted

McCarthy, Mary, "Apr. 30, 1898", 2, , , , Indenture Papers 1853, Out-Door Poor to AFGS #5073

McClain, Thomas W., "Nov. 13, 1870", 1 mo., "Shaffer, Louis", Newark , NJ, Commitments 1898-1900, Bound out

McClain, Thomas William, "Nov. 2, 1871", 6 wks., , , , Indenture Papers 1870-1871, "Surrendered by mother, Martha McClain"

McCleish, John, "Feb. 17, 1870", 13, "Banks, Charles", Warrenton (Fauquier Co.), VA, Indenture Papers 1865-1866, Apprenticed

McCloud, Lily Ann, "Nov. 4, 1871", 2 mo., , , , Indenture Papers 1870-1871, "Surrendered by mother, Christie Mccloud"

McClusky, Arabella, "Nov. 16, 1858", 4, "Kellogg, Alexander", Adams (Jefferson Co.), NY, Indenture Papers 1858, Adopted

McDermott, Mary Jane, "July 19, 1858", 12, "Griffin, Henry ", Roseville (Warren Co.), IL, Indenture Papers 1853, Clergyman/Bound out

McDermott, Mary Jane, "June 16, 1865", 7, "Joslin, Mrs. Sarah", Elizabeth City (Essex Co.), NY, Indenture Papers 1858, Adopted

McDermott, Rosanna, "Feb. 7, 1866", 8, "Carpenter, James", Union , NJ, Indenture Papers 1870-1871, Adopted

McDonald, Carrie, "June 22, 1871", 6 wks., , , , Indenture Papers 1870-1871, "Surrendered by mother, Margaret Jane McDonald"

McGuinn, Mary Jane, "Aug. 1, 1853", 12, "Wiley, Rev. A. Y.", Duanesburgh, NY, Indenture Papers 1854, Adopted

McGuire, John, "July 21, 1854", 11, "Veghte, Theodore", Griggstown (Somerset Cco.), NJ, Indenture Papers 1865-1866, Baptized Anna Blanche Truax

McIntyre, Harriet, "Jan. 28, 1870", 6, "Seymour, Henry", White Plains, NY, Indenture Papers 1853, Bound out

McIntyre, Margaret, "Jan. 28, 1870", 5, "Russell, Solomon", Pittsfield (Berkshire Co.), MA, Indenture Papers 1857, Name changed to William Thompson

McKenna, Maggie, "Nov. 21, 1900", 3, , , , Commitments 1898-1900, "City Magistrates' Court, 2nd District AFGS #6054"

McKenna, Margaret, "Sept. 28, 1900", 2, , , , Commitments 1898-1900, "Discharged Oct. 10, 1900 "

McKeon, Lizzie, "Nov. 20, 1900", 6, , , , Commitments 1898-1900, Out-Door Poor to AFGS #6052

McKeon, Maggie, "Nov. 20, 1900", 11, , , , Commitments 1898-1900, Out-Door Poor to AFGS #6050

McKeon, Mary, "Nov. 20, 1900", 7, , , , Commitments 1898-1900, Out-Door Poor to AFGS #6051

McKeon, Nellie, "Nov. 20, 1900", 3, , , , Commitments 1898-1900, Out-Door Poor to AFGS #6053

McKinzie, George, "Oct. 21, 1870", 8 mo., "Rogers, John", New York City (New York Co.), NY, Indenture Papers 1882, Adopted/AFGS Book 9.488

McMannis, Ann Marie, "Feb. 3, 1857", 1, "White, H. G.", Welleville, NY, Indenture Papers 1865-1866, Adopted

McMillan, Charlotte, "Jan. 19, 1900", 11, , , , Commitments 1898-1900, Commitment #6025

McMullen, Emma , "July 25, 1854", 13, "Brokaw, Henry E.", Harlingen (Somerset Co.), NJ, Indenture Papers 1857, Adopted

McWilliams, Sarah, "June 21, 1854", 7, "Hedden, Charles", Grotton (Thompkins Co.), NY, Indenture Papers 1858, Adopted

McWilliams, Thomasina, "June 21, 1854", 5, "Hedden, Charles", Grotton (Thompkins Co.), NY, Indenture Papers 1858, "Completed Sept. 4, 1862"

Meeker, George H., "Mar. 21, 1853", 4, "Scovill, Sylvester", Conesville (Schoharie Co.), NY, Indenture Papers 1854, Bound out

Meikle, Elizabeth, "Apr. 21, 1866", 5, "Randolph, John", Rahway (Middlesex Co.), NJ, Indenture Papers 1870-1871, Adopted

Meikle, Jane Harrison, "Apr. 18, 1866", 6, "Shawhan, R.W.", Tiffin, OH, Commitments 1898-1900, Bound out

Melmore, Mary, "Aug. 3, 1882", 8, "Polhemas, Samuel", Central Valley, NY, Indenture Papers 1870-1871, Adopted

Melzer(?), George Washington, "Aug. 31, 1871", 10, "Taylor, Benjamin", Anisin Creek(?)(McKean Co.), PA, Indenture Papers 1857, Adopted

Merrit, Maria Teresa, "Apr. 24, 1857", 5, "Scoville, Sylvester", Conesville (Schoharie Co), NY, Indenture Papers 1882, Adopted/AFGS Book 9.437

Merritt, Sarah Frances, "Oct. 1, 1858", 10, "Fellows, Rev.", Durham (Green Co.), NY, Indenture Papers 1854, Bound out

Meyers, Jane Louisa, "Aug. 22, 1870", 13, "Voorhies, ", Richburg (Alleghany Co.), NY, Indenture Papers 1870-1871, Adopted

Miller, Bertha, "June 27, 1871", 2, , , , Indenture Papers 1870-1871, "Surrendered by mother, Mary Miller"

Miller, George Augustus, "Apr. 27, 1874", , "Jones, Mrs. Martha", Canton, IL, Binder

Miller, Lena, "Mar. 27, 1874", , Thompson, Jersey City, Nj, Binder

Miller, Sarah Catherine, "Aug. 1, 1853", , "Reynolds, John E.", Perth Amboy, NJ, Indenture Papers 1854, Adopted

Minor, Joseph, "Nov. 28, 1863", 13, "Hughey, William", Abingdon (Knox Co.), IL, Indenture Papers 1854, Adopted

Monehan, Thomas John, "June 21, 1854", 5, "Ramsey, Charles", West Hartford (Hartford Co.), CT, Indenture Papers 1853, Ship Carpenter/Adopted

Monroe, Richard, "Jan. 9, 1854", 2, "Fisk, Ephraim (Jr.)", China (Wyoming Co.), NY, Indenture Papers 1854, Adopted

Moore, Mary Jane, "Dec. 30, 1868", 9, "Snell, Thomas", Hornellsville (Steuben Co.), NY, Indenture Papers 1870-1871, Adopted

More, Charles, "June 15, 1865", 12, "Thurston, George", Lakeland (Suffolk Co.) Long Island, NY, Indenture Papers 1858, "Completed Mar. 20, 1863"

More, Charles, , , , , , Indenture Papers 1865-1866, See AFGS history book 5 pg. 59

Morison, Freddie, "Oct. 29, 1875", , "Mulvey, John", Jackson, PA, Binder

Morrell, Ophelia, "July 10, 1854", 6, "Rogers, Jonathan", Waterford (New London Co.), CT, Indenture Papers 1853, Bound out

Morris, Emily, "May 18, 1874", , "Vinton, H. N.", Southbridge, MA, Binder

Morrison, Celia, "Apr. 21, 1866", 11, "Wilson, J. K.", Vermont P.O. (Chatauqua Co.), NY, Indenture Papers 1858, "Completed Oct. 1, 1863"

Morrison, Frederic, "July 9, 1862", 3, "Mead, Martin", Berkshire (Tioga Co.), Ny, Commitments 1898-1900, Adopted

Mulligan, Maggie, "Aug. 14, 1882", 6, "Lloyd, Thomas", Milltown, NJ, Indenture Papers 1882, Adopted/AFGS Book 9.416

Murdick, Charlotte, "Sept. 23, 1871", , , , , Indenture Papers 1870-1871, "Surrendered by mother, Jane Murdick"

Murdock, Charlotte E., "Dec. 7, 1871", 1 mo., "Bragg, Isaac", "Brooklyn, Long Island", NY, Indenture Papers 1857, Adopted

Murer, Mary Frances, "Sept. 15, 1853", 2, "Robertson, James", New York City (New York Co.), NY, Indenture Papers 1865-1866, Adopted

Murphy, Ann, "June 22, 1858", 5, "Benton, Mrs. Mary", Andover (Alleghany Co.), NY, Indenture Papers 1854, Adopted (See Brown)

Murphy, Hattie, "Feb. 16, 1882", 1, "Meyers, Marcus", North Adams, MA, Indenture Papers 1854, Adopted

Murphy, Susanna, "June 12, 1857", 8, "Olds, Calvin", Beloit (Rock Cco.), WI, Indenture Papers 1854, Adopted (See Gurtin)

Myers, Catherine, "May 25, 1858", 6, "Webber, Rev. Henry", Orange (Essex Co.), NJ, Indenture Papers 1857, Adopted

Noble, John, "Sept. 16, 1853", 10, "Boughton, John F.", Red Creek (Wayne Co.), NY, Indenture Papers 1870-1871, Adopted

Nugent, Mary, "July 10, 1854", 5, "Yano, Joseph W.", Sargeantville (Hunterdon Co.), NJ, Indenture Papers 1857, Bound out

O'Brien, Ann, "July 21, 1857", 4, "Thompson, John", Cleveland (Cuyahoga Co.), OH, Indenture Papers 1865-1866, Adopted

Okey, Helen, "May 25, 1858", 1, "Ladd, Rufus", Norwich (New London Co.), CT, Indenture Papers 1858, Adopted

Olds, Emma, , , , , , Indenture Papers 1857, See Susanna Murphy

Olson, Susanna, "Feb. 6, 1871", 2, "Gregg, Robert", Harlem, NY, Indenture Papers 1865-1866, Adopted

O'Rourke, Rosa, "Oct. 27, 1882", 15, "Hartzheim, Charles", Freehold, NJ, Indenture Papers 1882, Adopted/AFGS Book 9.540

Orr, Robert James, "Dec. 10, 1856", 11, "Thomas, Freeman", Hanover (Luzerne Co.), PA, Indenture Papers 1857, Adopted

Osborn, Sarah Louisa, "June 21, 1854", 2, "Beebe, Isaac", Lisbon (Kendall Co.), IL, Indenture Papers 1858, Adopted

Otten, Edith, "Apr. 16, 1870", 6, "Irving, Washington", New York City (New York Co.), NY, Indenture Papers 1882, Adopted/AFGS Book 9.42

Owens, Bessie, "Apr. 18, 1898", 4, , , , Indenture Papers 1853, Out-Door Poor to AFGS #5071

Owens, Georgie, "Apr. 18, 1898", 2, , , , Indenture Papers 1853, Out-Door Poor to AFGS #5072

Parker, Ann, "June 21, 1854", 10, "Livington, Peter", Moricher (Suffolk Co.) L.I., NY, Indenture Papers 1870-1871, Adopted

Parr, Minnie, "Oct. 26, 1875", , Burnham, Monticello, NY, Binder

Paterson, John Henry, "Apr. 18, 1866", 13, "Johnston, Robert", Westfield (Essex Co.), NJ, Indenture Papers 1857, Adopted

Paterson, Thomas LeRoy, "Jan. 25, 1866", 8, "Prentice, Charles", Easton, CT, Indenture Papers 1870-1871, Adopted

Paul, Frederic, "Oct. 2, 1899", 5, , , , Commitments 1898-1900, Out-Door Poor to AFGS #6017

Payne, Julian, "Sept. 13, 1871", , , , , Indenture Papers 1870-1871, "Surrendered by mother, Addie Payne"

Pearson, Nellie, "Feb. 15, 1882", 14, "Foote, Theron L.", Lee (Berkshire Co.), MA, Indenture Papers 1870-1871, Bound out

Peck, Edward, "Sept. 10, 1866", 2, "Parsons, Mr. & Mrs.", Oil City, PA, Indenture Papers 1865-1866, Adopted

Pemberton, William, "May 15, 1858", 10, "Robinson, David", Wythe (Hancock co.), IL, Indenture Papers 1865-1866, Adopted

Perham, Kate Amelia, "May 25, 1858", 3 mo., "Briarwood, John", New Brunswick (Middlesex Co.), NJ, Indenture Papers 1865-1866, Adopted

Perry, Eliza, "Aug. 1, 1854", 11, "Thomas, Freeman", Hanover (Luzerne Co. ?), PA, Indenture Papers 1857, Now Freddy Albert Barnes

Perry, John, "July 21, 1854", 12, "Lake, Ransom", Wayne (Du page Co.), IL, Indenture Papers 1865-1866, Adopted

Perry, William, Feb. 1857, 13, "Thomas, Freeman", Hanover (Luzerne Co.), PA, Indenture Papers 1865-1866, Adopted

Plunkett, Jane, "Dec. 21, 1871", 1, , , , Indenture Papers 1870-1871, "Surrendered by mother, Mary Plunkett"

Pollicy, Bertha Cecelia, "Oct. 22, 1874", , "Vincent, Joshua", Tonawanda, NY, Binder

Potter, Alice, "Dec. 20, 1882", 9, "Sargent, Judson N.", Jasper, NY, Indenture Papers 1865-1866, Adopted

Potter, Ida, "Dec. 20, 1882", 11, "Sargent, Judson N.", Jasper, NY, Indenture Papers 1853, Bound out

Power, Bridget, "Aug. 4, 1854", 6, "Brown, David P.", Noark (New London Co.), CT, Indenture Papers 1854, Bound out

Price, Wm. Ellsworth, "Apr. 11, 1866", 3, "Cooper, William", Brooklyn (Kings Co.), NY, Indenture Papers 1858, Adopted

Proctor, Lily May, "June 13, 1882", 6, "Lees, Susanna P.", High Bridge, NY, Indenture Papers 1882, Apprenticed/AFGS Book 9.554

Purdy, Ida Louisa, "Nov. 16, 1857", 7, "Peck, Rev. Jesse", New York City (New York Co.), NY, Indenture Papers 1882, Adopted/AFGS Book 9.465

Putnam, Mary, "Mar. 26, 1863", 12, "Bonton, Edwin", South Salem (Westchester Co.), NY, Indenture Papers 1854, Adopted

Quigley, Albert, "Mar. 3, 1898", 7.5, , , , Indenture Papers 1853, Out-Door Poor to AFGS #5060

Quigley, Laura, "Mar. 3, 1898", 3.5, , , , Indenture Papers 1853, Out-Door Poor to AFGS #5062

Quigley, Lester, "Mar. 3, 1898", 6.5, , , , Indenture Papers 1853, Out-Door Poor to AFGS #5061

Quinton, Eliza Jane, "May 24, 1870", 13, "Bradly, Charles", Greenfield (Fairfield Co.), CT, Indenture Papers 1858, Adopted

Radisch, Elsie, "Dec. 5, 1898", 6, , , , Indenture Papers 1853, Admit to Children's Fold & Physician's Statement

Radisch, Elsie, "Nov. 5, 1902", , , , , Indenture Papers 1853, Transfer Children's Fold to AFGS #6097

Ramsey, Seth Thomas, , , , , , Indenture Papers 1854, "See Monehan, John"

Rasmunson, George, "Dec. 3, 1875", , "Sisson, Porter", East Springfield, PA, Binder

Reardon, Ann, "July 10, 1857", 2, "Copeland, Henry", Franklin Mills (Portage Co.), OH, Indenture Papers 1857, Bound out

Reavey, Sally, "Aug. 26, 1898", 5, , , , Indenture Papers 1853, "Childrens Fold/AFGS #7003/Disc. May 16, 1905"

Reiley, Annie, "June 13, 1882", 8, "Weller, Fred", East New Durham, NJ, Indenture Papers 1857, Bound out

Renke, Louisa, "Aug. 8, 1882", 8, "Reynolds, Edward", Bedford Station, NY, Indenture Papers 1854, Adopted

Reynick, Elizabeth F., "Apr. 21, 1866", 9, "Freeman, Clarissa", Snccasuma(?)(Morris Co.), NJ, Indenture Papers 1882, Adopted/AFGS Book 9.344

Reynolds, Harriet, "Feb. 20, 1875", , "Griffith, Edward", Delhi, NY, Binder

Roberts, Mary Ann, "Apr. 11, 1865", 4, "Mixan, Andrew", Poughkeepsie, NY, Indenture Papers 1865-1866, Bound out

Robinson, Eliza Jane, "Dec. 29, 1858", 7, , , , Indenture Papers 1857, Surrendered by Abigail Stubes

Roff, Charles, "Aug. 17, 1871", 2 wks., , , , Indenture Papers 1870-1871, "Surrendered by mother, Mary Abby Roff"

Ross, Lizzie, "Apr. 18, 1899", 8, , , , Commitments 1898-1900, Commitment #6004

Russell, Maud, "Jan. 5, 1882", 1, "Demarest, Nicholas B.", New Bridge (Bergen Co.), NJ, Indenture Papers 1865-1866, Apprenticed

Sandoll, Isabella, "Aug. 1, 1854", 8, "Smith, John E.", Newark Valley (Tioga Co.), NY, Indenture Papers 1865-1866, Adopted

Saunders, Ellan, "July 9, 1862", 3, "Williams, Isaac P.", Astoria (Queens Co.), Ny, Indenture Papers 1870-1871, Bound out

Schella, Dorothea, "Sept. 14, 1858", 5, "Howey, Thomas", Walnut Grove (Knox Co.), IL, Indenture Papers 1882, Adopted/AFGS Book 9.509

Schmidt, Ernest, "May 31, 1898", 4, , , , Indenture Papers 1853, "#5082 stamped ""Discharged"""

Schmidt, Walter, "May 31, 1898", 2, , , , Indenture Papers 1853, "#5083 stamped ""Discharged"""

Schroeder, Willie, "Sept. 23, 1871", 3 wks., , , , Indenture Papers 1870-1871, "Surrendered by mother, Augusta Schroeder"

Schultz, Louisa, "July. 14, 1900", 6, , , , Commitments 1898-1900, Commitment #6038

Seal, Mary, "Dec. 7, 1871", 4, "Cary, William", Gansevoort (Saratoga Co.), NY, Indenture Papers 1858, "Completed March 26, 1863"

Sealer, Mary, "Nov. 22, 1899", 6, , , , Commitments 1898-1900, Out-Door Poor to AFGS #6020

Seely, Mary, "Sept. 25, 1871", 6, "Ludington, George", Williamsburgh (Kings Co.), NY, Indenture Papers 1858, "Completed Mar. 26, 1863"

Seidell, Augusta, "Aug. 14, 1854", 11, "Bradford, Rev. Thomas", Waterford (Erie Cco.), PA, Commitments 1898-1900, Identure 1863

Senior, Frank, "Mar. 2, 1882", 1, "Bailey, Wm. H.", Middletown, CT, Indenture Papers 1857, Adopted

Shawcross, Alice, "Oct. 24, 1871", 2 wks., , , , Indenture Papers 1870-1871, "Surrendered by mother, Kate Shawcross"

Sheehan, William, "Jan. 23, 1862", 8, "Smith, Rev. Edwin", Fremont (Tazewell Co.), IL, Indenture Papers 1865-1866, Adopted

Sheufele, Mary, "Mar. 25, 1875", , "Skidmore, J. L.", "Franklinville, Long Island", NY, Binder

Shields, Mary, "Oct. 15, 11858", 15, "Butler, Lysander", Oberlin (Lorain Co.), OH, Indenture Papers 1858, Adopted

Skogland, Dagmar, "Sept. 19, 1899", 8, , , , Commitments 1898-1900, Out-Door Poor to AFGS #6015

Skogland, Ethel, "Sept. 19, 1899", 3, , , , Commitments 1898-1900, Out-Door Poor to AFGS #6016

Smeddick, Margaret, "Nov. 16, 1857", 3, "Hill, James", Cleveland (Cuyahoga Co.), OH, Indenture Papers 1865-1866, Adopted

Smith, Elsa, "May 31, 1898", 5, , , , Indenture Papers 1853, "#5084 Discharged Mar. 21, 1902"

Smith, Emma , "Nov. 10, 1853", 1, "Skinner, E. L.", Elmira, NY, Indenture Papers 1854, Adopted

Smith, Emma , "May 31, 1898", 3, , , , Indenture Papers 1853, "#5085 Died June 24, 1898 at W.P. Hospital"

Smith, Florina, "Mar. 17, 1882", 1, "Ross, Charles Howard", New York City (New York Co.), NY, Indenture Papers 1857, Adopted

Smith, Henrietta, "Apr. 15, 1866", 4 mo., "Brower, Morris", New York City (New York Co.), NY, Indenture Papers 1858, Bound out

Smith, Ida, "Oct. 21, 1881", 7, "Herring, Cornelius A.", Hackensack, NJ, Indenture Papers 1858, Adopted

Smith, Isabella, "Jan. 18, 1875", , "Brown, Thomas", New York City (New York Co.), NY, Binder

Smith, james, "Mar. 1, 1882", 4, "Cowles, S. N.", Otisco (Orion Co.), NY, Indenture Papers 1865-1866, Adopted

Smith, Josiah, "Nov. 6, 1871", 1 mo., , , , Indenture Papers 1870-1871, "Surrendered by mother, Annie Brown"

Smith, Lena, "Sept. 11, 1863", 1, "Wright, Aaron", Newark (Essex Co.), NJ, Indenture Papers 1858, Adopted

Smith, Lilly, "Mar. 15, 1875", , "Randell, Morris", New York City (New York Co.), NY, Binder

Smith, Margaret, "Mar. 26, 1863", 3, "Jones, Robert", Jersey City (Hudson Co.), NJ, Indenture Papers 1858, Adopted

Smith, Mary Ann, "July 10, 1862", 2, "Hice, John", Newtown Centre (Luzerne Co.), PA, Indenture Papers 1858, Adopted

Smith, Millicent, "Oct. 25, 1900", 9, , , , Commitments 1898-1900, "City Magistrates' Court, 7th District AFGS #6049"

Smith, William Henry, "Oct. 25, 1875", , "Morrison, Martin", Bearsville, NY, Binder

Smythe, Laura, "Apr. 17, 1863", 6, "Hauk, George W.", Mt. Vernon (Knox Co.), OH, Indenture Papers 1854, Bound out

Southard, Jacob Henry, "Dec. 1, 1870", 6, "Foster, Henry J.", Palmyra (Wayne Co.), NY, Indenture Papers 1853, Bound out

Spaden, Albert, "Feb. 3, 1858", 9, "Hall, Foster V.", Depansville (Jefferson Co.), NY, Indenture Papers 1854, Adopted

Spriggs, Elizabeth, "Sept. 22, 1862", 2, "Freeland, John", West Hoboken (Hudson Co.), NJ, Indenture Papers 1882, Adopted/AFGS Book 9.527

Spring, Charlotte, "July 15, 1898", 6, , , , Indenture Papers 1853, #5098 treated for contagious eye disease

Stanley, Isaac, "Apr. 29, 1857", 4, "Barnes, Joseph", Cleveland (Cuyahoga Co.), OH, Indenture Papers 1870-1871, Bound out

Stein, Lavinia, "Aug. 21, 1900", 6, , , , Commitments 1898-1900, "Children's Fold to AFGS #7000/Dis. Jan. 11, 1905"

Stein, Lavinia, "July 3, 1899", 5, , , , Commitments 1898-1900, Out-Door Poor to AFGS #6008

Steinmetz, George S., "Jan. 14, 1857", 6, "Myers, Christopher", Monroe (Monroe Co.), MI, Indenture Papers 1870-1871, Adopted

Steinmetz, John, "Jan. 14, 1857", 4, "Myers, Christopher", Monroe (Monroe Co.), MI, Indenture Papers 1853, Farmer/Bound out

Steinmetz, John E., "Jan. 15, 1857", 4, "Myers, Christopher", Monroe (Monroe Co.), MI, Indenture Papers 1853, Farmer/Bound out

Steinmetz, Madeline, "May 9, 1899", 2.5, , , , Commitments 1898-1900, "City Magistrates' Court, 7th District AFGS #6006"

Stevens, Thomas, "Mar. 20, 1875", , "Norton, A. C.", Robertsville, CT, Binder

Stock, William H., "May 9, 1874", , "Young, G.", Calicoon, NY, Binder

Stone, Arthur, "Feb. 14, 1870", 3, "Macarchuin, John", New York City (New York Co.), NY, Indenture Papers 1854, Adopted

Sullivan, John, "May 30, 1857", 4, "Hays, John", Knoxville (Knox Co.), IL, Indenture Papers 1857, Adopted

Swallow, Florence, "Jan. 8, 1898", 8, , , , Indenture Papers 1853, "b. Chicago, IL/Out-Door Poor to AFGS #5044"

Swallow, Mabel, "Jan. 8, 1898", 3, , , , Indenture Papers 1853, "b. Corona, NY; Admitted to AFGS #5045"

Swan, Henry, "Nov. 24, 1876", , "Johnson, Julia", Monsey, NY, Binder

Swan, Johanna, "Feb. 9, 1875", , "Smith, Linnains", Newark, NJ, Binder

Swartmont, Frank Elvestine, "Apr. 18, 1866", 13, "Ryder, Aaron", Sing Sing (Westchester Co.), NY, Indenture Papers 1865-1866, Adopted

Swartz, Louis, "Feb. 23, 1870", 13, "Fenn, John", Mount Hope (Westchester Co.), NY, Indenture Papers 1882, Adopted

Swift, George, "July 1, 1898", 6, , , , Indenture Papers 1853, Out-Door Poor to AFGS #5090

Swift, Reina, "July 1, 1898", 9, , , , Indenture Papers 1853, Out-Door Poor to AFGS #5089

Taylor, Marietta, "July 11, 1870", 7, , , , Indenture Papers 1870-1871, "Surrendered by mother, Eliza Taylor (handwritten)"

Telley, George, "June 12, 1857", 6, "Bundy, David", Beloit (Rock Cco.), WI, Indenture Papers 1857, Adopted

Thompson, David, "June 22, 1858", 10, "Kelsey, Solomon", Naples (Ontario Co.), NY, Indenture Papers 1853, Bound out

Thompson, Flora, "June 21, 1871", 2 mo., , , , Indenture Papers 1870-1871, "Surrendered by mother, Phebe Sarah Thompson"

Thompson, Jennie, , , , , , Indenture Papers 1857, See Martha Jane Farlow

Thompson, Lydia Maria, "Mar. 26, 1863", 12, "Rogers, Henry", New London (New London Co.), CT, Indenture Papers 1870-1871, Bound out

Thompson, Sidney Doty, , , , , , Indenture Papers 1854, "See Barton, James M."

Thompson, William, , , , , , Indenture Papers 1857, See William Robert Farlow

Thomson, Elizabeth, "Mar. 30, 1875", , "Rodgers, George", "Huntington, Long Island", NY, Binder

Thornton, Emma, "Mar. 11, 1870", 5, "Beatty, Claudius", Brooklyn (Kings Co.), NY, Indenture Papers 1854, "Cancelled Nov. 7, 1855"

Thring, Jennie, July 1865, 14, "Young, Alpheus", Fairhaven (New Haven Co.), CT, Indenture Papers 1882, Adopted/AFGS Book 9.434

Tichnor, Frederick, "Nov. 29, 1864", 3, "Newton, Betsy", Durham (Green Co.), CT, Indenture Papers 1854, Adopted

Tilford, Hattie, "Mar. 27, 1882", 5, "Saunders, Sarah ", Brookfield, NY, Indenture Papers 1882, Adopted/AFGS Book 9.562

Topping, Emma, "Nov. 13, 1875", , Montagnami, Albany, NY, Binder

Truax, Anna Blanche, , , , , , Indenture Papers 1865-1866, See Lottie Allchin

Turcotte, Alice, "July 12, 1882", 7, "Menzie, John W.", Plankinton (Dakota Territory), , Indenture Papers 1854, Bound out

Tusete, Louisa, "Apr. 8, 1875", , "Miner, Alfred", North Stonington, CT, Binder

Umberfield, Mary, "June 2, 1854", 7, "Smith, Adon", New York City (New York Co.), NY, Indenture Papers 1882, Apprenticed/AFGS Book 9.464

Valley, Jennie, "July 11, 1898", 6, , , , Indenture Papers 1853, "Childrens Fold/AFGS #6099/ Disc. May 1, 1905"

Van Kuin, Ann Jane, "Nov. 11, 1853", 6, "Wheeler, Dr. Edward", Schnectady, NY, Indenture Papers 1858, "Completed Oct. 1, 1863"

Van Ness, Adolphus Peter, "Feb. 5, 1857", 11, "Raynor, John", Southampton (Suffolk Co.) L.I., NY, Indenture Papers 1882, Adopted/AFGS Book 9.530

Vedder, Anna M., "May 30, 1857", 10, "Stillman, Maxon, Jr.", Alfred Centre (Alleghany Co.), NY, Indenture Papers 1865-1866, Adopted

Vedder, James Albert, "Nov. 16, 1857", 7, "Potter, Ezra", Alfred (Alleghany Co.), NY, Indenture Papers 1857, Adopted

Veighler, Susan, "Mar. 16, 1899", 4, , , , Commitments 1898-1900, "City Magistrates' Court, 2nd District AFGS #6000"

Verden, Margaret, "Sept. 14, 1858", 9, "Fairchild, Abiel", Cameron (Warren Co.), IL, Indenture Papers 1858, "Completed Jan. 10, 1862"

Verdier, Isabella Bepplier, "July 8, 1871", , , , , Indenture Papers 1870-1871, "Surrendered by mother, Esther Verdier"

Vouthay, Caroline, "aug. 1, 1853", 11, "Pancoast, Wm. L.", Mullica Hill, NJ, Indenture Papers 1870-1871, Bound out

Wade, Lulu, "Feb. 17, 1898", 12, , , , Indenture Papers 1853, Out-Door Poor to AFGS #5053

Wagner, Ella, "Jan. 26, 1900", 6, , , , Commitments 1898-1900, Commitment #60226

Wagner, Harry, "Jan. 26, 1900", 2, , , , Commitments 1898-1900, Commitment #6027

Walford, Benjamin, "July 31, 1882", 8, "More, John A.", Findley's lake (Chaut. Co.), NY, Indenture Papers 1865-1866, Bound out

Walford, John, "July 31, 1882", 8, "More, John A.", Findley's lake (Chaut. Co.), NY, Indenture Papers 1882, Adopted/AFGS Book 9.357

Wall, Carrie, "Sept. 4, 1875", , "Ferris,", Yorktown, NY, Binder

Wallace, Ada, "Feb. 14, 1898", 4, , , , Indenture Papers 1853, Out-Door Poor to AFGS #5051

Wallace, John, "Feb. 25, 1898", , , , , Indenture Papers 1853, Com. #5048 held by NYJA by order

Wallace, Lizzie, "Feb. 5, 1898", 7, , , , Indenture Papers 1853, Out-Door Poor to AFGS #5049

Walters, Catherine, "Feb. 22, 1853", 12, "Voorhees, John, Jr.", Centerville, NJ, Indenture Papers 1858, "Completed May 20, 1862"

Walters, Samuel R., "July 11, 1882", 6, "Weyant, John", Fort Montgomery, NY, Indenture Papers 1854, Bound out

Walton, Charles, "Mar. 20, 1863", 9, "Knowles, Benjamin", Smyrna (Chenango Co.), NY, Indenture Papers 1865-1866, Bound out

Ware, Jane Elizabeth, "Nov. 3, 1882", 7, "Fry, James W.", Rochester, NY, Indenture Papers 1853, Bound out

Warren, Priscilla, "Mar. 20, 1875", , "Hendricks, Charles", Onondaga Co., NY, Binder

Watson, Charles, "June 7, 1871", , , , , Indenture Papers 1870-1871, "Surrendered by grandmother, Mrs. Edna Valentine"

Watson, John Henry, "Nov. 16, 1870", 2, "DeWolf, Luther", Sanask(?)(Carroll Co.), IL, Indenture Papers 1854, Bound out

Watson, Wilhemina, "Oct. 3, 1859", 1, "L'amoureux, Edwin K.", New York City (New York Co.), NY, Indenture Papers 1858, Adopted

Webb, John, "Apr. 18, 1866", 9, "Stebbins, Thomas", Utica (Winona Cco.), MN, Indenture Papers 1857, Adopted/Name changed to Wm. Edwin Corburier

Webb, Mary Isabella, "June 13, 1882", 6, "Swift, James B.", Peekskill, NY, Indenture Papers 1858, "Completed June 10, 1862"

Webster, Charlie, "Aug. 18, 1882", 4, "Binder, George J.", Rochester, NY, Indenture Papers 1858, Bound out

Weed, Sarah, "Nov. 17, 1858", 5, "Holmes, david", Coldwater (Branch Co.), MI, Indenture Papers 1865-1866, Adopted

Wehlburg, Alice, "Feb. 1, 1900", 4.5, , , , Commitments 1898-1900, Out-Door Poor to AFGS #6031

Wesela, Rosa, "Nov. 24, 1875", , Schneider, Hoboken, NJ, Binder

West, Mary , "Nov. 16, 1858", 9, "Allen, Robert", Fredericksburg (Wayne Co.), OH, Indenture Papers 1870-1871, Incomplete papers

Westerfield, Alfred, "Aug. 11, 1863", 10, "Havens, Ezra", Blue Ball (Monmouth Co.), NJ, Indenture Papers 1865-1866, Returned by Mrs. Carpenter

Westerfield, Emma, "Aug. 11, 1863", 5, "Havens, Ezra", Blue Ball (Monmouth Co.), NJ, Indenture Papers 1858, "Returned May 12, 1870"

Westfall, Harry, "Sept. 15, 1882", 3, "Martin, Daniel", Brooklyn (Long Island), NY, Indenture Papers 1882, Adopted/AFGS Book 9.504

Wheeler, Rose Delaney, , , , , , Indenture Papers 1854, "See Donnelly, Elizabeth"

Whelpley, Ada Mary, "Dec. 19, 1874", , "Lawrence, Daniel", New Boston, MA, Binder

Whigam, Elizabeth A., "Dec. 19, 1853", 11, "Brown, Joel", "Medford, Millers Place, L.I.", NY, Indenture Papers 1858, Bound out

Whigam, Horace, "Dec. 19, 1853", 8, "Brown, Joel", "Medford, Millers Place, L.I.", NY, Indenture Papers 1858, Bound out

Williams, Eva, "June 22, 1858", 4, "Squires, Nehemiah", Hamilton (Madison Co.), NY, Indenture Papers 1870-1871, Adopted (?)

Williams, Letitia, "Mar. 25, 1875", , "Osborn, Roby", Pawlings, NY, Binder

Williams, Sophia, "Apr. 5, 1875", , "McClaughry, Matthew", Fountain Green, IL, Binder

Wilson, Annie, "Nov. 16, 1858", 2, "Beckley, William", New Haven (New Haven Co.), CT, Indenture Papers 1865-1866, Adopted

Wilson, Maria, "July 21, 1854", 9, "Bigelow, John", Jacksontown (Licking Co.), OH, Indenture Papers 1882, Adopted/AFGS Book 9.517

Winchell, Charlotte, "Sept. 14, 1882", 7, "Porter, Belden", Liberty, NY, Indenture Papers 1870-1871, Adopted

Wise, Jacob, "May 25, 1858", 4, "Beaty, Eleazor", Croton (Licking Co.), OH, Indenture Papers 1882, Adopted/AFGS Book 9.500

Wise, William, "May 25, 1858", 5, "Winslow, william", Croton (Licking Co.), OH, Indenture Papers 1857, Now Emma Olds

Wood, Eva, "Apr. 21, 1866", 5, "Breckenridge, Elias", West Meriden, CT, Indenture Papers 1858, "Completed Mar. 25, 1862"

Wood, Sarah, "Mar. 28, 1882", 6, "De Baum, John", Wyckoff, NJ, Indenture Papers 1870-1871, Adopted

Woods, Ella, "May 6, 1898", 4, , , , Indenture Papers 1853, Out-Door Poor to AFGS #5079

Woods, Thomas, "May 6, 1898", 8, , , , Indenture Papers 1853, Out-Door Poor to AFGS #5078

Wright, Andrew, "Nov. 24, 1871", 3 wks., , , , Indenture Papers 1870-1871, "Surrendered by mother, Helena Wright"

Wultz, Maggie, "Nov. 8, 1875", , "Brown, Hetty", Banksville, CT, Binder

Young, Caroline, "Feb. 3, 1858", 12, "Prutsman, Adam", Princeton (Burean Co.), IL, Indenture Papers 1865-1866, Adopted

Young, Susan O'Neal, "Nov. 16, 1857", 12, "Stevens, Broadstreet", Oberlin, OH, Indenture Papers 1857, Indentured

Young, William Henry, "Feb. 3, 1858", 8, "Prutsman, Adam", Princeton (Burean Co.), IL, Indenture Papers 1882, Adopted/AFGS Book 9.167

Young , Susan, "May 17, 1858", 10, "Henrich, Lewis", Woodhull (Steuben Co.), NY, Indenture Papers 1853, Bound out

Zachanias, Leopold R., "Mar. 27, 1899", 3, , , , Commitments 1898-1900, Out-Door Poor to AFGS #6002

AMERICAN FEMALE GUARDIAN SOCIETY
HOME FOR THE FRIENDLESS
MORE INDENTURES

(Note: This list is in alphabetical order by surname, even though the first name appears first)

First name, Last name, Age, Date, Indentured to or adopted by:, City, County, State, Notes

Freely Martha, Allen, 4, "June 13, 1882", Mrs. Mirabel E. Denneston, South Elizabeth, , NJ, "See book 9.540, part 2 sent July 20, 1882"

Lizzie Shepherd, Allinger, 12, "Mar. 27, 1882", M/M James Degarimo, Newark Valley, , NY, "See book 9.148, part 2 sent apr. 22, 1882"

Annetta Marion, Anderson, 12, "July 11, 1882", M/M Henry Smith, Port Monmouth, , NJ, "See book 9.476, part 2 sent Nov. 3, 1882"

Edith, Anderson, 6, "Mar. 1, 1882", M/M R. Willis Lampman, Schnectady, , NY, "See book 9.437, part 2 sent Apr. 10, 1882"

Rosa, Appel, 11, "June 13, 1882", M/M Fred Brown, Newark, , NJ, "See book 9.557, part 2 completed and sent June 21, 1882"

Maggie, Armour, 11, "June 14, 1882", M/M George L. Rundell, Greenville, , NY, "See book 9.554, part 2 sent July 6, 1882"

Catherine, Boyle, 2, "June 3, 1861", John L. Peake, Hudson, Columbia Co., NY, "Born Jan. 4, 1859"

Kate Hall, Bryan, 4, "Dec. 20, 1882", M/M Stephen Andrews, Osborn Hollow, , NY, "See book 9.539, part 2 sent March 20, 1883"

Mary, Burns, 11 mo., "Jan. 5, 1882", M/M John Hayhurst, New York City, , NY, "See book 9.465, part 2 sent Jan. 20, 1882"

Wm. Henry, Butler, 10, "Dec. 6, 1862", Moses Hammond, Warsaw, Hancock Co., IL, "Born Nov. 10, 1852"

Geo. Wash., Chamberlin, 6, "Sept. 14, 1882", M/M Orlando M. Putnam, Dover, Kent Co., DE, "See book 9.378, part 2 sent Sept. 27, 1882"

Latimer, Clark, 9 mo., "Mar. 2, 1882", M/M Axel Ernest, New York City, , NY, "See book 9.553, part 2 sent Mar. 14, 1882"

Amanda, Cornell, 1, "Aug. 4, 1882", M/M Robert B. Burleson, Cambridge, , NY, "See book 9.509, part 2 sent Oct. 6, 1882"

Frederick, Donelson, 4, "Aug. 8, 1882", Rev. & Mrs. Peter A. Seguin, New York City, , NY, "See book 9.591,part 2 sent Aug. 14, 1882"

Agnes Louise, Farrell, 9, "Nov. 15, 1882", M/M John C. Berger , Somerville, Somerset Co., NY, "See book 9.610, part 2 sent Aug. 22, 1884"

Sallie, Fentz, 9, "June 14, 1882", Mrs. M. A. Hoffman, Claverack, , NY, "See book 9.231, part 2 sent June 30, 1882"

Annie, French, 13, "Aug. 9, 1882", M/M Henry C. Phelps, North Greece, , NY, "See book 9.418, part 2 sent Sept. 6, 1882"

Anna, Gallagher, 3, "June 13, 1882", M/M William Bray, Birmingham, , CT, "See book 9.498, part 2 sent Aug. 7, 1882"

Margaret, Genter, 4, "July 11, 1882", M/M Frederick Feierabend , Bridgeport, , CT, "See book 9.426, part 2 sent July 21, 1882, resent Apr. 18, 1884"

Robert, Greenwood, 4, "Aug. 14, 1882", M/M Joseph A. Linden, Milltown, , NJ, "See book 9.527, part 2 sent"

Alexander, Hall, 7, "Sept. 14, 1882", M/M Orrin Sason, Windom, , MN, "See book 9.600, part 2 sent Nov. 24, 1882"

Lizzie, Hall, 11, "Nov. 17, 1882", M/M Thomas L. Park , White Plains, , NY, "See book 9.612, part 2 sent Mar. 20, 1883"

Edward, Hannon, 2, "Mar. 8, 1882", M/M Edmund L. Osgood, Stittman Valley, , IL, "See book 9.492, part 2 sent May 15, 1882"

Amy, Harder, 7, "June 13, 1882", M/M William B. Dermott, Flemington, , NJ, "See book 9.563, part 2 taken Dec. 18(?), 1882"

Arthur, Hayes, 5, "June 22, 1882", M/M Emerson Hayes, Harvinton, , CT, "See book 9.312, part 2 sent Nov. 24, 1882"

Charles , Hesse, 5, "Mar. 1, 1882", M/M Felix Martian, Brooklyn, Long Island, NY, "See book 9.244, part 2 sent Mar. 3, 1882"

Elva, Horton, 14, "Aug. 8, 1882", M/M J. O. Austin, Unionville, Orange Co., NY, "See book 9.464, part 2 sent Aug. 8, 1882"

Minnie, Hughes, 8, "Nov. 9, 1882", M/M John Davison, Hopeville, , NJ, "Part 2 completed and sent Aug. 28, 1883"

Lizzie, Lambert, 2, "June 12, 1882", M/M Sheldon W. Center, Center White Circle, , NY, "See book 9.528, part 2 sent June 22, 1882"

Richard, Lynch, 11, "Sept. 22, 1860", Elijah Rice, Wallingford, , CT, "Born July 10, 1849"

John, Marshall, 4, "Aug. 9, 1882", M/M Richard W. Reichers, New York City, , NY, "See book 9.167, part 2 sent Dec. 11, 1882"

Annie, Mattel, 9, "Mar. 1, 1882", M/M Israel Gibbud, Union City, , CT, "See book 9.517, part 2 sent mar. 22, 1882"

Mary, Melmore, 8, "Aug. 3, 1882", M/M Samuel Polhamus, Central Valley, , NY, "See book 9.42, part 2 sent Oct. 16, 1883"

Maggie, Mulligan, 6, "Aug. 14, 1882", M/M Thomas Lloyd, Milltown, , NJ, "See book 9.344, part 2 sent"

Hattie, Murphy, 1, "Feb. 16, 1882", M/M Marcus E. Meyers, North Adams, , MA, "See book 9.529, part 2 sent Feb. 20, 1882"

Rosa, O'Rourke, 15, "Oct. 27, 1882", M/M Charles Hartzheim, Freehold, , NJ, "See book 9.57, part 2 completed & sent Aug. 23, 1883"

Nellie G., Pearson, 14, "Feb. 15, 1882", M/M Theron L. Foote, Lee, Berkshire Co., MA, "See book 8.164, part 2 sent January 8, 1883"

Alice, Potter, 9, "Dec. 20, 1882", M/M Judson Sargent , Jasper, , NY, "See book 9.504, part 2 completed and sent Jan. 2, 1883"

Ida E., Potter, 11, "Dec. 20, 1882", M/M Judson Sargent , Jasper, Stuben Co., NY, "See book 9.503, part 2 sent Jan. 2, 1883"

Lily May, Proctor, 6, "June 13, 1882", Mrs. Susanna P. Lees, High Bridge, , NY, "See book 8.416, part 2 sent June 22, 1882"

Annie, Reiley, 8, "June 13, 1882", M/M Fred Weller, East New Durham, , NJ, "Part 2 sent June 29, 1882"

Louisa, Renke, 8, "Aug. 8, 1882", M/M Edward Reynolds, Bedford Station, , NY, "See book 9.252, part 2 sent Sept. 6, 1882"

Maud, Russell, 1, "Jan. 5, 1882", M/M Nicholas B. Demarest, New Bridge, Bergen Co., NJ, "See book 9.538, part 2 sent Jan. 16, 1882"

Frank, Senior, 1, "Mar. 2, 1882", M/M William Bailey, Middletown, , CT, "See book 9.500, part 2 sent Mar. 14, 1882"

Florina, Smith, 1, "Mar. 17, 1882", M/M Charles Howard Ross, New York City, , NY, "See book 9.530, part 2 sent Apr. 10, 1882"

Ida, Smith, 7, "Oct. 21, 1881", M/M Cornelius A. Herring, Hackensack, , NJ, See book 9.339

James, Smith, 4, "Mar. 1, 1882", M/M S. N. Cowles, Otisco, Onon Co., NY, "See book 9.340, part 2 sent June 7, 1882"

Lena, Smith, 1, "Oct. 1, 1863", Aaron W. Wright, Newark, Epex Co., NJ, "Born April 24, 1862"

Mary Ann, Smith, 2, "July 10, 1862", John Hice, New Town Center, , PA, "Born Dec. 18, 1859"

Laura, Smythe, 6, "April 17, 1863", George W. Hauk, Mount Vernon, Knox Co., OH, "Born May 28, 1856"

Elizabeth, Spriggs, 2, "Sept. 22, 1862", John L. Freeland, West Hoboken, , NJ, "Born July 22, 1859"

Frederick, Ticknor, 3, "Nov. 29, 1862", Mrs. Betsy Newton, Durham, , CT, "Born April 6, 1861"

Hattie, Tilford, 5, "Mar. 27, 1882", Miss Sarah E. Saunders & Sisters, Brookfield, , NY, "See book 9.291, part 2 sent Apr. 28, 1882"

Alice, Turcotte, 7, "July 12, 1882", M/M John W. Menzie, Plankinton, Dakota Territory, , "See book 9.434, part 2 sent Mar. 20, 1883"

Benjamin, Walford, 8, "July 31, 1882", M/M John A. Moore, Findley's Lake, Chataqua Co., NY, "See book 9.400, part 2 sent Dec. 11, 1882"

John, Walford, 8, "July 31, 1882", M/M James C. Moore, Findley's Lake, Chataqua Co., NY, "See book 9.401, part 2 sent Dec. 11, 1882"

Samuel R., Walters, 6, "July 11, 1882", M/M John Weygant, Fort Montgomery, , NY, "See book 8.492, part 2 sent Sept. 6, 1882"

Jane Elizabeth, Ware, 7, "Nov. 3, 1882", M/M James W. Fry, Rochester, , NY, "See book 9.224, part 2 sent Nov. 7, 1882"

Mary Isabella, Webb, 6, "June 13, 1882", M/M James B. Swift, Peekskill, , NY, "See book 9.488, part 2 sent Sept. 22, 1882"

Charlie, Webster, 4, "Aug. 18, 1882", M/M George J. Binder, Rochester, , NY, "See book 9.562, part 2 sent Sept. 6, 1882"

Harry, Westfall, 3, "Sept. 15, 1882", M/M Daniel Martin, Brooklyn, Long Island, NY, "See book 9.491, part 2 taken Sept. 20, 1882"

Charlotte, Winchell, 7, "Sept. 14, 1882", M/M R. Belden Porter, Liberty, , NY, "See book 9.357, part 2 sent Sept. 25, 1882"

Sarah, Wood, 6, "Mar. 28, 1882", M/M John J. D. Baum, Wyckoff, , NJ, "See book 9.544, part 2 sent May 17, 1882"

Made in the USA
Middletown, DE
21 December 2019

Move Beyond Childhood Trauma

Identify the Roots of Emotional Turmoil

Liberate Your Inner Child, Move Past Dysfunction

Reject Unhealthy Patterns in Relationships

Discover the Authentic Life You Deserve

Freeman Publishing

Contents

Introduction

As a young child, did you ever find yourself struggling to make sense of the emotional turmoil around you? The weight of unresolved trauma can be carried for years, which manifests in relationships, self-image, and overall well-being. Young children often think they are the ones doing something wrong or undeserving of love. You can stay deep in a dip of self-doubt or finally take control of your own self-discovery and healing, reflecting on the complexities of the past and its impact on the present.

This book is designed to lead those who want to examine childhood trauma, identify the roots of their emotional pain, liberate their inner child, and move beyond the dysfunction that has held them back for so long.

Approximately 61 percent of adults in the United States have experienced at least one adverse childhood event, such as abuse, neglect, or household dysfunction (CDC 2021). The effects of these experiences can be far-reaching, creeping into one's mental health, relationships, and overall quality of life well into adulthood. While the past can't be undone, acknowledging childhood

trauma can catalyze an individual's healing process and help them break the cycles of intergenerational trauma.

There are a lot of factors that make up someone's trauma-driven inner world. We'll unravel the intricacies of your experiences and explore concepts such as emotional triggers, inner child work, and the impact of trauma on the brain and body. By the end of it all, you will better understand how your past influences your present and you'll have a few practical tools to help you navigate the challenges that arise.

Healing is not always easy, but it is a process filled with personal insights, discovery, and opportunities to reclaim your authentic self. This book is meant to guide the path you'll walk, offering a blend of emotional resonance, therapeutic guidance, and actionable exercises that will help you develop greater self-awareness and emotional resilience so you can break free from unhealthy patterns.

As we move through each chapter, you'll discover how to recognize and manage emotional triggers, engage in inner child work to heal past wounds, and cultivate self-compassion and empowerment. Each exercise is tailored to address different healing needs. You'll be able to engage in journaling, mindfulness, and expressive arts to help you process and release pent-up emotions.

While dealing with trauma can be an incredibly lonely process, I want you to know that you are not alone. Together, we'll uncover the strength of self-discovery, emotional healing, and the courage it takes to break free from the grip of the past.

By the end of this book, you'll have gained a deeper understanding of yourself, your emotional landscape, and the tools needed to navigate life's challenges with resilience. You'll find

yourself at the intersection of self-compassion and support, creating a life for yourself that aligns with your true desires.

Take a deep breath, open your heart, and join me on the first steps toward the rest of your life. The strength, wisdom, and resilience already lie within you; they're just waiting to be discovered. The best time to begin the process of healing, growth, and self-discovery is now, and it happens one page at a time.

Chapter 1

Understanding Your Emotional Landscape

Sometimes, just an offhand comment from someone can send you spiraling into self-doubt or anger. Regardless of whether these triggers come from a friend, a colleague, or even a stranger, you suddenly get caught up in a whirlwind of emotions that feel overwhelming and hard to control. While our loved ones may have good intentions, their comments can strike a chord deep within you, triggering a flood of emotions and memories you can't quite place. It's not always easy to identify why you feel so strongly, and it may stem from various sources. We'll unravel the complicated web of emotional triggers that shape your daily experiences, giving you insight into yourself and the patterns that no longer serve you.

Mapping Your Emotional Triggers

Emotional triggers that go unacknowledged remain in your life, like hidden landmines, lying dormant until something or someone steps on them and causes an explosion of feelings. These moments can seemingly come out of nowhere, but they

are deeply embedded in our psyche and are often linked to past experiences and unresolved emotions. Feeling criticized, rejected, or ignored are common triggers that can provoke a strong emotional response. When you feel that your feelings or values are being overlooked, it's easy to get flooded with feelings of inadequacy and anger. These reactions might seem out of proportion, but they're rooted in past experiences where similar situations shaped your frame of mind.

A quick self-assessment exercise can help you begin to understand your unique emotional triggers. This is a great time to invest in a journal, giving you space to document your experiences, insights, and reflections during your growth process. Your journal can be as simple as a spiral notebook or as fancy as a hardback pre-printed journal with various prompts. Once you have a notebook or personal log, find a quiet space where you can reflect. Here are a few prompts to get you started:

1. Recall a recent instance where you felt an intense emotional response. What was happening, and who was involved?
2. Think about a time when you felt unexpectedly overwhelmed by a feeling. What occurred right before this, and how was your body reacting?
3. Reflect on a situation where you suppressed your feelings instead of expressing them. What stopped you from sharing, and how did it affect you afterward?

Journaling is an opportunity to unload your thoughts without judgment. This exercise is meant to bring your attention to patterns you might not have consciously acknowledged. When you're reflecting on past experiences and responses, it's helpful to have a baseline knowledge of some common emotional triggers:

1. Feeling Unappreciated
2. Being Misunderstood
3. Encountering Conflict
4. Facing Criticism
5. Experiencing Loss of Control

This list can act as your guide to deeply comprehending your emotional reactions. The roots of these triggers lie within our brains' biological and psychological framework. A small almond-shaped cluster of nuclei located in the temporal lobe called the amygdala plays a significant role in processing emotions. Often referred to as the brain's emotional hub, it acts swiftly, sounding alarms when it perceives a threat, real or imagined. This can lead to an "amygdala hijack," where rational thinking is bypassed and emotions take over. Coined by psychologist Daniel Goleman, this term captures the essence of how our brain can react disproportionately to stimuli based on past experiences and learned responses (Guy-Evans 2023).

Understanding this process can empower you to manage your emotional reactions more rationally. When you feel triggered, your body might react with a rapid heartbeat, shallow breathing, or a rush of adrenaline. These are classic fight-or-flight responses; recognizing them is the first step to regaining control. When you're feeling yourself entering fight-or-flight mode, controlled breathing can soothe your busy mind. When you sense a trigger, try to pause and take a few deep, slow breaths, focusing on the rhythm of your breathing to calm your nervous system. Grounding is another technique that involves bringing your awareness to the present moment. To ground yourself during an intense emotional response, take a moment to look around you and notice the colors, textures, and sounds. This can help anchor you and reduce the power of the emotional surge.

Incorporating these tools into your daily life takes practice, but they can become second nature over time. You'll start to notice patterns and triggers that have been quietly affecting you. **This awareness is the foundation for change, enabling you to respond rather than react.**

The Science Behind Emotional Responses

There are several processes occurring within our bodies when our emotions flare up. The nervous system has a way of gearing up like a well-oiled fighting machine when we face stress or danger. This is the fight-or-flight response at work, a survival mechanism that dates back to our earliest ancestors. When triggered, your heart races, muscles tense, and senses sharpen. This is prompted by the hormones cortisol and adrenaline that prepare you to confront or flee the threat. This process is a physiological marvel that served us well when we were exposed to the elements of the world. In the modern world, the threats we experience look a bit different, and they might be as simple as an upcoming presentation or a difficult conversation. While these aren't life-threatening, our bodies don't differentiate, leading to the same intense physical reactions.

Childhood trauma can leave a lasting imprint on how we manage emotions. When the brain is still developing, traumatic incidents can alter its very structure, leaving individuals more prone to emotional dysregulation. This can manifest in adulthood as intense emotional responses that seem uncoordinated with the reality of the situation. Unresolved childhood wounds are often the hidden reason behind those disagreements that spiral into a full-blown argument. The amygdala, responsible for processing emotions, becomes hyper alert to perceived threats, leading to overreactions. These responses often reflect a time when

emotional neglect or abuse taught the developing brain to remain on high alert. In a traumatized individual, this heightened state becomes the new norm, making emotional regulation a challenging feat.

Managing your responses and avoiding emotion-driven consequences requires a sense of emotional intelligence. We'll review the details of building emotional intelligence at a later time, but it generally starts with being aware of your emotions and evolves into mastering them with skill and empathy. Self-awareness enables you to recognize your emotions as they arise, naming them and acknowledging their root. Conversely, self-regulation is about keeping those emotions in check, preventing them from dictating your actions. Empathy completes the trio, making it easier for you to relate to others' emotions and respond with care. Together, these components make up a framework that shifts emotional chaos into clarity.

Cultivating emotional intelligence starts with mindfulness. Being mindful invites you to be present with your emotions without judgment so you can observe rather than react. Here's a quick mindfulness exercise to get you started:

1. Find a quiet spot, close your eyes, and focus on your breath.
2. Acknowledge thoughts and feelings gently as they surface.
3. Visualize your strong emotions drifting away like clouds in the sky.

This exercise is simple, but it creates emotional awareness over time. Mindfulness is a power that enables you to manage your emotions from within. For an approach that uses your journal for

reflection, take a moment at the end of each day to review your emotional highs and lows by reviewing the following questions:

1. What triggered your intense emotional responses?
2. How did you react to your emotional highs and lows?
3. Did your reactions serve you well?

Reflecting on your own reactions and patterns builds your self-regulation skills while you learn from each experience and adjust your responses accordingly.

Emotional responses are complex and deeply rooted. A traumatized person may be called "dramatic" or "overly emotional," but each reaction is shaped by past experiences and the physiological processes within our bodies. Recognizing these mechanisms and using them to develop our emotional intelligence can allow us to better manage the unpredictability of our emotions, ultimately leading to a more balanced and fulfilling life.

Recognizing Patterns of Dysfunction

We all have patterns in our behavior, some of which are deeply ingrained in our psyche. These patterns can often be traced back to unresolved trauma from childhood, influencing the way we interact with the world around us. You might notice you have a tendency to withdraw when conflict arises in a relationship, as you prefer to avoid confrontation rather than face it head-on. Maybe there's a recurring theme of self-sabotage, where you find yourself procrastinating on projects that matter or ending relationships before they truly begin. These behaviors can be frustrating, but they're often mechanisms developed in response to past hurts and unmet needs.

The origins of self-destructive patterns can usually be found in our early interactions with caregivers and the environment we grew up in. Attachment theory is a psychological model that describes the dynamics of long-term relationships, offering insight into how these early bonds shape adult behavior. If you experienced a secure attachment with your caregivers and your needs were consistently met, you likely developed a positive view of yourself and others. If your early attachments were insecure due to neglect or inconsistency, you're more likely to have grown into an adult who struggles with trust or intimacy. This manifests in various attachment styles: anxious, avoidant, or disorganized. Each of these comes with its own challenges that impact how we connect with others.

Recognizing dysfunctional patterns is the first step toward making change. Developing your Emotional intelligence (EQ) requires a willingness to look inward and examine your behaviors with a critical eye. Your journal can be handy during this process; as you go through your day, note down any situations that trigger strong emotional reactions or cause you to behave in ways you're not proud of. Use this opportunity to answer the following questions:

1. What were the circumstances of this behavior?
2. How did you feel while you were acting out?
3. What thoughts or beliefs surfaced in the moment that may have influenced your reaction?
4. How did your response impact the situation or the people involved?
5. What alternative way of responding may have led to a more positive outcome?

Over time, your reflections may reveal patterns that offer clues to the underlying issues at play. When certain behaviors keep recurring, unconscious beliefs may be driving them. Your goal is to determine whether these beliefs are rooted in reality or are remnants of a past that no longer serve you.

Once you've identified these patterns, it's time to determine how to change them. One effective approach is cognitive restructuring, a technique used in cognitive behavioral therapy to challenge and alter negative thought patterns. The process looks like this:

1. Identify a recurring negative thought, like "I'm not good enough."
2. Examine the evidence for and against this negative thought.
3. Determine whether there is a more balanced perspective you can adopt.
4. Reframe the thought into something more positive and constructive, like "I am learning, and that's enough."

It may not come naturally at first, but with practice, this technique can help shift your mindset and behavior in a more positive direction. Breaking free from ingrained patterns of negativity takes time and effort, but it's a rewarding endeavor. **Growth is gradual and requires a bit of patience. Change doesn't happen overnight, and setbacks are a natural part of growth.** No matter how slow it may feel at the time, each step forward brings you closer to healing past wounds and creating a more fulfilling present.

"The journey of a thousand miles begins with one step"

— **Lao Tzu Philosopher**

The Role of Memory in Emotional Turmoil

Do you ever wonder why a whiff of a certain smell can suddenly teleport you back to a childhood memory or how a particular song can evoke emotions from events that happened years ago? Our memories are powerful, and they shape the way we respond to the world around us. Even unacknowledged memories influence our current emotional states. The brain uses both explicit and implicit memory to reflect on previously lived experiences. We can consciously recall explicit memories, like a birthday party or a family trip. Implicit memories, on the other hand, are more elusive, often affecting our behavior without us even realizing it. They can include the skills we've learned or the emotional responses we've developed over time. Implicit memories often drive our emotional reactions, especially when we're unaware of their origins.

Repressed memories can make memory recall even more complex. Memories that are repressed have been pushed out of our conscious awareness because they are too painful or upsetting to confront. These can resurface unexpectedly, triggered by a seemingly innocuous event. A conversation about loss might bring back the emotional weight of a long-forgotten family tragedy, or a particular location can stir up emotions tied to an event you thought you'd moved past. When these repressed memories come back to you, they can destabilize your emotional health, impact your sense of self, and intensify your interactions with others. A sudden flood of emotions is likely to leave you feeling unmoored and uncertain about how to process or integrate these old wounds into your current life.

To manage emotional turmoil, your memories should be engaged with in a way that promotes understanding and healing. **Guided imagery exercises can provide a safe space to explore**

these past experiences. These practices can be done sitting in a comfortable chair, eyes closed, as you imagine walking through a memory as an observer rather than a participant. This technique lets you revisit past events with distance and perspective to avoid becoming overwhelmed. Journaling is also useful for memory exploration. Here's a helpful exercise:

1. Write about a memory that frequently comes to mind.
2. Describe what emotions this memory stirs up.
3. Explore how this memory may connect to your present life.

Making these considerations when analyzing your experiences can help you unravel the emotional connections that tie past feelings to current responses, offering insights that might not have been apparent before.

Working through difficult memories can be an intense process. If the exploration itself causes you to experience inner turmoil, you'd likely benefit from professional guidance. Therapists and psychiatrists are trained to create a supportive environment where you can safely reflect on your memories and their impact. They can help you uncover the links between your past and your present and offer techniques to manage the emotions that arise. Therapy is particularly beneficial when you're dealing with deeply buried memories that resurface unexpectedly, building a framework for you to process and integrate your experiences into a healthier emotional state. Despite what you may have been conditioned to believe, it's important to remind yourself that seeking therapy is not a sign of weakness but rather a proactive step toward understanding and healing.

Identifying Hidden Emotional Wounds

Hidden emotional wounds are the silent forces of our psyche, often manifesting in subtle ways that we might not associate with past trauma. These wounds can make their way into our everyday lives, coloring our perceptions and interactions with a lingering darkness. You might be actively carrying around chronic feelings of guilt or shame, letting it constantly weigh down your spirit. These feelings often arise without any apparent trigger and they sometimes disguise themselves as feelings of being inadequate or failing in your roles. **Unexplained anxiety or depressive symptoms can also be indicators of hidden emotional wounds, presenting as a general sense of unease or a persistent gray cloud that obscures joy**. Many people learn to live with these feelings and never realize that they are echoing unresolved experiences from the past.

Hidden wounds are constantly impacting your self-perception and relationships. Your repressed experiences distort the lens through which you see yourself, often leading to a negative self-concept. Someone who internalizes guilt from past events might see themselves as inherently flawed and unworthy of love or success. This distorted self-image puts a filter over how you interpret the actions and words of others. These wounds can erode trust and intimacy in relationships, as you might expect rejection or betrayal, even when none is present. Think of the last time a partner or friend sent a delayed text, causing spiraling thoughts of abandonment when, in reality, they were simply busy. These assumptions are rooted in past hurt, and they can create barriers and misunderstandings that make it difficult to forge deep, meaningful connections.

Uncovering your hidden pain requires introspection and a willingness to examine your emotional history. Reflective exercises can be instrumental in this process. When you can set aside time in a quiet space, free from distractions, begin to consider moments when you felt disproportionately upset or anxious, asking yourself what memories or emotions these situations evoke. Then, use your journal to document these reflections, tracing your feelings back to their origins. This exercise is designed to help you understand how your past influences your present.

Healing psychological scars involves acknowledgment and active steps toward emotional repair. Compassion-focused therapy provides an approach centered on fostering kindness toward oneself. It teaches you to counteract self-criticism with nurturing thoughts, supporting an internal dialogue that is encouraging rather than punitive (Swee et al. 2024). Practicing self-compassion shifts the way you relate to yourself, replacing harsh judgments with understanding and care. This shift in perspective is liberating and essential for healing. **Forgiveness, both of yourself and others, is another significant part of healing from traumatizing experiences.** You don't have to make excuses for past wrongs, but releasing the hold they have over you frees you from the chains of resentment and guilt.

The healing process is gradual, and it might involve seeking help when you need it. As you gear up to learn more, make sure you've surrounded yourself with supportive people who understand and respect your journey. Each time you acknowledge and vow to heal a hidden wound, you take a step toward a future where you are no longer defined by past trauma. You'll stand empowered and have a clear understanding of who you are and what you deserve in life. This path may be challenging, but it

leads to a place of greater self-awareness and emotional freedom so you can build relationships grounded in trust and authenticity. In the next chapter, we'll review a few exercises and strategies that take you a few steps closer to emotional freedom by reflecting on childlike perspectives within you.

Chapter 2

Liberating Your Inner Child

Reflect on the last time you felt completely free. Maybe you were racing your bike down a hill with the wind in your hair or building a fort out of blankets and cushions. These moments capture the essence of our inner child, a part of us that remains untouched by the challenges of adult life. Your inner child embodies innocence, curiosity, and pure joy, but it's also where your earliest pains and unmet needs reside. Connecting with this aspect of yourself is not easy, but it's an important part of healing. Your inner child allows you to address the root of emotional pain and rediscover your capacity for wonder and joy, like meeting an old friend who knows you better than anyone else.

Meeting the Child Within You

Meeting your inner child starts with a simple meditation designed to bridge the gap between your past and present self. Here's a quick exercise to get you started:

1. **Preparation:** Find a quiet space where you can sit comfortably without distractions. Close your eyes and take a few deep breaths, grounding yourself in the present moment.
2. **Visualization:** Imagine yourself as a child, perhaps five or six years old, full of life and curiosity. Picture this child playing in a safe, beautiful place.
3. **Observation:** Notice the child's demeanor, expressions, and actions.
4. **Connection:** Gently introduce yourself and convey a sense of love and safety.
5. **Exploration:** As you sit together, allow any emotions or thoughts to surface without judgment.

This meditation gives you a space to be present and offer yourself love while letting your inner child know they are seen and valued. As you move through this process, you might encounter resistance. It's not uncommon to feel a sense of fear or vulnerability when reconnecting with past experiences, especially if they're painful. You might find yourself reluctant to revisit specific memories and worried about the emotions they could stir up. These feelings are a natural protective mechanism developed over time to shield yourself from pain, but you shouldn't let them hold back your healing. These memories are just echoes of the past, and they no longer define your present unless you allow them to. Allow yourself to feel uneasy; this is part of the healing process, and acknowledging your emotions is a significant step forward.

Many individuals use affirmations as a tool to work against resistance and encourage openness and acceptance. Simple phrases can be used with positive intention and consistency to ground you, reinforcing a sense of security as you explore these tender

areas of your psyche. When repeated, affirmations gradually dissolve the barriers keeping you from connecting with your inner child. These statements should apply to your personal situation, but I've provided a few to get you started:

1. I release my fear of uncovering past wounds, and I trust my ability to heal.
2. I welcome my emotions with compassion and curiosity, knowing they will guide me where I need to go.
3. It is safe for me to explore my past, and I do it with love and patience.
4. I embrace discomfort as a sign of growth and transformation.
5. My inner child deserves to be seen, heard, and nurtured.

Don't forget to take a few moments each day to write about your thoughts and feelings. Let the following prompts guide your reflection while you jot down a few notes about your inner child work:

1. What memories arise when you think of your childhood?
2. What emotions do your most prominent memories stir up?
3. When do you remember feeling most misunderstood as a child?
4. In what ways do you seek comfort, validation, or reassurance in similar ways that you did as a child?
5. What did you need from the adults around you that you didn't receive?

When you put pen to paper, you give voice to the parts of yourself that have been silent for too long, opening an inner dialogue

that can lead to growth. These meditative and reflective practices can be revisited whenever you feel the need to connect with your inner child or enter a space of healing and self-compassion.

Healing Through Play: Embracing Childlike Wonder

As adults, we're often conditioned to think that "playing" is an activity that is only allowed for children. In reality, mindful efforts to play throughout the day can support emotional healing and offer a reprieve from the stress and anxiety that accompany adult life. Play is a therapeutic technique that can dissolve emotional barriers and facilitate a deeper connection with oneself. Studies have shown that engaging in playful activities can significantly reduce stress and anxiety, giving individuals a mental reset that enables clearer thinking and emotional resilience (Pietrangelo 2019). Play therapy has long been used with children to help them express and process their emotions in a safe and non-verbal way, but adults can also benefit from these techniques, reconnecting with the carefree spirit that often lies dormant within.

When you're looking to integrate play into your life, consider activities that reignite the innocent energy of childhood. Adults commonly use building blocks or LEGO to engage their imagination, solve problems, and get lost in the moment. These activities are designed to evoke creativity and relaxation. Imaginative role-play, like acting out a scene from your favorite movie or pretending to be an explorer in your own backyard, gives you a space to step outside of yourself and experience the world through a different lens. This practice can be freeing, allowing you to experiment with different aspects of your personality in a safe and playful environment conducive to healing.

Structured play activities can address specific emotional issues, such as fear or anger. This may look like reenacting a situation that usually triggers fear, but this time, giving yourself the power to change the outcome. Through imaginative play, you can explore different responses, practice new coping strategies, and rewrite the narrative to empower your perspective. Using play to express anger can give you a much-needed outlet for pent-up emotions that converts them into energy to be redirected positively. Engaging in play that mirrors real-life challenges supports a natural healing environment without the pressure of formal therapy.

There are plenty of playful exercises that can spark joy and introspection. Let's explore a few:

1. **Building with Blocks or LEGO:** Set up a space where you can create without restrictions and build something that reflects your current mood or dreams for the future.
2. **Imaginative Role-Play:** Choose a character or scenario you'd like to explore and act it out with friends, family, or on your own. Take note of how it feels to step into this new role.
3. **Dancing to Childhood Songs:** Create a playlist of songs that remind you of happy times. Dance freely and let the rhythm guide you.
4. **Creating a Collage of Memories:** Collect images that represent joyful moments or aspirations. Arrange them on a board or paper to create a visual story of happiness and hope.

Engaging in playful activities may feel a bit funny at first, but it's a way to connect with a part of yourself that knows how to find

joy in the simplest of things. When you allow yourself to play without judgment, your mind and heart open up and invite transformation into your life.

Inner Child Dialogues: Conversations for Healing

Think back to the younger version of yourself who used to believe in magic and hold dreams untouched by the weight of reality. Holding a dialogue with your inner child is possible when you open a line of communication with this part of yourself. This conversation is likely to uncover hidden emotions and unmet needs. Strategic mindfulness lets you speak directly to the inner child so repressed feelings and desires can surface. Throughout your discussions with your inner child, you may find yourself unlocking parts of your psyche that have long been dormant.

Initiating dialogues with your inner child can be a simple process that looks similar to this (Ward and Ward 2024):

1. Find a quiet space where you feel comfortable and undisturbed.
2. Hold an object that connects you to your childhood, like a photograph or a favorite toy, or reflect on a favorable memory.
3. Set an intention to listen with empathy and respond with kindness, supporting a safe space for your inner child to express themself freely.
4. Close your eyes and visualize the inner child sitting across from you. Picture their face, their expression, and their body language.
5. Gently ask questions to encourage dialogue, like "What are you feeling right now?" and "What do you need from me?"

6. Let these questions guide the conversation, and listen patiently for the answers.

You shouldn't feel like you're forcing a response; instead, simply remain open to whatever arises. It may feel strange at first, but these conversations can reveal surprising insights into your emotional world over time.

Maintaining a safe emotional space is a necessity for these dialogues. Regardless of your situation, a few adaptations can contribute to a place where the inner child feels at ease. Consider implementing a few fresh flowers in your meditating space or include some soft pillows to lean on while you converse. Even if your physical space doesn't align with your comfort goals, visualizing such an environment can help you relax and trust the process.

The relationship you have with your inner child should be built based on understanding and acceptance. Asking questions like "What made you laugh today?" or "What scared you?" can help you tap into emotions often buried under the weight of adult responsibilities. These questions encourage your inner child to speak openly without judgment or fear of reprimand.

There are plenty of therapeutic benefits to engaging with your child within. Your conversations are likely to give you a sense of self-awareness so you can recognize patterns and emotions that influence your current behavior. You may experience emotional breakthroughs or moments when a long-held misunderstanding suddenly makes sense. Some realize that the anger they feel in certain situations is rooted in a childhood experience of being unheard. It's possible to uncover a deep-seated longing for approval that has shaped your interactions with others. These

realizations can be incredibly freeing, illuminating a gentle and uplifting path to healing.

Engaging in inner child dialogues isn't always smooth sailing. You may encounter overwhelming emotions or memories that feel too intense to face. When this happens, it can be helpful to have strategies in place that keep you grounded. We'll touch on many of these techniques later; deep breathing exercises, for example, can help calm your mind, while grounding techniques can bring you back to the present moment. If you find yourself struggling, it's okay to take a break and return to the conversation when you feel ready. Healing is a process that unfolds in its own time.

Transformative Storytelling: Rewriting Your Past

Though you can't change what's already happened, it's possible to rewrite your own past by taking the stories that have shaped you and giving them a new meaning. This process requires taking the narrative of your life and reshaping it in a way that empowers you rather than hinders you (The Dulwich Centre 2025). Narrative therapy suggests that by altering our personal stories, we can transform how we perceive past events and, in turn, change our emotional responses to them (Schroeder 2025). **When you're the editor of your own life story, you can decide which parts to focus on and which to let go.** This is particularly healing for those of us who have experienced trauma, allowing us to move beyond the role of victim and step into a place of agency and self-compassion.

Writing a letter to your past self is a straightforward way to start crafting a new narrative. This exercise can be incredibly cathartic. Here's a quick guide for beginning this process:

1. Picture yourself at a challenging moment in your life.
2. Address that version of you with understanding and love.
3. Acknowledge the emotions and struggles you faced, and offer the wisdom and support you wish you had at that time.
4. Consider what you would say to comfort your younger self and how you could reframe the difficulties you went through to highlight resilience and growth.

I'm not asking you to change the facts, but altering the lens through which you view them and showing compassion to your past self makes it easier to heal old wounds and develop a kinder relationship with your present self.

Another storytelling exercise could involve crafting a story where your inner child is the hero so you can reimagine past experiences from a perspective of strength and courage. Here's what it may look like:

1. Think about a time when you felt small or powerless.
2. Rewrite the scene emphasizing the bravery it took to endure instead of focusing on the hopelessness.
3. Highlight each moment of triumph, however small it may seem.

When you celebrate your resilience during difficult times, you empower your inner child and acknowledge their role in your survival and growth.

Journaling can heighten the effectiveness of this process. When you're reflecting on stories and using perspective to rewrite your past, use the following prompts to explore alternative life scenarios:

1. What if things had been different?
2. How did I grow from this experience?
3. What did this moment offer me that I wouldn't have had otherwise?
4. How did I support myself during this experience?
5. How did my resilience shape who I am currently?

Reflecting on the positive aspects of stressful or sad memories opens new possibilities for personal growth. As you journal or mentally reflect, your imagination should guide your expression. The exploration of "what could have been" can result in powerful insights that show you new perspectives and emotional clarity.

Real-life stories of emotional growth through narrative include valuable lessons for those on their own healing journeys. Jennifer Fox, a documentary filmmaker, used storytelling to confront her own childhood trauma. Her film, *The Tale*, is a narrative exploration of her own experiences with abuse. This expression allowed Fox to process and reframe her past, shifting her perspective from victimhood to empowerment (Democracy Now! 2025). Testimonials like these remind us of the potential each of us has to rewrite our stories and turn past struggles into sources of strength.

Storytelling is a powerful resource for change and healing. Emotional expression through art and writing invites you to become an active participant in your own life, reclaim the narrative, and make it your own. Engage with these exercises with a

goal of progress rather than perfection. Give yourself room to explore, imagine, and grow through the stories you tell.

As we progress into the next chapter, we will explore how to identify and break free from patterns of dysfunction that constantly impact your daily life.

Chapter 3

Breaking Free from Dysfunctional Patterns

Take a moment to reflect on the first serious relationship you ever had. For many of us, this connection was filled with promise and excitement until patterns that seemed all too familiar began arising. You may have felt an overwhelming fear of being left or a constant need to check in with your partner to feel secure. These behaviors can feel frustrating and puzzling, especially when they seem to appear out of nowhere. These responses often have their roots in our early experiences and challenges in childhood that left lingering emotional scars. Knowing how these early experiences impact our adult relationships can give struggling individuals a roadmap to healthier connections.

Becoming Acquainted with Trauma-Based Patterns

Whether you've experienced neglect, emotional maltreatment, or other adversities, childhood trauma can leave lasting imprints on how you interact with others. Those who have experienced **neglect** might find themselves constantly seeking validation in

their relationships, driven by a need to fill a void left by those unmet needs from childhood. This can manifest as over-dependence on partners as they look to them to provide the emotional security that wasn't received as a child. Those suffering from experiences related to **abandonment** might subconsciously seek out emotionally unavailable partners, recreating a dynamic where you feel perpetually on edge and fearing the next time they might walk away.

Recognizing trauma-based relational patterns is the first step in breaking free from them. As you engage in activities that connect with a deeper version of yourself or your inner child, you might notice that you avoid intimacy, keeping others at arm's length due to a fear of vulnerability. This could be a defense mechanism developed early on to protect yourself from getting hurt. While it may have served a purpose back then, using this mechanism in your adult life can lead to loneliness and isolation. Similarly, constantly needing reassurance from your partner can lead to a dynamic where you feel dependent on their approval, creating power imbalances that strain the relationship. When one partner holds the reins of emotional validation, it can leave the other feeling less empowered, producing resentment and dissatisfaction over time.

Unresolved childhood trauma can seep into every interaction and contribute to dysfunctional dynamics that are hard to break. A relationship with power imbalances often includes one partner dominating decision-making or emotional expression while the other may feel sidelined or unheard. These disparities can create a cycle of unmet needs, where neither partner feels fully satisfied or understood. This interplay slowly erodes trust and connection, making it difficult to build a foundation for a supportive partnership.

You may find that relational self-assessment questionnaires reveal hidden qualities about your own personal relationship patterns. These tools are designed to give you valuable insights into your behaviors and tendencies, highlighting areas that might be influenced by past trauma. This can be conducted within your reflection journal to help you explore your relational experiences. Here are a few related prompts that you can use to get started:

1. How do you typically respond to conflicts in relationships (i.e., withdrawing, becoming defensive, seeking resolution)?
2. How comfortable do you feel with expressing your needs or setting boundaries?
3. Do you find yourself drawn to certain types of people? If so, why do you think that is?
4. When faced with emotional discomfort in a relationship, how do you usually cope?
5. Can you identify any connections between these patterns and your early experiences?

Guided introspection can illuminate aspects of your relational dynamics that you might not have been aware of before so you can make efforts to break the cycle and forge healthier connections. You might try setting aside time each week to revisit these questions, noting any new insights or shifts in perspective. This reflection is the first step to fundamentally transforming your relational dynamics.

Unpacking Self-Sabotage: Why We Hurt Ourselves

Traumatized individuals often find themselves shutting down when things are going well or doing anything but completing a goal they had set for themselves. This is the work of self-sabotage,

an act of undermining one's own success. If you're affected by self-sabotage, you likely feel like there's an invisible force holding you back, even when you know what you want. At its core, self-sabotage is driven by internalized negative beliefs, many of which take root in childhood experiences (French 2023). **If you were told you weren't good enough or that success was out of your reach, these messages can be buried deep into your subconscious, creating a feedback loop that makes failure feel inevitable.** The cycle of negativity makes it difficult to accept success, as the fear of potential failure always lurks in the background.

Common forms of self-sabotage manifest in various behaviors that chip away at personal success and happiness. **Procrastination** is a common form of self-sabotage that involves putting off tasks that bring you closer to your goals, often replaced by less important activities. If you ever find yourself cleaning the house instead of working on an important presentation that's due, you've been a victim of procrastination. **Self-criticism** is another feature of self-sabotage, and it occurs when you undermine your achievements by focusing on perceived shortcomings. It may look like brushing off a compliment by saying, "It was nothing," or fixating on minor mistakes rather than celebrating your larger successes. These behaviors create a cycle of inaction and self-doubt, which can be challenging to let go of.

The emotional drivers behind self-sabotage often boil down to fear and guilt. Fear of success can sometimes be as paralyzing as fear of failure. With success comes change, and the unknown is inherently intimidating. You might find yourself worrying about what could happen if you're not able to maintain your success or how you'd react if it leads to more pressure or scrutiny. It's not uncommon for these fears to keep you rooted in place, even when

you consciously desire progress. Guilt and unworthiness may also be significant factors that are holding you back. Past experiences might have left you feeling undeserving of success, making it difficult to pursue your goals confidently. This feeling can lead to self-punishing behaviors, where you unconsciously sabotage good things to affirm these negative beliefs.

Breaking free from self-sabotage requires a substantial shift in mindset that moves from limiting beliefs to those that encourage growth. When you're looking to develop a growth mindset, it can be helpful to use positive affirmations, starting each day with statements that challenge your inner critic. Here are a few that might help you get started:

1. I am capable of achieving my goals.
2. I deserve success and happiness.
3. I release old patterns that no longer serve me, and I embrace my successes.
4. Mistakes are opportunities for growth, and I welcome the lessons they bring.
5. Seeing myself succeed and do well brings me joy.

When repeated consistently, positive affirmations can gradually rewire your brain to approach challenges with optimism instead of fear. When you're looking for opportunities to grow, make sure you're setting realistic goals, making success seem possible rather than unattainable. You don't have to take on a massive project all at once; breaking it into smaller, manageable tasks makes the goal more achievable and encouraging. Your mindset can make the process less daunting, allowing for small victories that boost confidence and motivation.

Practical exercises can help you to reinforce the impact of these strategies on your mindset. Here are a few steps you can take to

make sure you're taking action in your pursuit of undoing self-sabotage:

1. Create a list of goals and break each one into actionable steps.
2. Set deadlines for each step and hold yourself accountable, perhaps by sharing them with a trusted friend or mentor.
3. Celebrate each milestone, regardless of how small, to reinforce positive progress.
4. Take time to reflect on your achievements regularly, focusing on what went well and how you overcame obstacles.

This reflection is a short and quick way to solidify new patterns, shifting acts of self-sabotage into self-support. The goal is to replace the narrative of fear and inadequacy with one of courage and capability.

Boundary Setting: Protecting Your Emotional Space

Those who have experienced hardships in their childhood often feel overwhelmed by someone else's demands. Some of us have felt burdened by a friend who constantly calls at all hours or a colleague who assumes we'll cover their workload. These instances can feel like subtle invasions into your emotional space. This is where personal boundaries are required, defining where you end and where others begin. Personal boundaries are necessary for maintaining healthy relationships and ensuring self-care (Lauren 2022). **Healthy boundaries are firm yet flexible so you feel comfortable interacting with others without losing yourself in the process**. On the other hand,

unhealthy boundaries might be too rigid or too porous, leading to strained relationships and emotional burnout.

Setting boundaries can feel incredibly intimidating, especially if you've struggled with social rules and expectations in the past. The fear of rejection or conflict often looms and makes it hard to assert your needs. You might worry that standing up for yourself will push others away or lead to confrontation. This fear is understandable, especially if asserting yourself in the past has led to negative outcomes. Traumatic experiences can leave you convinced that your needs are secondary or even invisible, making the prospect of setting boundaries feel daunting. If setting boundaries feels like stepping into a role you're unaccustomed to playing, it's likely a sign that this is an even more important step to take toward reclaiming your emotional space and building healthier relationships.

To help manage the challenges of boundary setting, it might be helpful to have a few practical techniques to help you establish and maintain boundaries. Some individuals even use scripts when communicating their needs. These scripts can be rehearsed and adapted to fit various situations, offering a framework that makes it easier to voice your boundaries clearly. You can tailor these scripts to apply to your own situation or emotional needs, but they may look something like this:

1. **Setting Boundaries with a Friend:** I really value our friendship, but I need to take some time for myself right now. This is just something I need for my well-being.
2. **Declining Extra Work:** I appreciate the opportunity, but I won't be able to take on extra tasks at the moment. I want to be able to give my best efforts to what I'm currently working on.

3. **Addressing Unwanted Advice:** I know you mean well, but I'm making decisions based on what feels right for me. I'd appreciate your support even if you don't fully agree.
4. **Managing Difficult Conversations in a Relationship:** I need some space to process my feelings before we continue this conversation. I want to communicate openly, but I also need to feel emotionally ready to do so.
5. **Handling a Pushy Acquaintance:** I'm not comfortable discussing that topic, but I'd love to discuss something else. Let's focus on [alternative topic].

Role-playing exercises can also be beneficial. You might practice asserting your boundaries with a trusted friend or in front of a mirror to build confidence or help you anticipate potential responses and refine your approach.

Boundaries often bring the immediate relief of not being overburdened, but their benefits stretch even further. Emotional limits contribute significantly to your well-being, supporting increased self-respect and autonomy. When you set boundaries, you're telling yourself and others that your needs and feelings matter. This boosts self-esteem and reinforces your sense of self-worth. In relationships, boundaries encourage mutual respect and understanding, creating a space where both parties feel heard and valued. When partners understand and respect each other's limits, conflicts are less frequent and relationships become more fulfilling and supportive.

Boundaries act as a protective barrier that shields you from emotional exhaustion and resentment. When you define what is acceptable and what isn't, you prevent others from draining your energy or taking advantage of your kindness. This protection is

particularly important if you tend to prioritize others' needs over your own. Establishing clear boundaries means that you have control over your emotional needs being met so you can nurture yourself without guilt or anxiety. Over time, you'll become more comfortable with setting and maintaining boundaries. You'll find that they eventually become an integral part of your interactions, improving your relationships and overall quality of life.

The Cycle of Codependency: Breaking Free

A codependent relationship often includes two people who are so intertwined that they struggle to see where one ends and the other begins. **Codependency occurs when you prioritize someone else's needs above your own to the point where your well-being becomes secondary.** It's characterized by difficulty in recognizing and expressing your personal feelings because you're so focused on the other person's emotions and needs (Evolve Therapy 2023). This might mean staying late at work to help a colleague even when you're exhausted or ignoring your own stress to console a friend. While these actions can seem selfless or compassionate, they sometimes stem from a deep and unhealthy compulsion to serve others at the expense of self-care.

The core of codependency is frequently traced back to childhood, where family dynamics determine how you interact with others. If you grew up in an environment where roles were blurred, or responsibilities were misplaced due to unclear boundaries, you might have learned to associate love with caretaking. You may have found yourself stepping into an adult role early on by caring for siblings or emotionally supporting a parent. This can create a pattern where you seek validation through helping others or believe that your worth is tied to

your ability to care for and please those around you. A dynamic like this can quickly evolve into codependency, where your identity becomes entwined with the needs and happiness of others.

Breaking free from codependent patterns in your relationship starts with recognizing them. You might choose to use your journal to reflect on your relationship dynamics. The following prompts can guide this assessment:

1. Do you often feel responsible for other people's feelings?
2. Are you uncomfortable when others are upset with you, even when you haven't done anything wrong?
3. Do you find it hard to say no, fearing that it might lead to conflict or rejection?

Saying yes to these questions is a common sign of codependency. Conducting regular self-assessments can help to highlight areas where you might be unconsciously sacrificing your own needs for those of others, presenting a clearer picture of your relational dynamics.

Breaking the cycle of codependency is not always easy, and it involves supporting your own independence and developing healthier relationship patterns. Some would recommend establishing self-care routines that stay completely separate from your partner's needs. This could mean dedicating a specific time each week just for yourself and engaging in activities that nurture your spirit and well-being. Self-care could look like anything, including taking a long walk, meditating, or reading a book. Relaxing and independent moments of self-care allow you to reconnect with your own needs and desires. To take this a step further, you could even seek individual therapy or join support groups for codependents. These spaces are a safe place to explore your feelings with

others who grant you guidance and support as you work toward more balanced relationships.

Engaging in therapy or support groups can help you develop a stronger sense of self that is separate from your relationships. A therapist may give you insights into the origins of your codependent behaviors and help you build strategies for change. These groups or professionals can encourage you to practice setting boundaries, say no when necessary, and express your feelings honestly. These practices may feel challenging at first, but they lead to a newfound sense of empowerment and autonomy. As you implement these changes, you'll likely notice a shift in your relationships. Your interactions might feel more reciprocal, with both parties contributing equally to the dynamic. The result is healthier and more fulfilling connections where your needs are valued just as much as those of others.

Breaking free from codependency uncovers an opportunity to rediscover yourself as an individual who is capable of standing on your own while still maintaining meaningful relationships. **Your worth isn't measured by how much you do for others but by your inherent value as a person.** This realization might not come immediately, but the rewards are abundant: a stronger sense of self, healthier relationships, and a more balanced life.

Building Healthy Attachment Styles

Your early years served as a blueprint of your future self, quietly shaping how you connect with others. Attachment styles are developed during childhood, and they constantly influence the way we relate to partners, friends, and even ourselves. Our earliest interactions with caregivers make their way deeply into our identity, even when we don't notice their effects. There are

four main attachment styles: secure, anxious, avoidant, and disorganized. Each one explains how we engage in relationships:

1. **Secure Attachment:** Often developed through consistent and loving care, this attachment form often results in a sense of trust and balance.
2. **Anxious Attachment:** Emerging from inconsistent caregiving, this style leads to clinginess and an intense fear of abandonment.
3. **Avoidant Attachment:** This attachment style may lead you to distance yourself emotionally, stemming from a history of unresponsive caregiving.
4. **Disorganized Attachment:** Confusion and fear often dictate interactions, typically a result of chaotic or neglectful childhood environments.

These attachment styles manifest in distinct ways that impact your relationships. If you lean toward an anxious attachment style, you're more likely to be constantly seeking reassurance from your partner, driven by a deep-seated fear of rejection. This often leads to a cycle of dependency that strains the relationship, as your need for validation might become overwhelming. Those with avoidant attachment may struggle to open up emotionally, creating a wall between themselves and their partners. Emotional withdrawal can lead to misunderstandings and an emotional gap that is hard to bridge. Disorganized attachment can lead to a tumultuous dynamic, where fear and confusion disrupt the flow of a healthy relationship and produce unpredictable emotional responses and conflict.

Transitioning from an unhealthy to a secure attachment style takes conscious effort and reflection. This process is easier when you examine your past attachment experi-

ences, reflecting on your early relationships with caregivers and how they might mirror your current interactions. Determining whether your needs were met consistently or if you found yourself questioning your worth are insights that can be used to understand how your attachment style took shape.

Developing a secure attachment style occurs when you practice having one. Focus on open communication, expressing your needs and feelings honestly and without fear. This behavior builds trust and contributes to a nurturing environment in your relationships. As you develop your emotional regulation skills, you'll learn to manage your feelings without becoming overwhelmed, making it even easier to direct your emotional responses in a way that supports a healthy and open relationship.

Personal growth and relationship development are ongoing processes. Setting personal and relational goals can help you achieve attachment growth. If you struggle with anxiety in relationships, you would likely benefit from developing self-soothing techniques that reduce dependency on your partner for reassurance. If you suffer from patterns of avoidance, practice vulnerability by sharing your thoughts and feelings gradually. These goals should be realistic and tailored to your unique experiences and needs. Growth is a journey that includes every step along the way, and it's okay if your process looks different from someone else's. Every time you make an effort to understand and adjust your attachment style, you're a bit closer to healthier and more fulfilling relationships.

Building a secure attachment style is the surest way to maintain balanced, respectful, and emotionally fulfilling relationships. Your interactions should benefit you and leave you feeling safe, valued, and understood while you and your partner thrive both individually and together. Changing your emotional attachment style is

possible with patience and perseverance. Regardless of your past, you are capable of cultivating the relationships you've always desired. **Transitioning to a secure attachment style will change your relationships, but it will also give you an opportunity to transform yourself and offer a life where connection and love are rooted in mutual respect.**

With this chapter, you've taken a significant step toward understanding and reshaping your dysfunctional relational patterns. As we continue into the following chapter, we'll look into a few practical exercises that will guide you in releasing emotional baggage. Taking advantage of these actionable steps will inevitably lead to healthier interactions and personal growth.

Chapter 4

Practical Exercises for Emotional Release

When you have a few techniques and practices incorporated into your life, alone time can feel as supportive as sitting down with a trusted friend who is always ready to listen without judgment. Activities that offer you the space to express whatever's on your mind can unlock insights and emotions you didn't even know were there. Incorporating journaling practices, mindfulness, artistic expression, and breathwork into your daily routine will help you to unearth patterns, dissolve emotional blockages, and bring you greater clarity.

Writing as a Path to Emotional Clarity

Journaling is a prime example of a powerful tool for emotional processing and self-discovery. Writing down your feelings and memories can help you to make sense of complex feelings or experiences, like having a conversation with yourself where you feel comfortable exploring thoughts that might be too tangled or intense to articulate aloud. Writing down your thoughts organizes

them into a coherent narrative, which can be incredibly therapeutic and enlightening.

There is a well-established connection between expressive writing and emotional health. When you put pen to paper, you engage in a process of exploring and releasing deeply rooted emotions. Writing about stressful experiences has proven to improve both physical and psychological health (Baikie and Wilhelm 2018). Journaling can benefit your mental resilience while dealing with any stressor, such as handling a breakup or dealing with job stress. **If you maintain a focus on honesty and expression, writing can reduce symptoms of anxiety and depression while improving immune function.** Don't waste any time worrying about grammar or structure; allow yourself to release your thoughts in a judgment-free way.

To help you get started, I've provided a few guided journaling prompts designed to encourage deep reflection and emotional exploration:

1. Consider a recent situation that triggered strong emotions. Write about it in detail, exploring what thoughts and feelings it evoked and how you responded.
2. Write a letter to your past self. Imagine speaking to yourself at a difficult moment in your life, offering compassion and understanding.
3. Name one belief you hold about yourself that no longer serves you. Track where this belief originated.
4. Reflect on how you typically respond to stress or discomfort. Determine whether these coping mechanisms are helping or hindering your growth.
5. Think of a time when you silenced your emotions or

needs. Brainstorm how you can show up for yourself differently in the future.

These exercises are designed to cultivate a sense of self-compassion and offer a perspective on your growth and resilience over time. Different journaling techniques can cater to various needs and preferences. **Stream-of-consciousness writing** is a common approach that allows for uninterrupted emotional flow. This activity prompts you to write whatever comes to mind without stopping to edit or censor yourself. This is particularly freeing if you're looking to tap into subconscious thoughts and feelings. If you prefer a more structured or gradual approach, **gratitude journaling** might be a great option for you. This involves taking a few moments each day to jot down things you're grateful for, shifting your focus to the positive aspects of life and developing a mindset of appreciation and abundance. With time, this simple practice can completely reframe your perspective, making it easier to see the good amid the challenges.

Journaling produces the most benefits when done with regular practice. Consistently writing your thoughts or using prompts to reflect leads to enhanced emotional clarity and self-awareness. You only need to set aside a few minutes each day for journaling until it becomes a natural part of your routine, like brushing your teeth or having a coffee. If possible, it's ideal to choose a time when you're least likely to be interrupted so you can fully immerse yourself in the process. Once you've found what time works for you, stick to it. Your commitment to regular reflection is likely to produce surprising insights as patterns and themes emerge and guide you through the difficulties you're facing.

Mindfulness Practices to Ground Your Emotions

If you've ever wished you could hit the pause button on the chaos of life, I might have the answer for you: mindfulness. **Being mindful means being fully present without any judgment**. Practicing mindfulness allows you to move with purpose, aware of each moment as it unfolds. This will inevitably bring a sense of calm and balance, helping you manage stress and emotional ups and downs. When you practice mindfulness, you improve your self-awareness skills and notice thoughts and feelings as they arise (Mayo Clinic 2022). **Being aware creates space between stimulus and response so you have time to choose how you react rather than being swept away by impulsive reactions**. Over time, mindfulness becomes an instrument for emotional regulation, reducing the spontaneous reactions that often lead to regret or misunderstanding (Guendelman et al. 2023).

There are a variety of simple exercises that work to ground you in the present moment. Integrating mindfulness into your life can take as little as a few minutes. Let's explore a couple of these practices (Baker 2024):

Body Scan Meditation

1. Find a comfortable position, close your eyes, and take a few deep breaths.
2. Slowly bring your awareness to different parts of your body, starting from your toes and moving upward to the crown of your head.
3. Notice any sensations, tension, or areas of relaxation.

5-4-3-2-1 Technique

1. Find a quiet space and take a few deep breaths to center yourself.
2. Engage your senses by identifying five things you can see around you, four things you can touch, three things you can hear, two things you can smell, and one thing you can taste.
3. Allow yourself to fully experience each sensation and anchor yourself in the present moment.

These exercises help you connect with your physical self and provide a sense of calm and presence. Regularly engaging in these practices can completely shift the way you handle emotions. Consistency supports the creation of a habit of mindfulness while you learn to observe your thoughts and feelings without immediately reacting to them. With time, you'll develop better emotional control and the ability to pause and consider your response to a situation. Instead of snapping back when someone criticizes you, mindfulness gives you the space to process the comment and choose a more measured response. Mindful responses reduce the likelihood of impulsive reactions that escalate conflicts or exacerbate stress, giving you a chance at a more peaceful and balanced life.

Incorporating mindfulness into everyday activities can advance its impact. There are a few ways to do this:

1. **Mindful Eating:** Pay attention to the taste, texture, and aroma of each bite. Focus on the experience of eating while savoring each moment without distraction to enhance your appreciation of food and encourage a healthier relationship with eating.

2. **Mindful Walking:** As you walk, notice the sensation of your feet touching the ground, the rhythm of your steps, and the world around you. Observe the sights, sounds, and smells, immersing yourself fully in the experience.
3. **Mindful Listening:** When you're engaging in conversation, give your full attention to the speaker. Notice their tone, expressions, and words without planning your response in advance.

These practices are intended to remind you of the richness of the present, grounding you in the here and now. Being mindful supports a lifestyle that gives you emotional clarity in each moment. Committing to small and mindful actions promotes a more centered and intentional way of living and invites you to slow down, breathe, and appreciate the nuances of your day. Regardless of the demands of your busy schedule, mindfulness can turn each mundane task into an opportunity for reflection and presence. With time, you'll become more attuned to your emotions, managing their intensity with a newfound sense of resilience. This approach is simple, but it holds the potential to substantially improve your emotional well-being and overall quality of life.

Breathwork Techniques for Emotional Release

When you're in a stressful situation, your heart likely starts racing, your thoughts start swirling uncontrollably, and your body can't stop moving. Many people suffer from constant stress without the knowledge that just a few deep and intentional breaths can shift their chaos into calm. Breathwork is a powerful technique that is commonly used for emotional healing. Breathing practices are

rooted in the simple act of controlling your breath to influence your emotional and physical state. **Breathwork taps into the body's nervous system, regulating stress responses and promoting a sense of inner calm.** When you control your breathing, your parasympathetic nervous system becomes activated, counteracting the body's fight-or-flight response and reducing anxiety as a result (Khoddam 2022). Focusing on your breath slows everything down so you can give your emotions a space to be processed and released rather than suppressed.

There are a variety of common breathwork exercises designed to guide you toward emotional balance:

Box Breathing

1. Find a comfortable seat and inhale slowly through your nose for a count of four.
2. Hold your breath for another four counts, then exhale fully for four counts.
3. Finally, pause and hold your breath again for four counts before repeating the cycle until stress levels and emotions are stabilized.

Alternate Nostril Breathing

1. Close your right nostril with your thumb, inhaling deeply through your left nostril.
2. Close your left nostril with your ring finger and exhale through the right nostril.
3. Continue this pattern, alternating sides, for several minutes to harmonize the left and right hemispheres of the brain, promoting a sense of equilibrium.

4-7-8 Breathing

1. Find a relaxed position and place the tip of your tongue against the roof of your mouth, just behind your front teeth.
2. Inhale deeply through your nose for a count of four and hold it in for a count of seven, allowing your body to fully absorb the oxygen.
3. Exhale slowly through your mouth for a count of eight to release any tension.
4. Repeat the cycle for at least four rounds to activate the parasympathetic nervous system, reduce anxiety, and support relaxation.

Regular practice of breathwork can substantially enhance your emotional resilience and overall well-being. Mindful breathing practices can be used anytime to manage stress and emotional upheaval. Breathwork is another way to focus your attention on the present moment and away from the worries that produce emotional distress. Controlling your breathing grants you the strength to cope with life's challenges. Strategic breathing supports your emotional health, presenting a pathway to clarity and peace when emotions threaten to overwhelm you.

Integrating breathwork into your daily life is both simple and effective. Many choose to start their day with a brief morning breathing ritual to ground themselves. Before you even get out of bed, spending a few minutes focusing on your breath sets a calm and centered tone for the day ahead. You can also incorporate breathwork during work breaks to alleviate stress and recharge using a quiet space, even if it's just a few moments in the restroom or a walk outside. Having small,

intentional pauses during the day can make a significant difference in how you navigate the demands of daily life so you can approach tasks with a clearer mind and calmer disposition.

Breathwork gives you the power to influence your emotional state right at your desk, a comfy chair or bed. The value of this practice lies in its accessibility and adaptability; no special equipment or extensive time commitment is required. If you're at home, at work, or on the go, you can tap into the calming effects of breathwork anytime you need. **Your breath can be used as a bridge, connecting your mind to your body and allowing emotions to flow through you instead of getting stuck or bottled up.** With time, you'll develop a regular breathwork practice and find yourself more in tune with your emotions, better equipped to handle stressors, and ultimately, more at ease within yourself.

Meditation and Visualization for Emotional Freedom

Meditation is often perceived as a practice reserved for those with ample time and discipline. In reality, meditation is a flexible and accessible technique that gives anyone the space to sit quietly with their thoughts, letting the noise of the day fade into a gentle hum. Regardless of your physical surroundings, meditating offers a sanctuary for your mind and body to find calm. This is a practice of focusing inward to calm racing thoughts and ease tension, supporting a sense of peace that flows through your entire being. Meditation shields you from the chaos and gives your mind the chance to reset. **As you meditate, your body responds by releasing tension and promoting relaxation.** These qualities make meditating a valuable asset for emotional release and

clearing away the clutter that clouds judgment and amplifies stress.

Visualization takes meditation a step further by shifting negative emotions into positive energy. When you picture yourself in a place where you feel completely at ease, you replicate a sense of calmness that replaces anxiety or anger with tranquility. Find your happy place, whether it's a beach chair on a tropical island, a mountain cabin surrounded by nature or a zen garden by a babbling creek, your mind is a powerful place, and even simple mental imagery can shift your emotional state and provide a fresh perspective on challenging situations. Using your imagination, you can visualize a future where your goals are achieved to change your perspective and see things in a different light. Visualization empowers you to take advantage of the mind's creative potential and turn inner turmoil into a source of strength.

Guided meditation and visualization exercises have been known to reduce anxiety levels and promote a sense of emotional clarity (Beard 2025). Let's explore a few of these:

Loving-Kindness Meditation

1. Sit comfortably, close your eyes, and take a few deep breaths.
2. Focus on sending warm, loving thoughts to yourself, perhaps repeating phrases like, "May I be happy, may I be healthy, may I be at peace."
3. Gradually extend these wishes to others, such as friends, family, or even strangers, expanding the circle of compassion outward.

This exercise is designed to amplify feelings of self-love while strengthening your connection with others.

Peaceful Place Meditation

1. Picture a setting that evokes tranquility for you, like a quiet beach, a lush forest, or a cozy room.
2. Engage all your senses as you imagine being there, conjuring stimulations like the sound of waves, the smell of pine, and the warmth of sunlight.
3. Allow yourself to linger in this scene, absorbing its serenity.

This visualization provides you with mental refuge that you can return to whenever stress threatens to overwhelm you.

Light Visualization Meditation

1. Sit comfortably, close your eyes, and take a few deep breaths to calm your body.
2. Visualize a warm and radiant light above your head, glowing with a soothing energy.
3. Imagine this light slowly descending, entering through the top of your head and moving down through your body. Watch as it dissolves any negativity, tension, or heaviness, replacing it with calm and healing energy.
4. Let the light expand and surround you in a protective glow.

This visualization works to release emotional burdens and prompt a sense of inner peace and renewal.

These practices remind us that peace is always within reach, waiting to be tapped into when needed. When we have the time, we can take meditation a step further in an environment that supports calmness and clarity. A space that is conducive to meditation adds to the experience, making it more enjoyable and effective. To create this space, you might include calming music or nature sounds to aid relaxation, setting the mood for meditation. These auditory elements can contribute to your chosen mental landscape, deepening the sense of immersion. **Aromatherapy with essential oils can also enrich the practice.** Scents like lavender, chamomile, or sandalwood are often used for soothing purposes, and they can be misted using a diffuser to keep you grounded and center your mind. **Experiment with different combinations to find what resonates with you until you have created an environment that feels personal and restorative.**

Meditation and visualization techniques require consistency in order to have a long-term impact on your mental resilience. Committing to regularly practicing can produce meaningful changes in your emotional well-being. You only need to set aside a small amount of time each day for meditation, but it's important to treat it as a nonnegotiable part of your routine. With time, you're sure to notice a shift in how you handle stress and emotions that leaves you feeling more balanced and resilient.

Creative Expression: Art as a Healing Tool

Sometimes, emotional expression looks like doodling absentmindedly or perhaps splattering paint without a care for the mess. Art has the unique ability to express what words often can't. Art inherently encourages you to connect with your emotions on a deeper level in a safe and non-judgmental space.

Creative expression is often used to explore feelings and memories that might be too painful to articulate otherwise. Art therapy, in particular, has shown remarkable effectiveness in processing trauma (Kids First 2025). Painting, drawing, performing, or creating gives artists a chance to externalize their internal experiences using a tangible outlet for emotions that might otherwise remain buried.

Any form of art is a valid avenue for self-expression and healing. Drawing or painting allows your hand to move freely across a canvas or paper, giving your subconscious the freedom to speak. This self-exploration may reveal insights into your emotional state that you weren't even aware of. Creating visual representations of your feelings can help you understand and process them. Colors have a surprising impact on how you feel; red might symbolize anger or passion, while blue might evoke calmness or sadness. Art can represent emotions while you create a visual diary that captures your path through healing (Nash 2022).

A common way to get started with creative expression as an emotional outlet, creating a mandala is an ancient art form that involves drawing circular designs to promote relaxation and focus. Here's a quick way to do it:

1. Draw a large circle on a piece of paper.
2. Inside, create patterns using simple shapes like lines, dots, or curves.
3. Allow your design to evolve naturally, focusing on the rhythm of your movements rather than the final product.

Drawing mandalas encourages mindfulness and draws your attention to the present moment, away from intrusive thoughts. When you're engaging in creative processes, allow yourself to

embrace each imperfection and mistake. The value of art lies in its ability to reflect the artist's inner world, and that world is rarely tidy or predictable. Focus on the emotional release that comes from creating rather than the skill or outcome. There shouldn't be any pressure to produce art worthy of a gallery. You only need to focus on letting your emotions flow through your hands and onto the page. **Try to let go of any preconceived notions of what art should look like and allow yourself to be guided by intuition and emotion, trusting that the process itself is what's most valuable.**

Art presents a unique way to manage the challenges of emotional healing, crafting a language for the unspeakable and a space for growth. Creative expression is a way to explore, reflect, and transform your inner experiences in a personal and insightful way. You'll begin to notice how your perception of yourself and your past begins to shift. When you're healing from trauma, creating acts as a form of liberation and a way to rewrite the narrative and reclaim your story. **Making a commitment to self-care and emotional expression serves as a foundation that supports you through life's ups and downs**. In the following chapter, we'll review a few more ways that healing practices can be integrated into your daily life.

Chapter 5

Integrating Healing with Daily Life

Healing happens in therapy sessions and moments of deep reflection, but it also occurs continuously through your everyday choices and habits. To truly see progress in your emotional growth, you have to consistently make decisions that support your healing. Integrating healthy processes into each facet of your daily life contributes to a foundation of emotional stability, resilience, and improved well-being. Daily healing activities don't always come naturally, but they can easily become a part of your routine if you put the work in.

Establishing Routines to Support Emotional Growth

The structure of your day should promote both predictability and balance. Routines are a psychological anchor that can ground you amid life's uncertainties, giving you healthy habits to fall back on when everything else seems out of place. The predictability of a daily routine gives you a sense of control, which is especially advantageous when you're in the process of

healing from trauma or emotional upheaval. Having a structured daily schedule has proven to reduce anxiety and stress, presenting a semblance of normalcy regardless of outside circumstances (Cherry 2022).

Your personalized healing routine should include little therapeutic practices in each part of your day, starting right in the morning. **Morning rituals set a positive tone and offer a gentle transition into the demands of daily life.** Starting your day with a few moments of stillness, whether it's a short meditation or a mindful cup of coffee, can center you and provide clarity for the day ahead. You might even use your journal to engage in the gratitude practice we discussed earlier, where you list things you're thankful for to uplift your mood and shift your mindset to positivity.

Evening practices should focus on reflection and relaxation. Before bed, taking a moment to journal about your thoughts, feelings, and insights gained throughout the day can help you process emotions and clear your mind, promoting restful sleep.

When it comes to healing, one size definitely doesn't fit all. Each individual has their own distinct lifestyle that's filled with its own set of demands and opportunities. When you're trying to make new healing practices stick, the trick is to integrate them into habits that are already present. If you're not interested in completely overhauling your day, you'll need to analyze your current schedule, finding pockets of time where these practices naturally fit. If you're especially busy, you may have to use your commute as an opportunity for breathing exercises. As you travel, you can use short periods of downtime to focus on your breath, observing its rhythm and allowing it to calm your brain and body. It doesn't take long to turn a mundane commute into a moment

of peace. Lunchtime is a perfect time for midday reflection, where you can spend a few minutes journaling about how your day is going and noting any challenges or triumphs. This brief pause is like a mental reset that prepares you for the afternoon ahead.

Flexibility and adaptation are the main pillars of designing a healing routine. Life is unpredictable, and your emotional needs can vary from one day to the next. It's important to listen to your body and mind and use each signal to adjust your practices as needed. If you're feeling particularly stressed, you might extend your evening journaling session or add an extra breathing exercise to your lunchtime routine. On days when you're feeling more balanced, you could focus on gratitude or visualization exercises. As long as you remain open to change and avoid rigidity in your approach, your routine will remain supportive and relevant instead of becoming another source of stress.

Your routine should be tailored to your needs, goals, and existing schedule, but I've provided a basic example to get you started:

1. **Morning:** Complete a five-minute meditation or a gratitude practice after waking up. In your journal, reflect on what you're thankful for and set an intention for the day. Do your body a favor and drink 8 ounces of pure water.
2. **Commute:** Use your travel time to listen to a guided meditation, uplifting podcast, or calming music.
3. **Lunchtime:** Take a break from screens to eat mindfully, paying attention to the flavors and textures of your food. Engage in breathwork to calm your body and mind.

4. **Evening:** Journal a reflection of your experiences, emotions, and any insights gained. Avoid screens for at least 2 hours before bedtime. The blue light interferes with the normal production of melatonin and your ability to unwind.

When you structure your day around healing, you build a nurturing environment that supports your stability and growth. This routine supplies a refuge from the turbulence of life and guides you toward a balanced and fulfilling existence.

Building Resilience: Strengthening Your Emotional Core

Resilience is the quiet strength that helps you bounce back from life's challenges. A resilient person doesn't avoid difficulties but faces them head-on and grows through the experience. Emotionally strong individuals possess a unique blend of traits: optimism, adaptability, and a strong sense of purpose. **Resilience requires viewing adversities as opportunities for personal growth rather than insurmountable obstacles.** This perspective enables the maintenance of emotional equilibrium even when life throws curveballs. Developing resilience is necessary for healing as it empowers you to manage emotional turmoil with grace and strength (Mayo Clinic 2025).

Building emotional resilience requires proactive strategies that build your inner strength. Developing a solid support network during this process can be incredibly uplifting. Make sure you're surrounding yourself with people who uplift and encourage you, whether they're friends, family, or support groups. These connections act as a safety net when you encounter hardships, giving

you perspective and empathy when you need it most. Engaging in activities that push you out of your comfort zone also supports you in building resilience. Experiences like trying a new hobby, taking a solo trip, or learning a skill produces confidence and adaptability. Each challenge you face and overcome bolsters your resilience, solidifying your emotional core (Chowdhury 2019).

Resilience has an immense impact on emotional health. Emotionally strong individuals tend to have improved coping mechanisms that guide them through handling stress and setbacks with greater ease. When a resilient person loses a job, they might initially feel the sting of disappointment, but they're likely to quickly shift their focus to new opportunities and use the setback as motivation to pursue a new career. The ability to see beyond the immediate challenge supports a balanced emotional state, reducing the likelihood of becoming overwhelmed by negativity (NCTSN 2025). Resilience is like a buffer that protects you from the debilitating effects of stress and anxiety.

When you're on a mission to build inner resilience, it's easy to feel discouraged when your progress seems slow. Maintaining hope and commitment during this time is vital. Persistence and patience are the pillars of successful healing. Every time you find yourself responding more slowly and thoughtfully instead of letting an emotional outburst take over your day, you build a bit of momentum that reinforces your progress and motivates you to keep going.

Support systems greatly impact one's ability to build resilience. We'll explore the power of community and mentorship more later, but knowing that you have someone to lean on when you need encouragement or perspective can make your resilience journey exponentially easier. When you're facing a challenge that tests your emotional strength or ability to keep trying, don't be

afraid to reach out to your network of people. Friends who listen without judgment or mentors who offer guidance can be a lifeline in your healing process.

Having a solid recovery plan can help you tap into your resilience when you're faced with difficulties. **You can take a proactive approach to this by identifying potential challenges ahead of time and brainstorming strategies to overcome them.** If stress has a tendency to derail your daily progress, plan a few specific activities that help you relax, like deep breathing or a quick walk. Self-compassion goes a long way during this time; luckily, we'll review a few ways to engage in positive self-talk during tough times in our next chapter.

Regular self-reflection and personal growth are essential parts of building resilience, presenting opportunities to adapt, learn from challenges, and manage adversity with greater confidence. Reflective exercises can support this goal, helping you learn from past experiences and apply those lessons moving forward. Consistent reflection is a must; you may consider setting aside some time each week to think about a recent challenge and how you handled it. If you're inclined to use your journal for this reflection, feel free to use the following prompts:

1. What do you learn about yourself when you analyze how you handled a difficult situation?
2. Think of a time when you felt like giving up but pushed through. What motivated you to keep going?
3. Jot down three personal strengths that have helped you overcome adversity in the past. How can you intentionally rely on these moving forward?

Reflecting on your resilience reinforces your ability to adapt and grow. In essence, resilience starts with cultivating a mindset that embraces change and uncertainty with open arms. A resilient person doesn't avoid setbacks. Rather, they know what to do to bounce back from them with wisdom. **An emotionally healthy person knows that obstacles are actually just stepping stones to the next achievement they'll make.** The goal is to be able to trust in your ability to survive life's storms and emerge stronger on the other side. With time and consistency in your practices, you'll likely find that resilience becomes a natural part of who you are. It will become easier to face challenges with courage and confidence over time. When you view obstacles as opportunities to learn instead of setbacks, you're setting yourself up for positive change and emotional growth.

The Role of Nutrition and Exercise in Emotional Health

It may not always be the first thing you think of when you're thinking of emotional health, but what you eat and how you move can make a significant difference. **There's a strong connection between your physical well-being and your mood, and what you put into your body can greatly impact your neurotransmitters, the chemicals that help regulate your mood.** A diet rich in omega-3 fatty acids, for example, can promote mood regulation. These healthy fats are found in foods like salmon, walnuts, and flaxseeds and are known to support brain health and emotional balance. Omega-3 has a role in neurotransmitter function, helping to stabilize mood swings and reduce the symptoms of depression. Antioxidant-rich foods, like berries, leafy greens, and nuts, are also beneficial. These help to combat oxidative stress, which can lead to inflammation and affect your mental health. Consuming various

colorful fruits and vegetables supports overall health while reducing stress and anxiety levels behind the scenes.

Regular physical exercise is another valuable mechanism for emotional well-being. **Physical activity releases endorphins that act as natural mood lifters, supporting your emotional state and building resilience.** Exercising regularly is known to reduce anxiety and depression while presenting an immediate sense of accomplishment and motivation. Yoga is a common practice that is particularly beneficial to individuals suffering from trauma. Combining physical movement with mindfulness and relaxation, yoga involves deep breathing and meditation to calm the mind and reduce stress. If you don't feel like attending a class, you will find just as many benefits in following an online video at home. Incorporating mindful walking or running into your routine can also promote relaxation and enhance your emotional well-being. Cardiovascular exercises, like running, cycling, or swimming, are excellent for mental health as they increase your heart rate, release endorphins, and provide a sense of achievement. Just a short walk around the block can immediately elevate your mood and clear your mind.

Healthy eating and exercise can't have an impact on your mental health unless they are done consistently. You don't have to make any drastic changes overnight, but introducing small and sustainable shifts over time can lead to big changes. You might incorporate a balanced meal plan into your weekly schedule to support your health and verify that you're receiving the nutrients your body and mind need. It's best to include a variety of foods that provide healthy fats, lean proteins, and complex carbohydrates. These elements work together to maintain energy levels and support brain function. Your goal in balancing elements of diet and exercise is achieving moderation. It can be uplifting to enjoy

treats occasionally, but regularly opting for whole and nutrient-dense foods will better support your emotional well-being.

When you're introducing physical activities into your routine, make sure you're including practices that you enjoy and can fit into your lifestyle. You're never too late to start a new dance class, engage in a daily bike ride, or try pilates. As long as you're moving regularly and choosing activities that bring you joy, you're on the right path. Consistency is more important than intensity, so it's ideal to aim for at least thirty minutes of moderate activity most days of the week. The goal is to support a healthy relationship between your body and mind rather than punishing yourself with grueling workouts. Listen to your body and give yourself grace on days when rest is needed. Maintaining a healthy balance includes being kind to yourself.

When you learn to make mindful choices about what you eat and how you move, you produce emotional stability that supports your overall well-being. A few daily changes can help you feel more balanced, resilient, and ready to face whatever comes your way.

Digital Detox: Creating Space for Healing

Modern times are a bit strange. For starters, our phones' incessant pinging seems to be the soundtrack of our lives. In our hyper-connected world, the constant barrage of notifications, emails, and social media updates can be overwhelming, even if you don't notice it at first. It's no surprise that the relentless connectivity ramps up stress levels and contributes to feelings of anxiety. Many individuals have conquered this stress by consciously stepping back from screens and creating a more balanced relationship with technology. When digital consumption is reduced, there's more room for real-world interactions and

personal reflection. It would be nearly impossible to cut off technology completely, but a few changes can help you find a healthier balance that produces mental clarity and reduces stress. Taking breaks from digital devices can significantly reduce stress levels and improve mood, presenting a much-needed respite from the constant digital noise (Sreenivas 2023).

Implementing a digital detox might sound a little out of reach, but you can start reclaiming your time and focus with just a few steps. Creating a structured routine for your digital use can be beneficial. Instead of constantly scrolling, designate a couple of slots in your day when you allow yourself to check in, setting specific times for looking at emails and social media. Over time, this will dramatically reduce the compulsive need you feel to be always connected, allowing you to be more present in the moment. You can determine tech-free zones in your home where screens are not allowed, encouraging genuine face-to-face interactions and promoting rest and relaxation. These buffer zones give your mind a break from the constant influx of digital information.

Stepping back from digital devices isn't without its challenges. You might initially struggle with the anxiety of missing out on digital interactions or falling behind in the fast-paced world of social media. Acknowledge these feelings as they come, but consistently remind yourself of the benefits that come with a digital detox. To avoid feeling discouraged, start small, like dedicating an hour a day to being phone-free, and gradually increase the time as you become more comfortable with the disconnect. **Replace screen time with activities that nourish your soul and body, like reading a book, going for a walk, or engaging in a creative hobby. These activities are likely to fill the void that digital interactions leave, giving you fulfillment and joy without unnecessary stress.**

Throughout your digital detox, take a few moments each day to reflect on your online habits. Journaling can help you to explore how digital use affects your emotional health. Set aside time each day to jot down your feelings and observations, guided by the following prompts:

1. How do you feel when you're away from your phone?
2. What emotions arise during your detox?
3. What feelings do you miss from being on social media?
4. When do you feel the strongest urge to check your phone?
5. How do your focus and productivity change when you limit screen time?

The self-awareness your reflection brings can help you to identify patterns and make more informed choices about your digital consumption in the future. Becoming conscious of your habits empowers you to create a relationship with technology that supports your well-being rather than weighing down on you.

Incorporating a digital detox into your life makes space for healing and reflection, presenting a counterbalance to the demands of modern technology. As you learn more about your habits and digital consumption, you'll become more present, balanced, and emotionally resilient. This chapter is just one step in the broader exploration of integrating healing into daily life. Self-compassion and empowerment are pillars of achieving success in this process; in the following chapter, we'll explore these concepts further.

Chapter 6

Cultivating Self-Compassion and Empowerment

When you're standing in front of a mirror, your reflection should be looked at with the same warmth and understanding you'd offer a friend. Being kind to yourself is an effort that can be incredibly transformative. Self-compassion involves treating yourself with the same empathy and care you would extend to others, acknowledging your struggles without judgment, and recognizing that everyone makes mistakes. **Self-compassion is built on three pillars: being kind to yourself, understanding your shared humanity, and maintaining mindfulness.** Embracing these qualities can improve your mental health and improve your happiness levels while inherently reducing anxiety and depression (Best Day Psychiatry & Counseling 2022).

Using Affirmations to Reframe your Mindset

You may have noticed that affirmations have been mentioned a few times within our explorations of mental growth. When repeated, these statements have the ability to completely reshape

your self-perception and internal dialogue. Affirmations are used to create new neural pathways that promote optimism and confidence. Their beauty lies in their simplicity and accessibility; they can be incorporated into any busy schedule with ease. If you're looking to give yourself a regular reminder of your worth or a declaration of your strength, affirmations can shift how you see yourself and navigate the world (The Head Plan 2025).

Crafting impactful affirmations requires intention and personalization. You'll want to start by identifying areas where you seek growth or support. When you're writing, use present tense and positive language to frame your statements, focusing on achievable and specific goals. Instead of throwing out a simplistic statement like, "I will be happy," try something specific and intentional like, "I am finding joy in each moment." This subtle shift grounds your statement in the here and now, making it even more impactful. Tailoring your affirmations to resonate with your unique needs and desires keeps your efforts aligned with your personal values and aspirations. This guarantees the effectiveness of your affirmation practices, making them a powerful catalyst toward self-compassion and empowerment.

Much like any other practice, consistency is key when it comes to affirmations. Integrating them into your morning routine sets the tone for a day rooted in self-kindness. As you wake up, give yourself a moment to repeat your affirmations, letting their positive energy guide you. Visual reminders can also be used to reinforce these messages throughout the day. You might place sticky notes with your affirmations on your mirror, fridge, or computer screen, serving as constant reminders of your commitment to self-compassion and keeping your intentions front and center as you navigate daily challenges.

Your journal is an excellent place to record affirmations that can be used throughout the day. As you reflect on areas where you seek growth or support, write down a few affirmations using present tense and positive language. For the visual reminder, place them where you'll see them daily, like on your bathroom mirror or beside your bed. If you repeat them each day, their positive energy is likely to infuse your day, even if it's in small ways. These statements should be tailored to your situation and needs, but I've provided a few samples to get you started:

1. I am resilient and capable.
2. I embrace my unique journey.
3. I trust myself to manage challenges with grace.
4. I grow stronger and more confident every day.
5. I release feelings of self-doubt and welcome self-compassion.

Incorporating affirmations into your daily life builds self-compassion that supports every facet of your being. Regularly repeating positive statements invites a shift from self-criticism to self-acceptance, strengthening your resilience and empowering you to take action over your own outcomes. The path toward self-compassion is ongoing, but every step forward contributes to a kinder and more empowered version of yourself.

Empowerment Through Vulnerability: Embracing Your True Self

Being vulnerable can feel like standing on a stage with the spotlight on you and nowhere to hide. Your heart races, your palms sweat, and every instinct tells you to recoil back into the shadows. These instincts are often rooted in an unhealthy mindset that's encouraging you to retreat back into isolation. When you lean

into the discomfort and allow yourself to be vulnerable, you take on great power. Vulnerability is often misunderstood as weakness, but it's actually a strength that allows you to show your true self, flaws and all, and find strength in this authenticity. Every time you're open, you forge deeper connections with others and possibly make realizations about yourself in the process. Sharing your authentic self creates a bond built on trust and understanding, as people resonate with your honesty and courage. Vulnerability enables you to make fundamental connections grounded in mutual empathy and respect (Brown 2010).

Sharing your stories is a valuable way to express vulnerability and release emotional tension simultaneously. Regardless of whether you're in a support group or chit-chatting with a close friend, expressing your personal experiences can give you an opportunity to lay down any facades and let others see the real you. Sharing stories of vulnerability is a catalyst for healing, benefiting you and those who listen. When you unapologetically speak your truth, you invite others to do the same, creating a ripple effect of openness and acceptance (Jagiellowicz 2024).

Incorporating practices of vulnerability into your daily life requires a delicate balance between openness and protection. You want to set boundaries that keep you safe while still allowing room for genuine expression. Consider who to trust with your vulnerabilities and choose your moments consciously. **Active listening in conversations can also enhance vulnerability; fully engaging with others and providing your undivided attention creates an environment where your conversation partner feels valued and heard**. This reciprocity makes it easier for you to share in return, completing a cycle of empathy and connection. Empathy bridges this exchange so you can wholeheartedly understand and share the feelings of others.

With vulnerability as your guide, living authentically naturally produces self-acceptance and empowers you to do your best. When you strip away the masks and live in alignment with your values, you embrace your true self. You no longer need to conform to external expectations, and this realization can bring a sense of freedom and confidence. Consider the story of Carolyn Wonders, who initially left behind her love for art to pursue a corporate career in marketing. After feeling unfulfilled for decades, she rediscovered her passion for painting and felt drawn to create a dedicated studio space. Eventually, this shift brought her the personal fulfillment she had been looking for and led to a successful art career, demonstrating the long-term impact of aligning your life with your true passions (Mills 2025).

As you continue to handle the complicated dilemmas of daily life, remind yourself regularly of the power that lies in vulnerability. Choosing to be open when you're comfortable doing so invites opportunities for growth, understanding, and change. Each time you allow yourself to be seen, you strengthen your capacity for connection and resilience. Vulnerability is a courageous act that can change how you relate to yourself and others. Embracing this strength will result in the emergence of your truest self, ready to engage with the world in a way that's empowering and liberating.

Self-Love Practices for Lasting Change

Think about being a true friend to someone, do you treat them kindly, or are you critical? Do you offer encouragement or constantly put down their dreams? Would you consider someone who was critical and negative to be a true friend? You wouldn't act that way to anyone you cared about so it only follows that you shouldn't act that way toward yourself. If somewhere in your past

you didn't get the love and support you needed, you may have grown up thinking you don't deserve love. If you recognize these behaviors in yourself or others, they may be a person who didn't get love as a child:

1. Constantly seeking approval in Relationships - craving validation
2. Over Apologizing - linked to low self-worth
3. Constantly seeking to prove their worth - the need for validation
4. Struggle to accept compliments - causes discomfort/suspicion because they didn't get compliments as a child
5. Feel responsible for other's emotions - be what others need in order to feel safe
6. Need to be the Strong One - don't want to be a burden, inadequate, rejected
7. Connecting their self-worth to how much they're needed - if they aren't needed they question their worth

Recognizing these feelings and addressing their origins can help find the self-love that's missing.

Self-love is the glue that holds your emotional world together. A healthy relationship with yourself doesn't require gazing upon your reflection with adulation or placing yourself above others, but your inner connection should be nurturing, supportive, and accepting. Self-love starts with understanding your worth and treating yourself with kindness, even when things don't go as planned. **When you love yourself, you create a shield of emotional resilience and well-being that can withstand life's challenges.** You'll never be completely immune to life's difficulties, but practicing self-love does mean you can manage

them with more confidence. While this mindset may initially feel out of reach, it's more than possible with a series of small actions that remind you of your inherent worth.

Cultivating a mindset of personal value starts with developing a self-care routine that prioritizes your personal needs. This might mean carving out time each week for activities that bring you joy and relaxation, like a long bath, a walk in nature, or reading a book that gives you a mental reset. There's a common misconception that self-care is selfish; in reality, it's a necessary investment in your well-being.

It might sound silly, but writing a love letter to yourself can be a great introduction to practices that support self-love. **Within your journal, dedicate a space to expressing appreciation for who you are.** Write about your strengths, your achievements, and the qualities you admire in yourself. This can be incredibly affirming, reinforcing a positive self-image and enhancing your connection with yourself. When you've been feeling down, your inner self often needs a warm hug and a reminder that you are deserving of love and care.

When you embrace self-love, the benefits naturally spill over into your relationships and elevate your interactions with others. **Loving yourself gives you the strength to build healthier boundaries, guided by a heightened sense of self-awareness.** Understanding your needs means you can communicate them more effectively, reducing misunderstandings and fostering mutual respect. Self-love shouldn't make you become rigid or inflexible; instead, you'll learn to articulate your limits in a way that honors your needs and those of others. As you cultivate self-love, you also become more empathetic and compassionate toward yourself and those around you. You'll start to see others' struggles through a lens of under-

standing, knowing that everyone is on their own path to self-acceptance.

Self-love is an ongoing process that requires continuous reflection and growth. Make sure to use your journal as you progress, giving yourself a space to explore your thoughts and feelings about yourself. Set aside time each week to write about your self-love journey, noting any progress or challenges you encounter. Here are a few prompts you may want to consider as you make this reflection:

1. Analyze how your perception of yourself has evolved over time.
2. Consider which practices have been most beneficial to your relationship with yourself.
3. Name three qualities you love about yourself and why.
4. Reflect on how you speak to yourself in difficult moments. Would you say the same words to a close friend?
5. Describe a time when you prioritized self-care. Take note of how it impacted your mood, confidence, or well-being.

Reflecting on your self-love progress can help you identify areas where you may need to focus more attention. You should regularly adapt and refine your practices to better support your evolving needs. The commitment you make to self-reflection keeps your self-love practices dynamic and effective, contributing to a positive relationship with yourself that lasts a lifetime.

Overcoming Negative Self-Talk

When the voice inside your head is a persistent critic, it's constantly echoing doubts and insecurities. This internal dialogue usually stems from past experiences, particularly those from childhood. **Moments when we have been criticized or compared to others have a way of lodging deep in our psyche, shaping how we interact with ourselves**. Society's voice has an impact on your own, too, with its constant reminders of who we should be. Media, peers, and casual remarks from acquaintances can reinforce feelings of inadequacy. Over time, this negative self-talk becomes a default setting, constantly whispering that you're not enough or that you'll never succeed. These thoughts can be persistent, but they are not truths. They are narratives we've unconsciously accepted that are rooted in moments when we were most impressionable and vulnerable.

To shift the narrative of negativity your mind has become accustomed to, you need to challenge and reframe these thoughts. Cognitive restructuring is a technique that can be particularly effective for achieving this. This method involves identifying negative beliefs and questioning their validity. Here's a breakdown (Stanborough 2020):

1. Write down a self-critical thought that pops up in your mind, like "I always mess things up."
2. Examine the evidence for and against this belief. Question whether it's really true, for example, that you always make mistakes or if there are instances where you've succeeded.
3. Rewrite the thought using positive language that counters the inaccuracies in the self-critique.

Using evidence-based reasoning makes it easier to dismantle blanket statements and replace them with more balanced perspectives. Instead of claiming that you always mess things up, remind yourself that you make mistakes like everyone else and, more importantly, meet your goals and achievements. This shift might seem small, but it lays the groundwork for more positive internal dialogue.

Practicing compassionate self-talk can counteract learned negativity. When you respond to yourself, speak with the same kindness as you would to a friend who was feeling down. You'd likely offer words of encouragement and empathy, a kindness that you don't always provide to yourself. Having a list of compassionate responses to common self-criticisms can make this process easier. When you catch yourself thinking you're not good enough, counter it with the thought that you're doing your best, and that's more than enough. Being compassionate in your responses provides a buffer against negativity and gradually shifts your internal dialogue toward one of support and kindness. Over time, this can completely change how you perceive yourself, gifting you a mindset of growth and acceptance.

Positive self-talk has an abundance of benefits for emotional health. Changing the way you talk to yourself can lead to improved self-esteem and resilience. Natasha Hastings, a former Olympic sprinter, once faced significant self-doubt during her athletic career. When her performance suffered due to her lack of confidence, she knew something had to change. Natasha began adopting positive affirmations and self-talk patterns that focused on her achievements. With time, her resilience grew, and she was able to turn her career around. When she returned to sprinting, her performance was improved and she had developed a healthier mindset with herself (Hastings 2022). **Anyone is capable of seeing themselves in a new light by**

consciously replacing negative thoughts with positive ones.

Self-talk habits change gradually, and it's not always easy to shift your perspective. There will be days when your old inner critics creep back in, and all you can do is try your best to challenge them. Each time you catch a negative thought and choose to reframe it, you're building yourself a more fulfilling life. Be patient with this process and celebrate each of the small victories along the way. A lifetime of self-empowerment is a reward far worth the work.

Celebrating Small Wins: The Path to Empowerment

When you reach the finish line of a marathon, you rarely think about the countless small steps that got you there. Celebrating every small win is an important aspect of healing. **Even if it's minor, each achievement builds motivation and empowerment along the way. Internally recognizing these moments releases dopamine, a neurotransmitter associated with pleasure and reward, which reinforces positive behavior and encourages you to keep going.** Don't feel compelled to wait for the big milestones to celebrate. Take a moment, no matter how small, to acknowledge your everyday victories. If you get through a challenging day or you complete a task you've been putting off, bringing your attention to your resilience in these moments can fuel your progress and boost your self-esteem.

Keeping track of what needs to be celebrated is easier when you use your journal to track success. In your own words, you should try to track each of your grand achievements as well as the little things you accomplish throughout each day. When you manage a difficult conversation with grace or stick to a new healthy habit in

your routine, these moments should go in your journal. Over time, you'll have a tangible record of your growth that reminds you of your capabilities and resilience. In addition to journaling, consider setting up a reward system for your efforts. You can make this process feel a little more exciting by providing yourself with mini-rewards for reaching personal goals. These can be simple, like your favorite treat or an extra hour of leisure time. Rewarding your efforts creates a positive association that amplifies your motivation levels.

Celebrating your wins will immediately boost your self-esteem and drive. As you practice self-acknowledgement, you'll build confidence in your abilities to take on new challenges that enrich your life. Validating your hard work is an impactful way to shift your focus from what's left to achieve to what you've already accomplished, contributing to a more balanced and positive outlook. Shifting to this mindset is especially important when you face setbacks or moments of self-doubt. Revisiting your successes reminds you of your strengths, which can be incredibly reassuring and motivating.

Integrating acts of gratitude into your celebrations strengthens their positive effects. Similar to the love letter exercise, writing letters of gratitude to yourself is a way to acknowledge your achievements and express appreciation for the journey. This is a chance to reflect on your growth with kindness and develop a deeper connection with yourself. When you write these letters, focus on the qualities that helped you succeed, like your determination, creativity, or resilience. Reminding yourself of these qualities reinforces a positive self-image and creates a cycle of encouragement and empowerment. Gratitude is a lens that highlights the good in yourself and your life.

Celebrating each of your small successes completely shifts how you perceive your progress and potential. With time, you'll find yourself feeling more motivated, confident, and ready to take on whatever comes your way. Personal growth needs a positive mindset and environment to grow, and it all starts from within. In the next chapter, we'll explore how generational trauma shapes your emotional well-being, uncovering inherited patterns that might be influencing your relationships and personal goals.

Chapter 7

Navigating Generational Trauma

When you're sitting at a family dinner, stories are exchanged, laughter echoes, and everyone seems to play a part in the familial script. Shared moments and experiences bring families closer together, but these bonds sometimes hide past traumas that have quietly shaped each person's role around the table. Generational trauma influences our lives in ways we might not even realize, guiding our behaviors, emotions, and interactions. Trauma can be passed down without anyone consciously intending to do so. When left unacknowledged, significant events of trauma leave a lasting imprint on both direct survivors and their descendants.

Unraveling the Legacy of Trauma

Sometimes referred to as transgenerational trauma, the concept of inherited trauma has been studied extensively in psychology. The effects of trauma are sometimes transmitted from one generation to the next (Impossible Psych Services 2024). These patterns are especially prominent following signif-

icant traumatic events like the Holocaust or slavery. Distressing experiences can change the way genes are expressed, potentially affecting offspring through mechanisms like epigenetics. Studies on Holocaust survivors' children, for example, have revealed that they often exhibit behavioral and psychiatric issues, possibly due to their parents' trauma (Dashorst et al. 2019). The events themselves can be psychologically scarring, but their effects also seep deeply into family dynamics and relationships.

Signs of generational trauma within families reveal themselves through recurring patterns of behavior. Substance abuse or addiction are telling indicators of unacknowledged familial wounds. Recurring themes of anxiety or depression are also common, suggesting an inherited emotional burden that weighs heavily on those directly affected and those who come after. Intergenerational patterns of trauma can manifest as a constant feeling of unease that affects how family members interact and cope with stress. When one generation struggles with these issues, it often sets a precedent for how subsequent generations manage (or fail to manage) their own emotional health.

Generational trauma impacts family dynamics in a variety of ways. Communication can become dysfunctional, filled with misunderstandings and silences where there should be dialogue. **Unresolved trauma can result in unhealthy coping mechanisms like avoidance or denial, perpetuating a cycle that repeats with each new generation.** When emotions are rarely discussed openly, it leads to a lack of emotional intimacy and support. Alternatively, it may result in volatile interactions where emotions are expressed destructively or even aggressively. Once made, these patterns are difficult to break, as they become deeply ingrained and normalized over time.

Trauma guides the beliefs and behaviors that seem to run in your family like an unbroken thread. These patterns can be so deeply set that you may not even notice them consciously. Recognizing inherited beliefs and behaviors requires taking a close look at the recurring themes in your family's history. This process can begin by reflecting on the stories you've heard around the dinner table or during family gatherings.

Acknowledging personal and familial trauma is the first step in breaking the cycle. Exploring your family stories and histories to identify traumatic events that have shaped current dynamics can reveal opportunities for growth, benefiting your mental state and your relationship with your loved ones. Using information from extended family members and information stored away in boxes, try to learn as much as you can about the people who came before you. You may even choose to create a family tree, which can be a helpful visual mechanism for recognizing known trauma events and how they link across generations. Interviewing family members about their experiences can also reveal valuable information that gives you a broader context for present behaviors. These conversations might inform you of hidden stories or perspectives that have been lost or ignored, creating a more holistic picture of the family's emotional landscape.

Once you've learned more, don't forget to take time to reflect on your family's history. Consider these questions as a starting point for your journaling:

1. What stories have been passed down through the generations?
2. Did you notice any recurring themes or patterns in your family, such as addiction or mental health issues?
3. How have these experiences shaped your family's interactions and communication styles?

Use these reflections to guide your observations, noting key events and their impact. This exercise can help you understand the broader context of generational trauma in your family, marking the first step of positive change and healing.

Cultural and societal influences are also significant factors that shape and reinforce intergenerational patterns. Societal pressures, found in social media discussions and modern trends, are a driving factor of universal expectations that subtly guide family roles and behaviors. Societal expectations about gender roles, for example, can influence how family members perceive and interact with each other, perpetuating certain dynamics through generations. Cultural traditions can also reinforce certain behaviors and standards, embedding them deeply within the family structure. While these traditions can provide a sense of identity and continuity, they could also perpetuate outdated or harmful patterns. External factors continuously shape internal dynamics within an affected family.

To break the cycle of inherited patterns, it's essential to remain open to growth. Change is inevitable as you learn more about your family dynamic. It will benefit you to adapt to new ways of thinking and behaving, even if they initially feel uncomfortable or unfamiliar. You can start this process by setting family goals that are aimed at breaking negative cycles and promoting positive change. These goals might include encouraging open communication, supporting each other's growth, or challenging old beliefs that no longer serve the family. As long as these goals are realistic and approached with patience and compassion, gradual change is inevitable.

Healing the Family Tree: Strategies for Change

Your family tree is shaped by the experiences and hardships of every member. To support the integrity of this tree, you must tend to its roots, addressing the traumas that have been ignored and passed down through generations. Healing and adapting to healthier family dynamics can be made possible through family therapy sessions (Savage 2023). Giving your family members a safe space to come together, explore their shared history, and resolve conflicts helps everyone understand each other's perspectives, strengthening empathy within your connections. Making the healing process a collective effort makes it easier to confront past traumas and work toward healthier and more supportive relationships (Tuffs 2025).

Establishing new traditions that are centered around positivity and support can effectively replace bad habits that are present within your family. These practices build a sense of unity within the home and reinforce the importance of nurturing each other emotionally. Encouraging your loved ones to engage in these activities contributes to a basis of trust and support that will guide you through future challenges together. The traditions you set should vary according to your family's needs and schedules, but I've provided a few examples for your reference:

1. Host a weekly family dinner where everyone comes together to share their highs and lows. With no preset expectations, create a safe space to share without judgment.
2. Create a gratitude jar where family members write down things they're thankful for and read them aloud at the end of each month.

3. Establish a tech-free hour each evening and encourage meaningful conversations or quality down time.
4. Plan a monthly outdoor activity like a hike, picnic, or gardening project.
5. Start a family storytelling night where members share personal memories or ancestral stories.

Open dialogue is necessary for breaking the cycle of generational trauma. When family members discuss and process their shared history, everybody can benefit from the knowledge of how past events have shaped their present behaviors and relationships. Active listening and reflective questioning are pillars of successful conversations about trauma. We've discussed the importance of active listening in mindfulness, enabling a listener to fully focus on the speaker without thinking of what they'll say next. Similarly, reflective questioning encourages family members to explore their thoughts and feelings more deeply. It involves responding to information by asking open-ended questions like, "How did that experience affect you?" or "What do you think could help improve our relationship?" Being part of an environment that encourages and rewards empathy paves the way for familial healing and growth (Hurley 2016).

Cognitive behavioral techniques are commonly used to help people challenge negative patterns as they arise. Using these strategies, you can encourage your family to reframe negative beliefs and replace them with more positive and empowering ones. Using CBT to target negative thoughts starts with identifying a belief within your family that you find limiting, like the idea that you should always put others' needs in front of your own. Once you've identified an unhealthy thought, examine its validity by gathering evidence for and against it. Use these insights to construct a new, balanced belief that better aligns

with your family's values and goals. Group discussions are instrumental in addressing these patterns openly. **Make sure you're working to create a safe environment where everyone shares their perspectives and experiences. Allow for completely honest dialogue, focusing on understanding rather than judgment.** A collective reflection results in a sense of unity and shared commitment to change.

Breaking generational trauma is not always easy, but it has numerous benefits for family relationships and individual emotional well-being that make it well worth it. Families who work together to address generational wounds experience improved cohesion and support systems. Over time, your household will become more attuned to each other's needs and emotions, strengthening connections. In the meantime, the increased emotional resilience that comes with shared support gives each individual the tools they need to cope with future challenges. Confronting past traumas creates a more positive and nurturing environment where all members feel valued and supported.

Many families have been impacted by the positive change of breaking generational cycles. Andre Morrow once grew up in fear of his father, Sam, and his violent rages that were rooted in PTSD from the Vietnam War. Despite the deep-seated pain and estrangement, Andre became his father's full-time caregiver when Sam's health declined as a result of dementia and heart disease. This decision shifted their relationship and prompted a period of growth and healing (Dodd 2024). Through daily care and shared experiences, Andre and Sam effectively rebuilt their relationship and broke a cycle of trauma, setting a precedent of empathy for future familial generations. This personal anecdote is one of many that serve as a testament to the resilience and strength of

families who commit to healing their past and building a healthier future.

Building a Legacy of Healing for Future Generations

Every person leaves a legacy behind. Their life and relationship affects not only their children and family but also the generations that follow. Investing in a positive family legacy requires building an intentional environment where growth is prioritized. It doesn't matter if your future generations inherit flashy possessions; emotional well-being is the most valuable asset you can give them. "Legacy building" is a concept that involves taking conscious actions to shape your family's emotional and psychological landscape. Embedding values of healing and connection influences how your descendants navigate their own lives, potentially breaking cycles of trauma and replacing them with support.

Embedding healing and growth in the values of future generations starts with educating your family about mental health and well-being right now. Encourage open discussions about emotions and mental health, making these topics feel as normal as discussing plans for the weekend. Some families initiate regular family check-ins, giving each member a chance to share their current emotional state and seek support where needed. You may implement this concept into a tradition that you established earlier, like discussing highs and lows at a family dinner. **Regular check-ins promote emotional literacy and present a safe space for expressing feelings so family members can support each other through life's challenges.** Over time, these little moments will result in increased trust and empathy, making everyone more prepared to manage emotional ups and downs in a productive way.

Storytelling enables families to build a legacy of healing. When one member shares a family story with another, their connection becomes rooted in understanding, bridging any gap between past and present. Collecting and preserving stories of healing and resilience honors the struggles and triumphs of those who came before and reveals a roadmap for those who come after. To create a visual representation of these stories, creating a family memoir or scrapbook that documents these stories can help to capture moments of growth and joy. Having a tangible record of familial resilience gives current and future members a representation of how past generations overcame adversity. This sends an inspiring message: The road ahead may be challenging, but strength and resilience run deep in your family's veins.

Nurturing the emotional state of future generations starts with supporting the psychological development of your children and grandchildren. While these topics often fly under the radar among the stress of parenthood, teaching emotional intelligence and coping skills from a young age is crucial to breaking cycles of trauma. Simple acts like naming emotions, practicing deep breathing, or openly discussing feelings can help children recognize and manage their emotions from a young age. To take this a step further, invite children to participate in family healing rituals and activities, like mindfulness exercises or gratitude journaling. As they learn to encounter their emotions in an intentional way, these practices become part of their daily lives. Encouraging curiosity and questions enables children to explore their emotions without judgment. **Being proactive about their psychological development establishes a groundwork for emotionally healthy adults who are comfortable with vulnerability and capable of building meaningful relationships.**

Incorporating children into family healing activities creates a shared experience that reinforces the importance of emotional well-being. When you're engaging in your Sunday ritual of sharing gratitude or participating in a project aimed at helping others, involving your family spreads the value of empathy and community outward. Healing does not have to be a solitary endeavor; it can be a collective effort that binds your loved ones together. These efforts support the present generation while planting seeds for a legacy that prioritizes healing, growth, and connection for years to come.

Teaching Resilience to the Next Generation

Resilience is like a sturdy bridge that allows individuals to cross the choppy waters of life. Teaching this skill to children equips them with the strength to handle adversity without giving up. Emotionally healthy individuals possess a positive outlook, adaptability, and the ability to manage stress effectively, characteristics that empower children to deal with life's inevitable ups and downs. While it's never too late to learn resilience, developing this trait early reduces the long-term impacts of stress and supports emotional well-being. Every parent has the opportunity to instill resilience in their children so they can thrive despite obstacles.

Building resilience in children starts with implementing practical strategies that are designed to build emotional strength and adaptability. Problem-solving and critical thinking skills go hand in hand with resilient individuals. **When a child faces a challenge, resist the urge to provide a solution immediately. Instead, guide them through identifying the problem, brainstorming possible solutions, and evaluating the outcomes.** These extra steps instill valuable problem-solving skills as well as an immediate sense of agency and confidence. A

growth mindset is essential for resilient children; it celebrates effort over outcome and emphasizes that mistakes are opportunities for learning rather than failures. Reassuring your child with regular statements like, "You're improving," or, "Look at how far you've come," can support a mindset where obstacles are chances to grow rather than obstacles to fear.

Adults have the unique responsibility of modeling resilience through actions and attitudes. Children learn from what we say, but, more importantly, they learn from what we do. When you share personal stories of overcoming adversity, you demonstrate that setbacks are a natural part of life. This shows children that resilience takes persistence, creativity, and sometimes asking for help. When faced with stress or challenges, lead by example by handling them calmly and constructively. Show them how you pause to take a deep breath before responding to a difficult situation or how you prioritize tasks to manage a busy schedule without panicking. These actions are tiny, but they loudly convey the message that resilience is within reach and can be developed over time.

Ongoing support and mentorship are invaluable resources for building resilience in younger family members. Mentorship relationships within the family provide children with a supportive network where they feel safe to explore their emotions and challenges. You could be the mentor yourself, or you could connect children with other family members who are willing to provide guidance and support. Mentors supply wisdom, encouragement, and a listening ear for younger individuals who are working to build confidence and mental fortitude. An environment of support and mentorship is the most productive place for a child to grow, instilling the resilience needed to thrive in an ever-changing world.

Teaching resilience enriches the futures of children. When they learn to view challenges as opportunities, they develop a stronger sense of self-worth and capability. In our fast-paced, modern world, resilience enables us to adapt, innovate, and grow, regardless of the hurdles we face. Once you've nurtured these qualities in your family, they'll come easier within your growth process, too. Change starts with small, consistent efforts. The seeds you plant today become strength and courage that your children carry with them throughout their lives. You've now done the work to support your family and provide a safe space for their emotions. Progressing into the following chapter, we'll review how to build support networks for ourselves, too.

Chapter 8

Building Supportive Networks and Safe Spaces

When you find a community that truly gets you, it feels like stumbling upon a warm and inviting cabin in the wilderness during a chaotic storm. Every person deserves to be part of a group that supports their healing and shows empathy for their experiences. Your tribe is somewhere out there, waiting to offer the kind of support and acceptance you're looking for. Shared experiences often form the foundation for these groups, enriching your path toward recovery. It's one thing to have people to talk to, but having a space where you feel validated and understood by those who've walked a similar path is life-changing. Communal support aids in building resilience and promotes recovery through a shared sense of belonging.

The Power of Community in Healing

Support systems bring multitudes of psychological benefits to those within them. When you're surrounded by a community of people that resonate with your struggles, it eases the burden of isolation. Supportive groups remind you that you're not alone in

your journey and that your emotions are valid. They also often supply practical advice and emotional encouragement to help you manage the obstacles that come with trauma recovery. Community connections that are built in trust and shared experiences bring the validation needed to support your self-esteem and empower you to take steps toward healing (Stand Together 2025). Once you've found people who support the path you're on, you can work toward building an environment where growth is celebrated and setbacks are met with compassion rather than judgment.

Finding and connecting with like-minded individuals sometimes feels daunting at first, but there are many practical ways to get involved. Online forums on websites like Reddit or social media groups dedicated to trauma recovery can be valuable resources when you're looking for support or insight (Griffin et al. 2013). These platforms make it easy to engage with others, share your story, and learn from the experiences of those who've faced similar challenges. Seek out groups that resonate with your personal experiences and values so they're more likely to be a comfortable fit.

Looking beyond the internet, there are likely plenty of resources in your community that allow for face-to-face connections. Participating in local meetups or workshops puts you right in the center of a passionate group of like-minded individuals. These gatherings are your chance to meet others in person, creating relationships right within your area.

Choosing the right support group is an integral part of the process that starts with researching the focus of potential groups. Some might cater specifically to trauma survivors, while others could be more general. It's important to feel comfortable with the members so you can easily adopt a mindset of openness and

trust. Once you've narrowed down your options, try to attend a trial session if possible. This lets you get a feel for the group dynamics so you can determine if the environment aligns with your needs. Pay attention to how the group is facilitated and whether the discussions are constructive and relevant to your life. Finding a group where you feel safe and heard will maximize the benefits of your participation.

Community support groups can hold you accountable to your goals and habits. When you're part of a group that shares your aspirations, there's an inherent sense of accountability that encourages your personal development. Setting goals within or in front of this group can motivate you to stay committed to your healing process. **Attending regular meetings, participating in group activities, or simply checking in with one another are simple efforts that contribute to a shared sense of purpose and progress**. It doesn't hurt that you get to watch others grow and succeed; witnessing the resilience of your peers can inspire you to push through challenges, knowing that change is within reach.

Hosting or participating in community-building activities further strengthens the connections you make in these spaces. Look out for opportunities to volunteer or attend events within the group so you can contribute meaningfully and reinforce your sense of belonging. Each time you engage with your community, you develop new skills and expand your network, both of which are fulfilling rewards. Organizing group activities like workshops or social outings can also extend feelings of bonding and support. Group meetings can be insightful, but collaborating in a way that uses your creativity gives you a chance to engage with others in a relaxed and enjoyable setting. Immersing yourself in these communal experiences keeps your relationships nourished, making them vital sources of strength and encouragement.

As you work to create a support group online or in your area, your journal can be a handy way to reflect on your current network and identify areas for growth. Let the following prompts guide your thoughts:

1. Who are the individuals or groups that provide positive support in your life?
2. How can you deepen these connections or expand your network?
3. What steps can you take to engage more actively in community-building activities?

Once you've gathered insights from your reflections, set a few intentions for how you can strengthen your current support network. Opportunities for connection and growth are within reach, waiting for you to be part of a supportive community that aligns with your healing goals.

Creating Safe Spaces for Emotional Expression

When the chaos of the world seems to ramp up every second, a cozy refuge can give you space to escape it all and reset. Everyone could use a place to breathe and be themselves without pretense, and this is particularly true for someone healing from trauma. A safe space doesn't have to be flashy or covered in pillows; it just needs to be an environment where you feel free to express your emotions without any fear of judgment or misunderstanding. These environments provide the security necessary for vulnerability, characterized by being non-judgmental, comfortable, and private. Your inner thoughts and feelings can surface without reservation when you feel completely comfortable being yourself. When you enter your safe haven, you should feel

blanketed by a sense of peace, knowing that whatever emotions unfold are valid and welcome.

Investing in new furniture and decor is not a requirement of a safe space. Creating sanctuary at home or work begins with a few intentional changes that shift the mood and comfort. You might dedicate a space to setting up a quiet, comfortable area for reflecting and relaxing. This can be a corner of a room with a soft chair or a spot by a window with natural light. If the mood isn't calming on its own, add a few elements that soothe your senses, like a plush throw blanket, a calming scented candle, or a plant that brings a touch of nature indoors. Small and personal touches make the space more inviting for you and any others you invite in. Make sure to establish a few boundaries to protect your space. When you want the area to remain private, find a way to clearly signal to others that this is a time for your self-care and emotional processing. If you communicate your need for privacy clearly, interruptions will be minimized in your space and you'll be able to engage fully with your emotions.

Having your own designated safe space brings many benefits beyond immediate comfort. When you spend time in a secure and inviting space, you're more likely to let your guard down and explore the full extent of your emotions. This exploration may lead to uncovered insights and emotional release that leads to reduced anxiety and stress. **Safe spaces are your buffer against the pressures of daily life, giving you a retreat where you can recharge and regain perspective**. When you make time to regularly visit this space, you instill a habit of self-care that supports your mental health and your ability to cope with life's challenges.

Don't forget to take care of this space as it takes care of you. Keep the area fresh by personalizing it with items that bring you

comfort and joy. Include your favorite book, a piece of art that inspires you, and your journal for capturing thoughts during reflection. These personal touches make the space uniquely yours and reinforce its role as a refuge for emotional expression. Regularly tidying and refreshing the area can add to its calming atmosphere, guaranteeing that it remains a place you look forward to visiting. With time, this part of your living space will become an integral part of your healing process and a constant reminder of the importance of prioritizing your emotional well-being.

The Role of Mentorship in Healing

When you've gone through difficult times, it hasn't always been easy to reach out to others for help. For a long time, it's likely that you didn't even know that it was an option. Now, finding a mentor has never been easier. Reaching out to someone who has been through similar struggles to your own or someone who can offer a guiding light on your path can add another layer of support as you manage the challenges of healing. Mentorship is invaluable in the personal growth process. A confidant acts as a trusted ally who can supply you with wisdom, encouragement, and practical advice from their own experiences. When you have someone to walk alongside you, confronting trauma feels a little less daunting. Suddenly, your hardships become part of a shared journey where you feel unconditionally supported and understood. Emotional leaders show you your potential when you might doubt it yourself, presenting a perspective that can be incredibly grounding. Developing a connection with a mentor has emotional and psychological benefits that provide you with a validated sense of empowerment and direction.

Finding the right mentor takes a bit of matchmaking. If someone is the right fit for you, their experience and approach will resonate with your own needs and goals. Individuals who display empathy, experience, and a genuine willingness to listen make great advisers, as they are more likely to be able to connect with you on a personal level and process your struggles without judgment. A mentor who has personal experience in overcoming trauma may be a strong choice, as they likely can talk you through relatable and actionable insights. Any good adviser possesses the patience to listen actively and create a safe environment to express yourself without fear of dismissal.

When seeking potential mentors, start within your existing networks or communities. You might be shocked to find someone within a professional setting, a support group, or even a friend who has demonstrated resilience and wisdom in their own life and would be willing to guide you through your own struggles. Once you've identified a potential adviser, it's important to approach them with a clear expression of what you hope to gain from the relationship. Stay open about your intentions and expectations, expressing your desire for their guidance in specific areas of your life. Maintaining clarity sets the tone for a successful mentorship and demonstrates your commitment to personal growth, making it more likely that they'll want to engage with you.

Once you've established a mentorship relationship, actively participating in it offers an enriching experience every time. Regular check-ins with your adviser can help to make sure you're maintaining momentum and keeping both parties aligned in their goals. These meetups don't have to be formal or lengthy to be effective. Even a fifty-minute Zoom call can give you valuable insights and encouragement to keep going. During these interactions, stay open to feedback, discussing your progress and any

challenges you've encountered along the way. Setting goals together gives you a roadmap for your development, outlining clear milestones to work toward. Never forget to celebrate your successes along the way, giving yourself moments to reflect on your growth and identify areas for further improvement.

The relationship with an emotional adviser is dynamic and ever-evolving as you both grow and learn from each other. Both parties serve to benefit from the productive exchange of knowledge and experience. Engage with your mentor with an open mind and heart, and you'll likely see that the relationship becomes a source of strength and inspiration that supports you throughout the entirety of your healing process. **The bond formed through mentorship has lasting impacts, influencing your personal growth and ability to contribute positively to the lives of others.**

Navigating Therapy as a Guided Approach to Healing

Stepping into a therapy session sometimes feels like discovering a new language that speaks directly to your experiences and emotions. Therapists and counselors are sources of structured support and insightful perspectives who can completely rewrite your healing path. While you're perfectly capable of handling the challenges in your life, therapy helps you to take a more personalized approach in a private setting where you can safely explore your specific issues. You may not realize it, but even therapists have a therapist that they can talk to and get feedback for personal situations. Therapists tailor their treatment and discussions to your specific and unique needs, analyzing the best possible path for individualized care based on your goals and experiences.

Many people think that engaging in therapy means that you'll be healed after a few short sessions, but it requires a bit more effort than that. **In reality, finding success in therapy requires being proactive and setting clear goals for what you hope to achieve in your sessions.** You may need help managing anxiety, understanding past trauma, or improving relationships. Having specific objectives and discussing them within your sessions will guide your therapeutic journey and keep your growth on track. As you continue with your sessions, make sure that you and your therapist remain on the same page about your intentions. It might feel uncomfortable to be so open and honest at first, but sharing your thoughts and feelings without reservation gives the therapist more context so they can respond with relevant guidance. The therapist is a professional who is trained to help you, but they can only do so if they have a full picture of your experiences. These sessions are your time to ask questions or seek clarification on anything that feels unclear. Your relationship with therapy should be a collaborative one that enriches your own self-care routines and your personal values.

Attending a session or two of therapy can be enlightening, but the benefits don't really reveal themselves until you stay consistent. Regular attendance builds trust and rapport for both you and the professional you're working with, qualities that are essential for nurturing a supportive environment. If you start to find yourself dreading therapy sessions, it might be a sign that it's time for a mindset shift or maybe to find a new therapist altogether. Not every therapist will be the perfect match for your situation. When you look forward to healing and stay engaged with the process, you give yourself a steady source of encouragement and accountability. When you follow a regular schedule with your therapy sessions, it reinforces the progress you make, enabling you to make continuous development and adjust your strategies

as needed. It's similar to maintaining a fitness routine, where the more consistent you are, the stronger the results. Prioritize these meetings as you would any other important commitment, acknowledging their worth in supporting your well-being.

Your journey to healing may not look the same as others, but you'll never feel truly alone when you're with the right support system, mentor, or therapist. Never feel ashamed to seek out spaces where you feel seen and empowered to keep pushing toward wholeness. In the following chapter, we'll take an even closer look at the nuances of your healing progress, revealing areas for personalization that may bring you even closer to your goals.

Chapter 9

Personalized Healing Journeys

If everyone designed a road map for their personal healing journey, each path would be unique, marked by personal milestones, challenges, and the occasional detour. This is the reality of personalized healing plans; when you know your needs, goals, and boundaries, you can become the cartographer of your own emotional and psychological process. Taking a tailored approach to healing enables you to focus on what truly matters to you, making your progress more meaningful and effective. The guide to recovery is not one-size-fits-all. Rather, it's a living and breathing plan that adapts to your life, goals, and rhythms. **Being specific in your goal setting enables you to create a plan that guides you forward and keeps you motivated and grounded**.

Designing a Roadmap for Growth and Healing

Creating a personal healing plan starts with identifying your goals for emotional and psychological well-being. **Focus on what you truly want to achieve, like cultivating more self-**

compassion, reducing anxiety, or building healthier relationships. Remember, these goals should be specific and measurable so you can easily track their progress. Instead of saying you want to be happier, you might make a goal to write in your gratitude journal three times a week. Being specific about the outcome you desire and the timeframe you hope to achieve it within makes it easier to see how far you've come and what steps to take next. When you begin setting goals, you should take your current emotional challenges and strengths into consideration. Identify which areas where you struggle most and where you already feel strong. This assessment will help you set achievable goals that are relevant to your personal growth (DBT of South Jersey 2024).

Once you've established the specifics of your goals, you can then implement a comprehensive healing strategy. The strategies you use should fit easily into your schedule, comfort levels, and lifestyle. It may take some trial and error to figure out what works for you, but once you make mindfulness practices, physical exercise, or creative expression a regular part of your routine, it will become something you look forward to. Instead of trying to force yourself to do things you aren't interested in, choose activities that you find enjoyable and sustainable, making it more likely that you'll stick with them. The possibilities are limitless; you could decide to start your day with meditation, followed by a morning walk. At lunchtime, you can find solace in journaling accompanied by painting or playing music in the evenings. Whatever you decide, make sure it resonates with your healing goals and works in cohesion with the rest of your routine. Personalizing the methods you choose to engage in makes your healing routine feel a bit more familiar and natural, keeping you motivated.

Many healing methods work well in harmony with one another. Combining different techniques allows you to address multiple facets of your well-being in one swift motion. Pairing mindfulness practices with physical activities like running can help you simultaneously gain both mental clarity and physical vitality. Creative expression, like journaling or art therapy, beautifully complements traditional therapy, presenting a way to explore emotions in a non-verbal and intuitive manner. There's nothing to lose from taking a holistic approach to your practices. Healing is multifaceted, and addressing different areas can lead to lasting change. By the end of it all, your daily routine should support you and your goals on multiple levels.

Flexibility and adaptability are requirements of any successful healing plan. Everyone's life is at least somewhat unpredictable, and our needs tend to change over time. Periodically revisiting your plan gives you an opportunity to adjust your methods or goals as circumstances and priorities shift. A year from now, you may find that a certain practice no longer serves you or that you've developed new interests that you'd like to incorporate. This is okay, and it's usually a sign that you're growing. **Being open to change keeps your plan relevant and fresh so you have room to continue evolving**. This plan belongs to you, and it should reflect where you are now and where you hope to be in the future. Every up and down in the process is meant to be embraced. There are no obstacles, only opportunities for growth. The lessons you learn along the way are what make your plan a dynamic tool that supports your healing every step of the way.

For your reference, I've provided a quick checklist for designing your own personalized growth plan:

1. **Identify Goals:** Develop five to ten specific, achievable, and measurable goals related to your emotional and psychological well-being.
2. **Assess Current State:** Dedicate time to reflecting on your emotional challenges and strengths, using your observations to guide the prioritization of different strategies.
3. **Prioritize Activities:** Identify several healing activities that resonate with you and fit into your lifestyle, considering practices that can be done at the beginning, middle, and end of each day.
4. **Integrate Modalities:** Combine elements of mindfulness, physical activity, and creative expression within your practices for a holistic approach.
5. **Stay Flexible:** Make plans to revisit and revise your plan regularly to make sure that it is adapting to your changing needs.

Embracing Cultural Perspectives in Healing

When you think about healing, your cultural background sits behind you, silently influencing your perception of trauma and recovery. The culture and environment we are raised in shape the way we express emotions and how we process them. For many, cultural beliefs are the lens through which experiences are interpreted, influencing how they understand emotional pain and the approaches they would take to heal (Bryant-Davis 2019). In many cultures, empathy and emotional openness are highly encouraged, developing an environment where individuals feel comfortable asking for support or taking time to tend to their mental

health. In some cultures, openly expressing emotions is a bit taboo. In many groups, stoicism is highly valued, affecting how trauma is processed. It's not uncommon for a culture to perceive individuals who reach out for help as weak, especially when they've been taught to believe so. It's not always easy to say where these beliefs root, but recognizing the prevalence of these nuances can make a world of difference in your healing process, enabling you to select approaches that actually resonate with your personal and cultural identity.

Regardless of whether each and every cultural expectation aligns with your personal story, you can still honor your background by incorporating practices and rituals into your routine. Embracing your customs can add a few layers of comfort and a sense of continuity to your efforts, making you feel more connected to your roots and community.

Some cultures use ceremonies for emotional release. The Native American sweat lodge, for example, involves a ritualistic steam bath to purify the mind and body (Aaland 2018). This practice is meant to be a physical and spiritual detox that encourages reflection and renewal. Engaging in storytelling is another method that can be observed in cultures around the world. Much of the world has rich oral traditions where stories are shared to impart wisdom, teach lessons, or simply comfort each other. When you participate in or listen to these stories, you can identify the lessons and find parallels in your own experiences that give you a bit of perspective about the path you're taking.

Even if you don't resonate with any traditions from your own background, it can be enriching to explore diverse healing traditions from other cultures. Doing this can reveal new ways of understanding and addressing emotional well-being. Indigenous practices like talking circles present a communal space where individuals can

speak openly, share their experiences, and receive support without judgment. Eastern traditions, such as yoga and meditation, are designed to help you cultivate inner peace and balance, presenting new ways for practicing mindfulness and self-awareness. With time, these traditions strengthen the connection between your mind and body, making it easier for you to listen to your inner voice and honor your emotional needs. Engaging in well-loved traditions also brings a sense of belonging and mutual respect. Integrating a variety of traditions enriches your overall healing experience, tapping into historical wisdom that transcends any cultural boundaries.

A culturally informed healing process presents numerous benefits. Most importantly, it brings you a sense of identity and belonging at a time when you may sometimes feel like you're on your own. Engaging with practices that reflect your cultural heritage or the well-loved traditions of other communities elevates your connection to a history of self-care and inner growth. The connection you make with shared tradition can act as a source of support, reminding you that you are part of something larger than yourself. **As you practice new strategies and integrate elements of different cultures into your routine, you'll learn more about your own identity so you can manage your emotions with the utmost clarity**. Embracing a variety of perspectives in healing enables you to honor your roots while forging a fresh path forward that aligns with who you are today.

Monitoring Progress: Growth Through Reflection

When you take the time to reflect on your experience and the lessons you learned throughout the day, you're documenting some of the most important moments of your life. When you

look back at all that you have written, you'll begin to uncover shifts within you that might otherwise go unnoticed. Regular reflection gives you a pause in the hustle and bustle of life to enhance your self-awareness and willingness to grow. Noticing patterns and moments of success can be enlightening and motivating, especially when you reach a point where you feel like you haven't made much progress. Journaling is like reading the story of your own life, chapter by chapter, and finding meaning in the narrative. The insights you gain will guide you to make informed choices about your path forward.

Tracking and evaluating your personal growth can happen in any format that works for you. Your journal is a great tool for keeping all of your progress in one place, but there are also several apps that are designed for goal setting and reflection. These are built with structured prompts and tracking features that make it easier to stay organized and focused. They can even remind you to check in with yourself to make sure you're staying committed to your goals. For your reference, I've provided a few apps currently available that are designed to help with goal setting, reflection, and growth tracking:

1. **Daylio:** A mood and habit tracker app that gives you space to log your activities and feelings with just a few taps to help you uncover patterns in your well-being.
2. **Journey:** A digital journaling app with prompts and reminders that encourage daily reflection and goal progress tracking.
3. **Fabulous:** A habit-building app designed to help you create structured routines and track your progress toward personal goals.
4. **Reflectly:** A guided journaling app that uses AI to

generate prompts that encourage regular self-reflection and mindful exercises.

5. **Mindfulness Coach:** An app designed to support mental well-being by offering guided meditation, breathing exercises, and mindfulness tracking.

The more often that you choose to engage in self-reflection, the more clarity you gain as changes happen within you. You may not always want to track every step of the way, but these reflections give you an immediate boost of motivation and encouragement to continue your efforts. You're giving yourself opportunities to celebrate what went well while embracing what didn't. This appraisal should be as honest as possible, presenting a more balanced view of your progress that highlights each of the lessons learned from your experience.

To make self-assessment a regular part of your routine, use reflective questions and prompts like the ones provided throughout this book to guide your thinking at the end of each day. The questions you choose to expand on will impact the realizations and insights you gather from them. Generally speaking, asking questions like, "What have I learned about myself this week?" or, "How have my responses to triggers changed over time?" are great ways to explore your inner world, regardless of what is going on in your external spaces. Personalizing these prompts to your specific situations allows you to take an even closer look at your habits and patterns. Don't be afraid to uncover shifts in perspective or new approaches to handling emotions. While change may have scared you before, it now acts as an indicator of your personal growth. Intentional introspection nurtures your sense of self-awareness and enables you to understand the underlying motivations of your actions and reactions.

Not everyone loves to write or express their emotions creatively. If you struggle to feel inspired by typing your feelings away, a structured approach, like filling out a table outlining your daily experiences, can be enough to prompt a reflective mindset. Tracking your healing progress in a simple and organized way is a valid technique for observing progress over time, identifying patterns, and noticing emotional shifts. The way you conduct this should be personalized to keep you accountable to creating a tangible record of your resilience. To get you started, here's a sample of a quick table and an example to note key aspects of your healing:

Date	Emotional State (1–10)	Triggers/ Challenges	Coping Strategies Used	Progress & Insights	Next Steps
2/11/2025	*7*	*Felt anxious after a difficult conversation*	*Practiced deep breathing*	*Realized that open communicat ion reduces anxiety*	*Focus on expressing needs more calmly in future conversations*

Feel free to use the open spaces to include your own experiences or customize the categories based on your preferences. Reflection is a dynamic practice that evolves as you do and prompts you to engage with your feelings in a constructive and compassionate way. **When you make journaling a regular part of your life, you choose to improve your understanding of yourself while strengthening your ability to manage the more difficult parts of healing with grace and composure.**

Healing is a deeply personal journey that is constantly evolving. You're now prepared to create your own roadmap for growth, integrating cultural perspectives and reflection activities to keep your routine fresh and productive. **Taking intentional steps toward healing empowers you to break old cycles and support your emotional health.** There is no single correct path to emotional well-being; what matters is that your story reflects your values and needs. Some days will feel full of progress, while others may challenge you to keep going and dig deeper. As we move into the final chapter of our exploration, we'll explore how to translate the healing practices we've discussed into real-life applications, guaranteeing that the work you've done becomes an integral part of your life instead of remaining theoretical.

Chapter 10

Translating Healing into Real-Life Applications

Healing can only become powerful when it moves beyond theoretical discussions and becomes an active part of your daily schedule. Throughout this book, we've reviewed a variety of practices that are designed to support self-awareness, resilience, and emotional well-being. Now, it's time to put these insights into action. This chapter will help you translate your healing goals into tangible and lasting change that reflects your growth, authenticity, and emotional strength.

Harnessing Emotional Intelligence for Lasting Growth

Emotional intelligence (EQ) is a skill that many people don't even know could benefit them. **EQ is defined as the ability to manage challenges with clarity and rational thinking, enabling individuals to manage their own emotions while recognizing and influencing the emotions of others.** EQ is a valuable asset that can enact change in both the personal and professional spheres of your life. It encompasses

self-awareness, self-regulation, motivation, empathy, and social skills, all of which determine whether you are capable of making meaningful connections and achieving personal growth.

EQ, in essence, is learning to be smart about your feelings and the feelings of others. EQ is needed to respond to the nuances of everyday interactions. This intelligence isn't fixed or measured by a concrete number; it can be developed and refined through intentional practices. In personal settings, EQ helps you connect more empathetically with loved ones while elevating your capacity to lead, collaborate, and innovate effectively in professional environments. Within your family, the heightened sense of empathy and emotional understanding can contribute to stronger relationships that are based on honesty and trust. In the workplace, EQ encourages colleagues to communicate openly, support each other, and approach challenges with a sense of shared purpose. Regardless of where you are, practicing EQ elevates your experience and connections.

Improving EQ requires self-regulation, a skill that you've been building this entire time. When you're self-regulating, the goal is to manage your emotions constructively, especially in distressing situations. There are a few ways to do this, but the simplest is the "pause and reflect" approach, which prompts you to take a moment before making a decision or replying to an interaction to pause and think about your feelings and the possible outcomes of various responses. This brief pause can make a world of difference when you're in a heated mindset, preventing rash decisions and allowing for more thoughtful and deliberate actions (Ackerman 2019).

Another self-regulating technique, referred to as the "reframe and redirect" approach, involves consciously shifting your perspective on a situation before reacting emotionally. When

you're faced with a distressing or frustrating moment, it can be helpful to take a step back and ask yourself the following:

1. Is there another way to interpret this situation?
2. What is within my control right now, and what isn't?
3. How can I respond in a way that aligns with my values?

A personal stress-reduction kit can also be beneficial. You might carry a bag around that includes activities or items that help you calm down when you encounter a triggering or distressing scenario. Having a few familiar items readily available can calm you enough to effectively handle emotional disturbances in a healthy manner. Here are a few examples of what you might include in your stress-reduction kit:

1. **Sensory Items:** Stress balls or fidget toys are commonly used to redirect nervous energy.
2. **Aromatherapy:** A small bottle of essential oils like lavender or peppermint can relax your body immediately.
3. **Journal:** Keeping your journal on you can give you constant access to your reflections, reminding you of what works when you're feeling overwhelmed.
4. **Comfort Objects:** A sentimental item like a smooth stone, piece of fabric, or a stuffed toy can ground you during difficult moments.
5. **Distraction Items:** A book, crossword puzzle, or coloring pages can shift your focus from stressors.

Empathy is the core of EQ, enabling deeper connections, genuine trust, and compassion within relationships. Empathy defines our ability to understand and share the feelings of others. Being an empathetic person requires stepping into someone else's

shoes and seeing the world from their perspective. There are plenty of ways to build empathy:

1. **Active Listening:** Referring to our discussion from earlier, this strategy includes giving your full attention when someone speaks while resisting the urge to formulate any judgments.
2. **Perspective Taking:** Consciously put yourself in someone else's shoes and imagine their emotions.
3. **Practice Open-Ended Questions:** Ask yourself questions like "How did that make you feel?" to prompt further conversation.
4. **Read Fiction or Personal Narratives:** Engaging with diverse stories gives you an opportunity to experience life from different perspectives.
5. **Engage in Acts of Kindness:** Small gestures, like offering help or showing appreciation, can strengthen your ability to relate to others and their needs.

These exercises build your capacity for empathy, enabling you to connect more deeply with others and deepen your relationships.

When you're struggling to find empathy for someone in a specific instance, don't worry; it doesn't make you a bad person. Empathy is a skill that needs to be practiced, and this doesn't always come as easily after facing significant trauma. To address these moments, find a quiet space, close your eyes, and take a few deep breaths. Imagine the scenario that you're trying to gain empathy for, visualizing the scene in your mind. Now, place yourself in their position, asking yourself the following questions:

1. What were they feeling?
2. What would I want to hear in that moment if I were them?
3. What do I know about this person that may be impacting how they responded?

Taking extra steps to place yourself in someone else's position can make empathy feel a bit more natural.

Social skills are the final piece of EQ, encompassing the ability to manage relationships and build networks. These skills are the cornerstone of effective communication, conflict resolution, and collaboration. Improving your social skills takes time, especially when you're healing from inner wounds, but practicing clear and assertive communication helps you to build confidence and set healthy boundaries.

Being able to express your thoughts and feelings honestly while respecting others' perspectives is the core of EQ. When you're conversing with others, you should aim to always lead with mutual respect and understanding. Take the time to build and maintain your social networks in intentional ways, expressing to others that you respect and care about their friendship. An emotionally intelligent person reaches out to their friends and colleagues regularly, giving them support and seeking to understand their experiences. EQ also enables you to see when someone fails to show you the same respect or care that you offer them, giving you the cues you need to make distance or set clearer boundaries if the situation requires it. Building connections that honor and support an emotionally healthy mindset means you'll be left with a stronger support system that is there when you need it.

Developing EQ is an ongoing process of growth and learning. Working on these skills will inevitably make you a more resilient and fulfilled person, supporting your healing goals along the way. With the strategies we've discussed in your arsenal, you're prepared to make meaningful relationships and create a positive impact in your personal and professional interactions. Continue practicing activities related to self-awareness, self-regulation, empathy, and social skills. This is your commitment to building a more fulfilling and connected way of living.

Integrating Healing Practices at Work and Home

Let me guess: when you step into the office or workplace, your anxiety heightens and you're typically met with a hefty rush of chaos. Fortunately, healing isn't confined to a spa or a yoga class. Even if it's for only a moment, you can create an environment from anywhere that feels like a calm oasis. When there's a small plant on your desk, a gentle scent of lavender in the air, and a few personal items that make you smile, your mood can instantly shift. There are plenty of ways to adjust your workspace to make it more supportive of your emotional well-being and, in turn, your productivity. Bringing healing practices into professional settings can rewire how we feel at work and how we interact with others, resulting in improved performance and stronger workplace relationships (Craig 2019). Mindfulness strategies are commonly used to improve focus and reduce stress. When you're mindful, you're present and fully engaged in the task at hand and less likely to be overwhelmed by external pressures. Maintaining focus with mindfulness can happen from anywhere, resulting in improved decision-making and creativity. With time, these qualities will make you more effective and satisfied in your role.

Incorporating healing practices into your work environment starts by personalizing your physical space. If you're able to, try to include elements that bring you peace, like a photo of a loved one or a piece of art that inspires you. These small touches make a world of difference in setting a positive tone for your day. Scheduling brief mindfulness breaks throughout your workday can provide you with regular moments of relief and clarity. These don't have to be lengthy; even a five-minute pause to breathe deeply and center yourself can give you a mental reset. Find a quiet place, close your eyes, and focus on your breath, letting go of any tension or stress. These breaks are also effective for preventing burnout, allowing you to return to your tasks with a renewed sense of energy and focus.

Creating a calming atmosphere to retreat to during the chaos of the working day does wonders for your emotional health. Consider incorporating calming colors or natural elements, like a small desk plant or a water feature. These have a naturally soothing effect and instill a sense of balance. If you can, try to arrange your workspace to allow natural light to enter, as it can have a significant impact on your mood and energy levels. Don't forget to set boundaries for your work environment. If you're working from home, designate a specific area as your office so that there's a mental separation between work and personal life. If you do all your work from your bedroom, you're less likely to feel refreshed when you enter this space at the end of the day. Setting a physical boundary can help you reduce stress and maintain focus during work hours.

At home, establishing family meditation or relaxation times can be a wonderful way to connect and unwind together. Choose a time that works for everyone, like in the evening before bedtime, and gather in a quiet space. Use this time to follow a guided meditation or simply sit in silence together, focusing on your

breath. This practice provides each family member with a chance to relax before shutting down for the night. Simultaneously, these practices bring your family closer together, creating a shared experience of peace. You can adapt this practice to fit your needs, making it a simple yet impactful way to end the day on a positive note.

Meal preparation is another mindfulness exercise that often flies under the radar. Cooking can be extremely meditative, especially when it's approached with intention. For the next few days, while you're preparing a dish, take a moment to focus on the colors, textures, and aromas of the ingredients and engage all your senses as you prepare the meal. Pay attention to the rhythm of your movements, the sound of chopping, or the scent of spices. Not only are you nourishing your body when you prepare a meal, but you're also turning a routine task into an opportunity for presence and gratitude that makes mealtime more enjoyable and fulfilling. After you're done cooking, sharing a meal prepared with care with friends, family, roommates, or colleagues can advance a sense of connection and warmth.

Balancing work and personal life is not always easy, especially if you're someone who is used to having their limits pushed. This can be made easier by setting clear boundaries and confirming that one aspect doesn't overshadow the other. You'll want to define specific work hours and make a conscious effort to unplug outside of those times. This separation can help you maintain your focus and productivity during work hours while allowing for genuine relaxation and time with loved ones afterward. Be sure to communicate your needs and expectations clearly with your family and colleagues to keep everyone on the same page regarding your boundaries. If you need to, don't feel guilty about letting your family know when you need quiet time to work or informing colleagues about your availability.

Incorporating healing practices into your work and home life can bring a sense of balance and harmony that supports your overall well-being. When your day looks a bit more difficult than you had hoped, prioritizing these practices protects your emotional health and your relationships with those around you. Inevitably, integrating healing into every aspect of your life will improve your quality of life and bring a sense of peace and fulfillment to your everyday experiences.

Living Authentically: Embracing Your Empowered Self

When you love who you are, you wake up each day with a sense of alignment, and every one of your actions and decisions reflects who you truly are. This is the reality of living authentically. When you live as your genuine self, you can shed all the masks you wear for societal approval and step into the world with a renewed sense of confidence. Authentic living leads to greater fulfillment and self-confidence; when you're true to yourself, you feel more at ease and connected with your emotional well-being. This connection forms the basis for a life that feels meaningful and fulfilling. When your actions align with your true self, you're met with harmony, reduced inner conflict, and improvements in your overall happiness.

When you feel ready to begin living authentically, engaging in self-reflection is your next step. The self-reflection exercises mentioned throughout the book are designed to help you identify your core values and beliefs. When you reflect in your journal, it should feel like taking a step back from the noise of daily life and asking yourself what truly matters. Developing and drafting a personal mission statement can provide you with a single statement that serves as a compass to guide your decisions and

actions. A personal mission statement should primarily consider your core values and the principles that you hold dear. Next, think about your long-term goals and how they align with these values and use this information to craft a statement that encapsulates your purpose and what you hope to achieve. This quick exercise clarifies your values and provides a sense of direction, helping you stay true to yourself even when faced with challenges.

Reflection should be a regular process. Someone who lives authentically may set aside time each week to jot down their thoughts and feelings about different aspects of their life. To guide your regular check-ins, here are a few prompts you may use:

1. What makes you feel fulfilled?
2. What drains your energy?
3. What do you stand for?
4. What brings you joy?
5. When do you feel most like yourself?
6. What habits make you feel grounded?
7. What is something you've learned about yourself recently?
8. What is one small thing you do to take care of yourself?
9. What emotions have been showing up for you lately, and what are they trying to tell you?
10. When do you feel like you're at your best?

These questions are simple, but they encourage introspection and self-discovery to help you uncover the layers of your identity and what truly matters to you. Over time, you'll have clarity about your values and how they shape your decisions.

Once you've identified your values, the next step is aligning your daily actions with them. This means making choices that reflect your true self rather than conforming to external expectations. When you begin setting goals, your priority is confirming that they resonate with your core values. If one of your values is creativity, for example, you may set aside time each week to engage in creative pursuits like painting, writing, or cooking. Regardless of what you do, make sure your goals align with what you genuinely enjoy. When you love your routine, you're constantly filled with fulfillment and motivation to pursue activities that are meaningful to you.

Decision-making based on your authentic goals and desires requires mindfulness and self-awareness. Before making a choice, you should pause and ask yourself whether it aligns with your values, considering how the decision might impact your sense of self. When you practice intentional decision-making, your life reflects your true identity and produces greater satisfaction and confidence. Living authentically means making choices that honor who you are, even when faced with external pressures or societal norms.

Embracing vulnerability is an integral part of living authentically. You can't be your true self without being open and honest about your thoughts, feelings, and experiences, even when it's uncomfortable. Vulnerability strengthens your personal connections and supports your self-growth. Sharing your personal stories invites others into your world, creating opportunities for sincere connections. This openness furthers your empathy, building trust within your personal relationships. Engaging in activities that challenge your limits of comfort can also promote growth. If public speaking, trying a new hobby, or initiating a difficult conversation scares you, it might be signaling that it's time to take a few steps into discomfort to support your resilience and self-discovery.

Living authentically is a process that works alongside self-discovery, growth, and empowerment. When you embrace your true self, flaws and all, your life suddenly becomes deeply aligned with your values. The more you learn about yourself, the more you'll experience greater fulfillment, confidence, and emotional well-being. Even when it's challenging, making decisions that reflect your true self contributes to an existence that feels genuine, meaningful, and fulfilling. As our exploration of healing from trauma comes to a close, take a moment to reflect on how embracing your authentic qualities can shape your choices, relationships, and sense of purpose. Though our conversation may be coming to an end, you will continue to learn more about yourself each day, letting it carry forward into the way you live your life.

Conclusion

We've come to the end of our journey together, but your growth and reflection are far from over. Throughout this book, we've explored the impact of childhood trauma and the transformative potential of structured emotional healing. We've looked deeply into your emotional landscape to identify your trigger, liberate your inner child, and help you break free from dysfunctional patterns. It's been a long path of self-discovery, courage, and growth to get where we are now.

At the heart of this book lies my vision of guiding others to achieve emotional resonance and practical healing. When you make a conscious choice to engage in the exercises and strategies outlined in each chapter, you take significant steps toward understanding your own emotions and embracing self-compassion. You've learned to recognize and manage emotional triggers, cultivate mindfulness, and integrate healing practices into your daily life. Now, these are your building blocks for a life beyond trauma, filled with authenticity, connection, and joy.

Reflection is now an essential part of your daily routine. As you take time to write about your emotions or creatively express them, take a moment to remember the key takeaways from each chapter. Being in touch with your emotional landscape is the foundation for healing; mapping your triggers, exploring the science behind emotional responses, and recognizing patterns of dysfunction gives you the insight needed to create lasting change. Liberating your inner child through play, dialogue, and creative expression strengthens this process, resulting in deep healing and self-discovery. As you identify and break free from unhealthy relationship patterns and self-sabotaging behaviors, you build a path for more fulfilling connections and personal growth.

Central to your personal story is the practice of self-compassion. Treating yourself with kindness, understanding, and forgiveness is a revolutionary act that has the potential to completely change your relationship with yourself and others. You offer yourself a sense of empowerment and resilience every time you work toward nurturing your authentic self, celebrating your strengths, and honoring your vulnerabilities. This self-compassion is the foundation upon which lasting growth is built.

When you close this book today, don't let this be the last time. I encourage you to continue applying the lessons and exercises we've discussed. Healing is an ongoing process that will require commitment, patience, and self-love. As long as you're integrating practices like journaling, mindfulness, and creative expression into your daily routine, you're on your way to a life that supports your emotional well-being. Beyond your own actions and mindset, make sure you're surrounding yourself with supportive people, engaging in activities that bring you joy, and prioritizing communities that uplift you.

The end of this book is just the beginning of your progress. You've gained tools and insights from this book that can now be shared to create a ripple effect of healing and growth. Don't be afraid to share your experiences, triumphs, and challenges with others. Opening up about your own experiences on a public platform creates space where others can do the same, contributing to a community of support and empathy. Together, we can break the silence around childhood trauma and create a world where healing is possible for all.

Your courage in embarking on this journey is a testament to your strength and resilience. The moment you picked up this book, you took a powerful step toward reclaiming your life and your emotional well-being. From now on, you will never be alone in your journey, and you'll never have to question whether your experiences matter or if healing is a possibility.

A life where you are free to be your authentic self, build meaningful connections, and experience the fullness of joy and love is waiting for you on the other side of healing. Never stop working and healing; you are worthy of all the love and happiness this world has to offer. When you need this book again, for reference or support, it'll be here, waiting for you to continue learning more about yourself and your future.

Your Review can Illuminate the Path for Others

"I think we forget sometimes how blessed we are to be able to help others and make a difference!"

— Gautam Rode

You've just embarked on a journey of self-discovery and relationship building.

The purpose of this book is to give you the tools you need to understand your own childhood trauma and help those around you at the same time

There are other people out there like you—and the goal of Freeman Publishing is to reach as many of them as possible. If we can do that, we can help not only the people who are doing the work to improve their childhood trauma anxieties, but also improve their overall communication with others.

Now, it's time to share your insights with those who may be feeling lost.

By leaving a review on Amazon, you're not just expressing your gratitude, but you're also offering a beacon of hope to others who are seeking guidance. Your honest feedback can help them find the support and inspiration they need.

Please scan this QR code to leave a review.

Bibliography

Aaland, Mikkel. 2018. "Chapter Six: The Native American Sweat Lodge." mikkelaaland.com. 2018. Accessed February 19, 2025. https://mikkelaaland.com/the-native-american-sweat-lodge.html.

Ackerman, Courtney E. 2019. "13 Emotional Intelligence Exercises, Activities & Worksheets." Positive Psychology. February 4, 2019. Accessed February 19, 2025. https://positivepsychology.com/emotional-intelligence-exercises/.

Affordable Counselling. 2024. "Narrative Therapy—Rewriting the Way We View Ourselves." April 23, 2024. Accessed February 19, 2025. https://www.lighthearts-uk.com/new-blog/2024/4/23/narrative-therapy-rewriting-the-way-we-view-ourselves.

Baikie, Karen A., and Kay Wilhelm. 2018. "Emotional and Physical Health Benefits of Expressive Writing." *Advances in Psychiatric Treatment* 11, no. 5 (2018): 338–46. Accessed February 19, 2025. https://doi.org/10.1192/apt.11.5.338.

Baker, Sandy. 2024. "Mindfulness Practices for Daily Life." Willow Creek Behavioral Health. May 10, 2024. Accessed February 19, 2025. https://willowcreekbh.com/mindfulness-practices-for-daily-life/.

Beard, McKenzie. 2025. "Meditation Changes Brain Waves Linked to Anxiety, Depression." New York Post, February 14, 2025. Accessed February 19, 2025. https://nypost.com/2025/02/14/health/meditation-changes-brain-waves-linked-to-anxiety-depression/.

Best Day Psychiatry & Counseling. 2022. "Self-Compassion and Your Mental Health." January 3, 2022. Accessed February 19, 2025. https://bestdaypsych.com/self-compassion-and-your-mental-health/.

Brown, Brené. 2010. "TED Talk: The Power of Vulnerability." June 1, 2010. Accessed February 19, 2025. https://brenebrown.com/videos/ted-talk-the-power-of-vulnerability/.

Bryant-Davis, Thema. 2019. "The Cultural Context of Trauma Recovery: Considering the Posttraumatic Stress Disorder Practice Guideline and Intersectionality." *Psychotherapy (Chicago, Ill.)* 56, no. 3 (September 2019): 400–8. Accessed February 19, 2025. https://doi.org/10.1037/pst0000241.

CDC. 2021. "Preventing Adverse Childhood Experiences." Centers for Disease Control and Prevention. August 23, 2021. Accessed February 19, 2025. https://www.cdc.gov/vitalsigns/aces/index.html.

Cherry, Kendra. 2022. "The Importance of Maintaining Structure and Routine During Stressful Times." Verywell Mind. August 29, 2022. Accessed February

19, 2025. https://www.verywellmind.com/the-importance-of-keeping-a-routine-during-stressful-times-4802638.

Chowdhury, Madhuleena Roy. 2019. "What Is Emotional Resilience? (+6 Proven Ways to Build It)." Positive Psychology. January 22, 2019. Accessed February 19, 2025. https://positivepsychology.com/emotional-resilience/.

Craig, Heather. 2019. "Mindfulness at Work: Create Calm & Focus in the Workplace." Positive Psychology. March 9, 2019. Accessed February 19, 2025. https://positivepsychology.com/mindfulness-at-work/.

Dashorst, Patricia, Trudy M. Mooren, Rolf J. Kleber, Peter J. de Jong, and Rafaele J. C. Huntjens. 2025. "Intergenerational Consequences of the Holocaust on Offspring Mental Health: A Systematic Review of Associated Factors and Mechanisms." *European Journal of Psychotraumatology* 10, no. 1: 1654065. Accessed February 19, 2025. https://doi.org/10.1080/20008198.2019.1654065.

DBT of South Jersey. 2024. "Healing Trauma: Creating a Personalized Healing Plan." August 12, 2024. Accessed February 19, 2025. https://dbtofsouthjersey.com/healing-trauma-creating-a-personalized-healing-plan/.

Democracy Now! 2025. "'The Tale' Filmmaker Jennifer Fox on Surviving Childhood Sexual Abuse & Finally Naming Her Abuser." Accessed February 19, 2025. https://www.democracynow.org/2023/3/30/jennifer_fox_the_tale.

Dodd, Johnny. 2024. "Son Who Lived in Fear of Dad's Abuse Has Now Stepped Up to Be His Caregiver: How Their Relationship Healed (Exclusive)." People.com. November 22, 2024. Accessed February 19, 2025. https://people.com/veteran-with-ptsd-was-abusive-dad-now-son-is-his-caregiver-8749069.

Evolve Therapy. 2023. "Co-Dependency and Attachment Style," August 18, 2023. Accessed February 19, 2025. https://www.evolvetherapymn.com/post/co-dependency-and-attachment-style.

French, Mandy. 2023. "Self-Sabotage: How to Overcome Self-Defeating Behavior." MedicalNewsToday. October 19, 2023. Accessed February 19, 2025. https://www.medicalnewstoday.com/articles/self-sabotage.

Griffin, Siobhán M., Alžběta Lebedová, Elayne Ahern, Grace McMahon, Daragh Bradshaw, and Orla T. Muldoon. 2023. "PROTOCOL: Group-Based Interventions for Posttraumatic Stress Disorder: A Systematic Review and Meta-Analysis of the Role of Trauma Type." *Campbell Systematic Reviews* 19, no. 2 (May 13, 2023): e1328. Accessed February 19, 2025. https://doi.org/10.1002/cl2.1328.

Guendelman, Simón, Sebastián Medeiros, and Hagen Rampes. 2023. "Mindfulness and Emotion Regulation: Insights from Neurobiological, Psychological, and Clinical Studies." *Frontiers in Psychology* 8 (March 6, 2017): 220. https://doi.org/10.3389/fpsyg.2017.00220.

Guy-Evans, Olivia. 2023. "Amygdala Hijack: How It Works, Signs, & How To

Cope." *SimplyPsychology* (blog), September 18, 2023. Accessed February 19, 2025. https://www.simplypsychology.org/amygdala-hijack.html.

Hastings, Natasha. 2022. "Hanging Up My Spikes." The Players' Tribune. August 29, 2022. Accessed February 19, 2025. https://www.theplayerstribune.com/posts/natasha-hastings-usa-track-field-retirement.

Hurley, Katie. 2016. "Creating an Emotionally Supportive Home Environment." PBS KIDS for Parents, May 2, 2016. Accessed February 19, 2025. https://www.pbs.org/parents/thrive/creating-an-emotionally-supportive-home-environment.

Impossible Psych Services. 2024. "How Generational Trauma Influences Family Dynamics," June 7, 2024. Accessed February 19, 2025. https://www.impossiblepsychservices.com.sg/our-resources/articles/2024/06/07/how-generational-trauma-influences-family-dynamics.

Jagiellowicz, Jadzia. 2024. "Five Ways to Be More Vulnerable and Authentic." Greater Good, December 2, 2024. Accessed February 19, 2025. https://greatergood.berkeley.edu/article/item/five_ways_to_be_more_vulnerable_and_authentic.

Khoddam, Rubin. 2022. "Breath and Trauma-Healing Exercises." Psychology Today, March 31, 2022. Accessed February 19, 2025. https://www.psychologytoday.com/us/blog/the-addiction-connection/202203/breath-and-trauma-healing-exercises.

Kids First. 2025. "Top Art Therapy Techniques to Heal from Trauma." Accessed February 19, 2025. https://www.kidsfirstservices.com/first-insights/art-therapy-techniques-for-processing-trauma.

Lauren. 2022. "Boundaries Are Essential for Healing Trauma." *LMV Counseling* (blog), January 25, 2022. Accessed February 19, 2025. https://lmvcounseling.com/boundaries-and-trauma/.

Mayo Clinic. 2022. "Can Mindfulness Exercises Help Me?" October 11, 2022. Accessed February 19, 2025. https://www.mayoclinic.org/healthy-lifestyle/consumer-health/in-depth/mindfulness-exercises/art-20046356.

Mayo Clinic. 2025. "Resilience: Build Skills to Endure Hardship Sections." Accessed February 19, 2025. https://www.mayoclinic.org/tests-procedures/resilience-training/in-depth/resilience/art-20046311.

Mills, Paige. 2023. "From Corporate Misery to Artistic Bliss: Carolyn Wonders' Journey Back to Art." Artwork Archive, June 30, 2023. Accessed February 19, 2025. https://www.artworkarchive.com/blog/from-corporate-misery-to-artistic-bliss-carolyn-wonders-journey-back-to-art.

Mirgain, Shilagh A., and Janice Singles. 2016. "Therapeutic Journaling—Whole Health Library." General Information. Veterans Affairs, 2016. Accessed February 19, 2025. https://www.va.gov/WHOLEHEALTHLIBRARY/tools/therapeutic-journaling.asp.

Nash, Jo. 2022. "Expressive Arts Therapy: 15 Creative Activities and

Techniques," October 16, 2022. Accessed February 19, 2025. https://positivepsychology.com/expressive-arts-therapy/.

Pietrangelo, Ann. 2019. "Play Therapy: What Is It, How It Works, and Techniques." Healthline, October 11, 2019. Accessed February 19, 2025. https://www.healthline.com/health/play-therapy.

Savage, Lisa. 2023. "Healing Intergenerational Trauma Through Family Therapy." *Clinicians of Color Directory* (blog), March 4, 2023. Accessed February 19, 2025. https://www.cliniciansofcolor.org/clinician-articles/25527/.

Schroeder, Wilma. 2025. "How to Rewrite Your Own Story—Lessons from Narrative Therapy." Crisis and Trauma Resource Institute (CTRI), 2025. Accessed February 19, 2025. https://ctrinstitute.com/blog/how-to-rewrite-your-own-story-lessons-from-narrative-therapy/.

Sreenivas, Shishira. 2023. "Digital Detox: What to Know." WebMD, May 5, 2023. Accessed February 19, 2025. https://www.webmd.com/balance/what-is-digital-detox.

Stanborough, Rebecca Joy. 2020. "Cognitive Restructuring: Techniques and Examples." Healthline, February 4, 2020. Accessed February 19, 2025. https://www.healthline.com/health/cognitive-restructuring.

Stand Together. 2025. "Healing from Trauma: How Community Helps Survivors." Accessed February 19, 2025. https://standtogether.org/stories/strong-safe-communities/healing-from-trauma-how-survivors-find-resilience-through-community-support.

Sun, Lining, Amy Canevello, Kathrine A. Lewis, Jiqiang Li, and Jennifer Crocker. 2021. "Childhood Emotional Maltreatment and Romantic Relationships: The Role of Compassionate Goals." *Frontiers in Psychology* 12 (November 29, 2021): 723126. Accessed February 19, 2025. https://doi.org/10.3389/fpsyg.2021.723126.

Swee, Michaela B., Allison G. Corman, Jessica M. Margolis, and Alexandra M. Dick. 2024. "Compassion-Focused Therapy for the Treatment of ICD-11–Defined Complex Posttraumatic Stress Disorder." *American Journal of Psychotherapy* 77, no. 3 (September 2024): 135–40. Accessed February 19, 2025. https://doi.org/10.1176/appi.psychotherapy.20230019.

The Dulwich Centre. 2025. "Collection: Evidence for the Effectiveness of Narrative Therapy." Accessed February 19, 2025. https://dulwichcentre.com.au/collection-evidence-for-the-effectiveness-of-narrative-therapy/.

The Head Plan. 2025. "The Transformative Power of Affirmations : Rewiring the Mind for Success." Accessed February 19, 2025. https://theheadplan.com/blogs/mindset-elevation/the-transformative-power-of-affirmations-rewiring-the-mind-for-success.

The National Child Traumatic Stress Network (NCTSN). 2025. "Resilience and Child Traumatic Stress." Accessed February 19, 2025. https://www.nctsn.org/resources/resilience-and-child-traumatic-stress.

Travers, Mark. 2024. "3 Reasons Why Self-Love Fuels Romantic Love—From a Psychologist." Forbes, June 22, 2024. Accessed February 19, 2025. https://www.forbes.com/sites/traversmark/2024/06/22/3-reasons-why-self-love-fuels-romantic-love-from-a-psychologist/.

Tuffs, Rowan. 2025. "Breaking Generational Trauma: A Guide." Transformations Care Network. Accessed February 19, 2025. https://www.transformationsnetwork.com/post/breaking-generational-trauma.

Ward, Peggy Rowe, and Larry Ward. 2024. "A Meditation to Heal Your Inner Child." Lion's Roar, May 21, 2024. Accessed February 19, 2025. https://www.lionsroar.com/heal-your-inner-child-meditation/.

Wellness Road Psychology. 2024. "Effective Strategies for Trauma Healing: A Comprehensive Guide," June 14, 2024. Accessed February 19, 2025. https://wellnessroadpsychology.com/strategies-for-trauma-healing/.

Yehuda, Rachel, and Amy Lehrner. 2018. "Intergenerational Transmission of Trauma Effects: Putative Role of Epigenetic Mechanisms." *World Psychiatry* 17, no. 3 (October 2018): 243–57. Accessed February 19, 2025. https://doi.org/10.1002/wps.20568.

Made in the USA
Coppell, TX
03 January 2026

68154449R00090